A History of American Education

Joseph Watras

University of Dayton

Boston • New York • San Francisco
Mexico City • Montreal • Toronto • London • Madrid • Munich • Paris
Hong Kong • Singapore • Tokyo • Cape Town • Sydney

Executive Editor and Publisher: *Stephen D. Dragin*
Series Editorial Assistant: *Katie Heimsoth*
Marketing Manager: *Weslie Sellenger*
Production Editor: *Mary Beth Finch*
Editorial-Production Service: *Omegatype Typography, Inc.*
Composition Buyer: *Linda Cox*
Manufacturing Buyer: *Linda Morris*
Electronic Composition: *Omegatype Typography, Inc.*
Cover Administrator: *Elena Sidorova*

For related titles and support materials, visit our online catalog at www.ablongman.com.

ISBN-10: 0-205-47026-2
ISBN-13: 978-0-205-47026-6

Library of Congress Cataloging-in-Publication Data

Watras, Joseph.
A history of American education / Joseph Watras.
p. cm.
Includes bibliographical references and index.
ISBN-13: 978-0-205-47026-6
ISBN-10: 0-205-47026-2
1. Education—United States—History. I. Title.
LA205.W38 2008
370.973—dc22 2007017466

Printed in the United States of America

10 9 8 7 6 5 4 3 2 1 11 10 09 08 07

Photo Credits: p. 1, 15, 38, 87, 113, 138, 165, 190, 240, 267, 293, 320, 368, Library of Congress; p. 62, John Hancock Mutual Life Insurance Company; p. 216, National Library of Medicine; p. 346, Ronald Reagan Presidential Library.

Contents

Preface

This book is about the effects, influences, and implications of globalization on education in the United States. The relations between globalization and schools are complex. People changed their thinking about schools as the society underwent transformations, and they used those new ideas to alter curriculums to hasten social transitions.

In a short period, isolated colonies in America gave way to small towns in a new republic. In a few years, railroads linked rural villages together with cities. These changes happened rapidly in the United States. My aim is to explain how educators changed their ideas of the appropriate subject matter or the best method of teaching and how these ideas about curriculum moved around the world.

In making these explanations, I have tried to accomplish three things. First, I wanted to explore the ideas that educators proposed. Many of these recommendations were insightful, offering important perspectives about what constituted a good education. Second, I have attempted to show how people's definitions of ideals such as democracy interacted with ideas of appropriate social organization and curriculum reforms. Third, I have sought to demonstrate how reforms introduced new and different problems more than they improved education.

The composition of this book began during a breakfast conversation. A few years ago, I sat with Steve Dragin, Executive Editor and Publisher for Allyn and Bacon. He wanted to publish a history of education, and I wanted to write one. As we drank coffee, he described the situation as he saw it. Although the number of history of education courses in university catalogues had declined, the market for such texts appeared to be robust, particularly for a book that was balanced and coherent.

As I listened, I thought that he was describing a book that I could write. First, I knew the material because I had been teaching the history of education since 1972. Second, I knew the competing texts. The problem was finding a theme within which I could organize the enormous amount of information about the history of American education. The answer came to me when I attended a conference of the Comparative International and Education Society (CIES). One of my former professors, Victor Kobayashi, was president of the CIES, and I had a chance to talk with him. We spoke about the problems that resulted when people tried too hard to solve social problems. For example, when health workers tried to exterminate mosquitoes, they used such powerful pesticides that the chemicals disrupted the environment. Kobayashi feared that the belief that the scientific method was the means to improve the world had caused people to consider things from a narrow perspective. They discounted other ways of knowing.

When I went to the CIES conference, I heard scholars read papers about the need to reform educational efforts to improve the living conditions of people in underdeveloped countries. As I collected information for the book, I realized that American educators had tried to solve many social problems, and I linked this attitude to the changes that some authors considered as globalization. These authors disagreed about the causes of globalization. Some attributed it to the expansion of industries. Other commentators pointed to the spread of trade and the development of means of communication across political borders. Another view was that the changes in the twentieth century derived from the military dominance of the United States. Nonetheless, most writers seemed to agree that, by the twentieth century, people changed their ways of thinking. They did not look to traditions to determine policies. They tended to focus on concrete ways to enhance everyone's standard of living.

This change in perspective seemed to come out in various ways in education. For example, some people wanted schools to emphasize vocational training to help students cope with new ways of life. On the other hand, some educators believed that teachers should build lessons on the students' interests and thereby inspire them to reshape society to line with humane desires. Thus, my book would use the settlement of America and the development of a worldwide culture as the context in which to explore the ways people changed their thinking about schools.

Acknowledgments

Completing a work of this size, I incurred many debts. My biggest obligation is to the many scholars who compiled works about education and social change. Their names and their contributions appear in the text in the hundreds of citations filling each chapter. Many librarians in my own university and neighboring institutions helped me assemble the materials that I needed. These trained professionals gave me extensive aid in finding sources. Without them, I could not have accomplished anything. At the same time, with the permission of my editor, I presented some parts of the book to conferences of learned societies. The resulting criticism and comments were most helpful. I also tried some of the ideas in my own classes with my students. Although they never read the full text, I explained some of the things I was writing when those elements fit our classroom work. Their suggestions were always enlightening. Finally, I would like to thank the following reviewers for their helpful comments: Vincent A. Anfara, Jr., The University of Tennessee; David Bair, Grand Valley State University; Randy Cromwell, Averett University; Arthur Ellis, Seattle Pacific University; Gina M. Giuliano, University at Albany, State University of New York; and Connie Titone, Villanova University.

About the Author

Joseph Watras has been a professor of the history and philosophy of education at the University of Dayton in Ohio since 1979. After serving with the U.S. Peace Corps in West Africa, he completed his doctoral work in the history of education at The Ohio State University. He has published two previous books with Allyn and Bacon: *The Foundations of Educational Curriculum and Diversity from 1565 to the Present* and *Philosophic Conflicts in American Education, 1893–2000.* For ten years he served as editor of the *Journal of the Midwest History of Education Society.*

Acronyms

AAAS	American Association for the Advancement of Science
ACL	American Classical League
AMA	American Missionary Association
CAHSC	NEA's Committee on the Articulation of High School and College
CAP	Community Action Program
CCC	Civilian Conservation Corps
CEC	Council for Exceptional Children
CETE	Committee on the Economy of Time in Education
CIE	Civil Information and Education
CRSE	NEA's Commission on the Reorganization of Secondary Education
EPC	Educational Policies Commission
ESEA	U.S. Elementary and Secondary Education Act
ERIC	The U.S. Office of Education's Educational Research and Information Center
FERA	Federal Emergency Relief Administration
HEW	U.S. Department of Health, Education, and Welfare
MAA	Mathematical Association of America
MFLS	Modern Foreign Language Study
MLA	Modern Language Association
NAACP	National Association for the Advancement of Colored People
NANE	National Association of Nursery Education
Narkompros	Commissariat of Enlightenment in the Union of Soviet Socialist Republics
NCEE	National Commission on Excellence in Education
NCLB	No Child Left Behind
NDEA	National Defense Education Act
NEA	National Education Association
NSSE	National Society for the Study of Education
NSF	National Science Foundation
NTA	National Teachers' Association (an early version of the NEA)
NTE	National Teachers Exam
NYA	National Youth Administration
OCD	Office of Child Development
ODE	Ohio Department of Education
OEEC	Organization for European Economic Cooperation
OEO	U.S. Office of Economic Opportunity
PEA	Progressive Education Association
SCAP	Supreme Commander for Allied Powers
SEC	U.S. Securities and Exchange Commission
SMSG	School Mathematics Study Group
SNCC	Student Nonviolent Coordinating Committee
TVA	Tennessee Valley Authority
UNESCO	United Nations Educational Scientific and Cultural Organization
US	United States of America
USOE	U.S. Office of Education
WPA	Works Progress Administration

1

Introduction

One-room schoolhouse from the 1930s

This book is a history of education in the United States. It covers the changes in school organization, curriculum, and teaching practices that took place for more than 450 years. Because this is such a long stretch of time, the chapters illustrate how Americans reacted to changing social conditions, how they borrowed practices from other countries, and how they influenced those countries. Thus, the text suggests several relationships between American schools and globalization.

To prepare the reader for the chapters that follow, this introduction will consider how different authors have defined globalization and its relation to education. In an effort to provide a brief outline of the book, this introduction will offer summaries of each chapter explaining how it suggests something about schools and globalization. Finally, because the topic could be overly broad, the introduction sets out limits within which the narrative proceeds.

What Is Globalization?

There is no simple explanation of globalization and how it came to be. Commentators have used various terms to describe the ways that humanity has spread over the earth and how they have tried to form a universal culture. As a result, these authors have different explanations for the origins of contemporary conditions.

In 1899, John Dewey delivered a speech to parents of children who attended his elementary school; he described the transformations that had taken place in the past century. These changes constituted a description of globalization and an accounting of possible benefits as well as the problems that might result. In his speech, Dewey claimed that there had been a profound revolution. Instead of small villages, there was a worldwide market. Vast manufacturing centers churned out goods. Cheap methods of transportation and communication distributed those products among the parts of the newly interconnected society. To Dewey, the results were extensive. He noted that political boundaries had weakened or disappeared. People gathered into cities from the ends of the earth. Habits of living changed abruptly. Dewey claimed the force that lay behind these innovations was the application of science, and he thought the school should adopt curriculums that taught students to understand these changes and to think in scientific ways themselves.[1]

Although Dewey claimed the rise of modern industries had reshaped the world, he did not associate progress with the increased materialism derived from technical advances. Dewey acknowledged that roads, machines, and electricity ranked among the accomplishments of civilization. Nonetheless, he thought that progress would come from the application of those accomplishments in ways that would advance the shared and associated life by making cultural improvements through scientific thinking. Dewey decided this would be possible if people could absorb science into their imaginative and emotional dispositions in ways that would help them advance their views of morals and values. Because science had made it possible to imagine a world without poverty or disease, he hoped that science could advance people's taste in music, drawing, and sculpture.[2]

Because modern factories achieved their efficiency through bureaucratic organization, Dewey approved of such arrangements to divide labor and arrange tasks even though these conditions could make it difficult for most people to participate in the affairs of the society. For example, in *The Public and its Problems,* Dewey noted that modern urban societies became complex and this complexity prevented people from understanding what was taking place. They needed experts to illuminate the issues. The problem was these experts ignored common interests and formed their own classes. Despite this tendency, Dewey thought that experts could work to improve the methods and conditions of public debate by performing inquiries and disseminating information that enabled people to have intelligent discussions about public issues. As a result, the public could cast intelligent votes during elections for particular policies, and they could oversee the execution of those plans.[3]

As the twentieth century advanced, other commentators noted that the material wealth of the United States offered its citizens opportunities to use that wealth to improve human conditions around the world. Such errands of mercy constituted a second form of globalization. For example, a few months before the United States entered World War II, the American journalist Henry R. Luce wrote an extensive editorial in the February 1941 issue of *Life* magazine. He urged his readers to recognize that they lived in the American Century and to accept the responsibilities that attended such a position of leadership. Reminding readers about the stories and pictures they had read and seen about the German bombing of London, Luce argued that the United States could not remain neutral in World War II. Predicting that the United States would be involved, Luce claimed that the people should decide what they wanted to achieve in this conflict. He derived his answer from four points that he thought were true about the twentieth century. The first point was that, for the first time in history, the more than two billion human beings around the world depended on each other. The second point was that everyone hated and feared war. The third point was that technology had made it possible for the world to produce enough material goods for everyone on earth. The final point was that the twentieth century had to become the American Century, and the people around the world should derive the benefits it promised. To Luce, this meant that the people of the United States had to share with everyone their conception of democracy, their industrial wealth, and their technical skills.[4]

Although Luce wanted people in the United States to overcome provincial feelings of isolationism for the benefit of the rest of the world, some commentators argued that the United States entered international diplomacy through World War II and subsequent military affairs to protect its material attainments. This represented a third form of globalization. For example, in 1970 John M. Swomley, Jr. argued that since 1939 the direction of American foreign policy was to thwart any political change that interfered with narrowly conceived national interests. Thus, he argued that national officials chose to engage in wars and to garrison troops in ways that expanded American control. He noted that American leaders disavowed selfish aims by claiming they sought to defeat fascism or to contain communism.[5]

Swomley claimed that the United States used its military might to protect large companies as they expanded to other parts of the world. Consequently, he considered the United States to be an empire. It had conquered other peoples and established agencies to extract wealth from the subjugated peoples. At the same time, he warned that such dominance was tenuous. Other nations could come to hate the United States because of such impositions.[6]

Some prominent officials in the United States agreed with Swomley's assessment that military might had caused globalization, and they called for renewed military power to guarantee continued worldwide economic domination by the United States. For example, in 1997 officials, including William J. Bennett, Dick Cheney, and Jeb Bush, formed the Project for the New American Century. According to the Project's statement of principles, the United States had won the Cold War and defeated communism. Thus, the statement urged the national government to shape the new century in ways that favored American interests. This meant that politicians should accept the responsibilities of global leadership by creating and maintaining a strong military, and they should pursue foreign policies that supported continued American prosperity.[7]

When commentators concentrated on the spread of culture rather than military power, they offered a fourth definition of globalization. For example, in 2005 John Agnew argued that the word *hegemony* better described the relationship of the United States with the rest of the world than did the word *empire*. To Agnew, empire represented a binding of people around cultural norms that emanated from seats of power occupied by people with authority. This definition implied that the power came from some particular place, whereas the concept of hegemony separated the power from a geographical location. For example, the Roman Empire extended control from a specific city over a particular region for a particular length of time. In contrast, the hegemony of the United States led to what Agnew called globalization. He claimed that economic and cultural activities sped across space and such sharing led to changes and innovations that went beyond the control of authorities in the United States. As a type of globalization, Agnew described the tendency for people in most countries to look to the marketplace to determine what would or should happen. Agnew thought that officials in all societies believed citizens would approve of policies depending on how those practices would influence their material prosperity. Agnew believed the worldwide trend was for officials to eschew moral principles and seek signs of popular acceptance when they advocated policies. He added that levels of mass consumption had risen to the point that people around the globe measured the quality of their lives by the commodities they owned. At the same time, class distinctions remained disguised behind the rhetoric of equal opportunity. Most important, people held visions of themselves as consumers living private lives without the responsibilities to pursue public goods that they had held as citizens.[8]

Agnew acknowledged that United States officials caused many of these changes. For example, during the Cold War, they defended U.S. economic interests. In a similar manner, after the fall of communism, U.S. officials had advanced globalization by seeking to spread capitalism into the former Soviet Union and the People's Republic of China. Ironically, Agnew noted that the changes had weakened U.S. influence. As a result, the United States withdrew from global environmental treaties, it refused to participate in the International Criminal Court, and it invaded Iraq on its own. Consequently, Agnew believed globalization derived from American hegemony rather than from an American empire.[9]

Although the commentators described above disagreed about the nature of globalization, their definitions of globalization shared following three characteristics. The processes of modernization brought about industrial development with concurrent expansion of bureaucratic organization. At the same time, a free economy helped spread these methods and the resulting increases in wealth turned people's attention toward material satisfactions and away from spiritual achievements. Because several commentators associated these tendencies with American democracy, they wrote about an American empire or the American century.

How Does the History of American Education Describe a Process of Globalization?

Although many historians consider colonization as the beginning of globalization, other historians consider the process of more recent origin, mainly reflected in the growth of bureaucratic organizations. Previously, before the U.S. Civil War, Americans distrusted the central government and had a limited faith in education. For example, as the twentieth century opened, Americans began to believe in the benefits of big government. A significant number of Americans hoped that large cities with centrally organized schools would improve conditions for everyone. In part, the growth of large corporations such as railroad companies suggested that the bureaucratic ethos could work for the common good as well as for private gain. Similar changes took place around the world although some authors contended that the United States led the way.

One author who made such a claim was Brooks Adams. In 1903, shortly after the war with Spain, Adams wrote that, in a period of about one hundred years, the United States had risen from a being wilderness on the outskirts of world power to become the heart of civilization. According to Adams, the supremacy of America came from the application of science that created great American corporations. Most important, Adams praised scientific schools for opening the minds of the business leaders who fashioned the industrial success he admired. At the same time, Adams warned that although education enhanced the energy that empowered the United States, colleges could dissipate that force by concentrating on classical academic studies; such lessons taught young people to revere the past rather than to adjust to the future.[10]

In making his claims, Adams expressed his view of a law of historical development. Adams believed that throughout history the center of trade and industry had progressively moved westward, from Constantinople to Venice to Amsterdam to London. Each location became the center as population increased and new techniques of trade and industry appeared. In line with this prediction, Adams argued that the center would be the United States during the twentieth century. He warned that the shift could move further west and Russia might share this dominance.[11]

Adams could not convince other historians that he had found the law of historical change in some western movement. Nonetheless, his ideas had a significant impact and several foreign observers reinforced Adams' perception. For example, in 1902 William Thomas Stead, a British journalist who founded the *Review of Reviews,* noted that the United States had grown into an empire that exceeded the British Empire. Stead claimed there were several causes. The Americans were a young and vigorous race of people who lived in a rich, virgin continent. Because Americans were an amalgam of many other races, they lacked traditions or prejudices that restrained their efforts. Stead praised the ways that Americans concentrated their efforts on industrial pursuits rather than military endeavors or artistic achievements. He believed the Puritan heritage had developed tendencies to work hard and to adopt personal restraint. Above all, Stead considered the American faith in education to be the most important factor. He found that people in the United States looked on education as an investment. As a result, wealthy men contributed to the advancement of schools and poor people sacrificed to provide educations for their children. In the United States, workers were productive because they were educated, Stead wrote. They were energetic because they believed that anyone could rise in wealth and prominence through hard work.[12]

According to Lawrence Cremin, in the twentieth century the United States exported and imported many educational ideas. Among famous American educators who traveled to other lands, Dewey was one of the most well known. There was a wide appeal to the hope that Dewey expressed about schools protecting individual freedoms and establishing the basis for human growth and development. Carrying the message of American progressive education to other countries, Dewey visited Japan and China from 1919 to 1921 where he delivered lectures and visited many schools. Cremin claimed that Dewey's visits made such an impression in China that his views dominated educational discussions until the 1949 revolution. At the same time though, Cremin noted that Americans imported the educational ideas of such figures as Maria Montessori and Sigmund Freud.[13]

Cremin listed three important and related ways that different views went out from and came into the United States. The first was by individuals who moved between countries. Although these individuals included noted figures, many obscure people, such as American missionaries, lived and worked in places around the globe. At the same time, many exchange students came into the United States from continents such as Africa. Whereas they brought their cultural viewpoints to American schools, they returned to their home countries with American educational ideas. The second method of exchange was through the efforts of organized philanthropies, such as the Phelps-Stokes Fund that took the ideas of Booker T. Washington to Africa in the 1920s. The third was the efforts of private businesses such as the many book publishers who sought markets overseas for American books and who imported foreign works to sell in America. After World War II, the federal government spread a circle of libraries overseas filled with American books and printed materials through the United States Information Agency.[14]

This book agrees that the United States enjoyed rapid growth to prominence, but it breaks with Adams' view because it does not try to show that any particular historical law determined the process. Although it agrees that there was a relation between education and increasing world dominance, it does not contend that one sort of educational method or another was most influential. Instead, the book points out how the ideas of a good education changed as education spread across the United States. For example, although classical education became less popular as schools offered more vocational or practical studies, Adams and Stead may have overstated the benefits of vocational training as the fundamental contribution of the United States. The reason is that as shifts in the ideas of education took place, academic education retained its hold as many Americans, including John Dewey, tried to find ways to blend vocational and academic preparation.

What Is the Arrangement of the Various Chapters of This Book?

This book consists of sixteen chapters, including this introduction, that illustrate how Americans borrowed ideas from Europeans, how Europeans took notions from the United States, and, after World War II, how American educators sought to impose their ideas on Japan and Germany. Although the chapters describe events in chronological order, some chapters cover different aspects of the same general period. For example, Chapter 2 covers the colonial period. Chapters 3, 4, and 5 consider different regions of the United States during the new republic and the antebellum period. Once the narrative reaches the end of the nineteenth century and the beginning of twentieth century, regional differences give way to different topics that influenced schools across the country. Thus, although some of the chapters cover the same periods as other chapters, they focus on different types of educational reforms. Perhaps the following brief summary of each chapter will make clear the book's organization and the reasons for any apparent overlapping of chapters.

Although Chapter 2 covers the colonial period, it does not try to describe the efforts of each European country to settle in the New World. Instead, the book suggests that two models stand on opposite ends of a continuum with other colonial powers falling somewhere between them. On one end were the Spanish missions and on the other end were the English colonists. The differences were striking. Whereas the Spanish considered Native Americans as subjects of the Spanish crown, the English treated Native Americans as independent nations. After the War of Independence, officials in the new republic followed the English precedent. As a result, many of the subsequent problems and promises of education of American Indians derived from their unique status as members of foreign nations living within the United States. In short, this chapter offers two important insights. The first is to link globalization with education by identifying the efforts to expand imperial control by educational missions. The second is to suggest that the contradictory influences from these colonial powers may have led to an increasing concern for materialistic goals rather than spiritual development.

In Chapter 3, the reader will find a discussion of education in the new republic that begins with an explanation of the Northwest Ordinance. Although many historians contended that this act set the precedent for state funding and control of public elementary and secondary schools, this chapter disagrees. Instead, this text treats the ordinance as the first effort of the new republic to expand its borders. Although schools played important roles in these efforts, the ordinance may have influenced people's perception of the role of schools more than the ways to support them. In 1789, the national government considered schools a means to attract the proper type of settler to the West. By 1830 settlers in cities such as Cincinnati, Ohio, considered schools as means to reform the newly arrived Catholic immigrants. Although both hopes failed, they depended on the development of a central state authority to control education.

Chapter 4 covers what many historians called the "common school" movement in the North. In this part of the United States, advocates of common schools sought state control of education. Their critics argued that state administration of schools violated the democratic principles of local control. Rather than confront these arguments directly, common school advocates made efforts to improve the architecture of schools, the design of curriculums, and the training of teachers. According to the common school supporters, local districts could not respond to these needs. The point is that the common school movement moved schools in the direction of wider state control and bureaucratic organization that became the mark of modernization and globalization even though advocates of common schools did not make these choices clear to the public.

Chapter 5 considers the same historical period as the previous chapter and the same effort to establish common schools. The difference is that Chapter 5 concentrates on the antebellum South. Although many historians complained that Southerners did not establish educational systems, this chapter contends that there were many different types of schools available. Furthermore, many friends of education in the South sought to create a state system of schools in ways that imitated the efforts of common school advocates in the North. Although the South was unique in that it lacked the manufacturing and urban centers that sped the common school movement in the North, reformers in the South sought to establish state-supported schools by concentrating on the need for trained teachers and regular curriculums. In this way, advocates of common schools made acceptable bureaucratic organization and uniformity later associated with globalization.

Chapter 6 opens a new period. After the American Civil War, the former Confederacy underwent three phases of change. During Reconstruction, the federal government sought to reorganize the Southern states. Because white Southerners perceived the radical Republicans in the U.S. Congress as imposing Northern systems on them, they called for home rule. Northerners believed their actions protected the newly freed slaves from exploitation. After federal forces withdrew in 1877, Southerners considered the return to self-rule as "the Redemption." Since the term *self-rule* applied only to white men, racial antagonisms increased and conservatives limited industrial development and education. By the 1890s, boosters of the New South claimed the racial problems had ended. Although reforms were limited and the entire area suffered from underdevelopment, Southerners made significant strides in advancing the development of cities and manufacturing that were the marks of the new industrial age and subsequent globalization.

In Chapter 7, readers will find descriptions of the attempt to build a new order in the North and the Midwest after the Civil War. In organizing schools, reformers sought to change the definition of democracy from an emphasis on local relationships to a way of life that encompassed the entire nation. Although these efforts were not entirely successful, educators formed a national organization to spread information about schools. The federal government established a national office to aid in this effort. At the same time, school curriculums expanded. Educators claimed the best way to solve the problems in urban and rural schools was through the training of teachers and the bureaucratic organization of schools that followed the same rules in all places. Thus, the shifts served the development of impersonal ways of acting that are associated with globalization.

Chapter 8 describes the drive for consolidation and rational planning to solve social problems that characterized the period from 1880 to 1917, sometimes called the Progressive Era. The model for progressive urban reform was the business trusts that had developed, and educators adopted the same idea. School districts grew through consolidation. Although the public had less control over boards of education, those board members thought they could expand curriculums in ways that served the interests of the citizenry. Thus, the drive to overcome the problems of large business trusts was that all aspects of life including schools adopted the bureaucratic methods that made trusts possible.

Chapter 9 covers the same general period as the previous chapter. It describes how W. T. Harris and John Dewey offered coherent philosophies of education to shape instruction. Borrowing heavily from German idealism, Harris and Dewey shared many central concepts that they hoped could turn schools in humane directions. Other educators, such as Marietta Johnson of the Organic School and William Wirt who constructed the Platoon School in Gary, Indiana, wanted to change public schools but did not offer coherent ideas of education. As a result, their rebellions could not spread beyond a limited scope or they reinforced the problems of bureaucratic organization that they sought to reduce. Margaret Naumberg, who studied in Germany and Italy, adopted a psychoanalytic model; she founded the Children's School because she found excessive authoritarianism in the traditional ideas of Harris and in the progressive schools of Dewey and Johnson. In short, although European ideas influenced American schools in many ways, they did not deter the general progress toward increased bureaucratic control of schools and in some ways advanced it.

Chapter 10 extends the discussion of progressive education to the Great Depression by covering a different reform effort than the type discussed in Chapter 9. Seeking to relieve administrators from political pressure by concentrating on scientific aspects of education, Edward L. Thorndike and Charles H. Judd created educational psychology. To some extent, Thorndike and Judd followed the work of G. Stanley Hall. They applied German psychological ideas in ways that would make traditional academic teaching more effective. In their hands, educational psychology focused on the ways that children learned, thereby ignoring the relation the school had to its social setting. In making this effort, educational psychologists followed a conception of science that became popular in Britain during the Victorian Age, which was the view that narrow scientific improvements would accumulate in ways to bring about morally beneficial results to society. Although the scientists wanted to protect educators from political interference, their search for the best way to conduct classes and arrange curriculums may have increased administrators' demands that teachers adhere to bureaucratic requirements.

Chapter 11 extends the discussion of progressive education reform to describe the efforts of reformers who sought to use findings of educational psychologists to revise the system of elementary, secondary, and professional education. Although the movement for the "economy of time" began with complaints that students had to stay in school too long, the reformers expanded their efforts to broaden the curriculum and diversify studies. In seeking to shorten school programs and to make the classes relevant to social life, these educators enjoyed the most success in influencing the organization of secondary schools. They developed a uniquely American model called the *comprehensive high school* that was to allow students to pursue their particular vocational interests while learning skills and attitudes essential to life in a democracy. Because the committees for the economy of time concluded that many academic subjects such as classical languages served no purpose, Latin teachers, mathematics instructors, and teachers of modern foreign languages formed their own associations and conducted their own studies to show how those subjects could meet the needs of the community. As a result, these academic teachers changed curriculums to coincide with the drive for efficiency and social relevance.

In Chapter 12, readers will find a discussion of educators who sought to allow students to follow their own interests. Although these educators wanted to apply science to education, they took a different definition of science and democracy than did the reformers described in Chapter 11. Instead of trying to make the curriculum socially relevant, these educators designed a curriculum to enable students to acquire democratic attitudes. Applying the name *project method* to their model, these educators advanced the widely popular activity movement that influenced curriculums in elementary schools in the United States and around the world. For example, the Soviet Union adopted a version of the project method to consolidate the gains of the revolution. It appeared in several schools in Britain and France. In 1932 the Progressive Education Association (PEA) wanted to show that high school students could profit from the model. They constructed an experiment to see if students could succeed in college if their school had followed such a curriculum. From the PEA's study, the model became part of efforts during the New Deal to bring about reforms for Native Americans. In these ways, American educators spread an American conception of democracy to other peoples.

During the Great Depression and the postwar years, educators sought to rectify social ills. In this campaign, educators imitated the approach that the popular U.S. President Franklin Roosevelt took to cope with domestic and international problems. They formed independent commissions. The story of the efforts of such commissions from 1930 to the late 1950s is the subject of Chapter 13. Although not directly involved with educational organizations, these commissions, such as the EPC, sought to gather information from a wide variety of sources and to recommend practical policies educators could adopt. Educators also served on educational missions with the U.S. forces of occupation seeking to impose American models of the comprehensive high school and socially relevant curriculums on the defeated countries of Japan and Germany as antidotes to dictatorships. Another independent agency, UNESCO, sought to apply ideas from the Progressive Education Association to the problems of adult literacy in developing countries. In these ways, prominent American educators attempted to spread American conceptions of democracy and appropriate schooling to other parts of the world.

In Chapter 14, readers will find descriptions of three types of educational reforms that took place in the United States from the end of World War II to the time of the civil rights movement. Unlike the efforts to spread American educational ideals, such foreign affairs as the Cold War instigated these domestic reforms. The first was to encourage an appreciation for democracy among students. The second reform was to change the curriculum to produce elite scientists who could improve military defenses. The third reform was to end the racial discrimination found in schools so that people in foreign countries could see that Americans lived up to their ideals. This required that schools racially desegregate. The link between poverty and segregation encouraged the federal government to pass the Elementary and Secondary Education Act (ESEA) offering financial support to help schools break the cycle of poverty. Although the forms and content of these three reforms differed from each other, they shared the same inspiration to defeat communism at home and abroad.

In 1969 the national mood changed and people turned away from concerns for civil rights and away from the belief that the United States should act as the guardian of world peace. Despite this shift, federal officials continued to recommend educational reforms that they thought would address foreign affairs. Thus, Chapter 15 describes the ways that the racial desegregation of schools slowed and how political leaders recommended that teachers pay increased attention to basic academic instruction. The hope was that increased attention to academic skills would produce effective workers who could help enable American factories and businesses to compete with foreign industries. When these recommendations failed, political leaders sought mechanisms to enable parents to select their children's schools. During the 1990s, advocates of parent choice claimed that these reforms would enable schools to advance democracy. As in Chapter 14, federal officials suggested educational reforms to strengthen the position of the United States in the world market.

Chapter 16 is a summary of the ways historians and historians of education approach their work. The chapter shows that both groups changed their methods and their aims as times changed and that they changed in parallel fashions. Thus, during the civil rights movement, some historians tried to explain the situations of disenfranchised groups and several historians of education focused on the development of education for those groups. Because the methods the author used in this book derive from some of the approaches to the study of history described in this chapter, the reader can see how this effort builds on other similar endeavors.

Through this collection of brief summaries of the various chapters, the reader should recognize that the relation between education and globalization was not simple or direct.

These chapters do not describe the transition from one form of schooling to another to directly facilitate the spread of industries and the domination of corporate capitalism. Instead, during many periods, various forms of educational reform developed simultaneously. It is not fair to say that these reformers competed with each other. Although each curriculum model sought to reinforce democracy, advocates held different conceptions of what democracy was and how schools should reinforce it. Nonetheless, the various groups of advocates sought to cooperate with each other and produce a model that incorporated all their different ideas. For example, while one group of educators wanted to make school subjects socially useful, another group wanted to build lessons on children's interests. Both groups thought they held democratic ideals. The former, or adult-centered theories, depends on a notion of democracy where students learn skills that adults need to contribute to society. The latter, or child-centered theories, follows a conception of democracy wherein adults pursue their interests. With the model of the comprehensive high school, educators tried to blend both views of democracy by arranging the curriculums so that students could pursue their interests in ways that advanced the common good.

Although it may appear that Americans exported institutional arrangements and their rationales, the exchanges may have taken place naturally because every government had to face similar conditions. For example, by 1918 every state then in the United States adopted laws requiring children to attend elementary schools at public expense. The hope was that free compulsory elementary education would enable children to adapt to and flourish in a rapidly changing industrial country. This idea became an explicit belief among Americans who came to think of schools as institutions that could solve social problems ranging from automobile driving to teenage pregnancy. In line with the faith that education could relieve social problems, the United Nations formed its Educational, Scientific, and Cultural Organization (UNESCO) in 1946 to promote education as a human right. UNESCO's initial emphasis was to rebuild the schools, libraries, and museums destroyed during World War II. When less-developed countries joined the United Nations, UNESCO devoted more of its resources to enhance economic development through literacy programs. Thus, UNESCO linked the fight against poverty with increased education.

In its origins, UNESCO's effort to make education a human right suggested that people of all ages should receive such training. In 1990, UNESCO and other organizations changed the emphasis at the World Conference on Education for All (EFA). The following organizations sponsored the conference: UNESCO, the United Nations Children's Fund (formerly the United Nations International Children's Emergency Fund, UNICEF), the World Bank, and the United Nations Development Programme (UNDPE). At this conference, participants accepted the plan of EFA. They agreed to turn the emphasis of educational aid work to ensure that children received primary education.[15]

The mandate for EFA increased in 2000 during a meeting held in Dakar, Senegal, when delegates from 164 governments approved six goals. The first was to expand and improve early childhood care and education. The second goal required that by 2015 all children, particularly girls, would have access to free compulsory primary education. The third goal was for the training to be appropriate in helping children develop important life skills. To ensure that education was for all, the fourth goal required that all countries improve adult literacy rates by 50 percent, especially among women. The fifth and sixth goals called for an end to gender disparities in elementary and secondary school attendance and for education to focus on improving basic academic skills so that all children became literate and numerate. In agreeing to these goals, the conference members accepted the notion that schooling would advance the economic, social, and political development of the countries. It would enhance human capabilities, lead to improvement in health, increase family planning, and reduce such ills as poverty and AIDS.[16]

The proposal of the World Conference on Education for All repeated the faith that had fueled the drive for compulsory, public supported education in the United States. Unfortunately, the American model may be a faulty plan. For example, Henry Perkinson noted that educators in the United States claimed schools would solve several individual and social problems. When he compiled accounts of how educators had urged the spread of schools from 1865 to 1990, he found that people asserted that schools would reduce the problems of racial inequality, urban blight, inequitable distribution of wealth, and political corruption. More interesting, failure did not dampen the faith. Although racism, suburban sprawl, poverty, and political ineptitude continued unabated, Perkinson noted that educators continued to assert that the answer was to increase educational efforts rather than try another direction.[17]

According to Maxine Greene, schools did not reduce social problems in the United States because the motive for the spread of education was an unexamined form of freedom. Greene complained that everyone in the United States seemed to agree that education could increase people's freedom and this would make the world better. Unfortunately, people seemed to equate improvement with material gains. Educators spoke about the various things schools could teach as increasing freedoms. In reality, educators considered helping children to adjust to the demands of society and enabling them to be productive citizens as means that would give them the freedom to possess increased wealth. As a result, Greene contended that educators proposed solutions for the problems of poverty or AIDS that ignored shared norms and values except material prosperity. She concluded that those difficulties would continue until there was serious talk of reconstituting a civic order permeated by feelings of community.[18]

What Limits the Discussions in This Book?

Although this text reinforces Greene's observation about the direction of educational change, it cannot evaluate whether Greene is correct in her prescription to remedy the ills that beset reform efforts. Instead, the text explains how educational ideas have changed and spread around the world.

Because the book seeks to trace the educational ideas within the United States that fed into the movement toward the current conditions of globalization, the book has to cover a wide range of material. Ironically, the approach restricts the material the book can cover. For example, the book does not offer a wide-ranging description of the educational practices found throughout the country or the world. For example, it cannot celebrate the different educational practices of diverse cultures such as extensive descriptions of the ways that some Native Americans passed their culture to young people before the European colonists arrived. Although such descriptions are valuable, this book focuses on the ways that some forms of schooling advanced social changes that took place. Other forms of schooling may appear as they resisted those patterns that survived and spread.

At the same time, the book follows the changes in ideas about education. As a result, it draws on other historians' works and general assessments of changes that went on in society. Instead of collecting evidence of what happened in the many classrooms, many of the original sources come from papers or accounts of leading educators of the times. Thus, the book offers an intellectual history that records views of curriculum, philosophy, and school architecture to show shifts in educational perspectives.

In the accounts of educational reforms, the book describes the ways educators and members of minority groups influenced each other. These include the treatment of Native Americans and efforts to end racial discrimination. In selecting appropriate language for such descriptions, the author followed *The Chicago Manual of Style* that suggests a text should not display biased language because anything suggesting the author harbors prejudices may distract or offend readers. *The Chicago Manual* adds that calling attention to efforts to avoid bias by using stilted and awkward constructions can offend readers as well. The manual recommends that authors avoid biased language unless the terms are central to the meaning of the passages.[19]

In following these simple rules, the author tried to use terms the Chicago Manual listed as appropriate. Thus, readers will find terms such as *Native American, American Indian,* or *African American*. In a few places that refer to the writings of Puritans, the word *Indian* appears because this was the term those writers used. This word also appears when the popular term for government policies included it, such as the *Indian New Deal.* Similarly, the word *gentleman* appears in chapters on colonial education to refer to men of particular rank, and in those chapters that include paraphrases of work of W. E. Burghardt Du Bois, the word *Negro* appears in the manner that Du Bois used this term.

In a similar manner, the author adopted the Chicago Manual's list of appropriate historical terms. For example, readers will find the terms *American Civil War* and *the War between the States* referring to what some historians once called the *War of Rebellion.* Similarly, the text uses terms such as *American War of Independence, American Revolution,* and *Revolution* to refer to the break that took place between the colonies and Britain.

Some geographical names follow the conditions of the period the passages describe. For example, descriptions of events that took place before 1707 when England, Wales, and Scotland joined to form the United Kingdom of Great Britain may carry the term *English* whereas discussions that concern events after 1707 carry the term *British.* Finally, explanations of education after the Russian Revolution of 1917 may carry the term *Soviet Union* and events before 1917 or after 1991 may refer to Russia.

Many readers will notice that this book covers roughly the same material found in other texts on the history of education. As described in Chapter 16, one popular approach among these texts is to demonstrate that schools have advanced various forms of cultural domination. Another common approach is to describe a wide range of efforts that educators made to improve schools, suggesting that whatever domination occurred may not have arisen from racism or elitism. Although the former method offers coherence, it omits considerable evidence that might weaken the point. The latter method compensates by giving a more comprehensive view of educational changes at the expense of a coherent theme.

The view that directs this work is that although schools may have participated in some forms of cultural domination, this was not the intended result of many reforms. Instead, this book argues that oftentimes cultural domination was the unintended consequence of an effort to use technology and bureaucracy to increase people's freedoms. The effort was ironic because technology limits personal choices to the most effective and bureaucracy implies that superiors control the behavior of their subordinates. Thus, this book will turn away from attempts to show that particular notions of education grew to reinforce the position of one group or another. Although this may have happened, the more interesting alternative is that people selected new models to handle social difficulties without realizing the problems that could ensue.

The descriptions of how American educators interacted with teachers in other countries, such as the Soviet Union, Japan, and Germany, derive from explanations of the changes in the philosophy and the science of education and the rise of bureaucratic systems of schools. As a result, this book offers considerable information about changes in curriculum, educational administration, and teaching practices. Although curriculum and instruction are central to school life, educational history texts often omit such subjects, and curriculum texts treat superficially the development of ideas about what constitutes proper teaching.

To aid readers, the book offers three features. First, questions introduce the sections of each chapter. The table of contents lists these questions to form a sentence outline of the book. Second, each chapter has a theme that offers a pattern so readers can fit particular pieces of information into a meaningful whole. To aid in such integration, the introductions and the conclusions to each chapter point out the relationships the chapters have to the whole book. Third, at the end of each chapter, a summary repeats the argument in condensed form.

Endnotes

1. John Dewey, *The School and Society and the Child and the Curriculum* (Chicago: University of Chicago Press, 1990), 8–9.
2. John Dewey, *Democracy and Education: An Introduction to the Philosophy of Education* (1916; reprint, New York: Free Press, 1997), 36–37, 223–225.
3. John Dewey, *The Public and Its Problems.* (New York: H. Holt and Co., 1927), 205–209.
4. Henry R. Luce, "The American Century," *Life* (17 February 1941): 61–65.
5. John M. Swomley, *American Empire: Political Ethics of Twentieth Century Conquest* (London: Macmillan Co., 1970), 230–231.
6. Swomley, *American Empire,* 244.
7. Project for the New American Century, *Statement of Principles,* www.newamericancentury.org/statementofprinciples.htm (accessed 12 September 2004).
8. John Agnew, *Hegemony: The New Shape of Global Power* (Philadelphia: Temple University Press, 2005), 1–3.
9. Agnew, *Hegemony,* 3–8.
10. Brooks Adams, *The New Empire* (New York: The Macmillan Co., 1903), xi–xxxvi, 210–211.
11. Marquis W. Childs, "Evaluation," in *America's Economic Supremacy,* ed. Brooks Adams (1947; reprint, Freeport, N.Y.: Books for Libraries Press, 1971), 2–8.
12. William Thomas Stead, *The Americanization of the World or The Trend of the Twentieth Century* (New York: Garland Publishing, Inc., 1972), 7–14, 147–150.
13. Lawrence A. Cremin, *American Education: The Metropolitan Experience, 1876–1980* (New York: Harper & Row, Publishers, 1988), 10–12, 675–679.
14. Cremin, *American Education,* 679–684.
15. Colette Chabbott, "Constructing Educational Consensus: International Development Professionals and the World Conference on Education for All," *International Journal of Educational Development* 18, no. 3 (1998): 207–218.
16. EFA Global Monitoring Report Team, *Literacy for Life: Summary* (Paris: UNESCO, 2006), 1–3.
17. Henry Perkinson, *The Imperfect Panacea: American Faith in Education, 1865–1900* (New York: McGraw-Hill, 1991).
18. Maxine Greene, *The Dialectic of Freedom* (New York: Teachers College Press, 1988), 2–4.
19. University of Chicago Press, *Chicago Manual of Style,* 15th ed. (Chicago: University of Chicago, 2003), 233.

2

Education in Colonial America

Spanish Southwest mission-style chapel, seventeenth century

To justify establishing colonies in the New World, Europeans claimed it was an educational effort. For example, Isabella and Ferdinand, rulers during part of the Hapsburg dynasty in Spain, contended that they sent Christopher Columbus across the seas as part of their efforts to spread Christianity. In keeping with this spirit, other Spanish Hapsburg emperors required that soldiers, who invaded the villages and cities of indigenous peoples, and *encomederos,* who forced captives to labor on farms, provide spiritual enlightenment to the Native Americans in their charge.

In a similar manner, the English colonial effort began as an educational mission. Those settlers who sought to populate Virginia expressed the desire of evangelizing Native Americans. Although the Puritan settlers who came to New England had a different motive, they expressed an educational desire as well. In England, they feared the Reformation had not gone far enough. Unable to remove the remaining influences of the Catholic faith, the Puritans conceived of their errand into the wilderness as an effort to reinforce among themselves their own views of appropriate religious practices and thereby shine over the world as a light upon a hill.

Dutch and French settlers followed variations of the educational missions of Spain and England when they came to the future United States. The different approaches to colonial education might be said to fall on a continuum, with Spain and England illustrating the two distinct poles of European efforts to transmit their culture to the New World. For this reason the rest of this chapter considers the Spanish missions and the English colonists.

Although historians acknowledged that Spanish colonialists established schools and universities before and more extensively throughout South America and Mexico than did the English in the United States, the general view was that education came to the United States from England and spread westward. This view overlooked the influence of Spanish missions in the Southwest. This oversight was unfortunate because the differences between the colonial efforts of Spain and England may have led to the vacillations that took place in the nineteenth and twentieth centuries when the federal government sought to establish schools for Native Americans. That is, according to some historians, the effect of the Spanish view of Native American education, that the American Indians learned to advance their cause within the larger society. The English view, on the other hand, caused Americans to consider the Native Americans as belonging to separate nations that lived within the same country.

What Was the Spanish Colonial Empire?

According to Edward Gaylord Bourne, the Spanish thought of colonies as part of an empire. Thus, the Spanish crown considered indigenous people to be subjects, and they applied this conception to all groups who came under Spanish control. Consequently, when Spanish explorers conquered a tribal group that had ruled over other Native Americans, everyone that tribe had controlled came under the protection of the Spanish crown. On the other hand, Bourne noted, England established small settlements of colonialists who acted on their own. Consequently, English colonists tended to consider the Native American groups to be independent nations that took their chances in a struggle for survival with other tribal groups and with the English themselves.[1]

The rulers of Spain, Ferdinand and Isabella, described their educational aims when they wrote a letter informing Pope Alexander VI, who was a Spaniard, of Columbus's voyage and its results. Unable to send an expedition across the seas while engaged with the war in Grenada, they had issued Columbus a patent for the voyage when they succeeded in driving out the last armies of the Moors and unifying the Iberian peninsular under the Catholic faith. They told the pope that they had sent Columbus to search for islands not known to Europeans; to search for gold, silver, and spices there; and to introduce Christianity to the inhabitants.[2]

Seeking to spread the gospel, Spanish rulers moved the process of colonization along quickly. In 1493, Columbus brought the news to Europe that he had sighted the Bahamas.

Although Columbus may not have brought a priest on his first voyage, on his second trip he returned to the islands in seventeen ships carrying 1500 men, a few horses, some cattle, various vegetables, quantities of seeds for crops, and four priests with the necessary equipment to set up a church. As a result, the religious celebrated their first mass in the colony named Isabella, on the island that Columbus called Española, which is today divided between the Dominican Republic and Haiti. From this settlement, explorers made further excursions into surrounding areas, spreading the faith as they went.[3]

In recognition of the evangelical educational efforts of the Spanish crown, Pope Julius II issued a bull, or papal decree, *Universalis ecclesiae,* in 1508 granting the kings of Spain the authority to oversee the construction of all churches and the right to select the priests who would preside over those churches. Queen Isabella having died in 1504, the pope expressed the hope that Ferdinand and his daughter Juana would purge the lands now called New Spain of what he termed false and pernicious rites and plant the true religion.[4]

Although Charles V (1516–1556), grandson of Ferdinand and Isabella, gave full liberty to the subjects of his realms all over Europe to enter the colonies, by the time of Phillip II (1556–1598), son of Charles V, no one was supposed to enter the colonies without permission from the crown. The aim of this policy was to prevent foreigners from spreading error among the Native Americans.[5]

According to Anthony Pagden, the Hapsburg rulers of Spain wanted to unify the world as had the Roman emperors. Since the Spanish crown acquired, in one generation, more new territory than Rome conquered in five centuries, it seemed possible that the Spanish empire could extend across the entire globe. Although Spain never attained world domination, the Spanish colonial empire lasted three centuries in the Americas. This was almost as long as imperial Rome had dominated Western Europe. In that time, Spain transplanted its language, religion, culture, and political institutions to an area that was about twenty times larger than it was.[6]

The pattern of colonization was simple. From the islands where Columbus had begun, the colonists followed the military to the mainland that they called New Spain. By 1574 poverty reigned over the islands while comfort and civilization prevailed in the city of Mexico (Mexico City), as evidenced by public buildings, churches, high schools, and hospitals. The city of Lima, capital of Peru, enjoyed substantial wealth as well although with fewer institutions of formal education. From these centers, the empire spread north and south as settlers sought to discover wealth and to Christianize the indigenous peoples.

How Did Spain Transmit Its Culture?

Within mainland cities, formal schools played an important role in spreading Spanish culture. In 1553, the Spanish colonists created the Royal and Pontifical University of Mexico. Designed to imitate the University of Salamanca in Spain, the new university had seven academic chairs—theology, scripture, canons, the arts of logic and metaphysics, laws, decretals or the study of papal decrees, and rhetoric. Some of the professors occupying these chairs had studied under prestigious scholars in Spain. A similar institute of higher learning opened in Peru, and these two universities served as the models for the twenty-one universities that Spain established in the New World during the colonial period. In addition, some colleges and seminaries provided formal education without granting university degrees.[7]

In addition to religious education, the universities established chairs of medicine. In 1570, Phillip II of Spain sent royal physicians, *protomédicos,* to govern the medical profession in New Spain. Seeking to create a natural history of medicine, he charged these *protomédicos* to collect and send back information about local herbs and medicines. By 1579 they held the power to examine and license physicians, surgeons, and people who drew blood from patients; later, this authority went to a committee of civil servants. At least by 1585 a board led by a professor who occupied a university's chair of medicine assumed the power to grant medical credentials.[8]

Native Americans of pure race could enter the universities and the colleges because they were subjects of His Catholic Majesty. Some institutions barred the admittance of people with mixed parentage until 1804. Finally, all racial restrictions on university entrance ended in the Spanish colonies by 1812.[9]

In addition to institutions of higher learning, the crown and the church established primary schools beside churches. As in the case of medieval churches in Spain, a considerable amount of the religious instruction took place through pictures and drawings. At the same time, the missionaries sought to produce written forms of the native languages and use these to teach indigenous people to read and write. Workshops taught Native Americans trades of carpentry, blacksmithing, and painting.[10]

Despite the concern for schools, the primary means by which Spain transmitted its culture to Native Americans was through its notions of imperial domain. As the empire spread, the crown demanded that explorers and settlers recognize the humanity of the Native Americans and to affirm their status as subjects of the crown. By 1514 the Spanish authorities found a way to reconcile their military ventures with Christian aims. They made every military leader carry a copy of a message called the *Requerimiento* into battle. Before hostilities began, a Spanish soldier read this message in Spanish to the Native Americans. It presented a short summary of Christian history and demanded that the Native Americans recognize the authority of the Catholic Church, the pope, and the Spanish crown. The document warned that if the Native Americans failed to accept these conditions, they would be traitors and soldiers could seize their property and imprison them.[11]

By defining warfare as a punishment for traitors, the *Requerimiento* sought to make conquest an educational effort. Nonetheless, critics such as Bartolomé de Las Casas found the idea misguided. Believing that force was unnecessary in education, Las Casas offered to settle a section of what became Guatemala without military assistance. In the 1530s, Las Casas and his colleagues took a few months to win a peaceful conversion. This impressed Charles V who halted further conquests in 1550 and heard testimony about the need for military force. In 1573, Philip II issued the Royal Orders for New Discoveries prohibiting conquest or violence against the indigenous peoples and calling for pacification by members of religious orders instead.[12]

The alternative to military conquests came from a system started by Columbus to extract wealth from the colonies and to convert the Native Americans to Christianity. In punishment for a revolt, Native Americans had to provide labor on the Spanish farms of the Spanish settlers. The system of *encomienda* meant that a Spanish colonist held in trust the land and the labor of the Native Americans who lived in the towns clustered on that tract. The Spanish colonists as *encomederos* had to render military protection, education, and spiritual guidance to the Native Americans. Unfortunately, the *encomiendas* turned into a form of slavery. In 1512 to 1513, Ferdinand issued the Laws of Burgos to limit excessive cruelty and exploitation on the *encomiendas*. Unfortunately, local officials could not enforce the laws. After a series of extensive protests by Las Casas, Charles V issued an order in 1520 forbidding the establishment of new *encomiendas*.[13]

To strengthen the appeals, Pope Paul III issued *Sublimis Deus* in 1537 to reaffirm the human capacities of the Native Americans and their spiritual equality with Spaniards. In his declaration, the pope wrote that Christ had told the preachers of the faith to go and teach all nations. The pope added that Christ considered all people, without exception, capable of receiving the doctrines of the faith. He accused anyone who asserted that Native Americans were dumb brutes suitable for service to Spaniards of being an enemy of the human race.[14]

Despite the legal efforts to eliminate slavery, the practice of issuing *encomiendas* continued. Local conditions slowed their use, though. On the one hand, soldiers demanded *encomiendas* as rewards for their services in conquering new territory for the empire. The system of *encomiendas* worked easily in areas where Native American had established towns. A Spanish colonist could take control of an area, leave the Native American organization untouched, and rule through the tribal chieftains. On the other hand, problems arose on the frontiers of the empire where there were no fixed villages, where wild tribes threatened settlers, and where no one grew crops. In these areas, missions took the place of *encomiendas*. Although the two institutions followed similar systems of organization, a Spanish colonist governed an *encomienda* while a vowed religious directed a mission.[15]

How Did the Missions Play an Educational Role?

In the twentieth century, American historians devoted attention to the educational roles the missions played in the Southwest. During the 1850s, shortly after the United States had acquired California and the large New Mexico territory, authors characterized this area as a place lacking in history. To correct this oversight, Hubert Howe Bancroft, a wealthy bookstore owner, decided in 1859 to collect information about the region. Bancroft amassed an enormous collection of manuscripts, newspapers, and recorded interviews with pioneers. From this information, Bancroft wrote thirty-nine volumes of a history of the area.[16]

Part of the reason that historians ignored the Southwest was that they concentrated on the American Revolution and the development of democracy. In general, they advanced the idea that civilization came to the United States from Teutonic origins through England and spread like germs from the Atlantic colonies.[17]

In 1893, Frederick Jackson Turner proposed that the peculiarity of American institutions arose from the fact that people had to develop their societies anew as they spread across the country. Although Turner accepted the view that European life entered the continent from the Atlantic, he argued that the various frontiers that pioneers encountered modified what he called European "germs" and changed them into uniquely American institutions. Turner added that, as the frontier moved westward, the resulting institutions became more and more American as settlers exchanged European methods for the simpler ways of planting and fighting used by Indians. According to Turner, the various frontiers enhanced feelings of individualism and individual initiative. At the same time, he noted that New England preachers and schoolteachers shaped the hearts, minds, and consciences of the settlers across the land by establishing missions and Western colleges.[18]

In the 1940s, historians criticized Turner for ignoring larger economic and industrial issues or for relying on vague terms.[19] Nonetheless, Turner was instrumental in helping historians overcome excessive concern with developments that spread exclusively from the Atlantic region. In 1917, Herbert E. Bolton proposed a modest revision of Turner's thesis. Using the information that Bancroft had collected, Bolton argued that the people who settled the frontiers had not marched across empty wilderness. Those wildernesses had often previously been the frontiers of other European countries.[20]

In a paper entitled "The Mission as a Frontier Institution in the Spanish-American Colonies," Bolton suggested that the broad area that stretched from Florida to California shaped the development of American economic and political institutions in ways that differed from the influences Turner described as part of the advance of the Anglo-American frontier. Moving into the Southwest from Mexico, Spanish missions advanced the purposes of the Spanish crown toward the Native Americans. Bolton claimed these purposes included the desire to convert the Native Americans, the wish to civilize them, and the need to exploit them.[21]

Bolton noted that three groups of missionaries established the borderland missions: Franciscans who worked in New Mexico and Texas, Jesuits who worked in western Mexico and California, and Dominicans who worked in Lower California. Although they had religious aims, they performed more than religious duties. In addition to spreading faith, they served as agents charged by the state to civilize and educate the Native Americans. Since Native Americans tolerated their presence, missionaries could go into inhabited areas where soldiers would be attacked. Thus, missionaries often explored regions. Once missionaries constructed a mission, it could serve as a fort protecting a region against hostile tribes. Bolton claimed that every well-built mission consisted of a great court protected on all sides by buildings with walls that were eight feet thick. From these fortresses, missionaries sent reports about activities in their areas. According to Bolton, this did not mean the missionaries were hypocritical in their religious efforts. It was only by serving the government that the missions could acquire aid to continue, although they also tried to support themselves through agriculture and raising livestock.[22]

According to Bolton, there were not enough Spanish colonists to move into the borderlands. Consequently, the Spanish missionaries sought to change the Native Americans into civilized Spanish residents. The essence of the mission was to impart to the indigenous peoples discipline in moral, religious, social, and industrial forms. For this reason, the Spanish mission could not work as the French did by moving with transient groups. The central feature of a Spanish mission was a Native American pueblo or village. Thus, in places such as California where the Native Americans lived in small nomadic groups, the missionaries moved them into large congregations similar to the *encomiendas*.[23]

Although missions had different religious sponsors and existed in distinct regional conditions, they shared many characteristics. In each case, the missionaries wanted to create communities of Native Americans who obeyed the priests in secular and spiritual matters. When a missionary moved Native Americans who lived in open, unregulated conditions into towns or villages, the first building they erected was a church. At the same time, the missionary organized the community by appointing a Native American to be governor or mayor and selecting judges who maintained law and order.[24]

In many cases, the missionaries introduced an entirely new economic order. They brought in horses, sheep, and cattle; they introduced irrigation systems and planted new crops of beans, cotton, and corn. As the mission grew, they opened blacksmith shops to make farm implements such as plows and weaving shops to make cloth that could become European clothes. In these ways, the missions strove to be self-sufficient communities that paid tribute to the Spanish crown. In many cases, they avoided such taxes, though.[25]

The missions grew rapidly. By 1762 missions in Texas offered extensive farms, workshops, metal works, and textile shops. Houses on the mission had high beds, chests, and domestic utensils such as pots and kettles. Four missions in Texas held about 5,000 cattle and 12,000 sheep and goats.[26]

Most missions had similar types of inhabitants. As a rule, each mission had two missionaries, although many missionaries lived alone. When soldiers lived with the missionaries, they were to provide protection and discipline for the Native Americans. Unfortunately, these soldiers could cause trouble when they acted in immoral or insubordinate ways. Most missions included about three Native American families who had lived on other missions to act as teachers and as examples to the new recruits.[27]

Bolton concluded that the Spanish missions in the borderlands spread the Christian faith, taught the Native Americans Spanish, disciplined them in good manners, and introduced self-government. Thus, he decided that the missions were an educational institution that preserved the American Indians. In these ways, he found the approach the missions took toward the Native Americans to be superior to the way that English settlers treated the American Indians.[28]

Despite Bolton's appraisal of the educational role the missions played, the missions faced four dilemmas that made it impossible for them to succeed. These included resistance from the Native Americans that necessitated military force, changes in the Spanish administration of the colonies, the deaths of the Native Americans from cross-cultural contact, and a conflict of means and ends.

The first factor that weakened missions on the Spanish borderlands was the resistance of Native Americans. To some extent, the missionaries incited the rebellions they faced. In 1962, the anthropologist Edward H. Spicer claimed that although well-organized missions functioned as peaceful nondisruptive instruments of cultural change, this ideal pattern did not exist everywhere. For example, in New Mexico, Native Americans had their own villages and their own agriculture. In these regions, the priests lived apart from the towns and brought religious instruction. Although the law of the Indies enjoined the missionaries to learn the language of the people and seminaries set up professorships in indigenous languages, it was no easy task when there were many different distinct dialects in the same region. Worse, some Christian concepts did not exist in native languages. For such reasons, many missionaries in New Mexico used Spanish as the language of instruction and asked interpreters to translate their words. Worse, they engaged in a rigorous practice of destroying Native American religious objects and prohibiting native rituals.[29]

According to Spicer, such impositions by priests led to acts of resistance; every group violently resisted the Spaniards at some time. Spicer found that Native American and Spanish encounters passed through a general pattern containing three phases. At first, the Spanish established themselves in forts or in missions, enjoying friendly relations with the indigenous peoples. As the Spanish instituted controls over the Native Americans, some potential converts resisted and violence followed. To quell the revolts, the Spanish military entered to regain control, and the defeated American Indians accepted domination.[30]

Although Spicer blamed the revolts on impositions from the priests, Catholic historians attributed the problems to recalcitrant elements among the indigenous peoples. According to the Catholic historian John Gilmary Shea, priests built at least eight churches to bring the blessings of religion to the Hopi pueblos in the region of New Mexico. However, some Native Americans remained apart from the conversions and opposed the missionaries' efforts. The problems began in 1680, Shea added, when the unconverted rebels spread dissension among other Native Americans. They killed several missionaries and destroyed all but one church. About ten years later, the Spanish army returned to the area. When the soldiers had defeated the Native Americans, some missionaries restored a few of the missions.[31]

The second reason for the decline of the mission was changes in the attitude of administrators. By the late eighteenth century, the Spanish government had abandoned the idea of missions as unworkable. In some cases, the missionaries themselves suggested that the missions become parishes with the congregations supporting the priests. They recommended dividing the mission lands among the remaining Native Americans because they recognized that the missions were serving only white people. The population of Native Americans had declined and extensive intermarriage had taken place. This process, called *secularization,* spread widely. In Texas, it ended in the 1820s.[32]

The shift to secularization that took place after 1700 reflected the changed perspectives of the Bourbon dynasty that took control of the Spanish government. Although Bourbons held the same enthusiasm for the religious conversion of Native Americans that characterized the former Hapsburg rulers, the Bourbons appointed professional administrators who questioned the missionaries' skill in integrating the indigenous people into Spanish society. Thus, as American Indians mixed with Spanish settlers in the more settled areas of Mexico, the Bourbons sought more integration in the borderlands where the missions predominated. For example, some colonial administrators expressed the enlightenment view that the mission robbed the indigenous people of initiative because the missions prohibited the Native Americans from acquiring property. Since the Bourbons distrusted the missionaries, they came to depend on towns, markets, and Spanish settlers to convert Native Americans. They placed faith in the Spanish language as an instrument of conversion, and they pointed out that the missionaries had failed to teach the indigenous people to speak Spanish. Nonetheless, the administrators appointed by the Bourbons had difficulty convincing the missionaries to allow the indigenous people to own property and remain outside the mission while attending churches.[33]

When the war for Mexican independence broke out in 1810, the Viceroy of New Spain stopped sending the annual stipend of 400 pesos to each missionary. At the same time, the provincial government taxed the missions and requisitioned supplies from them. With the end of the war in 1821, the newly formed Mexican government offered some financial support to the missions. In a short period, though, the revolutionary government dismantled the missions, arguing they contradicted an ideology of individual freedom. For example, in 1826, the governor of California issued a proclamation ordering the missionaries to set free those Native Americans who could support themselves. In 1833, the Mexican government ordered the missions to be secularized. A year later, the governor of California decreed that the missionaries had to relinquish secular control over Native Americans. At the same time, he converted the missions into pueblos allowing the resident Native Americans to assume ownership of the lands. Because many Native Americans had no interest in taking over the mission property, they left so rapidly that the population on the missions in California declined from about 30,000 in 1834 to less than 5,000 in 1843.[34]

The third reason for the failure of the missions was that Native Americans often died shortly after joining a mission. Using the same archives that Bolton had used, Sherburne F. Cook published a series of essays in 1943 arguing that the missions contributed to the decline in the population of indigenous people. Cook estimated that in 1770 the Native American population in California reached approximately 135,000 individuals. During the next seventy years, until 1834, when the missions ceased to function, the Native American population declined to less than 98,000 individuals. More important, changes in the population of Native Americans within the missions indicated that they died on the missions. For example, the mission population in California rose from 100 in 1770 to 21,000 in 1821 and fell to 15,000 in 1834. The increase came from the numbers of new converts who entered the missions. During these same years, the rate of deaths in the missions was about 70 to 85 per thousand while the birth rate never exceeded 45 per thousand. In part, the premature deaths of large numbers of adolescent Native American girls and young women caused the low birth rate.[35]

According to Cook, the deaths on the missions came from disease enhanced by cross-cultural contact and further exacerbated by the fact that the missions drew Native Americans together into large aggregations, restricted them to an inadequate diet, and required them to labor in new and unaccustomed ways. Although epidemics of measles, pneumonia, and diphtheria played roles, more deadly were such venereal diseases as syphilis. To illustrate relative influences, Cook estimated that out of the 15,000 Native American deaths possibly caused by disease, about 3,000 deaths came from swift killers such as measles and about 5,000 deaths came either directly from syphilis or indirectly by syphilis weakening the Native Americans' constitutions. In addition, venereal disease affected the birthrate. Although Spanish soldiers may have introduced the disease, syphilis could spread quickly through Native American populations because American Indians held different ideas of sex than did the missionaries. The missions crowded the Native Americans together, and Cook found there was no obstacle to the spread of syphilis except ineffective preaching from the missionaries.[36]

In part, the high death rate may have come from receiving an inadequate diet. Although Cook claimed the missionaries did not force the Native Americans to labor excessively, the missionaries expected six to eight hours of work per day for five or six days per week. According to Cook's calculations, the missionaries fed the Native Americans on about 2,600 calories per day. He claimed this was inadequate when compared to the 3,000 calories per day he found appropriate in modern diets. Further, the mission diet consisted of corn, wheat, beans, and beef. These meals were monotonous, unappealing, and lacking in several important vitamins needed to prevent scurvy and pellagra. Although the regions around the missions contained fish, game, and wild fruits and nuts, the missionaries prevented Native Americans from hunting or fishing on the fear that Native Americans would return to their pagan ways if allowed to pursue traditional ways of gathering food.[37]

Since life on the missions was difficult, Cook wondered why Native Americans came to the missions. He determined that from 1770 to about 1790, the Franciscan missionaries avoided using force. Instead, they attracted large numbers of converts through kindliness, persuasion through spiritual arguments, and material inducements. To aid in these endeavors, the missionaries sought to make mission life as attractive as possible. When missionaries found it difficult to attract those Native Americans who lived several miles from the mission, they used coercive measures. Sometimes, soldiers brought in unconverted Native Americans. Other times, groups of converts kidnapped resistant Native Americans.[38]

Despite Cook's criticisms, students of Bolton repeated his favorable views of missions. For example, in 1955, John Francis Bannon, a Jesuit priest, concluded his account of the mission frontier in Sonora by claiming that the Jesuits built churches and planted faith through labor and pain. Bannon claimed that in doing this, the Jesuits worked within a policy that embraced Indian souls as well as Indian bodies.[39]

Bannon's optimistic conclusions met increased criticism. In 1959, Homer Aschmann published the results of his field research and documentary investigations using the Bancroft collection. Aschmann concentrated on missions in the central desert of Baja California constructed by Jesuits and found that the missions caused the deaths of many Native Americans.[40]

According to Aschmann, food production became a problem because missionaries imposed European ideas of gender distinctions. Before the missions arrived, Native Americans devoted almost all their efforts to procuring food. Once on the missions, the Jesuits demanded that women engage in such tasks as carding, spinning, and weaving wool and cotton because the missionaries considered clothing morally essential. The missionaries required the men to build roads and to perform construction tasks that provided no food supplies. When the men took on agricultural labor, they may not have worked well because women performed such tasks in traditional societies. Aschmann found that the Jesuits did not ignore the bodily needs of the Native Americans while ministering to their spiritual requirements. They sought to offset inadequate food supplies by importing grain from missions across the gulf.[41]

The fourth problem was that the missions used means that contradicted the ends they sought. According to David J. Weber, the goal of the missions was to transform the Native Americans into taxpaying Christians, yet the missionaries separated the Native Americans from the society they were supposed to enter. Worse, the missionaries did not prepare the Native Americans under their care to become self-reliant members of Hispanic communities. For example, when the missionaries collected the indigenous people onto the mission lands, the missionaries compared the Native Americans to young children and controlled their movements.[42]

As contemporary scholars attended to concerns of native cultures, they expressed antipathy toward Spanish borderland missions. For example, in 1987, Rupert Costo and Jeannette Henry Costo edited a collection of essays detailing what they called a legacy of genocide. Several essays in the book claimed that Native American culture flourished in California before the arrival of the missions. These essays described a cornucopia of wild, available foods, and they castigated the Spanish for starving, raping, beating, and killing Native Americans. To show the views of indigenous peoples, the editors collected several statements from various Native American tribes opposing the canonization of Father Junipero Serra, the Franciscan priest who established missions in California from 1769 to 1782.[43]

In addition, some authors claimed the missions cooperated with the Spanish government to rob and exploit Native Americans. For example, in 1993, George E. Tinker, a member of the Osage Cherokee nation teaching in a Lutheran theological seminary, described what he thought was a symbiotic relationship between the California missions and Spanish political structures. According to Tinker, the military forced the California natives into the missions and the missionaries pacified them so the Spanish could occupy their lands.[44]

In the face of such criticism, a group of historians calling for a new Latin American mission history published in 1995 a volume of essays in which they sought to revaluate the effects that missions had on native societies. In the essay, "The Ibero-American Frontier Mission in Native American History," David Sweet pointed out that although the missions destroyed native cultures, they offered four opportunities. First, the missions offered some promise of survival. Although most Native Americans perished on the missions, the missions offered an alternative to the sufferings of famine, disease, or intertribal warfare in the native villages. The Native Americans most likely to survive arrived in large groups, maintained their coherence, and withdrew shortly to remote locations or adapted gradually on particularly American Indian terms. Second, the missions taught the Native Americans about new tools, such as the ax, and new types of fruits and vegetables, such as melons and grains, suitable for temperate zones. Third, the missions provided Native Americans new forms of community that bridged the traditional divisions of tribe or clan. For example, by teaching Native Americans to speak Spanish, the missions opened the possibility of participation in wider social circles. Fourth, the Native Americans took the ideals of justice and charity found in Christianity and turned them to their own advantage. In these ways, Sweet concluded that the mission experience offered benefits to indigenous peoples that differed from what the missionaries intended. Those advantages may have enabled Native Americans in later years to survive and protect their heritage.[45]

What Was the Nature of English Colonialism?

According to Jack P. Greene, the English never achieved a colonial empire although the rulers entertained imperial ideas similar to those enjoyed by Spain as they commissioned colonists to spread across the globe. Greene listed four difficulties the English faced in their quest for empire in the New World. First, the king did not have adequate resources to control the colonies. Second, the great distance across the Atlantic Ocean prevented the central state from overseeing activities in the colonies across the sea. Third, although the desire for economic profit predominated, England never gained the resources to support close supervision. Fourth, after the colonists built homes and established communities, they developed more affection for their local area than they had for the home country. Although Greene thought these problems affected Spain, he found the difficulties to be most obvious in the case of England.[46]

Greene noted that Spain and England, like the other European colonizing powers, allocated the tasks of colonization to private agents. Since private adventurers found it difficult to mount such efforts, organized trading companies took on this struggle. Once these private individuals created their own dominions, they did not want to cede control to the home country. The Spanish found adequate sources of wealth to enable the central government to create a semblance of colonial administration. Consequently, the Spanish could weaken the control of local owners whereas the English were unable to extract enough revenue to enable the king to displace the private companies. Thus, although the English kings tried to consolidate their control over the colonies, colonial merchants frustrated these efforts. Local tradespeople created in the colonies representative institutions that could direct the affairs of the colony.[47]

While the maintenance of independent colonies prevented the English from establishing an empire, some commentators thought this model was England's strength. For example, educational historian Lawrence Cremin claimed the English achieved hegemony in America by 1620 because it established separate independent colonies. He asserted that although Spain, France, and Holland had established churches, missions, and schools in America, the educational innovation of the English was the development of colonies as permanent self-sustaining communities that propagated English customs, ideas, language, law, and literature.[48]

The English colonization of the Americas began in 1584 with an ill-fated adventure in Virginia. Hoping to offset this failure, two cousins, both named Richard Hakluyt, wrote to Queen Elizabeth I, recommending that she support colonization in the area of Virginia. The younger of the two Hakluyts had already collected information about the colonizing efforts of France, Spain, and Portugal. As a result, the manuscript that he completed in 1584 was convincing.

In his tract, Hakluyt gave religious, economic, and social reasons why such colonization should be undertaken. The religious reason was to spread the gospel to indigenous people. In his explanation, Hakluyt recalled the Acts of the Apostles wherein Paul planned to go to Asia to preach, but in a vision, Paul had perceived a man from Macedonia calling him to come to his country. Instead of referring to a personal vision, Hakluyt noted that England's efforts to spread the gospel in such areas as Brazil and Florida had met with failure. To Hakluyt, this suggested that the Divine Spirit was sending the English to a different place, such as the area around Virginia. The economic reason was that such colonies could establish English trade in a safe direction. In the recent past, England had carried on trade with Flanders and the Low Countries. Since these were Spanish dominions, Phillip II had restricted such endeavors. Other opportunities awaited in Virginia because the Spanish had no influence there. Further, Virginia contained unused resources that would make England richer. The social reason was that the enterprise would offer employment to numbers of idle men.[49]

In these arguments, Hakluyt built upon the severe economic and social upheavals of his day. From 1500 to 1600, the population of England had grown from about three million people to over four million. Other parts of the world underwent similar increases in population. Although most English people had lived in rural areas where they farmed parts of large estates, aristocratic owners had expelled them and fenced in large sections of land to raise sheep. Many of these displaced peasants moved to cities. As a result, the population of the city of London grew from 120,000 people in 1550 to over 200,000 in 1600 and to 375,000 in 1650. Unfortunately, life was difficult in the cities because the English cloth trade to the European continent had declined, and English economic growth had slowed.[50]

Although it is not clear that either Elizabeth or James I read Hakluyt's manuscript, James extended to a group of merchants, including the younger Hakluyt, a charter to establish colonies in Virginia in 1605. In this charter, James approved the desire of the members of the company to propagate the Christian faith among the people who lived on those distant shores. He added that he wanted the settlers to occupy the area, to fortify it against incursions, and to exploit the available wealth.[51]

The charter incorporated two companies. One of them, the London Company, could settle the Southern coast that became Virginia while the other, the Plymouth Company, could settle the Northern coast that became Massachusetts. In 1607, a group of settlers, including an Anglican minister, a doctor, 40 soldiers, 35 gentlemen, and a variety of laborers, took authority from this charter to establish Jamestown. Unfortunately, the colonists met with repeated failures until 1614, when they began growing tobacco for export.[52]

While economic motives dominated the settlement of Virginia, colonists came to New England to avoid religious conflict. The question concerned the extent that bishops appointed by the English crown should influence local church practices. As Elizabeth I and James I sought uniformity, the Separatists, who wanted independent churches, went to Holland first and later to Cape Cod to escape the bishops' control.

Writing in 1702, Cotton Mather, whose grandfather Richard came to the colony in 1635, claimed that the migration to the New World began with a group of devout and serious Christians who sought to give themselves to God and to each other. Fearing that the Church of England retained several practices from Catholicism, they wanted to extend the influence of the Reformation. Consequently, they obtained a patent from King James I to establish a colony where they could follow their own religious ideas, advance the dominions of his Majesty, and enlarge the interests of the gospel. Although directed to Virginia, they came to New England. Mather asserted that God had sent the colonists to those shores to spread His Divine Providence through the Indian wilderness.[53]

What Was Colonial English Education?

The English colonists brought with them from the home country a belief in the value of education. According to Cremin, a connected series of changes in England under the Tudors and the Stuarts made education important. The Reformation made reading an essential part of religious observances. Thus, clerics in local parishes taught parishioners to read the Book of Common Prayer that guided Anglican services, and a variety of schools and colleges opened to enroll the people who desired to learn about the Bible. At the same time, Parliament passed a series of acts requiring that every individual live within a family or family surrogate and demanding that each family provide religious and vocational training to children. As literacy spread, many English citizens sought in printed matter the answers to practical questions. In this way, they came to see learning a means to improve life. At the same time, the English tended to see themselves as agents fulfilling God's designs and this vision infused efforts in education and colonialism with a sense of purpose.[54]

In addition to faith in education, the English colonists brought with them a pattern of how to provide this education. According to Cremin, the colonists transplanted from England an educational configuration of household, church, and school. Although Cremin noted that the institutions worked somewhat differently in the colonies than they had in the home country, he argued that the institutions cooperated with each other and built on what he called didactic literature to teach piety, civility, and learning. Of the three educational institutions, Cremin thought the family was most important in the colonies because within it young people served a type of apprenticeship where they participated in essential activities with adults. In addition, in some households, they undertook structured lessons. In general, the families in a community gathered in a church that instructed them on the best ways to live. Of the three educational institutions, the school was the weakest. Most colonial children did not attend schools. Some students attended a petty or dame school where they learned to read and write. A few boys may have attended a local grammar school to learn Latin. In addition, all of these institutions depended on printed matter. Although most literature served the church, some literature dealt with secular matters.[55]

In each of the colonies, the home, the church, and the school took on different emphases. For example, in Virginia, the household had the most influence. Parishes covered more than a hundred square miles. Although schools existed in the few densely populated areas, there were frequent calls for more schools to be established. Finally, in 1730 printing presses arrived in Virginia. In New England towns, schools, churches, and printing presses were already available. Thus, these institutions reinforced the same knowledge and values of households. In the middle colonies, different groups of Quakers, Mennonites, and Moravians formed their own isolated communities around their own meetinghouses or churches. As a result, the same town could have various but separate configurations of families, church, and school. In each case, though, colonists maintained that education should advance piety, civility, and learning.[56]

When Cremin contended that the English configuration of family, church, and school reinforced piety, civility, and learning, he made two assumptions. The first was that the institutions of family, church, and school reinforced each other. The second was that the ideals of piety, civility, and learning were compatible. Other historians drew conclusions from their researches that questioned these assumptions.

First, although historians agree that church teachings influenced family life, Edmund S. Morgan suggested that the ideal of family weakened the influence of the church. According to Morgan, the founders of New England staked the success of their efforts on the church. Therefore, they confined political rights to church members, making the existence of the state dependent on a continued supply of church members. When their children did not express feelings of conversion, the founders offered in 1662 the Half-Way Covenant so that unconverted children of church members could remain incomplete members. Morgan attributes the unwillingness of the Puritans to look for converts outside of the circle of their own children to the importance they ascribed to the family. The ideal of the family made them think that parents passed on to their children the church as an institution. Although the Puritans quoted biblical justifications for this practice, Morgan concluded that they had placed the love of their children above the love of God, with the result that the Puritans deprived their church of its meaning.[57]

Second, the experience of a revival movement in the colonies implied that an advance of piety could weaken civil authority. For example, when Richard Bushman traced the changes that took place among the Puritans in Connecticut from 1690 to 1765, he found that the religious Puritans turned into ambitious Yankees. Although Bushman found that the shifts took place gradually, there were defining aspects that brought into question the compatibility of piety and civility. According to Bushman, the Great Awakening, a revival movement that swept the colonies in the second quarter of the seventeenth century, released people from civil restraints. According to the revivalist preachers, God's grace saved people. This meant that peoples' spiritual destinies were unrelated to their obedience to civil authority. Bushman added that this claim implied that people could resist civil authority when they believed that they should. An ironic result was that self-interest replaced idealism. Thus, instead of elections going to magistrates of ability and faithfulness, the victories went to candidates who complied with the popular will. As a result, by the 1760s the rulers had to cater to people who were determined to enhance their worldly possessions by opening new lands for settlement and providing increasing supplies of money for trading. These were measures the churches and the civil government avoided in 1690 in efforts to contain the people's avarice.[58]

Another historian, Paul R. Lucas, reinforced Bushman's contentions about the corrosive nature of piety. Studying the churches that grew up along the Connecticut River from 1636 to 1735, Lucas found the various church leaders who settled the river valley hoped that their particular church would provide the moral basis for an orderly and communal society. Because they wanted each church to be independent, they broke into factions that supported one theological arrangement or another. As the ministers fought among each other, the lay members came to believe that clerical disagreements weakened the community, and they searched for a more stable system. Ironically, this attitude aggravated the dissensions leading finally to the disruption of traditional patterns of authority and the weakening of institutional relationships in the Great Awakening.[59]

In fairness, it is difficult to determine the effect of the contradictions in Puritan beliefs. The decline of Puritan communities may have come from the successes the Puritans enjoyed. Writing a review of historical research, Jack P. Greene noted that the New England colonies profited from their stability. Entire families from a range of social classes moved to New England; also, the leaders came with the settlers from England. Further, the immigration took place quickly. Between 1630 and 1642, roughly 25,000 immigrants came to New England. Because few immigrants came to the area after that initial period, these colonies resembled established societies from their beginnings. Nonetheless, the population grew rapidly so that by 1660 New England contained about 60,000 settlers. Throughout the eighteenth century, population growth remained around 28 percent per decade so that by 1760 the population reached approximately 450,000. Such increases in population caused towns to spread through the region. Thus, after the battles with Native Americans called King Phillip's War in the middle 1660s, land development and speculation became a profitable business to accompany the commerce and shipping that had reached across the Atlantic. In these ways, the population in the New England colonies tended to resemble the socially divided, economically minded, upwardly mobile towns in England. This had to bring about a decline in religious solidarity.[60]

Although people in every colony expressed a desire for learning and schools, New England was able to act on those wishes. Writing in 1901, Edward Eggleston claimed that New England colonists had more zeal for schools than did other colonists for several reasons. The communities were compact; the local governments were vigorous; the people had come for religious reasons; and they wished to preserve the reforms they had enacted. According to Eggleston, a series of laws enacted in New England from 1642 to 1650 established the pattern for modern school systems by instituting laws for compulsory schooling. These laws required the towns to set up schools and ordered the children to attend. He added that the colonists established these laws because they worried that learning was leaving the colonies. Although the first settlers had been well educated in England, the children born in New England had lost interest in learning. They were more engaged in the demands of the rough life in the forests that required knowledge of canoe building rather than a facility in Latin or an ability to spell correctly.[61]

The environment may have inspired contradictions in the attitudes that the colonists had toward learning. For example, John Demos pointed out that although historians disagreed about the level of literacy among the Pilgrim colonists in Plymouth, they had considerable evidence that the Pilgrims valued books highly. In at least one case, a Pilgrim listed carefully the books he owned. Instead of signing the will, though, he made his mark. The controversies that resulted turned on the question of whether the fact of making a mark instead of signing was evidence of illiteracy. Nonetheless, Demos claimed that many of the men in the Plymouth colony were illiterate as were most of the women.[62]

A similar ambivalence existed about the establishment of schools. On the one hand, the General Court of Massachusetts tried to enforce the requirement to establish schools. For example, in 1668 the constable served a warrant on the selectmen of Topsfield requiring them to provide instruction to youth who lived with their families in reading English, in understanding the laws, and in learning the catechism.[63]

The General Court may have cited the community of Topsfield, but many New England townships ignored regulations demanding schools. For example, during his extensive research through the records of colonial Sudbury, Massachusetts, Sumner Chilton Powell could not find any mention of a schoolmaster or of any free scholars in the town. Powell noted that instead of a school, the town leaders appointed four men to visit the families in the town to verify that the children and the servants were following the ways of God. It was not until 1692 that residents of Sudbury appointed a master to teach writing and bookkeeping.[64]

Relying on an extensive survey of the impact of New England's school laws, Cremin claimed that from 1647 to 1657, the eight towns with more than one hundred families created grammar schools, and one third of the towns with fifty families created petty schools as required. Adherence to the law changed, Cremin added. After 1657, as towns reached the stipulated sizes, their selectmen ignored the regulations.[65]

As far as the printed material on which schools depended, teachers used texts that reinforced religion. One instrument was a page of written script fastened to a board and covered with a translucent film of horn that was therefore incorrectly called a *hornbook*. Another text was the *New England Primer* that contained 88 pages and measured about 3½ inches by 4½ inches. Containing religious aphorisms and catechism, this primer remained popular until 1806, and customers may have bought three million copies. From this primer, students may have moved to the Psalter, the oldest part of the Old Testament; to the New Testament, the section of the Bible that Christianity is based on; and to the complete Bible.[66]

Although printed matter reinforced religion, it changed its emphasis as time passed. According to Gillan Brown, the *New England Primer* underwent several changes during the time it remained in use. Despite these changes, she contended that the aim of the *Primer* was to enable children to know who they were, to describe the society that surrounded them, and to illuminate the choices they should make. Brown contended that the *Primer* reinforced an image of society similar to the one John Locke had envisioned, in which members joined by agreeing to share a condition. Thus, during the colonial period, the *Primer* indicated to the readers that they shared with Adam the fall from God's grace and that constant attention to the Bible could mend their lives. The *Primer* expressed the sinful state of humankind with the maxim, "In Adam's fall, sin we all." The redemptive power of the Bible came out in the following refrain: "Thy life to mend, this book attend." A picture of the Bible accompanied this saying. To give urgency to the choices, the *Primer* described various punishments for sin but cautioned against resentment as in the following rhyme: "Job, who feels the rod, blesses God." By the time of the Revolution, the *Primer* substituted patriotic rhymes for religious themes. For example, the letter *W* referred to "George Washington brave" who saved his country. At the same time, the *Primer* opposed monarchy in the following rhyme: "Kings and queens are gaudy things." In all cases, though, Brown found that the *Primer* encouraged its readers to know their origins and to choose to be part of the adult society that was around them.[67]

How Did the Puritans Offer Education to Native Americans?

Unlike the Spanish who considered indigenous people to be subjects of the king, the Pilgrims approached the Native Americans as members of independent nations. For example, on March 22, 1621, Captain Standish and Master Williamson concluded a treaty with Massasoit, whom they described as king of Pokanoket. In this treaty, each side agreed to protect the other's followers from harm or unjust invasion. In addition, the treaty stated that if any members of Massasoit's tribe harmed the colonists, he would send the malefactors to the colonists to meet justice. Evidence of the Pilgrims' sincerity in this mutual defense pact came shortly after forming this accord. Ten Pilgrims went on a short military expedition to protect Massasoit and their translator, Squanto, from threats by neighboring enemy villages.[68]

Further evidence of the English colonists' sincerity in honoring the treaty with the Native Americans came in 1638 when Plymouth magistrates tried and executed a colonist, Arthur Peach, and two of his colleagues for killing an American Indian. According to James H. Merrell, the Puritan practice of treating Native Americans justly served as a means to assimilate the indigenous people until King Phillip's War. Before this conflagration, some Native Americans took advantage of English law and registered their lands, seeking the protection of the colonists. For example, when the corn of a Native American was destroyed by a colonist's cattle, he captured the cattle, took them to the town, and sought legal retribution. In addition, Native Americans served as constables, gave testimony, and sat on juries. By 1669, though, the Plymouth colonists reacted to what they thought was excessive litigation by Native Americans and banned them from towns on court days. Finally, after King Philip's War, in 1676, the colonists reduced the Native American legal rights and promulgated restrictions on Native Americans.[69]

In treating the Native Americans as members of separate governments, the Pilgrims set a precedent that became part of U.S. law. In 1832, when U.S. Supreme Court Justice John Marshall wrote the decision in *Samuel A. Worcester v. the State of Georgia,* he referred to the English precedent of considering Native American tribes to be independent nations. From this idea, Marshall decided that state governments could not decide the fates of indigenous people. The U.S. Constitution gave the authority to make treaties to the U.S. Congress.[70]

Although the English colonists established settlements that were separate from the Native Americans, those settlements disrupted Native American life. The expansion of the colonies took up large tracts of land. A plantation established in Massachusetts in 1668 contained about five thousand acres and supported about sixty families. Moreover, the colonists sought to control interactions with Native Americans. For example, in 1639, the Plymouth colony forbade settlers to set up trade with the surrounding Native Americans. Similarly, in 1651, Rhode Island forbade any purchase of lands from indigenous peoples without the approval of the state.[71]

The Puritan treatment of Native Americans did not enable the indigenous peoples to retain their cultures. An important reason was that most of the American Indians died from the cultural contact. According to historians estimates, in 1610, the population of Native Americans in the area that became New England may have totaled around 80,000. One hundred years later, the population of Native Americans was closer to only 4,000. The foremost reason for the rapid decline was probably a smallpox epidemic that swept through New England around 1633. Other epidemics may have played roles as well as warfare with Europeans and competing indigenous groups.[72]

According to James H. Merrell, increased mortality of Native Americans took place throughout the colonial region. He added that the colonists looked upon these epidemics as signs of God's favor. To some extent, Native Americans shared this view because they generally emigrated when Europeans entered an area, usually within one generation, as the only way to avoid calamity. At the same time, Merrell noted that those Native Americans who chose to remain near Europeans lost their cultures as they developed appetites for European goods. Many Native Americans turned from their traditional crafts and used European tools. Other indigenous people who maintained their crafts, such as traditional pottery or carvings, traded those artifacts with the colonists for European materials.[73]

There was also violence between colonists and Native Americans. From England, Reverend John Robinson sent a letter to the members of his former congregation who had settled in Plymouth in which he complained that they should have converted the Indians instead of killing them. Robinson warned that although the colonists felt justified in committing violence, they should consider two problems: the Pilgrims might have slighted the Native Americans to instigate the violence, and the violence would spread across the colonies.[74]

In keeping with the idea that Native Americans lived under separate governments, the Puritans did little to Christianize them during the 1620s and 1630s. According to William Kellaway, the Pilgrims' theology made it difficult for them to act as missionaries to the Native Americans. Kellaway pointed out that in New England, the church covenant formed the basis of a society that distinguished between the elect members, or saints, and those who were unregenerate. The saints commissioned a pastor to tend to their needs, but they did not expect their pastor to cater to those people who had not joined the covenant. Kellaway added that Presbyterians in England complained strongly against such a theology that considered most of the population unfit to receive ministry. As a result, New Englanders had to defend themselves against these criticisms when they sought material aid from the mother country. Kellaway contended that the only available example they had to refute these attacks was the ministry of John Eliot.[75]

In 1631, Eliot arrived in Boston, and the following year, the congregation of the church in Roxbury ordained him as the teaching elder. By 1643, Eliot began to devote attention to the Indians who lived near his community and to learn their language, Algonquian. Although other English colonists had tried to master the language, Eliot may have been the first to use the language to preach to the Native Americans. In 1646, he began to organize a reservation system. Setting up the first praying town in Natick in 1651, Eliot had fourteen such towns by 1674, making it the most ambitious Christianizing effort in the English colonies.[76]

In addition to using the indigenous language to preach to American Indians, Eliot translated the Bible and other religious works into Algonquian. In 1649, Eliot expressed his goals to a member of the then newly formed Society for the Propagation of the Gospel. For the next fifty years, the Society expended about half of its funds in supporting an Indian library. The first endeavors were to translate and print copies of a primer and a catechism. By 1655 Eliot had finished and printed the Book of Genesis as a trial piece. He had completed the translation of the Bible by 1658.[77]

It is not clear how successful Eliot was in his translations. On the one hand, the commissioners of the Society had little faith in his abilities as a translator. They sought to have other individuals whom they regarded as experts in the native tongues verify the translations and watch over the printing. On the other hand, during the nineteenth century, an expert evaluated Eliot's translation of the Bible and declared it to be as good as any first version of the Bible had been. Nonetheless, some reviewers found the materials that formed the Indian library to be turgid and incomprehensible.[78]

To at least one of his contemporaries, Eliot appeared to have been most successful. Writing in 1687, Increase Mather described a meeting Eliot had in 1646 with a group of Native Americans. Opening with a prayer and sermon, Eliot began a conversation with the Native Americans in which he answered their questions about creation, salvation, and the commandments. Mather praised Eliot for translating the Bible and founding Natick, a praying town. Although Mather blamed obdurate infidels for the scarcity of such reservations, he noted that many Native Americans had joined such towns after smallpox epidemics spread through their ranks.[79]

The praying towns that Mather praised were important elements of missionary efforts. Eliot and the members of the Society believed that the Native Americans had to accept European civilization before they could convert to Christianity. The idea was that Native Americans had to change their lifestyles before the words in the Bible could bring about the necessary conversion. At the same time, many Native Americans adopted the English lifestyle to improve their own lives.[80]

According to Kenneth M. Morrison, Native Americans joined Eliot's praying towns because they admired the material superiority of European culture and they feared stronger enemy tribal groups. At the same time, although they feared the threat of eternal damnation, they sought to form social ties with the Europeans. Unfortunately, the praying towns were separate from the Puritan communities, and Eliot did not desire to form friendships as much as he wanted his pupils to accept salvation. As a result, Morrison claimed that the Indians and Eliot misunderstood each other, and neither recognized the destruction that would follow the meeting of the cultures.[81]

Part of the problem came from American Indians who adopted the material ways of the Europeans. For example, Morrison argued that wearing sparse loincloths and smearing the skin with grease offered protection against parasites. If the indigenous people adopted the European custom of wearing woolen clothes, they became infested with lice and disease followed. Despite such problems, Eliot considered the adoption of European dress to be a sign of progress, and he urged Native Americans to adopt English ways. Unfortunately, such changes did not earn them a welcome among the Puritans. Consequently, converts became a rootless group.[82]

In 1665, a Royal Commission visited and reported on the praying towns. The commission declared the effort a failure. The commission members could not distinguish the Native Americans in the towns from the indigenous people outside the towns except that those within listened to sermons. Although Eliot had translated the Bible into the language of the Native Americans, the commission members found that few American Indians learned to read and those who could read Eliot's Bible had only a superficial understanding of the English culture.[83]

In Massachusetts, the praying towns declined after King Philip's War in 1676. In securing their victory, the Puritans killed many American Indians, and they sold into slavery those Native Americans they captured. After these events, only four of the praying towns reopened, and many of the Native American survivors of King Phillip's War moved to New York. In 1677, Edmund Andros negotiated a treaty of peace that placed the Iroquois and their dependent tribes out of reach of land-hungry English colonists. Establishing the Covenant Chain, the treaty granted the western regions of New York to the so-called Five Nations of Native Americans who used the peace to replenish their populations and to build their material resources by trading furs with the English. For almost a century, the Covenant Chain brought peace enforced by the English on one side and by a militant confederation of Iroquois on the other side.[84]

Similar efforts took place among the other English colonies, and in 1763 Parliament established a line separating the American Indians from the English settlers with the aim of protecting the hunting grounds of Native Americans. According to Michael Leroy Oberg, those members of parliment who made these efforts held to the vision of dominion expressed by Hakluyt in 1584. They believed that the settlers and the American Indians could live together in peace and that the Native Americans would come to accept the blessings of Christianity and European culture. Oberg added that the English who lived on the frontier did not share this vision of a larger metropolis that included the different groups. The colonists on the frontier competed with the Native Americans for the same lands and wanted to use the land in ways that were incompatible with the desires of indigenous people. For example, when the settlers cleared the land for agriculture, they destroyed the hunting grounds. When the colonists brought in livestock, these animals ruined the corn the Native Americans had planted in unenclosed fields.[85]

Oberg contended that the competition engendered by the intercultural contact led logically, although tragically, to the Indian removal demanded by U.S. President Andrew Jackson in the 1830s. At the time, those Americans who retained the English vision of dominion protested the decision to remove the American Indians to Oklahoma because the Cherokees and the rest of the so-called Five Civilized Tribes had adopted Christianity, spoke English, and followed American lifestyles. Nonetheless, Oberg added, most people came to accept the removal of the Native Americans as the only way to bring peace to the frontier and as the best way to protect the Native Americans from the incursions of frontier settlers until the establishment of a more benevolent social order.[86]

Conclusion

In colonizing the area that became the United States, Europeans viewed their mission in educational terms. In this way, they made connections between imperial expansion and education. In fulfilling these ideas, they followed variations of two different models. One model of colonization came from the Spanish who regarded the Native Americans as subjects living within the Spanish empire. To fulfill the obligations of empire, Spanish missionaries set up missions within the area known as the Spanish borderlands that stretched from Florida to California. On these missions, the Native Americans practiced European ways of life and the Christian religion. The other model of colonization came from the English who viewed the Native Americans as belonging to separate nations. Consequently, the colonists established treaties acknowledging the rights and duties of the different sides, and few colonists participated in missionary work.

Despite the different attitudes of the Spanish and the English, both systems led to unfortunate results for the Native Americans. The intercultural contact brought epidemics that decimated the indigenous populations. In addition, colonists forced the Native Americans to move westward from the Atlantic coast. Finally, Native Americans who survived the contact with Europeans had to surrender aspects of their culture and their religion. This did not mean that Native Americans disappeared. According to some historians, Native Americans used European culture and language to advance a version of their traditional perspectives.

Although some historians contend that the English configurations of family, church, and school transmitted European culture to the New World, other historians suggest that these institutions and the values they represented contradicted each other. The result was that the formerly religious colonies adopted secular aims. Similar changes took place in the Spanish missions as the Bourbon kings expressed distrust for the missionaries and moved the religious missions toward more secular, materialistic goals. Thus, European countries may have ultimately established colonies because of modern pressures to increase material wealth, and the colonies advanced those materialistic concerns in the place of religious impulses.

While concerns from times long past differ from contemporary attitudes, European colonialism in the New World influenced the way we think about globalism today. One manner in which this occurred was through the expansion of imperial control. The second and more complex way was through the contradictory nature of colonial adventures that allowed people to place more emphasis on materialistic goals than on spiritual development.

Endnotes

1. Edward Gaylord Bourne, *Spain in America, 1450–1580* (1904; reprint, New York: Barnes and Noble, Inc., 1962), 202, 253–254.
2. Bourne, *Spain in America,* 29–30.
3. John Tracy Ellis, *Catholics in Colonial America* (Baltimore: Helicon, 1965), 28–29.
4. Pope Julius II, "Universalis Ecclesiae" in *Documents of American Catholic History,* ed. John Tracy Ellis (Milwaukee: Bruce Publishing Co., 1962), 4–6.
5. Bourne, *Spain in America,* 244–247.
6. Anthony Pagden, *Lords of All the World: Ideologies of Empire in Spain, Britain, and France, c.1500–c.1800* (New Haven: Yale University Press, 1995), 29–62.
7. John Tate Lanning, *Academic Culture in the Spanish Colonies* (1940; reprint, Port Washington, N.Y.: Kennikat Press, 1971), 12–33.
8. Lanning, *Academic Culture,* 112–116.
9. Lanning, *Academic Culture,* 40–43.
10. Bourne, *Spain in America,* 308–309.
11. Charles Gibson, *Spain in America* (New York: Harper and Row, 1966), 38–39.
12. David J. Weber, *Spanish Bourbons and Wild Indians* (Waco: Baylor University Press, 2004), 37.
13. Gibson, *Spain in America,* 49–57.
14. Pope Paul III, "Sublimis Deus," in *Documents of American Catholic History,* ed. John Tracy Ellis (Milwaukee: Bruce Publishing Co., 1962), 7–8.
15. Herbert E. Bolton, "The Mission as a Frontier Institution in the Spanish-American Colonies," *American Historical Review* 21, no. 3 (1917): 44–45.
16. John Walton Caughey, "Hubert Howe Bancroft, Historian of Western America," in *The Idea of Spanish Borderlands,* ed. David J. Weber (New York: Garland Publishing, 1991), 203–214.
17. Richard Hofstadter, *The Progressive Historians: Turner, Beard, Parrington* (New York: Alfred A. Knopf, 1968), 3–43.

18. Frederick Jackson Turner, "The Significance of the Frontier in American History," in *The Early Writings of Frederick Jackson Turner,* ed. Everett E. Edwards (1939; reprint, Freeport, N.Y.: Book for Libraries Press, 1969), 185–229.
19. George Wilson Pierson, "The Frontier and American Institutions: A Criticism of the Turner Theory," in *The Turner Thesis: Concerning the Role of the Frontier in American History,* 3rd ed., ed. George Rogers Taylor (Lexington, Mass.: D.C. Heath and Co., 1972), 70–97.
20. John Francis Bannon, "Introduction," in *Bolton and the Spanish Borderlands,* ed. John Francis Bannon (Norman: University of Oklahoma Press, 1964), 3–19.
21. Bolton, "The Mission as a Frontier Institution in the Spanish-American Colonies," 42–43.
22. Bolton, "The Mission as a Frontier Institution," 47–52.
23. Bolton, "The Mission as a Frontier Institution," 52–53.
24. Edward H. Spicer, *Cycles of Conquest: The Impact of Spain, Mexico, and the United States on the Indians of the Southwest, 1533–1960* (Tucson: University of Arizona Press, 1962), 290–291.
25. Spicer, *Cycles of Conquest,* 291–293.
26. Bolton, "The Mission as a Frontier Institution," 57–58.
27. Bolton, "The Mission as a Frontier Institution," 53–54.
28. Bolton, "The Mission as a Frontier Institution," 61.
29. Bolton, "The Mission as a Frontier Institution," 56; Spicer, *Cycles of Conquest,* 293–298.
30. Spicer, *Cycles of Conquest,* 15–17.
31. John Gilmary Shea, *History of the Catholic Missions among the Indian Tribes of the United States, 1529–1854* (New York: Edward Dunigan and Brother, 1855), 81–82.
32. David J. Weber, *The Spanish Frontier in North America* (New Haven: Yale University Press, 1992), 306.
33. Weber, *Spanish Bourbons and Wild Indians,* 37–49.
34. George Harwood Phillips, "Indians and the Breakdown of the Mission System," in *New Spain's Far Northern Frontier,* ed. David J. Weber (Albuquerque: University of New Mexico Press, 1979), 257–272.
35. Sherburne F. Cook, *The Conflict between the California Indian and White Civilization* (Berkeley: University of California Press, 1976), 3–5, 8–12, 197–206.
36. Cook, *The Conflict between the California Indian and White Civilization,* 22–30.
37. Cook, *The Conflict between the California Indian and White Civilization,* 42–47.
38. Cook, *The Conflict between the California Indian and White Civilization,* 73–77.
39. John Francis Bannon, *The Mission Frontier in Sonora, 1620–1687* (New York: U.S. Catholic Historical Society, 1955), 142.
40. Homer Aschmann, *The Central Desert of Baja California: Demography and Ecology* (Riverside, Calif.: Manessier Publishing, 1967), xv–xvi.
41. Aschmann, *The Central Desert of Baja California,* 234–236.
42. Weber, *The Spanish Frontier in North America,* 306.
43. Rupert Costo and Jeannette Henry Costo, eds., *The Missions of California: A Legacy of Genocide* (San Francisco: Indian Historian Press, 1987).
44. George E. Tinker, *Missionary Conquest: The Native American Cultural Genocide* (Minneapolis: Fortress Press, 1993), 42–68.
45. David Sweet "The Ibero-American Frontier Mission in Native American History," in *The New Latin American Mission History,* ed. Erick Langer and Robert H. Jackson (Lincoln: University of Nebraska Press, 1995), 1–48.
46. Jack P. Greene, "Transatlantic Colonization and the Redefinition of Empire in the Early Modern Era," in *Negotiated Empires: Centers and Peripheries in the Americas, 1500–1820,* ed. Christine Daniels and Michael V. Kennedy (New York: Routledge, 2002), 267–282.
47. Greene, "Transatlantic Colonization," 272–273.
48. Lawrence A. Cremin, *American Education: The Colonial Experience, 1607–1783* (New York: Harper and Row Publishers, 1970), 22–23.
49. Richard Hakluyt, "Discourse of Western Planting," in *New American World: A Documentary History of North America to 1612,* vol. 3, ed. David B. Quinn (New York: Arno Press, 1979), 70–72.
50. Alan Taylor, *American Colonies* (New York: Viking, 2001), 120–122.
51. "First Charter of Virginia, April 10, 1606," in *Foundations of Colonial America: A Documentary History,* vol. 3, ed. W. Keith Kavenagh (New York: Chelsea House Publishers, 1973), 1698–1703.
52. Richard Middleton, *Colonial America: A History, 1607–1760* (Cambridge, Mass.: Blackwell, 1992), 23–29.
53. Cotton Mather, *Magnalia Christi Americana or The Ecclesiastical History of New England,* Vol. I (1702; reprint, New York: Russell and Russell, 1967), 46–53.
54. Lawrence A. Cremin, *Traditions of American Education* (New York: Basic Books, Inc., 1977), 7–10.
55. Cremin, *Traditions of American Education,* 11–15.

56. Cremin, *Traditions of American Education,* 19–20.
57. Edmund S. Morgan, *The Puritan Family: Religion and Domestic Relations in Seventeenth-Century New England* (New York: Harper Torchbooks, 1966), 161–188.
58. Richard L. Bushman, *From Puritan to Yankee: Character and the Social Order in Connecticut, 1690–1765* (Cambridge, Mass.: Harvard University Press, 1967), 267–288.
59. Paul R. Lucas, *Valley of Discord: Church and Society along the Connecticut River, 1636–1725* (Hanover, N.H.: University Press of New England, 1976), 202–206.
60. Jack P. Greene, "Colonial New England in Recent Historiography" in *Interpreting Early America: Historiographical Essays* (Charlottesville: University Press of Virginia, 1996), 240–281.
61. Edward Eggleston, *The Transit of Civilization from England to America in the Seventeenth Century* (New York: D. Appleton and Co., 1901), 227–233.
62. John Demos, *A Little Commonwealth: Family Life in Plymouth Colony* (London: Oxford University Press, 1970), 22.
63. "Violation by the Town of Topsfield on the Massachusetts School Law of 1642," in *Historical Documents in American Education,* ed. Tony W. Johnson and Ronald F. Reed (Boston: Allyn and Bacon, 2002), 6–7.
64. Sumner Chilton Powell, *Puritan Village: The Formation of a New England Town* (New York: Doubleday and Co., 1965), 136.
65. Cremin, *American Education: The Colonial Experience,* 182.
66. Ellwood P. Cubberley, *Public Education: A Study and Interpretation of American Educational History* (Boston: Houghton Mifflin Co., 1919), 29–33.
67. Gillian Brown, *The Consent of the Governed: The Lockean Legacy in Early American Culture* (Cambridge, Mass.: Harvard University Press, 2001), 36–57.
68. Dwight B. Heath, ed., *A Journal of the Pilgrims at Plymouth* (1622; reprint, New York: Corinth Books, 1963), 56–75.
69. James H. Merrell, "'The Customes of Our Countrey': Indians and Colonists in Early America," in *Strangers within the Realm: Cultural Margins of the First British Empire,* ed. Bernard Bailyn and Philip D. Morgan (Chapel Hill: University of North Carolina Press, 1991), 117–156.
70. Katherine Jensen, "Civilization and Assimilation in the Colonized Schooling of Native Americans" in *Education and the Colonial Experience* 2nd ed. (New Brunswick: Transaction Books, 1984), 155–179.
71. W. Keith Kavenagh, ed., *Foundations of Colonial America: A Documentary History,* vol. 1 (New York: R. R. Bowker Co., 1973), 444, 591, 601.
72. Sherburne F. Cook, *The Indian Population of New England in the Seventeenth Century* (Berkeley: University of California Press, 1976), 13–14, 28, 84.
73. Merrell, "The Customes of Our Countrey," 117–156.
74. William Bradford, *Of Plymouth Plantation, 1620–1647,* ed. Samuel Eliot Morison (New York: Alfred A. Knopf, 1952), 374–375.
75. William Kellaway, *The New England Company, 1649–1776* (New York: Barnes and Noble, Inc., 1962), 5–7.
76. Taylor, *American Colonies,* 197.
77. Kellaway, *The New England Company,* 122–125.
78. Kellaway, *The New England Company,* 125–134.
79. Cotton Mather, *Magnalia Christi Americana: The Ecclesiastical History of New England* (1702; reprint, New York: Russell and Russell, 1967), 562–575.
80. Michael Leroy Oberg, *Dominion and Civility: English Imperialism and Native America, 1585–1685* (Ithaca: Cornell University Press, 1999), 124–126.
81. Kenneth M. Morrison, "'That Art of Coyning Christians': John Eliot and the Praying Indians of Massachusetts," *Ethnohistory 21* (Winter 1974): 77–81.
82. Morrison, "That Art of Coyning Christians," 82–84.
83. Morrison, "That Art of Coyning Christians," 84–92.
84. Oberg, *Dominion and Civility,* 212–216.
85. Oberg, *Dominion and Civility,* 217–226.
86. Oberg, *Dominion and Civility,* 227.

3

The Expansion Westward

Lyman Beecher

After the American War of Independence, many leaders of the new republic feared that problems would result from the open lands that lay to the west. It was not clear who would control the area. There were fears the frontier would attract undesirable people, incite lawless behavior, and protect Indians who could help Britain win back the former colonies. In efforts to manage these difficulties, the members of the Continental Congress took control of the area and adopted policies to regulate the development of the territory in ways the members believed would preserve the virtues of democracy. In this way, the new republic moved into new areas spreading its way of life. An important instrument in this effort was education.

Because the Northwest Ordinance enabled the national government to administer the area in the same ways England had controlled its colonies, it set the pattern for the federal government to act as an imperial power. The Congress divided the area into townships and promised tracts of land to support schools in hopes that these conditions would attract settlers who held the virtues thought essential to democracy. By 1830 immigrants from countries such as Germany settled in the territories. Protestant leaders claimed that these immigrants were Catholics who held attitudes contrary to republican ideals. These religious authorities used this complaint to raise support for the spread of schools, seminaries, and colleges in the West. In this way, the competition among religious denominations advanced education.

Advocates for common schools made similar appeals to state legislatures seeking support. They claimed that without education the settlers would not be productive, responsible citizens. Thus, from 1787 to 1841, the conception of education held by political leaders changed from treating schools as a means to attract virtuous people to a method to imbue the settlers with republican virtues. Despite these changes, people seemed to think that schools might solve social problems and spread virtue as the republic expanded. Thus, national expansion appeared to benefit everyone except the displaced Native Americans.

How Did the Continental Congress Resolve the Problems of the Western Frontier?

In 1763, with the signing of the Treaty of Paris to end the Seven Years War, the British won control of the nearly 250,000 square miles that lay between the Ohio River, the Mississippi River, and the Great Lakes. Proclaiming that this territory was to belong to the Native Americans, George III forbade governors to issue charters or establish surveys of the lands west of the Appalachian Mountains. Setting out the line of demarcation in South Carolina in 1765, surveyors extended the line into North Carolina, and by 1768 had drawn the line from Canada to Florida. The proclamation prohibited settlement in the area and ordered any settlers to leave. According to Francis Paul Prucha, this proclamation appeased British leaders who wanted to restrict colonial settlement to the coastline, and it also pleased leaders in Britain who favored westward expansion of the colonies, because the proclamation afforded time to pacify the Indians and to regulate the flow of settlers into the new lands.[1]

In 1780, while the Continental Army and the state militias were fighting the American Revolution, the Continental Congress adopted resolutions to the effect that New York, Virginia, Massachusetts, and Connecticut should cede their claims to the frontier lands so that the Congress could use the land to pay war debts. Congress promised to dispose of the land in ways benefiting the United States and to recognize the states formed from the territory as equal to the other states. Although New York, Virginia, Massachusetts, and Connecticut affirmed a willingness to make such donations, their delegates asked the Congress to grant certain concessions, such as providing free land to soldiers and building military forts in the area to protect settlers against Native Americans. Thus, the Congress began to set up procedures to regulate dispersion of the Northwest Territories though the states did not cede their claims to the land that became Ohio, Indiana, Illinois, Michigan, and Wisconsin until 1786.[2]

Although the frontier lands gave the Congress a way to pay the debts incurred in fighting the American War of Independence, members feared that colonists flooding into those areas would cause problems. According to Peter S. Onuf, the leaders of the new republic feared that the open land beyond the Allegheny Mountains would attract illegal settlers, called squatters, and speculators who would fight with each other and incite disorder among the Native Americans. They also feared that the fertility of the area would cause settlers to become concerned with their own private profits to the point that they forgot the common good. At the same time, they feared that the British and the Spanish, seeking to unseat the new republic, waited outside the borders to take advantage of any problems on the frontier. Finally, some policy makers believed these new lands would make the country too large for effective democratic government.[3]

Congress wanted to avoid the problems they thought the new territories presented, but the members also wanted to use the resources of the Northwest Territory. Consequently, the Congress accepted in 1784 a report from Thomas Jefferson describing how to manage the Northwest Territories. After debating Jefferson's suggestions and adding several new parts, Congress adopted the resolution although there was some doubt as to whether Congress had the authority to make such resolutions. Although the Congress did not register the action as an ordinance, settlers looked to the plan as if it was law, and historians refer to the recommendations as the Land Ordinance of 1785.[4]

Jefferson did not create the plan by himself. David Howell of Rhode Island and Jeremiah T. Chase of Maryland served with him on the committee to decide how to manage the new lands. Jefferson, Howell, and Chase thought Congress should mandate a survey in which they divided the land into townships consisting of six square miles and divide each township into sections of one square mile. Although Jefferson's committee had not mentioned schools, the Congress stipulated that one square mile tract of each township be dedicated to raising funds for the maintenance of schools within the township. In these ways, the Land Ordinance of 1785 set the pattern for all other states seeking admission to the Union. In each case, states agreed to dedicate one thirty-sixth of the land to the maintenance of common schools.[5]

According to Peter Onuf, the act of surveying the land was an important step in establishing the national government's title to the property and regulating its development. Without prior surveys, individuals could wander into choice areas, set up claims, and argue that they had as much right as anyone else to hold the land. The idea of dividing the land into townships served two functions. It suggested an appropriate level of population density, and it recommended that the settlers be groups of immigrants with prior communal bonds. Although the Congress removed from the ordinance any proposals that supported religion, members hoped the promise of an orderly development that included building schools and churches would encourage industrious, peaceful farmers to venture into the wilderness.[6]

When the members of the Continental Congress adopted the New England system of compact townships, they may have desired the townships to serve as instruments of socialization. According to Dennis Denenberg, the Congress expected settlers in these areas to be foreign immigrants who would need to learn the ways of a new country. As a result, they did not want to allow individuals to select their own locations without provisions for schools. In some parts of the South, the patterns of settlement had been unrestrained. Despite congressional efforts to control the frontier, the revised ordinance did not lead to increased sales of the land. Consequently, the Congress drafted the Northwest Ordinance of 1787 and sold the land to the Ohio Company headed by Reverend Dr. Manasseh Cutler of Massachusetts on the promise that he would develop the area. In making the agreement with the U.S. Treasury, Cutler urged a grant of areas equal to two townships in each state for universities.[7]

According to Peter Onuf, the Congress chose to disperse the land through Cutler's private Ohio Company because this method seemed the best way for the Congress to raise money to pay its debts. In the rush to obtain cash, the Congress sold the land at less than fifty cents per acre, though it originally asked a dollar per acre. Congress sold at reduced rates to Cutler because he promised to populate the area with industrious, enlightened people who would generate prosperity for everyone. In his private correspondence to the members of Congress, Cutler explained that he would sell the portions of land to New Englanders because they would be good settlers. He thought New Englanders were diligent people with robust physical bodies. Onuf claimed that Southerners supported Cutler's regional favoritism. A congressman from Virginia noted the Ohio Company included the best men from Massachusetts and Connecticut; he predicted that they would introduce the type of settlers who would spur economic improvements. Because schools would not be necessary to turn this type of settler into a productive citizen, the calls for education found in the Northwest Ordinance may have been intended to make the area appear attractive to people from New England.[8]

The early investors in the Ohio Company intended to emigrate west. Agents who were to sell the shares for the Ohio Company predicted that more than one thousand families would move from Massachusetts and Connecticut to the Northwest Territories seeking respite from the distressed economic conditions. Part of the difficulties arose from New England's dependence on maritime trade and industries that suffered when Britain, France, and Spain would not allow New England ships to enter their colonies. Another part of the problem was that Massachusetts had extensive war debts. When the legislature raised taxes to repay those obligations, farmers lost their land through foreclosures. In 1786, Daniel Shay, a former army captain, led 1200 men in an armed rebellion.

Veteran officers represented a significant portion of the settlers. Fearing that the materialistic desires of people in the settled states threatened the social order, these soldiers wanted to go west to affirm republican values. In 1788, they founded Marietta, Ohio. Unfortunately, the economy in New England remained poor and the Ohio Company dissolved in 1796.[9]

The Continental Congress took three approaches to maintaining peace in the Northwest Territory. First, the ordinance arranged the administration of the area so that the settlers had to assume the roles of colonists who were working toward statehood. In the process, the settlers would develop the mechanisms and the qualities necessary for self-government. Second, the ordinance encouraged the development of schools to train children in the ways of government and social activities. Third, the Congress forbade the settlers to treat the Native Americans unjustly.

The first approach was to regulate the administration of the area. In writing the Northwest Ordinance, the authors devoted the most attention to the proper arrangement of government that should appear in the territories. It arranged for two stages of control. At first, the Congress would appoint a governor and a secretary. The governor would appoint judges, establish a militia, and assign officers to maintain peace and order. Such authoritarian rule would continue until the region had a population of 5,000 free adult men. At this time, the residents could elect a legislature. The governor would create the pattern and extent of representation. At no time, though, was there to be slavery in the territory. When the Congress specified that this area would become three to five states, it gave approximate boundaries for those states and promised to admit any one of those areas as a state on equal footing with the other states when it had a population of 60,000 free inhabitants. On their part, the residents had to adopt a state constitution that shaped a republican form of government.[10]

According to Beverly W. Bond, Jr., the Congress established stages of colonial rule through the Northwest Ordinance that were roughly parallel to British efforts. Unlike British colonialism, the Northwest Ordinance specified the point at which the territories could become free and equal states. By describing the conditions needed for the settlers to become self-governing, the ordinance circumvented the possibility of revolutions. Bond claimed that the first governor of the territory, Arthur St. Clair, fulfilled the functions of a colonial agent. He appointed judges quickly, drew up a code that prescribed crimes and punishments, and mandated that militias form and assemble each Sunday.[11]

Governor St. Clair aroused considerable opposition when he claimed that the settlers were subjects of the Congress. In his eyes, they would not become citizens until Congress accepted the area as a state. According to the ordinance, St. Clair and three judges would have absolute control until the territory contained 5,000 free adult males who could convene a general assembly. Even with such a legislature, the ordinance gave St. Clair the power of veto. Since St. Clair considered the settlers unqualified for self-government, his dictatorial methods caused some settlers to complain about oppressive rule. Despite these controversies, Ohio was the only section where resistance to federal authority was strong enough to advance the move toward statehood. In Michigan and Wisconsin, for example, territorial governors did not exacerbate such controversies and the transition was less contentious.[12]

The second approach Congress used to maintain peace was to encourage the development of schools. The first sentence of Article Three of the Northwest Ordinance affirmed that education should be encouraged forever because religion, morality, and knowledge were necessary for good government and social happiness. Although the only mention of education in the ordinance appeared in the first sentence of Article Three and critics complained that it was a vague exhortation lacking specificity, William E. Sparkman argued that this was not a problem. First, the article set a precedent concerning the importance of schools. As a result, when Ohio, Alabama, and Mississippi adopted constitutions, they took the language from the Northwest Ordinance stating that education should be forever encouraged. Second, Sparkman added that state constitutions did not have to describe how schools should be organized or funded. He asserted that constitutions did not grant power to a legislature; they limited the power of legislatures. Thus, any legislature could establish schools whether an article appeared in the constitution or not. Sparkman believed this principle applied to the U.S. Constitution, but he acknowledged that eventually every state adopted an article directing the legislature to require free public schools. Not one of them described how the schools would be organized or supported.[13]

The third approach to peace in the territory was to forbid settlers to treat the Native Americans unjustly. The bulk of Article Three of the Northwest Ordinance of 1787 affirmed the need to observe the utmost good faith toward American Indians. It forbade taking Native

American lands without their consent, and specified that American Indians had rights and liberty. Although the ordinance allowed settlers to invade Native American villages in the case of a just and lawful war authorized by Congress, it forbade any other attacks.[14]

The Continental Congress expressed concern for Native Americans because James Duane sent a report from his committee on Indian affairs recommending that emissaries tell the Native Americans about the desire of the leaders of the new republic to act generously. The report added that the Congress should offer to draw a boundary line between the Native American villages and the new settlements although this view contradicted the feelings of many people. Some members of Congress felt that the Congress could remove the Indians to areas north of the Great Lakes because the Indians had fought on the side of the British and the British had ceded the Northwest Territory to the United States. This was not the view Duane's report recommended, though.[15]

According to Reginald Horseman, the Congress acted with caution toward Native Americans because the members faced a dilemma. On the one hand, the members wanted to acquire land from the Native Americans. On the other hand, they desired to keep the peace. Military leaders such as George Washington warned that American Indians could become allies of the British in Canada and invade the territories. Horseman noted that when Anthony Wayne won the Battle of Fallen Timbers in 1795, twelve American Indian tribes agreed to the Treaty of Greenville wherein they ceded to the United States the southeastern corner of the Northwest Territory. Thus, the national government acquired land. Unfortunately, Horseman added, the national leaders could not maintain friendly relations because Congress could not protect the American Indians' homes from the settlers who spread into the fertile valleys. In fact, Congress could not have prevented this westward expansion.[16]

In 1999, Colin G. Calloway offered a more critical interpretation. He claimed that emissaries from the British soldiers and from the American revolutionaries petitioned aid from the various Native American tribes during the American Revolution. Although many Native American groups tried to remain neutral, some tribes broke from their confederations to side with the British or with the Americans. The hostilities between settlers and many Native Americans did not end with the Revolution, and American settlers and soldiers destroyed many Indian communities. Calloway argued that the Americans came to believe that all the American Indians had supported the British, and they used this fiction to justify mass dispossession.[17]

Although there is truth to Calloway's accusation, it overlooks various efforts of governmental agencies to control the westward migration. Until the end of the War of 1812, the dispersal of federal land was slow. Up to that point, Congress admitted one state, Ohio, from the Northwest Territory. After the war ended, migration became so rapid that within the next four years, Indiana, Illinois, Alabama, and Mississippi joined the Union. Settlers without cash to buy land wandered into public lands, destroyed precious timber, and planted crops. When the land became available for sale, the land offices accepted credit from these illegal settlers to buy the titles to their farms. At various times, U.S. presidents sought to forbid settling on frontier lands, tried to remove illegal settlers, and attempted to require cash payment for the purchase of land. These measures would have controlled the migration into the frontier lands, but each president that tried had to relent in the face of public protests. As a result, the migration into the western lands continued unabated.[18]

Commentators at the time and historians writing after the fact blamed speculators for the rapid spread of population, the abuse of the land, and the poor treatment of American Indians; speculators bought land cheaply, demanded military protection, and made profits by charging high prices to the farmers who turned the virgin soil into farms. According to Daniel Feller, this was not the case. Feller claimed that land speculation was endemic in the new republic. All the farmers treated the land as a commodity, and everyone made profits from its sale. Thus, land speculators did not act any differently than did farmers. More important, the cost of the land could not influence the rate of migration because the initial price of land was a fraction of the cost of building a farm. Thus, Feller concluded that although politicians debated about how to control westward migration before the Civil War, the task was beyond the power of any governmental agency.[19]

How Did the Continental Congress Enhance the Spread of Schools?

Although the Northwest Ordinance of 1787 did not provide for the public support of schools, the Land Ordinance of 1785 had stipulated that one tract of a square mile of each township would be dedicated for schools. In addition, Manasseh Cutler had convinced the U.S. Treasury to devote two townships in each state to develop universities. The idea of such land grants for schools derived from an English tradition.

According to Joseph Schafer, the tradition of donating state-owned land for education began in England with Edward VI. Using the land that he and Henry VIII had taken from churches and monasteries, he endowed schools. In 1551, for example, the king acceded to a petition and used sequestered church land to create the Royal Free Grammar School of King Edward VI at Shrewsbury. Whereas Schafer noted that all the colonies followed the custom of land grants for schools, the practice of land grants developed into a system in Massachusetts, Connecticut, and New Hampshire. When the national government had a stretch of wilderness in 1785, it followed the practices these colonies used from the 1640s. It reserved open lands for the support of schools.[20]

At the time, land grants may have been the only way the Continental Congress could raise funds to support free public schools. As Thomas P. Slaughter pointed out, when Americans resisted the Stamp Act, they argued that the Parliament of Britain lacked the authority to impose such taxes. Consequently, when the Americans established their own central government, the Continental Congress, the Articles of Confederation reserved all taxpaying authority to the states. Further, as the states debated ratification of the Constitution, spokespeople complained that the power of taxation should never go to a central government. Slaughter noted that critics predicted a civil war would break out if the federal government tried to collect taxes. This prophecy seemed accurate in 1791 when the federal government imposed a tax on whiskey and a rebellion began.[21]

The feeling against taxes was so great that leaders from the original states asked for support for their own schools from funds derived by the sale or rent of the lands in the Northwest Territories. For example, in 1821, a senator from Maryland proposed that the thirteen original states receive funds from the federal government derived from frontier land sales to support the schools in their states. The logic of the proposal from Maryland was that, since the federal government had acquired the frontier lands with the aim of serving the good of the country, it should disperse some of the funds from the land to serve the citizens in states without frontier lands. This proposal failed because of resistance from the newly founded frontier states. Their representatives argued that the land for schools was not a donation from the federal government. In accepting the land set aside for schools, the state government had to agree not to tax any formerly federal land for five years after its sale. They contended that these forgone taxes represented payment for the land.[22]

Although land grants were extremely valuable, they did not provide significant support for schools. Because the Continental Congress did not monitor the trusts, the newly formed state governments could use the monies as the state officials pleased. According to George Knight, because the members of the Congress thought about the unsettled lands as resources to pay present debts, they included the idea of the land grants for schools in hopes of appealing to future settlers, without thinking of the worth of the school funds for future generations. Knight described the process as follows: When Congress admitted a state into the Union, the authorities in the state took control of the reservations of land. In Ohio and Illinois, responsibility to guard the funds fell to the state legislatures whereas in Indiana the townships received the lands. In Michigan the governor controlled the grants, and the people of Wisconsin appointed a board of commissioners to oversee the funds. According to Knight, no matter which type of supervision a state chose to exercise, the authorities squandered the monies from these school funds rather than dedicate them to education.[23]

To illustrate the extent of the corruption, Knight claimed that in 1821 the Ohio General Assembly authorized trustees to lease some land adjoining Cincinnati permanently for the price of forty dollars per year. Because this was a permanent lease, the renters paid the same price of forty dollars per year in 1839 when the value of the property exceeded one hundred thousand dollars.[24]

In constructing a history of the use of land grants for education in the Northwest Territory, Knight found several reasons why the states did not direct those resources toward education. For example, officials acted hastily in selling the lands. Sometimes, state legislatures adopted laws carelessly, thereby allowing opportunities for fraud and unfair appraisals of the value of the land, and the legislatures failed to invest the monies received from the land sales or rentals. The legislatures could make laws to favor certain individuals and misuse the money because citizens in the states were indifferent to schools. To Knight, the result was the waste of an opportunity of immeasurable worth. He claimed that, with proper management, the funds would have supported the needs of all levels of education for all time.[25]

The Northwest Territory was not the only area to squander school funds. According to Fletcher Harper Swift, the problem appeared throughout the United States during the nineteenth century. Writing in 1910, Swift found that many states had no records for educational funds. When Swift sent letters of inquiry to state department of educations, he received incorrect information or officials ignored his requests. Looking at state financial reports, Swift noted that these documents did not mention school funds for many decades. In California, the townships took control of fifty thousand acres in the 1860s. Although townships sold the land to support common schools, the funds disappeared. When Maine separated from Massachusetts in 1788, Massachusetts deeded parcels of land for schools to several Maine townships. A century later, by 1898, those funds disappeared. In Louisiana and Mississippi, the state officers sold extensive amounts of land, yet they could not account for the funds because they lost the records of the sales. Similarly, in Alabama the state superintendent of schools acknowledged in 1891 that there could be no accurate record made of the money relating to school lands; someone lost the documents or failed to record them properly. In addition to the almost universal lack of information, Swift found that some state land officers not only refused to answer his questions, they took actions to make him stop his investigations.[26]

Besides land grants, states had other ways to establish permanent funds for schools, but it was not clear they would have worked. Although a state government could establish taxes, such a fund might have retarded the development of schools. For example, in 1700, Connecticut required towns of more than seventy families to hold schools for eleven months and to levy taxes that would support the schools. In 1801, the state adopted the School Fund Act to provide additional support for the towns' schools. An unintended result of the School Fund Act was that virtually no town in Connecticut levied local taxes for schools from 1821 to 1854. Since the legislation of 1801 included a provision allowing local officials to close schools if funds were unavailable, they kept schools open only as long as state funds allowed. Similarly, the Indiana School Fund that began in 1816 with the admission of the state to the union did not provide support for schools until the state adopted a new constitution in 1851. Thus, in Connecticut and Indiana, the existence of permanent state funds for education ended the development of local schools and gave only the appearance of a wider concern for education.[27]

Although the land grant system did not enhance the development of schools, the failure of the land grants did not prevent the development of schools. Two factors enhanced the spread of schools in the West. The first factor was the efforts the settlers exerted as they developed urban centers. The second factor was a change that took place among spokespeople from the East who began to see the West as a place of promise rather than as a problem to solve.

The founding families in townships, including Cincinnati, Louisville, and St. Louis, created private schools for their children. Generally, the children stayed long enough to learn basic academic skills and then withdrew to an occupation. The newspapers of these towns carried advertisements about the opening of different new schools, indicating that teachers competed for scholars. According to one teacher, the way to maintain a school was for the instructors to avoid any modesty and claim that their new methods could impart twice the knowledge in half the time.[28]

By the first years of the nineteenth century, the Lancaster system arrived in the West. Developed more extensively in the Eastern cities, this method promised to teach children to read, write, and do arithmetic at little expense. The cost-saving factor was that one teacher taught a group of older children who acted as monitors and taught the same lessons to younger scholars. By 1815 most communities in the West had a school that followed such a system.[29]

According to Richard C. Wade, Cincinnati had the strongest educational offerings in the West. In 1829, the city had forty-seven private schools enrolling about 1,600 students. Although the city's leaders petitioned the state capitol to establish a statewide system of public education, nothing came of the request. As a result, the city amended its charter in 1829 to give the city council the authority to establish a system within the city. The resulting legislation divided the five wards of the city into two districts, and within each district, there were two brick schoolhouses, and each schoolhouse was two stories high. The city levied a property tax to pay for the school construction and the teachers' salaries. In the first year, the trustees claimed that two thousand children registered to attend the schools; average daily attendance was about 1,500, and the schools employed twenty-two teachers. Although Louisville had a weaker system, the city established a school at public expense a year earlier. Generally, city leaders in St. Louis resisted local pleas for public free schools. Nonetheless, a Catholic academy in the city had six priests who provided instruction for seventy students.[30]

The second factor to encourage the spread of schools was that conservative spokespeople of New England changed their views of the West. As Rush Welter pointed out, in the 1800s, conservative religious leaders viewed the West as a place for people who would never have the virtues for self-government. According to Welter, by the 1830s, these leaders began to recognize the West as a place of hope and promise that required the care of Easterners. To illustrate the change in conservative Eastern leaders, Welter contrasted the ideas of Timothy Dwight, Congregational clergyman and president of Yale University for twenty-one years, to those of Lyman Beecher, who had studied with Dwight.[31]

In 1800, Dwight portrayed the settlers of Vermont as typical of the class of frontier people; they were idle, talkative, passionate, prodigal, and shiftless. Worse, Dwight claimed that they were unwilling to support the ministers or the teachers who could aid in their conversion. By 1830 Lyman Beecher claimed that the West contained the promise of the republic. He urged New England clergy to recognize the potential power and wealth in the West and to support educational endeavors to ensure the settlers used those riches to emancipate the world.[32]

In part, the difference between these leaders derived from the fact that Dwight stayed in New Haven whereas Beecher moved to Cincinnati, Ohio, in 1832 in response to an invitation to head Lane Seminary. Founded in 1822 and incorporated by the Ohio legislature in 1829, Lane Seminary began to prosper when Theodore Dwight Weld selected it as the site to train a new generation of clergy through a combination of manual labor and theological training. Weld was acting as an agent for Lewis Tappan's philanthropy, the Society for Promoting Manual Labor in Literary Institutions. Tappan's money was to set up the seminary in the Walnut Hills section of Cincinnati. The students were to support themselves and improve their health through three or four hours of mechanical or agricultural labor each day. In addition, the students pledged to give up such luxuries as tea and coffee.[33]

Weld found additional support for the idea of a manual training model for the ministry from Charles Finney, a prominent revival preacher. During the summer of 1832, Weld and Finney traveled on a revival tour to recruit students for Lane Seminary. About forty older men enrolled in the seminary, and Weld joined them and resigned from Tappan's society. At the same time, Lyman Beecher moved to Cincinnati to become president of the seminary and professor of theology. Although Weld was an ardent abolitionist, Beecher held moderate views on the slavery question. He feared that the issue would splinter the denominations and destroy the seminaries he thought would win the West for democracy. In 1834, with Beecher's permission, the students held a series of debates about slavery and organized evening schools to teach the African Americans living in the city. During the summer, while Beecher was away, the trustees forbade further discussions or actions about slavery. In response, the students withdrew from the seminary, established a community in

Kentucky, and later founded a theology department at Oberlin College. Beecher remained at Lane until 1851 when he retired.[34]

When Beecher agreed to come to Cincinnati, the city was enjoying newly regained prosperity. The depression that swept the United States after the War of 1812 had crippled Cincinnati; the city spent all municipal funds on such relief as soup kitchens. By 1825 river traffic increased and manufacturing took hold in the city. By 1830 Cincinnati held a monopoly on river traffic and canals tied together other avenues of commerce. Located at such a crossroads, the city developed the strongest economy among such Western cities as Pittsburgh, Louisville, and St. Louis. Its population grew rapidly. In 1796, the city had a population of about 500. By 1820 the population reached to almost 10,000. Many of these residents came from the South and the Middle States. By 1830 the population jumped to about 25,000 as the demand for canal workers led to a significant flow of foreign immigrants into the city. Of all religious groups, Catholics prospered the most in this period. For example, in 1826, Cincinnati Catholics dedicated a new cathedral that could accommodate 1,000 communicants with a fine organ and paintings by a Roman master. Most of the immigrants came from Germany so that by 1841, when the population of the city grew to about 50,000, the German population comprised about 30 percent of the total. This percentage, when combined with the fractions of the population made up of British, French, and Italian immigrants, meant that half of the adults in the city were foreign born.[35]

Although Cincinnati was an urban island surrounded by the forests that covered Ohio, Beecher recognized it as the opening to a vast expanse of resources. Consequently, when he had the opportunity to travel through cities on the East Coast raising funds to support Lane Seminary, he played on this theme of possibility. In 1835, Beecher expanded these fund raising speeches into a short book entitled *A Plea for the West.*

Beginning with Jonathan Edwards' prophecy that America would lead the way to political and moral emancipation for the world, Beecher argued that the West could make Edwards' prediction come true. This region had the wealth and would soon hold the population to become the central political power in the nation. Beecher was amazed at the speed with which the West was growing, and he praised the settlers for developing an intellectual and moral culture. Unfortunately, he added, because the churches and the colleges in the West came from New England, they were uniform whereas the West contained a diverse population. To bring the people together, the frontier needed seminaries to prepare young men from the Western communities to establish locally based churches and schools in the West. Calling on his listeners to contribute to institutions such as Lane Seminary, Beecher asserted that such contributions would aid in stemming two dangers the republic faced from the West. The first was uneducated youth who would grow into ignorant and malleable voters. The second was the immigration of Catholics who depended on priests for guidance.[36]

In *A Plea for the West,* Beecher spent about a third of the 170 pages on the opportunities offered by the West and the need for seminaries of learning. In the other two-thirds, he described why Catholic immigrants threatened republican virtues. Beecher claimed that three-fourths of the immigrants coming to the West were Catholic. To Beecher, the problem was Catholics accepted the domination of priests. The church censured books; the pope claimed infallibility; they wanted to limit the control of the government. Thus, he feared their church would dominate the state. Beecher claimed that Catholics were working to change the nation into a Catholic country by spreading Catholic schools. Because the teachers were vowed religious, such as priests, nuns, or brothers, costs were low. Beecher did not think there was any way to stop immigration; he refused to restrict the rights of Catholics. He criticized people who burned churches or harmed Catholics. Beecher's answer to what he saw as the Catholic threat was education in common schools under the care of well-trained teachers.[37]

According to Kathryn Kish Sklar, in his speeches, Beecher portrayed the citizens in Cincinnati as requiring New Englanders to introduce the culture and sensitivity that could overcome the Catholic presence. Beecher told the Bostonians they could be a leaven to produce a saving and enduring influence. Sklar added that a Cincinnati journal published Beecher's remarks, in which the editor ridiculed Beecher for criticizing the cultural accomplishments of Cincinnati residents. Consequently, before *A Plea for the West* appeared in print, Beecher removed the passages Cincinnati residents had found insulting.[38]

It is not clear what effect Beecher's pleas had. Historian Robert Dunne claimed the anti-Catholic writings of Beecher served as the basis for nativist movements in the 1840s and 1850s. Dunne argued that Beecher placed one group in opposition to another with the result that some citizens wanted to restrict the immigrants' abilities to participate in American life.[39] Another historian, Lawrence Cremin, complained that Beecher's first public lectures in Boston in 1825 inspired the destruction of the Ursuline convent in Charlestown.[40] For his part, Beecher claimed he did not incite a mob to burn a convent. Although he acknowledged that he had given a speech in Boston condemning Catholicism the same night the convent burned, he did not believe the arsonists heard his words because the convent was three miles from the church where he spoke.[41]

In part, the reason the effect of Beecher's speeches is not clear is that he worked within a tradition of revivalist preaching in which denominational rivalry was a tool to spread education. In 1793, when Beecher entered Yale College, Ezra Stiles was president. Beecher characterized Stiles as urbane, polite, and learned, but uninspiring. In 1795, Timothy Dwight became president. Beecher noted that Dwight was a revival preacher who changed the college from an ungodly seat of infidelity where students read Thomas Paine, Francois Marie Arouet Voltaire, and Jean Jacques Rousseau into an orthodox institution where students read Jonathan Edwards, John Locke, and Isaac Newton. In all, Beecher credited Dwight with continuing the work of preachers such as Jonathan Edwards who had led the Great Awakening of the 1740s. Since the American War of Independence had interrupted their efforts, Dwight initiated a Second Great Awakening in which he baptized Beecher into the revival spirit. This meant that Beecher had foreseen the conversion of the world to Christ, and he tried to convey this insight to his listeners through emotional appeals to avoid the dangers of free or liberal thought.[42]

While Beecher condemned liberal thought, he depended on denominational rivalry. In July 1832, before he moved to Cincinnati, Beecher explained to his parishioners in Boston that he wanted to turn Lane Seminary into a training ground for revivalist preachers to do for the West what Andover Seminary had done for Massachusetts.[43] In making this promise, Beecher referred to the fact that Andover developed out of a disagreement among Congregationalists. Conservative Calvinists founded the seminary in 1808 as an outgrowth of Phillips Academy because they felt Harvard was excessively liberal. To enter Andover, students had to show proficiency in the classical languages of Greek and Latin.

To graduate, they had to take courses in such subjects as sacred literature, ecclesiastical history, and homiletics. Until the academy took over the grounds and the buildings of the seminary in 1908, the two institutions shared grounds and faculty members to the extent that they could not be distinguished easily. From this conservative training at Andover, the students went to Congregational pulpits in the New England area that otherwise might have been occupied by Harvard graduates.[44]

Beecher reflected his admiration of Andover and his experiences in Yale in 1836 in an address he made at Miami University in Oxford, Ohio, to the Union Literary Society. In his speech, entitled *A Plea for Colleges,* Beecher described the curriculum he thought appropriate for colleges in the West. Beecher contended that colleges were the guardians of liberty because they developed and disciplined the minds of students in ways that prepared them for life in a republic. This required the careful study of Latin, Greek, and mathematics. Although Beecher acknowledged that students liked the study of literature, he claimed this could not tax their mental powers as much as did the classical languages. He believed students should pursue science to learn about God's creation. In these courses, the students would acquire precision of thinking, accuracy of verbal description, balance of mind, and condensation of thought. In addition to such mental exercises, Beecher wanted students to undergo studies in mental philosophy, logic, physiology, and the Bible. When he came to questions of school governance, Beecher concluded that the trustees and the faculty members had to govern the college, although he suggested that committees of students could evaluate the benefits of policies before the trustees enacted them. As for social activism, he warned that college was not a time for the youth to become embroiled in public controversies. He wanted students to acquire beneficial habits of mind. Finally, on questions of school organization, he decided that men, women, and children should have their own institutions because they had to learn different things.[45]

In describing his plan for colleges, Beecher had his own experiences in mind. At Yale, he had pursued a classical curriculum, and Lane Seminary included manual labor in the curriculum. Further, at Lane, Beecher was embroiled in questions of student governance and of student involvement in social crisis. The controversy over abolitionism had threatened his institution. As a result, Beecher offered ways and reasons to contain student power.

How Did Controversies over the Bible in Classrooms and Women as Teachers Influence the Spread of Schools?

In *A Plea for the West,* Beecher claimed that libraries, schools, and Bibles were the important tools in preserving republic virtues.[46] When the trustees of Lane Seminary hired a faculty member from Andover, Calvin Stowe, they began the process of purchasing books suitable for the library of an academic and theological seminary. As president, Beecher agreed with this effort and raised funds to support the library. When Stowe found that he could not buy the books he wanted in the United States, he obtained permission and about $6000 to sail to England, France, and Germany. As Stowe purchased libraries of volumes and sent them to Lane, the trustees sent him more money with which to augment the collection. As a result, Lane Seminary acquired a library of more than 10,000 volumes, making it the largest collection west of the Alleghenies. Stowe remained committed to his library although the seminary began to face a series of financial difficulties in 1836. He served as librarian without pay while performing teaching duties. Further, for thirty years, no one added books to the library. Despite the privations, Stowe and other instructors required students to use the library. At the time, in other colleges students used libraries rarely.[47]

Before Stowe left for Europe to buy books, the Ohio legislature and the governor asked him to investigate teaching practices in several countries and submit a report to the general assembly. In 1837, Stowe offered the *Report on Elementary Public Instruction in Europe* in which he praised the Prussian system, urging the people of Ohio to adopt it. The aim of Prussian education was to awaken in the students a national spirit. Although Prussia was a monarchy, Stowe claimed that a republic such as the United States had to foster similar feelings of patriotism in citizens. Stowe claimed that an important aspect of this training was religious instruction. Although the students came from different religious denominations, teachers agreed that students acquired the desire to act morally by reading the Bible. In manual training schools, he found students singing religious hymns while they worked. Stowe recounted several instances where instructors directed students who had engaged in mischief to read the New Testament, bringing about remarkable transformations. In this way, religious training served the public good by developing virtues within the students.[48]

Stowe praised the Prussian system for including subjects such as reading, writing, arithmetic, and language study permeated throughout with moral instruction. The frequent Bible readings in the schools contained no sectarian bigotry, Stowe added. He thought that private academies or high schools could offer courses to train teachers in Ohio to do as well. He believed communities should pay teachers adequate salaries. Most important, the chairs and rooms in the schools should be comfortable, and lessons should attract the attention of all of the children. In this way, there was no need for corporal punishment to establish order in the classrooms.[49]

In his report, Stowe supported Beecher's evangelical aims. Buying books and creating the library gave Beecher a tool that he believed important in advancing the moral education of the West. By determining how states could support schools and train teachers, Stowe described one of the tools that Beecher called for in saving the West. Finally, when Stowe asserted that Bible readings did not advance any religious denomination, he made Protestantism an aspect of the common school curriculum. While Catholics rejected the notion that biblical values transcended denominational differences, Evangelical Protestants such as Beecher held that individuals could read and understand the Bible on their own. Although Catholics wanted people to read the Bible, they viewed priests as intermediaries who prevented parishioners from misinterpreting the Gospels. To Beecher, the fact that different people held different interpretations was a sign of the vitality of the democratic republic, and he thought the Catholic view denied democracy. Catholic leaders had a chance to respond to this view in a series of meetings in Cincinnati, as discussed in later paragraphs.

In 1829, a group of teachers formed an Academic Institute and in 1831, the institute sponsored a convention of teachers from the West. The convention took the name, Western Literary Institute and College of Professional Teachers, to indicate a meeting for people interested in education to discuss a variety of issues rather than to train teachers.

Members came from several parts of the former Northwest Territory and from the Southern states to attend the convention. After more meetings, in 1840, the members of the institute stated the aims of their organization. These included encouraging public interest in education, elevating the profession of teaching, providing opportunities for open exchange among teachers and advocates of education, collecting facts about education, and arranging those facts so that a science of education could develop.[50]

According to a historian who compiled an account of the organization, Allen Oscar Hansen, the objectives reflected the frontier temperament. The men who formed the Western Literary Institute and College of Professional Teachers were used to facing new situations and taking action. They realized that the public had to appreciate the value of education if the profession was to be elevated. Most important, Hanson contended, the institute had to base its decisions on facts if it was to influence public opinion or initiate legislative action. Consequently, the institute created a system of committees to research certain questions, to prepare reports, and to meet regularly to hear the reports and to decide on courses of action.[51]

The question of Bible reading was the first problem that confronted advocates of public schools. Following the procedures it had outlined, the Western Literary Institute and College of Professional Teachers received in 1838 two reports from a committee the institute had commissioned to consider whether it was reasonable to ask students in the common schools to read selections from the Bible. Beecher and Stowe had made the question an issue. In addition, such prominent members of the institute as Albert Pickett and William Holmes McGuffey had made collections of reading materials that they felt were appropriate for schools. In these collections, Pickett and McGuffey had included biblical tracts.

The first report came from the Rt. Reverend John Baptist Purcell, Archbishop of Cincinnati. He began by noting that Catholics approved of reading the Bible, and he accepted the conclusion that in Prussia the students read the Bible as part of character training. At the same time, though, Purcell warned that Bible reading had to prejudice one denomination or another. Since he thought denominational differences had to play a role in correct moral training in schools, he recommended that students read the Bible under the instruction of their own pastors. To prevent misuse of biblical passages, he added that Protestant Bibles not be placed in the hands of Catholic youth.[52]

B. P. Aydelott presented the view of the Protestant ministers at the same meeting. Aydelott noted that the word *Bible* meant the King James Version of the Bible rather than the Douay version that Catholics favored. Although he agreed with Purcell that it was impossible to introduce selections without favoring one denomination or another, he saw this as a problem if reading the selections were to take the place of reading the Bible itself. He argued this was not the case. Pointing out that textbook compilers such as Pickett and McGuffey included selections from the King James Version of the Bible in their books so that the children would begin to study their own Bibles, Aydelott recommended continuing the practice of encouraging Bible study in common schools.[53]

During the business meeting of the convention, the delegates accepted a motion to allow teachers and students in the common schools to read the Bible as religious exercises without denominational comment. Surprisingly, Purcell accepted this motion although it violated the Catholic position that the Catholic students should read a Catholic version of the Bible with appropriate notes of commentary. In 1842, Purcell realized the problem and wrote to the president of the board of common schools complaining that Catholic children had to read textbooks with selections from the King James Version of the Bible and, in some cases, Catholic children in common schools had to read that Bible itself. The board replied by accepting a motion to expunge any offensive selections from the textbooks and to prohibit teachers from requiring any children to read the Bible if their parents requested exemption.[54]

Although the motion represented the board's effort to forge a compromise, this proved impossible. By 1869 some Protestants demanded and won the imposition of the Bible as part of classroom exercises. At the same time, Purcell moved away from his conciliatory stance because he found that his complaints about the common school imposing the King James Version of the Bible encouraged the growth of separate Catholic schools. As Purcell hardened his opposition, the issue went to court. In 1872, the Ohio Supreme Court decided that the school board could not impose the Bible in public schools. In a unanimous verdict calling for religious tolerance, the Justices claimed that the state was establishing a state religion when laws required public school children to read the Protestant Bible. To the court, religious freedom meant that all religious doctrines had a free and fair field so that the best would triumph.[55]

In the course of what F. Michael Perko called the Bible War of 1869, school enrollments grew rapidly in Cincinnati. Although public schools and Catholic schools maintained their shares with increased numbers of students, private school enrollment declined in real numbers and in percentages of total enrollment. This pattern changed after the Bible War ended. In 1857, public schools enrolled about 13,000 students, Catholic schools held about 5,000 children, and private schools had about 2,400. In 1861, the provincial council of Cincinnati insisted that Catholic parents had an obligation to send their children to Catholic schools. Perhaps in response to the council's pastoral letter and then current controversies, enrollment in Catholic schools reached almost 16,000 by 1868, whereas public school enrollment rose to 27,000. Private school enrollment dropped to 1,900. After this point, enrollments in Cincinnati Catholic schools remained steady despite the fact that various Catholic councils made increasingly severe demands on Catholic parents to send their children to Catholic schools. On the other hand, enrollments in Cincinnati public schools rose to almost 45,000 in 1900.[56]

The second problem confronting advocates of common schools for the frontier was finding qualified teachers. To Catharine Beecher, this problem represented an opportunity to advance the education of women. When Lyman Beecher traveled to Lane Seminary, his daughter Catharine went with him. In the spring of 1833, she advertised the opening of an academy for women. The Western Female Institute opened with Catharine and her sister Harriett, who later married Calvin Stowe and wrote *Uncle Tom's Cabin,* as associate principals. Mary Dutton served as teacher. According to her biographer, Catharine assumed light responsibilities at the school, spending most of her time on social and intellectual affairs. Among those intellectual efforts was an essay she read in 1835 to the American Lyceum in New York. Entitled "An Essay on the Education of Female Teachers," the speech called for funds to support her institute and to turn it into a model of training teachers across the nation.[57]

In her essay, Catharine claimed that the country faced a crisis because thousands and thousands of degraded immigrants and their ignorant families were pouring into the country. She complained that these people would become voters and control the nation. She asserted that in countries such as Prussia, school children read the Bible and learned about their present and future duties to legally constituted authority and to God. In the United States, though, citizens wanted to remove the Bible from the classroom. As a result, the education of the lower social classes deteriorated. Worse, few men wanted to become teachers. Because Catharine believed that women had the natural dispositions, habits, and circumstances to be teachers, she asked every pious woman to dedicate some time to teaching before assuming the position of wife and mother. In turn, she asked men to offer women opportunities to pursue carefully taught academic courses, to have access to well-equipped laboratories and libraries, and to pay the expenses of such education. In this way, she thought that women would be able to follow a course of study appropriate to shaping the health and the character of children.[58]

Catharine's essay on the education of women failed to attract funds for her institute. According to Kathryn Kish Sklar, the effort failed because Catharine alienated the people whom she asked to contribute. When she repeated her father's belief that New Englanders had a moral mission to raise the intellectual and moral sensibilities of the citizens of Cincinnati, wealthy people in Cincinnati refused to contribute. This may not have bothered Catharine. In 1837, the institute closed while Catharine was traveling to attract women to come to the West to be teachers. According to her biographer, during this national tour Catharine disregarded the failing fortunes of her school.[59]

Catharine continued to recommend that women become teachers. She held that such duties would emancipate women and improve the nation. In 1837, she published "An Essay on Slavery and Abolitionism," directed to Angelina Grimké, the wife of the abolitionist Theodore Dwight Weld, a former student at Lane Seminary. Grimké had suggested that Northern women should unite and form an Abolition Society to fight against slavery in the South. Catharine's response was that such a strategy was unwise because it denied the strengths that women possessed as the subordinate sex. Catharine noted the unique opportunity that women had to become teachers. Catharine estimated that two million children could not read and had no schools, and she suggested that thirty thousand teachers should open schools for them. Because there were not enough men interested in the task to take up such a challenge due to their work in agriculture and mechanics, she predicted that the task would fall to women. As women would need training to assume this role, their status in society would rise as they acquired the necessary education. At the same time, for women to agitate directly for abolition would jeopardize this possibility, because men might then take a less benign view of women's education. Catharine suggested the best course of action was for women to suggest that their husbands, brothers, or fathers join abolitionist societies. If such persuasion failed, the women should advance the virtues of charity and discretion that would turn men toward Christian virtues rather than act directly as critics of an inhumane policy.[60]

Catharine wanted to form an agency that would recruit women to serve as teachers in the West. Among her plans were to have a committee of clergy appoint a director and a board of managers made up of clergy from the important Protestant denominations to create such an institution. By 1846 she had accumulated enough financial support to pay for a full time director or agent. William Slade, governor of Vermont, accepted the position; yet, he chose to remain separate from her to the extent that, in 1848, Catharine left the organization. Slade renamed the agency the National Board of Popular Education. It remained in operation for five years.[61]

Catharine Beecher was not alone in wanting to send women to the West to be teachers. In 1820, alumnae of Emma Willard's Troy Female seminary in New York had invited graduates to teach in places such as Ohio. In 1845, the Ladies' Society for the Promotion of Education in the West in Boston began sending women to the West, and, in 1852, it merged with the National Board. Together these organizations sent about 600 women to teach in the West. During its peak, the National Board admitted about fifty applicants to training each year in Hartford, Connecticut, where they underwent academic study, calisthenics, and inspirational lectures about the job that lay ahead.[62]

In keeping with Beecher's view that Protestants had to save the country from Catholic domination, the National Board of Popular Education required that each woman who wished to be trained at Hartford belong to an evangelical church in addition to being unmarried. Further, the candidates had to write a personal essay explaining how they had experienced a spiritual conversion. They had to submit supporting letters from their ministers with their applications. Women who could not meet this religious test had to wait until they were converted.[63]

Some critics disparaged this effort as simply providing brides for the West. Disagreeing with this view, Polly Welts Kaufman concluded the results were more complicated. Kauffman followed the careers of 250 of the women who went West with the National Board of Popular Education. She found that two-thirds of the women stayed in the West, although they had agreed to remain only two years. Although several recruits stayed single their entire lives, about 80 percent of them married after they left teaching. More women married in the West and remained there than returned to the East to start their families. Those women who stayed became settlers, attracted other women to come and open schools, and found release for themselves from the constraints of New England life. Thus, Kaufman concludes that through the National Board of Popular Education, some women established communities and achieved personal autonomy.[64]

How Did the Northwest Ordinance Influence State Control of Education?

Some historians contended that the Northwest Ordinance and the policy of establishing permanent state funds for education provided precedents for state support and state systems of education. In 1986, David Tyack and Thomas James claimed that the Northwest Ordinance set the stage for the state control of public education. Noting that nineteenth-century Americans distrusted governmental regulation, Tyack and James argued that citizens of the republic accepted the principle of state governments distributing the monies derived from the rental or sale of federal lands. Because most states adopted constitutions that expressed the belief that a democracy depended on an enlightened citizenry, the people recognized the need to establish an office of a state superintendent of education and a state board of education to ensure that these funds served an educational purpose. Tyack and James added that, once in place, the common school system grew after the Civil War to include high schools, textbook selection, and teacher certification.[65]

When some historians studied the experiences in Ohio, they took a different view. Ohio was the first state in the territory where efforts to construct a centralized system of education took place. According to Richard Wade, some historians believed that transplanted Yankees developed public schools in Ohio. However, Wade found some historians who suggested that the agitation for tax supported common schools came from urban centers; this suggested the urban experience inspired the movement.[66]

A fourth possibility came from Wayne Urban and Jennings Wagoner; they argued that the movement toward a publicly supported school system was part of a general movement toward what they called "modernization." Defining this as a movement toward a stronger role for the federal government, they claimed that this process accelerated after the U.S. Civil War and that it changed the nature of the country.[67]

If this idea is correct, the efforts of the Western Literary Institute and College of Professional Teachers, Calvin Stowe, and Catharine Beecher came too early. They sought to create an educational bureaucracy at a time when most Americans distrusted large organizations. As a result, critics at the time worried that campaigns to improve schools were self-serving. Despite such complaints, the people who expanded this movement, such as the first superintendent of Ohio schools, Samuel Lewis, thought of themselves of making schools effective and running them efficiently. Consequently, they concentrated on such things as school funding, school construction, and teacher qualifications. Similar to the criticisms they received, these advocates considered their critics as being selfish or politically motivated. Although selfish motives existed everywhere, narrow or unfair processes of rationalization could raise reasonable opposition. A description of Lewis's efforts will illustrate this situation.

In 1836, at the annual meeting of the Western Literary Institute and College of Professional Teachers in Cincinnati, Samuel Lewis, Albert Pickett, and Elijah Slack presented a report they had drawn up about the state of education in Ohio. Using rough estimates, they determined that the methods used were inadequate because many children were left without instruction. Because they believed that in a democracy all students should receive equal educations, they called for the adequate funding of common schools. About three-fourths of the total number of eligible children in a township should have a school. The teachers needed adequate salaries, and the supervisors had to be dedicated to their tasks.[68]

From Lewis's report, the institute adopted a motion to request legislative bodies in the Western states to enact laws providing universal education. In 1837, a representative from Franklin County introduced to the Ohio General Assembly a bill creating the office of state superintendent of schools. The legislation passed and Lewis accepted the position for a term of one year.[69] As superintendent, Lewis followed the procedures the institute had made for its members. He accumulated information about schools in Ohio; he presented a report to the General Assembly, and he suggested courses of action the legislature could follow.

In his first report, Lewis began by noting that the state constitution imposed on the legislature the obligation to provide for effective education. To Lewis, this requirement meant children should learn to read, write, and do arithmetic. The students should learn about their government and about sound principles of Christian morality. Such instruction was the basis of good citizenship. Unfortunately, Lewis concluded that reasonable schools did not exist outside of Cincinnati. Although the city of Cleveland had recently begun a system of common schools, the teachers faced classrooms of eighty pupils. Some districts sent children to private schools and gave some money toward tuition. In some districts, the teachers were incompetent. Other districts kept schools open for three months during the year. Lewis added that in Ohio over 3,000 school districts lacked schoolhouses, and many districts had buildings that were unfit for children.[70]

When he considered finances to pay for the improvement of education, he pointed out that the legislature sold or leased about half of the land grants to Ohio for excessively low prices. In part, this took place because county auditors lacked the staff and resources to oversee the processes. To prevent further waste, he suggested that each county appoint a superintendent to supervise the school districts. He urged that the state distribute funds to districts according to enrollment, but he discouraged thoughts of requiring school attendance. Although the Ohio General Assembly did not create the office of county superintendent, it did pass the Ohio School Law of 1838 that made Lewis's office permanent and established a common school fund supported by taxes on property in each county. In addition, the law made the township clerk the superintendent of schools, set up three school examiners for each county, and required each teacher to obtain a certificate from the examiners.[71]

Although the Ohio General Assembly gave Lewis most of the reforms he requested, he encountered increasing opposition. He traveled throughout the state to explain the law to people in hopes they would not overturn the reforms. One author, Loretta Petit, argued that Lewis encountered the most opposition on three issues: the reappraisal of school lands, the question of taxes to support schools and libraries, and the certification of teachers.[72]

On the question of school lands, Petit implied that people selfishly resisted reassessment. Because information about the state of school lands came from the districts, the easiest way to defeat reform efforts was to protest the creation of a county superintendent of schools. She added that resistance to taxes for common schools developed around complaints that middle-class parents would have to send their children to school with lower-class children. Taxes for libraries seemed an unnecessary expenditure in rural Ohio. When Lewis commended a county for offering licenses to teachers graded qualified, well qualified, and eminently qualified, critics complained that this was too difficult.[73]

In addition to traveling around the state explaining the need for increased financial support for schools in order to hire competent teachers, Lewis printed and mailed circulars expressing his views. At the annual meetings of the Western Literary Institute and College of Professional Teachers, the members voted to support Lewis's proposals.[74]

In the midst of his efforts, Lewis's health failed. At the same time, the Ohio General Assembly considered proposals to abolish the office of superintendent. In 1840, Lewis resigned the position of state superintendent of schools. After his resignation, the legislature reduced the value of the school fund and eliminated the office of state superintendent. Lewis could claim success because during his short term, the number of schoolhouses in the various districts in Ohio increased from over 4,300 to about 7,300 and the number of students enrolled increased from about 150,000 to more than 250,000; however, the number of teachers decreased from about 7,500 to about 7,200. Unfortunately, by 1844, the available figures indicated that the number of schools had declined to 3,300, the number of students declined to about 49,000, and the number of teachers had declined to 3,389.[75]

At the same time, the Western Literary Institute and College of Professional Teachers began to fade. In 1845, because few people attended the last meeting in Cincinnati, the members did not publish the proceedings. Although there was no simple explanation for the demise of the society, one author linked it to the repeal of school laws in Ohio that frustrated reformers and to the rise of abolitionism that attracted the attention of reformers away from school issues.[76]

In 1849, Beecher and Stowe resigned from Lane Seminary and returned to New England. In the fifteen years Beecher had presided over Lane, he had raised more than $50,000 for the institution. As a result, he left the seminary in a strong financial position. Although noting this accomplishment, Vincent Harding claimed that Beecher failed in his effort to unite Calvinist churches in an evangelization movement in the West. Instead, Beecher's pleas for unity among the evangelicals seemed increasingly impossible; Beecher's hope of training ministers to carry the message seemed to fail as well. Lane seminary never attracted a significant number of students. In fact, when Beecher died in 1863, the largest single denomination in the United States was the Roman Catholic Church.[77]

Beecher's biographers contend that his ideas were mutually contradictory in ways that led to social dissolution. For example, Stuart Henry pointed out that the family members split apart, each following different denominations or religious ideals they considered as affirming the central assumptions of the father. For example, Catharine had Lyman's desire to affirm conventional religious principles in ways that changed the social order. Although Catharine did not question the secondary roles women played to men, she published more than two dozen books indicating how women could lead social reforms. Eventually, these complex drives led Catharine to turn on her father's faith; she published a book criticizing her father's ideal, Jonathan Edwards.[78]

On the issue of forming common school systems, Lewis may have failed in reforming Ohio school law because the ideas of education he promoted did not fit the circumstances that farmers faced. Although commentators blamed Lewis's failure on public apathy, the public must have had reasons for not taking an interest in educational reform. For example, in a biography of William Holmes McGuffey, the author described the problems McGuffey faced in 1841 trying to get the land that was to support Ohio University reappraised. Although McGuffey won the support of the Ohio Supreme Court, the farmers never capitulated. They had used the land to graze their cattle, and the college did not serve their interests. The Ohio General Assembly protected the farmers by changing the laws to serve their interests. Although Lewis did not seek support for a college, he did call for libraries, high schools, and teacher training. This could have been more education than farmers wanted.[79]

Indeed, Lewis's arguments that schools would protect the virtues of students may have seemed bizarre to citizens. The communities in the Northwest Territory did not need schools to socialize the children. The idea of dividing the territories into townships provided arrangements wherein ties of family, home, and church ensured civil order. For example, when Robert P. Swierenga created a cultural geography of the territory, he found that the immigrants born abroad and those born in the United States settled in clusters. Thus, homogeneous groups who shared the same religious denomination settled a particular area close to other homogeneous groups. Within this cultural patchwork, the German, Dutch, and Scandinavian farmers tended to expand geographically. The father in a family would buy surrounding farmsteads, thereby replacing his former neighbors with the families of his grown children. On retirement, the farmer bequeathed his farm to a grown son in exchange for care and support. Thus, Swierenga concluded that the Northwest Ordinance enabled immigrant groups to create a rich mosaic of cultural traditions within states that differed from the ethnic composition on the Atlantic coast, where different immigrant groups tended to occupy entire states.[80]

The other complaints that people made against Lewis and the school law may have been reasonable. For example, teachers could complain about having to pass examinations given by examiners who lacked qualifications to evaluate teaching. In addition, parents who could afford to pay taxes may have reasonably objected to the fact that their children would be together with lower-class children in schools. Such concerns remained obstacles to the common school movement throughout the twentieth century.

Conclusion

When the Continental Congress adopted the Northwest Ordinance in 1787, the new republic began marching westward. In this effort to spread American virtues into the wilderness, members of Congress considered schools as means to attract the type of settlers who would bring peace and productivity to the region. In the 1830s, Protestant leaders such as Lyman Beecher, Catharine Beecher, and Calvin Stowe saw schools as the means to teach immigrants to accept republican virtues. Although the schools did neither of these things, the hope that education could solve social problems was an important element in the effort to settle the West. In part, the problem may have been that the effort to spread civilization and enforce some form of civil conformity required allegiance to a larger central authority. Because people in the new republic feared efforts to build central governments, they resisted taxes for schools. They refused strict accounting of funds from land granted to support schools, and they would not support the efforts to improve the quality of teacher training. Despite this resistance, educational reforms appeared to be inevitable if schools could solve social problems. Furthermore, the policies of land grants implied that there should be central control of schools even if those policies did not require such administrative arrangements. In the twentieth century these views would advance globalism.

Endnotes

1. Francis Paul Prucha, *The Great Father: The United States Government and the American Indians,* vol. 1 (Lincoln: University of Nebraska Press, 1984), 24–28.
2. George W. Knight, "History and Management of Land Grants for Education in the Northwest Territory," *Papers of the American Historical Association,* 1, no. 3 (1895): 7.
3. Peter S. Onuf, *Statehood and Union: A History of the Northwest Ordinance* (Bloomington: Indiana University Press, 1987), 1–20.
4. Richard P. McCormick, "The 'Ordinance' of 1784," *The William and Mary Quarterly* 50, no. 1 (January 1993): 112–122.
5. Knight, "History and Management of Land Grants for Education," 10–13.
6. Onuf, *Statehood and Union,* 21, 22, 39.
7. Dennis Denenberg, "The Missing Link: New England's Influence on Early National Educational Policies," *New England Quarterly* 52, no. 2 (June 1979): 219–233.
8. Onuf, *Statehood and Union,* 42–43.
9. Timothy J. Shannon, "The Ohio Company and the Meaning of Opportunity in the American West, 1786–1795," *The New England Quarterly* 64, no. 3 (September 1991): 393–413.
10. "The Northwest Ordinance: An Annotated Text," in *The Northwest Ordinance, 1787: A Bicentennial*

Handbook, ed. Robert M. Taylor, Jr. (Indianapolis: Indiana Historical Society, 1987), 31–77.

11. Beverly W. Bond, Jr., "An American Experiment in Colonial Government," *The Mississippi Valley Historical Review* 15, no. 2 (September 1928): 221–235.
12. Onuf, *Statehood and Union,* 67–87.
13. William Sparkman, "The Legal Foundations of Public School Finance," 35 B.C.L. Rev 569 (May 1994).
14. "The Northwest Ordinance: An Annotated Text," 61–63.
15. Reginald Horseman, "American Indian Policy in the Old Northwest, 1783–1812," *The William and Mary Quarterly* 18, no. 1 (January 1961): 35–53.
16. Horseman, "American Indian Policy in the Old Northwest," 46–53.
17. Colin G. Calloway, "The Continuing Revolution in Indian Country," in *Native Americans and the Early Republic,* ed. Frederick E. Hoxie, Ronald Hoffman, and Peter J. Albert (Charlottesville: University Press of Virginia, 1999), 3–36.
18. Daniel Feller, *The Public Lands in Jacksonian Politics* (Madison: University of Wisconsin Press, 1984), 14–38.
19. Feller, *The Public Lands in Jacksonian Politics,* 197–198.
20. Joseph Schafer, *The Origin of the System of Land Grants for Education,* Bulletin of the University of Wisconsin, no. 63 History Series, vol. 1, no. 1 (1902): 1–53.
21. Thomas P. Slaughter, "The Tax Man Cometh: Ideological Opposition to Internal Taxes, 1760–1790," *William and Mary Quarterly,* 3rd ser., 41, no. 4 (October 1984): 566–591.
22. Feller, *The Public Lands in Jacksonian Politics,* 40–48.
23. Knight, "History and Management of Land Grants for Education," 27.
24. Knight, "History and Management of Land Grants for Education," 62.
25. Knight, "History and Management of Land Grants for Education," 162–168.
26. Fletcher Harper Swift, *A History of Public Permanent Common School Funds in the United States* (New York: Henry Holt and Company, 1911), 129–159, 201–202.
27. Swift, *A History of Public Permanent Common School Funds,* 166–168, 199–202.
28. Richard C. Wade, *The Urban Frontier: Pioneer Life in Early Pittsburgh, Cincinnati, Lexington, Louisville, and St. Louis* (1959; reprint, Chicago: University of Chicago Press, 1971), 136–137.
29. Wade, *The Urban Frontier,* 137.
30. Wade, *The Urban Frontier,* 245–246.
31. Rush Welter, "The Frontier West as Image of American Society: Conservative Attitudes before the Civil War," *Mississippi Valley Historical Review* 46, no. 4 (March 1960): 593–614.
32. Welter, "The Frontier West," 595–598.
33. James W. Fraser, *Pedagogue for God's Kingdom: Lyman Beecher and the Second Great Awakening* (Lanham, MD: University Press of America, 1985), 108–109.
34. Fraser, *Pedagogue for God's Kingdom,* 106–123.
35. Wade, *The Urban Frontier,* 172, 189–190, 263; Allen Oscar Hansen, *Early Educational leadership in the Ohio Valley* (1923; reprint, New York: Arno Press and *New York Times,* 1969), 10–13.
36. Lyman Beecher, *A Plea for the West* (1835; reprint, New York: Arno Press, Inc., 1977), 7–47.
37. Beecher, *A Plea for the West,* 48–172; Conrad Cherry, *God's New Israel: Religious Interpretations of American Destiny* (Chapel Hill: University of North Carolina Press, 1998), 114–115.
38. Kathryn Kish Sklar, *Catharine Beecher: A Study in American Domesticity* (New York: W. W. Norton & Co., 1973), 116–117.
39. Robert Dunne, "A Plea for a Protestant American Dream: Lyman Beecher's 'A Plea for the West,'" *Old Northwest* 16, no. 3 (Fall 1992): 189–197.
40. Lawrence A. Cremin, *American Education: The National Experience, 1783–1876* (New York: Harper & Row, Publishers, 1980), 36.
41. Barbara Cross, ed., *The Autobiography of Lyman Beecher,* vol. 2 (Cambridge, Mass.: Harvard University Press, 1961), 251–252.
42. Barbara Cross, ed., *The Autobiography of Lyman Beecher,* vol. 1 (Cambridge, Mass.: Harvard University Press, 1961), 44–46.
43. Cross, ed., *The Autobiography of Lyman Beecher,* vol. 2, 204–205.
44. Claude M. Fuess, *An Old New England School: A History of Phillips Academy Andover* (Boston: Houghton Mifflin Co., 1917), 140–156; Cremin, *American Education,* 363.
45. Lyman Beecher, *A Plea for Colleges,* 2nd ed. (Cincinnati: Truman & Smith, 1836).
46. Beecher, *A Plea for the West,* 23.
47. Earle Hilgert, "Calvin Ellis Stowe: Pioneer Librarian of the Old West," *Library Quarterly* 5, no. 3 (July 1980): 324–351.
48. Calvin Stowe, "Report on Elementary Public Instruction in Europe" in *Reports on European Education,* ed. Edgar W. Knight (New York: McGraw-Hill Book Co., 1930), 243–269.
49. Stowe, "Report on Elementary Public Instruction in Europe," 270–313.

50. Hansen, *Early Educational Leadership in the Ohio Valley,* 13–15.
51. Hansen, *Early Educational Leadership in the Ohio Valley,* 15–18.
52. Rt. Rev. J. B. Purcell, "Report on the Expediency of Introducing Selections from the Bible instead of the Bible Itself into Our Schools," *Transactions of the Seventh Annual Meeting of the Western Literary Institute and College of Professional Teachers* (Cincinnati: James R. Allbach, 1838), 118–120.
53. Rev. B. P. Aydelott, "Report on the Expediency of Introducing Selections from the Bible instead of the Bible Itself into Our Schools," *Transactions of the Seventh Annual Meeting of the Western Literary Institute and College of Professional Teachers* (Cincinnati: James R. Allbach, 1838), 121–128.
54. F. Michael Perko, *A Time to Favor Zion: The Ecology of Religion and School Development on the Urban Frontier, Cincinnati, 1830–1870* (Chicago: Educational Studies Press, 1988), 124–126.
55. Perko, *A Time to Favor Zion,* 190.
56. Perko, *A Time to Favor Zion,* 156–159, 208–209.
57. Kathryn Kish Sklar, *Catharine Beecher: A Study in American Domesticity* (New York: W. W. Norton & Co., 1973), 112–115.
58. Catharine Beecher, "An Essay on the Education of Female Teachers," in *Pioneers of Women's Education in the United States: Emma Willard, Catharine Beecher, Mary Lyon,* ed. Willystine Goodsell (New York: McGraw-Hill Book Co., 1931), 165–188.
59. Sklar, *Catharine Beecher,* 130–131.
60. Catharine E. Beecher, *An Essay on Slavery and Abolitionism with Reference to the Duty of American Females* (repr. 1837; reprint, Freeport, N.Y.: Books for Libraries Press, 1970), 104–109, 146–152.
61. Sklar, *Catharine Beecher,* 183.
62. Polly Welts Kaufman, *Woman Teachers on the Frontier* (New Haven: Yale University Press), xvii, 6–23.
63. Kaufman, *Woman Teachers on the Frontier,* 17–18.
64. Kaufman, *Woman Teachers on the Frontier,* 45–48.
65. David Tyack and Thomas Jones, "State Government and Public Education: Exploring the 'Primeval Forest,'" *History of Education Quarterly* 26, no. 1 (Spring 1986): 39–69.
66. Wade, *The Urban Frontier,* 245.
67. Wayne J. Urban and Jennings L. Wagoner, Jr., *American Education: A History* 3rd ed. (Boston: McGraw Hill, 2004), 159–160.
68. Samuel Lewis, "Report on the Best method of Establishing and Forming Common Schools in the West," in *Transactions of the Fifth Annual Meeting of the Western Literary Institute and College of Professional Teachers* (Cincinnati: Executive Committee, 1837), 151–176.
69. Arthur Taylor Carr, *Samuel Lewis: Educational and Social Reformer* (Ph.D. diss., Western Reserve University, 1938), 44, 65–66.
70. William G. Lewis, *Biography of Samuel Lewis: First Superintendent of Common Schools for the State of Ohio* (Cincinnati: Methodist Book Concern, 1857), 131–151.
71. Carr, *Samuel Lewis,* 80–89.
72. Sister Mary Loretta Petit, O.P., *Samuel Lewis: Educational Reformer Turned Abolitionist* (Ph.D. Diss., Western Reserve University, 1966), 83–86.
73. Petit, *Samuel Lewis,* 83–86.
74. Lewis, *Biography of Samuel Lewis,* 182–184.
75. Lewis, *Biography of Samuel Lewis,* 262–265.
76. Thomas R. Rich, *The Western Literary Institute and College of Professional Teachers and the Common School Movement in the West, 1830–1840* (diss., Northern Illinois University, 1973), 173.
77. Vincent Harding, *A Certain Magnificence: Lyman Beecher and the Transformation of American Protestantism* (New York: Carlson Publishing Inc., 1991), 444–473.
78. Stuart C. Henry, *Unvanquished Puritan: A Portrait of Lyman Beecher* (Grand Rapids, Mich.: William B. Eerdmans Publishing, 1973), 267–282.
79. Dolores P. Sullivan, *William Holmes McGuffey: Schoolmaster to the Nation* (London: Associated University Presses, 1994), 70–72.
80. Robert P. Swierenga, "The Settlement of the Old Northwest: Ethnic Pluralism in a Featureless Plain," *Journal of the Early Republic* 9, no. 1 (Spring 1989): 73–105.

4

Educational Reform in the Northeast

Horace Mann presents to the Senate, nineteenth century

During the first half of the nineteenth century, educational reformers in the Northeast sought to reduce the reliance on private schools and to bring about state support and state control of schools. They faced resistance from a variety of religious groups such as Catholics who argued that public money should support church-sponsored education and from Democrats who felt that state boards of education would administer the district schools in ways that diminished local control. Public school advocates did not confront these accusations directly. Instead, reformers complained about widespread neglect of schools resulting in derelict school buildings, inappropriate curriculums, and unqualified teachers. Since most people could support these changes, the reformers reinforced an organized and rational system without drawing attention to the problems of bureaucracy.

Why Did Reformers Think There Was the Need for State Control of Education?

Many religious groups opposed common schools, claiming that secular studies threatened the formation of the children in faith. As Chapter 3 explained, Catholic educators agreed that schools should teach the children to be moral and that children should read the Bible. Catholics complained that common schools used a Protestant version of the Bible and removed the denominational guidelines Catholics thought essential for proper understanding. Another religious group that shared this view was the Calvinists who complained that knowledge of the type imparted by common schools would not help individuals become moral. The Calvinists feared that when people gained the little knowledge available from a nonreligious school, the students would turn away from the truth of the religion and the salvation it offered.[1]

According to Merle Curti, conservative politicians pointed to Benjamin Franklin to show that education was a local or private matter.[2] Franklin served as an example because he had set out to learn the virtues that he needed to succeed in the world and he had spread the means of such self-improvement through the publication of *Poor Richard's Almanac* as well as his autobiography and his sponsorship of subscription libraries. Although Franklin sponsored an academy, he claimed that he did not seek public support for these institutions. He sought philanthropic support, suggesting that the wealthy patrons would gain the satisfaction of knowing they advanced the common good.[3]

Most important, the idea of state-supported common schools violated the tradition of local control that had developed in New England towns after the War of Independence. In the sixteenth century, a colonial settlement in New England was a unit of about forty square miles with a town at the center. In each town, there was a church that residents used for meetings and as a school. As the population spread away from the center, settlers could not attend church, participate in meetings, or send their children to school. Thus, parishes opened away from the centers providing the services the towns had offered. After the War of Independence, settlers in what had been parishes assumed the legal right to form school districts, elect school trustees, levy district school taxes among themselves, select a teacher, and establish the school. Although this model started in Massachusetts, it spread quickly to other states because it fit the attitudes of the people. Those communities whose residents wanted schools could have them, pay for them, and direct what happened within them. Communities whose residents did not want schools did not have to support them. According to Elwood Cubberley, the election of Andrew Jackson as president in 1828 solidified public sentiment in favor of the district model of school administration. Jackson represented popular democracy, and the school district was the smallest unit of civic management where people could learn to protect their interests through simple forms of parliamentary procedure.[4]

Although the principle of local control of schools was established, educational reformers in New York and New England conducted a propaganda campaign from 1827 to 1847 to bring about state control of district schools. According to Sydney Jackson, the district schools, also called common schools, were institutions of primary or middle-level education. He noted that the reformers called themselves friends of education. Because they sought allies among a wide range of social groups, they maintained positions of neutrality on such important issues as religion. Unwilling to pinpoint specific enemies, they made vague complaints about people's apathy and the neglect schools suffered. At the same time, they boasted about the positive social benefits that would accrue from the spread of education.[5]

When Jackson reviewed the many periodicals and books that flourished in the early 1800s, he found that education was never a central issue during the Common School Revival. For example, although most political speeches mentioned education, other topics such as slavery or temperance were the central issues. Horace Mann focused on education, he addressed teachers in Massachusetts. According to Jackson, organizations such as the American Institute of Instruction raised issues concerning unhealthy school buildings, irrelevant curriculum offerings, and inadequate training of teachers caused by local inattention to education. The institute published lectures on these subjects, but they seemed to have less political effect than popular stories such as Warren Burton's *The District School as It Was*. Published in 1833, Burton's book did more for reform of common schools than all the treatises that came from the American Institute of Instruction. At least, this was the claim the editors of the *New York Mirror* made.[6]

Burton began his story in 1804 when he was three-and-one-half years old and started attending a district school in Wilton, New Hampshire. The school was set in the geographic center of the district so that it was equally distant from all the people who built it and paid for the teacher. This placed the building on top of a hill. It was an unattractive building consisting of one room with six windows in considerable disrepair. The exterior walls were unpainted; some of the window glass was broken and replaced with shingles. The shutters were useless. The roof leaked, and the bricks in the chimney had lost their mortar. The teacher's desk sat upon a platform. The fireplace was on the right near a door leading to a closet that served as a coatroom and as a place of punishment. On each side of the room were five or six long seats with writing benches. Burton recalled that, in winter, the room was cold, but the heat coming from the fire was hot enough to draw pitch from the plank on which he sat. Thus, while the front of his body roasted, his back froze. Worse, he could not move on this bench. Although he was very young, he had to sit quietly, memorize a list of letters or words that excited no interest, and stare forward until the teacher called on him.[7]

In his account of life in the district school, Burton described the various teachers he had. The first woman teacher was kindly although she taught material the children found tedious. Several male teachers had such sadistic tendencies that they devoted their attention to maintaining order by means of threats and beatings. One of these teachers hit a young child so hard on the head with a ruler that blood appeared. The older students rose up in anger, carried the teacher outside on a snowy day, and cast him down the hill. The best teacher that Burton had was a young man who came from a nearby academy. He required students to write compositions about things they knew, such as pressing cider or hunting squirrels. In that way, the teacher showed the children that academic studies related to life. Under this system, the teacher had little problems with order and control.[8]

At the end of the term, the students had to pass final examinations in front of the town minister. Burton thought these tests were meaningless exercises. For example, in grammar, the students demonstrated their abilities to parse the same sentences they had studied in the class. Because they had memorized the different parts of speech and their relations to each other, they were reciting what they memorized instead of showing analytical skills. Nonetheless, when the students performed, the minister praised them on their accomplishments. It would have been difficult for a minister to criticize the children of his parishioners.[9]

Although the editors of the *New York Mirror* thought Burton's book did more for school reform than the professional lectures, the lectures concentrated attention on three issues that had appeared in Burton's account. These were the unhealthy school buildings, irrelevant curriculum offerings, and inadequate training of teachers. According to Burton and professional educators, these problems derived from local school officials' inattention to or ignorance of education. The remedy was some form of central or state control. Burton complained about these difficulties in rural sections. Philanthropists contended that similar problems beset urban schools as cities grew and changed.

Between 1820 and 1860, about five million immigrants came to the United States. The bulk of this immigration occurred in the 1840s and 1850s when more than four million Irish and German immigrants arrived. Earlier, before this rush, free African Americans and some impoverished European immigrants moved to Northern cities in the early 1800s. Faced with newcomers unfamiliar with urban living, citizens organized schools where the children could learn to adapt to their new surroundings.[10]

The result was that in many cities different types of schools existed together. For example, by 1790, New York City had an extensive network of private schools that children of either sex could attend for small tuition fees. As former slaves and foreign citizens immigrated to the city, free school societies provided schools for these children. When the free schools became public schools, the Catholics set up their own network of institutions. By 1860 New York City had a varied configuration of schools that made education widely available. The public schools enrolled about 153,000 children. Catholic schools contained about 14,000 students, and independent schools had several thousand children. At the same time, some charitable organizations, such as the Children's Aid Society, continued to operate schools.[11]

Beginning as early as 1787, free schools opened in New York City to serve destitute African Americans, and in 1801 schools began to serve poor white children. Although the state chartered the Children's Aid Society, private philanthropists paid subscriptions of $200 per year to support its endeavors. Until 1853, this society built schoolhouses, trained teachers, and supplemented the work of private and church schools in efforts to turn the children of poverty into what the organization considered useful and responsible citizens.[12]

In 1806 in New York City, the Free School Society opened a school dedicated to using the monitorial method devised by Joseph Lancaster. This method offered a complete rationale for curriculum development, teacher training, and school architecture. It promised efficiency by providing instruction in basic academic skills at low prices. Because a graduate of the system could become a teacher, it included a form of teacher training. In addition, manuals of instruction gave complete directions for setting up and running such schools. Most important, the system appeared humane because it forbade corporal punishment, depending on shame and praise to motivate the children.[13]

The model began in the 1790s when two educators, Andrew Bell and Joseph Lancaster, separately developed systems of instruction that used older students who acted as monitors carrying out instruction among younger students. According to Ellwood P. Cubberley, the monitorial or mutual system was more efficient than the individual method used by rural schoolteachers. Cubberley claimed that, in rural schools, most teachers catered to individual students or to small groups of students while the other children waited. Despite Cubberley's assertion, many rural schoolteachers had older students teach younger students in ways that occupied the entire class. For example, in 1727, when the Ursiline Sisters founded a school for young women in New Orleans, they imported from France a method that depended on student-teachers, called dizainiéres, that was similar to the monitorial method Lancaster and Bell each claimed to have created about a half century later.[14]

Shortly after the first Lancaster or monitorial school opened in New York City, other cities, including Cincinnati, Detroit, and Louisville, opened schools using the Lancaster method. In 1826, Maryland instituted a statewide system that followed Lancaster's model. An important aspect of Lancaster's popularity in the United States was that he incorporated a form of moral training wherein children read gospel passages without denominational lessons, whereas Bell, on the other hand, had added the liturgy and catechism of the Anglican Church. Because the Church of England supported Bell's system, the method was unpopular in the United States.[15]

According to Lancaster, the monitorial system provided efficient and orderly instruction. For example, instead of providing each child with a book, Lancaster printed the pages of texts on large cards. The monitors took those cards to stations where groups of twelve to twenty students stood around the cards. In this way, 200 students could follow the same lesson in the space of three hours. Further, the lessons flowed along rapidly and quietly. In spelling, for example, the card contained a list of words. The first student would read the first word sounding out each syllable. If the child made an error, the monitor turned to the second student to read the word correctly. At no time, did the monitor correct the students' pronunciation. Instead, the monitor would award a medal to the child who read the word correctly.[16]

To prevent children from repeating lessons they had learned, Lancaster appointed one monitor to become an inspector-general. This monitor surveyed the different groups, took attendance, and examined the students' proficiency in the tasks assigned. Students who had mastered a particular lesson moved to another group and received an award for accomplishment.[17]

The monitors supervised the behavior of the students in their groups. If a child was idle or chattered with the other students, the monitor took out a card with the offense written on it and gave it to the offender who turned the card into the teacher. If the child repeated the offence, the teacher hung a log weighing six pounds around the child's neck to act as a pillory. If the offences continued to accumulate, the teacher placed the child in a cage suspended in front of the class. Although Lancaster lamented the need to punish children, he argued such public humiliation was less severe than the methods teachers used with other methods of instruction.[18]

Because the monitors were central to the Lancaster model, the teacher had to choose them with care and examine their mastery of the lessons they would teach. In this way, the teacher could be confident the monitors knew the subject matter well enough to fulfill their duties. Further, the teacher had to write the duties of the monitors on cards. Each monitor had to be able to recite the list of duties from memory before taking a place in the schoolroom. In addition, Lancaster required the teacher to have been a student in a monitorial school and be familiar with its principles.[19]

In addition to teacher training, Lancaster specified architectural models. According to Dell Upton, the ideal Lancaster classroom was a large undivided space. In 1840, following this recommendation, the New York Free School Society built Public School 17. It was a two-story rectangle about eighty feet long and forty-two feet wide. The teacher's desk was on a platform at one end. The students sat at desks with benches bolted to a sloping floor facing the teacher's platform. Lancaster allowed sufficient space between the desks so students could move to the aisles without disturbing each other. Lancaster argued that, because a thousand pupils could fit into such a classroom, the cost per student declined to as little as $2.50 per student per year.[20]

When Lancaster recommended large classroom spaces, American school boards tried to comply by building spacious schools. In 1818, Philadelphia built a model school for boys. They constructed another building for girls in 1820. The classrooms in these buildings were eighty feet by forty feet, and the teachers' desks were in the middle of a long wall while the students sat at three rows of desks separated by three-foot aisles. Although the board claimed that about 400 boys and 300 girls used the schools, critics complained that there were never enough students to fill them and that the board had inflated attendance figures to hide the waste.[21]

Believing instruction should inculcate morality, Lancaster created a nondenominational catechism for children to memorize. For these lessons, Lancaster adapted gospel passages into patterns of questions and answers. For example, he selected questions such as the following: "What will be the end of a perfect and upright man?" The answer the students were to learn came from a Psalm: "Mark the perfect man, and behold the upright: for the end of that man is peace."[22]

Lancaster claimed that when children memorized such questions and answers, the knowledge would serve them into adulthood because the children would remember these passages when they faced temptations. Not only would such reminders help the children retain moral virtue, he thought their value was more than the mechanical learning indicated. He was convinced that the students would recognize the truth in the passages they had memorized when they understood more about life.[23]

Using a nonsectarian approach to the Bible, Lancaster's method of moral training was similar to that witnessed by Calvin Stowe in Prussia. In 1837, when Stowe advocated that children in common schools read the Bible without commentary, Catholic Archbishop Purcell complained that this was a Protestant practice. In some places, though, the nonsectarian approach of the Lancaster school caused few problems. For example, in 1818, St. Peter's Catholic School in New York City adopted the monitorial model. In fact, Lancaster visited the school because he was in the city as the time. The difference was that Stowe wanted the nonsectarian reading of the Bible to go on in public schools attended by Catholic and Protestant children whereas St. Peter's was a Catholic school. Thus, the teachers could incorporate Catholic teachings with the Lancaster method. When other Catholic schools adopted aspects of the monitorial model, they described their type of teaching as a mixed method.[24]

At the time that the Lancaster system spread through the United States, advocates went to South America to demonstrate its superiority. In 1818, the British and Foreign School Society sent James Thompson to Hispanic America to create Lancaster schools and to sell Bibles. Traveling through Argentina, Chile, Brazil, Uruguay, Peru, Columbia, and Mexico, Thompson sought aid from political and religious leaders to create monitorial schools. At first, Thompson met with success, although he encountered problems finding qualified students to act as monitors. Later, Catholic leaders condemned what they considered a Protestant bias permeating the Lancaster model. As a result, in 1822, Thompson turned exclusively to the task of distributing Bibles.[25]

According to David Hogan, although Lancaster designed his monitorial system to aid lower-class children, the lessons served the rising middle class. Hogan argued that Lancaster placed the students in groups in hopes that the pressure from the group would control the students. At the same time that the students worked together, they competed to excel individually. Since the Lancaster system offered a rational organization or a self-regulating machine, it was similar to the marketplace described by Adam Smith. The Lancaster system prepared children to advance themselves in the ways the members of the middle class envisioned their own successes. Hogan concluded that Lancaster replaced the old system of education based on piety, subordination, and social estates with a new vision of education in which students earned rewards for their accomplishments.[26]

If Lancaster's system served middle class aspirations, this might explain why the model failed when applied to Native American education. In 1818, Reverend Cyrus Kingsbury opened the Brainerd School in Tennessee to serve forty-seven Cherokee Indians. Kingsbury's plan was to teach students academic skills through Lancaster's method while the students learned carpentry, agriculture, and cooking through manual labor. After the first year, the monitorial system had almost disappeared because the students spent most of their time at manual labor. A similar school for Native Americans, the Choctaw Academy that opened in Kentucky in 1825, went through a similar pattern of change. At first, teachers used the Lancaster method to teach academic skills. By 1832, after receiving reports that the academic studies produced little effect, the curriculum at the Choctaw Academy turned exclusively to manual labor.[27]

By the 1840s, enthusiasm for the Lancaster movement ended. In part, the method was impractical. For example, although Lancaster believed that order was most important, he wanted the students to move to different stations for their lessons and he asked the inspector-general to shift individuals to different groups. Unfortunately, a thousand students could not move around in a large room easily or quietly. Similarly, although Lancaster thought that students would pursue more education on their own after they mastered the basic instruction, there was nothing in the system that encouraged such growth. The system taught rudimentary skills and information; it did not encourage students to master complex methods of thinking.[28]

According to Carl Kaestle, the monitorial movement was a victim of its own success. Because the model promised efficiency and simplicity, the monitorial movement made people comfortable with the idea of public education. Once the Lancaster ideal encouraged people to think of teachers as having professional training, though, it caused problems for itself. The method depended on young, untrained monitors. As a result, other methods of teacher training and curriculum formation became popular.[29]

When Horace Mann wrote his seventh report to the Massachusetts State Board of Education in 1844, he described his visits to monitorial schools in England, Scotland, and Ireland. Mann explained that some countries, such as Holland and the German states, had abolished this system. According to Mann, the problem was that the instruction given by the older students, the monitors, was hampering, blinding, and misleading to the younger children. He added that the limited range of monitorial instruction became clear when compared to the creative power of an accomplished teacher.[30]

How Did Teacher Training Develop in the Early Nineteenth Century?

While the Lancaster movement gained popularity, educators in academies established a movement of teacher training built on classical education. According to Theodore R. Sizer, more than 6,000 academies established themselves during the eighty years that began with the War of Independence and ended with the American Civil War. Sizer noted that academies admitted students who had finished training in district schools, adding that academies did not offer college training but provided a variety of curriculum options. In colonial Massachusetts, for example, children leaving the district school attended a Latin grammar school, if there was one near their home, to learn Greek and Latin before entering a college such as Harvard. Academies mixed classical training in Greek and Latin with some sort of practical studies. In addition, while school districts supported Latin grammar schools, the academies received government subsidies and charged students tuition.[31]

Sizer believed the hybrid nature of the academies fit the ambivalent attitudes of early nineteenth-century Americans. For example, Sizer noted that academies offered a mix of classical and practical curriculums. Americans held people with the ability to read or write Latin in high esteem. At the same time, though, they expected graduates to be able to do something to earn a living. In addition, although academies could not exist without some form of government support, the heart of the Jacksonian movement was the enhancement of small private businesses. Thus, Sizer noted, the owners of the academies presented their institutions as private schools that depended on some form of student payments.[32]

Although neither Lane Seminary in Cincinnati, Ohio, nor Andover Seminary, the model Beecher used for Lane, were academies, they shared common origins and functions with the academies. Phillips Academy at Andover, Massachusetts, was one of the first academies, and it became the model. Phillips opened in 1778; Andover Seminary began in 1808 on the same grounds. For more than one hundred years, the two institutions had the same board of trustees. Nonetheless, not until 1830 did Phillips Academy fulfill its promise to provide practical training. It opened the English Department for teacher training. Calvin Stowe recalled this model when he returned from Prussia in 1837 and recommended that academies offer teacher training.[33]

According to Claude M. Fuess, the constitution of Phillips Academy adopted in 1778 had called for classical studies, such as Latin and Greek, mixed with practical courses, such as geometry and science. Together these studies would reveal to the students something of their final destiny and something about the business of life. The constitution added that the scholars were to engage in gardening and manual labor to preserve their health and develop habits of industry. Despite these mandates, the academy had concentrated on classical studies. Fuess contended that the trustees' decision in 1830 to include teacher training brought Phillips back to the original intentions of the founders.[34]

Phillips appointed the Reverend Samuel Read Hall to be the first principal of the English Department in 1830. Hall had experience in this area because in 1823 he opened a teacher-training program in Concord, Vermont. To help the trainees, Hall wrote a manual for teachers to follow. Published in 1929, Hall's manual was entitled *Lectures on School-Keeping* because it contained thirteen lectures he had given in his own teacher-training school. The first three lectures explained the ways that common schools provided the basis for a democratic society, the obstacles that reformers faced in advancing common schools, and the talents teachers had to perfect in themselves to succeed in their work. Written with rural schools in mind, Hall used these lectures to offer practical reasons for a person to want to be a teacher. He thought that teachers should see their mission as one of introducing moral behavior among children left to run wild in the country. In his lectures, Hall suggested that teachers use simple language the students could understand, that the teachers be patient and forgiving with derelict students, and that they know the subjects they taught. He also noted the difficulties schools faced, suggesting that farmers were unnecessarily parsimonious when they refused to buy inexpensive books for the scholars. He complained that the people in school districts refused to accede to one another and, as a result, they built schools in the geographic center of the district. Unfortunately, this could result in selecting inclement sites such as the top of a treeless hill where winter winds buffeted or summer sun baked them.[35]

In his specific suggestions, Hall quoted such philosophers as Pestalozzi, who made the schoolroom be pleasant for the children and advocated that teachers endeavor to do the same. He urged teachers to ensure that students understood the work they did and to devote their complete attention to helping students succeed. In one example, Hall described a teacher who wanted his students to love their subjects but went about it the wrong way. When a young girl asked him why she had to carry a number when doing addition, the instructor answered that was because numbers move from right to left in a decimal ratio. Although the words puzzled the girl, the instructor turned to help another student. According to Hall, the teacher could never repair the damage done to the girl. She had not understood the answer, and she decided that she could not do arithmetic because it was too complicated for her.[36]

Hall developed his interest in teaching while training for the ministry, as his father had done. In 1796, one year after Hall's birth, his father, Samuel Read Hall, Sr., set off to establish a farm in Canada. While traveling to the farm site, he found the seller had cheated him. Consequently, instead of becoming farmers, the family settled in Vermont. Because his father had trained for the ministry, Hall read these textbooks as a child. In 1811, Hall Sr. accepted a post as church minister in Bethel, Maine, but he died only three years later. Hall went to the local school, studied for the ministry, and began to teach school. Introducing new methods of instruction, Hall encountered difficulties but overcame them. For example, when Hall asked his students to write original compositions, they rebelled and Hall had to explain the reasons for such work to the parents. In a few days, the students completed their assignments.[37]

In 1818, Hall entered Kimball Union Academy in New Hampshire and remained three years while teaching in district schools in the winters. He brought to the schools several innovations such as the study of geography and the use of new texts. When the Vermont Domestic Missionary Society asked him to accept assignment to a church in Concord Corner, Hall agreed, provided the Society would allow him to establish a school to prepare young men and women for teaching. According to Mason Stone, the idea of teacher training was unusual at that time, as was the concept of a woman teacher.[38]

In an advertisement for his school, Hall mentioned that he was willing to omit instruction in classical languages. Despite his desire to offer practical information, Hall did not attract many students. Further, Hall suffered for being a mason. Until 1829, there was considerable hostility against masons in Vermont because advocates of freemasonry eschewed attachment to any religious denomination, although they embraced many religious beliefs, including faith in a supreme being. As a result, when Phillips opened its English Department, Hall recognized an opportunity to leave Vermont, and he accepted the appointment.[39]

Mason Stone believed that Hall's school was the first normal school in America. Ellwood Cubberley disagreed. According to Cubberley, the curriculum in Hall school followed the typical academy training in mathematics, chemistry without a laboratory component, astronomy, logic, moral philosophy, and Christianity. Teacher training came in the form of lectures in the third year and some practice teaching in district schools in the winter. Cubberley claimed that in 1836 Massachusetts applied the name *normal school* to a program to prepare teachers. He added that this was the first use of the term and the first state supported teacher-training institute. The name came from the French term designating a school where teachers learned to teach according to the best standards or norms.[40]

As the name implied, the English Department at Phillips excluded studies in Latin and Greek. Although the English Department accepted only men, they could enroll for lengths of time ranging from one term to six years. In addition to the teacher's class where the students sought to master pedagogy, the students could enroll in a general department where they prepared for life. The department had a model school that enrolled children who provided practice for the teachers in training. To make its curriculum practical, the English Department offered a varied curriculum that included six courses in mathematics, several scientific courses, surveying, civil engineering, moral philosophy, history, and the art of teaching.[41]

The teacher-training component at Phillips was never popular. In 1835, the trustees of Phillips Academy changed the name of the English Department to the Teachers' Seminary, and they sought to regularize attendance by extending the program over three years and shaping the courses so that they fit together and advanced each year. In this way, the trustees hoped to draw attention to the value of the program for young men preparing to become teachers in district schools. However, these changes did not increase enrollment. Consequently, in 1837, Hall left. When Reverend Lyman Coleman succeeded him, he emphasized general education or practical courses. Although this direction attracted some students, the improvement was inadequate. In 1842, the Teachers' Seminary changed its name back to the English Department, merged with the Academy, and offered a similar curriculum but omitting the language studies found in the classical program. Thus, instead of offering a significantly different form of training through teacher preparation, the English Department became the less rigorous, less prestigious of the two programs found at Phillips.[42]

In addition to programs at academies such as Phillips, there were two other types of teacher preparation. One of these was the teacher institute. It remained popular until the American Civil War. Started by Henry Barnard in 1839, an institute offered several weeks of meetings focusing on such subjects as mathematics, reading, geography, and the practice of teaching. The participants visited schools to watch teaching methods in action, and they discussed how to create teacher associations in various parts of the country. The other type of teacher preparation institution was the state supported normal school similar to Hall's innovation.[43]

Although institutes and normal schools appeared early in the nineteenth century, the normal schools did not become popular until after the War between the States. According to Paul Mattingly, the change came about because a new generation of educators became more concerned about the specific professional abilities of teachers. Before the American Civil War, the educators wanted teachers to possess appropriate character traits. Since no one could measure these traits, the inspirational nature of the teacher institutes appeared to offer adequate preparation.[44]

In 1842, Henry Barnard and Emma Willard created what they called a permanent Normal Institute. They wanted teachers to take classes for a month twice a year, once in April and again in August, for four years. These sessions took place before the summer sessions began in district schools and before the winter sessions started. In between these visits, the participants taught in elementary schools.[45]

The idea of teacher institutes spread quickly throughout New England. In most cases, a single person, such as Emma Willard, dominated a particular institute. This happened because the educators believed it was the integrity, the character, and the moral perspective of the distinguished person that made him or her into a fine teacher. The institutes repeated the need for the participating teachers to develop these qualities. Most important, since many prestigious educators accepted the idea of the institutes, advocates raised substantial funds to pay for them. By 1860 though, the institutes had changed from schools of teacher preparation into opportunities for convivial professional meetings, methods of raising public awareness about educational problems, and entertainment.[46]

In Massachusetts, Horace Mann contended in 1838 that academies, colleges, normal schools, or any other method could provide adequate teacher training. Refusing to advance any particular method, he wanted the Massachusetts legislature to support the necessity of teacher training in some form and he used his position as secretary to the newly formed state board of education to make this plea around the state.[47]

Mann had this opportunity because in 1837, Governor Edward Everett, urged the Massachusetts senate to approve legislation authorizing him to appoint eight persons to a state board of education. The secretary, Mann, was to collect information needed to make recommendations for educational improvements. The legislation required that Mann travel to each county and also deliver an annual address to the state's common school convention. During these lectures, Mann made many of his pleas for reform. He had accepted the position although he had expressed doubts that he could make many changes as he rode from county to county appealing for reform. He changed his mind when he read about education in other countries and decided that common school reform was necessary. The popularity of his lectures suggested there was a receptive audience for his ideas.[48]

When Mann delivered his second address or lecture, he spoke about teacher training. He noted that at the time there were three women teachers for every two men teachers. He believed that more women should serve as teachers because they had the natural talents to understand and correctly lead young children. Nonetheless, he wanted the women to go through some sort of training so they would develop their talents correctly.[49]

In 1838, when the legislature agreed to support teacher training, they set up three normal schools in rural areas spread around the state. They chose rural schools because the enrollments in rural schools exceeded the enrollments in urban schools. Further, the resources available in the rural districts were low. When historian Jurgen Herbst collected measures of the students who attended these three normal schools, he found that almost 85 percent of them were women. The average age of the women students was about 18 years and the men students had an average age of about 21 years. About half of the women came from farm families whereas seven out of ten of the men did.[50]

Although the Massachusetts State Board of Education reported in 1844 that the normal schools had succeeded in producing qualified teachers, Horace Mann recommended that the state expand its efforts. When Mann delivered his report of 1844, he recommended that the Board adopt the system of teacher institutes that Barnard and Willard had begun in New York. Arguing that these institutes offered the characteristics of a good normal school, he thought that the institutes would complement the progress shown by the normal schools.[51]

Unfortunately, the normal schools may not have improved the rural schools as much as hoped. The problem was that many students used the normal schools as vocational training centers that helped them prepare for jobs elsewhere. Although the women were more likely to remain teachers than were the men, they moved into the cities where pay was better. The male students used normal school training to compensate for inadequate district school educations. After graduation, they moved into other unrelated occupations. As a result, by 1873, although the normal schools were in the rural sections, almost half of the teachers with normal school training taught in the eighteen cities of Massachusetts.[52]

It may have been that those normal school graduates who moved to the cities to apply their education denied the rural areas the benefits of their education, and the male graduates who sought other employment ignored the problems of schools. Nonetheless, these graduates were participating in a social change that was affecting American society. In 1790, about 5.1 percent of the population lived in towns of more than 2,500 people. By 1860, the percentage of people in such towns, defined as cities by the U.S. Bureau of the Census, rose to 19.8 percent. At the same time, the percentage of workers involved in nonagricultural work rose from 28.1 percent in 1820 to 41 percent in 1860. According to Maris Vinovskis, this commercialization of the economy forced more Americans to look beyond their local community for their livelihoods. As a result, the normal schools may have helped graduates acquire the education needed to move from rural areas to more urban centers and to take on occupations unknown in farming communities.[53]

How Did School Architecture Influence Curriculum Formation?

In 1830, William Alcott, brother of Bronson Alcott, published an essay on the construction of schoolhouses. Credited with being the first discussion of this subject, Alcott's essay recommended that country schoolhouses follow Lancaster's model except the floor should not slope. He thought a school should consist of one room about 48 feet long and 35 feet wide. The school should have seats and desks for about sixty students set into rows with aisles of about two feet separating them. The teacher sat in front of the students. Horace Mann approved of this model.[54]

In his first annual report, in 1838, Mann had complained that school facilities were inadequate. He appended a subsequent report describing some of the improper conditions that he had observed. A year later, Mann noted that some towns had improved their buildings. Nonetheless, he repeated his complaints in his second annual report in 1839. The children sat upon hard benches. Between recitations, they did nothing more than look straight ahead. The schoolroom lacked adequate ventilation. In this report, Mann noted that a physician had compared the rate of illnesses in two similarly constructed school buildings with relatively similar student bodies. One building had poor ventilation while the other building had adequate windows and vents. At the end of forty-five days, the school with poor ventilation had nineteen students who missed twenty days of school because of illness. In the school with good ventilation, five scholars missed twenty days of classes because of illness. To Mann, the evidence was clear that proper ventilation and clean surroundings were essential to promote student health.[55]

In his sixth report, delivered in 1843, Mann devoted attention to the curriculum in the schools. The state had required schools to teach spelling, reading, writing English grammar, geography, and arithmetic. Since teachers could offer other subjects, Mann collected a list of the courses found in schools and the numbers of students in each class. The most popular course was American history. Algebra enrolled about 2,500 students, about 1,500 children studied bookkeeping. Latin classes enrolled about 1,000 pupils, and Greek was last with nearly 200 students. As Mann considered this list, he could not see any reasonable pattern. The decisions to offer courses seemed capricious. Practical courses enrolled fewer students than abstract ones. Worse, the course that Mann thought most important, physiology, never appeared. This omission was important to Mann because he thought physiology taught the laws of health. Although he thought that there was no problem observing such laws, people had to understand them before they could follow them. He believed the aim of the common schools was to help people improve their health.[56]

Mann connected school architecture and curriculum because they promoted health. He also noted that the organization of school districts could influence curriculum selection. For example, he suggested merging school districts so they could build separate schools for children of different ages. In this way, one of the schools could become a high school.

When Mann made these suggestions, there was little stratification by age in schools. The most common distinction in rural district schools was between the summer term, when young children attended, and the winter term, when the older children came. In urban schools, the model tended to be primary schools for children aged five years to twelve and intermediate for older children. In 1847, John D. Philbrick worked out a system in Quincy, Massachusetts, for graded instruction that followed two principles. First, the subject matter was standardized and organized in a progression of increasing difficulty. Second, administrators assigned teachers to teach different parts of this course of studies. To some extent, the teachers divided the children into grades by age. More frequently, teachers placed children in different grades according to the students' abilities to master the material.[57]

Writing in 1848, Henry Barnard sought ways that intelligently designed buildings could reinforce the entire education of the children, no matter what system of separating the different levels of students the districts followed. To make this point, Barnard wrote his book, *School Architecture.* By 1855, readers in New York, Massachusetts, Connecticut, Rhode Island, Vermont, New Hampshire, Ohio, Indiana, and Upper Canada bought more than 125,000 copies of this book. In his volume, Barnard considered location and type of construction of the school, the size, the available lighting, the ventilation, the heating, the seats and desks, the arrangements for the teacher, instructional aids, the library, and the landscaping. Barnard believed that some school designs aided the instruction of the children. Other designs hindered good teaching.[58]

Barnard suggested that the exterior of the school exhibit proportion calculated to inspire respect in the students. Within the school building, each student should have 150 cubic feet of air. They needed space to move freely, and teachers required aisles to pass among the students comfortably. All rooms had to have adequate ventilation. To ensure adequate heating, the building had to be strong enough to keep out winter winds. Barnard recommended using Franklin stoves in place of fireplaces because the stoves were much more efficient. He provided several examples of comfortable, sturdy, and inexpensive desks and chairs for the students so they need not sit with their feet dangling in the air or leaning over to reach a desk placed far from the bench. Although he recommended that the teacher have a large desk situated on a platform, he noted that teachers had to move about the classroom in order to keep order. Barnard added that every classroom should have blackboards, clocks, counters, globes, pictures, and magic lanterns that were a type of slide projector. He thought these devices would enable children to learn on their own. The school had to have a library providing books to reinforce the teaching in the classroom. The yard should offer a playground. The school's landscaping should enhance the students' tastes for beauty and appreciation of nature.[59]

Although Barnard approved of the model of a rural school described by Alcott, he offered several variations. For example, in Windsor, Connecticut, he found a brick building 34 feet by 22 feet that was fashioned in a style he called Greek Revival. Its plain classical lines offered a graceful appearance. The front of the building had one door. Within the building, the twenty-six students sat in one large room at individual desks set in four rows. The students faced the teacher's desk behind which were two doors. One of them was for boys to enter the building and the other was for girls.[60]

In other areas, Barnard found a range of designs of one-room buildings with adequate space for each child and one teacher. Barnard explained that they were comfortable, attractive, and pleasant. One model was a rustic, octagonal schoolhouse that had a glass-covered opening in the center of the roof, called a lantern, providing light and ventilation. Barnard recommended this idea because the lighting spread evenly through the room. The ventilation was good because the air moved up the high walls. The shutters on the side windows closed to prevent the distractions of glass windows. Another model was a board and batten building. Although inexpensive, it was a serviceable model about 30 feet long and 20 feet wide.[61]

In addition to one-room schools, Barnard offered designs for those rural districts that had merged as Mann suggested so that they could offer advanced studies to some pupils. In these cases, the buildings followed the same general patterns, but they contained one section for the primary school, another section for the intermediate schools, and a third section for the high school. The example from Woonsocket, Rhode Island, housed 160 pupils in an elementary school on the first floor in the front of the building. Behind this area, two intermediate schoolrooms held 64 students each. The third floor was devoted to 170 high school students with a recitation room and a room to store teaching apparatus.[62]

Urban schools offered the most opportunity for specialization although the categories followed those found in rural districts. These included primary schools, intermediate schools, grammar schools, and high schools. In the cases that Barnard described, the spaces were large. For example, in the grammar school, the rooms held 200 students. In the high school, chemical experiments took place as demonstrations in lecture rooms holding 250 pupils. Although boys and girls attended the same buildings, they used separate entrances, played in different yards, and sat on opposite sides of the rooms.[63]

From Barnard's description of such large classrooms, two questions arise. The first is whether enrollments were high enough to warrant such classrooms at the high school level in 1848 when Barnard wrote his book. The second is whether the high schools served a restricted group of people. One set of answers is that the enrollments were not large and the students came from a narrow class of people. Michael Katz gave these responses when he discovered the records of an election held in Beverly, Massachusetts, in 1860. At that time, the leaders of the town held a vote whether to abolish a high school they had recently built. Massachusetts had passed the first compulsory education law in 1852 and required the town to build a high school. Opponents of the high school wanted to redistribute the money to the school districts. The city leaders wanted to use the election results to challenge the law in court. In 1968, Katz compiled a survey of the occupations of the people who voted in this election. The majority agreed to disband the high school and these voters came from a lower social class than did the voters who supported the high school. Thus, Katz concluded that high schools in early nineteenth-century Massachusetts served a few rich families and ignored the larger group of working class families.[64]

Since no statewide records exist about high school attendance in Massachusetts in 1860, historians could not easily verify whether the high school was popular or not. Nevertheless, in 1995, Maris Vinovskis compiled surveys of the lives of individuals who had lived in Essex County, Massachusetts, in the 1860s. He found that about 20 percent of them had completed some sort of high school education. More surprising, when he listed the occupations of the fathers, he discovered that one out of six children of unskilled workers had attended a public high school. Because Essex County included a medium sized city, Newburyport, Vinovskis looked outside the city to small towns where a high school was available. In those settings, at least four out of ten of the children had attended high school. Thus, it may be that Barnard was correct and that, at least in the Northeast, high schools had to be spacious enough to accommodate large numbers of students.[65]

How Did European Models Influence Curriculum Formation and Teacher Training?

In his seventh annual report, delivered in 1844, Horace Mann described what he had seen when he visited Prussia. Comparing his observations to those Calvin Stowe had made, Mann proclaimed that the United States should adopt the Prussian system. Although Mann recognized that the Prussian model served an aristocracy, he was convinced that it could reinforce a democratic republic.[66]

Mann was impressed with the lessons that consisted of conversations between teachers and pupils about objects that surrounded them. In the youngest classes, these took the form of descriptions of the schoolroom. The students described the materials used in constructing the classroom. They listed its different parts and the objects it contained. They went on to speak about their food, their duties as children, and their relation to their maker. For older children, the discussions were about objects that were remote or abstract such as different kingdoms of nature or various occupations people pursued.[67]

Mann thought these object lessons exercised the children's thinking, and he disagreed with critics who claimed children recited the answers from memory. Quoting a teacher who claimed it was a sin for a teacher not to encourage the students to think, Mann noted that the teacher did not use books, but instead encouraged the children to observe objects closely and find a multitude of aspects in them. For example, a lock could have different parts or it could be made of certain materials and those materials, such as iron, could have certain qualities such as malleability. Mann decided the opportunities were endless. Most important, the discussions interested the children; they delighted in the exercise of their perceptive powers.[68]

Although Mann was impressed with the ways that the Prussian schools encouraged children to develop the powers of reason and to become moral beings, he accepted the then common view that the Prussian people did not make many mechanical inventions, appeared sluggish, and retained such vices as sexual promiscuity. Mann explained that the Prussian people did not engage in intelligent thought because the government and the religion were authoritarian. Although the children learned to think independently in school, they left school to enter a society where they could not exercise such freedoms and the children lost the abilities. He added that vice remained because the upper classes displayed personal depravities, thereby setting examples that contradicted the lessons of the schools. His conclusion was that a republic where virtue permeated the social order could adopt the Prussian system.[69]

When Mann presented his report in Massachusetts, several Boston schoolmasters contended that their textbook method was superior to the Prussian model of discussions between teachers and pupils. They argued that the textbook method did not depend on the teacher to lead the student to make discoveries. With texts, the children learned to learn on their own. Further, the schoolmasters contended that when teachers offered interesting lessons, the children did not learn to discharge their duties. The schoolmasters argued that children should acquire the habit of deriving their pleasures from fulfilling their responsibilities.[70]

The controversy between Mann and the Boston schoolteachers escalated into extensive controversies. Although the teachers modified some of their views, they retained their argument that classroom teachers had to employ some corporal punishment in order to maintain positions of authority. Mann may have profited from the publications that resulted from this debate. In a short time, though, the controversy turned into a political battle in which Mann's supporters tried to remove the protesting teachers from their positions and the teachers tried to establish teacher organizations to remove Mann as secretary. The fight exhausted Mann. Nonetheless, Jonathan Messerli claimed that Mann influenced public opinion and Mann's supporters preserved their gains quietly through teacher training, licensing arrangements, and the adoption of administrative rules in schools.[71]

In his report, Mann did not explain the sources of the system that Prussian schools used. In fact, the Prussian schools followed the ideas of a Swiss educator, Johann Heinrich Pestalozzi. This influence began in the eighteenth century when Frederick the Great and Queen Louisa read Pestalozzi's book, *Leonard and Gertrude.* In Berlin and Frankfort, schools opened that followed Pestalozzi's model of educating children and fitting them for life. By 1809, after Prussia suffered military defeats, the Prussian leaders organized a primary school system based on Pestalozzi's principles, determined the aim of this education was to train the students' abilities to make judgments and to develop their moral senses, and established methods to train teachers. This was the system Mann viewed and praised.[72]

Before Prussia built its primary school system, a French citizen, Francis Joseph Nicholas Neef, brought Pestalozzi's ideas to the United States. Previously in 1796, Neef suffered a wound at the battle of Arcole when Napoleon extended French control of Italy. While recuperating, he read Pestalozzi's work and decided to become a disciple. Neef went to Burdorf, Switzerland, to learn the method. In 1809, Neef traveled to the United States to open a school outside Philadelphia at the falls of the Schuylkill financed by the philanthropist, William Maclure, who later invited Neef to move to the utopian project in New Harmony, Indiana.[73]

To encourage Americans to accept Pestalozzi's ideas, Neef in 1808 wrote *Sketch of a Plan of Education Founded on an Analysis of the Human Faculties and Natural Reason Suitable for the Offspring of Free People.* Describing his indebtedness to Pestalozzi and to Maclure, Neef defined education as the unfolding of human powers. To Neef, this meant that the pupils had to begin with things they knew and proceed to things they did not. In explaining how to help the children unfold the power of speech, Neef described how he would ask them to describe the human body by examining its external form. In this exercise, the students had to determine when an object was a part of a larger whole and when it was independent. In this way, he listed several exercises that led the students to describe their bodies and the parts. He claimed that in this manner, the students learned the four ways people acquire knowledge: from immediate perceptions, from their own thoughts, from comparisons or analogies, and from testimony of other people.[74]

During moral lessons, Neef asked students to discover what he considered truths. For example, the recognition that their bodies needed food, clothing, and shelter led them to discover the need for society and government. When the students considered that God created them, they determined that God endowed them with human rights and prescribed duties, the supreme one being the following mandate: Do not do to other people what you do not want them to do to you. These discussions between Neef and his students culminated in a constitution for the school. To him, these exercises seemed more educative than asking the students to memorize a catechism or read the Bible.[75]

In summarizing his model, Neef claimed that he did not teach the students anything. He learned along with them. For this reason, he would not accept more than forty students. Disparaging the idea that teachers would set pupils to work individually, he wanted all the students to hold discussions with him as a class. Consequently, he wanted the students to be of about the same age, between the ages of six and eight years old. Above all, Neef refused to use any form of punishment because he thought the teacher should be a friend of each student. The students would spend four hours per day at their studies or discussions, although they might spend longer periods when they matured. Finally, he wanted the students to be prepared to take exams each month to ascertain their progress.[76]

Although American schools did not adopt Neef's methods, other educators brought Pestalozzi's ideas to public attention. For example, Henry Barnard described Pestalozzi's ideas in his journal and in at least one volume. The most significant influences in spreading the doctrines of Pestalozzi were Edward Austin Sheldon and the Oswego Normal School.[77]

According to Hariklia Efthimiou, the method of object teaching developed at Oswego dominated teacher training in normal schools during the second half of the nineteenth century. Although prominent educators such as William Torrey Harris preferred the textbook method of teaching, object teaching depended on pedagogical principles that became central in the progressive education movement of the twentieth century.[78]

In 1861, Sheldon was the secretary of the board of education of Oswego, New York. As the chief administrator of the schools, he arranged for Margaret E. M. Jones of the Home Colonial Training Institution in London, England, to open a teacher-training school in Oswego. She introduced what she called the new methods to teachers in the city schools. Sheldon claimed this was the first teacher-training school organized in America. Although he knew about earlier examples of normal schools, he thought Ms. Jones's innovation was that she concentrated on training teachers in the actual practice of their work.[79]

Sheldon became interested in the work of Home Colonial Training Institution because he was dissatisfied with his initial efforts in organizing the Oswego schools. In 1853, Sheldon had created the school system. On taking office, Sheldon had arranged the city into twelve primary districts with schools to cover the first three years of the children's school life. This pattern divided the children equally and distributed them to appropriate buildings. In addition, he made up four junior school districts for the fourth, fifth, and sixth years of the children's school life. Finally, he opened two high schools that enrolled students for three years. He weeded out poor teachers, installed a qualifying exam for teachers, and hired candidates who scored well on the tests as new teachers. When he brought in several teachers from Syracuse where he had worked earlier, critics complained of hiring teachers from out of town instead of employing home talent. Sheldon's defense was that he wanted good, experienced teachers in the schools no matter where he had found them.[80]

Sheldon had taken care to spread the school buildings around the town to facilitate attendance. In one case, though, all three divisions occupied the same building. In the high schools, Sheldon arranged for teachers to offer all the courses taught in other high schools in New York. With this accomplishment, he claimed that the schools offered a continuous course of study that extended through all levels from the beginning of primary school to the end of high school. To serve the different schools, he opened a central library and acted as the librarian. When Sheldon found that some pupils did not meet the qualifications for the branch they should attend because of their ages, he created an unclassified school that gave those students opportunities to improve in the areas that kept them from being with their age mates. Every Saturday, he met with his teachers to discuss principles of education and methods of teaching. Despite, or perhaps because of, this organization, he complained that the system was like a machine, and he called for a change.[81]

In 1859, seeking to bring life to his schools, Sheldon began touring neighboring cities that had reputations for having good schools. In Toronto, Ontario, Sheldon saw the charts of objects, colors, and forms that the Home and Colonial Training Institution had distributed. Along with the materials were complete sets of instructions in their proper use. After purchasing three hundred dollars worth of these materials, he installed them in the schools. They became the subject matter of his Saturday meetings with the teachers. After two years, he found that teachers were taking his training and leaving the Oswego schools to teach for other city schools. Deciding to set up a training school charging tuition to teachers from outside Oswego, Sheldon wrote to the London institution to hire one of their representatives to run the training school. The institution sent Ms. Jones.[82]

The training school opened with nine prospective teachers enrolled. It was located in a primary school building with about 200 children. After one year, Ms. Jones returned to London. Hermann Krüsi, who had worked with Pestalozzi, took her place.[83]

In 1861, during the first year that Ms. Jones taught at the Oswego training school, the board of education invited prominent educators to examine the system of object teaching that Sheldon had introduced. The participants included the secretary of the board of regents for New York, state superintendent of Connecticut, superintendents of Syracuse and Rochester, principals from high schools in Albany, New York, and Trenton, New Jersey, and directors of several institutions in Indiana and New Jersey.

The committee examined the primary schools for three days in February 1862. The committee's report began with a description of the system. Quoting Pestalozzi, the report noted that he based his method on faith and love, that he sought the harmonious development of every faculty in the children's minds, that he wanted instruction to begin with the perception of external objects, and that he wanted every lesson to be about form, number, and language. Finally, Pestalozzi found the basis of moral teaching to derive from the children's ability to express love, gratitude, veneration, and confidence. After noting these principles, the committee witnessed several different lessons carried out by the teachers and children. These included a lesson on form wherein the children described the shape of a stovepipe and a lesson on size where children measured such things as the distances between their fingers, the length of lines on the blackboard, and the sizes of torn sheets of paper.[84]

When the examinations ended, the committee agreed that the principles of the system harmonized with the laws of human development. They added that the demonstrations they witnessed illustrated that harmony. As a result, they approved of the work done in Oswego and recommended school districts adopt the system.[85]

The report of the examination committee fueled the spread of the object method. In 1863, Sheldon explained his work to the National Teachers' Association (NTA), and in 1865, a committee on object teaching for the organization reported that skillful teachers enjoyed success with object teaching in elementary schools. For the following decade, object teaching was a part of most conventional teaching.[86]

When Ms. Jones taught the training school, she described the principles of object teaching. She thought teachers should begin by allowing the child to discover things, because this would exercise the child's senses. Jones thought it was important for the teacher to begin with sensory exercises because she wanted the teachers to train the child to act, to offer variety in the lessons, and to cultivate the faculties of the children's minds in their natural order. She wanted teachers to reduce each subject to its elements, presenting one at a time and proceeding systematically. She added that each lesson should have a point. When teaching terms, the teachers should develop the idea before giving the name of the concept or thing. In general, teachers should proceed from simple things to difficult tasks, from things the children knew to those they did not. The direction should follow from the particular to the general and from the concrete to the abstract. The idea was that there was a particular order in which the teacher had to move in order for the children to develop their mental abilities or what Jones and Sheldon called mental faculties [87]

In 1866, Sheldon arranged an edition of the Home and Colonial Training Institution's book, *Lessons on Objects.* Originally written by Elizabeth Mayo, the book offered models for teachers to follow in designing lessons for a class. The text recommended that teachers write a sketch of each lesson before trying it. The sketch was to begin with a statement of the single point the lesson was to make. The next part was a description of the method or plan of the lesson. This would include a description of the steps the teacher would follow in order to draw out the information from the students. Since the way children learned something was as important as what they learned, each lesson had to exercise the children's minds, and the way this happened should be in the sketch. In addition, the sketch should describe how the teacher would introduce what is abstract, would illustrate what students do not understand, and would resolve the complex into simple elements. Finally, the title of the lesson should appear at the top.[88]

The text contained five series of lessons arranged in order of increasing difficulty. The aims of the lessons were to develop the students' capacities of perception, to call each sense into action, and to enable students to make correct judgments. The hope was to link ideas to words in ways that provided a ready command of language. The text warned the teacher not to tell the students too much and not to give the students a term before the student felt the need for it.[89]

In the first lesson, the children held a basket, named it, and distinguished its parts. They had to describe the uses of the basket and the use of each part. Finally, the teacher asked the students what would happen if various parts were missing. This series of lessons continued through twenty-two objects, such as a needle, a penknife, a picture of a pig, a cube of wood, and finally an orange. In the last exercise, the students noted the peel of the orange, the rind of the peel, the white of the peel, the juice, the pulp, the seeds, the eye, the divisions, the membrane, the inside, the outside, and the surface. For each part, they had to tell the qualities they noticed. For example, the quality of the peel was its color. The quality of the pulp was its juice.[90]

Although the first series in Sheldon's text had twenty-two lessons, the last series extended through ninety-four individual lessons. The final series was to become exercises in composition. After the students worked through the analysis of an object in a discussion with the teacher together as a class, the students would write individual essays describing the object. One such lesson was making comparisons of different types of glass, pointing out their differences, their different uses, their advantages over other substances, their method of manufacture, and the history of their construction. Because students could not guess some of the answers by looking at the objects, the text indicated what the teacher should tell the students.[91]

One member of the examination committee that had praised object teaching in 1862 apparently dissented. Although the original report did not contain any attachment, H. B. Wilbur criticized the Oswego system in a report to the New York State Teachers Association and to the National Teacher's Association. Complaining that object teaching held dubious standing in England, Wilbur pointed out that separating children by age prevented younger children learning from older children. Another difficulty was that children had to discover every truth for themselves. Wilbur did not believe children could recreate the advances of human knowledge by this process. A third difficulty was the overly complicated way the object method presented simple steps. For example, the process asked a child to develop an idea and then learn a term for it. He thought that these processes happened together. He added that, when teachers tried to separate an idea from the term that named it, they gave the children overly advanced words, such as *amorphous, serrated,* and *hyaline.* In all, Wilbur called for more study into the wisdom of object teaching before it spread further.[92]

Despite Sheldon's continual mention of Pestalozzi, the Oswego method of object teaching did not conform to Pestalozzi's model. According to Gerald Lee Gutek, the type of object teaching found in Oswego was overly formal. Nonetheless, the Oswego method had several benefits. Because the teacher planned and organized the instruction for the entire class, the method offered reduced discipline problems.[93]

Ironically, Sheldon may have failed in bringing about the changes he wanted. He turned to the object method in order to break away from the mechanical atmosphere he had created when first placed in charge of the Oswego schools. Unfortunately, in adapting English object teaching to his school, he made it into a mechanical process that teachers could follow in a lock-step pattern. For example, the lessons he placed in his book gave answers that students might offer and it listed explanations that teachers could make. Although Sheldon noted in the preface that he offered the outlines as suggestions, not as plans to be blindly followed, the process could devolve into a series of memorized questions and answers.

How Did Schools Change during the Common School Movement?

In 1980, two historians, Carl Kaestle and Maris Vinovskis, used extensive statistical analyses to determine several changes that took place during the common school movement. Because the analyses revealed correlations, the historians could not determine what caused the changes. Nonetheless, what they found was important.

Concentrating on Massachusetts, Kaestle and Vinovskis noted that enrollment levels measured by percentage of school-age children who attended school declined from 1840 to 1880. This did not signal a defeat of the common school movement because the population grew at such a rate and students transferred from private to public schools in such numbers that the numbers of children in common schools increased considerably. Nor was the increased attendance concentrated in cities. Kaestle and Vinovskis found that sparsely populated towns had the highest percentage of children in schools, but these school terms were short, giving fewer schooldays to rural children. Commercial towns had longer school sessions and higher enrollments than did towns dependent on manufacturing. Although older children tended to leave school, adolescents living in rural areas tended to stay in school longer than teenagers in urban settings, perhaps because the school offered a social role absent in rural children's lives. Although there were many factors involved, Kaestle and Vinovskis concluded that increased population and industrialization did not bring about increased schooling.[94]

Kaestle and Vinovskis found a way to measure the sources of resistance to the common school movement. In 1840, the representatives in the Massachusetts House held a vote to decide whether to retain or abolish the newly founded board of education, with Mann as secretary, and newly erected normal schools. The vote failed and the board and the normal schools remained. Analyzing the votes in this contest, Kaestle and Vinovskis found that the issue fell along party lines. The Whigs, the party to which Mann belonged, supported the expenditure of state money to support teacher seminaries. The opposing party, the Democrats, did not want to support those institutions because they felt that private academies could train teachers and they did not believe teachers needed special training. More important, the Democrats feared the extent to which the state board of education could interfere in local district school affairs. They complained that such a body could determine the curriculum in each district school, thereby undermining local autonomy. When Kaestle and Vinovskis looked at other factors such as religion or occupations of the voters in a representative's district, they could not find that these factors influenced the votes, although they did find more support among representatives of economically developed areas of the state for the board and normal schools than among those from less-developed areas. Because the issue fell along party lines, Kaestle and Vinovskis concluded that the controversy was more about the best way to protect liberty in a republic than about the value of public schools. The Democrats saw the state board as a threat to local control whereas the Whigs considered state support for public schools necessary for raising intelligent citizens who would protect the republic.[95]

Conclusion

In the first half of the nineteenth century, common school reformers in New England and New York sought to change traditions of local school control. Facing opposition from a variety of people, the so-called friends of education concentrated on three areas of improvement: school buildings, curriculum advancement, and teacher training. To improve conditions, reformers recommended models they found in European countries. Early in the nineteenth century, models such as the Lancaster system developed in Britain offered ways to integrate building design, curriculum change, and teacher training. Although academies and teacher institutes offered opportunities for teacher training, advocates of common schools sought to create normal schools as in France to offer direct training. Some normal schools such as those in Oswego, New York, followed the object lesson model that was devised in London. Although it is not clear that these changes improved education, the reforms brought the United States more in line with developments in Europe. More important, the new patterns of education prepared people to adjust to the social changes taking place. For example, the move to incorporate teacher training in academies strengthened the place of vocational training in higher education. Although many graduates of normal schools did not become teachers, they acquired the education needed to move from rural areas to cities and take up occupations not found on farms. Finally, changes in building design, curriculum development, and teacher training that reformers brought about made school life appear efficient and reasonable. Critics who opposed the common school reforms preferred the local control found in small school districts. Although the reforms led to increased regimentation because of graded school plans and strict curriculum divisions, school attendance increased. The regularity associated with modern industrial societies was more widespread, and the differences between rural and urban schools diminished. Thus, the common school movement moved education in the direction of bureaucratic organization and uniformity that became the mark of modernization and globalization, although advocates of common schools did not make these choices clear in their campaigns.

Endnotes

1. Sidney Jackson, *America's Struggle for Free Schools: Social Tension and Education in New England and New York, 1827–1842* (Washington, D.C.: American Council on Public Affairs, 1941), 40–54.
2. Merle Curti, *The Social Ideas of American Educators* (1935; reprint, New Jersey: Littlefield Adams, 1978), 30–31.
3. Benjamin Franklin, *The Autobiography of Benjamin Franklin* (1771; reprint, New York: Airmont Books, 1965).
4. Ellwood P. Cubberley, *Public Education in the United States: A Study and Interpretation of American Educational History* (Boston: Houghton Mifflin Co., 1919), 43–44, 155–156, 240–241.
5. Jackson, *America's Struggle for Free Schools,* 80–84.
6. Jackson, *America's Struggle for Free Schools,* 80–84.
7. Warren Burton, *The District School as It Was* (1928; reprint, New York: Arno Press, 1969), v–19.
8. Burton, *The District School,* 137.
9. Burton, *The District School,* 138–154.
10. Maris Vinovskis, *Education, Society, and Economic Opportunity: A Historical Perspective on Persistent Issues* (New Haven: Yale University Press, 1995), 108–109.
11. Lawrence Cremin, *American Education: The National Experience* (New York: Harper Row, 1980), 444–445.
12. Cubberley, *Public Education in the United States,* 86–89.
13. Carl F. Kaestle, "Introduction," *Joseph Lancaster and the Monitorial Movement: A Documentary History* (New York: Teachers College Press, 1973), 37–40.
14. Rev. J. A. Burns, *Principles, Origins, and Establishment of the Catholic School System in the United States* (New York: Benziger Brothers, 1912), 77–79.
15. Kaestle, "Introduction," 17–24.
16. Joseph Lancaster, "Improvements in Education as it Respects the Industrious Classes of the Community," ed. Carl F. Kaestle, *Joseph Lancaster and the Monitorial Movement: A Documentary History* (New York: Teachers College Press, 1973), 67–71.
17. Lancaster, "Improvements in Education," 74–79.
18. Lancaster, "Improvements in Education," 79–83.
19. Lancaster, "Improvements in Education," 89–90.

20. Dell Upton, "Lancasterian Schools, Republican Citizenship, and the Spatial Imagination in Early Nineteenth-Century America," *Journal of the Society of Architectural Historians* 55, no. 3 (September 1996): 238–253.
21. Upton, "Lancasterian Schools," 238–241.
22. Lancaster, "Improvements in Education," 85–87.
23. Lancaster, "Improvements in Education," 85–87.
24. Very Rev. J. A. Burns, Bernard J. Kohlbrenner, and Most Rev. John B. Peterson, *A History of Catholic Education in the United States: A Textbook for Normal Schools and Teacher's Colleges* (New York: Benziger Brothers, 1937), 79; Joseph J. Panzer, S.M., *Educational Traditions of the Society of Mary* (Dayton, Ohio: University of Dayton Press, 1965), 156–157.
25. Webster E. Browning, "Joseph Lancaster, James Thompson, and the Lancasterian System of Mutual Instruction, with Special Reference to Hispanic America," *The Hispanic American Historical Review* 4, no. 1 (February 1921), 49–98.
26. David Hogan, "The Market Revolution and Disciplinary Power: Joseph Lancaster and the Psychology of the Early Classroom System," *History of Education Quarterly* 29, no. 3 (Autumn 1989): 381–417.
27. Ronald Rayman, "Joseph Lancaster's Monitorial System of Instruction and American Indian Education, 1815–1838," *History of Education Quarterly* 21, no. 4 (Winter 1981): 395–409.
28. Upton, "Lancasterian Schools," 249–251.
29. Kaestle, "Introduction," 43–45.
30. Horace Mann, *Seventh Annual Report Covering the Year 1843* (1844; reprint, Washington, D.C.: NEA, 1950), 60.
31. Theodore R. Sizer, "Introduction," *Age of the Academies* (New York: Teachers College Press, 1964), 2–3.
32. Sizer, "Introduction," 2–6.
33. Claude M. Fuess, *An Old New England School: A History of Phillips Academy Andover* (Boston: Houghton Mifflin Co., 1917), 140, 206–207.
34. Fuess, *An Old New England School,* 204–206.
35. Samuel R. Hall, *Lectures on School-Keeping* (1829; reprint, New York: Arno Press, 1969), 2–40.
36. Hall, *Lectures on School-Keeping,* 78–80.
37. Mason S. Stone, "The First Normal School in America," *Teachers College Record* 24, no. 3 (May 1923): 263–271.
38. Stone, "The First Normal School in America," 265–267.
39. Stone, "The First Normal School in America," 268–271.
40. Cubberley, *Public Education in the United States,* 287–291.
41. Fuess, *An Old New England School,* 207–212.
42. Fuess, *An Old New England School,* 212–218.
43. Paul H. Mattingly, *The Classless Profession: American Schoolmen in the Nineteenth Century* (New York: New York University Press, 1975), 62–63.
44. Mattingly, *The Classless Profession,* 63–64.
45. Mattingly, *The Classless Profession,* 64–65.
46. Mattingly, *The Classless Profession,* 65–83.
47. Horace Mann, "Special Preparation, A Pre-Requisite to Teaching," ed. Lawrence Cremin, *Lecture on Education* (1838; reprint, New York: Arno Press, 1969), 63–116.
48. Jonathan Messerli, *Horace Mann: A Biography* (New York: Alfred Knopf, 1972), 239–252.
49. Horace Mann, "Special Preparation," 72–82.
50. Jurgen Herbst, *And Sadly Teach: Teacher Education and Professionalization in American Culture* (Madison: University of Wisconsin Press, 1989), 74–83.
51. Board of Education, *Eighth Annual Report of the Board of Education* (1845; reprint, Washington, D.C.: NEA, 1950), 19–45; Horace Mann, *Eighth Annual Report of the Secretary of the Board of Education* (1845; reprint, Washington, D.C.: NEA, 1950), 69–74.
52. Herbst, *And Sadly Teach,* 83–86.
53. Vinovskis, *Education, Society, and Economic Opportunity,* 108–109.
54. Henry Barnard, *School Architecture; or Contributions to the Improvements of School Houses in the United States* (1848; reprint, New York: Teachers College Press, 1970), 115–117.
55. Horace Mann, *Second Annual Report Covering the Year 1838* (1839; reprint, Washington, D.C.: NEA, 1948), 29–32.
56. Horace Mann, *Sixth Annual Report Covering the Year 1842* (Boston: Dutton and Wentworth, 1843), 51–64.
57. Maris Vinovskis, David L. Angus, and Jeffrey E. Mirel, "Historical Development of Age Stratification in Schooling," *Education, Society, and Economic Opportunity: A Historical Perspective on Persistent Issues* (New Haven: Yale University Press, 1995), 171–193.
58. Jean and Robert McClintock, "Introduction," *Henry Barnard's School Architecture* (New York: Teachers College Press, 1970), 1–29.
59. Barnard, *School Architecture,* 54–81, 131.
60. Barnard, *School Architecture,* 119–123.
61. Barnard, *School Architecture,* 135–142.
62. Barnard, *School Architecture,* 145–150.

63. Barnard, *School Architecture,* 150–181.
64. Michael B. Katz, *The Irony of Early School Reform: Educational Innovation in Mid-Nineteenth Century Massachusetts* (Cambridge: Harvard University Press, 1968), 19–20, 80–85, 122.
65. Vinovskis, *Education, Society, and Economic Opportunity,* 142–151.
66. Horace Mann, *Seventh Annual Report of Secretary of the Board of Education* (1844; reprint, Washington, D.C.: NEA, 1950), 23.
67. Mann, *Seventh Annual Report,* 117–118.
68. Mann, *Seventh Annual Report,* 118–125.
69. Mann, *Seventh Annual Report,* 150–160.
70. Messerli, *Horace Mann,* 412–414.
71. Messerli, *Horace Mann,* 415–422.
72. J. A. Green, *The Educational Ideas of Pestalozzi* (1914; reprint, New York: Greenwood Press, 1969), 165–168.
73. Gerald Lee Gutek, *Joseph Neef: The Americanization of Pestalozzianism* (University, Al.: University of Alabama Press, 1978), 5–22.
74. Joseph Neef, *Sketch of a Plan of Education* (1808; reprint, New York: Arno Press, 1969), 1–15.
75. Neef, *Sketch of a Plan of Education,* 74–85.
76. Neef, *Sketch of a Plan of Education,* 161–168.
77. Gutek, *Joseph Neef,* 133.
78. Hariklia Efthimiou, "Object Teaching," in *Historical Dictionary of American Education,* ed. Richard J. Altenbaugh (Westport, Conn.: Greenwood Press, 1999), 265.
79. Mary Sheldon Barnes, ed. *Autobiography of Edward Austin Sheldon* (New York: Ives-Butler Co., 1911), 138–139.
80. Barnes, ed. *Autobiography of Edward Austin Sheldon,* 99–103.
81. Barnes, ed. *Autobiography of Edward Austin Sheldon,* 99–115.
82. Barnes, ed. *Autobiography of Edward Austin Sheldon,* 116–135.
83. Ned Harland Dearborn, *The Oswego Movement in American Education* (1925; reprint, New York: Arno Press, 1969), 14–15.
84. Board of Education of Oswego, *Proceedings of the Educational Convention Held at Oswego, N.Y.* (New York: Harper & Brothers, 1862), 2–12.
85. Board of Education of Oswego, *Proceedings of the Educational Convention,* 26–28.
86. Cubberley, *Public Education in the United States,* 296–297.
87. Dearborn, *The Oswego Movement,* 69.
88. E. A. Sheldon, *Lessons on Objects, Graduated Series; Designed for Children of Six and Fourteen Years: Containing also Information on Common Objects* (New York: Charles Scribner & Co., 1866), 3–21.
89. Sheldon, *Lessons on Objects,* 22–25.
90. Sheldon, *Lessons on Objects,* 25–46.
91. Sheldon, *Lessons on Objects,* 208–211.
92. Dearborn, *The Oswego Movement,* 81–88.
93. Gerald Lee Gutek, *Pestalozzi and Education* (New York: Random House, 1968), 163–165.
94. Carl F. Kaestle and Maris A. Vinovskis, *Education and Social Change in Nineteenth Century Massachusetts* (New York: Cambridge University Press, 1980), 34–40, 136–138.
95. Kaestle and Vinovskis, *Education and Social Change,* 230–231.

5

Education in the Antebellum South

Men's physical education class, Antebellum South

In the period before the American Civil War, the section of the United States called the South was unique. It enjoyed a long growing season, had stable crop patterns, and depended on black laborers. Accentuating these differences, the wealthy planters traded directly with Britain, thereby weakening the local development of manufacturing and commerce. In contrast, manufacturing and commerce grew in Northern states. In the 1830s, these differences grew into antagonisms as abolitionists flooded the nation with pamphlets and notices condemning slavery. Southern spokespeople rose to defend their system, and war followed. To justify the violence, Northerners claimed that Southerners had rejected democratic institutions. For some years, historians debated whether the people in the South had disparaged such innovations as popular education. The answers were not clear. Although advocates of common schools in the South faced different conditions than did such advocates in the North, they campaigned to build statewide systems of reasonably designed schools with regular curriculums and trained teachers. Such efforts reduced the unique character of South, making it more similar to the rest of the country.

How Did Commentators Disagree about the Common School Movement in the South?

Writing in 1941, newspaper editor W. J. Cash called the Southern states "Uncle Sam's other province." He added that the Belgian Congo could not have been more different from New England. Cash claimed that there was one South although he did not think this was what political commentators in the 1940s referred as the Solid South. There were economic and political differences between the southeastern and the southwestern regions. According to Cash, the South extended beyond the old Confederate states into such border states as Kentucky. Within this area, though, the white residents shared a social pattern that was aristocratic, held to habits of thought based on ideals of honor and chivalry, and retained prejudices that led to such brutalities as lynching. Cash claimed that these sentiments separated Southerners from the rest of the Americans and that Southerners developed these attitudes before the War between the States. Despite their unique nature, Cash contended that these beliefs derived from the common American heritage to such an extent that the South could not have existed outside the United States.[1]

Cash's book enjoyed a wide readership throughout the 1940s, 1950s, and 1960s. Although he appealed to a popular audience, many college instructors assigned his book for their courses. Some of his phrases, such as the "hell-of-a-fellow" ideal, became stock descriptions of Southern characters. By the 1970s, though, historians questioned his generalizations. For example, C. Vann Woodward complained that Cash and his admirers had overstepped the bounds of reasonable scholarship. Although Woodward agreed the South was unique, he did not believe the people had retained the same sets of attitudes over three centuries. Woodward noted that, in the seventeenth and eighteenth centuries, the largest and richest slave society in world history had grown in what became the heart of a bourgeois, puritanical republic. It produced leaders of skill and ingenuity. When the crisis came, these leaders chose to fight. When they lost, the society was ruined. What bothered Woodward was Cash's contention that Southerners retained essential ways of thinking and acting throughout these drastic historical changes.[2]

According to Woodward, the unique aspect of the South was that it had suffered through more periods of change and instability then other regions in the United States. He argued that other sections, such as New England, enjoyed continuous development. In comparison, he added, the South went through periods of slavery and secession, independence and defeat, emancipation and reconstruction, and redemption and reunion. In each successive regime, the economic and industrial order of the South changed along with the political and social arrangements.[3]

Woodward described major changes that occurred with the War between the States. One result of the conflict was that commentators outside the region interpreted the South in ways that justified their particular orientations. For example, in 1865, the year the American Civil War ended, the opening speaker for the National Teachers Association's meeting in Harrisburg, Pennsylvania, characterized the conflict as a war of patriotism against ignorance and barbarism. He added that slavery had persisted in the South because most people lacked contact with culture that would have come through a coherent system of education. Consequently, he warned that another civil war would occur unless everyone worked to spread education through the South.[4]

To a Southern historian, Edgar Wallace Knight, this view was fallacious. He claimed that the origins, the organization, and the results of schooling in such Southern states as North Carolina, Virginia, and Alabama were similar to those found in New York, Pennsylvania, or Connecticut. He asserted that the development of public education was similar across the United States before 1850.[5]

In his text, *Public Education in the South,* written in 1922, Knight explained that the South had borrowed ideas from the North. For example, of the five Southern states in the Union before 1800, North Carolina and Georgia included provisions for education in their constitutions. Knight claimed that North Carolina's statement came almost directly from Pennsylvania, where a similar provision had appeared. Other states such as Georgia acted similarly.[6]

Other historians disagreed with Knight's arguments about the common school movement in the South. For example, in 1935, Merle Curti wrote that except for two or three states and the larger cities, the South did not make educational progress. Southern policy makers felt the state governments should not interfere in such private matters as education.[7]

In 1951 in *The American Common School,* Lawrence Cremin contended that the people in the South took a different attitude toward education than did people in other parts of the United States. The cause of the difference was the plantation system, wherein owners dealt directly with traders in England. Because the South enjoyed little commercial activity, cities did not grow. Instead, the area maintained three social levels. A landed aristocracy occupied the highest level. In the middle was a class of yeoman farmers who were proud and independent. At the bottom were poor whites and Negroes. In such a setting, a monarchical republicanism that advanced liberty without equality replaced the radical ideas of Jefferson. Claiming that most Southerners considered education to be private affair, Cremin noted that the states supported only charity schools enrolling children from poor families.[8]

In 1962, another historian, Rush Welter, extended the views of Curti and Cremin. Welter claimed that the South's dedication to slavery made it difficult for leaders to adopt universal education. To illustrate his point, Welter quoted Southern spokespeople who argued that social equality and universal freedom could not exist together. Welter thought that Southern people accepted the view that a few white people should direct everyone else because the society accepted the inequality implicit in slavery. To support his argument, Welter quoted some Southerners who considered universal education to be Northern error because workers had little time or ability to reflect on matters of social policy. Although schooling would give the workers the ability to read written propaganda, Southerners believed the workers could not think deeply about what they read, and demagogues could lead them astray. As a result, Welter concluded, Southerners believed that universal education would interfere with the proper arrangement of government by the privileged few.[9]

In 1965, Forrest David Mathews argued against Curti, Cremin, and Welter, returning to Knight's assertion that the common school movement was similar in the South and in the North. Concentrating on efforts in Georgia and Alabama, Mathews found that, as had been the case in the North, education was not an intensely important issue. Other matters, such as wars with American Indians, dominated public attention. Nonetheless, from 1830 to 1860, when state governors' gave addresses, the topic of education appeared frequently. Further, Mathews noted that the usual rationale for universal schooling was that it provided for the development of a responsible citizenry.[10]

Mathews completed his dissertation under the direction of Lawrence Cremin, and he may have influenced his teacher. In 1980, Cremin published *American Education: The National Experience, 1783–1876.* Unlike *The American Common School,* Cremin's earlier book, this book recognized that before the American Civil War, most states, including New York, Massachusetts, Virginia, and Michigan, had tried and failed to create systems of education. Although conditions differed among these states, the efforts led to general success after the war concluded.[11]

When Cremin described the configurations of education, he argued that each state had its own pattern. By configuration, Cremin meant the ways that such institutions as family, church, school, college, and newspapers formed patterns to acculturate children. In the nineteenth century, states added such new institutions as the factory, shop, office, orphan asylum, penitentiary, and lyceum, each influencing the educational configuration. He noted that in Massachusetts, the Lowell factories exerted a unique influence. In Sumter, South Carolina, Cremin found an Anglican, Presbyterian, and Baptist church blended with academies, farms, and newspapers to present an educational configuration. Thus, in comparing different systems and configurations of education during the national experience, Cremin claimed that education in the antebellum South was similar to other sections of the country, although aspects of development had been unique in each setting.[12]

In 1983, the editors of *The Journal of Thought* devoted the fall issue to the history of education in the South. They claimed that a book of essays, *Education and the Rise of the New South,* edited in 1981 by Ronald K. Goodenow and Arthur O. White, was the first general, comprehensive survey of education in the South written since Charles Dabney published *Universal Education in the South* in 1936. As a result, they called for new histories of schooling in the South before the war. Clinton B. Allison asserted that Knight's histories were the best sources available. Unfortunately, he believed Knight's works suffered from the author's bias in favor of state control of schools and from Knight's fixation on the errors of Reconstruction. Allison claimed that Knight opposed racially mixed schools to an extent that led him into racism. Finally, Allison noted Knight's view that Jacksonian Democrats favored common schooling and wealthy plantation owners disapproved of it. Allison argued that modern scholarship did not support such a clear distinction.[13]

According to Carl F. Kaestle, the common school movements in the South were the same as the North. Calvin Wiley in North Carolina, Samuel Lewis in Ohio, and Horace

Eaton in Vermont shared the same goals, made the same appeals, and worked the same ways. They faced the same resistance from rural communities who disliked property taxes and from urban dwellers who preferred charity schools for indigent children. In none of these regions did an overwhelming majority of voters favor state control of schooling, Kaestle noted. Yet, advocates in the North faced social conditions that they could use to more advantage than did the advocates in the South. As a result, by 1860, except in the South, state legislatures and local school committees had accepted such policies as state superintendents, tax support for schools, and teacher training.[14]

An example of the efforts by advocates of state-supported schools in the South comes from the campaign waged in North Carolina by Calvin Henderson Wiley. In this crusade, Wiley worked in ways that imitated the efforts of Horace Mann in Massachusetts. In 1853, the general assembly of North Carolina created the position of superintendent of schools and elected Wiley to hold the position. After studying the efforts that had taken place in Massachusetts, Wiley sought to imitate them. He began his efforts by visiting all the counties in a horse-and-buggy in the same way Mann had toured Massachusetts. In these travels, Wiley spoke to as many gatherings as possible. At each stop, he inquired about the state of education as Mann had done. As he traveled, he enlisted the aid of newspapers to distribute stories about the condition of schools and the need for improvements. As a result, he succeeded in having the general assembly pass laws permitting local districts to tax themselves to support schools. More important, he persuaded the voters in nearly every county to levy a tax for schools. Unable to create normal schools, he proposed methods for teachers to improve on their own and for superintendents to examine the teachers and bestow the best teaching assignments on those teachers who had mastered their material.[15]

Wiley conducted this campaign from 1852 to 1866. Following Mann's example, he wrote annual reports. In addition, at his own expense, he published a textbook, *The North Carolina Reader,* to explain the history and resources of the state. When war broke out, North Carolina maintained its common schools. Consequently, at the end of the war, Wiley claimed that his state had furnished the largest number of troops for the battles and had done the most for the cause of education. During Reconstruction, Wiley had to leave the office of superintendent.[16]

Although Wiley used the methods of Horace Mann, the situation he confronted in North Carolina differed from Massachusetts. Thus, although Wiley used arguments similar to those Mann advanced, he had to arrange them in ways that fit the Southern context. For example, Wiley advanced the claim commonly made in the North that common schools should enlighten the citizenry, unite them through an understanding of the laws, and help them work toward a common end. Unlike Mann, though, Wiley raised the specter of slave insurrections to encourage the spread of schools. He argued that discontented, impoverished white people might express hostility to other social classes and encourage the slaves to participate in a rebellion. Wiley told state lawmakers that the best way to avoid such antagonisms was to provide for the moral and spiritual development of the white masses. He argued that education would help poor whites recognize that elitism and slavery were parts of the proper order of society; otherwise, impoverished white people might try to take advantage of a slave rebellion.[17]

In the North, Mann had been an abolitionist, but he had promised wealthy people that schools would prevent social class conflicts because education was a ladder upon which aspiring children could climb. The result was that the public school movement in the North profited from the fears of established citizens that immigrants would upset the social order. In North Carolina, Wiley warned that uneducated white people might incite slave insurrections. Thus, Wiley's warning resembled the warnings about immigrants made in the North, although Wiley did not suggest that African Americans should attend schools.

Studies of school attendance showed that schools spread through such states as Tennessee under methods of local control. For example, Janice Price Greenough analyzed questionnaires of Civil War veterans describing their education before the war. She found that most children had walked less than three miles to school. She located eight or ten academies, subscription secondary schools, chartered between 1820 and 1860 in small counties. To support these schools, the parents provided money to hire a teacher and deferred the responsibility for instruction and discipline to the teacher.[18]

What Distinguished the Common School Movement in the South?

In the nineteenth century, the formal legal movement toward systems of public schooling underwent uneven progress throughout the United States. For example, Horace Mann was able to build a system of education in Massachusetts. Whereas, when the Connecticut legislature abolished their state board of education four years after creating one based on the Massachusetts board in 1838.[19]

In part, legislatures advanced state control and then withdrew it because policy makers disagreed about the benefits of sacrificing local control of the schools. According to Kaestle, the question of local control of schools provided the main dynamic in school reform throughout the new republic. He noted that there was a substantial rise in school enrollment during the first fifty years of the nation's history, prior to the common school movement of 1830. Furthermore, he added that there was virtually no public opposition to schooling. Resistance developed around 1830 over questions of state control and financing of schools. Thus, Kaestle concluded that the central disagreement about the expansion of education was whether schools should be locally controlled or governed through a statewide organization. Almost no one argued against the spread of schools.[20]

Because the controversies appeared to be ubiquitous, Kaestle argued that Southern states might have embraced state school systems more fully if the sectionalism between the North and South had not deepened in the 1850s. In the South during this decade, Northern influences came under attack. To illustrate the extent of this jealousy, Kaestle noted that in 1859, James Mason of Virginia spoke against Justin Morrill's proposal to the U.S. Senate to extend land-grant colleges throughout the states on the grounds that this would begin an effort to impose on the South the system of free schools found in New England. In the escalating conflict over slavery, the issue of local control of schools became a matter of sectional Southern pride.[21]

Kaestle claimed that, for the period before the American Civil War, the educational situations in the Midwest and in the South appeared similar. Land grants had failed to produce income for schools and the regions were sparsely populated and dependent on agriculture. Further, in both regions, there was resistance to property tax support of common schools. By 1860, however, he asserted that all the Midwestern states had established state regulated, tax-based systems of schools whereas few Southern states had.[22]

According to Kaestle, the difference came from the economic changes and the resulting ethnic diversity that developed in the Midwest. Although both regions had similar republican and Protestant origins, the development of industry caused, cities such as Chicago, Detroit, and Milwaukee to grow and attract immigrants from foreign lands. In these places, advocates claimed that common schools would enable these different ethnic groups to assimilate into the cultural patterns of their new home. On the other hand, the South remained tied to agriculture, experiencing little immigration and focusing on westward expansion. Although plantation owners disapproved of spread of education, small landholders and professionals wanted more schools. As a result, Kaestle argued that tensions emerged in the South that made it more difficult for state-supported systems to emerge.[23]

To some extent, Kaestle's interpretation differed from that of Rush Welter. Welter believed that the institution of slavery caused Southerners to deem social inequality as essential to life in a republic, and he found critics who complained that universal education would lead to insurrection. During the War between the States, slavery was the issue that divided North and South. Nonetheless, it is not clear to what extent the institution of slavery prejudiced Southerners against popular education. First, the institution of slavery was not unique to the South; some Northerners supported slavery as well. Second, people could believe that inequality preserved the social order without supporting slavery or denying the need for universal education. The following paragraphs explain these points in turn.

First, in the colonial period, slavery existed in the North as well as in the South. For example, in the 1700s, Jonathan Edwards, the Calvinist preacher from Massachusetts who took part in the Great Awakening, owned slaves. Edwards contended that slavery was acceptable if the slaveholder treated the slaves humanely and encouraged them to accept Christianity.[24]

After the War of Independence, however, many Americans had difficulty accepting slavery. For example, during the constitutional convention, the delegates set 1808 as the date to end the importation of slaves to all areas. According to W. E. B. Du Bois, the discussion over this compromise reflected the different moral attitudes people held about slavery. Du Bois contended that the South apologized for it, the middle states denounced it, and the Easterners tolerated it from afar. By agreeing to a date for its end, the delegates cast slavery as a temporary condition because they felt slavery had to end when the trade ended.[25] Unfortunately, slavery did not end when the importation of slaves ended.

In the South, the population of slaves grew to such an extent that by 1845 slavery had spread through fifteen states extending from the Delaware River to the Rio Grande. Although most Northern states provided for some sorts of gradual emancipation, it was not until 1846 that all Northern states made slavery illegal. The decisive point came in the 1830s when members of the abolition movement in the United States took inspiration from the success of antislavery leaders in England and flooded the country with propaganda calling for an end to slavery.[26]

Although feelings became more intense, the arguments about slavery remained constant from the colonial period until the American Civil War. According to Larry E. Tise, the abolitionist movement of the nineteenth century did not change the nature of the controversy; both sides repeated older themes. To illustrate his point, Tise quoted two justices in Massachusetts who engaged in a debate about slavery in the early 1700s. Although this exchange took place more than a century before abolitionism flowered, Tise found the views that dominated the later controversies within the few pages these justices wrote. On one side, Samuel Sewall disapproved of slavery and claimed that all human beings had a right to liberty. As a result, he called slavery "manstealing." He added that importing white servants would have better served Massachusetts. On the other side, John Saffin owned slaves and defended this practice by citing biblical sanctions permitting Christians to make lawful captives from heathen nations into slaves although Christians should not enslave each other. Furthermore, Saffin contended that slavery conformed to the inherited inequalities among people; those individuals with the talents needed to lead society should hold exalted positions and those persons who lacked those abilities should accept direction from their superiors. Most important, Saffin added that slavery had introduced Africans to Christianity and had restrained their primitive and wild passions. Tise noted that, in later years, Saffin's points became the view that slavery was a positive good.[27]

The point that Tise made was that proslavery advocates based their position on traditional American views about the need for the best people to rule. Although Tise acknowledged that Southern clerical and political leaders added justifications for slavery from the Bible and from the U.S. Constitution, the basis of proslavery ideology was that inequality was an essential aspect of life in a republic.[28]

On the other hand, some policy makers could assert the need for inequality without supporting slavery. For example, Thomas Jefferson and Benjamin Rush suggested that schools could justify inequality, but they did not extend their views to affirm the need for slavery.

In 1779, Thomas Jefferson proposed a plan for the general diffusion of knowledge in his home state of Virginia. Submitted to the Virginia General Assembly, Jefferson's bill called for aldermen to divide their counties into small sections of about five square miles with an adequate number of children conveniently distributed to support a school. Boys and girls would attend these schools free of charge, and they would study reading, writing, and arithmetic. The aldermen were to construct a grammar school for each hundred elementary schools. After an examination, the best and most promising boys from the elementary schools would proceed to a grammar school where they could lodge and study Latin, Greek, English grammar, geography, and mathematics. At least two boys whose parents could not support such study would be included at the grammar school. After four years, the best students as proven by extensive examination would proceed to William and Mary College.[29]

In a similar way in 1786, Benjamin Rush proposed a system of free schools for Pennsylvania. He recommended setting up free schools in every district that had a population of one hundred families. In these schools, he proposed that children would learn English, German, and mathematics. He suggested spreading four colleges through the state in the cities of Philadelphia, Carlisle, Lancaster, and Pittsburgh. After the young men completed the free schools, parents who wanted to extend their children's education could send them to these colleges. At the college, the young men would study mathematics and science. Those young men receiving testimonials from the colleges could attend the one university in the state where they could study law, physics, science, economics, or political science.[30]

In the models of Jefferson and Rush, students worked through hierarchical systems that selected the most able students to move to higher levels. Thus, each plan reinforced inequalities by offering different children different educational opportunities depending on their abilities.

Jefferson's hope was that the resulting elite would be composed of people from each social grouping because schools were in all parts of the state. He wanted every child to have the opportunity to receive basic instruction. Because each area of one hundred schools had a grammar school, the best students from the elementary schools went on to the grammar schools. Finally, the best students from the grammar schools proceeded to college where they received the training needed to become a social leader. The result was that the system trained representatives of each social grouping to move into positions of authority. In this way, Jefferson sought to create an aristocracy of talent instead of reinforcing family ties.

Although Rush may have been less careful than Jefferson to break family connections, both reformers believed that inequality was inevitable. Neither Rush nor Jefferson accepted proslavery ideologies. Although Jefferson owned slaves and did not urge immediate emancipation, he was uncomfortable with slavery. Because he felt that black people and white people could not live together, he thought that emancipated slaves should leave America.[31] In most cases, Rush opposed slavery. For example, in 1773, Rush urged the emancipation of slaves in the West Indies.[32]

How Did Education Spread among Slaves and Slaveholders?

The spread of education differed among slaveholders and slaves. Most slaves lived on large plantations in the Deep South, which includes the South Atlantic and Gulf coastal plains as well as the lower Appalachian Piedmont, under slaveholders who educated their children with private tutors. In the case of the slaves, Southern legislatures sought to limit literacy. Nonetheless, the ability to read and write was widespread, as discussed in later paragraphs.

Slavery suited an agricultural society, and the South was a rural area. In 1860, there was no city with more than 10,000 people in North Carolina, Florida, Mississippi, Arkansas, or Texas. The only big, truly Southern city was New Orleans. Nonetheless, slavery spread unevenly throughout the South. In 1860, about three-fourths of Southerners had no connection with slaves. Of Southern farmers who owned slaves, almost 90 percent had fewer than twenty and about 50 percent fewer than five. Most slaves in the South lived with the 10 percent of farmers who held more than twenty slaves on large plantations. The plantations were more numerous in the states of the Deep South, such as Alabama, in an area called the Black Belt because of its rich, dark soil that produced valuable cotton crops. Thus, in the Deep South, in 1860, there were about thirteen slaves per slaveholder whereas, in the upper South, there were about eight slaves per slaveholder.[33]

According to Edward and Elaine Gordon, the apparently haphazard education that wealthy patrons extended through private tutors provided excellent training to such prominent leaders as George Washington, Thomas Jefferson, and James Madison. The Gordons point out that Washington's mother received her education from a tutor. When Washington was old enough to receive instruction, his father brought a tutor from England as an indentured servant. After the tutoring, Washington attended an old-field school taught by a local minister. An explanation of such models of schooling appears below; it is sufficient to note here that Washington completed such instruction at age thirteen. In a similar manner, he eschewed local schools when his stepson was ready for instruction, complaining that literary instruction taught words, not things. He enlisted a tutor to make the boy into a gentleman rather than a scholar.[34]

The Gordons quote from the journals of Philip Vickers Fithian to illustrate that the work of the tutor could be rewarding and pleasant. Fithian spent thirteen months as tutor to seven children in the family of Robert Carter in Virginia. He taught English and arithmetic to the five girls and Latin, Greek, and composition to the boys. A special tutor taught the girls to play musical instruments and to dance. Except in classes on catechism, the boys received instruction separate from the girls. During his stay with the Carter family, Fithian enjoyed the same treatment extended to other members of the family, and he enjoyed prestige among the servants.[35]

Philip Freneau offered a distinctly different view of the life of a tutor. After graduating from Princeton in 1771, he served as a teacher before becoming a poet and journalist. To show the disadvantages of being a tutor, Freneau described a wealthy man who advertised for a tutor who could teach subjects ranging from foreign languages to meteorology for small salary. At the same time, the mother refused to permit the tutor to discipline the children. Once employed, the servants ignored the tutor and refused to feed or to help him any way. After a year, the wealthy man invited the physician, the country lawyer, and the clergyman to examine the children. When they determined that the children did not know much information or possess many academic skills, the wealthy man fired the tutor and refused to pay him the year's salary.[36]

Whereas the children of plantation owners worked with private tutors, slaves faced legal prohibitions against their learning to read. In 1740, fearing that slaves in South Carolina could exchange written plans to rebel, the colonial legislature forbade the teaching of reading or writing to any slave. In 1800, the legislature broadened the scope of forbidden activities to include any sort of mental instruction such as arithmetic and forbade such instruction to free blacks as well as slaves. Other states adopted similar laws. In 1830, Louisiana lawmakers made it a capital crime to teach slaves or free black people to read and write. In the same year, the legislature of North Carolina forbade anyone from teaching slaves to read because literacy excited dissatisfaction and incited rebellion. Policy makers in North Carolina allowed slaves to learn arithmetic, though, because with those skills slaves could perform such trades as carpentry.[37]

The rationale behind these laws was that literacy encouraged African Americans to seek freedom or equality. Although opponents argued that literacy was essential for the development of religious understanding, authorities resisted such arguments. For example, Heather Andrea Williams recounts that in 1853, a white woman, Margaret Douglass, went to jail for teaching free black children to read in Sunday school. While Douglass claimed the children had to read the Bible to gain their faith, the judge argued that literacy was not a prerequisite to moral behavior. He added that abolitionists spread inflammatory documents that could inspire slave insurrections.[38]

Despite the laws forbidding slaves to learn to read, literacy spread among slaves and free black people. One reason may have been that the laws were unpopular. For example, in 1850, petitions circulated in Georgia asking the legislature to withdraw the prohibition against teaching African Americans. Although the repeal was narrowly defeated, the law prohibiting education of slaves proved ineffective. According to the federal census of 1850, of the nearly 3,000 free black people in Georgia, almost 2,500 could read. Further, one report asserted that out of the 400,000 slaves in eastern Georgia, about 5,000 had learned to read.[39]

On obtaining freedom, most former slaves moved to cities or towns where they found independent African American churches. Often these institutions sponsored Sunday schools and day schools. In the Deep South, wealthy freedman started schools. Although these efforts were illegal, authorities in different cities responded differently. For example, officials closed a school in Raleigh, North Carolina, whereas several schools in Charleston, South Carolina, went undisturbed.[40]

In 1830, Daniel Alexander Payne founded a school for black children in Charleston, South Carolina. At the time, Payne was only nineteen years old. He had spent three years at a school where he learned to read, write, and do arithmetic. As a carpenter's apprentice, he had spent his few leisure moments with books. Opening his school, he enrolled three children. Because his teacher had not taught him geography, he studied it with his students. He acquired some understanding of astronomy, Greek, and biology in the same way. Within a year, Payne attracted sixty pupils. After Nat Turner's rebellion, the school closed; however, Payne went on to become the president of Wilberforce University and a bishop in the African Methodist Episcopal Church.[41]

Some slaves undertook extraordinary efforts to master reading, writing, and arithmetic. A famous example is Frederick Douglass. In his autobiography Douglass wrote that, when he was seven or eight years old, one of his mistresses, Mrs. Auld, taught him the alphabet. When her husband found out, he warned her that such teachings would make Douglass unmanageable, discontented, and worthless as a slave. On hearing this warning to Mrs. Auld, Douglass decided that he had to acquire the skills of literacy. One method he used was to meet white boys in the street and make trades with them. He would give bread from the kitchen to a white child in exchange for a lesson from the book he always had hidden in his clothing. As if to prove his former master, Mr. Auld, correct, Douglass read several denunciations of slavery and decided to seek his freedom. In the meantime, he learned to write by copying carpenters who wrote letters on boards to indicate where the boards belonged on a project. He perfected the skill by challenging young white boys to writing contests on pavements, walls, and fences.[42]

Douglass's story was not unique. When Eugene D. Genovese surveyed accounts of life on plantations, he found literate slaves everywhere. Most plantations had one or more literate slaves, and slaves who could read appeared in each locality. According to Genovese, in most cases, the slaveholders disregarded the law and public opinion and taught slaves to read because the owners needed someone who could read on the plantations. The greatest effort came from white children who taught black children. The slaves continued the process by teaching each other. Sometimes, these lessons took place late at night after work was finished for the day.[43]

According to Genovese, many accounts of slave life described slaves as wanting to read and understand mathematics. Although part of this ambition came from the belief that literacy would lead to freedom, another reason came from the slaves' wishes to be able workers. For example, Genovese told about a slave, assigned to be a carpenter, who complained that his master had not taught him the simple geometry he needed to perform his trade. Instead, the master left the slave to figure out measurements on his own. To Genovese, it was not important that many slaves refused to undertake what he called the Herculean efforts needed to learn to read or write; instead, the story was with the few slaves who mastered the skills.[44]

That black people in the South before the War between the States could learn to read is partly because the institution of slavery was complex. Although by the end of the American Civil War commentators agreed the practice of slavery was immoral, the details of the implementation of slavery caused historians to disagree about its nature and its effects.

In 1918, Ulrich Bonnell Phillips claimed that what he called the plantation regime provided an acculturating experience for the slaves and the slaveholders. Slaves were the workers on the plantation, Phillips asserted. As such, they represented valuable property to the slaveholders. When he looked at plantation records, Phillips found the owners concerned about the care and well-being of the slaves. They maintained order so that slaves could perform their chores efficiently. They cared for children and pregnant women. When listing the allowances for food and clothing, Phillips found the rations to be sufficient for health and vigor. In the work schedules, the slaves set off to work at sunrise. They had a break for lunch at noon, and they returned for dinner. At some plantations, the ringing of a bell tolled the schedule and signified the daily transitions, such as the time to rise and to go to bed. In addition to requiring orderly habits, the owners promoted domesticity among the slaves. Marriage was encouraged. The slaves could keep individual garden plots, and the owners set aside Sunday afternoons or evenings for Gospel preaching.[45]

Although Phillips found accounts of discipline, he noted that the plantation owners described the need to apply whippings or solitary confinements in an impersonal manner so the slaves understood the punishments were for acts of disobedience and thereby served as correctives. One plantation owner had a system of rewards to encourage the slaves to act and to work properly. To show that plantation owners did not lose their tempers while managing a large number of slaves, Phillips quoted travelers such as Harriett Martineau who complimented several Southern planters for their patience after seeing them in their fields with the slaves. Phillips noted that Charles Eliot Norton had not found neatly kept plantations, but Norton did find evidence of harmony and goodwill on the plantations.[46]

According to Robert William Fogel, most historians accepted the view that Phillips offered until the 1950s. Revisionists could not easily contradict the claims because Phillips had used original documentary evidence. The change came in 1956 when Kenneth M. Stampp published *The Peculiar Institution,* criticizing Phillips's interpretations.[47]

After consulting plantation records, archive collections, census data, records of births and deaths, and slave manuscripts, Stampp disagreed with most of Phillips's conclusions. Instead of finding moderate work schedules, Stampp found excessive labor with insufficient periods of rest. In the months of harvest, for example, slaves worked eighteen hours per day, seven days a week. The result was that slaves died in the fields. Instead of finding slaves content with their lives, he found them longing for liberty and striving to escape. Instead of reasonable and objective punishments, Stampp found horrible and cruel tortures. Rather than encouraging domesticity, he found slaveholders willfully breaking up families.

Looking at census data, Stampp found the life expectancy of the slaves to be lower than that of whites. Infant mortality among slaves was considerably higher. As for particular skills, Stampp found that the unlettered slaves could not easily develop intellectual interests, although they created an amazing repertory of music to express emotions, longings, and religious sentiments. Deprived of intellectual pursuits, the slaves accentuated physical abilities that included athletic skills and manual training. According to Stampp, slaves adopted a religion that promised a better time in the future.[48]

In 1966, Eugene Genovese wrote the introduction to a new edition of Phillips's book. Genovese acknowledged that racism blinded Phillips to important insights. For example, Phillips noted how contact with white people changed the Africans, yet he would not recognize that white people had changed as well. Although Genovese agreed with Phillips that the plantation system had produced some of the finest traditions and sensibilities in American life, he noted that historians had to understand the origins of these traditions if they were to separate the benefits from the injustice and brutality that existed on the plantations.[49]

In his book, *Roll, Jordan, Roll,* Genovese pursued his idea that the plantation system shaped masters and slaves. According to Genovese, the owners adopted aspects of the slaves' culture and the slaves adapted aspects of the owners' culture to serve their interests. According to Genovese, the bridge between the cultures was the paternalism implicit in plantation life. The masters were supposed to protect the slaves in return for the labor the slaves gave to the masters. Although most owners left immediate supervision of the slaves to overseers, they hired relatives to perform this supervision and they would dismiss or imprison abusive overseers. In return, the slaves identified with a particular master and a community. The slaves developed a religion that reminded them to care for one another, thereby reinforcing their sense of self-worth. Their version of Christianity enabled them to reject the proslavery ideology that asserted the inferiority of Africans. As the slaves increased their devotion to religion, the owners held more tightly to their own religion, which carried the message that they had to be kind to their slaves.[50]

Genovese did not believe that the paternalistic nature of slavery caused masters and slaves to live peacefully with each other. Sometimes they did. At the same time, though, Genovese pointed out that slaves learned to steal pigs, geese, and other foodstuffs. Further, slaves could take revenge for what they felt were wrongs, through such aggressive acts as arson or barn burning that could destroy a planter's profits.[51]

Many researchers who followed Genovese agreed that slavery was a paternalistic system. According to Peter J. Parish, because this meant that slaves could manipulate masters, studies tended to show compromise, contradiction, and compartmentalization on plantations, instead of pictures of total mastery on one side and surrender on the other.[52]

What Types of Schools Were Available in the Antebellum South?

Because slavery was concentrated in large plantations, it did not spread far among Southern farmers. In 1949, Frank Lawrence Owsley compiled census returns and tax lists from 1850 and 1860 for sample counties in the lower South and Tennessee. Owsley found that the core of the society was a large mass of what he called "plain folk" who were white but were neither rich nor poor. Although slaveholders comprised about one-third of the population, most of these were small landowners. About 60 percent of the slaveholders owned farms of fifty to three hundred acres and they had from one to five slaves. Few slaveholders owned large plantations with large numbers of slaves.[53]

The plain folk that Owsley studied were the dominant class in the antebellum South. Although derided as white trash, these people were landowners and they made up the bulk of lawyers, physicians, preachers, teachers, business people, and political leaders. On looking at the life histories of individuals who rose from poverty to local leadership, Owsley found that the parents had schooling beyond simple literacy. According to Owsley, the parents in these families held education in high regard and possessed some personal refinements. The sons accepted the pride of their parents and used every opportunity to acquire an education. An aspiring lawyer would read the law under the direction of a practicing attorney while he served as a secretary. A young man who wanted to be a physician might read medical books under a doctor's guidance and attend some lectures at a medical college. In the meantime, many of these aspiring professionals taught school to support themselves.[54]

Owsley contended that most of the young people in rural antebellum South, including the wealthy and the poor children, attended what he called "old-field schools." These were elementary schools supported by subscription, with each child paying about $2.50 for a five- or six-month term and one dollar for a six-week summer term. In these schools, the children learned to read, write, and do arithmetic. In towns, academies offered elementary instruction and high school subjects such as chemistry, logic, moral philosophy, Greek, Latin, French, algebra, and mechanical drawing, depending on students' interests and abilities to pay tuition. Among the fifty-seven academies in Georgia in 1860, the tuition was about $15.50 for elementary studies and $26 for the high school branches.[55]

When Janice Price Greenough studied the subscription schools in the antebellum Southern highlands, she found them to be rife with violence. Greenough claimed that whereas public school advocates in the North were able to reduce the teachers' reliance on corporal punishment, advocates in the South could not rival this accomplishment. In the North, Horace Mann could claim that the incidence of corporal punishments dropped 25 percent when Massachusetts required schoolteachers to report each incident. Requiring disclosure had induced restraint. According to Greenough, in the South, nothing could reduce corporal punishment as long as authority remained local.[56]

She found several accounts testifying that teachers exercised the right to beat children whenever they wanted. Parents supported the school and the teacher, and they tended not to interfere with what teachers did. In 1837, the Supreme Court in North Carolina upheld the teacher's right to inflict corporal punishment so long as no permanent harm came about to the children.[57]

According to Greenough, the violence escalated in Southern schools in ways not found in the North. Students in the North resisted beatings in the 1820s, and she noted accounts of district schools in the North in which students barricaded the doors and windows of the school, preventing the teachers from entering until the students gained some extra holidays. Thus, in the North, the extent of violence in schools seemed limited to teachers whipping children and students seeking some sort of revenge by throwing teachers down a snow covered hill. On the other hand, in the 1840s and 1850s, violence in Southern schools, according to Greenough, was at a homicidal level. Students in Tennessee and Kentucky used knives and guns to threaten and kill teachers. This came from the uniquely Southern code of honor, she claimed.[58]

Greenough said the Scotch-Irish tradition brought the virulent strain of violence to the antebellum Southern highlands and tied it to the code of personal honor. The result was that a man had to defend his honor against any insult. More important, Greenough contended that in the North white males retained a sense of dignity that allowed them to ignore insults. In the South, she argued, such tolerance was a sign of cowardice. As a result, parents in the South would urge children to stand up to an abusive teacher so that they would learn to fight for themselves. Students expressed this violence to female teachers as well as male.[59]

To restrict such practices as corporal punishment, Southern advocates of education sought to improve teacher training. In 1817, Archibald D. Murphey wrote a report about the schools in Prussia for the legislature of North Carolina. In his report, Murphey praised the methods of Lancaster and of Pestalozzi although he had not visited those schools. In 1839, after Calvin Stowe made his report to the Ohio legislature, Benjamin M. Smith submitted a description of Prussian schools to the governor of Virginia. In his report, Campbell called for teacher training and some form of certification. He thought such requirements would establish well-run classrooms.[60]

In 1840, teachers and so-called friends of learning formed the Alabama Educational Association. Around the same time, various educators recommended that colleges and academies add courses to train teachers. For example, in 1843, the president of Washington College in Virginia suggested that the state pay the tuition of young men to prepare to teach, providing the student agree to serve as a common school teacher for a number of years. In larger towns, different levels of common schools existed. There were normal schools where young men could learn the different subjects taught in the schools and the practical skills they would need to impart the information. In 1849, the governor of South Carolina recommended the establishment of a department in the college to train graduates to become teachers. He urged that the department enroll students equitably from throughout the state.[61]

In 1849, Braxton Craven explained how schools should be constructed and organized. Because he felt the need to recommend that schools include essential amenities, there must have been schools that were primitive or followed idiosyncratic curriculums. For example, Craven noted that schools should be enclosed and heated evenly so students did not have to huddle around the fire. He called for desks of various sizes to suit different-aged pupils and chairs with backs so students would be comfortable. The building should have water buckets, fire shovel, and axes. Instructional devices included a blackboard, a map of the United States, and an English dictionary. The class day should begin at 8 a.m., and end at 4 p.m., with a fifteen-minute recess at 10 a.m., dinner from 11:30 a.m. to 1 p.m., and recess at 2 p.m. During the lunch period, students could practice such things as sounds of letters, spelling, or number facts. In the class, everything should be orderly. The curriculum should include reading, writing, counting, bookkeeping, physiology, grammar, history, and natural philosophy. The teacher should read from the Bible to the students each day.[62]

In 1853, Craven established Normal College in North Carolina to effect the changes he sought in common school instruction. Although he sought state aid to support Normal

College, he was unsuccessful except for a small loan the state extended for a building. As a result, in 1859, the college became Trinity College of the Methodist Church and, subsequently, Duke University.[63]

In an effort to convince North Carolina's legislators to support normal schools, The *North Carolina Journal of Education* published articles affirming the need for a normal school. In 1858, after the legislature had agreed to support public schools, the *Journal* noted that this required the establishment of a state normal school. Otherwise, the *Journal* warned, teachers would come from outside the state to fill those positions in the common schools.[64]

Fear of Northern influence was common. As early as 1805, *The Richmond Enquirer* warned against sending Southern youth to the North for their education. The danger was that they would learn political and economic theories that opposed the Southern way of life. In 1835, Joseph Holt Ingraham complained that two-thirds of the planters in Mississippi sent their sons to Northern colleges, such as Harvard, Princeton, and Yale. Ingraham argued that this meant the planters sent large sums to support those schools while literary institutions languished in the South. Instead, he urged wealthy families to send their children to Southern schools, even if it meant hiring Northern teachers to raise educational standards. As abolitionist campaigns increased, state officials entered the controversy. In 1844, the governor of Mississippi warned that the practice of sending youth to other states for an education resulted in young men growing up with prejudices against their home institutions. In 1853, Jefferson Davis warned that teachers and textbooks opposed to slavery introduced false ideas to children.[65]

In 1859, the commissioners of free schools in Charleston, South Carolina, opened the Female High and Normal School with the aim of training women to become teachers in district schools. At the time, a common school offered instruction to about 800 pupils. The normal school and high school enrolled female students from around the state, taking about fifteen from each congressional district. A high school for men had already been operating in Charleston before the women's school opened. It received state funds as well as private subscriptions. The view of the founders was that women were the natural teachers of young children. In 1860, South Carolina legislators visited the female high school and normal school. This led to the confirmation of an appropriation to open a normal school serving the parishes of St. Philip and St. Michael.[66]

Critics of the normal schools claimed that the money should go into teacher salaries and this would attract better candidates. The danger was that school commissioners would never raise teachers' salaries until they thought the teachers' qualifications were sufficiently high. Worse, they may not have felt a need to raise teachers' salaries because instruction followed narrow paths. Few teachers knew enough geography, history, or grammar to teach those subjects. As a result, most schools imparted basic instruction in reading, writing, arithmetic, and spelling. Most schools were one-room affairs with a teacher, many different texts, and a mixture of class levels. Although many reformers recommended that school districts adopt some form of a graded school plan with uniform textbooks at each level, no state in the South adopted this model before the American Civil War, according to Edgar Knight. In spite of the resistance to uniform texts for students, some groups of teachers published lists of recommended texts for different subjects.[67]

Throughout the South, an important part of instruction was Webster's "Blue Back Speller." According to Knight, in the antebellum period, this book from New England was the first one placed in students' hands. As in other sections of the country, spelling bees were a popular school exercise. In some cases, the speller was the only book students knew. It served as a moral catechism and as a reader because it contained a collection of short stories.[68] Although teachers may have concentrated on spelling, they may not have had widespread success. For example, a description of life in North Carolina included a quotation from a notice distributed by a district's school committee in 1842 that read as follows: "Notis, the free scule comity has implowed Mr. Jones to tech sade scule."[69]

Knight pointed out that some Southern schools used texts in such subjects as geography that included pejorative descriptions of Southern states. He quoted from a geography text published in 1793 by Jedidiah Morse that enjoyed wide circulation. The text complained that in North Carolina, the rich planters had little taste for the sciences and people in the coastal regions suffered from diseases and wasted time drinking and gambling, neglecting their plantations and their minds. The text added that Southerners engaged in barbarous sports such as trying to gouge out each other's eyes. By 1844, though, Southern educational journals carried advertisements for textbooks that were carefully revised and free of such objectionable material.[70]

How Did Academies Serve the South before the American Civil War?

Middle class society attended academies. For example, in Sumter District, South Carolina, the members of the highest social classes did not attend academies; they tended to have their children tutored at home. In a similar pattern, beginning around 1811, the members of the lowest social classes who desired education for their children sent them to the public schools. In this district of about 30,000 people, in 1853, there were forty-three public schools with about 450 students. Although historians could not determine how many academies there were or how many students attended, it seemed that there were more academies than public schools. Although many of the academies were short-lived, the majority of secondary students attended academies.[71]

To some extent, the academy movement owed its origins to suggestions by John Milton. In 1644, Milton wrote his essay, "On Education," in response to entreaties about his ideas on the nature of proper schooling. Although he noted the aim of education is to know God as much as possible, he added that education should impart things useful in this life as well. He suggested that the academy should take place in a house large enough to accommodate 150 persons. The curriculum should include grammar and lead to readings in Greek and Latin by such authors as Plutarch to inspire love of virtue. The students should pursue arithmetic and geometry, history, and the natural sciences. In the evenings, the students would read Scripture. As the students moved through the classes, they could study philosophy and poetry. In addition to studies, Milton recommended military exercises as a form of physical activity. He included in this category fencing, wrestling, riding horses, and building fortifications. During the military exercises, the students would form the basis of such personal virtues as courage, trustworthiness, and discipline. Further, the students should eat good, substantial, healthful, but moderate meals.[72]

In 1749, Benjamin Franklin proposed to the citizens of Philadelphia that they apply for a charter to open an academy. Franklin claimed that Daniel Defoe's "Essay on Projects" influenced his thinking, and his proposal included many ideas found in Milton. Although

Franklin omitted the study of Greek and Latin and he avoided any mention of military exercises, he wanted the students to read the best English prose, study arithmetic and geometry, and engage in activities such as gardening and planting along with excursions to nearby farms to learn the best agricultural practices.[73]

According to Knight, there were two types of academies in the South. One class of academies included modest local efforts that had grown from old-field schools or through the efforts of tutors. The other type of academy was more prestigious, financially secure, and better equipped. Both types provided a liberal education. They were incorporated, which meant the state permitted the board of trustees to conduct the school, and the students paid fees, although some academies admitted a few charity cases.[74]

To illustrate how an interested individual might build an academy, Knight described the efforts of John Davis, an English citizen who stayed in the United States four years. Serving as a tutor, Davis accumulated recommendations from such prominent people as Thomas Jefferson and began a school in what Knight called a log hut. The farmers in the neighborhood brought their children and agreed to build a stone schoolhouse if Davis stayed seven years. The students were of various ages. The oldest was a man of thirty. Some of them came from comfortable circumstances. For example, a slave accompanied a young girl who came on horseback. The curriculum was an eclectic collection of essays and other works that Davis thought represented high thought. After three months, one of the farmers discovered that his son wrote a more careful script than did Davis. After a short controversy, the farmers asked Davis to resign and they appointed another headmaster.[75]

Manual labor schools were a variation of the modest types of academies. In 1787, *Columbia Magazine* published an article recommending that any settlement with about sixty families could contribute subscriptions, obtain grants from the state, and solicit charitable donations to buy a farm and stock it with livestock. In such a setting, boys and girls aged eight to fifteen could learn to manage the home and fields and pursue academic studies such as literature, botany, geography, and history.[76]

In 1833, Theodore Weld, one of the figures involved in Lane Seminary described in Chapter 3, published a report of the Society for the Promoting Manual Labor in Literary Institutes. Weld claimed that students should not pursue academic studies without opportunities to engage in manual labor. He found support from such individuals as Philip Lindsley, president of Nashville University, and Thomas S. Grimke of South Carolina. Since several reviews of his report praised the model, various denominations started manual labor seminaries. By the 1850s, the movement died in the South as students lost interest, neglected their work, and abused the livestock. The manual labor schools that continued served indigent boys.[77]

The various states arranged the control and support of academies differently. Some states divided a sum of state money among its academies. For example, from 1840 to 1861, Tennessee divided about $16,000 equally among the seventy-four counties to support academies. Louisiana created a University of New Orleans to establish a college in the state and one academy in each county. Each academy was to receive $2000 for initial construction and $500 per year for maintenance.[78]

Although most of the academies were for boys, some academies were for girls and other academies were coeducational. At first, the curriculum focused on Latin, Greek, and mathematics because these were the subjects needed for college admission. By 1847, when colleges required English grammar, geography, algebra, geometry, and ancient history, these courses appeared in the curriculums of Southern academies. Practical courses such as navigation, needlework, and surveying appeared as well.[79]

A unique aspect of Southern academies was the military training component in schools for boys. In 1802, the federal government established the U.S. Military Academy at West Point to train military leaders to defend the new republic. Graduates of this academy founded dozens of military academies throughout the South, meanwhile criticizing West Point for establishing a federal monopoly on military training. They claimed that private military academies provided soldiers who made state militias effective whereas West Point served the federal government. According to advocates of military academies, these private institutions served the states in two ways. They produced graduates who had received training in civilian professions, and they taught the students how to lead soldiers in times of emergency.[80]

In some cases, state legislatures created military academies to replace state troops stationed at arsenals. In Lexington, Virginia, and in Charleston and Columbia, South Carolina, citizens disliked the state troops assigned to guard the arsenals, calling them idle, dissolute, and odious. Supporters of state-supported military academies claimed that the academies could perform the job and provide the cadets with an education. In this way, the unreliability of existing militias became an important argument to advance academies in the South. Advocates of private military academies contended that if the United States hired mercenary troops to defend its borders, these mercenaries could rebel and cause internal strife. The supporters added that military academies were beneficial because they could strengthen character and inculcate in cadets habits of order, diligence, and punctuality, as well as fill idle time with military drill to avoid opportunities for dissipation.[81]

Parents found another advantage to military training. Because these academies promised to teach cadets to submit to lawful authority, the parents hoped the academies would discipline their unruly sons. Thus, headmasters of military academies promised to teach the cadets to be patriotic and to correct their waywardness. In similar fashion, advocates addressed state legislatures, promising that the free military education in an academy would provide the state with fifty worthy, valuable young citizens a year. Because military abilities required scientific and engineering knowledge, the cadets received training in useful arts. As a result, the curriculums emphasized science, engineering, and mathematics.[82]

In the 1830s, critics complained that the military academies inspired aristocracy. Officials in the Southern military academies took two steps to increase egalitarianism. The first was to admit financially handicapped cadets. For example, the Virginia Assembly required Virginia Military Institute to admit twenty indigent youth each year. By 1860, one-third of the academy's graduates fell into that category. They had incurred expenses of about $80 per year while other students paid around $225. In South Carolina, the indigent youth attended without any charge. The second step the academies took was to require uniforms, because they erased social distinctions.[83] Some states, including Virginia, North Carolina, Alabama, and Georgia, required the graduates who had received free or lowered expenses to teach in a public school or college in the state for two years. Thus, the academies served as normal schools.[84]

As the confrontation with the Northern states approached, the number of military academies grew rapidly. From 1845 to 1860, every slave state except Texas had a state-supported military academy. Dozens of private military academies received some state support. As a result, by 1860, the slave states had opened ninety-six military academies, colleges, or universities while the nonslave states had fifteen.[85]

A historian interested in the rise of military academies in the South, Rod Andrew, Jr., concluded that the sectional frenzy that led to the war was one of the least important factors contributing to the popularity of military academies. He found that military academies claimed a heritage of republican thought that stretched to antiquity. In this model of thought, an armed, trained, disciplined citizenry was an important aspect of democratic society. Ironically, although the military academies included strong elements of egalitarianism, they became centers of conservative resistance to abolitionism as the conflict approached. In fact, Andrew points out that, according to some graduates of the Citadel, a state military academy established in 1842 in Charleston, South Carolina, their cadets fired cannon shots at the ship, the *Star of the West*, sent in 1861 to bring supplies to Fort Sumter. With this action, the cadets started the American Civil War.

What Obstacles Prevented the Rise of State Supported Schools in the South?

Although efforts to provide state support for schools began in the first years of the nineteenth century, advocates did not enjoy success in many Southern states until the 1850s or even Reconstruction. For example, in 1811, state-supported schools opened in Charleston, South Carolina, to impart elementary education to all white children, with a preference for orphans and children of indigent parents. By 1834, the city had five free schools with 525 pupils. Unfortunately, most residents of Charleston considered the public schools to be charity schools and refused to support them. This remained the case until well after the American Civil War. Similarly, in 1806, Tennessee devoted extensive tracts of land to the support of schools; however, it was not until 1854 that Tennessee selected a state school board and superintendent and added a provision for tax support of schools.[86]

As noted in the beginning of this chapter, historians disagree on the reasons for sectional differences in the development of state supported schools. Historians have suggested at least five obstacles that prevented the rise of state supported education in the South before the War between the States. These included slavery, the problems of land grants as a way to support schools, a "laissez faire" attitude toward government, the rural nature of the South, and the affection for universities. These factors turned into obstacles because different social groups used them to reinforce the political differences that existed in the Southern states.

First, although slavery and the notion of aristocracy did not prevent Southerners from accepting universal education, these factors turned many proposals for state-supported education into plans for charity schools rather than for common schools. For example, from 1830 to 1850, Lancaster schools employing the monitorial method had been popular, and many Sunday schools opened to teach poor children to read so they could accept religious instruction. This served the critics of publicly supported education who feared the breakdown of class barriers if wealthy and poor children mingled in common schools.[87]

Second, many states in the South wanted to use land grants to support schools. As had been the case in the Northeast and the Northwest Territories, these land grants represented an indirect tax for schools. Although the state did not have to impose taxes on property holders to support schools, the funds derived from these lands were lost through mismanagement, bank failures, and poor administration. Another problem was that the land grants supported areas that did not need schools. For example, in Alabama, the first state superintendent of schools complained that the permanent school fund derived from land grants was an obstacle to school reform. He claimed that, in many of the school districts with families in need of educational services, the land devoted to the support of education was worthless. He noted that the valuable land grants were in the section of the state known as the Black Belt. Although wise managers guarded this money, it did not support schools because large plantations dominated the area.[88]

Third, a characteristic nineteenth-century concept, often called the "laissez faire" doctrine, held that government should not supply things that individuals can obtain on their own. Following this view, critics contended that if the state provided schools for everyone, it would have to levy taxes on people who did not want schools. According to this doctrine, the limit of state intervention should be to remove anything that prevented people from obtaining education on their own. Acknowledging that such a "laissez faire" view was strong in the South, Mathews pointed out that the initial system of land grants or literary funds implied that states should support schools. He found that opposition became serious when advocates of state schools sought to consolidate the financial aid implied in land grants or permanent school funds through the creation of a state board of education and a superintendent.[89]

The opposition to state support was sufficiently strong to impose conditions that made such control impossible even if a legislature had approved some form of centralization. For example, in 1829, the Mississippi governor suggested investing the literary fund derived from the sale of land grants in the Bank of Mississippi. Although the state followed this recommendation, officials squandered or left uncollected a great deal of the money. In 1843, a new governor, Albert Gallatin Brown, took office. Calling attention to the loss of the land grant funds, Brown sought to establish a statewide system of schools. When the law passed, it required that a majority of people in each township give written permission for any levy for schools. Thus, few townships set up schools. From 1846 to 1860, the legislature adopted five different systems of organization and passed twenty-six specific ordinances for schools in particular counties. According to one historian, these legislative efforts removed any trace of a public school system.[90]

Fourth, the rural nature of the South retarded the spread of schools. Although the schools in Southern cities may have been comparable to those in Northern cities, they were more isolated. Children who lived outside urban centers could not easily attend school. Comparisons of rates of literacy reinforce these conclusions. For example, in 1850, in New England, about 2 percent of the white population older than twenty could not read. In rural sections of New England, though, the rate of illiteracy was about 5 percent. Because illiteracy was higher in rural sections and the South was largely rural, it is no surprise that the rate of illiteracy in the South approached 8.5 percent. Nonetheless, the South enjoyed one advantage. A higher percentage of the white population attended college in the South than in the North. Out of 19,000,000 white people in the North in 1860, about 27,400 students attended college. In the South, out of a white population of 7,400,000, about 26,000 attended.[91]

Fifth, universities may have risen in the South at the expense of common schools. For example, Jefferson's efforts to diffuse education throughout Virginia resulted in the legislature eventually approving the founding of a university but leaving questions of elementary schooling to the caprice of fortune. In fairness to Jefferson, he did not intend to sacrifice schools to the university. Given the sentiments at the time, this may have been all that was possible.

In 1776, taking a seat in the Virginia legislature, Jefferson introduced several bills in an effort to democratize the state. The first were changes in the laws of inheritance. The practice had been that an estate passed entirely to the eldest son upon the death of the owner. Because estates remained in the hands of few people, they continued to be large. Jefferson argued that this process of disinheriting younger members of the families harmed their morals and prevented them from improving the lands. At the same session, he introduced his bill for the general diffusion of knowledge described above that the legislature refused to fund.[92]

Jefferson felt that his actions fit together to increase democracy. First, the removal of primogeniture and entail eliminated the feudal practice of inheritance wherein the eldest son received the entire estate and other family members got nothing. Second, he added to these changes the prohibition against establishing a national church. This freed less-wealthy people from supporting dominant faiths. Finally, Jefferson recommended the diffusion of education to give the less-wealthy people the training to understand and to change their situations. At the same time, Jefferson wanted the schools to enjoy local control because he feared centralizing tendencies from state or national support. It was this fear that caused him to vote against proposals to build a national university although he wanted to create a university in Virginia.[93]

The Virginia legislature did not act on Jefferson's bill for education; however, another opportunity arose after he left the presidency. In 1816, the federal government reimbursed Virginia $400,000 for debts incurred in the War of 1812. When added to the literary fund, the sum seemed to be enough to fund Jefferson's plan. Consequently, Jefferson modified his original plan and sent it to Joseph C. Cabell to reintroduce in opposition to a plan promoted by Charles Fenton Mercer to establish one university, four colleges, twenty-five academies, and many primary schools throughout the state. Jefferson opposed Mercer's plan because it did not place control of the schools in the local districts but in a state board of instruction. The threat of central control led Jefferson and his supporters to fight Mercer's ideas although they agreed to the idea of spreading educational facilities through the state.[94]

The result was a compromise. The legislature approved the founding of a university that became the University of Virginia, allocating $15,000 per year. For elementary schools, the legislature mandated that each county court appoint a board of fifteen commissioners to establish schools. Whether these boards would create any schools was a matter of local concern, though. To help create schools, the legislature divided $45,000 per year among the counties. Since each county had to ask for the money to receive it and they had to support more than charity schools, only four counties established schools by 1820. In those counties, the schools created by votes of the county commissioners were part of the pauper system.[95]

Although legislative approval of the University of Virginia hurt the common schools, policy makers in Georgia turned support for the university into aid for common schools.

In 1801, Georgia opened a state university. Since wealthy landowners wanted the university, supporters of common schools sought to use the university money for common schools. In 1830, the governor suggested that offering university scholarships to the poor met the demand for improving common schools because those indigent students would become teachers. In 1845, another governor repeated the argument saying the university was essential to ensure the proper training of common school teachers.[96]

Although the five obstacles listed above were not sufficient to block school reform, different groups could use them in efforts to support or oppose aspects of state support of schools. This became evident in some analyses of people's reaction to various proposals.

In 1914, when Knight considered who favored state support of schools, he determined that supporters came from different types of people. For example, in Virginia, an important source of support was a new middle class of professionals who had developed as population moved away from the large plantations near the coast into the western regions. Most colleges and academies were in the coastal region. Votes of representatives from the more newly settled regions helped pass legislation in favor of state-supported education. In South Carolina, Knight found that the wealthy citizens of cities such as Charleston patronized the public schools, thereby weakening the prejudice against them. In Tennessee, when the reforms centered on expanding financial support so that school terms could be longer, the money came from the larger towns of Nashville, Memphis, and Clarksville. In Mississippi, Knight found that the Whigs and the Democrats joined together to pass the 1846 law to provide local commissioners of education who would license teachers and control school curriculum.[97]

In 1937, Horace Mann Bond wrote that in Alabama, economic class distinctions determined political decisions. Describing an election in 1854 concerning the use of land grant funds, Bond claimed that representatives from the Black Belt, where the land was most valuable and cotton plantations dominated, proposed that funds remain in the sections where the lands were located. This proposal lost by one vote. In 1856, in a vote to amend the education bill, all the dissenting members represented the Black Belt. Although Bond recognized that there were at least five classes of white people in Alabama, he decided that the plantation system created divisions between white people who owned many slaves and white people who did not.[98]

In 1965, when Mathews considered voting patterns in antebellum Alabama and Georgia, he found the strongest support for common school reform came from what he called the professional class. This included doctors, lawyers, ministers, and small planters. In addition, support came from counties with a large group of owners of small, independent farms. These sections tended to vote Democratic. The opposition came especially from the counties with extremely wealthy planters, who tended to vote for Whigs, and from the economically deprived counties in the isolated areas of hill country. Although the votes seemed to fall along party lines, Mathews noted that voters tended to fall into four different groups on educational issues rather than simple partisan lines. These groups included wealthy individuals who supported charity schools, professionals who wanted state superintendents and normal schools, yeomen farmers in the hill country who wanted free schools without state superintendents, and backwoods people who objected to any form of education. Nonetheless, he noted that determining the patterns of support for reform were complicated because some proslavery advocates and some antiegalitarians supported common schools, although the reforms contradicted their social or economic positions.[99]

Conclusion

Because prosperous plantation owners in the South traded directly with Europe, they limited the growth of commerce and manufacturing. Although the South lacked the industrial urban centers that sped the development of common schools in the North, Southern advocates of common schools pushed for the improvement of school buildings, textbooks, and teacher qualifications as their Northern counterparts had done. In fact, in the North and South, the campaign for common school reform followed similar strategies and appealed to similar groups for similar reasons. In the North and South, common schools began as charity schools for what were called indigent youth. In the South, plantation owners employed private tutors or sent their children to the North or to England for their education. The middle classes valued education as a means of social advancement. Members of this social class tended not to hold slaves and they considered the reform schools to be in their interests. Since this middle class turned to academies for secondary school training rather than to public schools, reformers sought state support for private academies, arguing that military academies produced good citizens and valuable professionals. Despite these Southern campaigns for state-supported education, states in the North and the Midwest adopted more aspects of state-supported universal schooling than did the Southern states. Nonetheless, by the advent of the American Civil War, the South had adopted more of the characteristics of centralized schooling than many commentators recognized. Thus, people in Southern states adopted some aspects of education later associated with globalization.

Endnotes

1. W. J. Cash, *The Mind of the South* (New York: Alfred A. Knopf, 1941), vii–xi.
2. C. Vann Woodward, *American Counterpoint: Slavery and Racism in North-South Dialogue* (Boston: Little, Brown, and Co., 1971), 261–283.
3. C. Vann Woodward, *Strange Career of Jim Crow,* 2nd ed. (New York: Oxford University Press, 1966), 3–6.
4. Edgar W. Knight, "Some Fallacies Concerning the History of Public Education in the South," *South Atlantic Quarterly* 13, no. 4 (October 1914): 371–381.
5. Knight, "Some Fallacies," 372–373.
6. Edgar W. Knight, *Public Education in the South* (Boston: Ginn and Co., 1922), 112–143.
7. Merle Curti, *The Social Ideas of American Educators* (1935; reprint, Totowa, N.J.: Littlefield, Adams & Co., 1978), 74.
8. Lawrence A. Cremin, *The American Common School: An Historic Conception* (New York: Bureau of Publications, Columbia University, 1951), 24–27, 110–118.
9. Rush Welter, *Popular Education and Democratic Thought in America* (New York: Columbia University Press, 1962), 132–135.
10. Forrest David Mathews, "The Politics of Education in the Deep South: Georgia and Alabama, 1830–1860" (Ph.D. diss., Columbia University, 1965), 407–412.
11. Lawrence A. Cremin, *American Education: The National Experience, 1783–1876* (New York: Harper & Row, 1980), 148–163.
12. Cremin, *American Education: The National Experience,* 414–432.
13. Clinton B. Allison, "The Appalling World of Edgar Wallace Knight," *Journal of Thought* 18, no. 3 (Fall 1983): 7–14.
14. Carl F. Kaestle, *Pillars of the Republic: Common Schools and American Society, 1780–1860* (New York: Hill and Wang, 1983), 100, 216–217.
15. Charles William Dabney, *Universal Education in the South,* vol. 1 (1936; reprint, New York: Arno Press, 1969), 15–116.
16. Dabney, *Universal Education in the South,* 171–173.
17. James L. Leloudis, *Schooling the New South: Pedagogy, Self, and Society, 1880–1920* (Chapel Hill: University of North Carolina Press, 1996), 21.
18. Janis Price Greenough, "Resistance to the Institutionalization of Schooling in the Antebellum

Southern Highlands" (Ph.D. diss., University of California, Berkeley, 1999), 30–38.

19. Cremin, *American Education: The National Experience,* 173–175.
20. Kaestle, *Pillars of the Republic,* ix–xi.
21. Kaestle, *Pillars of the Republic,* 212.
22. Kaestle, *Pillars of the Republic,* 214–215.
23. Kaestle, *Pillars of the Republic,* 215–216.
24. Kenneth P. Minkema, "Jonathan Edwards on Slavery and the Slave Trade," *The William and Mary Quarterly* 54 no. 4 (October 1997): 823–834.
25. W. E. Burghart Du Bois, *The Suppression of the African Slave-Trade to the United States of America, 1638–1870* (1898; reprint, New York: Russell & Russell, Inc., 1965), 61–62.
26. Louis Filler, *The Crusade Against Slavery* (New York: Harper & Brothers, 1960), 10–12, 49–75.
27. Larry E. Tise, *Proslavery: A History of Slavery in America, 1701–1840* (Athens: University of Georgia Press, 1987), 16–19.
28. Tise, *Proslavery,* 347–362.
29. Thomas Jefferson, "Thomas Jefferson's 'Bill for the More General Diffusion of Knowledge' (1779)," ed. Sol Cohen, *Education in the United States: A Documentary History,* vol. 2 (New York: Random House, 1974), 739–744.
30. Benjamin Rush, "Benjamin Rush Proposes a System of Public Schools for Pennsylvania (1786)," ed. Sol Cohen, *Education in the United States: A Documentary History,* vol. 2 (New York: Random House, 1974), 756–758.
31. Nathan Schacner, *Thomas Jefferson: A Biography* (New York: Thomas Yoseloff, 1951), 153–154.
32. Tise, *Proslavery,* 22, 28, 288–289.
33. Kenneth Stampp, *The Peculiar Institution: Slavery in the Ante-Bellum South* (New York: Alfred A. Knopf, 1956), 29–31.
34. Edward E. Gordon and Elaine H. Gordon, *Literacy in America: Historic Journey and Contemporary Solutions* (Westport, Conn.: Praeger, 2003), 56–69.
35. Gordon and Gordon, *Literacy in America,* 63–66.
36. Philip Freneau, "The Private Tutor," in *The Work of Teachers in America: A Social History through Stories,* ed. Rosetta Marantz Cohen and Samuel Scheer (Mahwah, N.J.: Lawrence Erlbaum Associates, 1997), 23–27.
37. Heather Andrea Williams, *Self-Taught: African American Education in Slavery and Freedom* (Chapel Hill: University of North Carolina Press, 2005), 14–15.
38. Williams, *Self-Taught,* 28.
39. Mathews, "The Politics of Education in the Deep South," 150–152.
40. Catherine E. Cave, "Literacy and Freedom: The Changing Role of Literacy in the Lives of Southern Blacks, 1830–1895" (Master's thesis, University of Rochester, 1992), 28–32.
41. Daniel Alexander Payne, "The School Master in the Dark South," in *The Work of Teachers in America,* ed. Rosetta Marantz Ghen and Samuel Scheer (Mahwah, N.J.: Lawrence Erlbaum Associates, 1997), 57–61.
42. Frederick Douglass, *Narrative of the Life of Frederick Douglass: An American Slave* (1845; reprint, New York: New American Library, 1968), 48–58.
43. Eugene D. Genovese, *Roll, Jordan, Roll: The World the Slaves Made* (New York: Pantheon Books, 1974), 561–565.
44. Genovese, *Roll, Jordan, Roll,* 563–565.
45. Ulrich Bonnell Phillips, *American Negro Slavery: A Survey of the Supply, Employment, and Control of Negro Labor as Determined by the Plantation Regime* (1918; reprint, Baton Rouge: Louisiana State University Press, 1966), xxiii–xxiv, 260–270.
46. Phillips, *American Negro Slavery,* 270–290.
47. Robert William Fogel, *The Slavery Debates, 1952–1990* (Baton Rouge: Louisiana State University Press, 2003), 6–8.
48. Stampp, *The Peculiar Institution,* 3–26, 85, 139–140, 190–191, 266–267, 318–319, 416–418, 431–436.
49. Eugene D. Genovese, "Foreword: Ulrich Bonnell Phillips & His Critics," in *American Negro Slavery: A Survey of the Supply, Employment and Control of Negro Labor as Determined by the Plantation Regime,* Ulrich Bonnell Phillips (Baton Rouge: Louisiana State University Press, 1966), vii–xxi.
50. Genovese, *Roll, Jordan, Roll,* xv–xvii, 3–25, 183–193.
51. Genovese, *Roll, Jordan, Roll,* 585–622.
52. Peter J. Parish, *Slavery: History and Historians* (New York: Harper & Row, 1989), 73–92.
53. Frank Lawrence Owsley, *Plain Folk of the Old South* (Chicago: Quadrangle Books, 1949), 7–9.
54. Owsley, *Plain Folk of the Old South,* 139–146.
55. Owsley, *Plain Folk of the Old South,* 148–149.
56. Greenough, "Resistance to the Institutionalization of Schooling," 175–176.
57. Greenough, "Resistance to the Institutionalization of Schooling," 30–31, 177–178.
58. Greenough, "Resistance to the Institutionalization of Schooling," 184–188.
59. Greenough, "Resistance to the Institutionalization of Schooling," 188–195.
60. Benjamin M. Smith, "Report on Teachers in German Schools, 1839," in *A Documentary History of Education Before 1860,* ed. Edgar W. Knight

(Chapel Hill: University of North Carolina Press, 1953), 4:228–230.
61. Henry Ruffner, "President Henry Ruffner of Washington College, Virginia Discusses Teachers and Normal Schools, 1841," in *A Documentary History of Education Before 1860,* 5:231–234.
62. Braxton Craven, "Describes Proper School Practices, 1849," in *A Documentary History of Education Before 1860,* 5:239–243.
63. Dabney, *Universal Education in the South,* 168–170.
64. "Necessity and Practicability of Establishing a System of Normal Schools in the State of North Carolina," *The North Carolina Journal of Education,* in *A Documentary History of Education Before 1860,* 5:259–265.
65. "Southern Opposition to Northern Influences," in *A Documentary History of Education Before 1860,* 5:278–287.
66. C. G. Memminger, "Address at the Opening of the Female High and Normal School in Charleston, South Carolina, 1859," in *A Documentary History of Education Before 1860,* 5:268–277.
67. Knight, *Public Education in the South,* 269–304.
68. Knight, *Public Education in the South,* 270–273.
69. "Some School Practices in Western North Carolina are Described, 1842," in *A Documentary History of Education Before 1860,* 5:234–236.
70. Knight, *Public Education in the South,* 281–291.
71. Cremin, *American Education: The National Experience,* 425–432.
72. John Milton, "Of Education," in *The Age of Academies,* ed. Theodore Sizer (New York: Bureau of Publications, Columbia University, 1964), 50–65.
73. Benjamin Franklin, "Proposals Relating to the Education of Youth in Pennsylvania," in *The American Curriculum: A Documentary History,* ed. George Willis, et al., (Westport, CN: Praeger, 1994), 20–22.
74. Knight, *Public Education in the South,* 75–77.
75. Knight, *Public Education in the South,* 77–81.
76. "Agricultural and Manual Labor Schools Are Recommended, 1787," in *A Documentary History of Education Before 1860,* 4:64–68.
77. Theodore Weld, "Extracts from the Report of the Society for Promoting Manual Labor in Literary Institutions, 1833," in *A Documentary History of Education Before 1860,* 4:98–110.
78. Knight, *Public Education in the South,* 91–95.
79. Knight, *Public Education in the South,* 104–109.
80. Rod Andrew, Jr., *Long Gray Lines: The Southern Military School Tradition, 1839–1915* (Chapel Hill: University of North Carolina Press, 2001), 9–11.
81. Andrew, *Long Gray Lines,* 11–13.
82. Andrew, *Long Gray Lines,* 13–15.
83. Andrew, *Long Gray Lines,* 15–17.
84. Andrew, *Long Gray Lines,* 17–18.
85. Andrew, *Long Gray Lines,* 19.
86. Dabney, *Universal Education in the South,* 225–227, 288–295.
87. Knight, *Public Education in the South,* 265–267.
88. Knight, *Public Education in the South,* 181–183.
89. Mathews, *Politics of Education in the Deep South,* 415–417.
90. Dabney, *Universal Education in the South,* 342–345.
91. Owsley, *Plain Folk of the Old South,* 146–148.
92. S. E. Forman, *The Life and Writings of Thomas Jefferson* (Indianapolis: Bowen-Merrill Co., 1900), 22–25.
93. Dabney, *Universal Education in the South,* 6–8, 16, 20.
94. Roy J. Honeywell, *The Educational Work of Thomas Jefferson* (New York: Russell & Russell, Inc., 1964), 17–22.
95. Dabney, *Universal Education in the South,* 37–40.
96. Mathews, "The Politics of Education in the Deep South," 427–430.
97. Knight, *Public Education in the South,* 206, 228, 233, 235–237, 248–250.
98. Horace Mann Bond, *Negro Education in Alabama: A Study in Cotton and Steel* (1939; reprint, New York: Atheneum, 1969), 5–8.
99. Mathews, "The Politics of Education in the Deep South," 200–214, 423–426.

6

Education during Reconstruction and the New South

A school sponsored by the U.S. Bureau of Refugees, Freedmen, and Abandoned Lands

The term *Reconstruction* comes from the series of acts that the U.S. Congress passed from 1866 to 1868 over the veto of President Andrew Johnson. These acts, together with the Thirteenth, Fourteenth, and Fifteenth Amendments to the U.S. Constitution, released from bondage nearly 4,000,000 African Americans, gave these newly freed slaves the right to vote, and divided the South into five military districts each commanded by a general who had the authority to remove and appoint state officials. In 1886, after Reconstruction had ended, Henry Woodfin Grady, editor of the *Atlanta Constitution,* made a speech to financiers in New York describing the opportunities that awaited investors in the reconstructed South. When Grady made his speech, he used the term *New South.* The terms *Reconstruction* and *New South* describe conditions during specific periods in the eleven former Confederate states and sometimes Kentucky and the territory of Oklahoma.[1]

During the second half of the nineteenth century, the South underwent three major changes. The first was Reconstruction, which officially ended in 1877 when President Rutherford B. Hayes withdrew the remaining federal troops from Louisiana and South Carolina. In many ways, it ended earlier when the Republican state governments that advanced Reconstruction in the South collapsed by 1870. In their place, conservative white Democrats promised to redeem the region. The third change came by 1890 when the white owners of small farms formed a populist party and sought to replace the Democrats. However, proclamations of a New South weakened the Democrats and the populist regimes as advocates claimed business was more important than politics.

As noted in Chapter 5, historians such as C. Vann Woodward claimed these shifts in Southern life focused on the status of African Americans. Reconstruction derived from policies of the federal government to end slavery and to advance citizenship among African Americans. Conservative Democrats created policies designed to prevent African Americans from voting, and other white politicians enacted laws requiring racial segregation as part of the rise of the New South. By the beginning of the twentieth century, many prominent African Americans accepted these restrictions and sought economic progress.

Historians have devoted considerable attention to the periods of Reconstruction and the rise of the New South. In part, their interests derive from efforts in the 1960s by the federal government to end racial discrimination in housing, employment, and education. Historians who considered the 1960s and 1970s the second Reconstruction sought to determine what had happened during the first Reconstruction. Thus, the years after the American Civil War provided an opportunity for historians to consider whether or how a government could change people's moral attitudes and to what extent schools could advance efforts of social liberation.[2]

What Were the Effects of Reconstruction in the South?

According to Eric Foner, until the 1960s, historians took what he called the traditional view of Reconstruction. This was the notion that vindictive Radical Republicans forced the South to accept black supremacy and unleashed corruption by *carpetbaggers,* a pejorative term applied to Northern immigrants, and *scalawags,* an insulting name for native whites who became public officials, along with ignorant freedmen. In this view, the conservative Redeemers restored honest government. Although this view came from Southern Democrats who had campaigned in the 1870s against Reconstruction, William Archibald Dunning gave such interpretations historical legitimacy in the early years of twentieth century.[3]

Writing in 1897 about the military governments that controlled the South immediately following the hostilities, Dunning claimed that most military commanders acted efficiently and justly. Nonetheless, he argued that their authoritarian rule caused resentment among Southerners. Dunning added that, when the military imposed Negro suffrage, white Southerners were outraged. The subsequent election of representative governments caused disaster because the process of Reconstruction turned the social pyramid on its top. According to Dunning, the slaves who had occupied the bottom of the social pyramid came to occupy the top. He concluded that the federal government had been foolhardy to enthrone the freedman in positions of authority because the military force of the North could not protect them.[4]

In a similar manner, in 1906, writing his *History of the United States from the Compromise of 1850,* James Ford Rhodes justified the harsh treatment of the former slaves through the Black Codes. According to Rhodes, from 1865 to 1866, each state in the former Confederacy, through their provisional governments, adopted laws that forbade black people to vote, to hold public office, to meet together, to move about the state, and officials executed black men for such crimes as rape when white men would receive milder penalties. Rhodes argued that these Black Codes were necessary to restrain the former slaves who suffered from inferior mental development and who lacked a sense of the responsibilities associated with freedom.[5]

When Rhodes described how the federal government's Reconstruction Acts of 1866 had terminated the authority of the Black Codes, he complained that these federal laws pandered to carpetbaggers, the adventurers who descended on the South like vultures. He added that the laws helped the knavish white scalawags and ignorant Negroes defraud honest people. He claimed the extent of corruption was outrageous. Full relief did not come, he added, until the Democrats took control in various states and Hayes became U.S. President.[6]

In 1917, John Roy Lynch disputed Rhodes description of Reconstruction. Lynch had been a prominent actor in those events. Born a slave, Lynch served as the Republican speaker of the house in Mississippi. He won election to the U.S. House of Representatives and became an auditor for the U.S. Treasury. In 1884, he presided over the Republican Party's national convention. Lynch disputed Rhodes's characterization of the end of Reconstruction as the final restoration of home rule. According to Lynch, the region had never lacked home rule except for a brief period when military leaders exercised control. According to Lynch, the Reconstruction Acts forced the states to elect democratic governments. In fact, he believed that the governments formed during Reconstruction were more democratic than any that preceded the American Civil War. He added that states formed undemocratic governments after Reconstruction because new election laws prevented many residents from voting.[7]

Lynch accused Rhodes of misrepresenting important facts. For example, in making a larger point, Rhodes cited the example of a military officer who had appointed an illiterate, incompetent black man to the office of sheriff. Rhodes contended that this sheriff allowed a white deputy to do the work although the black man received the pay. Lynch knew this particular black sheriff personally. He pointed out that this man had demonstrated his honesty and his diligence in his previous service as a Baptist minister and Union soldier. Further, the Negro sheriff was still living and had sent a letter to Lynch showing that he was able to read and write.[8]

More important, Lynch argued that Rhodes's generalizations were inaccurate. Rhodes had described the Reconstruction Acts as attacks on civilization because they led to Constitutional Amendments that forced Southern states to grant newly freed slaves the right to vote. According to Lynch, the Radical Republicans imposed black suffrage in order to prevent the defeated Confederacy from reestablishing slavery. Because the Fourteenth Amendment extended federal protection to the newly freed slaves, Lynch contended that only people who approved of slavery could consider the Amendment an attack on civilization.[9]

W. E. Burghardt Du Bois made similar complaints about historians. Du Bois warned that Northern efforts to conciliate Southerners' antagonism to Negro suffrage caused the Northerners to render African Americans an injustice. According to Du Bois, the Southern policy makers forced the U.S. Congress to adopt the Reconstruction Acts by enacting the Black Codes that denied civil rights to African Americans. To the members of Congress, the former slaves had to have the right to vote so they could protect themselves. Although Southerners claimed that Negro suffrage led to extravagance, theft, and incompetence, Du Bois claimed these were exaggerations. Citing incidents such as the misuse of land grants for colleges, Du Bois argued that African Americans never committed fraud to such an extent. To illustrate the effectiveness of black policy makers, Du Bois noted that the state constitutions of Florida, Virginia, South Carolina, and Mississippi had formed by conventions with black delegates, yet they remained in force for twenty to thirty years after their adoption. Such longevity indicated the members of the conventions had carefully constructed the constitutions.[10]

Concerning schools, according to Du Bois, when former slaves received the right to vote, they created the foundation of what he called the Negro common school. Du Bois wrote that instruction for African Americans began with the Freedman's Bureau and with missionary societies. It continued, he added, when the governments in states such as Mississippi, Alabama, Arkansas, Florida, Louisiana, and the Carolinas formed during Reconstruction established uniform systems of free public schools for children between the ages of five and twenty-one years.[11]

Many historians ignored the arguments of Du Bois and Lynch. For example, in 1929, Claude G. Bowers wrote a bestselling account of Reconstruction entitled *The Tragic Era.* Bowers claimed that, during the twelve years following Lincoln's assassination, unscrupulous federal officials followed the policies of such people as Thaddeus Stevens; they tortured the Southern people, ignored the constitution, and treated the U.S. Supreme Court with contempt.[12]

This view became part of the conventional wisdom through popular movies such as *Birth of a Nation* by D. W. Griffith. Opening in 1915, Griffith's film portrayed blacks as evil people who were determined to destroy Southern society. Griffith cast the members of the Ku Klux Klan as heroes who saved society with their vigilante form of retribution. In 1939, David O. Selznick's production of the movie *Gone with the Wind* reproduced the image of the South torn apart by uncontrolled forces during Reconstruction.

In 1940, Howard K. Beale called for a reappraisal of what he called Reconstruction history. To Beale, the important change was not Negro suffrage or the personal corruption among conservative white Democrats who replaced Republican office holders. When

Beale considered the debts that Southern states contracted during Reconstruction and during later conservative rule, he found that the largest portion of these funds went to the construction of railroads. According to Beale, the same men owned the railroads in the South from the 1850s to the 1880s. Beale argued that state resources went to further the business enterprises of a few capitalists no matter which regime was in power. Thus, for Beale, capitalism and industrialism proceeded through the American Civil War, Reconstruction, and the rise of the New South.[13]

With the victory of the NAACP Legal Defense Fund in 1954 in the case of *Brown v. Board of Education,* historians reported with favor the black suffrage that resulted from Reconstruction. For example, in 1960, John Hope Franklin argued that the so-called Reconstruction Acts required that the former Confederate states form conventions and revise their constitutions in order to apply for readmission to the Union. In these conventions, he added, many delegates expressed views similar to those the common school advocates had repeated during their efforts to encourage state support of public education. They claimed that, in order to exercise the responsibilities of voting and of holding public office, the citizenry had to be educated. These delegates included white and black representatives. Although Franklin noted that some white members expressed doubts about the education of black people, he claimed that no convention considered measures that would have excluded the former slaves from schools. In the conventions, the delegates debated whether the public schools should be racially integrated or segregated. Those members in favor of racially mixed schools contended that the Fourteenth Amendment demanded equality and racially integrated schools. Despite the fear that the U.S. Congress would not accept separate schools, Louisiana and South Carolina were the only states that adopted provisions for racially integrated schools.[14]

Franklin added that, with the end of reconstruction in 1877, a group calling themselves the Redeemers began to institute policies that made it increasingly difficult for African Americans to participate in politics or to protect their legal rights. By adopting various strategies to prevent black adults from voting, these supposed Saviors of the South disenfranchised many white people as well. According to Franklin, the result was that a small political minority exercised political power.[15]

In 1964, Willie Lee Rose returned to the theme that Howard Beale had described in 1940. Emphasizing the role education played in Reconstruction, Rose focused her study on the events that followed the capture in 1861 by the U.S. Navy of the plantations and slaves on the Sea Islands of South Carolina. According to Rose, Northern abolitionists used these islands and the slaves that worked the plantations to launch an experiment proving that newly freed slaves could profit from education and from opportunities to work for themselves. In writing the history of the Port Royal Experiment, Rose showed that the abolitionists held a confusing variety of motives. For example, although some abolitionists wanted to erect a communal society, the leaders of the project thought they could use the effort to introduce capitalistic ways of thinking and acting among former slaves. Rose contended that people working at cross-purposes marred the Port Royal Experiment. Some men cheated the former slaves. Many government actions appeared to be half-hearted. Nonetheless, the Port Royal Experiment was influential in leading the U.S. Congress to create the Freedmen's Bureau and, Rose claimed, it reflected the goals and the ironies that followed in Reconstruction.[16]

In short, whereas some historians thought the North acted vindictively and imposed the models of New England on the former Confederacy, other historians thought the North had tried to alleviate the problems caused by the institution of slavery. A third group thought that the business mentality continued to grow despite the aristocratic tendencies of people before the war and the dislike of the North after the war. Finally, a fourth group of historians noted that all these descriptions held at least some truth.

How Did Reconstruction Policies Influence the Spread of Public Education?

Educational historians followed in the patterns of historians of Reconstruction. Although they agreed that Reconstruction introduced state-supported systems of education into the South, they offered different assessments of the success of those innovations. Some educational historians claimed that Reconstruction ended Southern efforts to create state systems of schools. Other historians claimed the newly freed slaves provided the impetus to create state systems of education. A third group complained that the Northern teachers who started the schools antagonized native white Southerners and thereby retarded the development of free schools.

As noted in Chapter 5, after victory, some Northern educators claimed that a cause of the War between the States was the South's lack of schools. Despite such aspersions against Southern education, there were many different educational arrangements in antebellum Southern states. In fact, when Albert Fishlow tried to determine if the common school revival had influenced school enrollments, he noted that, from 1840 to 1860, enrollment rates declined in New England while they expanded in the South Central and South Atlantic states. This pattern suggested that the common school movement did not have the effect in New England that its advocates claimed. From 1840 to 1850, the South experienced increased diffusion of education. The same was true for the Midwest although in both the South and the Midwest there was little effort to build state systems of education.[17]

Some historians who favored the common school movement complained that Northern imposition retarded the spread of public education in the South. For example, in 1922, Edgar W. Knight argued that Reconstruction interrupted efforts by politicians in the Southern states to create state-supported systems of public schools. Before the war ended, Arkansas, Louisiana, Tennessee, and West Virginia established provisional governments under what Knight called the "presidential plan" for reconstruction. After Lincoln's death, President Johnson asked the remaining states in the former Confederacy to set up provisional governments and establish conventions to draft new constitutions. Knight claimed that as the states began the processes, the legislatures adopted the Black Codes to regulate the behavior of the newly freed slaves. He added that, as the new state governments were considering how to establish public schools, the U.S. Congress imposed the Reconstruction Acts that invalidated those efforts.[18]

In 1935, W. E. Burghardt Du Bois took the opposite view. He asserted that the first mass movement for public education came from Negroes. While admitting that public leaders in the South before the war had urged general education, Du Bois contended these leaders were content to open some schools for paupers. According to Du Bois, in the South, "public education for all at public expense was a Negro idea."[19]

The reasoning that Du Bois followed was that the idea of publicly supported education began during the war when African Americans asked for instruction. Subsequently, philanthropic societies set up schools in such places as Port Royal, South Carolina. He added that Mary Peake, a free Negro from the North, established the first day school for African Americans in Hampton, Virginia, under the auspices of American Missionary Society. In a short period, African Americans built several schools and paid the teachers. In this way, many private schools opened that were supported by former slaves. In addition, the U.S. Army established schools for African Americans in Louisiana and elsewhere. The U.S. government contributed to the effort by establishing the Freedmen's Bureau. Although the bureau was not to establish schools, it gave financial and material support to teachers until 1866 when the legislation allowed cooperation with benevolent societies to develop schools for African Americans.[20]

Du Bois argued that events in Virginia demonstrated the influence of African Americans. He wrote that twenty-five Negroes attended the state's Constitutional Convention in 1867. Together with some of the white delegates, they proposed a uniform system of public schools. The voters approved this legislation in 1869, and Ruffner became superintendent in 1871. Enrollments showed the enthusiasm that black people had for schools. In Virginia in 1871, there were 2,900 schools. Of those, about 700 were for African Americans. At the same time, in Virginia, there were about 130,000 students enrolled in the schools. Of these about 39,000 were African Americans. Thus, Du Bois claimed that, in Virginia, "the Negroes were eager for the schools, but the whites were largely indifferent."[21]

Despite the fact that Southern states provided schools for African Americans, Du Bois contended that the politicians in most Southern states made schools for black children as bad as they could. According to Du Bois, when Northern philanthropies contributed to the establishment of Negro colleges, they saved public schools in the South because those colleges trained African American teachers who worked in the black schools.[22]

Whereas Du Bois praised the Northern philanthropies for the educational progress, more narrowly focused histories claimed that philanthropists from the North caused problems in the South. For example, in 1941, Henry Lee Swint published his book, *Northern Teacher in the South, 1862–1870.* Focusing on the work of missionary teachers from the North, Swint contended that white Southerners considered the white teachers as agents sent to control the votes of newly freed slaves. To show that the teachers favored Northern aims, Swint examined the written statements of the officers of several missionary societies that sent the teachers. These officers held a combination of views: they believed in abolitionism, they belonged to temperance societies, they sought women's suffrage, and several of them were industrialists who considered capitalism as an answer to sectional rivalry. These leaders chose teachers who shared these radical views.[23]

Swint claimed that, in 1869, half of the nearly 10,000 teachers working in freedman schools came from New York and New England. They wrote profoundly religious statements in their journals and letters. At the same time, their former homes lay along routes the slaves had followed when they escaped from bondage. This information plus quotes from their reports led Swint to conclude that the teachers had abolitionist feelings.[24]

Swint acknowledged that leaders of the missionary organizations advised teachers not to use materials that would alienate white Southerners, but he noted many of the books in the freedmen's schools came from the North. These included McGuffey's *Readers,* Webster's *Speller,* geography texts, and arithmetic books. Further, he complained that teachers extended lessons into political areas by having young students sing songs celebrating the end of slavery, and he cited catechisms that Northern teachers used with the children praising the North for bringing freedom and castigating the slaveholders for exploiting the slaves. Finally, Swint claimed that the teachers encouraged students to venerate Lincoln and to revile Confederate leaders, even while the missionary societies forbade them to encourage partisan feelings.[25]

According to Swint, white Southerners reacted strongly. Some whites poured hot tar and cotton on the teachers. Members of the Ku Klux Klan left threatening messages for teachers and drove them from the schools. Swint concluded that the teachers caused the violence from which they suffered by trying to advance the Radical Republican Reconstruction of the South. He contended the problems did not arise from Southern prejudice against the North because Northerners who came to the South with mercantile interests did not meet such resistance. Ironically, Swint added, Southern opposition to Northern teachers may have encouraged Southern support for public education of African Americans because the Southerners wanted to employ native whites to teach in the schools for black children.[26]

In a similar manner in 1955, George Bentley argued that the U.S. Bureau of Refugees, Freedmen, and Abandoned Lands, commonly called the Freedmen's Bureau, increased opposition to civil rights throughout the South. The U.S. Congress created the Freedmen's Bureau in March 1865 to help former slaves and white refugees and decide the fate of lands abandoned in war by former owners. Not surprisingly, Bentley found that the bureau suffered from a confusion of aims. Although Bentley did not focus on the educational work of the bureau, he described the schools the bureau sponsored as teaching the students subjects that the Southerners did not want taught in schools, such as to support the Republican Party and to believe in equal rights. Thus, Bentley concluded that the Freedmen's Bureau used methods that hurt African Americans because they increased racial antagonism. Instead of pushing Negroes to gain education and political power, the bureau should have tried to change the attitudes of Southern white people, Bentley concluded.[27]

In 1976, Robert C. Morris disagreed that missionary teachers had expressed radical aims. Morris examined educators' statements, class lessons, and textbooks to determine whether abolitionists dominated the Northern efforts to provide education to African Americans in the South. Instead of radical abolitionist societies, Morris found that the policy makers and the teachers sought the support of local citizens. Thus, they fashioned moderate policies that should have been acceptable to Southerners. The education emphasized black-self help, practical training, and the gradual improvement of racial conditions. For example, Morris found the officers mainly concerned with practical matters such as collecting and distributing funds and providing teachers with training in classroom techniques. Although many abolitionists belonged to the missionary societies, members tended to be more pragmatic than ideological.[28]

When Morris looked at the available records of the teachers' backgrounds and recruiting materials, he found that they did not conform to any stereotype, although he found the societies did not employ immigrants from foreign lands such as Germany or Ireland.

Morris noted that many of the missionary teachers were free, middle-class black men and women from the North. Although the wisdom of industrial training was controversial among these black teachers, they agreed with the aim of gradual, orderly change in the South. In addition, Morris found that the Freedmen's Bureau subsidized white Southern teachers. Although most of these teachers had prior experience and came from the middle class, there was a surprising range among them. Some white teachers had been wealthy Southern landowners. Some white Southern teachers expressed racial prejudice whereas some of them held idealistic goals for the newly freed slaves.[29]

According to Morris, the missionary societies held modest educational objectives. The teachers conducted lessons designed to prepare the newly freed slaves for productive life in the community. Instead of advanced academic training, the schools offered practical or industrial education. The instruction imitated the teaching found in Northern schools. Teachers reinforced order, morality, and forgiveness. Instead of encouraging radical reconstruction, they designed lessons to maintain stability in the society [30]

Morris noted an irony. When the nation accepted the end of Reconstruction, people repeated the faith in education that the missionary teachers had expressed. At the same time, though, the missionary teachers seemed to have lost it. Public officials such as Rutherford B. Hayes claimed that education would ameliorate the conditions of African Americans; however, Morris found the former missionary teachers expressed doubts that the freedmen could profit from schools. He quoted letters from missionary teachers stating that it was a mistake to have given African Americans the right to vote. The former missionary teachers explained that education did not help. White men could easily dupe black officials. As a result, the black politicians became corrupt as well.[31]

What Did the Experiences of the Missionary Teachers Suggest about Schools and Social Reform?

Several historians found an opportunity to test the value of schools as instruments of social change in the experiences of the missionary teachers and of the Freedmen's Bureau that partially supported them. In 1980, Ronald E. Butchart decided that the missionary societies and the African Americans had been victims of class conflict. In making this observation, Butchart suggested that education had served as a substitute for the sources of power such as land the newly freed slaves needed if they were to attain what he called full personhood.[32]

In describing the work of the Freedmen's Bureau, Butchart described it as a conservative organization that sought to lower the aspirations of the black people. Instead of giving captured plantations to former slaves, agents gave lectures on the necessity of former slaves learning obedience and respect for property. At the same time, the bureau increased its concern for education. Although expenditures for schools increased from $500,000 in 1866 to more than $5 million in 1871, Butchart argued these actions, showed that the bureau's "leadership lacked commitment to black power and pride."[33]

Butchart's accusation brought criticism. Writing a review of historical works about Reconstruction, Eric Foner cited Butchart's use of the phrase "black power." According to Foner, this concept from the Civil Rights Movement of the 1960s illustrated an unfair standard for historians to apply to the Reconstruction Era of the 1870s.[34]

Whether Foner was correct or not, Butchart was convinced that the missionaries had missed an opportunity to work for significant social change. Butchart complained that the missionaries set up schools for the former slaves instead of working for liberation. According to Butchart, the teachers knew that when the serfs left bondage, Russia had given them land confiscated from the nobility. Although Butchart quoted the missionaries as saying that unless the freedmen had land, they were powerless against the white society, he argued that the missionaries held to the ideology that education would solve the problems. It was an ideological point of view because the more education seemed ineffective, the more the missionaries tried to increase or improve their schools. According to Butchart, the missionaries would have done more good if they had tried to alter the social relations of production.[35]

In a similar manner, James D. Anderson claimed that white Southerners diverted the enthusiasm for education of the ex-slaves and created schools that served the needs and interests of the dominant class whites. According to Anderson, the freedmen's school movement was not the product of the missionary societies or the Freedmen's Bureau. It derived from the ex-slaves willingness to form educational associations and support private schools. He claimed that, in Louisiana, enrollment in these schools supported by voluntary associations of African Americans exceeded the enrollment in schools supported by the Freedmen's Bureau.[36]

Anderson argued that the missionary teachers participated in the diversion of black aspirations because they used texts that portrayed black people as inferior to white people and contended that the proper role of African Americans was to be subservient to white people. Such texts included *The Freedmen's Primer* and *The Lincoln Primer.* He added that white educators continued to use schools to teach African Americans to serve white peoples' interest after the American Civil War. In 1868, Samuel Chapman Armstrong founded Hampton Normal and Agricultural Institute in Virginia. Although most commentators considered the mission of the institute to be agricultural and mechanical training, Anderson claimed it was primarily a teacher training institution. After the students had imbibed the work ethic that Armstrong felt was desirable, they could leave the institute and teach other black students to work hard at their trades. As a result, about 84 percent of the 723 graduates of the first twenty classes became teachers. In 1900, this imbalance was still true, Anderson added. Only forty-five students were enrolled in the trade school division of Hampton out of a total enrollment of 656 students, and only four were in agriculture. Nonetheless, all these students worked at a trade or on the farm.[37]

Although Butchart and Anderson criticized the Freedmen's Bureau, other historians contended that the agents did not easily give up the idea of distributing captured lands to former slaves nor did they overwhelmingly support education in place of land ownership. For example, writing in 1997, Paul A. Cimbala contended that external tensions prevented the bureau from succeeding. This was particularly clear in Georgia where the freedmen should have been able to hold land captured by the Union forces.[38]

On the question of land, in January 1865, U.S. General William T. Sherman issued a field order setting aside land on the coast extending from Charleston to Florida for the freed slaves. Each black family could receive forty acres. Rufus Saxton carried out this order. Although the records disagree about the number of slaves involved, thousands of former slaves settled on thousands of acres. They organized militias to defend themselves and set up governments to run their societies. In September 1865, U.S. President Johnson nullified the bureau's capacity to distribute land to freed slaves, and in October 1865, the Commissioner of the Freedmen's Bureau, Oliver Otis Howard, ordered the land restored to the white owners after the former slaves harvested the crops they had planted. Although the agents in Georgia ultimately complied with this order, they tried to protect the crops of the freedmen. More important, in some cases, the agents enabled groups of freedmen to establish colonies of their own elsewhere in Georgia.[39]

Interestingly, in 1866, the bureau had another opportunity to distribute land to former slaves. President Johnson signed the Southern Homestead Act opening 46 million acres of public lands in Alabama, Florida, Louisiana, and Mississippi to settlement. Although agents of the Freedmen's Bureau tried to help former slaves settle on these lands, they faced several obstacles. For example, some white people sought to keep black people out. The land offices were understaffed and could not process the claims. Sometimes, the land officers were incompetent or unscrupulous and caused African Americans to settle on the wrong lands or to lose their holdings. Finally, a sizeable portion of the available land was unsuitable for settlement. Despite these problems, an estimated 6000 black families took legal possession of some land. Once on their homesteads, these families did as well as white families.[40]

Not only did the bureau have limited success in providing land for the freedmen, the agents did not provide free education either. According to Cimbala, the bureau's agents turned their attention to protecting the legal rights of freedmen more than they supported education. Unfortunately, the resources of the bureau did not reach far enough to protect black farmers against hostile white Georgia residents or to provide schools for former slaves. In the case of education, the bureau officials tried to facilitate education by meeting with former slaves, encouraging them to form educational associations and donate money for schools. If the associations formed schools, students would not need to pay tuitions. Free tuition made it easier for students to attend, and the agents thought that the African Americans would appreciate the work of the teachers if they paid for the schools through associations. Looking at records in Georgia, Cimbala found that black people accepted these obligations. Black churches and black teachers worked to set up their own schools. Although the agents of the Freedmen's Bureau considered the black teachers poorly trained, they acquiesced and in 1869 helped support the creation of a normal school in Atlanta sponsored by the American Missionary Association (AMA) to prepare African American teachers.[41]

Although the missionary schools may not have brought about social change for African Americans, Jacqueline Jones found that the experience of being a missionary teacher enabled the women who volunteered to use their talents in a spiritual realm and thereby counter ideas of the proper roles of women. Nonetheless, Jones did not begin by considering only women's contributions. Her study focused on the men and women who went to Georgia as teachers for the American Missionary Association. By 1865, the AMA had built a close association with the Freedmen's Bureau that enabled it to dominate education in Georgia.[42]

Jones found that the missionary teachers did not fit into any simple category except that they were hardworking and dedicated to their students. When these teachers went to the South to bring about wide social change, they were uncertain how long the process would take. Jones found that as they stayed in the South, they found the goal receding away from them. As a result, they focused on individual students who performed well in their schools and advanced to a normal school or university. In the mid-1870s, the AMA gave up its interests in common schools and focused its efforts on Atlanta University and other colleges for African Americans.[43]

Although the AMA withdrew from common schools in Georgia, Jones argued that the missionary teachers did not abandon their missions. She explained that the transition began in 1870 when the Georgia general assembly approved legislation creating the office of state superintendent of schools, establishing school districts in each county and specifying separate facilities for black and white students. Because the legislation did not enable the collection of taxes, public schools did not appear until members of the Democratic Party dominated the legislature and appointed a white conservative to the office of superintendent. As tuition-free public schools appeared in Georgia, the African Americans who had paid to attend missionary schools withdrew and enrolled in the state-supported schools. According to Jones, the missionary teachers responded with dismay, personal hurt, and sometimes anger. Despite feeling abandoned, many missionaries transferred to teach in the new public schools, consenting to the indignities of public examinations to prove their qualifications. Jones noted that eleven of the AMA missionary teachers remained as teachers twenty years after the end of the war in spite of the fact that life in the South had not been pleasant for them.[44]

Thus, historians seemed to agree that neither the Freedmen's Bureau nor the missionary schools enacted the wide social changes their advocates had imagined. It was not clear whether those failures resulted from implicit weaknesses in schools, conflicts among social classes, or the usurpation of the school by one group to dominate another. Some historians complained that the efforts to use education to bring about social change retarded the movement to create public education in the South.

How Did Public Education Spread through the South?

Historians disagreed about why state governments in the South did not support the spread of public schools during or immediately after Reconstruction. According to Knight, Reconstruction drained available resources from state governments. Knight contended that during Reconstruction there was extensive fraud and waste of funds that should have supported public education. For example, although Virginia adopted legislation to create public schools, there were three reasons why schools did not develop. First, financial support was unavailable and parents had to pay a subscription fee to send their children. Second, there were inadequate numbers of trained teachers. Donations from the North supported the two normal schools in the state, Hampton and Richmond, but they trained black teachers. There were no similar facilities for white teachers, he added. Finally, complicated state tax laws prevented schools from receiving appropriate aid. Although conditions in other states differed, all of the Southern states suffered from loss of property and the demise of what Knight called the distinctive Southern civilization during Reconstruction. He concluded that these conditions prevented the spread of schools until the beginning of the twentieth century despite the efforts of many friends of education.[45]

Another historian, Charles William Dabney, claimed that the advocates of public education in the South faced difficulties that were similar to those in the North. For example, Dabney argued that William H. Ruffner and John B. Minor laid the foundations for the development of a state system of public schools in 1870 by encouraging the Virginia legislature to adopt an act to create a system of free schools. Other Southern states adopted similar laws soon after Virginia did. Most important, on taking office as the first school superintendent in 1871, Ruffner toured the North. Finding graded schools, normal schools, and teacher institutes, Ruffner imported these ideas to Virginia and convinced the legislature to adopt a system with twelve county superintendents who collected taxes to support the creation of schools. This was similar to the manner that New England district schools had spread. Unfortunately, when the Virginia legislature allowed the county commissioners to levy specific taxes, they met such opposition that they had to repeal the levies. To change public opinion, Ruffner wrote circulars, made public addresses, and wrote annual reports. For example, in one report, Ruffner complained about twisted values because each Virginian spent $16 per year on alcohol but they allocated only eighty-five cents for each child's education in a year. He called on Virginians to engage in a moral revival and awaken themselves to such imbalances.[46]

Although Ruffner followed the example of Horace Mann by suggesting that common schools would preserve the social order, Ruffner turned Mann's arguments to fit the conditions in Virginia. For example, Ruffner believed that Virginians would never support racially mixed schools. Nevertheless, in his position as superintendent, he wanted the schools to be open to African Americans as well as white children. When his critics complained that education for blacks would elevate them from the laboring class and force whites to descend to it, Ruffner replied education would prepare African Americans for the civic and social roles they would have to play in the new economic and social order. When critics argued that racial integration of schools would lead to social amalgamation, Ruffner responded that education would instill in African Americans a pride in race that would prevent the social forms of racial mixing.[47]

Dabney explained that the success during Ruffner's leadership changed when he left office. According to Dabney, when Ruffner was superintendent of the schools of Virginia, he administered about $12 million. Although this money was unsecured and unregulated, no one accused Ruffner of wasting or losing any money. In 1887, Ruffner retired. Dabney noted with dismay that subsequent political administrations were less scrupulous.[48]

Dabney may have overestimated Ruffner's administration. According to C. Vann Woodward, historians writing before 1960 heaped praise on the so-called "Redeemers." For example, Woodward noted that the conservative Democrats were often called Redeemers after replacing the Reconstruction Republicans; however, they rarely kept close accounts or incorporated safeguards against corruption. Although they enjoyed high regard, many of these officials did not deserve such estimation. Woodward reported that in Virginia, in 1873, when Ruffner was in office, the state treasurer escaped trial for embezzlement by pleading insanity. In 1877, in Virginia, there was more embezzlement of school bonds, and people turned against state support of public schools.[49]

Although Southern states did not make substantial gains in sponsoring public education until the 1880s and 1890s, historians such as David Tyack and Robert Lowe contend that Du Bois was correct in noting that the constitutional conventions and legislatures held during Reconstruction laid the foundations for public schools. According to Tyack and Lowe, once the idea of state-supported schools was in place, the enrollment of black students in public schools increased from about 91,000 in 1866 to about 150,000 in 1870, reaching about 572,000 in 1877.[50]

The case of Alabama illustrated the difficulties common school advocates faced in trying to create state-supported free schools. The constitution of 1819 in Alabama and various legislative acts directed the townships to use the funds derived from land grants for education. Until 1854, when the legislature approved the appointment of Jabez Lamar Monroe Curry as state superintendent, there was no state supervision or any public taxation to support public schools. In 1868, a new constitution the state adopted created a state board of education and placed common schools under the direction of this body. Nonetheless, this revision had little practical effect until 1875 because the state board lacked the power to raise taxes or make appropriations supporting the schools.[51]

Economic problems retarded the development of state-supported schools in Alabama. From 1860 until 1900, Alabama suffered from decreased agricultural production, declines in the value of farm property, and reduced values of personal and real estate. Nonetheless, from 1860 to 1870, assessed valuation for taxes rose from $0.20 per $100 to $1.92. Although the state collected more money, fraud and the development of railroads added to public debts. Not surprisingly, illiteracy rates rose. In 1860, about 17 percent of the adults were illiterate. By 1870, almost 22 percent of the adults in Alabama could not read or write.[52]

Because most Southern states faced economic difficulties, the Peabody Fund began to support public schools in Southern cities. The agent of the fund refused to donate monies for private, sectarian, or charity schools because he wanted to bring about an increase in public schools. Further, in order for schools to qualify for this money, teachers had to hold classes for ten months, and the schools needed to be organized in grades.[53]

The fund began in 1867 when George Peabody of Massachusetts donated $1 million for the improvement of education in the South. The fund's trustees named Barnas Sears, then president of Brown University, to act as the general agent. Sears had previously worked on the Massachusetts Board of Education, succeeding Horace Mann as secretary. According to Earle H. West, when Sears was secretary of the board, he had found that many segments of the population of Massachusetts were dissatisfied with the common school legislation and sought to undo it. For example, some religious denominations complained that state schools were irreligious. Thus, he determined that educational progress could not alienate any group.[54]

Sears's aim was to use the money from the Peabody Fund to develop state systems of education throughout the South. Selecting cities that would influence other areas, Sears offered money for elementary schools providing that the community raised three or four times the amount given and that the schools were under some form of public control. In the first year, only thirteen towns in five states accepted Peabody money. Occasionally, Sears required that black and white children have schools; however, few African American communities could afford to set up schools. Because Sears wanted the schools to be nonsectarian, he refused to help missionary schools. Thus, the Peabody Fund directed its efforts to white education in the South. In efforts to ameliorate this bias, Sears devoted $1,000 for African American schools in each Southern state.[55]

In public statements, Sears took the view that the Peabody Fund would not meddle in politics and would not take a stand on whether schools were racially segregated or integrated. Thus, if the state supported mixed schools, the Peabody Fund would support them. Nonetheless, he added that if white students left the public schools, the fund would support the white schools and not the public schools attended by the remaining black students. Consequently, the fund contributed money to larger towns in Louisiana without giving any support to the racially integrated schools in New Orleans.[56]

Despite Sears belief that the racial integration of schools would fail, the desegregation of New Orleans schools could have been successful. Although the state constitution adopted in 1867 required racially mixed schools, critics brought legal suits to delay the process until 1870 when school authorities allowed black students to enter schools they wished to attend. At the height of desegregation, a thousand black students may have mixed with several thousand white students in about twenty-one schools. The desegregated schools accounted for about one-third of the city's schools. Because these were the most prestigious schools, integration did not cause white students to withdraw because they would have moved to schools with inferior instruction. The mixed schools were peaceful until 1874, when riots spread. The local White League incited rowdy white adolescents who did not attend the schools to attack the black students. More sober citizens prevailed upon the White League and peace returned. In 1877, the city board segregated the schools.[57]

Despite evidence that desegregation might work, Sears continued his campaign. He broke his promise not to meddle in politics and sought to convince national politicians of what he considered the dangers posed by racially mixed schools. In 1874, members of the U.S. Congress debated requiring racial mixing in schools within the pending U.S. Civil Rights Bill. Sears took the opportunity of his annual report to the trustees of the Peabody Fund to explain how he prevented the passage of such a requirement. He claimed that he foresaw the destruction of public education in the South if white children had to attend schools with black students. The white children would either not go to school or they would attend private schools. To prevent what he considered a calamity, Sears appeared before congressional committees and spoke to leading members of the U.S. Congress urging them not to force states to create mixed schools and require all students to attend them. He warned that such an amendment to the bill would cause the states to disband all public schools and to open private ones. This would leave black children without any educational opportunities. Sears went so far as to speak to the president, urging him to oppose such legislation. When the civil rights bill passed, it did not have a clause demanding that schools include students of both races.[58]

In addition to setting up public school systems, the Peabody Fund encouraged teacher training. In the last annual report that Sears wrote before he died in 1880, he told the board that he had promised to help the legislatures of the states establish normal schools. In 1878, Texas had opened a normal school in Huntsville in response to a Sears promise. Because this was for white teachers, Texas opened a normal school for black teachers in Prairie View as well. By 1880, Virginia had three normal schools, and North Carolina opened a normal and industrial school in 1891.[59]

In general, the aid that Sears and the Peabody Fund extended to African American normal schools was in the form of tuition payments to individual candidates for teacher training. Most African American schools, such as Hampton, Fisk, and Atlanta University, added teacher-training departments. Because Sears wanted to support regular normal schools, these universities did not receive the substantial help given to such schools as Nashville Normal that did not accept African American candidates. This was unfortunate, according to Earle H. West, because there was no effort to establish such high-level, regional normal schools for Negroes.[60]

Although Nashville Normal would not accept African Americans, the Peabody fund created it in 1875 to serve the entire South. On visiting the city, Sears proposed to the state governor a plan to develop a normal school. When the legislature refused to appropriate funds, the University of Nashville agreed to suspend its literary department and devote those facilities to a normal school if they could obtain Peabody funds. The school opened in 1875 with thirteen women as students and one classroom. Sears selected Eben Sperry Stearns to lead Nashville Normal because Stearns had been the head of a state normal school in Massachusetts when Sears was secretary to the board of education. In 1887, William H. Perry replaced Stearns and renamed the normal school as the Peabody College for all the Southern States.[61]

Because Nashville Normal could not provide enough white teachers to staff the many rural schools in the South, the Peabody Fund and the state of Tennessee cooperatively sponsored summer institutes for teachers from 1880 to 1898. Held at the University of Tennessee in Knoxville, the teacher institutes attracted about 200 white teachers of rural Tennessee schools each summer. The institutes offered lectures, poetry readings, and excursions to sights around the state. During the sessions, the teachers learned about such curriculums as the object method from Oswego, New York. They learned about new textbooks and methods of school discipline. Examinations were optional, but the teachers who took them received certificates indicating their readiness to teach. At the same time, African American teachers attended similar institutes. The programs for black teachers took place in Knoxville in a public school building that served African American students during the school year.[62]

To offset the limited assistance the Peabody Fund gave for training black teachers, John F. Slater established a fund in 1882 dedicated exclusively to training African American teachers. During the first year of the Slater Fund's operation, the trustees gave $16,500 to twelve institutions. Unlike the Peabody Fund, the Slater trustees directed their philanthropy to private and denominational schools training Negro teachers, although they used the same agent. J. L. M. Curry had succeeded Sears as agent of the Peabody Fund in 1880, just as he succeeded Atticus G. Haygood of the Slater Fund.[63]

Why Did the Idea of the New South Require Racially Segregated Schools?

At the end of the nineteenth century, Southern states adopted Jim Crow laws requiring racial segregation. In many states, these laws did not come onto the books until the twentieth century. Although they represented an unfortunate aspect of New South ideology, the segregation of the New South reduced the racial violence that had taken place earlier. For example, in 1877, the federal government arrested and charged hundreds of Ku Klux Klansmen in South Carolina for thwarting Reconstruction through murder and assault.

Segregation became the norm even though many prominent white citizens in the South considered laws requiring racial segregation affronts to well-behaved, well-educated African Americans. Somehow, as the South took on the elements of a modern industrial society, the alternatives for racial integration disappeared.[64]

The rise of education accompanied the increase of segregation. According to James Anderson, the South committed itself to systems of universal schooling because the former slaves campaigned to spread education. Anderson claimed that poor whites sought to attend schools when they realized that African Americans had gained the ability to read and write. In fact, white supremacy demanded some form of universal schooling or the black children would become superior. This attitude spread to the planter class, Anderson contended, and they became more amenable to demands for publicly supported schools than they had been.[65]

Whereas Anderson attributed the growth of public schools in the South to the jealousy of white toward blacks, another historian, Howard N. Rabinowitz, reversed the formula to explain the dominance of racially segregated education. According to Rabinowitz, the South had accepted public education by 1890. At the same time, Southerners wanted the schools to be segregated and African American teachers to teach black students. Rabinowitz added that, in the South, African Americans had accepted the necessity of segregation and advocated black schools for black students.[66]

In the schools in four Southern cities, Rabinowitz traced a progression of types of teachers who taught African American students. The first was the Northern white missionary. White Southerners replaced these teachers, and finally black graduates of local colleges and normal schools took the jobs. This progression did not result from the end of Reconstruction. The white conservative politicians who replaced the Republicans promised to send white teachers to black schools. The black communities sent petitions requesting the boards to hire black teachers and administrators for the black schools. Their hope was that these African American adults would be better able to prepare black children for adult roles and their presence would enhance black pride. At the same time, there was a fear that only incompetent white teachers would accept assignments to teach in black schools. By the time the school boards agreed, most of the white teachers were old enough to retire, and the boards could pay lower salaries to the black replacements. Thus, the decision was easier to make.[67]

The situation may have been more complicated than Anderson and Rabinowitz described. For example, when John William Graves studied the growth of segregation in Arkansas, he found that blacks and whites in cities resisted segregation more frequently than did rural whites. At least, this was the case until the 1890s when race relations hardened. For example, black and white voters rejected city ordinances requiring segregation in city parks, streetcars, and theaters until a state law forbade racial mixing. In the case of schools, racial segregation appeared in the school laws passed by the Reconstruction legislature. Although African Americans accepted this requirement, they refused to allow public carriers, hotels, or restaurants to deny services to black patrons. The Arkansas legislature in 1873 approved a civil rights act forbidding such denials. Although the laws remained in force until 1907, they were rarely enforced.[68]

Advocates of the New South proclaimed that the spread of state-supported education would mark the entry of the New South into the world of capital and industry. As part of this social change, educators embraced the graded school plan. Although Calvin Wiley and later the Peabody Fund had introduced the graded school plan, it spread through states such as North Carolina in the 1880s. According to James L. Leloudis, more than two dozen communities approved special taxes to support graded schools for black and white students. In Goldsboro, trustees of a black graded school established a private normal school. In a neighboring community, white officials did the same. Leloudis claimed that the popularity of the graded school plan derived from two sources. First, the instruction followed a scientific method. Second, the teachers rewarded the students for their accomplishments using uniform measures of evaluation. In these ways, the graded school plan was supposed to prepare children for life in an industrial world.[69]

Although teachers maintained accurate records of attendance and performance on tests, the function of the graded school was not to instill conformity as much as it was to help children solve problems on their own and to encourage them to distinguish themselves. Thus, instead of memorizing arithmetic facts, the students had to understand the relationships among such processes as addition and multiplication. In reading, the students learned to sound words out for themselves rather than depend on hearing another person read the new words to them. According to Leloudis, the teachers thought these methods encouraged the independence of mind and diligence needed in the world of work. Most important, he added, the teachers wanted to introduce their children to the various opportunities that waited for them beyond the limits of farm and town.[70]

At the same time, commencement speakers for normal schools predicted a coming social revival. For example, in 1897, Walter Page Hines, who became editor of the *Atlantic Monthly* the following year, addressed the State Normal and Industrial School for Women at Greensboro, North Carolina. Hines told his listeners that a revolution was in progress and their institution was one of its first and best fruits. He declared that the moral earnestness of the well-trained women seated before him would disperse the social illusions and worn out traditions that held back the South.[71]

Hines explained that the revolution in North Carolina was the rejuvenated movement for public education. At the time, he noted that North Carolina spent less on education per child than any other state except South Carolina. He added that the state spent $3.40 per child per year while Minnesota spent $30 per child per year. Contending that North Carolina had the wealth found in other states, Hines claimed the people in other states were willing to pay local taxes to support their local schools while people in North Carolina resisted such impositions. Nonetheless, Hines was heartened to hear politicians in North Carolina call out for the support of free preparatory schools, free high schools, free industrial schools, and free colleges. He predicted that such institutions would transform what he called forgotten men and women into a cultivated population.[72]

Hines gave his speech in Greensboro as part of a campaign for a referendum to centralize control of education. This legislation would give county commissioners authority to appoint boards of education who would then appoint county superintendents. Within the counties, the small school districts would merge into townships and the school board would appoint committees of five men to control those township schools. Thus, larger graded facilities could replace small district schoolhouses. In addition, the townships had to raise $1,500 through local taxes to pay for these school improvements. According to Leloudis, opposition to these changes came from parents who wanted to control their own local schools rather than depend on central administrators to act in their interests. Although newspapers across the state reprinted Hines' speech, the bill to reorganize schools suffered a resounding defeat as voters either avoided the polls or cast votes opposed to central control of schools.[73]

The voters in North Carolina did not act alone. In 1883, the U.S. Congress resisted federal support of education, claiming it represented excessive central control of schools. In 1883, Senator Henry W. Blair of New Hampshire proposed a bill to provide federal support to the states for education. Blair's plan was to distribute the federal funds according to the proportion of illiterate people in each state. Thus, the Southern states would have received more than Northern states. Although Blair's bill did not call for federal control of education, the U.S. Congress rejected it three times. According to Charles William Dabney, the opposition did not follow party or sectional lines. The congressional representatives expressed fears that the use of federal money would inevitably lead to central control of local schools.[74]

When Hines pointed out that North Carolina spent less per pupil per year than other states, he did not add that North Carolina spent the money unequally. That is, in 1899–1900, African American students received about 28 percent of the school funds although they made up about 35 percent of the school population. At the same time, the salary for black teachers was about $65 per year in North Carolina whereas white teachers received about $100 per year.[75]

The disparities in educational opportunities contradicted the optimistic expressions of the advocates for the New South. As noted in the beginning of this chapter, Henry Grady popularized the term "New South" in a speech he gave at a banquet held by the New England Society of New York in 1886. Because Grady was sitting beside U.S. General William Tecumseh Sherman, he took advantage of the opportunity to joke that Sherman had been careless with fire in Atlanta. Despite his barbed comment, Grady described how Southerners had forgotten their complaints and built a beautiful city from the ashes. He claimed that the South had planted schoolhouses and made them free for white and black students. Although Grady did not go beyond this point in New York, he added in later speeches that native white Southerners had taken charge since Reconstruction so that Negroes prospered and peace reigned.[76]

In 1895, Southern business leaders had the opportunity in the Cotton States and International Exposition in Atlanta to show Northern investors that the former slaves lived and worked as free citizens in the Old Confederacy. Although this exposition was a local affair held in a depression year, people from all over the country visited. Attendees included foreign representatives.

The part of the exposition that became most famous was a speech by Booker T. Washington to explain his educational ideas. Standing before an audience divided by race, Washington noted how African Americans were essential to the economic progress of the South. Noting how black slaves had been faithful to white slaveholders, he promised that this faithfulness would continue if white Southerners would give African Americans opportunities in education and in industry. In return for cooperation in economic affairs, Washington promised that, in social affairs, black people and white people could be separate.[77]

According to Louis Harlan, the speech that Washington gave in Atlanta offered nothing new. Washington had shared the same ideas with Henry Grady, who had approved of racial separation. Further, Washington had practiced the phrases and the metaphors in other addresses. In 1881, Washington had established an industrial training school in Tuskegee, Georgia, where students practiced such activities as agriculture, domestic service, and building trades. In order to gain support for this school, he had traveled extensively and spoken to many audiences.[78]

Although Tuskegee Institute was not a college, Washington's ideas became popular among the philanthropic organizations devoted to advancing colleges for African Americans. As a result, his speech encouraged the philanthropies to emphasize the focus they had been developing. For example, in 1882, Atticus G. Haygood became the first agent of the Slater Fund. Because he would not give money to any college that lacked an industrial training component, many colleges added such facilities. During Haygood's final year, the Slater Fund divided about $200,000 among twenty-one Negro colleges such as Atlanta, Fisk, and Howard. The second agent, J. L. M. Curry, was highly impressed with Tuskegee Institute, directed by Washington, and Hampton Institute, which had been Washington's model. As a result, from 1900 to 1903, Curry influenced the board of trustees of the Slater Fund to direct over half of the total appropriations of about $270,000 to these two schools that were exclusively industrial training schools. The Slater Fund divided the remainder among seven other institutions of higher learning.[79]

This change in philanthropic support appeared dangerous to W. E. B. Du Bois. In 1903, Du Bois agreed that a broad system of common schools supplemented by industrial training schools would help African Americans to profit from the industrial development of the South. Nonetheless, Du Bois argued that the industrial training schools or the common schools could not exist without Negro colleges that produced teachers and people of culture to staff those training institutes and common schools. Although most people thought that educational reform should begin with common schools, Du Bois believed that reform had to begin at the top. Instead of supporting common schools or industrial training schools, philanthropies should support colleges. If the colleges flourished, educated African Americans from the colleges would establish and spread common schools. Because white people would not teach black children, colleges had to train black people to become teachers.[80]

According to William Watkins, the influence that Washington and his teacher, Samuel Armstrong, had on African Americans in the South was to encourage the spread of an ideology of gradualism. This conservative view was rooted in religious faith and in a belief in the value of hard work. Although this view supported the objectives of white industrialists, it created a middle class of African Americans who served as a buffer between a people battered by sharecropping and violence and their oppressors.[81]

To some extent, when African Americans such as Washington expressed a willingness to accommodate the demands of white politicians, they protected themselves against violence. For example, in 1936, E. Franklin Frazier charted the numbers of Negroes lynched from 1882, the first year authorities gathered such statistics, to 1936. According to Frazier, the number of incidents of lynching increased from 49 in 1882 to 160 in 1892. Although most incidents of lynching involved black men accused of murdering someone, Frazier noted that at least 10 percent of the incidents of lynching resulted from such minor offenses as insulting a white person. When Washington made his speech in 1895, the number of such incidents declined rapidly. Frazier claimed that African Americans accepted their subordinate status, at least outwardly, and violence declined.[82]

The violence may have declined, but it did not disappear. In 1906, white mobs attacked a large community of respectable middle-class African Americans in Atlanta. To Frazier, the subsequent actions of conservative white leaders illustrated the impossible position of the black middle class. Although these politicians had made the African Americans defenseless by stripping away their power to vote, the remedy of these white leaders was to establish a fund to replace some of the property destroyed by the white mobs.[83]

According to Louis Harlan, African Americans could not seek help from reform-minded intellectuals in the North. Progressive reformers were unable to confront the racism of the New South because the climate of social Darwinism that flourished amid progressive reform suggested that groups should engage in a struggle to survive. Applied to racial groups, this metaphor justified the domination of white people over other racial groups. The result was that the nation accepted segregation, Harlan concluded, and African Americans had little choice but to bow to segregation, discrimination, and the threat of violence.[84]

The problem was that, as educational reform movements extended across the South, the segregation of schools encouraged racial discrimination. Between 1890 and 1915 in the South, the number of public schools increased. The length of the school terms increased. Most important, the number of children enrolled in the schools increased. According to Robert L. Church and Michael W. Sedlak, this expansion of public schools came at the expense of African Americans. The discrimination happened in the following way. Legislatures in Southern states permitted local school boards to collect taxes from all the people residing in the districts. Each board was to distribute the funds in ways that advanced the general educational welfare of the entire district. The aim of this policy was to avoid dividing the expenditures according to the amount that each group had contributed because it was impossible to identify the amounts each group had contributed. The effect was to enable politicians to deprive African Americans of their education. For example, when Democrats pledged to white supremacy controlled the state governments, they controlled the appointments to the school boards in the districts. Thus, even if the district was solidly Republican, the school trustees could collect taxes from black and white citizens and spend the money on white schools. The result was inequities in high school enrollments. In Virginia in 1915, African Americans made up about 35 percent of the school age population; however, African Americans represented about 7 percent of the high school enrollments in the state.[85]

Although white supremacists may have felt that they profited from African Americans, everyone suffered from the racial inequities. When Roger L. Ransom and Richard Sutch considered the economic results of racial discrimination in the South in the 1880s and 1890s, they noted African Americans lacked assets, education, and skills with which to improve their lives. Worse, white people created a system that seemed designed to cripple the region. Because most black farmers worked as tenants, they had no incentive to invest in the long-term improvement of the land. At the same time, the landowners were taking their share first and had no reason to improve the conditions that could make farmers more efficient. The merchants enjoyed monopolies and exploited white and black farmers. The result was that they took away capital instead of investing it in increased production. Thus, although advocates of the New South promised that increased industrial investments would improve conditions in the South, the South remained rural, agricultural, and impoverished. This should not have happened because the average per capita gross national product rose rapidly after the American Civil War. When Ransom and Sutch sought to discover what kept labor in the South and capital in the North, they decided that it was racial barriers that prevented what would have been a reasonable and profitable exchange. Black farmers could not afford to move, and the exploitive nature of the conditions threatened any investments by Northern capitalists.[86]

It may appear fitting that the entire South suffered when Southerners adopted racial discrimination as a way of life. Although such a moral may have been partly true, it did not reveal the entire picture. The South remained an agricultural region in the early parts of the twentieth century, but it made extensive strides in manufacturing and commerce. As C. Vann Woodward noted, by 1904, the South produced about 11 percent of the manufactured goods in the United States, which was roughly the same proportion the area had produced in 1860. Woodward contended that the fact the South retained the same proportion of manufacturing over fifty years did not mean the region stood still. The rest of the United States had spread across the continent and industrial development in other areas had been extensive. Thus, for a fixed region to hold its own was an impressive achievement. Further, by 1912, Southern politicians helped elect Woodrow Wilson as U.S. president and took a significant number of important positions in the federal government. Thus, it appeared the South was returning to a dominant position in American life similar to its status before the American Civil War.[87]

Conclusion

With the end of the American Civil War, the South had the opportunity to reconstruct its society. Instead of following a progressive path, Southern legislatures adopted laws designed to restrain the former slaves. In response, the U.S. Congress adopted several measures to protect the civil rights of African Americans. At the same time, the Congress established the Freedmen's Bureau to encourage humane development in the South, and missionary teachers moved to the former Confederacy to bring education to the former slaves. Within a dozen years, Reconstruction ended and white politicians ushered in a return to conservative politics. At the end of the nineteenth century, advocates of industrial and economic growth claimed they lived in a New South marked by increased investments in railroads, merchandising, and manufacturing. Unfortunately, the New South legalized segregation. Although the advocates of the New South disparaged discrimination, they could not prevent it. Even the educational reform movements that took place at the end of the nineteenth century reinforced the discrimination implicit in policies of racial segregation.

To many historians, these events offered measures of how much schools could encourage social reform. When the South surrendered slavery, educators hoped that they could usher in a new era of freedom and civil rights for all people. They could not and the South resisted the spread of public schools. Nonetheless, the Freedmen's Bureau, the missionary schools, the growth of public schools, and the industrial training schools of Armstrong and Washington did not cause the failure. These institutions faced handicaps of inadequate resources and conflicting policies, and the problems the institutions sought to rectify may have been outside the influence of the people who worked in them. It remains an unanswered question whether adequately staffed, given sufficient authority, and able to call on reasonable amounts of resources, those agencies could have reduced racial prejudices.

By some measures, it appeared that Southern people retained their prejudices and suffered economic penalties as a result.

Despite the problems that occurred during the rise of the New South, state-supported schools spread in the South as African Americans and white children attended schools. Although segregation and inequality marked those educational experiences, the drift was toward building systems in the South that were similar to the systems available in the North. In this way, the lives of people in different areas of the United States became more similar. Central administrations acquired authority and urban industrial centers replaced agriculture as the dominant way of life. These changes served the development of the impersonal ways of working, living, and learning later associated with globalization.

Endnotes

1. Paul M. Gaston, *New South Creed: A Study in Myth-making* (New York: Alfred A. Knopf, 1970), 17–18.
2. Eric Foner, "Reconstruction Revisited," *Reviews in American History* 10, no. 4 (December 1982): 82–100.
3. Ibid.
4. William Archibald Dunning, *Essays on the Civil War and Reconstruction, and Related Topics* (1897; reprint, Hallandale, Fla.: New World Book Co., 1971), 174–175, 250–252.
5. James Ford Rhodes, *History of the United States from the Compromise of 1850 to the McKinley–Bryan Campaign of 1896* (1906; reprint, London: Macmillan & Co., 1920), 6:41–43.
6. Rhodes, *History of the United States,* 7:232–233.
7. John R. Lynch, "Some Historical Errors of James Ford Rhodes," *The Journal of Negro History* 2, no. 4 (October 1917): 345–368.
8. Lynch, "Some Historical Errors," 353–354.
9. Lynch, "Some Historical Errors," 363–364.
10. W. E. Burghardt Du Bois, "Reconstruction and Its Benefits," *The American Historical Review* 15, no. 4 (July 1910): 781–799.
11. Du Bois, "Reconstruction and Its Benefits," 796–799.
12. Claude G. Bowers, *The Tragic Era* (Cambridge, Mass.: Riverside Press, 1929), v–vii.
13. Howard K. Beale, "On Rewriting Reconstruction History," *The American Historical Review* 45, no. 4 (July 1940): 807–827.
14. John Hope Franklin, *Reconstruction: After the Civil War* (Chicago: University of Chicago Press, 1960), 104–113.
15. Franklin, *Reconstruction,* 218–219.
16. Willie Lee Rose, *Rehearsal for Reconstruction: The Port Royal Experiment* (1964; reprint, New York: Oxford University Press, 1976), 176–178.
17. Albert Fishlow, "The American Common School Revival: Fact or Fancy?" *Industrialization in Two Systems: Essays in Honor of Alexander Gerschenkron,* ed. Henry Rosovsky (New York: John Wiley & Sons, Inc., 1966), 40–67.
18. Edgar W. Knight, *Public Education in the South* (Boston: Ginn and Co., 1922), 306–333.
19. W. E. Burghardt Du Bois, *Black Reconstruction: An Essay toward a History of the Part which Black Folk Played in the Attempt to Reconstruct Democracy in America* (New York: Russell & Russell, 1935), 638.
20. Du Bois, *Black Reconstruction,* 638–648.
21. Du Bois, *Black Reconstruction,* 657–658.
22. Du Bois, *Black Reconstruction,* 665.
23. Henry Lee Swint, *The Northern Teacher in the South, 1862–1870* (1941; reprint, New York: Octagon Books, 1967), 3–6, 23–34, 142.
24. Swint, *The Northern Teacher in the South,* 35–51.
25. Swint, *The Northern Teacher in the South,* 81–93.
26. Swint, *The Northern Teacher in the South,* 93–133.
27. George R. Bentley, *A History of the Freedmen's Bureau* (Philadelphia: University of Philadelphia Press, 1955), 48–49, 180–181, 214.
28. Robert C. Morris, *Reading, 'Riting, and Reconstruction: The Education of the Freedmen in the South, 1861–1870* (Chicago: University of Chicago Press, 1976), ix–xi, 45–53.
29. Morris, *Reading, 'Riting, and Reconstruction,* 83–84, 129–130, 143–148.
30. Morris, *Reading, 'Riting, and Reconstruction,* 172–173, 210–211, 248.
31. Morris, *Reading, 'Riting, and Reconstruction,* 245–249.
32. Ronald E. Butchart, *Northern Schools, Southern Blacks, and Reconstruction* (Westport, Conn.: Greenwood Press, 1980), 207–208.

33. Butchart, *Northern Schools, Southern Blacks, and Reconstruction,* 107–113.
34. Foner, "Reconstruction Revisited," 86.
35. Butchart, *Northern Schools, Southern Blacks, and Reconstruction,* 197–202.
36. James D. Anderson, *The Education of Blacks in the South 1860–1935* (Chapel Hill: University of North Carolina Press, 1988), 4–10, 31–32.
37. Anderson, *The Education of Blacks in the South,* 30–37.
38. Paul A. Cimbala, *Under the Guardianship of the Nation: The Freedmen's Bureau and the Reconstruction of Georgia, 1865–1870* (Athens: University of Georgia Press, 1997), xii–xx.
39. Cimbala, *Under the Guardianship of the Nation,* 166–192.
40. Michael L. Lanza, "'One of the Most Appreciated Labors of the Bureau': The Freedmen's Bureau and the Southern Homestead Act," in *The Freedmen's Bureau and Reconstruction: Reconsiderations,* ed. Paul A. Cimbala and Randall M. Miller (New York: Fordham University Press, 1999), 67–87.
41. Cimbala, *Under the Guardianship of the Nation,* 105–113.
42. Jacqueline Jones, *Soldiers of Light and Love: Northern Teachers and Georgia Blacks, 1865–1873* (Chapel Hill: University of North Carolina Press, 1980), 3–13, 199.
43. Jones, *Soldiers of Light and Love,* 207–208.
44. Jones, *Soldiers of Light and Love,* 191–194.
45. Knight, *Public Education in the South,* 337–381.
46. Charles William Dabney, *Universal Education in the South* (1936; reprint, New York: Arno Press, 1969), 1: 150–153.
47. Dabney, *Universal Education in the South,* 1: 154–160.
48. Dabney, *Universal Education in the South,* 1: 162–163.
49. C. Vann Woodward, *Origins of the New South, 1877–1913* (Baton Rouge: Louisiana State University Press, 1951), 66–69.
50. Louis R. Harlan, *Separate and Unequal: Public School Campaigns and Racism in the Southern Seaboard States, 1901–1915* (New York: Atheneum, 1968), 37; David Tyack and Robert Lowe, "The Constitutional Moment: Reconstruction and Black Education in the South," *American Journal of Education* 94, no. 2 (February 1986): 236–256.
51. Oscar W. Hyatt, *Development of Secondary Education in Alabama* (Nashville, Tenn.: Cullom & Ghertner, Co., 1933), 9–14, 44.
52. Hyatt, *Development of Secondary Education in Alabama,* 56–61.
53. Hyatt, *Development of Secondary Education in Alabama,* 62–65.
54. Earle H. West, "The Peabody Fund and Negro Education, 1867–1880," *History of Education Quarterly* 6, no. 2 (Summer 1966): 3–21.
55. West, "The Peabody Fund and Negro Education, 1867–1880," 9–11.
56. William Preston Vaugn, *Schools for All: The Blacks and Public Education in the South, 1865–1877* (Lexington: University of Kentucky Press, 1974), 147–151.
57. Louis R. Harlan, "Desegregation in New Orleans Public Schools during Reconstruction," *The American Historical Review* 67, no. 3 (April 1962): 663–675.
58. J. L. M. Curry, *A Brief Sketch of George Peabody and a History of the Peabody Education Fund through Thirty Years* (1898; reprint, New York: Negro Universities Press, 1969), 62–65.
59. Curry, *A Brief Sketch of George Peabody,* 87–89.
60. West, "The Peabody Fund and Negro Education, 1867–1880," 11–13.
61. Curry, *A Brief Sketch of George Peabody,* 121–129.
62. Clinton B. Allison, "Training Dixie's Teachers: The University of Tennessee's Summer Normal Institutes," *The Journal of Thought* 18, no. 3 (Fall 1983): 27–36.
63. Reid E. Jackson, "Rise of Teacher-Training for Negroes," *Journal of Negro Education* 7, no. 4 (October 1938): 540–547.
64. C. Vann Woodward, *The Strange Career of Jim Crow,* 2nd rev. ed. (New York: Oxford University Press, 1966), 31–45.
65. James Anderson, "Ex-Slaves and the Rise of Universal Education in the New South, 1860–1880," in *Education and the New South,* ed. Ronald K. Goodenow and Arthur O. White (Boston: G. K. Hall and Co., 1981), 1–25.
66. Howard N. Rabinowitz, "Half a Loaf: The Shift from White to Black in the Negro Schools of the Urban South, 1865–1890," *The Journal of Southern History* 40, no. 4 (November 1974): 565–594.
67. Rabinowitz, "Half a Loaf," 565–582.
68. John William Graves, "Jim Crow in Arkansas: A Reconsideration of Urban Race Relations in the Post-Reconstruction South," in *African Americans and the Emergence of Segregation, 1865–1900,* ed. Donald G. Nieman (New York: Garland Publishing, 1994), 127–154.
69. James L. Leloudis, *Schooling in the New South: Pedagogy, Self, and Society in North Carolina, 1880–1920* (Chapel Hill: University of North Carolina Press, 1996), 24–25.

70. Leloudis, *Schooling in the New South,* 30–35.
71. Walter Page Hines, *The Rebuilding of Old Commonwealths: Being Essays towards the Training of the Forgotten Man in the Southern States* (1902; reprint, New York: AMS Press, 1970), 46–47.
72. Hines, *The Rebuilding of Old Commonwealths,* 28–44.
73. Leloudis, *Schooling in the New South,* 127–132.
74. Dabney, *Universal Education in the South,* 2:13–14.
75. Harlan, *Separate and Unequal,* 12–13.
76. Gaston, *New South Creed,* 87–95.
77. Louis Harlan, *Booker T. Washington: The Making of a Black Leader, 1856–1901* (New York: Oxford University Press, 1972), 204–222.
78. Harlan, *Booker T. Washington,* 165; Gaston, *New South Creed,* 140.
79. Dwight Oliver Wendell Holmes, *The Evolution of the Negro College* (College Park, MD: McGrath Publishing, 1934), 167–169.
80. W. E. Burghardt Du Bois, *The Souls of Black Folk: Essays and Sketches* (1903; reprint, Greenwich, Conn.: Fawcett Premier, 1961), 74–87.
81. William H. Watkins, *The White Architects of Black Education: Ideology and Power in America, 1865–1954* (New York: Teachers College Press, 2001), 59–61.
82. E. Franklin Frazier, *The Negro in the United States,* rev. ed. (New York: Macmillan Co., 1957), 159–162.
83. Frazier, *The Negro in the United States,* 163–164.
84. Harlan, *Separate and Unequal,* 42–44.
85. Robert L. Church and Michael W. Sedlak, *Education in the United States: An Interpretive History* (New York: The Free Press, 1976), 147–152.
86. Roger L. Ransom and Richard Sutch, *One Kind of Freedom: The Economic Consequences of Emancipation,* 2nd ed. (New York: Cambridge University Press, 2001), 181–195.
87. Woodward, *Origins of the New South,* 140, 480–481.

7

Organizing Schools According to a New Definition of Democracy

Election propaganda cartoon, nineteenth century

During the decades that followed the American Civil War, politicians and educators sought to unify the country around democratic principles. Because social circumstances had changed, these officials altered the definition of democracy. As earlier chapters showed, before the War between the States, people resisted state control of schools because they believed that the best guarantee of democracy was the autonomy of their communities. Thus, they sought local control of schools, even though the informal, personal ways of interaction found in small towns and villages served the prosperous farmers or bankers who dominated less fortunate residents. After the war, the growth of railroads and the rise of large businesses brought new and impersonal ways of exchange. Because the residents of small towns could no longer exist apart from other communities, officials introduced managerial forms of administration to coordinate the activities of citizens who lived far apart. Although central administrations promised to treat people equitably, central management appeared to be autocratic and clashed with local forms of community participation.[1]

In schools, educators sought unsuccessfully to adjust older forms of local control to coincide with the more impersonal administrative efforts. School officials were unsuccessful because whatever compromises they made fell on the side that reinforced the secular, industrial order. As a result, although schools enrolled different types of students, they did so by preparing children to function in urban, industrial societies.

Because Americans in different regions came to face similar problems after Reconstruction ended in 1877, the book begins a different pattern with Chapter 7. Whereas earlier chapters discussed the ways schools developed in different regions of the United States, the remaining chapters cover issues that faced education generally. These include such problems as the development of school administration, the drive for consolidation, the efforts to construct educational philosophies, the ways educational psychology rose to replace philosophy, the effort to arrange an efficient, socially relevant sequence of grades, and the pursuit of a curriculum based on students' interests.

When educators built schools to help a new middle class take its place in the new nationwide society, they faced issues of appropriate organization, administration, and curriculum. Because the new order depended on large corporations, businesslike methods of producing goods and distributing services, and central planning, many educators adopted those patterns. Other educators resisted such uniformity and tried to preserve opportunities for individual initiative and creativity. At any rate, by 1918, every state in the Union adopted laws requiring children to attend schools, and educators tried to fulfill the responsibilities universal schooling implied. Although these efforts took place together, the reforms went in different directions. Seeking to make sense of a complicated series of changes, the following chapters discuss each of the issues separately.

What Was the Relation between Religion and Education?

According to Ward M. McAfee, before the American Civil War, the Republican Party claimed it wanted to protect free labor against the westward spread of slave labor. In these antebellum campaigns, the Republicans portrayed Southern agriculturalists as repressive slaveholders and described Northern industrialists and factory workers as freedom-loving entrepreneurs who created wealth. After the war, the Republican Party claimed that public schools could unify the United States, and to accomplish this goal and many others, they initiated Reconstruction. When Democrats attacked the Republicans for grasping power, the Republicans replied that the central government had to control the states if African Americans in the South and Irish Catholics in the North were to enjoy adequate public schools.[2]

The contest took shape in 1874, when Charles Sumner, an abolitionist senator from Massachusetts, spoke from his deathbed to urge his colleagues to rejuvenate the campaign for his Supplementary Civil Rights Bill. Sumner had proposed his version of the Civil Rights Bill during the depression of 1873, but it had not advanced through the Congress. According to McAfee, when the Republicans revived the bill, the Democrats complained that the Republicans wanted racially integrated schools. In response, the Republicans claimed that the bill would force Catholic children to attend public schools and thereby teach them to follow republican principles rather than the edicts of a foreign pope and the Catholic Church. Thus, while the Democrats appealed to racism, the Republicans tried to profit from religious intolerance.[3]

The public reaction to the threat of racially mixed schools was immediate and severe. In the elections of 1874, the Republicans lost control of the U.S. House of Representatives, making them unable to enact any further Reconstruction legislation. President Grant blamed the threat of racially mixed schools as the cause for his party's defeat. Newspaper reports in New York and Philadelphia agreed with this assessment. The white citizens in these Northern cities disapproved of any measure that would require their children to attend schools with black children. Thus, McAfee concluded that, in 1874, the racial biases of Protestant Northern voters were much stronger than their fears of Catholic leaders. The result was that the fear of racially integrated schools caused the end of Reconstruction.[4]

With the end of Reconstruction, the Republicans stopped trying to infuse their ideas of Christian values throughout the nation. According to McAfee, the Republican mission suffered from internal contradictions. On the one hand, Republican leaders had believed the spread of the common school would establish a national religion. On the other hand, they advanced their dream of unifying the nation under Christianity by discrediting Catholicism as sectarian and divisive.[5]

To avoid religious controversies, educators sought to separate religion from public education. For example, in 1867, when William Torrey Harris accepted the position of superintendent of St. Louis Schools, local newspaper articles attacked Harris and the St. Louis public schools for raising children to be radicals and infidels. The dispute began when Methodists and Presbyterians had complained that Harris did not want the schools to teach the Bible or religion. In response, Harris wrote a report to the board of education arguing that the mission of the school was to develop rational thought. Although he believed such ways of thinking could serve as the basis of religious faith, he urged that the schools be free from sectarian bias. He believed that the various churches should impart denominational teachings, and he thought churches would fulfill their own missions better if schools omitted specific sectarian ideas.[6]

Instead of religion, Harris preferred adding science to the basic curriculum. For example, in another report written in 1871, Harris acknowledged that studies of reading, writing, arithmetic, and geography were most important in public schools because these subjects enabled students to understand their culture. Although he warned against adding too many subjects to the school day, Harris added that natural science was important because it provided the basis of industrial change and thereby generated the wealth that most people enjoyed.[7]

The following year, in 1872, Duane Doty, superintendent of Detroit city schools, and Harris met with several leading educators to draft a statement of the fundamental principles of education to which school people could agree. Although reinforcing the authority of local school officials, the educators called for uniformity around a nonsectarian, literary education. The statement claimed the schools had to shape the character of the children; however, the source of such influence came from the school organization or secular subjects. Religion was not an essential aspect in school life.[8]

Doty and Harris's statement began with the assertion that schools had developed in the United States to satisfy social and political needs. As a result, the control of schools resided with the states and the local communities. Because citizens engaged in political functions, all people regardless of sex, social rank, wealth, or abilities required an education. Schools prepared people to participate in politics and enhanced the economic well being of the community as well. According to Doty and Harris, educated people could apply their increased intelligence to their property to increase its value. Consequently, as settlers developed commercial towns and manufacturing centers, schools spread through the frontier.[9]

Doty and Harris claimed that the role of the school was to draw children from the nurturing setting found among families and introduce them to the vocations and civil society. This meant that teachers had to form the moral character of the child by inculcating such traits as obedience and self-control. Instead of finding the basis for such discipline in religion, Doty and Harris argued that school organization could impart good character. For example, in rural sections, schools commonly enrolled less than fifty pupils, the subjects concentrated on agriculture, the atmosphere reflected family life, and the teachers depended on corporal punishment to maintain order. On the other hand, in city schools with as many as three hundred pupils in one building, the division and classification of students into classes of similar ability allowed a military style of organization stressing punctuality, regularity, attention, and silence. These were the characteristics needed in industrial or commercial life.[10]

Turning to matters of curriculum, Doty and Harris recommended that elementary schools on the frontier and those in the established cities follow a curriculum designed to introduce the students to the arts and accomplishments that could provide for further self-education. These included arithmetic, geography and natural history, reading and writing, grammar, and the history of the United States. The educators found that teachers in city schools added drawing, vocal music, and some oral presentations of natural science. For high school students, the educators recommended adding such subjects as algebra, natural philosophy, English literature, Latin, and a modern language.[11]

As for teaching methods, the Doty and Harris statement asserted that textbooks formed the basis of instruction because the printed page provided the means to obtain information about the recorded experience of humankind. In some cases, though, students performed investigations to verify theories or to discover new facts.[12]

Doty and Harris added three points that characterized American education. First, girls and boys attended the same schools from the primary grades through the high schools and studied the same courses. Second, racial integration took place in the Northern states whereas the larger numbers of black students who lived in the South attended separate schools. Third, almost 90 percent of the teachers in city schools were women. According to Doty and Harris, women monopolized teaching because most school superintendents believed that women could manage young children naturally, and they thought women could facilitate the children's transition to the classroom from the home. Another consideration was that the labor of women was comparatively inexpensive. These advantages did not extend outside the cities because men tended to be the country schoolteachers.[13]

Doty and Harris devoted four sentences to the instruction of religion in public schools. They wrote that public schools did not give sectarian education. Although Doty and Harris acknowledged that most schools began the day with Bible reading and prayer, they claimed that religious teaching should go on in families and Sunday schools. Thus, they decided that religion had a peripheral role in schools.[14]

Bearing signatures of approval from seventy-seven noted educators and public officials, the statement drafted by Doty and Harris appeared to represent the mainstream view of the free school in the United States. The statement noted that some religious denominations disapproved of the secular nature of public school instruction and created their own schools to infuse religion among the studies. Interestingly, Doty and Harris added that these denominations sought public school funds to carry on this education.[15]

How Could Catholic Schools and Public Schools Cooperate?

As noted in Chapter 3, Catholic schools became popular in Cincinnati, Ohio, after Catholic leaders disagreed with the ways public schools used the Bible in classes. The statement by Doty and Harris suggested another source of disagreement when Catholic bishops asked to share school funds. Many historians contend that Catholic schools arose in the United States when public school boards refused to provide financial resources for Catholic schools.

One historian who contended that Catholic schools arose from disagreements between church officials and public school boards about sharing financial resources was Vincent Lannie. According to Lannie, the development of Catholic parochial schools in the United States began during the 1850s when Archbishop John Hughes sought to obtain some of the public school funds of New York for Catholic schools. His efforts failed, and he accused public officials of creating a system of schools that separated religion from education. Although Catholic parents had to contribute taxes to these schools, they did not have to send their children to them. Consequently, Hughes called on them to erect Catholic schools where children learned religion in ways that better suited the republic. This experience set the model for Catholic school development, according to Lannie, because, when other bishops sought public school funds for their schools, they met similar disappointments. As a result, they turned against public education and encouraged each parish to create its own parochial school.[16]

Despite Lannie's assertion that Bishop Hughes's experiences foretold the failure Catholic leaders would confront trying to cooperate with state or local agencies in forming schools, some compromises took place that allowed Catholic leaders to integrate their schools with the public schools that were developing around them. Such compromises were possible because Catholics and other Americans shared the desire for schools. Furthermore, most people felt that education was a local responsibility and that the family and church should have the right to direct a school. Thus, although Americans developed systems of central control of schools, they accepted some limits that would protect the freedom of religious expression.[17]

Three examples illustrated the cooperation between public school officials and Catholic educators. These took place in Lowell, Massachusetts; in Savannah, Georgia; and in Poughkeepsie, New York. These compromises led to a school controversy when Catholic prelates who disliked cooperation with public schools called on officials in Rome to end the programs. The pope refused to make a choice. He supported the conservative prelates who wanted Catholic children to attend Catholic schools at the same time that he gave local ordinaries, the individual bishops, the authority to decide when Catholic children could attend public schools.[18]

The first example took place in Lowell, Massachusetts where members of the Irish middle class compromised with school committee members to use public funds to support Catholic schools for Irish children. In the late 1820s, Lowell had changed from a village into an industrial city. When Rev. Theodore Edson, an Episcopalian minister, obtained a seat on the school committee, he called for a townwide system of graded schools because small district schools no longer served the larger population. In the 1830s, after the school committee approved Edson's plan, the members designated a graded school building especially for the Irish children in the "paddy camps." Although the public graded school enjoyed adequate financial support, few Irish children enrolled. Instead, most of the Irish children attended classes in the basement of St. Patrick's Church. These basement rooms were overcrowded, and the church could not afford to improve them.[19]

In 1835, the priest from St. Patrick's approached the school committee to ask for help with the Catholic school. Making a compromise, the school committee agreed to open two classrooms in the Chapel Hill area where Irish families lived and to support two classrooms in the church basement. Although the school committee retained its authority to appoint instructors, regulate textbooks, and supervise instruction, the school committee agreed to appoint only Catholic teachers of whom the priests approved for these classrooms. To ensure the texts did not slander Catholicism, the committee allowed the priests to inspect the books in advance.[20]

The compromise was successful. In six months, over 450 Irish children enrolled and about 280 attended regularly. In subsequent years, enrollments increased and the committee opened another school and added more instructors who were Catholic. In fact, the Lowell school committee members and officials from the Massachusetts Board of Education agreed that in no other place were more Irish youth attracted to public schools.[21]

Although Irish children attended primary schools and grammar schools in Lowell, they did not go on to high school, even though they were welcome there, according to the school committee. Despite this promise of open enrollments, high school authorities rejected three of the four Irish students who applied to attend in 1850. The Irish students continued to be attracted to the lower grades because such an education made them eligible to work in the mills. This opportunity, in addition to the compromise with the priests, made the lower-level public schools attractive to the Irish students even if they could not pursue a higher education.[22]

Unfortunately, factionalism developed among the parishioners of St. Patrick's Church. When a newly appointed priest, Father James T. McDermott, sought to reduce the debts incurred by his predecessor, the parishioners who had favored the former priest opposed his fundraising efforts. When the Catholic schoolteachers joined the opposition, McDermott tried to replace the teachers, but the school committee refused to fire the teachers. Consequently, the priest urged Catholic parents to boycott the public schools. Although the bishop reprimanded the priest for weakening a helpful church–state relationship, subsequent priests appointed to St. Patrick's chose to build Catholic schools when the population of Irish immigrants increased. By 1850, the school committee complained and the compromise ended.[23]

The second example came from Savannah, Georgia, where, in 1870, Bishop Augustin Verot entered into a cooperative agreement with the public school board to form a Catholic public school. The negotiations for this agreement between the bishop and the board of education had begun in 1862, but the War between the States intervened. In 1866, federal troops established a public school system. Consequently, Verot asked that Catholic schools be included under the management of the public schools. He wanted the schools to retain Catholic teachers and the students to learn the Catholic catechism. Verot considered the proposal reasonable because Catholics contributed to the support of public schools, and he found the cost of Catholic education was burdensome. For example, in one year, Verot had spent about $7,000 to operate a school for 700 pupils.[24]

In part, Verot and the board of education could not resolve the discussions because the state legislature did not create a general, state-supported system until 1870. At the same time, school board members were unwilling to accept sectarian schools. Nonetheless, in the course of these discussions, Verot made several concessions. For example, he acknowledged that the state had the right and the duty to provide schooling for the citizens. At the time, this was a unique admission for a Catholic priest to make. In addition, he offered to give the board of education the authority to supervise the Catholic schools. In return, he asked that the teachers instruct the children about the Catholic catechism.[25]

In 1869, the school board agreed to the compromise. Although the board retained control over matters of instruction, they promised to prefer Catholic teachers for the Catholic schools. With the agreement settled, Verot left Savannah in 1870. His successor, Ignatius Persico, praised the cooperation with public schools and claimed that the arrangement was unique. By 1873, newspapers in Brooklyn, New York, heralded the liberal spirit and justice of the Savannah plan. Despite the warm praise, the idea did not spread widely. For example, in 1875, Verot sought to reproduce the same arrangement in St. Augustine, Florida, where he had gone to serve. Unfortunately, the legislature refused to act on his petition. Nonetheless, the plan continued to operate in Savannah until 1916, when a Savannah attorney complained to the state's attorney general that the state was supporting a church under this plan. When the attorney general agreed, the board of education terminated the Catholic public school.[26]

The third model was developed in Poughkeepsie, New York. In this case, cooperation grew out of the willingness of immigrants to participate in activities that the natives valued. For example, during the American Civil War, German and Irish immigrants showed their patriotism by enlisting in the Union army. The pastor of St. Peter's Church held a flag-raising ceremony when the Confederates fired on Fort Sumter. In addition, the Catholic Church took an active part in local campaigns for abstinence from alcohol. Thus, in 1873, when several Catholic boys advanced in their studies, the public high school admitted them and suspended religious services to avoid offending them.[27]

At the time, the separate Catholic schools in Poughkeepsie for boys and girls reported an average attendance of 820 students whereas the average attendance in the city schools was about 1,700. In addition, the Catholic schools were in a section of town where the public schools were already overcrowded. As a result, when the priest of St. Peter's announced to the public school board that the church would have to close the parish schools, a board member suggested renting the buildings and maintaining two parochial schools in addition to the public elementary schools. In this way, the school board could alleviate overcrowding without building new schools. The board decided that the parish could nominate the teachers, and the parish could use the formerly Catholic school building after school hours. This agreement made in 1873 became the Poughkeepsie plan.[28]

At first, there was some resistance because teachers in the formerly Catholic schools suspended Bible readings during the day. In reply to the flurry of complaints, the board members pointed out that the opportunity to Americanize the immigrants was most important. In addition, the board noted that reading the Bible without clerical supervision offended the Catholics. The board added that, although Bible reading was an important American custom, freedom from ecclesiastical imposition was also an American virtue. As a result, the plan stayed in effect until 1898 when a resurgence of nativism forced the board to abandon it.[29]

Despite the apparent success of such compromises as the Poughkeepsie plan, many conservative Catholics wanted Catholic parents to send their children to Catholic schools. For example, in 1874, James McMaster asked Vatican officials if Catholic parents could send their children to public schools not supervised by Catholic clergy. The answer came in the form of an eight-point document that stated such a practice was permissible if there was no Catholic school available. Although this answer avoided affirming either the opinion of McMaster or the views of the Catholic bishops who favored Catholic schools, the number of Catholic schools rose rapidly. In 1875, the number of parishes with Catholic schools was about 1,400. By 1885, the number of parish schools increased to more than 2,500. Most important, in line with instructions from the Vatican, U.S. bishops met in Baltimore in 1884 where they adopted a set of decrees that required every parish to build a school and that required all Catholic parents to send their children to Catholic schools.[30]

Despite the apparent stringent nature of the decrees of 1884, they did not end cooperative agreements with public schools. Some prelates continued to push for accommodations. For example, in 1890, Archbishop John Ireland addressed the annual meeting of the National Education Association in his home city of St. Paul. In his speech, he announced his support of universal compulsory education. Warning that state schools would be nonreligious, he offered a solution similar to the one found in Poughkeepsie. The city school board could rent the parish schools and control the teaching during the day so long as the Catholic teachers remained. Priests would teach Christian doctrine after school hours.[31]

Conservative Catholic bishops complained to Rome about Ireland's proposal. In an effort to conciliate the dispute, Pope Leo XIII asked U.S. Cardinal Gibbons for his opinion. This approach did not satisfy conservative critics because Ireland had submitted his speech to Gibbons for approval before he delivered it. In 1892, Rome replied again that the decrees of the U.S. bishops continued in force, but that Ireland's plan was acceptable. Because neither liberal nor conservative U.S. bishops were satisfied with this answer, the pope asked the American prelates to meet with an archbishop sent from Rome who was supposed to carry a set of proposals designed to solve the controversy. When the bishops and the archbishop from Rome met, the proposals did not seem to satisfy either side. Nonetheless, the complaints of the U.S. bishops had no further effect. The pope acknowledged that the ideals of public education were compatible with the ideals of the church, and Catholics did not have to decide between a secular education and a Catholic school. Various compromises were possible.[32]

According to Timothy Walch, the pope's decision enabled American Catholics to live in harmony with their neighbors and to meet the growing demands posed by state control of schools. For example, by the 1920s, American Catholics accepted such state demands as the uniform training and certification of teachers provided the Catholic schools were able to permeate the lessons and the life of the school with religious teachings.[33]

How Could Educators Encourage the Development of Uniform Schools under Systems of Local Control?

As the various state governments created departments of education, educators wondered if there should be some system to encourage uniformity among the states. In seeking to establish some sort of national organization to improve schools, educators debated a definition of democracy that depended on local control and an idea of democracy that derived from spreading education equitably. Unable to choose one, the educators adopted two related methods. First, they formed a national organization dedicated to spreading information about good schooling. Second, they endorsed the creation of a federal bureau to collect statistics and information about schools. Together, the national organization and the federal bureau sought to protect local control while ensuring that each state or school district adopted beneficial educational measures. They served these apparently contradictory aims in a simple manner. First, the bureau collected the then-current ideas concerning a good education. Second, the national organization distributed this information to leaders at the different levels of schooling. Thus, uniformity was to come from moral suasion rather than authoritarian imposition.

The process began with the formation of a national organization. During the early years of the nineteenth century, teachers formed organizations that held meetings to spread ideas about education. As the nineteenth century advanced, the spread of normal schools and teacher institutes trained more teachers. Publishers created a wide variety of textbooks and other materials. Nonetheless, most instructors worked in isolated one-room schoolhouses, and many teachers could not concentrate on teaching because they had to take up other occupations such as farming to compensate for the meager salaries they received as teachers. In such situations, teachers turned to regional and state organizations for professional guidance and encouragement.[34]

In 1857, ten teacher organizations in such states as Massachusetts, New York, Illinois, and Iowa sent out invitations for teachers to attend a meeting in Philadelphia in August. The purpose of the meeting was to form the National Teachers' Association, to provide a means to coordinate the work of various state organizations. The hope was that such an organization could provide an annual convention where educators could exchange ideas. Further, the association would publish the proceedings of the meetings to disseminate information about schools around the country.[35]

Once created, the National Teachers' Association held annual meetings attracting increasingly larger audiences and offering speeches that covered a wide range of topics. The most common topic was educational theory and psychology. Other speakers covered various courses of study and methods of instruction. Furthermore, from 1857 until 1867, the meetings of the National Teachers' Association included proposals or speeches endorsing the creation of a federal department of education to collect statistics. Such statements of approval seemed to be the extent of the organization's efforts in favor of a national bureau of education. Although the weakness of the educators' efforts made some politicians wonder if teachers understood American politics, the first president of the National Teachers' Association, Zalmon Richards, claimed that teachers did not petition actively for such a department because they were unsure that the national government should take part in the crusade to improve schools. Nonetheless, the movement achieved this aim in March 1867 when President Andrew Johnson signed the bill to create a federal department of education.[36]

Fearful of federal encroachment, Johnson signed the legislation to create the new department when supporters assured him that the creation of a federal education department would not threaten the control of schools by local or state officials. Johnson's fears were reasonable because neither supporters nor critics could determine what the department would do. On the one hand, the legislation charged the department to collect statistics and information about education. On the other hand, most of the legislators expected the department to be an active agency that improved schools across the nation.[37]

Johnson appointed Henry Barnard, former Connecticut superintendent of schools, to be the first commissioner. Interestingly, most prominent educators opposed Barnard's appointment because they feared that he was inefficient as an administrator and inept as a politician, although they admired him personally and found him to be brilliant as a scholar.[38] Some years earlier, in 1850, Barnard had presented a plan for a central national agency to advance education. The proposal called for the agency to collect information, statistics, and studies about schools and education. To advance his plan, Barnard offered to donate his extensive personal library as the foundation. Because Barnard had not considered how to staff or support the agency, few people embraced the proposal.[39]

In 1867, once confirmed as U.S. Commissioner of Education, Barnard set up an office, hired clerks, delegated his duties to the clerks, and left Washington for his home in Hartford, Connecticut. According to Barnard's biographer, Edith Nye MacMullen, he spent most of his time and effort working on his journal that he had founded some years before. When the department failed to produce reports, Barnard blamed his clerks. To meet his obligation of assessing the condition of education, Barnard planned a massive survey that went far beyond what Congress expected him to do and involved plans that he could not complete. In an effort to make up for failing to provide the basic information Congress wanted, Barnard wrote a 700-page report of education in Washington, D.C., in which he proposed centralizing the city schools.[40]

Although Barnard had hoped that his plan for Washington, D.C., would become the model for school reform nationwide, Congress acted before he could deliver the report. In 1869, the U.S. Congress approved legislation that removed the Department of Education as an independent department within the administration, placed it under the Department of the Interior as a bureau, and gave it the name Office of Education. Further, the salary of the commissioner dropped from $4000 per year to $3000.[41]

While the federal education office suffered declining fortunes, the National Teacher's Association grew by adding other state organizations to the original founding ten. In addition, the association absorbed other organizations to expand its range beyond common school teachers. In 1869, the National Teacher's Association absorbed an organization of school superintendents, an association for colleges, and another group for normal schools. In view of its enlarged focus, the National Teacher's Association changed its name to the National Education Association (NEA). To provide for the different interests of the various associations, the NEA created a department of higher education, another for elementary education, and one for teacher training.[42]

Meanwhile, at the federal level, Barnard resigned as U.S. Commissioner of Education when the Congress reduced his salary and downgraded the department. In 1870, President Grant appointed John Eaton to the position of commissioner. Although Eaton lacked qualifications and scholarly abilities, he had taught schools, served in various administrative posts in Ohio schools, worked as an assistant commissioner of the Freedmen's Bureau, and functioned as a superintendent of schools for Tennessee. His most important quality was that he was a politically astute friend of Grant. Once in office, Eaton warned against efforts to undermine the local control of schools and he called for efforts to spread schools fairly throughout the land. He chose to follow Barnard's manner and style of gathering information about schools in hopes that people constructing schools could do so intelligently; however, Eaton worked more efficiently and published the information more regularly. For example, less than eight months after his appointment, Eaton published his first report using material gathered or published by Barnard.[43]

Although critics complained that Eaton's report did not focus on common schools, most legislators appreciated the fact that Eaton had produced a report. To gather information about schools, Barnard and Eaton sent letters to school people around the country asking about school practices and enrollments. Because they could not compel the superintendents to reply, the information they received was unreliable. In addition, although Eaton could draw attention to problems, such as the fact that few black children attended schools, he could not directly address those issues. As a result, Eaton set about winning the friendship of educators in different parts of the country and forming cordial relations with congressional politicians.[44]

In 1885, after a Democratic president, Grover Cleveland, took office, Eaton resigned to become president of Marietta College in Ohio. When Eaton left Washington, he had been commissioner for sixteen years. In that time, the bureau had grown to a staff of thirty-eight. Although most staff members were clerks, some of them were qualified specialists whose duties included compiling and analyzing statistical information about schools. In addition, the bureau's library had grown to contain over 18,000 volumes and more than twice as many pamphlets and booklets.[45]

In 1886, President Cleveland appointed Nathaniel Henry Rhodes Dawson, a Southerner, as commissioner. Although trained as a lawyer, Dawson sought to advance common schools across the nation. Hampered by congressional budget cuts, Dawson had to reduce the staff and the responsibilities of the office. Nonetheless, he was able to draft and implement a plan for the organization of schools in the newly created district of Alaska. In Dawson's plan a territorial school board of three appointed officials made rules and regulations for common schools subject to the commissioner's approval, and local school districts retained control of their affairs. While Dawson's plan provided an outline for a common school system, he lacked adequate financial support to put it into practice.[46]

In 1889, after Benjamin Harrison defeated Grover Cleveland for the presidency, Dawson resigned his position as U.S. Commissioner of Education. At the recommendation of Nicholas Murray Butler, one of the founders of Teachers College and later president of Columbia University, Harrison appointed William Torrey Harris to be U.S. Commissioner of Education.[47]

Following Barnard's view of the role of the commissioner, Harris devoted considerable attention to writing scholarly papers. During his lifetime, Harris published more than 400 articles about various aspects of education. In addition, he wrote textbooks for schools, and he published a prominent journal of philosophy. During Harris' term as commissioner, the office of education received an increased volume of information, and it sent out a greater number of reports than it had done previously. Nonetheless, the methods of gathering information continued to be letters sent to superintendents around the country asking for information. Harris and the clerks continued to handle those reports as Barnard had when he created the office twenty-two years earlier.[48]

Barnard's example remained in place because it provided a way to encourage teachers and administrators to organize their schools without trespassing on the prerogatives of local officials. In fact, the commissioners avoided using political power to improve schools. For example, neither Eaton nor Harris used the NEA to raise the status of the U.S. Bureau of Education to a cabinet-level position. In the sixteen years that Eaton was commissioner, from 1870 to 1886, he addressed the NEA ten times. Further, he remained active in the association until 1898. Although Eaton complained about inadequate support, he never suggested that the association should do more than ask the U.S. Congress to appropriate more money for the bureau to do its work. Similarly, in the seventeen years that Harris remained as commissioner, from 1889 until 1906, he attended NEA meetings, delivering by one count 145 speeches. Although he served on NEA committees that asked for larger appropriations for the bureau, Harris seemed to have such faith that school leaders would follow his written reports that he did not recommend elevating the position of commissioner to the level of a secretary in the president's cabinet.[49]

Whereas the staff of the bureau had expected Harris to strengthen the role of the department, Harris proceeded at his own pace on his scholarly work. Considering direct requests for money to be unseemly, Harris depended on the NEA to petition the U.S. Congress for additional resources for the bureau. Nonetheless, Donald Warren concluded that Harris's views of education dominated the bureau and the NEA. Harris seemed to believe that his scholarly work represented a considerable step toward organizing schools across the nation.[50]

According to Harris's biographer, Kurt F. Leidecker, it was typical of Harris to lead by offering objective or scholarly analysis. According to Leidecker, in 1869, when Harris became superintendent of St. Louis, he chose to allow the building principals the freedom to direct their schools. He set up certain standards or goals the schools were to meet. Those principals who were successful received promotions to bigger schools or increases in salaries.[51]

Similarly, as a young man, Harris had adopted a view of unifying the country through the diffusion of philosophical understandings. Harris left Yale in his junior year and moved to St. Louis, Missouri, in 1858. Although St. Louis promised to become a wealthy metropolitan area, the city exhibited many contradictions. For example, the population expanded because different groups of people such as New England Protestants and German Catholics moved into the city. Further, although Missouri was a slave state, the people of St. Louis supported the Union cause. Living in the midst of these social contradictions, Harris met Henry Conrad Brokmeyer, who introduced him to the philosophy of Hegel. It was in Hegel's philosophy that Harris found ways to enable individuals to advance their freedoms and, at the same time, bring together various groups during a period of social growth.[52]

In 1870, Harris delivered a speech to the NEA that foreshadowed his view that ideas changed social conditions rather than leaders. In this speech, Harris described the War between the States that had recently ended. Harris claimed that the victors, the Union forces, had dominated because they held the view that industrial progress could further humanitarian goals. Although the South rejected this view, Harris claimed Southerners had come to accept the need for industrial development to advance their society. In the same way, Harris believed that educators would come to see that textbooks, not the leadership of the teacher, provided the means to advance human freedoms.[53]

According to Harris, eighteenth-century philosophers such as Rousseau and Pestalozzi encouraged teachers to ignore books and instead allow students to learn through their senses. When teachers in the United States tried to follow their principles, they created methods of oral instruction, such as object teaching, described in Chapter 4. In these systems, teachers asked questions aimed at helping students develop their powers of observation. Harris argued that the lessons had the opposite effect. First, pupils had to depend on the teacher. If the instructor went too fast, the pupils could not review the material on their own. They had to wait for the teacher to go over the lesson again. If the teacher was tired, the students could not move ahead by themselves. On the other hand, with a textbook, the pupils could reconsider difficult passages or they could move ahead as they chose. Second, the authors of text considered carefully what they wrote whereas teachers in the classroom might speak without thinking. Despite the possibility of teachers misspeaking, the teacher was the only source of information in systems of oral instruction. With the increased production of books, though, students learned to seek information from many sources.[54]

Harris claimed that, in the United States, schools introduced younger students to textbooks than did schools in other countries. This practice was in harmony with the country's affection for democracy, Harris added, because the students could study alone using the skill of reading. For example, Benjamin Franklin had learned philosophy while he held a job as a printer. In such a system, the ideal of culture filtered through the social classes whether or not the parents could afford to send their children to school for extended periods. In addition, the inventions of the telegraph and the growth of newspapers spread ideas so widely that they weakened sectionalism and sectarianism. Thus, Harris concluded, the tools of reading and information from the printed page enabled students to unfold their latent powers indefinitely.[55]

Under Harris's model, the teachers were not to govern the students. Instead of forcing children to obey, the teachers should provide examples by reading avidly and growing themselves. The students would imitate the teachers and take on the desire to grow. As the students acquired more knowledge from books and other printed sources around them, they would come to participate with the best and wisest members of humanity and, thereby, would feel it a disgrace to allow anyone to govern them except themselves.[56]

In his ideas of instruction, Harris depended on what he called the self-activity of students and colleagues. This was a faith in the ability of people to find their own best ways by coming to understand the best and most profound literary and historical works. Such a view of education corresponded to a belief that a commissioner of education could organize schools by encouraging the schoolteachers to learn more about education and about their own civilization.

Contemporaries of Harris praised him for trying to organize the schools by appealing to the intelligence of the educators. Writing for the Paris Exhibition of 1900, the president of the University of Illinois, Andrew Sloane Draper, praised Harris and the bureau of education for their presentation of information and their philosophic analyses of educational subjects. Calling the bureau the international clearinghouse of educational information, Draper stated that Harris had used the resources of the bureau to demonstrate how educators could change schools so that they promoted an improved culture. To Draper, this approach of disseminating information had been better than seeking the authority to supervise schools.[57]

How Did Educators Consolidate the Management of Schools, Make Student Attendance More Regular, and Improve the Curriculum?

As the nineteenth century advanced, educators organized schools in three related ways. The first was the effort to consolidate control. Such central control was essential because the development of larger, graded schools required more financial support than small communities could afford. The second line of development was to increase attendance because graded schools required a larger number of students than did smaller, one-room country schools. The third line of development was to arrange the curriculum in ways that attracted more students. On the one hand, graded schools required improved training of teachers. On the other hand, graded schools gave the teachers an opportunity to specialize more than was possible in the one-room schoolhouse. Thus, teachers undertook assignments tailored to their abilities.

As described in Chapters 3 and 4, the movement toward central state control took place in the Midwestern and Northern states before the American Civil War began. In Ohio, for example, the general assembly made its first effort to secure state supervision of schools in 1837 by creating the office of state superintendent of schools. The general assembly empowered the office to collect statistics and make reports and then abolished it in 1840. The general assembly restored the office in 1853, established a township system of governing schools to replace the smaller district schools, and expanded the powers of the state superintendent to control school funds. In 1873, the Ohio general assembly reinforced the process of centralization by authorizing boards of education to appoint local superintendents, required these superintendents to make reports to the local board, and pass these reports to the state superintendent. Such codes prepared the way to greater uniformity among schools in the state.[58]

As the control of schools shifted to state officers, the school buildings became larger and better equipped to offer a diverse number of studies. For example, in states such as Ohio, agents of the state teachers' association used the movement toward central control of schools to urge the construction of large, graded schools that would replace the small one-room district schools. By 1852, members of the state association congratulated themselves on the success of their campaign. One estimate held that in three-fourths of the towns with populations exceeding one thousand inhabitants, the citizens contributed to funds to build substantial schools that made a graded school possible. At the same time, the teachers sought to raise the qualifications of the teachers, to improve the classification of the students, and to introduce better methods of instruction.[59]

By 1899, all state constitutions contained provisions for popular education. In every state, the legislature had created a state department of education and a superintendent of public instruction or state school commissioner with authority to distribute state funds and to oversee the training and hiring of teachers. Nonetheless, the extent of the central control of schools differed among the states. By the late 1890s, New York had advanced the most in this direction whereas, in some states, officials worried that the trend discouraged individual initiative.[60]

By 1895, enrollments in elementary schools grew to over 14 million students out of a total school age population of about 20 million. On average, these schools remained open about 140 days per year. About 130,000 teachers were men and about 270,000 teachers were women. In all, enrollments totaled about 417,000 in the nearly 7,000 public and private high schools in the country.[61]

Although enrollments in elementary schools overshadowed high school attendance, the influence of compulsory education laws was not clear. About thirty-two states and territories had enacted such legislation by 1895, and all the states then in the Union had compulsory education laws by 1918. In general, these laws required children from eight to fourteen years of age to attend schools for some period. In Massachusetts and Connecticut, students remained in schools for the entire term. In other states, such as Kentucky, a student had to attend eight weeks of the term. When critics complained that these laws were inadequate and that the laws were rarely enforced, Harris responded that the laws had the beneficial effect of encouraging the majority of parents to send their children to schools. He thought that these parents abided by the law whether there was a punishment or not. For these parents, the laws for compulsory attendance represented recommendations by the state government to send the children to school. Nonetheless, Harris claimed such recommendations were sufficient. Worse, he added, without the laws, many of these law-abiding parents might not act in the interests of education.[62]

The enrollment figures for 1895 indicated that 70 percent of eligible children attended school. This represented an important increase from 1870 when about 7.5 million students attended school, comprising about 61 percent of school-age children. Harris attributed the bulk of the increased enrollment to social changes. The biggest change that made it easier for children to enroll in schools was the increased ease of transportation and the resulting growth of cities and towns replacing villages and isolated farms. He noted that from 1870 to 1890, miles of railway had doubled with the result that people living around cities could travel into urban areas. Harris complained that what he called the unsatisfactory practices of the district school continued in sparely settled districts. Unqualified teachers faced students of various ages and abilities in one-room buildings for a term that lasted sixty or eighty days. Because the teacher worked with each child individually, students spent most of the school day waiting to be called on by the teacher. In addition, teachers did not focus on education because they worked at other occupations for the greater part of the year. With the ease of transportation, communities could build larger graded schools in central locations. In the new schools, teachers divided the students by abilities, designed lessons for the common group, and kept each child working throughout the day. Thus, Harris estimated that by 1890, as a result of the growth of the railways, about half the school population attended graded schools with trained professional teachers who held classes for about 200 days or five days per week for forty weeks.[63]

Critics found the atmosphere of the graded schools to be mechanical, but Harris contended that the punctuality, silence, and order that typified graded schools served the educational aims of the school. Harris acknowledged that, in a mixed one-room school, individuality reigned whereas, in a graded school, the children learned to guide their behaviors for the well-being of everyone else. He considered this an improvement. For example, if the children gave in to the impulse to chatter or whisper, they would disturb the serious work of the class. Harris noted that in country schools children did not learn to work together. The teachers left the children alone in those one-room buildings while each child went individually to the teacher's desk to recite some lesson. Harris argued that in a larger, graded school with smaller but uniform classes, the students learned to work together.[64]

Harris claimed that reports to the bureau of education indicated that most elementary schools taught the academic subjects the NEA had recommended in 1894. These courses included reading, penmanship, spelling, grammar, Latin/French/German, arithmetic, algebra, geography, science and hygiene, history, physical culture, vocal music, drawing, and manual training. Of these subjects, arithmetic took up the most time because teachers spent an average of about 150 hours per year on the subject. Teachers spent almost the same amount of time on spelling, reading, and history when these subjects included citizenship, civics, and a study of the U.S. Constitution. Although general history did not appear among the subjects covered in schools, oral lessons on physiology, morals and manners, and natural science were common in most cities. Grammar took up about 38 hours per year, but singing and cooking were popular. Some form of physical culture or exercise appeared to take up almost 250 hours per year. Manual training was required in 149 cities and several state legislatures had mandated manual training in elementary and high schools.[65]

How Did the Curriculum Expand to Include More Subjects Than Academics?

As the nineteenth century ended, educators added subjects to the school curriculum that broadened the reach of the school to include aspects of life beyond academic training. Three examples illustrated this expansion. The first was manual training, the second was the kindergarten movement, and the third was the training of younger children who people called defectives. The paragraphs that follow will explain each case in turn.

The first example, manual training, entered school curriculums at the end of the nineteenth century. In 1876, advocates of manual training, Calvin M. Woodward and John D. Runkle, had found a method of preparing students for industrial training in an exhibit from the Moscow Imperial Technical School that appeared in the Philadelphia Centennial Exposition. In this model, the director, Victor Della Vos, had discovered that teachers could analyze the skills for each trade, organize them in order of ascending difficulty, and teach them in a program. Supervisors watched the students work through a graded series of exercises. In addition to using tools correctly, the students learned to follow drawings and models. To Woodward and Runkle, manual training taught students about the industries that characterized modern society. Therefore, they thought that all students should learn it. They added that manual training was an important aid for those students who would become craftspeople.[66]

Despite the faith that Woodward and Runkle expressed in manual training, Harris opposed manual training in the 1880s, claiming that children should learn academic subjects in schools. He contended that the place for manual training was in the shop or the farm. Advocates for manual training such as Woodward pointed out that students could not learn those skills in shops or small businesses because industrial changes had made it impossible for young people to obtain employment as apprentices. Consequently, Woodward and other advocates of manual training argued that the school should incorporate lessons that taught the students to use their hands as well as their minds. Since this was a compelling argument, the boards of education in many cities made manual training a compulsory subject.

The second way that schools expanded was to include a kindergarten for young children wherein teachers employed methods of teaching different from the techniques found in the primary school. In Europe, in 1838, Friedrich Froebel built his kindergarten around a series of gifts, objects such as balls, blocks, or cubes, and occupations. His hope was that when children manipulated a gift, they would develop a set of meanings that were associated with that object. For example, when the children would play with a ball, advocates of the kindergarten believed that this activity enabled the children to recognize the unity of the universe with the roundness of the ball reflecting human perfectibility.[67]

According to Barbara Beatty, the first kindergartens opened in the United States during the 1850s in efforts by German immigrants to preserve their language and their culture. Some of these teachers had studied with Froebel. When they moved to Wisconsin and Ohio with other German immigrants, they started their own schools. In 1872, kindergarten teachers displayed their ideas at the meeting of the German American Teachers Union in Cincinnati, Ohio.[68]

The success of the kindergarten movement in the United States depended on its avoidance of intellectual stimulation. Beginning in 1827, the idea of infant schools enjoyed popularity especially in states such as Massachusetts. By 1835, though, there were no such schools in the state because physicians disliked forcing young children to learn academic skills and information. The doctors contended that the children's minds might become susceptible to mental illness if they were overstimulated during infancy. Not surprisingly, advocates for the kindergarten built on this fear by claiming that they allowed children to develop naturally. These advocates noted that kindergartens followed the beliefs that young children were different from adults, and, as a result, the children had to learn differently.[69]

Although Harris was a strong advocate of academic preparation, he agreed with such advocates as Susan Blow and Elizabeth Peabody that kindergartens should provide education for the children without stressing intellectual development. In 1889, Harris addressed the kindergarten department of the NEA claiming that the methods of instruction found in kindergartens differed from those of primary schools. He added that the models were appropriate to the stages of growth through which the children passed. Thus, Harris argued that children should receive kindergarten and academic training in order to grow and mature properly.[70]

According to Harris, children who had not acquired language considered each event or object to be unique. Once the children learned about words, they searched for the universal reality to which they thought the names of objects referred. Thus, Harris called this period the symbolic stage of development because the children looked for the qualities shared by items in a class and learned to overlook less important differences. Most important to Harris, the kindergarten methods seemed to reinforce this pursuit of universal realities. For example, in many of the occupations, such as building, laying down sticks, or modeling in clay, the children learned about geometric shapes.[71]

Harris added that in kindergarten songs and pantomimes, the children reproduced the activities of the social world. By placing themselves in the roles of adult citizens, the young children attained a new and higher mode of thinking because they became acquainted with the laws of politeness and came to develop consciences. Consequently, Harris contended that the children sought the ideals behind these conventions and, in so doing, they moved toward the absolute or divine law.[72]

Harris believed that children passed through the symbolic stage as they ended their stays in the kindergartens, and they moved into what Harris called the conventional stage in which they regarded themselves as members of society. At this point, the children were ready to teach themselves about the world they were to enter. As a result, Harris concluded, the children needed the intellectual instruction offered by primary schools for two reasons. The practice of working at studies in the primary school took the children away from the play of the kindergarten, and the skill the students acquired in reading gave them the ability to learn by themselves. Consequently, whereas kindergartens fostered creative understandings, the primary schools fostered diligence and self-reliance. Harris concluded that when schools offered such a combination, the students could develop the various aspects of their personalities.[73]

The third example of the expansion of the schools beyond academic training was the care and education of children with disabilities. Before the American Civil War, New England, New York, and Pennsylvania opened schools for children with hearing, vision, or mental impediments. In a short period, similar schools opened in Ohio, Kentucky, Virginia, and Illinois. Interestingly, the superintendents of the schools for the deaf were ordained clergy while the superintendents for children with visual or mental problems were physicians. In both cases, though, the schools were boarding institutions. Although all these institutions received state aid, many took support from private donations and endowments.[74]

Systematic instruction of the children suffering from disabilities of hearing, vision, or thinking began in France, and teachers from the United States went to France to learn the techniques. Once these teachers returned, they set up schools that received international acclaim. For example, Dr. Samuel G. Howe returned from his studies in Europe to open a school to help six pupils with vision difficulties. As his school grew, his pupils gave public demonstrations of their accomplishments, and other schools opened to follow his methods. Thus, by 1899, there were about forty schools for children with vision difficulties in the United States. Every state made some provision for the education of the visually impaired, and total enrollments of blind students were about 3,600.[75]

Howe's efforts became famous. In 1842, Charles Dickens visited Howe's Perkins Institution and Massachusetts Asylum for the Blind. With effusive praise, Dickens claimed the success of Howe's school showed the superiority of publicly funded institutions over privately funded ones. In England, on the one hand, such institutions were the products of private philanthropy that placed the schools' financial support on the unreliable dispositions of a few wealthy individuals who could require foolish practices or ruin a school in a moment of unreasonable anger. On the other hand, in Massachusetts, Dickens found an orderly, clean, comfortable establishment. He was most impressed with the children who had profited from Howe's instruction. One of these students, Laura Bridgman, could neither hear nor see; yet, Dickens found her to be a merry, cheerful girl who communicated with a finger alphabet.[76]

In 1887, Helen Keller's accomplishments brought praise to Howe's school. Keller's teacher, Ann Sullivan, followed the methods Howe had used in teaching Laura Bridgman. When Keller was sixteen, she had progressed enough to enter Cambridge school for girls. A year later, she entered Radcliffe College. When she graduated, educators praised her as a genius.[77]

Stories such as those of Helen Keller fueled the movement to increase the education of those people called blind, deaf, and feebleminded. In 1878, a census proclaimed that the nearly 3,000 graduates of schools for the blind held jobs as teachers, piano tuners, storekeepers, and housekeepers. According to advocates for these schools, such statistics showed that increased efforts in education would save public monies. In 1880, the U.S. Census reported that almost 50,000 blind people lived in the United States and about 2,500 had been committed to almshouses. According to advocates, education would keep blind people from becoming public charges.[78]

How Did the Resistance to Annual Examinations of Elementary Pupils Enhance the Growth of Higher Education?

As the movement to expand and control education continued, resistance developed against two important reforms. The first concern was that efforts to expand systems of education to include high schools served few students and consumed resources better devoted to the lower social classes. The second concern was the extent to which graded schools depended on examinations to determine the proper placement of pupils. Ironically, educators asserted that the solution was to expand both tendencies.

In the first case, during the last part of the nineteenth century, public high schools began to replace private academies for advanced education. Actually, few states developed systems of higher education during the nineteenth century. According to reports from the U.S. Bureau of Education, Massachusetts was the most advanced. In 1896, the total taxes paid to support schools in the state reached about $12 million, of which about 20 percent went to high schools.[79]

The earliest example of state organization began in 1784 with the creation of the University of the State of New York. Following the model of France, a board of regents directed the university and their control extended to the secondary education in the state.

By 1898, New York had a system that allotted a portion of state money to each high school for each day's attendance by each student who had earned a preliminary certificate from the regents of the University of the State of New York. In addition, the state paid increased amounts according to the number of students who passed the regent's examination. In 1865, Maryland swept away a system of academies and replaced them with public high schools supported by county boards of education. In 1872, the state required that a county examiner and an instructor from the state normal school visit and inspect the high schools. In 1875, Wisconsin approved legislation allowing towns to merge to build high schools and support them through local taxation combined with some state aid.[80]

In most states, the creation of high schools was slow because they depended on concentrations of population, the schools were expensive, and they educated a small percentage of the students in any city. At the same time, some critics complained that colleges dominated the high school curriculums. Although few students advanced past high school, the colleges turned to high schools for students as academies diminished in popularity.[81]

Controversies over high schools increased as school districts opened public schools. For example, in 1873, citizens of Kalamazoo, Michigan, sued in state court to restrain the school board from levying taxes to support the local high school. In 1874, the Michigan Supreme Court heard an appeal and decided that the school board had the authority to decide how to organize the high schools once voters had agreed to open them. Although Jurgen Herbst contended that this decision provided the legal basis for the high school's place as a connecting link from the common school to the university, he acknowledged that complaints against high schools continued. In 1875, a superintendent of schools of Illinois, S. M. Etter, opposed building high schools and asserted that no board should sacrifice the interests of the large numbers of students in common schools for the few students who would profit from high schools. This resistance was short lived. By 1881, the Illinois supreme court rendered decisions that made high schools a legitimate part of the state public school system.[82]

Once high schools became part of the public schools, communities celebrated with elaborate designs of buildings. In the 1880s, in Ohio, school districts competed with each other to build the most attractive high school. The relatively small city of Newark built in 1885 one of the smaller high schools. About 100 feet square, the high school reached 106 feet to the top of a tower. Heated by steam, lit by gas, it had water connections to every room. There were four classrooms on each of the four floors and two large gymnasiums for physical exercise. In the same year, Akron opened a more elaborate building in Richardson Romanesque architecture with sandstone and terra cotta trim around doorway and window arches. The 160-foot entrance tower held a 2,000-pound bell and a clock with illuminated dials. On the main floor, there were eight classrooms. On the second floor, there was an assembly hall with 650 opera chairs. The building featured oak woodwork, bronze hardware, and floors of hard maple. In an apparent effort to appeal to civic pride, the Ohio legislature passed laws allowing boards of education to open or rent the high school buildings for literary entertainments, school exhibitions, singing schools, or religious exercises.[83]

Despite the official view that high schools provided a link to the colleges, the U.S. Commissioner of Education complained in 1897 that, in many states, there was little difference between high schools and colleges. Repeating the commissioner's remarks, another commentator added that more than half of the so-called colleges offered educations equivalent to those from high schools. Moreover, few people went on to college. In 1897, according to the U.S. Bureau of Education, when the total population was nearly 71 million people, the total enrollment in U.S. colleges and universities was about 85,000 students, of whom about 53,000 were men. Of these college and university students, about 70 percent attended institutions in the northeastern and north-central portions of the United States. This may have been because, at the time, these sections of the U.S. contained about 65 percent of the total population.[84]

In general, college officials conducted examinations covering material the college instructors prescribed to determine which students to admit. Although this should have compelled the high schools to present rigorous courses, the effect was to turn many high school courses into cramming sessions. Teachers concerned themselves less with problems of general education and sought to determine the nature and extent of the exams. To reduce problems associated with entrance examinations for colleges, the University of Michigan introduced a system in 1871 to admit students who had graduated from approved secondary schools and received a recommendation from the principal of the high school. By 1896, about 150 other universities across the United States adopted similar systems of accreditation.[85]

To accredit a high school, a group of university professors inspected the school to verify that the instruction was effective and intelligent. Some universities conducted rigorous investigations of the schools whereas others made cursory examinations. The University of California appointed a committee from the academic senate to coordinate the high school visits. Each year, instructors from various departments visited the high schools at the expense of the university to evaluate the teaching practices. The hope was that because the professors from the college performed the investigations of the high school teachers, they would make definite suggestions to improve the high school instruction. Released from definite examinations, the high school teachers could think about ways to improve education.[86]

Despite the benefits of the accreditation system, the effort cost universities considerable expense in money and time for the professors. More important, the investigations could not cover all high school departments equally well as investigators overlooked many areas of study in the high schools. Finally, the accreditation did not free high schools from the domination of colleges. Instead of considering the fundamental purposes of a high school education, the teachers in high schools using these systems of accreditation shaped their curriculums to match the entrance requirements of the colleges. In this way, they received the accreditation allowing their graduates to proceed to higher education.[87]

Another effort to reduce the difficulties of transition from high school to college began in New England when secondary school teachers formed an association in 1885 that recommended material in ancient and modern languages and literature that students should master in high school. Other, similar associations grew up in some middle states—Ohio, Tennessee, and Colorado. Meanwhile, the NEA sought to create requirements that were uniform across the nation for matriculation from high school to college.[88]

In 1892, the NEA appointed prestigious educators to the Committee of Ten and charged them to determine what subject matters high schools should cover and how extensive the coverage should be. Made up of nine subcommittees of ten members each, the committee considered such areas as ancient and modern languages, mathematics, physics and chemistry, history, and geography. Although the committee offered examples of four sample programs, some educators claimed these were of less value than the principles that led to the creation of the programs. For example, the committee of ten contended that all students, whether going to college or not, should pursue the four main lines of academic subject areas: language, mathematics, history, and natural history. In addition, the committee offered suggestions that unified the subjects and correlated them to each other. More important, the committee recommended that students should encounter all of the principal fields of knowledge during the first two years of high school in hopes that they would exhibit their abilities and develop their interests. In the last two years, students could specialize. Finally, the Committee of Ten recommended that colleges should accept applicants who passed through any of the suggested courses no matter what specialization the students followed.[89]

Although critics complained that higher education drained resources better spent on elementary schools, educators sought to create ways that the advanced training available in the high schools served the lower schools, one way of which was to direct higher education toward teacher preparation. Thus, by 1897 in Massachusetts, candidates for admission into the normal schools for teacher training had to be graduates of approved high schools. Although some other state normal schools followed the Massachusetts example, many states required less training for admission. The common standard was no more than two years of high school study to enter a normal school. Consequently, by the end of the nineteenth century, most of the high school students were women from the middle and upper classes who wanted to become teachers.[90]

In addition to making high school training necessary for admission into teacher training programs, educators sought to use certification or licensing laws to increase teacher qualifications. In 1898, the NEA undertook an investigation into the requirements for teacher certification in the various states. The investigators found that Massachusetts had no state system. Instead, each of the 353 school districts in the state set its own standards for issuing a teaching license that was valid in that district alone. Many other states issued certificates to the graduates of the liberal arts state university provided they took courses in pedagogy. Although these state certificates were valid across the state that issued them, they were not valid in different states. Despite the committee's acknowledgement that schools should be local institutions, the members recommended that all states approve statewide procedures granting licenses to college graduates who had studied pedagogy. Such centralization would remove many inconveniences for teachers who had to retake teaching examinations when they moved to a new school, and it would make teacher preparation more reasonable.[91]

The tendency of universities to include teacher training had begun as early as 1874 when the University of Michigan found that many of its graduates went to work managing large schools. Therefore, the administration concluded that lectures or studies in the art of teaching and the management of schools would help them with these duties. In line with this decision, the university established a chair in the science and art of teaching. It offered courses in comparative studies of educational systems, school supervision, and the history of education. Academic departments within the university, such as Latin, mathematics, and history, began to show university students how to teach the material. Other colleges followed Michigan's example.[92]

To many educators, increased educational qualifications of teachers would lead to the improvement of elementary schools. For example, writing in 1875, the superintendent of schools in Columbus, Ohio, contended that all opposition to the public graded school had disappeared. The institution had become so popular that people attended public examinations of the students and praised the results. He added that the system depended on two factors. The first was the qualifications of the teachers. In this case, the hope was that well-trained teachers would use better methods of instruction. The second factor was the classification of the students that enabled the school to divide into grades. In this second case, examinations were an important tool. Each year, the students took five to eight examinations in addition to an annual examination to qualify for promotion or transfer. According to the Columbus superintendent, in the 1860s, teachers averaged the students' daily recitations to decide whether to promote a student, whereas by 1875, Ohio schools gave several examinations during the year and an annual examination at the end of the year using questions written by the superintendents or their appointees.[93]

The change to annual districtwide examinations enjoyed popularity because it promised uniformity in instruction. In 1891, the U.S. Bureau of Education published a circular of information about the use of examinations in graded schools. Written by Emerson E. White from reports sent to the bureau by superintendents in seventy cities across the United States, the report contained information from such cities as Boston, Massachusetts; Cincinnati, Ohio; Denver, Colorado; Galveston, Texas; Los Angeles, California; and Wheeling, West Virginia. Most of these cities offered twelve years of public schooling divided into three equal periods. The primary school included grades one to four. Grades five through eight comprised the intermediate or grammar school, and the high school occupied the last four grades. Although in most cities these divisions occupied different buildings, some large cities, such as Wheeling, retained the high school grades in the district schools.[94]

Most cities required the pupils to move together annually from one grade to another. White complained that this system reduced the bright students to the level of the mediocre. He believed that more frequent reclassification of students might have offered capable students more opportunities to excel. Nonetheless, he acknowledged difficulties in arranging transitions more frequently. For example, rapid changes demanded more frequent examinations and shifting students to new teachers. Most important, students withdrew frequently from these classes. As a result, on average in all the cities, of the students who entered the first grade, about 60 percent passed on to the sixth grade and about 15 percent entered the ninth grade. About 5 percent of the students who entered first grade completed the twelfth grade. With such a high proportion of withdrawals, the schools consolidated classes and placed students in front of teachers who covered different materials. Although schools found it awkward to reclassify students after one term or less, White found the practice to be valuable for elementary schools.[95]

According to White, the biggest problem was that most cities based promotion decisions on the results of annual examinations given across grade levels. In some cases, newspapers published reports of student performance on these exams, and many boards of education and citizens considered the performances to be measures of the efficiency of the school or teacher. Consequently, under the pressure to have students perform adequately, the teachers reduced instruction to helping the students pass the exams. Teachers collected examples of tests used in previous years, drilled their students in answering these specific questions, and thereby enabled many students to pass with high marks because many districts used questions for more than one year. In addition, cheating became rampart because students could read each other's papers in the small classrooms, and some teachers chose not to interfere.[96]

If uniform examinations to decide promotions reduced teaching to drills, increased qualifications of teachers might improve schools. Not surprisingly, when White considered the solution to the problems posed by the exams, he recommended that schools depend on the reports of teachers about the work of the students to make decisions about promotion. It was easier to trust teachers who were well trained. White contended that teachers did not need to complete such markings daily. Weekly or monthly averages would suffice. He believed that such regular assessments discouraged biased reporting, and they offered parents opportunities to help their children remediate deficiencies before it was too late.[97]

Conclusion

After the industrial North defeated the agricultural South in the American Civil War, various groups tried to build systems of management that were appropriate to the new social problems. Members of the Republican Party believed that public schools would help people recognize the necessary changes. Unfortunately, their vision of democracy conflicted with another more traditional system of local control. To overcome this conflict, Republicans attacked the Catholic Church as an institution that weakened parishioners' patriotic feelings. Ironically, in this battle, the Republicans fought against a group that shared a similar conception of education as a social benefit. The Catholic clergy who sought to enlist public school officials in cooperative plans shared such a vision.

After the failure of the Republican campaign, educators realized the nation faced a set of changing social circumstances. They claimed that schools could help people adjust to these new developments. One effort was to spread uniform conceptions of education across the country. Since educators wanted to avoid the use of federal authority to force local schools to follow a prescribed curriculum, they formed a national association of educators to spread information about education through annual meetings and publications and they encouraged the creation of a federal office of education to amass the information that the national organization could disperse. The hope was that local administrators would use their authority wisely and follow the recommendations of nationally prominent educators.

To meet the needs of many different people, schools expanded their curriculums to include manual training for vocational preparation, the kindergarten movement to inspire children's spiritual growth, and the education of children called "defective." Unfortunately, as large numbers of children enrolled in public schools, instruction became excessively mechanical in nature. Many educators believed that continued growth of the system would solve the problems created by the expansion of education. They called for special classes in high schools and universities to train teachers to avoid overly mechanical methods of instruction and evaluation.

Thus, as Americans confronted the need to open isolated communities to wider national control, educators tried to introduce uniform procedures of school organization, curriculum development, and academic assessment. Seeking to avoid federal imposition, educators formed national organizations to spread ideas of appropriate changes among local school districts. Thus, they sought a new definition of democracy that maintained the localism of previous models but put new emphasis on a nationwide consensus. The hope of blending localism with nationalism proved futile as nationwide changes became increasingly more reasonable. By the end of the twentieth century, worldwide reforms seemed essential, thereby making national changes appear provincial.

Endnotes

1. Robert H. Wiebe, *The Search for Order, 1877–1920* (New York: Hill and Wang, 1967), xiii–xiv.
2. Ward M. McAfee, *Religion, Race, and Reconstruction: The Public School in the Politics of the 1870s* (Albany: State University of New York Press, 1998), 1–7.
3. McAfee, *Religion, Race, and Reconstruction,* 161–163.
4. McAfee, *Religion, Race, and Reconstruction,* 152–173.
5. McAfee, *Religion, Race, and Reconstruction,* 220–222.
6. Neil Gerard McCluskey, *Public Schools and Moral Education: The Influence of Horace Mann, William Torrey Harris and John Dewey* (New York: Columbia University Press, 1958), 145–160.
7. William T. Harris, *How to Teach Natural Science in Public Schools* (Syracuse, N.Y.: C. W. Bardeen, Publisher, 1895), 9–11.
8. John Eaton, "Letter," in *Statement of the Theory of Education in the United States as Approved by Many Leading Educators*, Duane Doty and W. T. Harris (Washington, D.C.: Government Printing Office, 1874).
9. Duane Doty and W. T. Harris, *Statement of the Theory of Education in the United States as Approved by Many Leading Educators* (Washington, D.C.: Government Printing Office, 1874), 9–13.
10. Doty and Harris, *Statement of the Theory of Education,* 12–14.
11. Doty and Harris, *Statement of the Theory of Education,* 15–16.
12. Doty and Harris, *Statement of the Theory of Education,* 16–17.
13. Doty and Harris, *Statement of the Theory of Education,* 17–19.
14. Doty and Harris, *Statement of the Theory of Education,* 18.
15. Doty and Harris, *Statement of the Theory of Education,* 18.
16. Vincent Lannie, "The End is the Beginning," in *Enlightening the Next Generation: Catholics and Their Schools, 1830–1980,* ed. F. Michael Perko, S.J. (New York: Garland Publishing, 1988), 245–258.
17. Timothy Walch, *Parish School: American Parochial Education from Colonial Times to the Present* (New York: Crossroads Publishing, 1996), 1–2.
18. Harold A. Buetow, *Of Singular Benefit: The Story of Catholic Education in the United States* (New York: Macmillan Co., 1970), 170–175.
19. Brian C. Mitchell, *The Paddy Camps: The Irish of Lowell, 1821–1861* (Urbana: University of Illinois Press, 1988), 50–52.
20. Mitchell, *The Paddy Camps,* 52.
21. Mitchell, *The Paddy Camps,* 113–115.
22. Mitchell, *The Paddy Camps,* 116–117.
23. Mitchell, *The Paddy Camps,* 60–65, 113–117.
24. Michael V. Gannon, *Rebel Bishop: The Life and Era of Augustin Verot* (Milwaukee: Bruce Publishing Co., 1964), 170–173.
25. Gannon, *Rebel Bishop,* 169–170, 174.
26. Gannon, *Rebel Bishop,* 182–191.
27. Clyde and Sally Griffen, *Natives and Newcomers: The Ordering of Opportunity in Mid-Nineteenth-Century Poughkeepsie* (Cambridge, Mass.: Harvard University Press, 1978), 27–28.
28. Griffen and Griffen, *Natives and Newcomers,* 28–29.
29. Griffen and Griffen, *Natives and Newcomers,* 28–29.
30. Walch, *Parish School,* 58–61.
31. John Ireland, "State Schools and Parish Schools," in *Catholic Education in America: A Documentary History,* ed. Neil G. McCluskey, S.J. (New York: Teachers College Bureau of Publications, 1964), 127–140.
32. McCluskey, *Catholic Education,* 141, 151–152, 161; Walch, *Parish School,* 90–99.

33. Walch, *Parish School,* 134–151.
34. Edgar B. Wesley, *NEA: The First Hundred Years* (New York: Harper and Brothers, 1957), 18–19.
35. Wesley, *NEA*, 20–24.
36. Wesley, *NEA*, 48–49; Donald R. Warren, *To Enforce Education: A History of the Founding Years of the United States Office of Education* (Detroit: Wayne State University Press, 1974), 52–54, 90–91.
37. Warren, *To Enforce Education,* 97.
38. Warren, *To Enforce Education,* 96.
39. Warren, *To Enforce Education,* 49–54.
40. Edith Nye MacMullen, *In the Cause of True Education: Henry Barnard and Nineteenth Century School Reform* (New Haven: Yale University Press, 1991), 259–279.
41. Darrell Hevenor Smith, *The Bureau of Education: Its History, Activities, and Organization* (Baltimore: Johns Hopkins Press, 1923), 4.
42. Wesley, *NEA*, 44.
43. Warren, *To Enforce Education,* 151–161.
44. Warren, *To Enforce Education,* 161–165.
45. Harry Kursh, *The United States Office of Education: A Century of Service* (Philadelphia: Chilton Books, 1965), 17–18.
46. Kenneth R. Johnson, "N. H. R. Johnson: United States Commissioner of Education," *History of Education Quarterly* 11, no. 2 (Summer 1971): 174–183.
47. Warren, *To Enforce Education,* 169–170.
48. Smith, *The Bureau of Education,* 20–21.
49. Wesley, *NEA*, 244–245.
50. Warren, *To Enforce Education,* 170–171.
51. Kurt F. Leidecker, *Yankee Teacher: The Life of William Torrey Harris* (New York: The Philosophical Library, 1946), 253–259.
52. Lawrence A. Cremin, *American Education: The Metropolitan Experience, 1876–1980* (New York: Harper and Row, 1988), 158–159.
53. William T. Harris, *The Theory of Education* (Syracuse, N.Y.: C. W. Bardeen, 1893), 12–13.
54. Harris, *The Theory of Education,* 13–40.
55. Harris, *The Theory of Education,* 41–47.
56. Harris, *The Theory of Education,* 47–54.
57. Andrew Sloane Draper, "Educational Organization and Administration," in *Monographs on Education in the United States,* ed. Nicholas Murray Butler (Albany, N.Y.: J. B. Lyons Co., 1900), 25.
58. Eli Tappan, "School Legislation," in *A History of Education in the State of Ohio: A Centennial Volume,* by Ohio Education Association, Centennial Committee, (Columbus, Ohio: Gazette Printing House, 1874), 70–79.
59. R. W. Stevenson, "Graded Schools," in *A History of Education in the State of Ohio: A Centennial Volume,* by Ohio Education Association, Centennial Committee, (Columbus, Ohio: Gazette Printing House, 1874), 118–121.
60. Draper, "Educational Organization and Administration," 19–21.
61. Draper, "Educational Organization and Administration," 30.
62. William T. Harris, "Elementary Education," in *Monographs on Education in the United States,* ed. Nicholas Murray Butler (Albany, N.Y.: J. B. Lyons Co., 1900), 98–99.
63. Harris, "Elementary Education," 52–53, 79–81.
64. Harris, "Elementary Education," 15–18.
65. Harris, "Elementary Education," 33–37.
66. Cremin, *American Education: The Metropolitan Experience,* 223–224.
67. Caroline Winterer, "Avoiding a 'Hothouse System of Education': Nineteenth-Century Early Childhood Education from Infant Schools to the Kindergartens," *History of Education Quarterly* 32, no. 3 (Fall 1992): 289–314.
68. Barbara Beatty, *Preschool Education in America: The Culture of Young Children from the Colonial Era to the Present* (New Haven: Yale University Press, 1995), 53–55.
69. Winterer, "Avoiding a 'Hothouse,' " 289–314.
70. William T. Harris, *The Kindergarten Methods Contrasted with the Methods of the American Primary School* (NEA, 1889), 3–4.
71. Harris, *The Kindergarten Methods,* 5–7.
72. Harris, *The Kindergarten Methods,* 8–9.
73. Harris, *The Kindergarten Methods,* 10–12.
74. Edward Ellis Allen, "Education of Defectives," in *Monographs on Education in the United States,* ed. Nicholas Murray Butler (Albany, N.Y.: J. B. Lyons Co., 1899), 1–5.
75. Allen, "Education of Defectives," 18–28, 47.
76. Charles Dickens, *American Notes* (Gloucester, Mass.: Peter Smith, 1968), 43–61.
77. Allen, "Education of Defectives," 32–36.
78. Allen, "Education of Defectives," 28–29.
79. Elmer Ellsworth Brown, "Secondary Education," in *Monographs on Education in the United States,* ed. Nicholas Murray Butler (Albany, N.Y.: J. B. Lyons Co., 1899), 191–192.
80. Brown, "Secondary Education," 150–152, 192–197.
81. William J. Reese, *America's Public Schools: From the Common School to "No Child Left Behind"* (Baltimore: Johns Hopkins University Press, 2005), 62–63.
82. Jurgen Herbst, *The Once and Future School: Three Hundred and Fifty Years of American Secondary*

Education (New York: Routledge, 1996), 62–64, 75–76.

83. Virginia E. McCormick, *Educational Architecture in Ohio: From One-Room Schools and Carnegie Libraries to Community Education Villages* (Kent, Ohio: Kent State University Press, 2001), 89–92.
84. Andrew Fleming West, "The American College," in *Monographs on Education in the United States,* ed. Nicholas Murray Butler (Albany, N.Y.: J. B. Lyons Co., 1899), 239–241.
85. Brown, "Secondary Education," 165–168.
86. Brown, "Secondary Education," 166–167.
87. Brown, "Secondary Education," 167–168.
88. Brown, "Secondary Education," 168–169.
89. Brown, "Secondary Education," 169–172.
90. Reese, *America's Public Schools,* 62–63; B. A. Hinsdale, "The Training of Teachers," in *Monographs on Education in the United States,* ed. Nicholas Murray Butler (Albany, N.Y.: J. B. Lyons Co., 1899), 371–372.
91. B.A. Hinsdale, Charles De Garmo, and Elmer Brown, "The Certification of College and University Graduates as Teachers in the Public Schools," *School Review* 7, no. 6 (June 1899): 331–371.
92. Hinsdale, "The Training of Teachers," 392–399.
93. Stevenson, "Graded Schools," 121–126.
94. Emerson E. White, *Promotions and Examinations in Graded Schools* (Washington, D.C.: Government Printing Office, 1891), 7–12.
95. White, *Promotions and Examinations,* 13–21.
96. White, *Promotions and Examinations,* 28–37.
97. White, *Promotions and Examinations,* 50–51.

8

The Growth of Bureaucratic Organizations

Large early twentieth century classroom

From the American Civil War until 1890, industries grew and the United States reached across the continent. Although the rapid expansion of business promised increased prosperity, it unsettled many occupations, exposed consumers to tainted processed foods, and destroyed considerable portions of the wilderness. As a result, from 1890 until 1917, a period often called the Progressive Era, reformers such as Theodore Roosevelt, Woodrow

Wilson, John Peter Atgeld, Eugene V. Debs, Jacob Riis, Jane Addams, and Robert La Follette sought to protect the public and the common good through rational planning. At the same time, educators applied similar patterns of reform to improve schools. Although the progressive reformers and the educators hoped that reasonable mechanisms could ameliorate the problems resulting from the rapid transformation of the nation from a rural to an urban one, they created bureaucracies that seemed to operate independently of human control.[1]

The men who created trusts during the 1880s, such as John D. Rockefeller and J. P. Morgan, wanted to bring order, predictability, and control to production and distribution. They believed the way to accomplish this end was to consolidate widespread but related businesses into enormous corporations. Because the result was to be steady profits, consolidation was not enough. In the large corporations such as U.S. Steel, managers had to organize the flow of materials, arrange production schedules, and coordinate shipping schedules. At each point, management had to have accurate information about cost in order to ensure that adequate profits resulted.[2]

The efforts of large businesses to consolidate and control production succeeded beyond expectation. Rockefeller came to control nearly every aspect of the refining, distribution, and sale of oil. U.S. Steel defeated workers' efforts to form unions and protect their jobs by introducing methods of production that did not require skilled labor. Profits increased, and the managers improved production, thereby providing more goods for the public.[3]

According to Steven J. Diner, in the 1890s, people in the United States turned to the federal government to restrain the giant corporations that had usurped the economic importance of workers, small entrepreneurs, and farmers. Large corporations such as U.S. Steel employed efficient methods of production that rendered workers increasingly replaceable, enabling the companies to lower wages and increase profits. Railroads and grain elevators could charge owners of small businesses and farmers high prices for transporting their products. In 1887, with the creation of the Interstate Commerce Commission and, in 1890, with the Sherman Antitrust Act, the federal government began to respond. Unfortunately, most official efforts were ineffectual.[4]

Although people wanted to control the trusts, many Americans admired the success that large corporations enjoyed. As a result, many reformers hoped that the mechanisms that enabled the large corporations to flourish could solve the social problems that the development of large corporations had created. This hope was ironic because the effect was to expand bureaucratic ways of thinking rather than to enhance democracy.

In fairness, the progressive movement was not original in hoping that bureaucratic techniques could reinforce democratic ideals. According to John Higham, the progressive hopes were part of longer process. Antebellum authors of success literature depicted personal advancement as a reward for controlling moral flaws. As the nineteenth century progressed, such morality tales changed. Higham pointed out that after the war, authors tended to portray success as the result of the protagonist's efforts to overcome external barriers. In this way, utilitarian techniques replaced ethical ideals as the important variables in the control of human affairs. Thus, Higham noted, it was not difficult for people to look to scientists to discover improved methods of arranging society to eradicate social injustices.[5]

Although Higham did not explain how the effort to solve human problems through rational means overthrew more democratic methods of directing social institutions, David B. Tyack claimed that the changes that took place during the Progressive Era, especially in urban schools, resulted from business leaders and experts forming conspiracies to wrest the control of schools from community members. Labeling some educational reformers as administrative progressives, Tyack complained that these educators created an interlocking directorate of experts who imposed a blueprint for reform on all schools. Tyack claimed that, by 1913, when officials in school districts wrote to professional educators seeking the names of experts to conduct school surveys making recommendations for improvement, they received recommendations to contact such prominent administrators as Ellwood P. Cubberley, Paul Hanus, Charles H. Judd, or Edward Thorndike. These were college professors who worked to make education a science.[6]

Tyack contended that the blueprint of reform for the administrative progressives followed the model of business corporations. The school board acted like the board of directors in a firm. It was made up of few members who had been elected at large by the all the voters in the city rather than within particular wards in the city, and the superintendent, who was trained in educational management, acted as a chief executive in carrying out the policies set by the board.[7]

Although the rationale for separating schools from particular wards was to reduce partisan politics, Tyack claimed that this pattern of reform represented as much a partisan view as the former ward based model. Tyack argued that organizing schools by wards allowed people to select board members and teachers from their neighborhoods. In this way, the ward schools functioned in the way that district schools had operated in rural settings with the voters in each ward in the city controlling their own schools. Tyack's complaint was that, because voters in the entire city elected the central school board members, a different group of people took control of school affairs. Although the reformers hoped that men of talent would take the positions of decision making, Tyack argued that the effect of the reforms was to reduce the possibility of minority groups controlling their own schools. Because the men of talent admired by the reformers tended to be successful business leaders, Tyack added that the slogans administrative progressives used, such as "keep the schools out of politics," disguised the transfer of power that took place.[8]

Other historians disagreed with Tyack. For example, when Paul Peterson surveyed the actions of superintendents in Atlanta, Chicago, and San Francisco during the opening years of the twentieth century, he found the superintendents to have been at odds with a range of groups that included business leaders, trade unionists, and conservative elites as well as the machine politicians and ethnic groups. Thus, Peterson claimed that the different groups were not simply supporters of educational administrators or their opponents as Tyack asserted. According to Peterson, the Progressive Era administrators undertook manysided efforts to use schools to improve the lives of individuals. Peterson added that because the administrators' efforts differed in various cities, changed in different contexts, and varied among several issues, they could not create a closed directorate whose members followed a simple blueprint for reform.[9]

Jacques Ellul suggested a way to accommodate Tyack's argument with Peterson's observations. Ellul contended that the social techniques adopted by the progressive reformers could not reinforce human values because the reformers had accepted efficiency as the primary value. According to Ellul, people in the United States during the nineteenth century began to apply rational techniques to solve complicated problems more than did people in other nations. This was possible, Ellul added, because the United States had a flexible social milieu with citizens who valued efficiency more than tradition. With such openness to innovation, people could search for the best way to accomplish any task. Unfortunately, when people focused on technical considerations, the drive for efficiency replaced other concerns. Consequently, any sort of ideal, such as local control, had to give way to any method that promised improved performance. For example, proponents of such methods as city planning promised that technical considerations, such as proper zoning, would serve moral ends. Ellul contended that the concerns about such efforts as housing regulations expanded to the point where the desire to organize the city became the moral quest. As a result, experts did not have to form a conspiracy to impose their ideas on other groups; the process of organizing bureaucracies augmented itself even when different people applied it to a variety of problems.[10]

Following Ellul's argument, the reformers' efforts to improve urban life led to consolidating small municipalities into large metropolises, removing the control of the cities from political processes, and seeking to solve problems through the objective collection of information through surveys. Not surprisingly, school people followed the same processes. They centralized the control of schools, placing the administration in the hands of appointed administrators and insulating them from political processes. Once freed from political influences, the administrators sought qualified teachers who would use improved methods of instruction. Finally, administrators depended on surveys to collect objective information about the schools and the need to broaden the curriculum. Thus, both improving city management and enhancing education demonstrated Ellul's belief in the self-augmenting nature of such rational solutions as bureaucracy. Each step toward more rational organization posed more difficulties that increased organization might solve.

Because these changes took place across the nation, this chapter will not focus on a particular region. Chapter 7, as well as this chapter, and those that follow, seek to explain the general concerns administrators faced across the United States. In this chapter, the following sections explain how the effort to solve the problems of bureaucratic organizations moved by its own logic and thereby affected schools everywhere.

How Did Urban Reform Encourage the Growth of Bureaucracies?

According to U.S. census statistics, the nineteenth century was a period of rapid urban growth in the United States. For example, from 1860 to 1920, the U.S. population tripled in size from 31 million to 105 million inhabitants whereas the urban population increased nine times from 6 million to 54 million. As a result, in 1920, more than half the population lived in cities, making the United States an urban nation.[11]

Although the census considered any town with 2,500 residents to be a city, large cities grew larger and more cities became large cities. In 1860, nine cities had populations of 100,000 or more; however, by 1920, sixty-eight cities had populations of 100,000 or more. Further, by 1920, about half of the 54 million urban dwellers lived in cities of 100,000 or more inhabitants. Furthermore, the industrial core that supported most of the cities in the United States stretched from Massachusetts southward to Maryland and westward to Illinois, southern Wisconsin, and eastern Missouri. This region continued to be the industrial and urban anchor of the United States until 1920, despite the growth of cities in the West and on the Pacific Coast. For example, Los Angeles was a city of 5,700 in 1870. It doubled in size by 1880, and doubled again within a decade. By 1920, Los Angeles contained over 500,000 inhabitants.[12]

Three factors led to the increase in the size of cities, including immigration from abroad, immigration from within the United States, and the amalgamation of municipalities into large cities.

The first factor that brought about the growth of many cities was immigration from abroad. For example, during the 1880s, a heavy flow of immigrants from Russia, Poland, Austria-Hungary, the Balkans, and Italy settled into the larger cities of Boston, New York, and Chicago. Consequently, by 1900, the total population of the United States was about 76 million people and nearly 10 million of these had been born in Europe.[13]

A second factor in the growth of cities was immigration from within the United States. In describing why people left rural areas and entered the rapidly growing cities, Arthur M. Schlesinger described the town of Xenia, Ohio, which in 1890 had about 8,000 inhabitants. It was a prosperous agricultural community with eight churches boasting steeples, a single police officer, schools, a newspaper, and a YMCA. Despite the apparent comfort, Xenia was too small for the young people who continually drifted to larger cities. Thus, nearby Columbus, Ohio, grew nearly 80 percent from 1880 to 1890. In the same time, Chicago grew from 500,000 to more than a million inhabitants, becoming the second largest city in the United States. Because the immigration moved from farms to cities, twelve of the fifty principal cities in the United States in 1890 were in the Midwest.[14]

According to Schlesinger, there were several reasons why people moved to the cities. In part, national land policy drove farmers off their lands because it forced them to live in solitude. In 1785, Thomas Jefferson and his committee had rejected the New England system of farm communities in the Ordinance of 1785 in preference for large, scattered individual holdings. In 1862, the Homestead Act had reinforced this concept of isolated individual farms. Thus, in sections of Minnesota and Wisconsin, families lived out of sight of other homes and lacked even such meetings that mail deliveries might offer. The cheerlessness and hardships of such life may have contributed to an abnormally high rate of mental illness, but many communities brightened life with infrequent but regular community diversions such as picnics, dances, and church services. Nonetheless, according to Schlesinger, cities attracted young people to the light and heat of civilization away from the loneliness of rural life.[15]

A third factor causing some cities to grow was amalgamation. The most important case is New York City. In 1898, the New York legislature created Greater New York by uniting Manhattan, Brooklyn, Queens County, Staten Island, and the Bronx. In all, the merger joined ninety-six governmental units into a city of over 3.5 million people. This was double the size of Chicago. Only London in Great Britain was larger. The legislature consolidated the cities because New York's share of foreign commerce had dropped and merchants believed that a reorganization of the port district and the transportation lines through the country would increase efficiency. At the same time, the chaotic growth of the business district and resulting transportation problems led New Yorkers to believe that coordinated planning could solve problems of water distribution, reduce pollution, and prevent fire hazards.[16]

As the creation of New York City indicated, rational and centralized planning promised to control the seemingly bewildering growth of human institutions because policy makers could apply objective techniques of management to large metropolises in ways that served democratic ideals. In the early nineteenth century, cities had grown chaotically. The idea of city planning grew as civic leaders tried to exert control of the environment on behalf of residents. From such initial efforts as the creation of New York's Central Park in the 1850s to the establishment of the first metropolitan park system around Boston, city planning grew into a discipline that by 1909 supported a National Conference on City Planning. In 1916, D. Appleton and Company published the first book on city planning. Whereas the British turned city planning to the creation of low-density suburban estates, experts in the United States created comprehensive plans that integrated the various aspects of city life into integrated wholes. Most important, in the United States, an office within the municipal government was to oversee the development of the city on a permanent and continuing basis.[17]

Because the effort to manage the city's development in a rational manner aggravated conflicts between the desires of individuals and the needs of the society, city planners sought to take the politics out of city government in hopes that unbiased deliberation would solve those conflicts. Thus, in 1894, the City Clubs of New York and Philadelphia called a national conference on good government. Convinced that established political machines made public administration impossible, attendees to the conference formed the National Conference on Good Government that became the National Municipal League. According to the members, the way to change the structure of city governments was for cities to adopt what they called a strong mayor plan. Under this model, the mayor appointed trained technicians to head departments and conduct civic affairs in businesslike ways.[18]

The strong mayor plan was popular because it promised to run the city as if it was a business. Another proposal, the city manager model, more closely aligned itself with business practices because the power was concentrated in a small city commission with members, elected at large, each of whom became the head of a city department. By 1911, more than 160 cities used this form of city government.[19]

The city of Stauton, Virginia, developed a new twist on the city commission idea in 1908. Called the city manager plan, this model had the commissioners serve as part-time elected officials. In turn, the commissioners appointed a full-time city manager to carry out the commission's policies and to supervise the various departments. Thus, the city manager acted as the president, or chief executive officer, of a business firm and the commissioners oversaw the actions of the manager and filled the advisory roles of the board of trustees. Supported by such progressive figures as Woodrow Wilson and Charles Beard, the city manager plan appeared in eleven cities by 1911, and Dayton, Ohio, was the first large city to adopt it in 1914. From 1918 to 1923, the period of the most rapid growth for the model, the number of cities with city managers rose to 251.[20]

In Dayton, the voters accepted a new charter with the city manager administration after a flood in 1913 killed more than 400 people and destroyed $100 million in property. Playing heavily on the alleged inefficiency of the city's efforts to help during the flood, business leaders such as John Patterson, then president of National Cash Register, urged voters to take advantage of a home rule amendment recently added to the Ohio Constitution to shape the city administration in businesslike ways. Nonetheless, according to reports gathered in 1919, the flood was not the cause of the change. These reports claimed that the flood accentuated the problems already present in the city. For some time, annual expenditures had exceeded revenues and there were inadequate controls over the services of the employees.[21]

When John Patterson championed the city manager plan in Dayton, Ohio, in 1913, he claimed that it would improve the quality of life in the city. The way that city managers were to solve problems was to use such supposedly scientific techniques as surveys to facilitate the formation of public policies. According to Barry D. Karl, sanitary engineers had collected social statistics to suggest the complex relationships involved in any effort of systematic reform at the beginning of the nineteenth century. Karl noted that during the American Civil War, medical researchers, architects, engineers, and transportation specialists cooperated to form the privately financed U.S. Sanitary Commission to oversee conditions in army camps, hospitals, and prisons. When philanthropists such as John D. Rockefeller took an interest in these methods, they created corporations, such as the Rockefeller Sanitary Commission, that followed the survey pattern.[22]

By 1900, social scientists had set the basic model of social reform based on surveys. According to Karl, the method depended on three steps. A core group of experts defined a problem, the experts called a conference to interest the public in the issues, and they conducted a survey to reveal the nature of the difficulties and to suggest remedies. The experts expected the government or the public to base any remedies they adopted on the reports they submitted. In these ways, the survey movement appeared to Karl to fit the requirements set out by John Dewey in *The Public and Its Problems* for democratic decision making in a modern urban society.[23]

Although Dewey acknowledged that experts tended to remove themselves from common interests and to become a class of their own, he did not want to remove expertise from efforts to solve social problems. Instead, Dewey argued that experts could be part of a democratic form of government. In a democracy, administrators had to consult with the majority of the people and determine their needs and troubles. Although Dewey thought that an election could be a form of consultation, voters may not cast their ballots according to their feelings on particular issues. For example, in elections where slander or personality dominated, the results might not reflect a majority view on particular issues. In order for majorities to form, people had to discuss issues and agree on solutions. With this condition in mind, Dewey contended that experts could improve the methods and conditions of debate. If experts performed inquiries and disseminated information that would enable people to have intelligent discussions, the public could cast intelligent votes for particular policies and oversee the execution of those plans.[24]

Although people may not have followed Dewey's ideal, the city manager model became popular. By 1974, more than half the cities in the United States with more than 5,000 residents followed the city manager/city commissioner model. Unfortunately, the system or style of city government did not seem to influence human concerns. For example, when Richard J. Stillman II surveyed the literature to determine the relative effectiveness of the manager–commission form of government, he found that the form of city government did not influence the quality of life in a city. The most obvious factors that influenced the quality of life in a city included such things as the per capita income of the residents, the median school years completed by these residents, the extent of home ownership, the rates of morbidity among citizens, and the extent of participation in cultural events. Although Stillman noted that the form of city government did not influence these factors, he urged prospective city managers to seek the advanced training required by their profession. He concluded that the rationale for being a city manager was that many cities had city managers.[25]

Thus, as Ellul predicted, once the city adopted a technological organization, such as the city manager plan, new problems arose, such as the training of city managers, that required programs within universities and the creation of professional organizations of city managers. Although neither the model nor the training of the managers improved the quality of life within the city, these changes fit together as part of a technological system. In this way, the process of rational organization or bureaucracy created inseparable systems that augmented themselves. For example, the organization revealed new problems for new methods of organization to solve.

Nineteenth-century school reform coincided with reform of city management in that the reformers sought to apply to schools the same methods of planning that had been successful in large corporations by such entrepreneurs as Rockefeller and Carnegie. Thus, reformers did not introduce any new or startling innovations. Instead, as with the case of the changes made in municipal affairs, educational reformers called for consolidation of the control of schools and subsequent increases in the preparation of administrators and teachers, the use of surveys to determine what changes to make, and the widening of the curriculums.

How Did the Consolidation of School Districts Lead to Bureaucratic Expansion?

As noted in Chapter 7, in 1857, when educators formed the National Teachers' Association, later renamed the National Education Association (NEA) and supported the creation of the U.S. Bureau of Education in 1867, they expected the NEA and the bureau to influence local schools by issuing reports on the procedures carried out in most schools. Because most reformers feared federal imposition in local school affairs, they agreed that such exhortations were the best means by which a national organization and a federal office could influence the organization of local school districts.

Throughout the last part of the nineteenth century, such reports served at least two purposes. On the one hand, they recorded the changes that were taking place. On the other hand, they influenced local schools to change. Because the bureau relied on such organizations as the NEA to make these reports, the content represented the view of most of the prominent educators in the United States. One point on which the reports seemed to agree was the need for central organization of the school districts in order to make planning as objective as possible. Although such central organization could prevent unnecessary duplication of efforts or simple oversights, reformers gave their appeals increased urgency by arguing that local citizens in small districts used the school funds for selfish purposes. Thus, the reformers referred to the need for central planning as taking politics out of schools.

An example of such a report appeared in 1885 when John D. Philbrick, former superintendent of Boston city schools, published a description of city schools in the United States. According to Philbrick, city school districts used different systems of administration. Defining a city as any municipality with more than 8,000 residents, Philbrick noted that local boards governed the administration of schools in these cities; these boards varied by name, by size, by method of election, by length of tenure in office, by powers, and by duties. In most cities, reformers whom Philbrick called intelligent friends of education sought to separate the selection of this board from party politics. Boards followed two directions to reduce the influence of politics. First, they gave the authority to appoint school board members to mayors or judges, thereby eliminating the electorate. A similar effort was to give local or ward boards the authority to appoint delegates to the central school board. Second, they held regular public elections. Some states expanded the electorate by giving women the right to vote in these elections, in hopes of reducing the possibility of corruption. Unfortunately, few women chose to exercise this franchise. For example, in New Hampshire, less than a hundred women chose to vote in school board elections in 1883. Thus, Philbrick contended that there was no universally satisfactory way to reduce the influence of partisan affairs.[26]

In general, school boards organized their work in two different ways. One way was to delegate responsibilities to a few committees or departments. Philbrick noted that St. Louis followed this pattern. The board appointed twelve committees, each one dealing with a specific aspect of school life such as course of study, library facilities, janitors, and salaries. The other system of organization that Philbrick found to be popular was to appoint several committees that covered more closely tailored aspects such as furniture, discipline, penmanship, and furnaces. Cincinnati followed the second system with twenty-two different committees. Philbrick contended that the St. Louis approach with fewer committees allowed for more comprehensive planning.[27]

School boards in different cities had different duties and varying sorts of authority. Philbrick noted that in most cities, the central school board managed whatever related to instruction and they controlled the expenditure of funds. In New York and St. Louis a moderate-sized central board had almost unlimited authority. In some cities, such as Philadelphia, Pittsburgh, and Hartford, the central board shared authority with the various local or ward boards that were part of the city.[28]

The recommendations that Philbrick made appeared in such reports as that of the NEA's Committee of Fifteen on Elementary Education released in 1895. Andrew Sloane Draper, president of the University of Illinois, served on the subcommittee for school organization along with the superintendents of schools for Washington, D.C., and for Trenton, New Jersey, schools. Draper and his colleagues defined a city school as any system too large for volunteers to administer. To facilitate the conduct of efficient and useful schools, the members of the subcommittee recommended six principles. The first was that school affairs should be nonpartisan, unrelated to any political party. Second, legislative functions and executive functions had to be separate. Third, a small school board should carry out legislative duties with members appointed rather than elected to represent the entire city. Fourth, the administration should have different parts. One department would oversee instruction and a separate department would manage business affairs. Fifth, each of these departments should have a chief executive officer to control its affairs. Sixth, the school board would appoint these executive officers. Thus, although the division of labors took away from board members the authority to appoint friends or family members as teachers, they were in a position to approve the criteria by which the administrators made such appointments.[29]

The same principles applied to the rural schools. Whereas Draper and his committee considered what principles urban schools should follow, the NEA's Committee of Twelve on Rural Schools extended those same ideas to solve the rural school problem. The committee recommended that small district schools merge to form larger centralized schools and pay for students' transportation to the schools from public funds. The problem was that rural schools in small districts served so few families that they could not afford to hire trained teachers who used reasonable methods of instruction. In the larger consolidated schools, the pupils would have opportunities to meet and socialize with children of their own ages. In small district schools, the few students may have been of different ages. Although the residents should pay a certain definite sum to support the consolidated schools, the committee recommended that the state should contribute part of the support because these payments would enable the state to demand that teachers possess certain qualifications. At the same time, the state could adjust the calendars and the content of the state normal schools in ways that would facilitate the improvement of the teachers already teaching in the rural schools.[30]

By 1900, in a report written for the U.S. Commission to the Paris Exposition, Draper claimed that a system of education had grown up in the United States because most cities were following the principles set forth by the National Education Association's Committee of Fifteen on Elementary Education that he had authored. According to Draper, although state legislatures had not mandated uniform systems of school administration among the cities, systems had emerged following predictable patterns. Although the ideal had been for the people to control their schools, the systems had become more centralized as towns and cities grew too large to allow the members of neighboring families to decide how to build, repair, staff, and control a small school as they had under the school district model. By the middle of the nineteenth century, township systems replaced school districts in many states, allowing for bigger schools, better teachers, and more diversity in the curriculum. At the same time, Southern states adopted county systems of school administration that usually consisted of a county superintendent and local trustees within subdistricts. Although there were some variations in the county system of the different Southern states, Draper argued that the model functioned in ways roughly similar to the ways that township schools operated in Northern schools.[31]

In addition to experts making reports, popular authors wrote magazine articles surveying the practices of schools, and they offered suggestions for improvement. Interestingly, such articles repeated the ideas of the reports that emanated from the NEA and the U.S. Bureau of Education even when the authors claimed to be working independently of school people. For example, from January to June 1892, Joseph Mayer Rice visited city schools across the country. In explaining his methods, Rice wrote that he ignored the information provided by school officials, relying instead on his own observations. As a result, he claimed that he spent every school day during the six months of his survey in school buildings. He added that he had observed over 1200 teachers in the schools of thirty-six cities, and he had visited twenty institutions of teacher training.[32]

Although Rice was most concerned with inadequate teaching techniques, he believed that changing school administration was the best way to reform teaching. For example, among the practices that Rice found were teachers conducting singsong recitations in spelling and arithmetic. No school operating by what he called scientific practices would tolerate such methods, he claimed. To bring about what he called scientific management, Rice recommended four steps. First, the public had to be interested in education. He claimed that if one parent in one hundred held an intelligent interest in schools the most flagrant evils would disappear. Second, the board members had to make their decisions unselfishly. This meant that the board members had to be divorced from politics in every sense. Third, superintendents had to be thoroughly versed in the best instructional practices so that they could ensure the teachers followed those models of teaching. Unfortunately, Rice added, superintendents rarely performed such services because they moved to other places quickly. A superintendent should be in office for four or five years in order to make reasonable improvements, Rice noted. Finally, he suggested that teachers had to graduate from good city training schools. Although Rice believed that normal school training in the United States was comparable to the best available in the world, he was saddened to note that few teachers had graduated from such preparatory programs.[33]

How Did Superintendents' Efforts to Improve Schools Increase Bureaucratic Controls?

In 1885, a few cities did not use superintendents. When John Philbrick noted this fact, he thought superintendents improved schools. When one person should hold the authority of the school administration, various assistants might aid the superintendent and a superintendent could serve as an expert who offered advice to the school board and executed the policies the board formed. Philbrick added that to occupy such a position, the superintendent needed special training, a sense of independence, and a feeling for moderation. Unfortunately, most superintendents had liberal educations instead of special training, successful experiences teaching, and some instruction in methods of economy in directing an institution. Further, Philbrick was distressed to note that many superintendents strove to be loyal servants of the board members. Without special training and expressing a servile attitude, superintendents might ignore the need to establish teacher training schools or encourage self-improvement among teachers. To Philbrick, the aim of supervision should be to ensure that the machinery or the organization of the system enhanced the intellectual and spiritual goals of the schools. He thought intelligent well trained superintendents could achieve this aim.[34]

According to educators such as Franklin Bobbitt, superintendents could improve the supervision of instruction if they imitated the methods of efficient organization found in large corporations. To Bobbitt, this meant that administrators in city schools should use standardized measures of student achievement to supervise instruction in the same way that factory managers would use rates of work to regulate employees. According to Bobbitt, the first step of this process was to determine the standards of production. In steel mills, the standard of production could be a particular number of rails shaped to certain measures. In schools, Bobbitt recommended that supervisors rely on such objective measures as the tests of mathematical abilities developed by S. A. Courtis and T. W. Stone. With these tests of the skills that students should perform at the various grade levels, teachers could determine the average proficiency of a class, the speed with which students could perform arithmetical computations, and the level of accuracy they could attain. Teachers could use the scores to determine which students need specific help and the areas in which the students required assistance. In addition, Bobbitt suggested that such measures offered supervisors simple means to compare the effectiveness of different teachers.[35]

Surveys were an important technique that superintendents used to determine policies or practices to implement. Although critics such as Tyack complained that surveys were devices to impose the values of a particular social class on the various school districts, the development of the surveys suggested that they offered ways to inform a central board of the needs or interests of a large district in the fashion that Dewey described in the *Public and its Problems.*

In 1914, the National Society for the Study of Education devoted the second part of its yearbook to the question of school surveys. H. L. Smith noted that school surveys followed the pattern set for social services by economists, political scientists, and city planners. They had become essential because there were demands to offer kindergartens, to provide moral and physical education, and to provide intellectual training. As a result, surveys offered means for school administrators to understand the complicated patterns of organization involved in modern education. Smith added that local organizations, such as a business organization, a Grange, or a woman's club, could conduct helpful surveys. Although Smith recommended that the surveys cover as much of the community life as possible, he noted that investigations could be limited if the board required information about specific problems such as excessive failure of students. In this case, the fact-finding might concentrate on the school accounting system, the physical conditions of the students, and visits to the students' homes to determine the cause of what he called backwardness.[36]

In addition to offering lists of concerns that the surveys might consider, Smith collected comments from a wide range of educators about the wisdom of importing experts to conduct the surveys. Educators who thought local officials could conduct surveys claimed that the employees knew the system and the community better than did experts from the outside. People who favored bringing in outside consultants argued that such experts knew what other school districts were doing and could measure local practices against national tendencies. Most educators thought that teams of evaluators composed of a combination of some local school officials and of some people from universities should conduct the surveys. In that way, the local school people could contribute their understanding of the local conditions and the university people could add information about the best practices found nationally. On receipt of the final report, which could be extensive, the school board and appropriate officials could decide what policies to make in line with the study's findings and recommendations.[37]

In rural schools, state supervisors sought to help county superintendents improve the efficiency of the elementary schools. By 1913, in thirty-eight states, a superintendent took charge of the district schools in an entire county. The elected trustees of the district hired the teacher of a one-room, one-teacher school. The trustees took care of the financial matters. The superintendent acted in an advisory capacity. In some states, the superintendent examined the teachers and granted them a license to teach in the schools in that county. The main duties of the county superintendent were to keep records, make reports, and improve the quality of teaching by organizing teacher institutes and visiting the schools. On average, a county superintendent in the United States visited each school once per year and stayed about two hours. The extent of supervision was low because in some states such as North Dakota, superintendents were responsible for as many as 150 schools. In comparison, a city supervisor was usually responsible for twenty teachers, and supervisors spent half their time visiting their classrooms.[38]

In seven states, including Massachusetts, two or more country towns could join to hire a superintendent for their schools. Such an officer would supervise between twenty-five and fifty different one-room schoolhouses. In comparison to states such as North Dakota where superintendents might cover 150 schools, this was a modest number that allowed the superintendent to become a trainer of the teachers who were young, inexperienced, or wholly untrained. As a sort of head teacher, the superintendent had to travel to each school making a visit of an hour and one-half each week to assist the teachers. Consequently, the superintendent's main task was to visit teachers. At these times, the superintendent could notice the physical conditions of the school and the progress of the students. At the same time, the superintendent could examine the instructional program and make suggestions to improve instruction.[39]

In the rural south, the county superintendent and the state superintendent worked together to improve the efficiency of the elementary schools. They did this in two ways. First, when state supervisors visited, they took advantage of the opportunities to participate in local movements to consolidate small district schools into a strong central building. Thus, in eleven states in the South in 1912, there were 103 consolidation efforts and 188 new buildings. Second, the state supervisors prepared teacher manuals that the state departments of education printed. These provided material for teachers to discuss among themselves and in summer teacher institutes.[40]

When the superintendent took on the authority of supervising teachers, this change disrupted the career path most teachers had followed in urban schools. Before superintendents held powerful roles, the school principal was the person who supervised the teachers' performances. Usually, the principal was someone who had been teaching in the building for a considerable period. Thus, the principal knew the school well. In New York, for example, an orderly pattern of promotion was for a teacher to move through the grades of an elementary school, rising to the office of the principal. If a ward board threatened to assign people to administrative positions without considering seniority, the teachers could appeal to the community and pressure the small local board to follow the more traditional pattern. Such political appeals were not possible when the board could not feel political pressure and a powerful superintendent made the decisions.[41]

According to Wayne Urban, in 1891 and in 1895, when educators such as Nicholas Murray Butler proposed a plan to adopt small central school boards, teachers opposed the proposals because the change would give superintendents the authority to make decisions about the appointment of principals. The teachers felt that senior teachers should become principals because such methods rewarded loyalty and guaranteed that the principals knew the established practices. The problem was that the new superintendents made appointments based on training, examination results, and ratings by supervisors. Despite the opposition from teachers, cities such as New York and Cleveland adopted the central board and superintendent model as part of the effort to reform schools. In Cleveland, critics had complained that teachers could make suggestions to the board. Reformers replied that teachers should not influence administrative policy because teachers tended to be overly conservative. The fear was that giving teachers a voice in administrative decisions would prevent the improvement of teaching practices.[42]

In addition to making the school board positions nonpartisan and insulating the members from political pressure, the reformers changed the composition of school boards. In the neighborhood or ward boards, the school trustees came from those neighborhoods. Thus, if the residents were workers or members of ethnic groups, these people could become school trustees. When the entire city voted for each school board member, the members tended to be prominent citizens. For example, in 1916, when Scott Nearing wrote the superintendents of the 131 cities with populations exceeding 40,000, he found that these cities had small school boards. Twenty-six cities had five members or less. Ten cities had boards ranging in size from ten to six members. Thirteen cities had school boards of eleven to fifteen members. Only six cities had boards with more than sixteen members. In addition to the boards being small, Nearing's sample of 104 replies showed that only 67 were women out of the 967 school board members. Further, more than three-fourths of the board members were business or professional men. Thus, few wage earners, clerks, or industrial workers occupied positions on school boards.[43]

When Nearing concluded that the school boards represented the business and professional interests of the communities, other studies confirmed his conclusions. In 1919, the Teachers Union of New York City sent questionnaires to superintendents of 204 cities with populations exceeding 40,000. Receiving replies from superintendents in sixty-seven cities, the union researchers found that only seventeen cities had school board members representing labor. In 1922, George G. Struble gathered information about board member from 169 cities. He found that about 60 percent of the board members were merchants, bankers, lawyers, physicians, or business executives. In 1920, George S. Counts solicited information about school board members from 1,654 boards of education. Although he included county boards, district boards, and city boards and subjected the results to more complete analysis, his results were similar to the other studies. He concluded that although the different communities had developed different school systems and had different arrangements of governance, the social composition of all the different boards was remarkably similar. Most boards were composed of college and university men who occupied favored positions in society. Thus, Counts concluded that the professional classes dominated the boards of education. He feared they could use this control to turn the schools into instruments of propaganda supporting their interests.[44]

At least one sociologist complained that Counts exaggerated the dangers because no one could predict how school board members would act by determining the social class to which they belonged. W. W. Charters, Jr. complained that analyses of the social class of educators could not demonstrate that a particular group controlled schools unless the studies demonstrated how the values of the social class had entered into the decision making. Charters pointed out that a variety of factors other than social class affiliation influenced school administrators when they made their decisions. For example, many different groups lived and worked in the cities. Because these people were interested in the events in schools, school board members and administrators sought their opinions through such mechanisms as surveys before making decisions.[45]

As noted above, Tyack thought that experts used those surveys to impose the same business model on all schools. Although Tyack may have overstated the case, those surveys led in a particular direction even though experts did not conduct the surveys by themselves. Ellul contended that, no matter who administered the surveys, the logic behind such a rational technique led in the direction of a strong, centralized organization, a nonpartisan administration, some form of teacher training, and an expanded curriculum. Although the people who instituted such reforms may have wanted to improve schools, the effect of these changes was to expand the educational system.

How Did the Growth of Bureaucracies Influence Teacher Preparation?

When surveys illuminated the need for centralized administration, those same survey techniques reinforced efficient ways of teaching. At first, the surveys suggested simple interventions. For example, in 1891, Emerson White wrote a report for the U.S. Commissioner of Education surveying the teaching methods of seventy cities. He noted that the lower grades were much larger than the upper grades because students left schools before completing all levels. Thus, in many cities, a total of about forty or fifty students were together in a room of primary or elementary classes. Often, the instruction in these large classes was individual recitations. One student might rise and say, "One plus eight is nine. Eight plus one is nine." When the student sat down, another rose and repeated the same sentences. This proceeded until everyone in the class had recited the sentences. In this way, the students memorized arithmetic facts; however, White noted that a simple lesson could take a class more than twenty-five minutes to complete and each student worked for only a few moments. White suggested incorporating a plan of two classes within the room. Although these students would be of the same grade level, they could pursue different exercises and one group could complete assigned studies while the other group could recite. In this way, individual students would complete more work in a day.[46]

In another report, White noted that the problems of instruction were different in country schools. In rural settings, a teacher in a one-room building faced forty pupils ranging in age from five to sixteen. In such situations, the pupils had unequal abilities and accomplishments, yet they needed instruction within the six hours allotted for the day. Writing in 1894, White noted that most teachers in such situations tried to work with individual students. White argued that under this method, students sat alone for too much time. Although a few bright students could teach themselves in such conditions, most students could not profit from the free time. Thus, he recommended what he called the three-grade solution. In this system, the pupils from five to eight years of age used the reader to master reading, writing, and arithmetic. For the next grade, children from eight to eleven years used separate textbooks to study reading, arithmetic, and geography. In the final four years, the teacher added such areas as grammar, history, and natural science. To White, the advantage of such a system was that exercises could be done simultaneously by the students in a grade. Thus, White considered the solution to the country school problem to be the adoption of methods of organization similar to those found in the cities.[47]

By applying the ideas of efficiency and science, educators sought to make classroom recitations reasonable. During the early years of the twentieth century, the term *recitation* covered classroom drills and a wide range of other activities. For example, writing in 1910, George Herbert Betts described four types of recitations: (1) the question and answer type wherein the teacher led the students to realize new subject material from information previously mastered, (2) the topical method in which the teacher asked a question that led to student to go off and find an answer, (3) the lecture method in which the teacher provided information by talking to the class, and (4) the written recitation in which students performed such tasks as completing arithmetic problems, writing essays, or making drawings. In all these cases, the room should be free from distractions, the teacher should be well-prepared and enthusiastic to incite student interest, the recitations should be judged by high standards, and a spirit of cooperation should pervade the classroom.[48]

Because teachers were responsible for inciting the students' interests, school improvement depended on the training of teachers. Most teachers had little training, and the surveys suggested increasingly extensive teacher preparation. For example, in 1895, the NEA released the report of the Committee of Fifteen described above. It recommended that teachers should have finished four more years of schooling than the pupils they taught. Although the committee members preferred that teachers be high school graduates, they approved several arrangements for training such as normal schools, professional courses in a high school, or training schools conducted by a school district. Although they worried that blending academic training and professional training would dilute the quality of academic courses, they wanted prospective teachers to have both types of knowledge. Under professional training, the committee recommended courses in psychology, in a study of children, in a study of teaching methods, in the history of education, and some form of practice teaching. The entire experience of teacher training should take about two years.[49]

Despite the calls for increased teacher training, the training prospective teachers received was rudimentary. For example, in 1895, Daniel Putnam published a manual that followed the content of courses in teacher training at Michigan State Normal School. Drawing on different sources for ideas of what constituted good teaching, Putnam applied them in his classes over many years. Consequently, Putnam quoted many philosophers, psychologists, and educators to show that the study of children's development led to an understanding of the laws of the mind and to the methods of teaching. Seeking to be prescriptive, Putnam suggested that the teacher prepare the students by bringing up some material previously learned and relate it to the new material. Because he believed the first law of mind was that students could understand material best when it was a coherent whole, he recommended that the second step of teaching was to begin lessons with overviews of the material. From these whole units, the students' minds could move to analyzing the parts. Thus, the third step of teaching was analysis of the new material aligning it with information already acquired. Putnam called the fourth step of teaching "abstraction." Following what he called the third law of the mind, the students formed some sort of general notion or rule from the material. The fifth step was application, in which the children associated it with something new. Thus, if the students learned the sentence, "I have a book," they could create new sentences such as "You have a book." Although these five formal steps provided the scientific basis for Putnam's approach, he cautioned teachers to use other techniques as well. He approved of teachers offering lectures, holding questioning sessions with the students, and allowing students to explore topics.[50]

It did not matter that the content of teacher-training programs seemed rudimentary. The number of state normal schools grew from 15 in 1865 to 103 in 1890. As the number of state normal schools increased, more state governments recognized graduation from a state normal school as qualification for teaching. By 1897, twenty-eight states accepted normal school graduation, and by 1921, only one state would not accept a normal school diploma as a teaching credential.[51]

In addition, city school districts sought to prepare a qualified teaching force and to tailor the instruction to the city's needs. For example, in 1913, the Cincinnati, Ohio, public schools and the University of Cincinnati joined together to form the College for Teachers, offering a four-year program granting a bachelor's degree as well as preparation for teaching in the city schools. A professor in the college, John W. Hall, supervised the practice teaching done by prospective teachers in the public schools. No only did the prospective teachers perform this supervised instruction before they graduated, they did it again after they graduated when they were employed by the city. In addition, newly hired city teachers trained at other schools had to complete a period of practice teaching supervised by the college staff.[52]

From 1894 to 1926, more states took over the certification of teachers. In 1893, three states issued all teaching certificates for the entire state. In 1936, thirty-six states issued all certificates. State departments of education curtailed the arbitrary authority formerly exercised by local school districts over teachers, and state officials wanted teachers to have the same training they had received. The county and state authorities who began issuing teaching permits had educational training themselves. As a result, they looked for teacher preparation as criteria for certificates. Previously, local authorities had administered examinations and granted teaching permits based on the results. Although the change in requirements added training, the shift benefited teachers because the certificates were valid in many school districts, allowing teachers to move more easily. Further, the state credentials were valid for longer periods than the annual certificates offered by local authorities. Although increasing standards threatened to reduce the number of available teachers, this did not happen. Because teachers with more qualifications received higher pay, more candidates sought the positions.[53]

Ironically, as more school boards sought teachers with normal school preparation, the normal schools broadened their programs, increased their appeal, and began working in areas other than the training of elementary school teachers. By the 1880s, principals of normal schools found that their programs offered weak preparation for elementary school teachers. Further, most of the women who finished normal school training left teaching after about six years. Thus, the principals began offering a wider range of professional courses to prepare candidates for high schools and for administrative positions. Many normal schools grew into state teachers colleges with four-year bachelor's degrees, abandoning the preparation of elementary school teachers. In some states, the normal schools turned themselves into liberal arts colleges. Once the normal schools included other fields of study, they could not turn back to their original aim of preparing elementary teachers because the task of training teachers seemed less important than preparing professional educators to serve as principals of high schools, instructors at teacher institutes, and leaders in educational reform.[54]

As Ellul had predicted, the process of teacher certification and training served itself more than it solved educational problems. The aim of normal schools was to provide training that could improve classroom instruction. Once those schools enjoyed some success, they expanded the concept of professional training to include the preparation of educational authorities who would supervise the growing educational system. Those graduates of normal schools who became authorities required increased training of teachers, believing such professionals would improve the elementary schools. Once teachers received their degrees, they tended to move out of the elementary school classroom to teach advanced grades or become administrators.

How Did the Growth of Bureaucracies Influence the Curriculum?

In the curriculum, as with other areas such as consolidation of control, statements from the U.S. Bureau of Education and the NEA recorded and influenced changes. The report of the Committee of Ten influenced the high school curriculum when the NEA issued it in 1893. As described in Chapter 7, this report recommended that students in high schools enroll in academic subjects whether they wanted to attend college or go to work. Although the committee offered four different programs, the programs tended to differ in the amount and type of foreign language study the students undertook.

At the time, many commentators approved of the committee's decision to shape a curriculum by considering what young men and women could learn about the culture. For example, writing shortly after the report appeared, J. G. Schurman praised the committee for ignoring subjects such as ethics and metaphysics that young minds would find to be overly introspective. Because Schurman thought some study of the ancient languages Latin and Greek was necessary, he was pleased to note in the report recommendations that students pursue those languages. At the same time, he thought the committee had wisely limited the extent students had to study those ancient languages. He believed that students should gain understandings of other more contemporary subjects as well. In general, he praised the committee for selecting programs that inculcated the students with the humanities.[55]

According to Sol Cohen, the NEA Committee of Ten's report was the last gasp of an age of academic instruction in public schools. Cohen argued that the report's pleas for more academic courses did not reflect the spirit of the period. By 1906, vocational education had replaced such overwhelmingly academic proposals.[56]

The authors of the report may not have ignored vocational studies as completely as Cohen contended. For example, the committee's report acknowledged that subjects such as drawing did not appear in any of the four curriculum plans they approved. Nonetheless, the members expected that students would make drawings in such classes as history, botany, zoology, and geography. Although neither industrial training nor commercial courses appeared among their selections, the report noted that bookkeeping and commercial arithmetic could take the place of algebra. Further, if high school officials wanted to introduce courses in trades or the useful arts, they could do this by substituting those practical subjects for some of the science courses in one of the less classical programs.[57]

When the NEA's Committee of Fifteen made its response in 1895 on the correlation of studies in elementary school curriculums, the subcommittee, chaired by William Torrey Harris, made a similar qualification. According to this subcommittee, an academic curriculum consisting of language studies, reading, penmanship, and grammar, arithmetic, geography, and history would correlate the children to their spiritual and natural environment. Thus, these studies should dominate elementary schools. Although Harris had been a member of the Committee of Ten, and he had been a strong advocate of academic courses, his report made room for practical courses in elementary schools. Noting that industrial or manual training, calisthenics, and science should appear in some forms in the elementary schools, Harris recommended that teachers allocate some time to these pursuits.[58]

Some historians refused to believe vocational pursuits appeared within the report of the Committee of Ten or the report of the Committee of Fifteen. For example, although Jurgen Herbst acknowledged that the report of the Committee of Ten suggested that high schools could add vocational subjects if it seemed desirable, he thought that this promise contradicted the report's aim. Herbst believed the report's strength lay in offering the same studies in the humanities to all students, no matter what the students wanted to do later in life. In this way, the authors of the report avoided setting up any sort of special classifications that could harm the children later in life. Herbst added that the report contradicted this strength when it suggested offering some vocational courses to those students who wanted to go to work after high school. According to Herbst, the students who were going to college had the time to take more of the academic courses that the committee had considered essential for a good education.[59]

Herbst may have been correct in assuming that schools could not offer vocational training and provide the same education for all students. Most schools retained academic programs. For example, in 1899, the Committee of Twelve for the American Philological Association released its report suggesting how to organize four-year programs in Latin and Greek in secondary schools. The reason for submitting such a plan was that reports for the school year of 1897–1898 showed about 275,000 students enrolled in Latin. This was almost a 174 percent increase from 1889–1890 when about 100,000 secondary students enrolled. This meant that about half the students in secondary schools were studying Latin while other academic courses, such as geometry, algebra, German, and physics, enrolled the rest. At the same time, the report noted that the preparation of Latin teachers and the available Latin textbooks had improved. From the increased interest in Latin, the committee predicted substantial increases in the study of classical Greek.[60]

Although the Committee of Twelve predicted that classical programs would remain popular, they did not. By 1904, the percentage of high school students preparing for college declined as more students entered high schools and enrollments mounted. The new students changed the percentages in various courses even though the numbers of students enrolled in classical programs remained high. In 1892–1893, when the Committee of Ten had made its report, about 15 percent of public high school students planned to go on to college. The percentage dropped to about 10 percent eleven years later. Although a higher percentage of students in private high schools planned to go to college, a similar decline took place among these students as the percent of college-bound students dropped from about 27 percent to about 22 percent. At the same time, the high schools offered more courses in applied economics, technical business subjects, and domestic science.[61]

According to reports that visiting commissions to the United States sent back to Europe, the elementary schools and high schools in the early 1900s offered extensive programs in vocational education in addition to academic courses. For example, in 1903, the Mosely Educational Commission came to the United States from Britain to determine four things. They wanted to know if the elementary schools influenced the students' individuality. They wondered about the social and intellectual effects of the wide distribution of education. They surveyed the results of instruction in business methods and in applied science. Finally, they considered people's opinions of the value of university instruction to the tasks of business.[62]

During the three months the committee spent in the United States, the members of the Mosely commission traveled to such cities as New York, Philadelphia, Washington, Chicago, and Boston and looked at a wide variety of schools. The commission members agreed that the prosperity of the United States derived from the extent of education the country enjoyed. They described the school buildings as magnificent and the equipment as lavish. Yet, the commission noted that teachers were not adequately paid and that women dominated the teaching force. Nonetheless, in schools of all levels, the Mosely commission members found the teachers possessed with the desire to help their pupils, and they found the pupils willing to learn. They did not encounter prejudices against specific social groups or classes and religious difficulties appeared to be absent, as a result of which a spirit of enthusiasm seemed to permeate the schools. They noted that practical studies had spread widely. Manual training appeared in the elementary schools and university professors stressed the practical applications of theoretical studies.[63]

When the director of the commission offered his remarks, he noted that American boys remained in school longer than did British children and that the American schools fitted the boys for their trades so that few fell into lives of poverty or crime. He noted with appreciation that Americans have shown that trade and technical training increases the productive value of workers. Thus, the workers and the factories gain from the time and money spent on schools. Nonetheless, he found the students learned little about art or music, and he found this lack of culture to be dismaying.[64]

Public commissions agreed with the Mosely commission about the benefits of separate vocational and technical training. For example, in 1906, the Massachusetts Commission on Industrial and Technical Education urged that all towns and cities modify the work of elementary schools so that the students had instruction in agriculture, mechanical arts, and domestic science. In high schools, work in mathematics and science should be altered to show the application of those subjects to local industries. At the same time, the commission recommended that cities and towns provide elective courses of high school instruction in agriculture, domestic science, and mechanical arts.[65]

Other cities made similar changes. For example, in the city of St. Louis, Missouri, public school enrollment went from 266 pupils in 1840 to almost 56,000 pupils by 1880. Schools touched only one of every fifty people before the War between the States. By 1880, one out of six people had contact with the schools. Although the schools in St. Louis increased in complexity and size, Selwen K. Troen found few changes in their functions from 1850 to 1880. Most of the students enrolled in the first three grades, and the teachers devoted attention to reading, writing, arithmetic, some geography, and group singing. This curriculum broadened in the 1890s and the enrollment grew.[66]

In St. Louis in 1894, the high school diversified its curriculum, offering courses in drawing, science, business arithmetic, commercial law, and pedagogy. In 1898, a few private citizens donated funds to support manual training for boys and domestic science for girls in elementary schools around the city. Although these practical courses occupied only one or two hours per week, they were popular. The high school curriculum widened again in 1904 when the school board opened two new high schools that offered what were called cosmopolitan or comprehensive curriculums. These buildings included large shops with machinery and tools. Although students had to enroll in such traditional courses as English, algebra, and history, they could select from twenty-five courses in subjects such as bookkeeping, typewriting, and commercial geography. At the same time, the high school enrollments increased. In 1900, about 2,400 students enrolled in grades nine through twelve. By 1912, high school enrollments increased to 6,255, and by 1920, the high school enrollment approached 12,000. Although girls outnumbered boys in the high schools, the percentage of male students increased. In 1900, about 30 percent of the students were boys, but, by 1920, over 42 percent of the students were males.[67]

According to Selwyn K. Troen, the school administrators wanted these increases in enrollments and they added vocational courses to attract more students and to keep the students already enrolled. Consequently, the St. Louis schools offered a variety of evening programs with vocational options and a series of one- and two-year courses in such crafts as cabinetmaking, printing, and automobile mechanics.[68]

Because administrators changed the high school curriculums, educators urged colleges to widen entrance requirements to include the popular vocational preparation. For example, in 1907, Henry W. Holmes, a teacher in a commercial high school, claimed that the tendency of colleges to require purely academic courses for entrance caused two opposing evils. On the one hand, the rules for college entrance encouraged high school students without any propensity for language to take classes in Latin. On the other hand, those requirements imposed stigmas on students who attended schools of manual training or commerce. According to Holmes, the colleges could rectify these problems by making modest changes in the entrance requirements.[69]

In fairness, many colleges had accepted vocational subjects for entrance. For example, Harvard College took drawing and music; Leland Stanford accepted manual training, drawing, and music; and Columbia accepted manual training, drawing, and music. Although no college accepted domestic science or domestic art as an entrance requirement in 1907, Virgil Prettyman of Horace Mann High School in Teachers College at Columbia University thought that colleges had begun to loosen entrance requirements. Furthermore, since 1882, college enrollments had increased. As a result, Prettyman thought that the purposes of college education would soon aim to satisfy the masses of people. Thus, he urged that colleges change their entrance requirements so that they could accept such courses as shop work, industrial history, commercial geography, and domestic science.[70]

The introduction of vocational education did not solve the problem of making schooling relevant to students as much as it introduced a new set of problems. When the schools offered academic subjects considered essential for all students, there was no need for students to choose their courses of study or to select an occupation for which they would prepare. With the introduction of vocational training, the vocational guidance of youth became a pressing need. In response, several educators concluded that they needed to institute new programs to confront this problem. For example, shortly after Boston, Massachusetts, opened commercial and manual training schools, these high schools attracted more applicants than they could admit. Faced with the problem of how to choose which applicants to accept, some principals selected students through a sort of lottery system and other principals asked the elementary schools to select the best prospects for them. Hoping to improve the process, the Boston School Committee opened a Civic Service Vocation Office with Frank Parsons as director. He found his office swamped with requests for counseling services. Since the task was more than he could accomplish, he recommended that the school committee open a special office staffed by counselors who would use scientific methods of analysis to help students make appropriate vocational decisions. When business leaders and social workers became interested, the school committee charged in 1909 a vocational bureau to submit a plan for vocational guidance.[71]

The director of this vocational bureau, Meyer Bloomfield, held conferences with the masters and the teachers of the high schools in Boston to suggest ways they could guide their students. After one year, each school had appointed a counselor, and each elementary school had completed vocational cards for each student indicating the student's interests and accomplishments. The elementary schools forwarded the cards to the high schools. At the same time, the vocational bureau offered a series of lectures to the elementary students about the vocational opportunities ahead of them. The bureau offered similar lectures to parents' associations to enlist the help of the children's family in appropriate vocational guidance.[72]

Because bureaucracies grow when people try to find reasonable solutions to problems, the effort to design a curriculum that served everybody changed school districts in similar ways. Whether the school districts covered urban or rural areas, school programs moved toward vocational training because the material rewards exceeded the benefits of cultural pursuits. When schools offered many different choices among programs, officials had to help students make selections. Adopting a reasonable solution, they added guidance counselors.

Conclusion

As cities grew from 1880 to 1917, policy makers believed that the best approach to solve the difficulties facing the new urban centers was through consolidation and rational planning. Reformers thought they could improve the quality of life for city residents by imitating the methods of organization that large corporations had followed to bring order to capitalism, to protect profits, to improve predictability, to control production, and to make distribution more routine. The corporations had achieved success by growing to enormous sizes and by collecting and using accurate information on each facet of their work. Consequently, business leaders and policy makers believed that some form of expert management could improve urban affairs. The result was the city manager form of government. A similar process took place in schools at about the same time.

The first step was consolidation of school districts, making the schools larger and thereby able to command increased resources. Although cities appointed school board members in different ways, the direction of the reforms was to remove control from the residents of specific areas served by the schools, ensure that the people serving on the boards had little opportunity to act in self-interested ways, and to put the daily operation of the schools in the hands of a trained supervisor. Similar changes took place in rural schools.

When the reformers consolidated school boards, insulated the members from political pressure, and placed increased authority in the hands of a superintendent, the teachers found themselves without a voice in school affairs. In addition, they found that administrators might overlook long and meritorious service. The new system seemed to focus on training, examinations, and supervisor ratings. Despite this apparent injustice, the reformers believed the changes to be beneficial because they considered that teachers preferred conservative methods of instruction.

Although the centralization of school administration resulted in elite professional men serving as school board members, it was difficult for critics to show that these individuals made selfish decisions. They used surveys similar to those conducted by urban planners and approved by such intellectuals as John Dewey to make decisions as democratic as possible. The surveys tended to lead in similar directions. The training of teachers was essential and the curriculum had to be broad.

An important component in school reform was teacher training. Many states created normal schools in hopes that such preparation would lead to improvements in elementary schools. As the normal schools increased in importance, those institutions abandoned their focus on teacher training. The normal schools became four-year institutions that prepared professional administrators, supervisors, and policy makers.

In a similar way, after 1900, schools opened programs of vocational education to attract and retain more students. At the same time that elementary and secondary schools broadened their curriculums, educators called on colleges and universities to broaden their entrance requirements. Although the educators created these programs in reasonable hopes of offering curriculums that were relevant to the growing industrial society, the new programs did not solve this problem as much as they created new problems of vocational guidance. The result was the creation of a new set of programs to help children select courses for themselves and to help educators choose which students were likely to succeed in vocational programs. In this way, the process of school organization and reform was self-augmenting.

According to some scholars, urban schools grew and took on corporate models of administration during the Progressive Era because the experts conspired to reduce formerly democratic methods of control. Although authoritarian methods may have replaced formerly pluralistic ones, the bureaucracies grew because the reformers hoped that rational efforts such as objective methods of gathering statistics would show what officials could do to improve human life.

Since bureaucratic organizations represented ways to solve problems, many school districts used them. Although the drive to organize school districts in reasonable ways accelerated with the end of the U.S. Civil War, the movement during the Progressive Era was greater still. In fact, Jacques Ellul noted that the United States led the world in adopting bureaucratic procedures. As those procedures spread around the world, they became part of one definition of globalization.

Endnotes

1. Richard Hofstadter, *The Age of Reform from Bryan to F.D.R.* (New York: Vintage Books, 1955), 3.
2. Steven J. Diner, *A Very Different Age: Americans of the Progressive Era* (New York: Hill and Wang, 1998), 30–31.
3. Diner, *A Very Different Age,* 31–49.
4. Diner, *A Very Different Age,* 3–29.
5. John Higham, "Hanging Together: Divergent Unities in American History," *Journal of American History* 61, no. 1 (June 1974): 5–28.
6. David B. Tyack, *The One Best System: A History of American Urban Education* (Cambridge, Mass.: Harvard University Press, 1974), 126–137.
7. Tyack, *The One Best System,* 137–147.
8. Tyack, *The One Best System,* 4, 147–167.
9. Paul Peterson, *The Politics of School Reform, 1870–1940* (Chicago: University of Chicago Press, 1985), 154–156.
10. Jacques Ellul, *The Technological Society,* trans. John Wilkinson (New York: Vintage Books, 1964), 58, 78–81.
11. Raymond A. Mohl, *The New City: Urban America in the Industrial Age, 1860–1920* (Arlington Heights, Ill.: Harlan Davidson, Inc., 1985), 8–9.
12. Mohl, *The New City,* 9–17.
13. Thomas H. Johnson with Harvey Wish, *The Oxford Companion to American History* (New York: Oxford University Press, 1966), 400–401.
14. Arthur Meier Schlesinger, *The Rise of the City, 1878–1898* (New York: Macmillan Co., 1933), 63–64.
15. Schlesinger, *The Rise of the City,* 58–60, 78.
16. Keith D. Revell, *Building Gotham: Civic Culture and Public Policy in New York City, 1898–1938* (Baltimore: Johns Hopkins University Press, 2003), 1–4.
17. Jon A. Peterson, *The Birth of City Planning in the United States, 1840–1917* (Baltimore: Johns Hopkins University Press, 2003), 1–3.
18. Harold A. Stone, Don K. Price, and Kathryn H. Stone, *City Manager Government in the United States: A Review after Twenty-Five Years* (Chicago: Public Administration Service, 1940), 3–5.
19. Stone, Price, and Stone, *City Manager Government in the United States,* 6.
20. Stone, Price, and Stone, *City Manager Government in the United States,* 5–10.
21. Chester E. Rightor, Don C. Sowers, and Walter Matscheck, *City Manager in Dayton: Four Years of Commission-Manager Government, 1914–1917; and Comparisons with Four Preceding Years under the Mayor-Council Plan, 1910–1913* (New York: MacMillan Co., 1919), 1–5.
22. Barry D. Karl, "Presidential Planning and Social Science Research: Mr. Hoover's Experts," in *Perspectives in American History,* ed. Donald Fleming and Bernard Bailyn (Cambridge, Mass.: Charles Warren Center), 347–412.
23. Karl, "Presidential Planning and Social Science Research," 350–351.
24. John Dewey, *The Public and Its Problems* (1927; reprint, New York: Swallow Press, Inc., 1954), 205–209.
25. Richard J. Stillman II, *The Rise of the City Manager: A Public Professional in Local Government* (Albuquerque: University of New Mexico Press, 1974), 102–103.
26. John D. Philbrick, *City School Systems in the United States* (Washington, D.C.: Government Printing Office, 1885), 9–16.
27. Philbrick, *City School Systems,* 16–17.
28. Philbrick, *City School Systems,* 17–19.
29. National Education Association of the United States. Committee of Fifteen on Elementary Education, *Report of the Committee of Fifteen on Elementary Education with reports of the sub-committees: on the Training of Teachers; on the Correlation of Studies in Elementary Education; on the Organization of City Schools* (New York: American Book Company, 1895), 128–129.
30. National Education Association, *Report of the Committee of Twelve on Rural Schools* (Columbus, OH: John L. Trauger Press, 1895), 19–20.
31. Andrew Sloane Draper, "Educational Organization," in ed. Nicholas Murray Butler, *Education in the United States: A Series of Monographs* (New York: American Book Co., 1910), 6–13.
32. J. M. Rice, *The Public School System of the United States* (1893; reprint, New York: Arno Press, 1969), 1–3.
33. Rice, *The Public School System,* 10–27.
34. Philbrick, *City School Systems,* 52–59.
35. Franklin Bobbitt, "Some General Principles of Management Applied to the Problems of City School Systems," in *Twelfth Yearbook of the National Society for the Study of Education, Part 1,* ed. Franklin Bobbitt (Bloomington, Ill.: Public School Publishing Co., 1913), 11–30.
36. H. L. Smith, "Plans for Organizing School Surveys," in *Thirteenth Yearbook of the National Society for the Study of Education,* ed. S. Chester Parker (Bloomington, Ill.: Public School Publishing Co., 1914), 7–10.
37. Smith, "Plans for Organizing School Surveys," 22–26.
38. A. C. Monahan, "The Status of the Supervision of Rural Schools in the United States," in *Twelfth*

Yearbook of the National Society for the Study of Education, Part 2, ed. S. Chester Parker (Bloomington, Ill.: Public School Publishing Co., 1913), 9–16.

39. Julius E. Warren, "Rural Supervision in New England Townships and Union Districts" in *Twelfth Yearbook of the National Society for the Study of Education, Part 2,* ed. S. Chester Parker (Bloomington, Ill.: Public School Publishing Co., 1913), 28–49.
40. Wallace Lund, "Work of the State Supervisors of Rural Schools in the South," in *Twelfth Yearbook of the National Society for the Study of Education, Part 2,* ed. S. Chester Parker. (Bloomington, Ill.: Public School Publishing Co., 1913), 50–57.
41. Wayne J. Urban, *Why Teachers Organized* (Detroit: Wayne State University Press, 1982), 29–31.
42. Urban, *Why Teachers Organized,* 32–36.
43. Scott Nearing, "Who's Who on Our Boards of Education," *School and Society* 5, no. 108 (20 January 1917): 89–90.
44. George S. Counts, *The Social Composition of School Boards* (1927; reprint, New York: Arno Press, 1969), 3–5, 9, 81, 97.
45. W. W. Charters, Jr., "Social Class and Control of Public Education," *Harvard Educational Review,* 23, no. 4 (Fall 1953): 268–283.
46. Emerson E. White, *Promotions and Examinations in Graded Schools* (Washington, D.C.: Government Printing Office, 1891), 24–27.
47. Emerson E. White, *The Country School Problem* (New York: American Book Company, 1894), 1–11.
48. George Herbert Betts, *The Recitation* (Boston: Houghton Mifflin Co., 1910), 27–52, 79–104.
49. NEA, *Report of the Committee of Fifteen on Elementary Education,* 19–39.
50. Daniel Putnam, *A Manual of Pedagogics* (New York: Silver, Burdett, and Co., 1899), 136–146, 180–199.
51. David F. Labaree, *The Trouble with Ed Schools* (New Haven: Yale University Press, 2004), 23.
52. John W. Hall, "Supervision of Beginning Teachers in Cincinnati," in *Twelfth Yearbook of the National Society for the Study of Education, Part 1,* ed. Franklin Bobbitt (Bloomington, Ill.: Public School Publishing Co., 1913), 97–109.
53. Michael W. Sedlak, " 'Let Us Go and Buy a School Master,' " in *American Teachers: Histories of a Profession at Work,* ed. Donald Warren (New York: Macmillan Publishing, 1989), 257– 290.
54. Jurgen Herbst, "Teacher Preparation in the Nineteenth Century: Institutions and Purposes," in *American Teachers: Histories of a Profession at Work,* ed. Donald Warren (New York: Macmillan Publishing, 1989), 213–236.
55. J. G. Schurman, "The Outlook for the Curriculum," *School Review* 1, no. 2 (February 1893): 67–73.
56. Sol Cohen, "The Industrial Education Movement," *American Quarterly* 20, no. 1 (Spring 1968): 95–110.
57. National Education Association, *Report of the Committee of Ten on Secondary School Studies with Reports of the Conferences Arranged by the Committee* (New York: American Book Co., 1894), 49–50.
58. NEA, *Report of the Committee of Fifteen on Elementary Education,* 40–113.
59. Jurgen Herbst, "The American People's College: The Last Promise of Democracy in Education," *American Journal of Education* 100, no. 3 (May 1992): 275–297.
60. American Philological Association, *Report of the Committee of Twelve on Courses in Latin and Greek for Secondary Schools* (Boston: Ginn & Co., 1899), 5–9, 44–45.
61. Cheesman A. Herrick et al., "Vocational Studies for College Entrance," in *The Sixth Yearbook of the National Society for the Scientific Study of Education,* ed. Manfred J. Holmes (Chicago: University of Chicago Press, 1907), 9.
62. Mosely Educational Commission, *Reports of the Mosely Educational Commission to the United States* (1903; reprint, New York: Arno Press, 1969), vii, xxiii.
63. Mosely Educational Commission, *Reports,* xxiii–xxiv.
64. Mosely Educational Commission, *Reports,* vi–xxii.
65. Commonwealth of Massachusetts, *Report of the Commission on Industrial and Technical Education* (Boston: Wright & Potter Printers, 1906), 20–21.
66. Selwen K. Troen, "Popular Education in Nineteenth Century St. Louis," *History of Education Quarterly* 13, no. 1 (Spring 1973): 23–40.
67. Selwyn K. Troen, *The Public and the Schools: Shaping the St. Louis System, 1838–1920* (Columbia: University of Missouri Press, 1975), 184–189.
68. Troen, *The Public and the Schools,* 190–191.
69. Henry W. Holmes, "Education Versus College Entrance Requirements," in *The Sixth Yearbook of the National Society for the Scientific Study of Education,* ed. Manfred J. Holmes (Chicago: University of Chicago Press, 1907), 16–35.
70. Virgil Prettyman, "Vocational Studies for College Entrance Requirements," in *The Sixth Yearbook of the National Society for the Scientific Study of Education,* ed. Manfred J. Holmes (Chicago: University of Chicago Press, 1907), 50–56.
71. Meyer Bloomfield, *The Vocational Guidance of Youth* (Boston: Houghton Mifflin Co., 1911), 25–33.
72. Bloomfield, *The Vocational Guidance of Youth,* 34–41.

9

W. T. Harris, John Dewey, and Progressive Educational Reform

Boy's Laboratory School, early twentieth century

In his survey of progressive education, Lawrence A. Cremin claimed that William Torrey Harris, the fourth U.S. Commissioner of Education, created the first systematic philosophy of education native to the United States. According to Cremin, during the 1880s and 1890s, increasing numbers of children attended schools. Seeking to accommodate the new students, Harris urged that schools adopt regular arrangements, supervise instruction, standardize textbooks, and collect statistics. Because Harris considered these efforts essential for the development of the people and the country, he fashioned his philosophy of education to explain his belief. According to Harris, when students entered graded schools, they undertook sequential academic lessons with regular examinations, and this discipline enabled students to become self-active individuals who could exercise their freedom within their own civilization. Thus, he concluded, the lessons connected the students' natural selves to the larger society. The difficulties arose when Harris contended that the students' freedom came from voluntarily obeying the constraints of justly organized institutions. In Cremin's view, Harris became an apologist for the bureaucratic models of school organization described in Chapter 8. Cremin asserted that succeeding educators fought against Harris's ideas because they seemed to reinforce the often grim, factory-style schools.[1]

Although Cremin thought that progressive education came from many sources, he noted that people associated John Dewey with the movement most frequently. Dewey's ascendancy was rapid. Harris died in 1909. Six years later, Dewey published *Schools of Tomorrow* with his eldest daughter, Evelyn. The book was a success. In ten years, after fourteen printings, publishers issued translations in Spanish, Russian, French, Rumanian, and Chinese. At the time, few other books enjoyed such a wide readership. *Schools of Tomorrow* presented progressive education as if it was a movement and Dewey was its leader.[2]

In *Schools of Tomorrow.* The Deweys described several experimental schools that shared three principles. First, they allowed the students to have greater freedom. Second, the teachers related the children's lives in school to their lives at home. Most important, the schools identified education with the advancement of democracy. For many readers, *Schools of Tomorrow* offered a way to break the bureaucratic model of schooling that had spread widely. Although many people believed that Dewey opposed Harris's ideas, Dewey did not oppose Harris as much as he found ways to turn Harris's principles in different directions.

Despite his lack of university training, Harris had acquired a strong background in philosophy. He believed that philosophy should provide the means to select the curriculum and to determine the best methods of instruction. On the other hand, Dewey finished graduate work in Johns Hopkins where he studied philosophy. Like Harris, though, Dewey believed that the philosophy of education could determine what people should study and how they should learn. In addition, the two men shared a profound understanding of the methods of thinking of German idealists. As a result, they built careful philosophies of education on conceptions imported from German universities adapted to the American environment.

Although Harris and Dewey offered ways to control the growth of bureaucracies, their ideas did not have such an impact. According to Cremin, Harris's dependence on German idealism allowed his followers to bend his views toward authoritarian positions that served the growth of bureaucracies more than they aided human development. If Harris could be guilty of encouraging conformism, Dewey had a similar influence for two contradictory reasons. Like Harris, he used a form of German idealism that gave primary importance to social needs. At the same time, Dewey supported such a wide range of reforms that his followers could twist his suggestions to mean that a progressive school was any institution that had adopted currently popular ideas.

To explain these problems, the following sections will proceed in two directions. The first is the ways that Dewey and Harris shared idealistic ways of thinking that made social growth important. Because this represents a discussion of ideas, this part of the chapter takes a philosophical direction. The second is the ways that followers of Dewey applied his ideas. These accounts show how some educators twisted Dewey's ideas to support bureaucratic methods and how other followers found Dewey's suggestions to be authoritarian. Because these are descriptions of what people did with or thought about Dewey's notions, they tend to be historical.

How Did German Idealism Become an American Philosophy of Education?

If Harris created the first American philosophy of education, he did not construct it on his own. He followed the work of Georg Wilhelm Friedrich Hegel, a German philosopher active during the late eighteenth century. Imitating Hegel's idealism, Harris claimed that people advanced their understanding in two ways. The first was to undertake analyses of their own ways of thought. The second was that people developed increasingly higher states of consciousness as they immersed themselves in the wisdom derived from the experience of the human race.[3]

For Harris, personal thought offered one method by which people could analyze consciousness. Harris claimed that intellectual growth took place because the levels of mind, which Harris called faculties, fell into distinct but advancing stages. For example, in learning about a thing, a person would begin by having some emotional reaction to the object. The second level was sense perception. The process continued to a third stage of memory, to a fourth stage of common sense, to a fifth stage of reflection, and, finally, to reason.[4]

Harris gave the name *self-activity* to the perceptions a person achieved when he or she blended the content of a stage with the contents from a higher mode. For example, the step of memory included the content of the sense perception as well as the recognition that the information came through the senses. When a person combined those contrasting methods of knowing, he or she could move from one level of thought to another. For example, when a person contrasted memories of sense perceptions with the information that had come through their emotions, the resulting contrast enabled the person to move to the higher level of cognition. Harris believed that when people followed this progression through the ways of knowing, they increased their awareness of themselves.[5]

Because thinking moved by its own logic, Harris argued that a study of the faculties of the mind would reveal the goal of the process of knowing. According to Harris, the growth of consciousness implied that people, who were born as animals concerned with material affairs, could become spiritual beings by lifting themselves above their particular existence toward some universal form. This happened when people directed their studies to knowing about consciousness.

It is important to recognize that Harris did not trust scientific analyses or experiments to accumulate in ways that would advance human understanding of the world. In fact, he held that an objective study of experience such as a scientist might undertake would not reveal the aim of knowledge because scientific studies reinforced the particularities of life rather than its universal quality.

Instead of science, Harris recommended that people analyze consciousness by seeking to understand culture. This was the most helpful method of education. According to Harris, children moved toward spiritual dimensions when they acquired the ways that their particular group had moved beyond specific activities. For example, by acquiring language, children learned about the culture of their groups. Since such learning moved toward a quality of universality, it lifted the children's spirits toward an ethical plane. Although a person could not reach a state of universality because the body remained particular, Harris believed that each of the institutions in civilized society, such as family, school, civil society, and church, had its own role to play in helping people to recognize the rational movement of history and thereby move closer to God.[6]

Because culture moved people toward universal understandings, it was the key to self-perfection. Consequently, Harris believed that students could learn the ethical or universal aspects of the culture when they followed academic subject matters arranged in separate but hierarchal order. Such an appropriate curriculum consisted of aspects that transcended experience and therefore were true for all conditions. For example, in kindergarten, the students would encounter a series of objects that illuminated geometric concepts and numerical concepts that would apply to later studies. In the elementary schools, they would begin to encounter the disciplines that would enable them to take up the rudiments of human civilization. Harris divided these school studies into five divisions that he called the windows to the soul. They included mathematics combined with physics, biology, literature and art, grammar as the technical study of language, and history concentrating on the study of institutions. The areas were separate because the students used different ways of thinking within each division. For example, in mathematics and biology, the students had to use the sense of quantity whereas, in grammar, they followed a sort of introspection in which they looked for the meanings of words and the roles the words played in sentences. As a result, in mathematics and biology, the students could look for equality or difference among objects, but in grammar, they had to look beyond the words themselves to the contexts in which they appeared.[7]

Although Harris thought the students should study the same subjects in the different grade levels that extended from elementary schools to universities, he wanted the students to pursue the subjects with increasing depth as they advanced. For example, students in elementary schools encountered arithmetic. In secondary schools, they moved into algebra and geometry. In college, calculus, physics, and chemistry appeared on the curriculums. The effect of such a progression was to strengthen the students' grasp of culture. Thus, for Harris, students who ended their educations at the elementary school barely understood their culture while students who proceeded to college acquired critical, comparative, and conservative attitudes of mind. That is, college students understood why established institutions existed, and they were less likely to act impetuously than were people who had not attended college.[8]

According to Harris, higher education illuminated the culture because it included the study of philosophy. To Harris, philosophy was the discipline that described the place and function of things within the absolute system. Although Harris praised science for collecting facts about existence under different conditions, he believed that it was the task of philosophy to determine the reason for the existence of all things. To achieve this goal, Harris counseled students of philosophy to follow five steps of thinking. These steps led from sense perception, to cognition of general classes, to an awareness of the unity of the causes of the classes, to careful consideration of the methods for determining the unity, and finally to the realization that the method of rational thought itself was the system or the cause behind the events in the universe.[9]

The important point about Harris's philosophy of education is that Harris constructed his view of the aim of education on his understanding of the nature of human consciousness. He thought that, when teachers recognized that truth lay beyond human experience, they could organize their courses in line with the progress of human understanding. For example, he recommended that teachers avoid thinking that the aim of education was to make good citizens or valuable workers. Instead of advocating such practical goals, Harris urged teachers to recognize that the aim of schools should be to enhance the spiritual natures of the students. For Harris, this was the most practical concern for school people because schools improved the students' citizenship or occupational skills by encouraging them to advance to ethical planes of thought. The practical benefits came indirectly from the study of the properly arranged subject matters.

How Did Idealistic Philosophy Become Science?

In creating his philosophy of education, Harris followed a European model that retained God as the central aspect. By the end of the nineteenth century, philosophers in American universities broke away from the religious traditions that Harris shared with other idealist philosophers. They adopted realistic perspectives from psychology.

Addressing the British Academy in 1918, Santayana explained how American philosophers had altered the ideas of their European colleagues. Since Santayana had been born in Spain, he was sensitive to differences in the ways Americans and Europeans thought. In part, Santayana thought the spacious environment of the United States changed people's ways of thinking. In these new spaces, young people forgot the moral restraints imposed by former generations. He added that the many immigrants adopted a similar independent social spirit, and philosophers adopted independent attitudes as well. According to Santayana, the academic philosophers of the early or middle nineteenth century had retained conservative ideas and defended religion. A new generation of professional philosophers, such as William James, Santayana's former teacher, replaced the more conservative and clerically oriented professors. While James and philosophers of his generation wanted to reform society, they did not use the religious tendencies of previous philosophies for this purpose. Allocating religion to the realm of private opinions, they sought practical evidence of the worth of any idea.[10]

According to Santayana, both groups, the older philosophers who held religious views and the socially minded academics, relied on German idealistic philosophy. As a result, an ironic process had taken place. German idealists during the eighteenth century, such as Kant, had held that consciousness was a faculty of mind that could bring together items that were logically and naturally different. For example, consciousness colored events with memories and added images to words. These idealists thought they could understand this faculty of consciousness if they studied it. Thus, idealists such as Kant encouraged a critical attitude toward consciousness and its attributes. Santayana claimed that, in the late nineteenth century, philosophers in the United States took the critical attitude toward consciousness, blended it with ideas from psychology, and claimed that consciousness was nothing but the sense impressions of which consciousness was aware. Thus, American philosophers had taken an effort to understand how consciousness operated and turned it into a way to claim that consciousness was simply the awareness of the things that made up experiences. It had no reality beyond the impressions it contained.[11]

According to Santayana, when philosophers such as William James concluded that consciousness, as an entity, did not exist, they thought they had made their work easier because they could study the world that surrounded them rather than debate the nature of consciousness. Santayana argued that they actually made their work harder because they had not answered the question of how people could know truth. For example, when James introduced psychology, he suggested that truth, as an independent body, did not exist. Santayana acknowledged that James did not deny that truth existed; however, he thought that James had adopted a stance that made the search for truth impossible. This happened because James identified an idea with an object. As a result, he could not claim that any idea was an aspect of a larger body of truth. Instead of asking what an opinion asserted logically, James's realism sought to identify the existential relations that surrounded true ideas. Santayana concluded that when James held that people could discover the objective world in things that surrounded them, he could not explain how an idea could be true if he could not compare it with some comprehensive reality. According to Santayana, when James identified an idea with its object, he proceeded to create lists rather than bodies of truth.[12]

Despite his criticisms, Santayana believed philosophers such as James had a faith that science would improve human life. Thus, although the traditional categories of consciousness and truth played no role in contemporary American philosophy, science offered an impartial accumulation of ideas. Americans may have had few abstract principles to follow, but they had mastered an array of facts. Santayana hoped the Americans would use their accumulated facts to bring about a better social order.[13]

How Did Dewey Revise Harris's Ideas of Knowledge and Curriculum?

At the same time Santayana described a shift in thinking among philosophers, a similar change took place among educational philosophers such as Harris and Dewey. Although Harris and Dewey differed about notions of consciousness and truth, Dewey did not reject Harris's ways of thinking. Dewey accepted the German idealism that fueled Harris's thought and agreed that educators had to understand the nature of consciousness. The important difference was that, although Dewey followed the principles of idealism, he rejected any notion of truth as a transcendent body of ideas separate from sense experiences. Thus, in ways roughly similar to those that Santayana found in William James's work, Dewey translated the concept of consciousness into the concept of experience. In spite of this similarity, Dewey did not seek to investigate the world; he wanted to know how people should think. Thus, in a manner similar to Harris's view that a study of consciousness could lead to the recognition of absolute truth, Dewey claimed that a study of experience revealed the best way to direct experience toward more and better or wider experiences. In this way, Dewey changed the concept of consciousness into the ability to solve problems, and, like consciousness, this experience took place within a person. Such a conclusion led Dewey to agree with Harris that truth was the process of rationality. For Dewey, at best, truth was the scientific process that brought about the growth or expansion of experiences.

When Dewey made experience the important object of study, he claimed that it involved action and thought. Noting that people could not profit from moving from one experience to another in some random fashion, Dewey contended that people had to think if they were to learn from experience. Thus, experience had an active phase and a passive part. The active phase involved some effort to try something. The passive part was undergoing the changes that resulted. When people connected these different aspects, realizing that certain actions led to certain consequences, they could direct their experiences in fruitful directions. Defining thinking as the recognition of these connections, Dewey concluded that the scientific method was the most effective way to predict the consequences of an action and to determine the influences those consequences would have. Although such a method could not predict all the consequences, it provided such a careful survey that it was superior to simple trial and error.[14]

In fairness, although Harris had believed that reason transcended experience, he had valued science. According to Harris, science was the systematized results of observation that followed three separate stages. The first was the observation of things and facts. The second was the investigation of interrelations. The third step was an effort to show how all of nature was part of a process of evolution. In this last step, Harris turned science into philosophy that sought the first principle or organizing idea of existence. In this step, science moved beyond experience to reveal the origin and destiny of the universe. The important aspect of Harris's ways of thinking was that he claimed the shift from science to philosophy could not come from the other steps. He argued that an inventory of events could not lead to an understanding of the origin of those events. Instead, because Harris thought all of nature was moving in the direction of rationality, he suggested that theology could show that God created nature to develop spiritual creatures who would share in His blessedness.[15]

Although Dewey did not bring up the existence of God when he discussed the ways that people should think, his method implied that God had created nature and that human beings should cooperate with nature. Arthur Wirth, one of Dewey's biographers, offered this interpretation of the ways Dewey developed his thought. According to Wirth, during a crisis of faith, Dewey recognized that nature would allow people to learn and grow even though nature could harm human beings. Dewey conceived of nature as beneficent because people could use their intelligence to alter natural conditions in ways that enhanced human life.[16]

Because Dewey had faith in the goodness of nature, he disliked philosophical theories that separated the workings of the human mind from events in the world. In what might have been a criticism of Harris, Dewey claimed that a tendency to focus on consciousness had developed in the sixteenth century when intellectuals sought to avoid the domination of religion that had restricted their freedom of thought. To avoid censorship, these philosophers had retreated into their minds where no one could dictate any conclusions. Dewey added that, on the educational side, the fear of intellectual imposition came out in philosophers such as Montaigne and Bacon who urged people not to accept any idea from authority. One solution to the problem appeared in German idealism. Dewey claimed that Hegel had taken Descartes's view of reason as the most important quality and integrated the reason present in the human mind with a quality of reason that permeated nature. In this way, Hegel overcame the problems that arose from separating consciousness from nature. Nonetheless, Dewey disliked the fact that Hegel claimed social institutions resulted from the workings of an absolute mind. To Dewey, in this way, Hegel reinstated the principle of authority.[17]

Despite his criticisms, Dewey followed Hegel's method of integrating apparently different concepts. Unlike Harris, though, Dewey argued that types of thinking did not need to change in order to advance toward the truth. That is, Harris thought scientific thinking changed into philosophy as it advanced, whereas Dewey claimed that scientific thinking maintained a consistent form when it became philosophy. Because one definition of philosophy was that it was an outlook on life, Dewey argued that philosophy might arise from the desire to report particular facts with scientific thoroughness and objectivity. Thus, for Dewey, philosophy was the willingness to view discoveries as opportunities to learn in the same way that unbiased curiosity fostered scientific explorations. A second definition of philosophy was that philosophy was thinking that had become self-conscious. Dewey turned this definition to mean that philosophy was the search for the ways that thinking could direct experiences. Thus, in these definitions, Dewey refused to distinguish between practical impulses and spiritual ideas as the bases for the search for truth. For Dewey, when people moved from science to philosophy, they did not change their method of thought at any point along the way.[18]

In matters related to education, four points illustrate the ways that Dewey began with ideas similar to those of Harris but took them in different directions. These include conception of the subject matter, views about manual training, the need for social organization, and the value of examinations. The following paragraphs in this section will explain each in turn.

First, although Dewey adopted Harris' view that the subject matters of school should introduce children to the wisdom of humankind, Dewey did not look upon the subject matters as means to lift students to spiritual realms. Instead, Dewey thought the academic subjects represented efforts that people had made in the past to overcome obstacles. For Dewey, the subject matters were the accumulations of the outcomes of the efforts, the strivings, and successes of the human race generation after generation. In order for people to profit from these accumulations of experience, scholars had arranged the information logically in textbooks. Thus, for Dewey, these texts served as maps indicating how the students could undertake activities in the most fruitful ways possible. For the teacher, the texts could indicate the directions that the students' present experiences should move in order for them to lead to more experiences that would broaden the students' outlooks and enhance their desires to learn.[19]

When Dewey defined subject matters as accumulations of human experiences, he made a technical definition of education possible. For him, education was the reconstruction of experience in ways that led from the children's present experience out into the organized experiences found in the subject matters. As this definition implied, there were no discontinuities between the experiences the children had in schools and the subject matters found in the schools. Because the content of the texts was the record of the experiences of the previous generations of human beings, teachers could arrange lessons so that children reconstructed those experiences.[20]

The second point comparing Harris to Dewey was the view toward manual training. Manual training was a model of education that taught children to engage in practical activities such as sewing or carpentry to master a set of skills rather than a trade. Although both Harris and Dewey believed that schools should concentrate on academic subjects, Dewey considered manual training a route into the academic subjects whereas Harris did not. As a result, Dewey began the lessons with some sort of manual training that would lead the students quickly to investigations into the subject areas. On the other hand, Harris chose to limit the emphasis that manual training had in schools.

Although Harris agreed that students should develop some sorts of manual skills to earn their livelihoods, he believed that the best places to learn these skills were in workshops and commercial establishments. Harris made some provision for acquiring these skills in schools, but he refused to consider such activities as substitutes or as enrichments to academic affairs. Harris thought that manual training taught specific useful skills whereas he believed that academic studies could lift people beyond their mortal conditions to an understanding of universal categories. Thus, Harris believed that manual training and academic training taught different types of understandings and aimed for different goals.[21]

Holding the view that manual training and academic subjects were qualitatively different, the best that Harris could do was seek to limit the intrusion of manual training into schools. Thus, as Chapter 8 described, Harris's ideas dominated the report of the National Education Association's Committee of Ten that appeared in 1893 and its report of the Committee of Fifteen that appeared in 1895. Although both of these reports emphasized that academic subjects should dominate school studies, they acknowledged that manual training and vocational training had places in elementary and secondary schools.

In this regard, Dewey could be more consistent. Sharing Harris's view on the importance of academic subject matters, Dewey placed manual training at the center of the school curriculum and turned it to serve the cultural insights that Harris wanted schools to convey. Dewey could do this because he believed that subject matters came from experiences of other people and students could learn the subject matters through their own experiences. To illustrate this view, Dewey gave the name *occupations* to the lessons that derived from his conception of manual training. Even though the name conjured images of vocational training, Dewey may have borrowed the term from Frederick Froebel who used *occupations* to describe the ways he wanted young children in his kindergarten to use the objects he designed to learn about size, shape, and colors. To Dewey, the value of occupations in schools was to help children understand how scientific thinking had changed society rather than acquire the technical skills to become carpenters, cooks, or tailors. As a result, in an activity such as sewing, the students' efforts, such as trying to use pieces of wool, cotton, and flax as part of clothing, led them to determine how technical inventions such as the cotton gin changed the ways that people carried on daily activities, such as manufacturing clothing.[22]

Thus, Dewey thought manual training could enable children to understand the technological and social changes that had taken place in the past hundred years; it could help the students acquire the moral training once available in farm life; and it could open children to the wide range of experiences made possible by industrial life. Manual training could aid in achieving these three goals, he added, if teachers conceived of work, such as weaving or sewing, in its social significance.[23]

When Dewey thought manual training could be adapted to teach the children about the industrial progress of human society, he believed that it could serve as the gateway to learning how to use the scientific way of thinking that had caused enormous changes in social life. It was science, Dewey noted, that enabled people to harness the forces of nature, to develop vast manufacturing centers, gather populations into cities, and distribute products throughout the world.[24]

Although Dewey wanted lessons to begin with the students' impulses, he sought to direct those instincts to a better form of expression. As a result, Dewey sought to lead the children through some sort of progression that seemed to recapitulate the progress of human society. For example, he noted that thoughts of hunting with a bow and arrow fascinated young boys. As a result, he offered the children opportunities to make stone arrowheads. This exercise led to a study of the composition of different types of rocks and eventually to the construction of a furnace to smelt iron. In these activities, the students followed their interest in hunting to the study of geology as they tried to shape stones. As the students sought to improve on stone arrowheads, they investigated physics in trying to regulate the drafts and the fuel for the furnace to smelt iron and make metal implements. Such movements from activities to subject matters were possible, Dewey contended, from the knowledge that because the subject matters were records of how previous generations had tried to overcome problems, the subject matters were tools the students could use to advance their own efforts.[25]

The third point of comparison between Dewey and Harris was the need for social order. Dewey believed that when children carried out the occupations, they cooperated with other students at the same time the teachers acted as guides offering suggestions and asking questions that enabled the children to realize their aims. Because the students proceeded from their own instincts, they learned to form plans and follow procedures to reach their aims and to adjust their aims to fit changing conditions. In the process, the students learned to apply themselves to their tasks, thereby developing the diligence or character training children had learned when life was lived on farms. At the same time, they learned to work with other students in ways that advanced their own goals and those of the other students as well. The lesson was that social organization enhanced their own freedoms to do things.[26]

Just as Harris justified the existing social arrangements, Dewey held similar conservative ideas. For Dewey, the occupations imposed organization on everybody. Although Dewey acknowledged that a busy kitchen could appear disorganized because bustle and confusion accompanied any activity, he claimed that the type of order permeating these occupations came from efforts to achieve goals. In seeking to accomplish something, the students had to divide the labor and cooperate. This meant that they had to select leaders and designate followers. Although such an order differed from the organization found in a school where forty or fifty students had to learn set lessons, the occupations provided the chance for the children to develop what Dewey called the spirit of cooperation and community life. It was a form of discipline.[27]

In general, Dewey did not consider human freedom or the tolerance of differences to be good things for their own sakes. That is, although Dewey was a proponent of academic freedom, he did not believe that human beings had the right to freedom as part of their essential dignity. Philosophers like Harris who held idealistic or religious ideas made arguments about human dignity. Although Dewey did not mention dignity, he considered human freedom an essential aspect of social progress because free people could develop their skills and abilities fully. For Dewey, individual improvement and social progress abetted each other. A person living with others thought more deeply about his or her experiences because a person who lived alone had no reason to reflect on his or her past. In fact, Dewey contended that social life existed in the transmission of ideas until those ways of thinking became common possessions. Although this meant that a person derived his or her human capacities by his or her membership in a group, Dewey was careful to caution against any excessive pressure on individuals to force them to conform to some shared set of ideas. Dewey pointed out that individual variation was the means by which society advanced because people who held different perspectives could suggest new ideas to solve pressing and common problems, and the members of the group could test those suggestions. Thus, he concluded, a democratic society had to protect intellectual freedom in order to progress.[28]

The last point of comparison concerned regular examinations. Although Harris approved of the graded schools with separate classes for separate studies conducted by teachers who held examinations or recitations, Dewey disapproved of recitations as opportunities for students to show how much they had learned. Nonetheless, Dewey wanted some regular form of evaluation. He achieved this by capitalizing on what he considered the children's impulses to communicate. As part of the occupations, the students would talk about what they tried to do, explain the successes they had, and describe the ways they could improve the work. Other students could join in the conversation, making the discussion into what Dewey called a social clearinghouse that corrected misconceptions and opened new lines of inquiry.[29]

How Did Dewey Initiate a Progressive Education Movement?

Dewey did not set out in his career to open a laboratory school. After graduating from the University of Vermont in 1879, Dewey accepted a position teaching high school courses in Pennsylvania. During the evenings, he read philosophy and submitted two articles to Harris who published them in the *Journal of Speculative Philosophy.* In 1882, he decided to make philosophy his life work, and he enrolled in the newly founded graduate school at Johns Hopkins University. After extensive studies of Kant's and Hegel's works, Dewey graduated and accepted a position at the University of Michigan in 1884 where he served on the faculty committees charged with evaluating the programs of secondary schools that sent students to the university. Realizing the quality of high school programs depended on the organization of elementary school programs, Dewey became interested in ways of designing a curriculum that integrated psychological and philosophical ideas into educational plans. In 1894, when Dewey moved to the University of Chicago, he had the opportunity to organize an elementary school program. At Chicago, Dewey became the chair of the combined departments of philosophy, psychology, and pedagogy.[30]

Although Dewey's position in the university justified his creating a laboratory school, he claimed that his motive was to provide appropriate training for his own children. Whatever his reason, Dewey opened a school in a private home with sixteen students and two teachers in 1896. Two years later, after moving twice, the school opened in a former residential home. Within this house, the school divided into departments roughly imitating the organization of the University of Chicago. At its height, the school enrolled 140 children with twenty-three teachers and ten graduate students who came from the university to act as assistants. Although Dewey served as director, Ella Flagg Young was the supervisor of instruction. Young went on to become superintendent of Chicago public schools and president of the National Education Association.[31]

For the first two years, 1896 to 1898, the teachers at the laboratory school experimented with various arrangements of lessons. By 1898, however, the teachers adopted the belief that schools should train children in cooperative and helpful living, and they sought to build lessons on the students' impulses to share experiences, to make things, to investigate, and to express or communicate discoveries. Because the teachers were to act as guides, teachers needed to have abilities in specialized areas of knowledge so they could work together, contributing from their strengths, to help the students carry out the occupations.[32]

In selecting the activities, the teachers looked for projects related to the children's present experiences that illuminated the ways social practices had come into being. For example, the youngest group of children, aged four to five years, reconstructed the homes of primitive people and expanded the activity into accounts of the homes of ancient Greeks. This led to reading literature, to writing stories, and to drawing pictures as the children sought to discover information and to express what they learned about houses. At all points, teachers avoided imposing the lessons. For example, in the artistic efforts, the children did not practice techniques of manipulating color, line, or texture. Instead, they sought to express the ideas they had, and the teachers suggested techniques to enhance that expression.[33]

As the school grew, children aged from fourteen to sixteen years enrolled. The older students in this senior division formed clubs to undertake specialized projects. A problem arose when they created a photography club and a debating society because the school lacked adequate space for them to do their work or to hold their meetings. Thus, they proposed building a larger clubhouse. This project involved architecture, construction, sanitation, interior decoration, and finance. Undeterred by the enormity of their tasks, the students formed committees to work on the different facets of home construction. They visited buildings in the city to determine what was possible on the land that was available, and they went to museums to consider the best architectural style. They debated questions of interior design and decoration. Although a professional mason constructed the fireplace, the senior students did most of the construction work. Whenever a particular task exceeded their abilities, they turned to teachers and to other people for help. As a result, they learned to cooperate with other people, to seek resources from experts outside the school, and to permit different children to contribute according to their talents and abilities.[34]

Because the laboratory school flourished, the University of Chicago took advantage of an opportunity to merge it with two other schools, the Southside Academy and the Chicago Manual Training School in 1903. At first, Dewey considered the combination advantageous.

He claimed that the manual training component offered the means to expand opportunities for students to make things whereas the academy and the laboratory school brought in elements of culture, and the university could provide ideas from educational theory. Expressing the hope that the resulting facility would demonstrate how to combine these diverse elements, Dewey predicted that the school would be a model for schools across the country.[35]

Unfortunately, Dewey's optimism was short-lived. In making the merger, the University eliminated the jobs of several staff people who had served in the laboratory school. Because Dewey had not realized that people would have to leave the school, he was upset with the changes. He resigned from the university and the combined school in 1904. Although the laboratory school continued, it lacked a director until 1909 when Charles Judd accepted the position. Under Judd, the school followed a different direction by emphasizing testing rather than curricular integration.[36]

Although Dewey had only been involved with the laboratory school for a short time, it led him to begin writing about education. One result was *Schools of Tomorrow,* described previously that he undertook with his daughter, Evelyn. In writing this book, the authors included accounts of a mix of public and private schools from across the country. For example, in the Phoebe Thorn Experimental School of Bryn Mawr College, teachers integrated the study of grammar with other activities. When the eleven-year-old students asked questions relating to sentence structure and meaning, the teachers and the students constructed their own grammar books with the result that the students learned to analyze sentences quickly. In the Elementary School of the University of Missouri at Columbia directed by J. L. Meriam, the children engaged in activities that allowed them to run and to play while learning about their community. Although the teachers in Public School 45 of the Indianapolis school system followed the state curriculum, they introduced ways to teach subjects such as arithmetic by having the students draw the plans for a house.[37]

According to William W. Brinkman, the tendency of John and Evelyn Dewey to praise each school that appeared in *Schools of Tomorrow* implied that progressive schools emphasizing freedom and student interest were superior to academic education. Brinkman argued that if Dewey had been more careful to pinpoint the weaknesses in these progressive schools, he might have been able to encourage progressive schools to adopt coherent theories of education instead of allowing children to engage in a welter of activities. Brinkman added that Dewey confronted the problem in 1938 in his text *Experience and Education,* in which he urged progressive educators to develop organized curriculums.[38]

Although Brinkman was correct in complaining that *Schools of Tomorrow* did not critically evaluate the practices of the schools, the book did offer some analyses. For example, although the description of the Montessori system claimed that Maria Montessori allowed the children the freedom to move around and the liberty to engage in activities that interested them, it added that this freedom was incomplete. The description added that Montessori designed the exercises to teach children to be independent, orderly, and cooperative. With these exercises, the children learned to tie their own shoes or button their shirts because Montessori had designed appliances that they could use by themselves. In a similar way, Montessori had designed didactic materials, each of which taught the children something. A set of letters and numbers shaped from sandpaper that the children touched while blindfolded taught the children those letters and numbers because the children would guess from feel which letters or numbers they were. According to the description, the teacher never corrected the children if they made a mistake or misused an object. Instead, the teacher put the materials away and started something else. Although the book concluded that the children in Montessori schools had complete liberty in their use of the materials, it noted that the children's freedom consisted in using the material properly. Because the children did not have to find ways to cooperate with other people to achieve the ends they wanted, the Montessori materials failed to teach them how to meet two sets of constraints that are found in real life. One was to adjust to limitations in materials. The other was to meet the demands of other people. Although students might learn one of these techniques in a Montessori school, they would not learn the other.[39]

Other progressive educators expanded the criticisms of Montessori found in *Schools of Tomorrow.* For example, writing in 1914, William Heard Kilpatrick complained that Montessori's didactic materials allowed only one line of activity. Citing the example of a cylinder box, Kilpatrick noted that the child could only take the cylinders out of the box and place them back in the proper order. Although Montessori claimed that the material controlled error, Kilpatrick claimed that if the children attempted to make a wagon out of the box and the cylinders, the teacher would prevent them. Further, the design of the box prevented the children from putting cylinders in the wrong holes. Kilpatrick's conclusion was that Montessori materials did not offer the type of instruction a child might receive trying to hammer a nail or ride on roller skates where the self-correction in the effort was part of some larger purpose such as building a table or skating with friends. Instead, in the Montessori system, the children responded to the wishes of the teacher even when the teacher was in the background.[40]

Why Did Progressive Schools Come to Adopt Any Currently Popular Idea?

When Dewey had described the educational theories behind his laboratory school, he noted that students should enjoy the freedom to move around and the liberty to explore things that interested them. Although he valued these concepts, freedom and interest, they were not central to his ideas. In keeping with his affection for the combination of opposite tendencies, Dewey noted that in any activity having an aim, freedom and interest were aspects of discipline and control. Freedom would be the ability to set aims for oneself rather than having to follow the commands of a person in authority. Interest was the recognition that certain objects served as means or as obstacles to completing the activity and achieving the aim. Discipline came from the attention that a person paid to succeed at an activity. Since freedom and interest were necessary for the experiences to unfold in fruitful ways, they were subservient to the advancement of experience.[41]

Other progressive educators did not pay as careful attention to educational theory. Although many of the school reformers may have had some experience with philosophy and psychology, they did not concentrate on theoretical works as Dewey had. Instead, these people tended to be practically oriented. They thought they were conducting educational experiments even when they lacked a hypothesis to test. They seemed to think that the practical efforts they made demonstrated their own worth to the extent that theoretical justifications appeared unnecessary. Two examples, each from opposite parts of the country, illustrate this tendency. One is from the work of Marietta Pierce Johnson. The other is from the efforts of William A. Wirt. In these cases, the accounts that John and Evelyn Dewey wrote in *Schools for Tomorrow* avoided the critical evaluation these efforts should have received.

In compiling the accounts of progressive schools for *Schools of Tomorrow,* Evelyn Dewey had visited several experimental schools that carried on her father's general ideas. She wrote accounts of what she saw and her father, John, wrote analyses of those practices. In one case, though, John Dewey visited a school. It was the Organic School of Marietta Johnson in Fairhope, Alabama. Johnson called her school "organic" because she sought to provide the activities necessary for the children at each stage of growth to develop.[42]

The Organic School grew out of the reformist principles that Johnson and her husband Frank shared. The Johnsons left St. Paul, Minnesota, in 1902 and moved to Fairhope, Alabama. Located on Mobile Bay, the village had a population of about 100 residents, most of whom were socialists who had come to establish a community in accord with the theories of Henry George. Dedicated to what they called cooperative individualism, Fairhope residents leased their land from a community cooperative. The residents' rent represented the single tax that supported parks, a beach, and a library.[43]

Marietta Johnson completed teacher training in 1885 at a state normal school. On graduation, she taught school in Minnesota, rising through the elementary grades, teaching some high school courses, and serving in normal schools. She turned against the traditional approach to education after reading Nathan Oppenheim's book, *The Development of the Child.*[44]

Although Johnson had the chance to experiment with her new ideas when she moved to Fairhope, she abandoned the effort when her husband wanted to start a pecan farm in Mississippi. In 1907, the farm failed, and Johnson returned to Fairhope and began teaching. Drawing inspiration from C. Hanford Henderson's *Education and the Larger Life,* Johnson committed herself to treat each child as a complete organism. This was the theme of Henderson's book, and Johnson borrowed the term when she opened the Organic School.[45]

In 1913, John Dewey visited Johnson in Fairhope. Impressed with what he saw, he showered praise on the Organic School in *Schools of Tomorrow,* bringing Johnson nationwide attention. Newspapers such as *The New York Times* wrote approving stories, and Johnson toured widely, giving lectures to explain her ideas. In 1913, a group of prominent women in Greenwich, Connecticut, formed a Fairhope League to support Johnson's school and opened the Edgewood School in Greenwich that Johnson directed along with her original school. When an industrialist, Joseph Fels, gave Johnson $11,000, she moved the school to a ten-acre site the community gave her rent-free. By the 1920s, the campus contained ten buildings.[46]

According to Joseph Newman, although Johnson claimed that she drew inspiration from Oppenheim, Henderson, and Dewey, she did not take her ideas from any source. Newman claimed that what Johnson took from Oppenheim was the view that children were not small adults. Oppenheim counseled that children needed special treatment. Newman added that Johnson defined the special treatment children needed as coming down to a set of simplistic principles she decided were true. For example, she argued that children should not learn to read until they were nine years old because younger children had inadequately formed nervous systems.[47]

Rather than think through a position, Johnson appeared to accept ideas that coincided with her views. Thus, at one time, she justified her stand against teaching reading by saying that Dewey showed children learning through activity rather than through reading. To a person who had read Dewey's essay, "School and the Life of the Child" such a statement would seem wrong.[48]

When her husband failed at farming, he returned to the Organic School and took charge of the shop. This became the biggest and best-equipped building on campus, and it impressed most visitors. Marietta Johnson claimed the shop was the most important place on her school's campus because the children had to learn to do before they learned to read and write. Nonetheless, academics had a place. As the students advanced toward high school, they enrolled in four years of literature, history, math, and science, as well as studying Latin and French.[49]

Robert H. Beck acknowledged that Johnson enjoyed widespread fame although critics agreed that she was not an intellectual. For example, Beck noted that when Johnson wrote about her efforts in the Fairhope Organic School, she wrote a naïve account that lacked any expert or studied thinking. According to Beck, this happened because Johnson wrote as she spoke. Instead of providing an internally consistent theory, she offered a sequence of anecdotes that were associated with her views. Ironically, Johnson's lack of coherence may have stemmed from her desire to retain independence. She refused to associate her ideas with any theory. For example, although most of her success came from the fact that progressive educators in the 1920s championed her school, she would not identify herself with progressivism as a movement even though she was among the founding members of the Progressive Education Association. She identified with her own organic school.[50]

Another educator that John and Evelyn Dewey praised in *Schools of Tomorrow* was William A. Wirt. Although Wirt had received considerable attention for introducing extensive opportunities for industrial training, the account in *Schools of Tomorrow* claimed that Wirt had approached the opportunity to build a school system from the beginning. According to *Schools of Tomorrow,* Wirt did not consult experts or hire architects. He did not visit other communities to gain ideas. Instead, Wirt stayed at home and thought about two questions. First, what did the students need to become good citizens as well as happy and prosperous human beings? Second, how could the school provide for those needs?[51]

In referring to the importance of industrial training, the account in *Schools of Tomorrow* claimed that Wirt had included such activities because they had superior educational value. In this effort, Wirt did not want to serve the interests of an elite class of industrialists by training workers for the steel mills nor did Wirt want to turn unpromising immigrants into self-supporting individuals. Instead, the account concluded that Wirt found ways to cooperate with the community and to form the students into alert and intelligent citizens.[52]

Although John and Evelyn Dewey claimed that Wirt derived his ideas without looking beyond his community, Ronald D. Cohen suggested that this was not the case. Cohen wrote that Wirt had studied in Chicago where he learned of Dewey's school, and he visited Hull House to learn the benefits of public playgrounds and William Morris's praise of craft industries. In 1906, Wirt accepted the position of superintendent of Gary schools although neither the city nor the schools existed. The U.S. Steel Corporation was building its plant and the adjacent city on nine thousand acres of Lake Michigan shoreline. Immediately, Wirt began hiring teachers, surveying possible school sites, and selecting William B. Ittner as architect for the new school buildings. Over the next two decades, all the schools in Gary followed Ittner's designs and he built over 500 schoolhouses across the country. These were large, impressive brick structures with multiple uses. They had several windows that brought in natural light and clean, sanitary interiors. Further, in 1907, before moving to Gary, Wirt toured Europe to visit schools where he was impressed with the industrial training available in Berlin. According to Cohen, from these efforts, Wirt fashioned a complex school system incorporating the latest in educational thinking.[53]

Because Indiana had adopted a state law making education compulsory, Wirt faced an urgent need to build schools. Approved in 1897, the Indiana law required children from ages eight to fourteen to attend school and directed each county to appoint a truant officer to enforce the statute. Although there were not enough schools for students to attend, Wirt found places for them by 1908. He made schools from a three-story building, several one-room portable buildings, and some church facilities. The truant officer appointed by officials in Gary made efforts to bring the children of immigrant workers to schools. In response, Wirt added kindergartens in an effort to expose the young children to English and introduce them to school life.[54]

In planning the schools in Gary, Wirt did not want to construct small buildings in the children's immediate neighborhoods. He argued that large buildings surrounded by playgrounds with libraries, gymnasiums, and recreation rooms could be used by children and parents alike. Such facilities were essential, he claimed, in a community that lacked such amenities. In one school, for example, Wirt held monthly programs of literary or musical entertainments. He hired physical education teachers to work year round supervising the playgrounds, and he provided summer programs in such things as sewing, cooking, chemistry, and commercial arithmetic. By offering a wide range of services for many people, Wirt argued that the per capita expense of his schools was low although the initial costs seemed high.[55]

When Wirt decided to extend manual training to the elementary schools, he hit upon the plan that made him most famous. Taking a three-story building, Wirt expanded the third floor into a playroom, equipped the basement with benches and tools for wood and metal shop, and left nine rooms for classes. To use this space efficiently, Wirt divided the students into two groups that he called "platoons." While one platoon was in the classrooms, the other group was in the playroom, the workshop, or the playground. During the day, the students changed places as they engaged in different activities. In this way, the students used the entire facility all the time. This innovation in Gary, called the platoon school, was admired by many people.[56]

According to Raymond E. Callahan, in 1912, Franklin Bobbitt proclaimed the Gary plan an example of scientific management. Bobbitt praised Wirt for building a thoroughly modern school system equipped with every modern necessity, designed to obtain maximum service from the buildings, the equipment, and the teaching staff. Although Wirt did not connect his innovation with efficient use of space, Bobbitt claimed that the classrooms, shops, and playgrounds were always full. Furthermore, Bobbitt added that the schools provided activities for the community during the evenings and the weekends. Because teachers taught similar groups, the teachers devoted attention to specialized tasks. There were no special supervisors to oversee the students' work. Bobbitt's praise led the school boards of New York City and of Troy, New York, to hire Wirt as a consultant to help them introduce the Gary plan in their schools.[57]

Bobbitt's praise increased Wirt's fame among school administrators, and Dewey's praise suggested that the platoon school was a progressive model. Randolph Bourne added to Wirt's popularity among progressives. According to Cremin, Bourne wrote a series of impressionistic articles in *The New Republic* in 1915 claiming that the Gary plan allowed children to learn by doing without introducing the danger that vocational education would simply prepare lower-class children to work in factories. Bourne added that the Gary plan was typically American and one that all cities should adopt. One year later, Bourne published a book, *The Gary Schools,* comparing Wirt's ideas favorably to those of Dewey.[58]

Bourne contended that Gary was unusual although the city had grown up in a short period. Within three years, an area covered by sand dunes and scrub oak swamps changed into a metropolis. The steel mill employed thousands of workers. As the population grew, the town built miles of paved roads and cement sidewalks. As homes rose throughout the area, the city added sewers, water and gas lines, and electric facilities. Despite the rapid development, Bourne claimed that Gary faced the typical problems of urban life. These included political corruption, a substantial immigrant population, and the domination by a large group of native-born white Americans.[59]

According to Bourne, the Gary schools bore out the ideal of integrating into the daily school day the diverse elements of work, study, and play. Because Wirt had adapted an old school building to these purposes, Bourne thought the Gary plan showed that any building could be adapted to what he called the varied life of a school community.[60]

Quoting Dewey's description of the school and society, Bourne claimed that Wirt had organized the Gary schools around the attempt to restore the natural education once found in rural farm life and to adapt it to modern demands. The school was to become a self-sustaining community wherein the manual training programs provided the maintenance of the school. Thus, vocational training came from carpenters, cabinetmakers, and machinists working in well-equipped shops with the children to make and repair anything the schools needed. In a kitchen, students learned domestic science by preparing lunch for the rest of the school. Students did the school's laundry and needlework on campus. Supplies came from a school store the students conducted. Furthermore, each of the departments saved the school enough money to cover the expenses of materials and teacher salaries. Thus, the children worked with artisans or businesspeople in the ways children had worked with their parents on farms.[61]

Despite the apparent uniqueness of the programs in the Gary schools, Bourne claimed the curriculum followed the course of study set out by the State Department of Public Instruction. Bourne claimed that the teachers taught all the subjects in the Gary schools in concrete ways that drew on experiences familiar to the children. Although the activities were practical, they were also cultural. For example, in a history class, the students compared the education available in the ancient city of Athens with the education offered by the city of Gary. In this way, the students came to understand the purposes of their school and recognize how schools contribute to the social and political life of the city. In physics classes, the lighting, heating, and ventilation systems of the school buildings provided practical lessons that led to theoretical understandings. In a similar manner, students in chemistry classes worked as the municipal laboratory to test the city water, various milk supplies, and produce. Not only did the students work as city health inspectors, they tested the materials supplied to the school, such as coal and cement, to ensure the products met specifications.[62]

Concluding that the Gary schools offered a synthesis of the best aspects of the schools that Dewey had described in *Schools of Tomorrow,* Bourne was most pleased that the program was flexible and could adapt to changing conditions. Most important, he believed the students could recognize that their work was similar to the occupations and the interests that adults pursued in the wider society. Bourne concluded that the Gary schools offered a simple plan of organization with ingenious financial economies that promised to serve all the children.[63]

Despite Bourne's praise, critics pointed out that Wirt's model was not a carefully thought out plan. For example, in 1924, Abraham Flexner and Frank P. Bachman released their report of the Gary schools for the General Education Board. Flexner and Bachman built their comments on an extensive, eight-volume analysis of the Gary schools by such experts as George Strayer and Stuart Courtis. They praised the Gary schools for attempting to offer the maximum instruction in the widest range of activities to the greatest number of students and for allowing the students to move freely while they pursued interesting activities. At the same time, Flexner and Bachman did not find that administrators had linked these various activities. They claimed that the students encountered a welter of rapidly changing activities with little apparent integration. For example, although the students undertook interesting activities in the auditorium, the classroom teachers did not build on those activities.[64]

Although Bourne had claimed that students learned practical skills by working in shops and kitchens with skilled artisans, Flexner and Bachman contended that this was not the case. They found that the students executed orders that the instructors gave them. As a result, when the students completed their assignments, they had not learned the basic principles or skills those tasks required. Nor did the students learn how people in businesses completed similar jobs. At times, the instructors had to tend to some emergencies in the building, and they left the pupils without guidance.[65]

Although Bourne had praised the science teaching in the Gary schools, Flexner and Bachman felt that the science teaching was haphazard. Although Flexner and Bachman agreed that teaching science from a textbook was dispiriting, they claimed the Gary schools had not found a reasonable alternative. In many of the schools, the classes were formless and aimless. Thus, while Flexner and Bachman found that teachers in science, English, and shop approached similar topics with an interdisciplinary focus, they noted that students encountered these lessons as disconnected diversions. The lessons did not progress in an orderly fashion. Instead, the students engaged in series of unrelated activities. Consequently, although the students were interested in their work and derived pleasure from these studies, they did not develop the capacities to intelligently deal with large problems.[66]

According to Flexner and Bachman, the administration was to blame for the failures in Gary. For example, the school buildings contained classrooms, shops, and auditoriums. Because the students moved together as classes through these facilities, some of them were in each part throughout the day. Although this was supposed to be an efficient use of space, the teachers did not have the training to use the schedule and the facilities properly. In short, Flexner and Bachman complained that instead of teachers holding to high standards of work, mediocre results satisfied them. Without the patient and careful attention of teachers, many children did not master such things as academic skills.[67]

Despite the severe complaints, Flexner and Bachman did not censure the Gary plan. Praising the innovative spirit that led to the creation of the plan, they noted that it could succeed if the efforts were carefully controlled and the results critically evaluated. Thus, they claimed the Gary plan might result in methods to prepare children for the demands of modern life if these efforts received more thought, more planning, and more control.[68]

Despite Flexner and Bachman's call for thoughtful planning, the Gary plan spread through the United States. By 1929, about 220 cities employed the Gary plan in about 1068 schools with around 730,000 students. Although advocates claimed that the model solved a range of problems, they did not call for the careful planning and integration of studies that concerned Flexner and Bachman. For example, in 1931, Roscoe David Case claimed that the platoon model relieved congestion in schools, provided opportunities for teachers to take regular rest periods, and offered flexibility in planning. Case, a former superintendent of city schools, noted that an important advantage to the platoon system was that classes held increased numbers of students and required fewer teachers. In setting out the steps for implementing the platoon school, Case noted that the model required considerable planning. Case recommended surveys to show the community the need for such a school, use of procedures to select teachers willing to work in such a setting, and implementation of adequate publicity to inform the community of the coming change.[69]

Case called the platoon school the most modern educational practice. According to Case, the philosophy of the platoon school consisted of four points that everyone within the building had to accept. First, the design of the school buildings followed the findings of psychologists about children's growth. This meant that children had to move around. Second, children had to learn to solve problems found in a community. Third, all parts of the school building were used efficiently. Finally, the people working in the platoon school had to agree to be part of an experimental program.[70]

Although Case's book demonstrated the popularity of the platoon model, it illustrated an unwillingness to recognize the shortcomings that Flexner and Bachman had pointed out in 1924. Although Case called for careful study before instituting a platoon model, he did not call for studies that organized the subject matters in reasonable sequences nor did he call for the platoon schools to follow a theoretical model such as Harris or Dewey had described. Instead, to Case, the philosophy of the platoon school was a commitment to follow whatever educational practices were considered to be most current.

Could Progressive Educational Reforms Encourage Individual Liberation?

Although philosophical disputations played an important role in the reform of schools during the 1880s and 1890s, most educators did not build their practices according to the philosophies of education. They based their practices on what they called common sense rather than on educational theories.[71] This was true of untrained teachers and reformers. As noted above, Marietta Johnson and William Wirt claimed to introduce new ways of thinking about schools even when they expanded long-accepted, practical models.

Despite the common reliance on common sense among educators, there were thoughtful progressive educators who disapproved of the excessive concern Dewey seemed to place on the individual's cooperation with other members of a group. It was Dewey's concern for social cooperation that bothered Margaret Naumburg, the founder of the Walden School.

Born in 1908, Naumburg was almost fifty years younger than Marietta Johnson. Whereas Johnson grew up on a farm, Naumburg was born in the city of New York, attended private liberal schools such as the Horace Mann School, and entered Barnard College where she majored in philosophy and economics. She studied with John Dewey. After graduation in 1912, Naumburg traveled to Europe where she met and studied with Maria Montessori.[72]

On returning to the United States, Naumburg opened a kindergarten in a public New York City school. Although she tried to introduce the Montessori techniques, she found the authorities unwilling to accept her innovations. After a short period, she decided that the didactic materials for which Montessori was famous prevented the children from doing anything creative. To Naumburg, the sole benefit of the Montessori techniques was to enable children to learn basic academic skills quickly. Naumburg found an antidote for the oppressive nature of schools in the work of psychoanalysis and in the recognition of the benefits of physical movement from experts such as F. Matthias Alexander.[73]

In 1914, Naumburg opened the Children's School with Claire H. Raphael in a rented room in the Lette School in New York City, for children aged two, three, and four years. According to Blythe Hinitz, a biographer of Naumburg, the Children's School was the first nursery school based on psychoanalytic theory. The program sought to enhance the physical coordination of the children through movement exercises and music. At the same time, Naumburg thought she could encourage the emotional and intellectual development of the children. To signify her desire to assert the rights of individuals against the pressure of conformity, Naumburg changed the name of her school to the Walden School, after Thoreau's adventures on Walden Pond.[74]

In 1914, Naumburg entered psychoanalysis with an analyst trained in the manner of Carl Gustav Jung. When she opened the Walden School, she expected the teachers to undergo analysis so that they could enable the children to achieve emotional and intellectual integration. In fact, one of her students was the child of A. A. Brill, a Freudian analyst, under whom Naumburg entered therapy later.[75]

According to Hinitz, the aim of the Walden School was to use the insights of analytic psychology to meet the developmental needs of the children during the first five years of their lives. Naumburg thought these beginning years of a child's life were the most significant. Thus, Naumburg believed that she could use children's play as a resource to understand and direct their growth. Following psychoanalytical theory, Naumburg and her staff wanted young children to learn about sex and reproduction in simple yet straightforward ways. Such instruction was part of a general effort to help children form habits that allowed them to preserve their identity.[76]

Although Naumburg's concern for children's habits appears similar to Dewey's ideas, Hinitz contended that Naumburg did not like the ways that teachers in Dewey's laboratory school had set up projects for the children. As noted above, it was through the projects that Dewey wanted children to form the habits of good thinking. Hinitz claimed that Naumburg disagreed with the way the teachers in Dewey's laboratory school created the projects and manipulated the children to take an interest in carrying out the activities. For Naumburg, such adult imposition prevented the children from developing a sense of their own independence.[77]

Although Naumburg wanted the children to develop their own identities and become independent, she wanted the students to acquire social skills. She resolved this apparent paradox through art. Along with other teachers in the Walden School, Naumburg decided that art was the means by which the children expressed energies that arose from within their psyches. They added that universal ideas such as beauty offered the children means to integrate those internal forces. As the children grew, they expanded their senses of art in ways that enabled them to develop into healthy socialized yet independent personalities.[78]

Because art was central to the child's development, the school had a quantity of paper, crayons, and paints that the children used in any manner they wished. As a result, the children painted what they felt and they frequently expressed complicated views of their relationships with other people. At best, the teachers considered the children's paintings as measures of changes in the children's perceptions. In this way, the art program led Naumburg into a study of art therapy and helped her accomplish pioneering work in the field.[79]

Naumburg left the Walden School in 1924, but the schools continued to grow. By 1928, Walden School had a nursery, elementary school, and high school. Total enrollment reached 200 boys and girls divided into thirteen groups ranging in age from two years to college age. In 1928, Naumburg published *The Child and the World,* in which she described her views about education and social reform. Complimenting Francis Parker and John Dewey for freeing the school from a monastic curriculum, she complained that they turned excessive attention to the social functions of the school. The problem was that the effort to orient children to life in the community turned into attempts to train children for the responsibilities of citizenship even though the civic order functioned badly. As a result, children learn to work within a society that allowed injustices to continue instead of learning how to reform it.[80]

According to Naumburg, some form of individual spiritual renewal would do more to transform America than the efforts of service clubs such as the Rotarians. If such a personal approach did not come about, she feared the extinction of individuality. Nonetheless, she found it difficult to convince people that they might be hurting individual development when they concentrated on serving society. Although reformers promised that improved organization and increased productivity would enlarge people's leisure and increase their freedom, Naumburg wondered what the leisure and freedom served. She wondered what could be the value of more cars, more jazz music, and more radios.[81]

Naumburg found the malleability of children to be a distressing and a hopeful thing about education. Although there was the danger that schools could shape children to adapt to a bad society, she thought that an intelligently designed school could produce extraordinarily differentiated individuals who would stand against the pressures of conformity and protect the interests of the individual. Noting that schools had produced such men as Henry David Thoreau, Bronson Alcott, and Henry Adams, she hoped that schools could do it again.[82]

After leaving Walden School, Naumburg became influential in the field of art therapy. Calling her model Dynamically Oriented Art Therapy, she thought it was appropriate for use with a wide range of neurotic and psychotic adults as well as some adolescents and children. The rationale of this process was that the images the patients painted or drew reflected what was going on their unconscious. In this way, the art therapy served as a form of free association to reveal to the therapist and to the patient what was happening. Aided by such insights, the patient could move toward personal independence and integration.[83]

Although art therapy may seem distinct from preschool education, Naumburg thought they were similar. A music and art critic, Paul Rosenfeld, suggested such connections when he included an essay about Naumburg in his collection of biographies of such famous American moderns as John Marin, the painter, and Carl Sandburg, the poet. Rosenfeld claimed that Naumburg had taken as her medium the education of children. He praised Naumburg for creating a school that freed children from the destructive social processes that crushed their integrity and their creative potential. According to Rosenfeld, the innovations of the Walden School came from the fact that Naumburg resisted the influences of conservatives who wanted the children to master academic skills and she avoided the dangers of liberals who disliked any concern for subject matter. Praising Naumburg for avoiding any ideology, Rosenfeld claimed that she acted as an artist who coaxed forth the identity that she knew to be within each child.[84]

Although Rosenfeld felt that Naumburg did not follow any educational theories, this was not true. Naumburg was familiar with many theories of education. She did not rely on common sense in the way that Johnson did. Nor was she as concerned with administration as Wirt was. Naumburg moved in intellectual circles. She invited famous writers and scientists to her school. Lewis Mumford taught English. Ernest Bloch taught music. Hendrick Van Loon taught history. When Agnes De Lima visited the school after Naumburg had left, she found that the staff sought to provide a rich variety of resources rather than to define syllabi for the different age levels. Although these efforts to stand aside from the children as they grew derived from psychiatry, they did not represent a lack of educational theory.[85]

Thus, although Naumburg criticized the values and the orientation of the educators around her, she found the direction for reform in a rekindling of images from the American past. At the same time that Naumburg employed the ideas of Harris and Dewey, she added an understanding of the European advances in psychiatry. Thus, although Naumburg emphasized the values of freedom and democracy that Thoreau, Alcott, and Adams expressed, she found ways to bring out the individual capacities of each student through Jungian psychiatry. Naumburg thought she could help children use art to integrate their personalities.

Conclusion

According to Cremin, during the latter part of the nineteenth century, the general movement called progressivism encouraged an educational protest. Until the advent of World War I, progressives believed that the application of reasonable plans could improve the world. Most important, Cremin claimed that most progressive reformers who worked from 1890 to 1918 believed that schools would aid these reforms.[86]

Although Cremin described differences between conservative educators, such as Harris, who worked before 1890 and the reformers who followed, such as Dewey, there were important similarities. For example, prominent progressive scholars such as Dewey did not introduce new models of thinking to replace Harris's ideas. Instead, Dewey continued to use the German philosophical methods that Harris had acquired. For example, Harris identified the nature of consciousness with the processes that went on in the mind, and he concluded that cultural practices represented ways by which the processes of thinking could move to higher levels. When Dewey adopted Harris's approach, he changed the concern for consciousness into a method of controlling experience. As a result, Dewey argued that stages or levels of thinking differed in their complexity, not in their qualities. Thus, for Dewey, the processes of thought about practical affairs were roughly similar to the processes of thinking about philosophy. The best method of thinking in all situations was the scientific method because it enabled people to change nature in ways that improved their lives.

In 1896, Dewey tried his ideas of learning in a laboratory school. In asking the students to master the scientific method of thinking, Dewey wanted students to understand the force that was changing the world. As noted in the introduction, Dewey believed that science had led to the growth of large industries, new methods of transportation, and improved ways of communication. By understanding science, the students could see the social transformations later called globalization.

Although Dewey introduced educational practices with which Harris would have disagreed, Dewey reinforced Harris's concern with such things as social organization and mastery of subject matter. As a result, Dewey appeared to foster a concern for social conformity as Harris had. In part, this tendency derived from the model of thinking that Harris and Dewey shared. The idealism expressed by German philosophers such as Hegel integrated contradictory tendencies in ways that explained social change, but the model of thinking seemed to emphasize social progress.

Following the spirit of American adventurers, some educational reformers tended to ignore educational theories. These drifted into meaninglessness as did the Organic School of Marietta Johnson or they reinforced the bureaucratic organization of schools as did Wirt's platoon school model.

Although European innovations seemed to reinforce social organization, some American reformers introduced ideas from European psychiatrists that encouraged the free development of individual children. For example, Margaret Naumburg turned to psychoanalysis seeking methods to free the children from pressures to conform. To an outsider, the innovations in the Walden School may have appeared discontinuous. They were not. Margaret Naumburg used her background in psychoanalysis to reject what she contended was a pervasive element of compulsion in Dewey's laboratory school. Consequently, she allowed the children complete freedom to express their feelings through art. In this way, Naumburg reinforced the concern for the development of more integrated, better-developed ways of thinking that Harris and Dewey had shown. She took her ideas from German thought as well. Instead of Hegel, though, she followed Freud and Jung.

The educational reformers described in this chapter sought to train children to become socially cooperative while providing for individual growth. They inspired educators to visit other countries to determine if those models had achieved such a synthesis. In some cases, such as the platoon school, the hope was that an efficiently organized bureaucratic administration would blend these goals. To some extent, bureaucratic arrangements did encourage students to develop a variety of practical skills. Unfortunately, this was a narrow definition of growth. It enhanced globalization when many educators expressed interest in those solutions.

Endnotes

1. Lawrence A. Cremin, *The Transformation of the School: Progressivism in American Education, 1876–1957* (New York: Alfred A. Knopf, 1964), 14–20.
2. William W. Brinkman, "Introduction," in John Dewey and Evelyn Dewey, *Schools of Tomorrow* (1915; reprint, New York: E. P. Dutton & Co., 1962), ix–xxvi.
3. Lawrence A. Cremin, *American Education: The Metropolitan Experience, 1876–1980* (New York: Harper & Row, 1988), 157–164.
4. W. T. Harris, *Psychologic Foundations of Education: An Attempt to show the Genesis of the Higher Faculties of the Mind* (New York: D. Appleton and Co., 1899), 228–229, 233–234, 239–240.
5. Ibid.
6. Harris, *Psychologic Foundations of Education,* 228–236.
7. Harris, *Psychologic Foundations of Education,* 323–326.
8. Harris, *Psychologic Foundations of Education,* 337–341.
9. Harris, *Psychologic Foundations of Education,* 376–400.
10. George Santayana, *Philosophical Opinion in America* (London: H. Miford, Oxford University Press, 1918), 1–3.
11. Santayana, *Philosophical Opinion in America,* 3–7.
12. Santayana, *Philosophical Opinion in America,* 7–9.
13. Santayana, *Philosophical Opinion in America,* 11.
14. John Dewey, *Democracy and Education: An Introduction to the Philosophy of Education* (1916; reprint, New York: Macmillan Co., 1966), 139–151.
15. Harris, *Psychologic Foundations of Education,* 376–383.
16. Arthur G. Wirth, *John Dewey as Educator: His Design for Work in Education, 1894–1904* (New York: John Wiley & Sons, Inc., 1966), 8–9.
17. Dewey, *Democracy and Education,* 291–305.
18. Dewey, *Democracy and Education,* 323–326.
19. Dewey, *The Child and Curriculum and The School and Society,* 12, 16, 20–21.
20. Dewey, *The Child and Curriculum and The School and Society,* 11.
21. Harris, *Psychologic Foundations of Education,* 266–267.
22. Dewey, *The Child and the Curriculum and The School and Society,* 9, 19–21.
23. John Dewey, *The Child and the Curriculum and The School and Society* (1915; rev ed. Chicago: University of Chicago Press, 1971), 12–14.
24. Dewey, *The Child and the Curriculum and The School and Society,* 37–38.
25. Dewey, *The Child and the Curriculum and The School and Society,* 47–54.
26. Dewey, *The Child and the Curriculum and The School and Society,* 29, 37–38, 40–41.
27. Dewey, *The Child and Curriculum and The School and Society,* 15–18.
28. Dewey, *Democracy and Education,* 4–6, 304–305.
29. Dewey, *The Child and Curriculum and The School and Society,* 55–56.
30. Wirth, *John Dewey as Educator,* 9–16.
31. Katherine Camp Mayhew and Anna Camp Edwards, *The Dewey School: The Laboratory School of the University of Chicago, 1896–1903* (1936; reprint, New York: Atherton Press, 1966), 7–9, 446.
32. Mayhew and Edwards, *The Dewey School,* 39–43.
33. Mayhew and Edwards, *The Dewey School,* 43–45.
34. Mayhew and Edwards, *The Dewey School,* 228–233.
35. Mayhew and Edwards, *The Dewey School,* 14–17.
36. Mayhew and Edwards, *The Dewey School,* 17–19; Wirth, *John Dewey as Educator,* 223.
37. Dewey and Dewey, *Schools of Tomorrow,* xxvii–xxviii, 31–33, 54–58, 62–63.
38. Brinkman, "Introduction," xxv.
39. Dewey and Dewey, *Schools of Tomorrow,* 104–120.
40. William Heard Kilpatrick, *The Montessori System Examined* (1914; reprint, New York: Arno Press, 1971), 31–35.
41. Dewey, *Democracy and Experience,* 137–138.
42. Dewey and Dewey, *Schools of Tomorrow,* 17–18.
43. Joseph Newman, "The Organic School," in *"Schools of Tomorrow," Schools of Today: What Happened to Progressive Education,* ed. Susan F. Semel and Alan R. Sadovnik (New York: Peter Lang, 1999), 67–69.
44. Newman, "The Organic School," 73.
45. Newman, "The Organic School," 73; C. Hanford Henderson, *Education and the Larger Life* (Boston: Houghton, Mifflin, and Co., 1902), 97–131.
46. Newman, "The Organic School," 75–77.
47. Newman, "The Organic School," 72–75.
48. Robert H. Beck, "Marietta Johnson: Progressive Education and Christian Socialism," *Vitae Scholasticae* 6, no. 2 (1987): 142–143.
49. Joseph Newman, "Marietta Johnson and the Organic School," in *Founding Mothers and Others: Women Educational Leaders during the Progressive Era,* ed. Alan R. Sadovnik and Susan F. Semel (New York: Palgrave, 2002), 19–36.

50. Beck, "Marietta Johnson," 157–158.
51. Dewey and Dewey, *Schools of Tomorrow,* 128–129.
52. Dewey and Dewey, *Schools of Tomorrow,* 130–149.
53. Ronald D. Cohen, *Children of the Mill: Schooling and Society in Gary, Indiana, 1906–1960* (Bloomington: Indiana University Press, 1990), 4–6, 21.
54. Cohen, *Children of the Mill,* 7–12.
55. Cohen, *Children of the Mill,* 12–17.
56. Cohen, *Children of the Mill,* 17–21.
57. Raymond E. Callahan, *Education and the Cult of Efficiency: A Study of the Social Forces that have shaped the Administration of Public Schools* (Chicago: University of Chicago Press, 1962), 128–135.
58. Cremin, *The Transformation of the School,* 156–157.
59. Randolph S. Bourne, *The Gary Schools* (1916; reprint, Cambridge, Mass.: The MIT Press, 1970), 3–5.
60. Bourne, *The Gary Schools,* 13–15.
61. Bourne, *The Gary Schools,* 35–56.
62. Bourne, *The Gary Schools,* 113–130.
63. Bourne, *The Gary Schools,* 175–177.
64. Abraham Flexner and Frank P. Bachman, *The Gary Schools: A General Account* (New York: General Education Board, 1924), 196–201.
65. Flexner and Bachman, *The Gary Schools,* 134–136.
66. Flexner and Bachman, *The Gary Schools,* 120–121.
67. Flexner and Bachman, *The Gary Schools,* 201–203.
68. Flexner and Bachman, *The Gary Schools,* 203–206.
69. Callahan, *Education and the Cult of Efficiency,* 130; Roscoe David Case, *The Platoon School in America* (Stanford: Stanford University Press, 1931), 101–117.
70. Case, *The Platoon School,* 11–12.
71. Cremin, *The Transformation of the School,* 20–21.
72. Blythe Hinitz, "Margaret Naumburg and the Walden School," in *Founding Mothers and Others: Women Educational Leaders during the Progressive Era,* ed. Alan R. Sadovnik and Susan F. Semel (New York: Palgrave, 2000), 37–42.
73. Robert Holmes Beck, "American Progressive Education, 1875–1930" (Ph.D. diss., Yale University, June 1942), 165–167.
74. Hinitz, "Margaret Naumburg and the Walden School," 42–43.
75. Hinitz, "Margaret Naumburg and the Walden School," 38–39.
76. Hinitz, "Margaret Naumburg and the Walden School," 44–45.
77. Hinitz, "Margaret Naumburg and the Walden School," 44–45.
78. Beck, "American Progressive Education, 1875–1930," 171–172.
79. Hinitz, "Margaret Naumburg and the Walden School," 49–50.
80. Margaret Naumburg, *The Child and the World: Dialogues in Modern Education* (New York: Harcourt, Brace, and Co., 1928), xvii–xix.
81. Naumburg, *The Child and the World,* xix–xxii.
82. Naumburg, *The Child and the World,* xxii–xxiv.
83. Margaret Naumburg, *Dynamically Oriented Art Therapy: Its Principles and Practices Illustrated with Three Case Studies* (New York: Grune & Stratton, 1966), 6–10, 162–165.
84. Paul Rosenfeld, *Port of New York: Essays on Fourteen American Moderns* (New York: Harcourt, Brace and Co., 1924), 117–134.
85. Agnes de Lima, *Our Enemy the Child* (New York: New Republic, Inc., 1925), 203–206.
86. Cremin, *The Transformation of the School,* viii–ix, 85.

10

Science, Professionalism, and Teaching

G. Stanley Hall

Although the last years of the nineteenth century gave rise to organized philosophies of education, educational psychologists working at the same time disdained these theoretical methods of organizing educational thought. Eschewing the general disciplines of philosophy and psychology as well, the educational psychologists created what they called a science of education. Borrowing their methods from Germany, educational psychologists sought to determine the most effective teaching practices, make education a professional field, and free teachers and school administrators from political interference.

As noted in Chapter 9, John Dewey held to an image of educational research that united education with wider fields of philosophy and psychology. Thus, when Ellen Condliffe Lagemann surveyed the development of educational research, she noted that John Dewey developed an innovative idea that connected educational research with important social changes. Although some educators were enamored of Dewey's ideas, Lagemann contended that Dewey's idea of education was not popular among educators. Instead, scholars in philosophy, sociology, and social psychology adopted Dewey's view that education could advance democracy. To Lagemann's surprise, she found that most public elementary and secondary school educators believed that educational scientists such as Edward Lee Thorndike would discover the ways to tailor instruction to the psychology of the child and to transmit those insights to teachers. The result was that scientists such as Thorndike turned the study of education into a technical field separated from philosophy.[1]

Although educational philosophy developed alongside educational psychology, the fields competed with each other and had different effects on schools and schoolteachers. Because each model followed different paths, this chapter will describe the ways that people's views of science changed and the effects those changed perspectives had on schools. The previous chapter described the development of educational philosophies.

How Did Popular Conceptions of Science Change in the Nineteenth Century to Make a Science of Education Appear Reasonable?

In the early years of the nineteenth century, commentators complained that strict adherence to empirical science limited understanding. For example, in 1835, Alexis de Tocqueville found on a visit from France that Americans had an interest in science although they appeared to dislike scientific theories. According to Tocqueville, Americans focused on those aspects of science that could save labor and increase profit instead of constructing theoretical explanations of phenomena. Tocqueville thought the desire to use scientific studies to illuminate practical affairs derived from the condition of equality found in democracies. In aristocratic societies, intellectuals tended to think of science as the pursuit of abstract understandings. This was an advantage, Tocqueville asserted, because a thinker such as Blaise Pascal could not have made his important discoveries in physics and mathematics had he pursued material gain. Because the practical emphasis on science could frustrate the development of important knowledge, Tocqueville recommended that policy makers support the development of theoretical sciences and allow the people engaged in practical affairs to use the sciences as they wished.[2]

As the nineteenth century unfolded, the benefits of empirical science expanded, and people claimed that technical achievements could improve society. Thus, they implied that practical improvements fulfilled a moral mission. According to Daniel Walker Howe, this broader faith in practical science resulted from a transmission of what he called Victorian attitudes from Britain. To illustrate the values of the period, Howe quoted a message that Queen Victoria, who ruled in Britain from 1837 to 1901, exchanged with U.S. President

Buchanan in 1858 to the celebrate the joining of Europe and America by a transatlantic cable. Written in Morse code, her message predicted the telegraph would bring peace on earth and good will among men. In her brief message, Victoria expressed excitement about the technological achievement, and, resorting to biblical language, she predicted that humankind could engineer a moral society through such feats. To Howe, Victorians in Britain and the United States had a similar faith that technical progress would lead people to organize society in rational ways. He added that these Victorian ideals were generally Protestant in nature and that they appealed to the members of the middle classes.[3]

Howe described the cultural attitudes that Americans borrowed from Victorian Britain; other historians noted that those shifts in the concept of science influenced higher education in the United States. For example, according to Laurence R. Veysey, in the early years of the nineteenth century, professors at universities applied the term science to any well-organized body of knowledge. After Darwin, university people began to speak about science as the application of specific evidence they had observed in nature. By the beginning of the twentieth century, university people expanded the notion of science and spoke about applying empirical evidence to determine how people should live. At the same time, universities came to honor the spirit of research as very important. By 1890, graduate schools opened at Harvard, Chicago, and Columbia. In order to acquire prestige, administrators in lesser colleges encouraged their faculty members to study at the more advanced graduate schools where they undertook research projects that promised to improve social life. As a result, graduates of this limited number of graduate schools that undertook research returned to their colleges to spread the hope that scientific studies could advance society.[4]

The changes in the ways people considered science appeared in publications aimed for a literate audience. For example, in 1904, Ira Remsen, then president of Johns Hopkins University, praised the members of the American Association for the Advancement of Science for the growth in scientific research that had taken place since the founding of the association in 1848. In his speech, Remsen noted that two motives had directed scientific research. The first was the desire to understand the universe. The second was the drive to increase the comfort of the human race. Remsen took a view that contradicted Tocqueville's; he claimed that these two motives worked together so that pure research led to practical applications. To verify his view, Remsen described advances in agriculture through the study of chemistry that brought about the development of fertilizers, improvements in health that came through biological studies of microbes, and industrial progress that resulted from studies of efficient fuels. Remsen went so far as to compare the ethical implications of scientific research to religious life. He claimed that honesty and fidelity to the work were essential in both cases.[5]

At about the same time that Remsen congratulated his audience for work they had done together, David Starr Jordan delivered a speech to the members of Sigma Xi, a society formed at Cornell University in 1886 with the aim of binding together scientific research and practical applications. Addressing the members as comrades in zeal, Jordan divided scientific research into four classes. These included experiments that tested laws and found out how things worked, descriptions that recorded things in the world and set them in some sort of order, inventions that applied the findings of the sciences to human ends, and the efforts to find the causes and relations among observed facts. Jordan believed that each type of science was equally valuable, and he thought the participants in different fields could aid each other by cooperating. Above all, to show the moral worth of scientific activities, Jordan reversed Tocqueville's observation about the influence of democracy on science. Whereas Tocqueville worried that democracy weakened the drive for pure research, Jordan claimed democracy strengthened the march of all forms of science because in a democracy neither tradition nor authority could justify the work; each discovery had to prove its worth. Jordan concluded that, as a result, scientists pursued their efforts to understand the world with religious fervor. They became worshipers of the god of things as they are.[6]

Although academic people praised scientific investigation as being an altruistic occupation akin to religion, Burton Bledstein complained that selfish motives inspired the university professors and the members of the middle class. According to Bledstein, the rapid changes to society in the last half of the nineteenth century brought about the growth of industries and the development of means of transportation. The new economy threatened farmers and owners of small businesses, which had served the middle classes. Bledstein argued that members of the middle class turned to American universities to secure their status. Perceiving that professional work was remunerative, they felt that the work was secure and beneficial to society because universities advanced the image of professionals as people trained in scientific knowledge who offered public service. As a result, middle class youth enrolled in the universities, graduated with degrees, joined the professional associations, and moved their careers relentlessly upward.[7]

On the other hand, some historians, such as David A. Hollinger, considered Bledstein's argument to be overly cynical. Although Hollinger acknowledged that some university presidents used the ideal of science as part of public relations campaigns to advance their institutions, he added that many people believed the notion was true. As a result, Hollinger contended that faith in professionalism was more than the result of a campaign by a few college administrators to hoodwink the public. To illustrate his point, Hollinger found many educated people not directly connected to universities, such as clerics, teachers, and writers, who believed that the technical advances offered by scientists enhanced social progress.[8]

According to D. H. Myer, the theory of natural selection challenged previous ideas of universal order the Victorians held dear. Myer claimed that religious thinkers took two different directions to ameliorate what he called a crisis of faith. One method found among writers in Europe was to declare science to be a narrow field that could not penetrate religious principles. In the United States, Myer found that writers tended to claim science would eventually support faith and morals. Myer added that the result was that Americans thought of science as a public endeavor and religion as a private domain that no one could explain. Consequently, Myer found that Americans used vague religious references in public. They implied that religion was a matter of the heart, and that they could not discuss it objectively.[9]

Some educators in the United States followed what Myer called the second alternative. Although they relegated religion to a private sphere, they thought that the theory of evolution offered people the opportunity to think more broadly about education. For example, when Nicholas Murray Butler addressed the National Educational Association in

1900, he noted that American educators had not settled on an educational theory. He complained that American secondary schools and colleges had embraced vocational education and rejected classical training in hopes of satisfying students' wishes. Made on narrow grounds, this decision turned education into opportunities for students to follow their interests without learning skills and knowledge they could use to improve the social order. He noted with optimism that the doctrine of evolution caused people to question this arrangement. According to Butler, the premise of evolution was that ideas followed a natural order and that there should be natural sequence of studies. Thus, educators hoped they could discover this order and use it to create curriculums that allowed particular students to fulfill their own desires in ways that would serve the life of the society.[10]

Whereas Butler thought the doctrine of evolution would impel educators to think more deeply about schools and society, educational psychologists adhered to a narrow conception of science. For example, Edward Lee Thorndike avoided any science derived from educational theory. When Thorndike wrote that science was important to education, he considered science to be studies focused on some practical end. He called this type of applied research the American variety of science. Within such a frame, Thorndike completed studies designed to answer some practical problem. He used statistical comparisons of various alternatives to show their worth, and he disparaged philosophical speculation. Thus, when Thorndike asserted that science was the only sure foundation for social progress, he meant a science that found which technical alternative was superior to others. Because he did not think that progress would come from a more inclusive interpretation of educational theory, he set strict limitations within which his findings could apply, and he discounted any studies that went beyond similarly circumscribed limits. For this reason, Thorndike's biographer, Geraldine Joncich, accused Thorndike of proudly proclaiming that he could not understand the writings of John Dewey. It was not that Thorndike could not understand philosophy, though. Thorndike followed a different way of thinking.[11]

According to Lagemann, the science of teaching, as Thorndike expressed it, rose in prominence after Dewey left the University of Chicago in 1909. The university appointed Charles Hubbard Judd to take charge of the aspects relating to education. Judd and Thorndike had studied together at Wesleyan University in Middletown, Connecticut. Judd had traveled to Germany to receive his Ph.D. from his studies with Wilhelm Wundt at the University of Leipzig. Unlike Dewey, who sought to create a science of philosophy through the study of education, Judd wanted to develop a field of study that would make education into a profession. Like Thorndike and other educational researchers, Judd hoped that science would provide the resources to enable educators to stand apart from political influence or public opinion. He wanted to turn education into a profession.[12]

How Did the Child Study Movement Initiate the Development of Educational Psychology?

Although no one person originated the science of education, Granville Stanley Hall had a significant influence on the process. As a student, Hall attended prominent universities in America. Like many of his fellows, he studied in Germany to find out how to carry out a science of psychology. Believing that teachers could help complete empirical studies of children's development, Hall took credit for starting the child study movement. Although Hall wanted psychology to follow empirical methods, he did not study children directly. Instead, he gathered opinions of mothers, teachers, and experts about children's behavior. In trying to discover the nature of children, Hall believed that his studies illuminated the proper organization of schools. As a result, he combined reports of his findings with criticisms of school practices.

Born in 1844 in a farming village in western Massachusetts, Hall attended Williams College where he studied literature and philosophy. In 1876, Hall entered Harvard University where he became a student of William James. Under James's direction, Hall turned toward a sort of physiological psychology that compared the maturation of an individual with biological evolution. In forming these ideas, Hall borrowed extensively from the German psychologist Wilhelm Wundt, who became famous for conducting experiments in which he recorded variations in the time it took subjects to react to stimuli. In 1878, Hall traveled to Germany, but he became disappointed because he believed that Wundt depended more on speculation than on empirical measurement.[13]

After Hall returned to the United States in 1880, Charles W. Eliot, president of Harvard University, offered Hall the opportunity to deliver some lectures to teachers. Held on Saturdays, the lectures proved wildly popular. According to Hall's biographer, Dorothy Ross, the lectures that Hall gave were successful. He lent the authority of science to the popular and romantic views of Pestalozzi and Froebel that advised teachers to be gentle, to impart practical skills to children, and to appeal to the children's interests. In his lectures, Hall described psychological principles, and he explained the most current German teaching methods. He claimed that such material was the foundation of an educational science because it enabled the selection of teaching practices according to an understanding of the natural development of children.[14]

Because of the lectures, Hall secured the assistance of four kindergarten teachers in the Boston schools to ask the children about matters considered common knowledge. For example, the teachers asked about cows, butter, milk, and certain wooden objects. The teachers reported that the children knew little about these things.[15]

In 1883, Hall published an article entitled "The Contents of the Children's Minds" in the *Princeton Review* that described his findings. Hall claimed that he took inspiration from a study conducted in 1869 by the Pedagogical Society of Berlin, Germany, in which schoolmasters asked over 2000 children a series of questions they thought surveyed common knowledge. The schoolmasters found the children did not know such things as the major buildings in their neighborhoods or fundamental religious ideas. To gather information for his article, Hall had recruited about sixty teachers to ask questions of three children apiece. These questions were similar to the ones the kindergarten teachers had asked. Putting everything together, he had results from about 200 children. When Hall determined the percentages of children who could answer simple questions about nature and about their bodies, he came to four conclusions. First, teachers could not assume children had certain prior experiences or knowledge. Second, the best preparation for school included trips to the countryside to become familiar with natural objects and attendance in kindergarten. Third, the teacher should try to determine what children knew before beginning instruction. Fourth, children in one area learned different things than did children in another locale.[16]

According to Naomi Norsworthy, the article that Hall published about his study in Boston became so famous that it was the beginning of the child study movement. She added that teachers accepted his conclusions to the extent that, by 1908, they made his rules basic to their instruction.[17]

While Norsworthy may have overstated the influence of Hall's article, "The Contents of the Children's Minds," Hall's article contained the elements of what Hall considered the empirical study of children. First, he did not study the children. Instead, he asked teachers to ask children questions and to report their answers. Second, he tabulated the results and used simple percentages to arrive at some conclusions. Third, he joined his conclusions with opinions or ideas he received from other experts. Fourth, he used his general conclusions to criticize the practices of then contemporary teachers.

At the same time, Hall's article foreshadowed the reasons other psychologists would give for rejecting the methods that Hall used. In listing the problems associated with the study, Hall noted that the teachers were not equally skillful in asking the questions. Some children repeated what they heard other children say while other children said what they thought the teacher wanted to hear. Not only did these complaints suggest the results of the interviews were unreliable, the method proved to be time consuming. Hall claimed that each interview with each child took several hours.[18]

To Hall, the time devoted to the study of education would advance the study of what he called genetic psychology. In 1881, Hall accepted a lectureship at Johns Hopkins University, and in 1887, he founded the *American Journal of Psychology.* Publishing the work of colleagues and students, Hall's journal sought to advance empirical or experimental psychology to the extent that his journal called his view of psychology a science and labeled any opposing view as superstition. To advance his cause, Hall founded the American Psychological Association in 1892. Because Hall wanted teachers to help him, he invited members attending the 1891 conference of the National Educational Association to visit sessions discussing the study of children. From these meetings, he recruited teachers to fill out questionnaires about such things as the ways that children played with toys, how or when they told lies, or what they feared.[19]

Hall's ideas about the relation of scientific research to practical school affairs came out in his plans for what he considered a true American university. This effort began in 1888 when Hall accepted the offer of a wealthy businessperson, Jonas Gilman Clark, to become the president of a newly founded college in Worcester, Massachusetts. Although Clark wanted the institution to begin as an undergraduate college bearing his name, Hall convinced his benefactor to found a graduate school. Hall's idea was that an undergraduate college could grow from the advanced studies, and the advanced programs would enable the younger students to recognize the importance of research. Upon accepting the position, Hall left to travel through Europe visiting various universities. While on this tour, Hall adopted the ideal of an international university community. When he returned to Worcester, he decided to build a university that would contribute to a worldwide search for truth although this had not been part of the more local interests of its founders.[20]

In the search for truth, Hall considered the publication of his two-volume work, *Adolescence: Its Psychology and Its Relation to Physiology, Anthropology, Sociology, Sex, Crime, Religion, and Education,* in 1904 to be a major accomplishment. In fact, Hall asserted that his *Adolescence* was as important as Charles Darwin's *The Origin of the Species* had been fifty years earlier. He explained that his work was new in two ways. He believed the first innovation was his contention that children passed through stages of growth that correlated with the stages through which humankind had progressed in its evolution. Calling this comparison the recapitulation theory, Hall claimed that it provided a way to recognize the errors in education. He thought the second innovation of the book was the method by which he had arrived at his conclusions. Claiming that most psychologists depended on theories, Hall asserted that he based his conclusions on empirical evidence. After seeking evidence of how children grew, Hall had surveyed the pedagogical practices commonly used for each age level, and he determined if or how those methods of instruction matched the conditions common to the children's stage of development. For example, he argued that the period from eight years to twelve was a unique time for children. During this stage, children wanted to roam the woods, to hunt, and to fish. Although Hall acknowledged that teachers could not allow children to run freely in urban school settings, he thought teachers should expose the children to stories of heroic adventures wherein they vicariously indulged their passion for adventure. Further, Hall noted the children were quick to learn simple things although they lacked the power of reason. Thus, he recommended that the instruction the children received during these ages would require them to memorize academic skills they could apply later in life. Adolescence was a new birth, he continued. The bones and muscles of the teenagers grew rapidly bringing new strength and vigor, but the desire for knowledge about sex threatened vice and disease. Although strict religious codes had protected adolescents from their desires in the past, Hall did not think it was reasonable to return to a dependence on such injunctions. A better solution was for teachers to accept direction from a science of education and provide youth with the objective information they craved about love and about life. In short, Hall added that American universities could provide guidance for parents and teachers if those institutions imitated the great universities found in Europe. Although Hall noted that few universities in the United States encouraged what he considered research, he hoped his book would provide a basis for understanding because it offered a full survey of the information available about adolescents between fourteen and twenty-four years old.[21]

Despite Hall's praise of his own work, *Adolescence* suffered mixed reviews. For example, H. Heath Baldwin did not think that Hall's contributions were equal to Darwin's theories. Although Baldwin acknowledged that Darwin and Hall had analyzed vast amounts of data, he added that many other psychologists did the same. Thus, Hall did not offer a new method for psychological work. Nor did Baldwin think that Hall offered a radical reformulation of ideas of child development. Baldwin claimed that most psychologists already agreed with Hall's contention that children passed through different stages following some rhythms and that adolescence was the most important of these stages of growth. Nonetheless, Baldwin praised Hall for his extended discussions of adolescence and sexual development. Although Baldwin acknowledged that Hall was frequently unscientific, he praised Hall for treating questions about sex in ways that would bring helpful insights to parents and teachers.[22]

Other reviewers were more critical. For example, Edward Lee Thorndike, who had studied at Harvard with William James as had Hall, praised Hall for accumulating a record of over 2000 references on the subject of adolescence. At that same time, Thorndike raised three significant objections. The most important was that Hall relied on unreliable evidence.

When Hall accumulated questionnaires and tabulated people's responses to questions about children's development, he had evidence of what people thought happened to children rather than evidence of how children grew. Thorndike added that Hall was one of very few scientists who had any confidence in such reports. Nonetheless, Hall was so confident about the value of questionnaires that he did not try to justify their use despite the fact that almost every other psychologist had rejected this method of accumulating evidence.[23]

Thorndike added two other serious complaints. One was that Hall could not consistently define what he meant by the theory of recapitulation. At times, Hall seemed to mean that the stages of child development were parallel to those of human evolution. At other times, the continuity was some sort of continuity between animal instincts and human characteristics. The third complaint was that Hall drew many important conclusions without any supporting evidence. For example, Thorndike cited Hall's conclusion that children disliked going to bed in the evening because prehistoric humans had feared the night and used fire to control the darkness. In this case, it appeared to Thorndike that Hall disguised speculation as science.[24]

Despite his objections, Thorndike praised Hall's criticism of science textbooks. Thorndike agreed with Hall that textbooks carried forward the interests of the authors rather than the interests of the students. Thorndike added that Hall's complaints were more valuable than his recommendations because most of Hall's suggestions focused on having students memorize facts and information.[25]

Because many reviewers complained about the poor composition of *Adolescence,* Hall offered a shortened version entitled *Youth.*[26] In a review of the condensed work, Will S. Monroe praised *Youth* for being more carefully proofread and for presenting an intelligent selection of the ideas from *Adolescence.* At the same time, Monroe marveled at the extent of the European following for Hall's works. He noted that publishers translated Hall's essays and books into more than six European languages as well as Czechoslovakian. As a result, Monroe added, Hall had spread the child study movement throughout the world.[27]

In 1911, Hall published a two volume work entitled *Educational Problems* that considered the years when children went to elementary schools. According to Hall, when he began his work, sonorous metaphysical platitudes from leaders such as W. T. Harris constituted the understanding of education. No one brought insights from Europe or engaged in empirical studies. Hall asserted that his efforts brought child study to the center of educational thought. Hall added that not everyone listened to him. For example, in the ideal education, schools should encourage the children to pass through the developmental stages as quickly and as fully as possible. Unfortunately, Hall believed that this was not what most teachers tried to accomplish. They coerced unwilling children to master academic lessons in which the children had no interest. Because he offered a different approach, he claimed that his volumes suggested how teachers could improve the schools.[28]

Reviewing *Educational Problems,* Charles De Garmo explained how Hall amassed extensive references about the development of children. Clark University was the only institution in the United States where the primary interest of the president, Hall, and the faculty and graduate students was the collection of information about child development available in the United States and in Europe. From this cooperative effort, Hall could publish extensive annotated bibliographies in his books. The references were so extensive and complete, De Garmo continued, that they could serve as the contents of an educational library. Despite this praise, De Garmo was disappointed that Hall's excessive focus on the individual development of children caused him to ignore the social settings within which people lived. Hall passed over these areas so completely that De Garmo complained readers would not know human beings were social and economic creatures from reading Hall's book.[29]

Dorothy Ross claimed that Hall's popularity began to decline after the publication of *Adolescence.* In part, the book caused problems because the extensive discussions of sexuality alienated teachers who had followed his ideas, and many libraries banned the book. Another factor was that many prospective teachers could not understand Hall's use of science. Despite these problems, Ross claimed that the most important factor explaining Hall's decline was that child study became more specialized and increasingly technical. She added that the momentum of the child study movement carried it beyond Hall and made Thorndike the chief exemplar of the more scientific approach to child study.[30]

How Did the Educational Psychologists Come to Adopt Narrow Methods of Research?

Ironically, G. Stanley Hall may have encouraged educational psychologists to adopt narrow technical orientations because Hall's work appeared amateurish. At least, this was a conclusion that Robert L. Church made after he surveyed the articles that had appeared in *The Journal of Educational Psychology* from 1905 to 1920. Church was surprised to find that educational psychologists ignored the work of psychologists such as James Mark Baldwin or George Hebert Mead, who followed a social view of learning. According to Church, educational psychologists narrowed their focus to what occurred in formal classrooms and how academic instruction should proceed.[31]

In part, Church thought that Edward L. Thorndike encouraged researchers to study particular problems because Thorndike's conservative political views prohibited him from advocating the reformist ideas found in social psychology. According to Church, the negative example of G. Stanley Hall was a greater influence because Hall made educational psychology appear unprofessional by enlisting teachers untrained in psychology to help in his work. Further, Hall made speculative pronouncements similar to what might appear in a religious revival.[32]

Church did not put all the blame on Hall because he offered three related influences that may have limited the vision of educational psychologists. The first was that educational psychologists depended on statistics. Using this form of counting, psychologists set out to determine what existed rather than what teachers should introduce. The second was that educational psychologists concentrated on what they called deficient children when they studied individual differences. In comparing normal children to children with difficulties, educational psychologists could determine how normal children developed. They did not seek ways to expand the range of children's abilities, as did progressive educators. Finally, the educational psychologists held simplistic ideas of how children learned. For example, Thorndike made a stimulus–response bond popular even though this model of learning obscured any social role for education.[33]

Although Church did not emphasize Thorndike's role in separating educational psychology from the wider field of social psychology, Thorndike had expressed the desire to narrow the field in order to raise the status of education and make it professional. Because Hall and Thorndike had studied with William James, they adopted the view that studies of how children learned were helpful in illuminating larger psychological concerns. Although Thorndike began his studies with animals, he turned to work with schoolchildren when such opportunities opened.

In 1899, when Thorndike began teaching at Columbia University, animal research had given way when opportunities opened to perform mental measurements of children that would engage his graduate students and use the statistical methods he had developed. Most important, Thorndike believed mental measurements of human learning could relate to his previous work with animals because Thorndike had determined that animals learned. That is, the previous experiences of animals influenced their abilities to form associations and thereby improved their responses in future efforts. For example, when a cat had escaped from several boxes, the animal developed the skills to escape from other containers. To Thorndike this seemed like a sort of intelligence. As a result, he began a series of experiments with R. S. Woodworth to determine if training in one set of skills enabled people to learn another.[34]

To explain why he chose this problem for his experiments, Thorndike offered anonymous quotes from supposed educators who suggested that learning mathematics developed the student's ability to pay attention and to use reason, or that the correct use of a foreign language developed the student's ability to concentrate. Thus, to Thorndike, the issue of the transfer of training appeared to be important because some educators used it to justify continued instruction in classical academic subjects.[35]

As Charles Judd showed, Thorndike overstated the extent that educators relied on the doctrine of transfer to justify classical studies. Indeed, many educators during the nineteenth century, such as W. T. Harris, had argued against such a simple rationale for classical instruction. Nonetheless, Thorndike asserted that the doctrine of transfer of training was an important educational matter and he began studying it.

At any rate, Thorndike's studies on transfer appeared in 1901. In this series of articles, Thorndike stated that improvement in one mental function did not influence a student's ability in other mental functions. To arrive at this conclusion, Thorndike and his coauthor, R. S. Woodworth, asked subjects to perform some task such as estimating the size of triangles. When the subject acquired mastery in this skill, Thorndike and Woodworth asked the subject to estimate the size of an object with a different shape. They found that the speed with which a subject mastered the ability to estimate the size of the different object depended on how similar the new object was to a triangle.[36]

Calling his view of psychology *connectionism,* Thorndike developed the Laws of Habit Formation. The first law was that the more emphatically a response was connected with a particular situation, the greater the chances that it would be repeated in such a situation in the future. The second law was the greater the satisfaction from giving a particular response, the greater the chances that it would be given again in that situation. From his studies of transfer, Thorndike noted that practice was beneficial in performing certain tasks. He added that there was no simple way for a person to develop general powers such as concentration from a particular exercise. Although the extent of any transfer of skill depended on the similarity of the elements in the activities, Thorndike was unsure which elements had to be identical or how many identical parts there had to be.[37]

In affirming Hall's belief that educational psychologists would contribute to the improvement of teaching if they used empirical studies to describe human nature, Thorndike focused his studies on behavior. He ignored the developmental psychology that intrigued Hall. In his major text, *Educational Psychology,* Thorndike claimed that educational psychology could offer knowledge about the original nature of human beings and describe the laws governing how to change human nature. Because he thought any behavior was a response to a situation, he believed that, once a person made a response, he or she formed a bond or connection in his or her mind between the situation and the response. Although Thorndike argued that these bonds were the bases of intellect, character, or skill, he did not think the bonds appeared arbitrarily. The response a person gave was somehow rooted in original tendencies present in human nature. For example, Thorndike argued that the fact that people could think was due to original human capacities to associate or analyze phenomena; however, the content of people's thoughts derived from the environmental conditions under which they used those capacities of thought. It was Thorndike's hope that teachers would use such information about children's original nature to change their behavior for the better.[38]

To some extent, Thorndike drew on a list of instincts that William James had proposed as basic to human nature. Nonetheless, Thorndike did not think that any instincts or tendencies acted independently to produce a response to a situation. He argued that the process was extremely complicated. For example, the sight of an approaching figure could promote a response to flee, but it could also promote a response to welcome the other person. Although the different responses could come from a variety of different tendencies in the subject, those internal tendencies could be excited, modified, or inhibited by a range of distinct environmental conditions. The internal tendencies and the external conditions related to each other in countless combinations. Further, because thousands of millions of neurons governed the connections that took place among the person's internal tendencies, they offered an infinite number of possible permutations. Consequently, Thorndike warned that a simple inventory of impulses and environmental conditions would not explain the connections that could take place.[39]

Although human behavior seemed to follow certain rules, Thorndike did not think people acted alike. He devoted considerable attention to questions of individual differences in part because he noted that American schools seemed to operate on the view that the children of different social classes and distinct genders had inherited the same mental capacities. Thorndike recommended constructing studies to compare the differences among groups of children from different ethnic groups of the same age and similar schooling. He thought a series of studies that made several different comparisons would show that children were not equal. More important, the studies could isolate some of the causes for individual differences.[40]

In addition to focusing on behavior, Thorndike made comparative experiments a popular model for educational psychologists. According to Joncich, since Thorndike disliked complicated machinery and intricate laboratory settings, he used experimental designs that were extremely simple. For this reason, she claimed, Thorndike introduced the extensive use of control and experimental groups. Using simple statistical comparisons, such comparative studies could illuminate what had taken place. Joncich noted that before 1901, when Thorndike and Woodworth conducted the experiments on transfer of training, few psychologists used control groups in their experiments. After the publication of these studies, the control group assumed a fundamental place in research design. Nonetheless, some critics complained that Thorndike's experiments were overly simple. For example, Nicholas Murray Butler complained about the popularity of the studies by Thorndike and Woodworth. According to Butler, Thorndike's few superficial experiments had undone the effectiveness of American education by undermining the place of classical studies.[41]

Thorndike conducted several experiments using the same simple designs. Perhaps because of their straightforward nature, they remained influential for many years. For example, in 1917, Thorndike published an article entitled "Reading as Reasoning: A Study of Mistakes in Paragraph Reading." In 1971, the journal, *Reading Research Quarterly,* published a retrospective examining the impact the article had on the teaching of reading. The answer was that the article continued to be one of the most frequently cited articles more than fifty years after its publication.[42]

In his article about reading, Thorndike wanted to show that reading was an act that involved all the characteristics of reasoning. He did not believe that reading was a simple act requiring a compound collection of certain habits. To prove his point, Thorndike asked his subjects to read a simple paragraph and answer several questions about its content. In reviewing the responses, Thorndike showed that understanding a paragraph was similar to solving a problem in mathematics. The reader had to select the important elements, put them together into the proper arrangement, and attribute the appropriate weight each element should have. Because understanding even simple paragraphs required considerable skill, he cautioned teachers to recognize the difficulties that reading involved.[43]

In the 1971 issue of *Reading Research Quarterly* that reprinted Thorndike's article, Wayne Otto warned that the influence of Thorndike's view of reading was not a measure of its quality. For example, Thorndike omitted the information from his description of the results that would make it possible for researchers to replicate his results. He reported only some of the data, and he failed to explain how he categorized the responses as he did. Further, he told nothing about the subjects. He did not reveal the directions he gave them. He did not suggest why he had selected the questions and the paragraphs. As a result, Otto concluded that reviewers in 1971 would reject Thorndike's article.[44]

Whether Thorndike's views were overly simple or not, they were popular. By 1915, the idea of stimulus–response bonds became the core of educational thought. John Dewey used the idea to explain how people think. William Heard Kilpatrick used Thorndike's laws of learning to explain the effectiveness of the project method. Most important, according to Harold Rugg, from 1913 until the Great Depression, teachers colleges throughout the United States used Thorndike's *Educational Psychology* as the standard text.[45]

How Did Educational Psychology Replace Philosophic Thinking as a Guide to Effective Instruction?

As noted in Chapter 9, when Dewey organized his laboratory school, he tried to follow a set of procedures that would enable teachers and students to use science in ways that helped them understand the direction in which they wanted to work. His plan was to enable college professors, elementary school teachers, parents, and students to cooperate in discussing how to teach the subject matters. In this way, Dewey developed an idea of educational research that originated from the particular concerns of specific classrooms but asked everyone who was involved to consider the aims of education that were implied in the proposed solutions. Although professional distinctions existed in Dewey's laboratory school, the different assignments represented the primary concerns of different individuals rather than a hierarchal order of authority. Thus, teachers focused on classroom interactions and administrators considered ways to facilitate those activities. Dewey claimed that, as principal and chair of the university's philosophy department, he selected the different subject matters, showed how they were related, and demonstrated the theory that justified the selections. He called these tasks the philosophy of education. Nonetheless, he believed that everyone in the laboratory school functioned as a student of education though each person approached the broader topic from his or her particular area of concern.[46]

When Dewey left Chicago, Judd came to the university and took charge of the laboratory school. Judd had made it clear when he arrived in Chicago that he had a different view of a science of education than Dewey had. According to Judd, teachers and college professors were to cooperate in the study of education to find answers to problems that Dewey might consider overly narrow. For example, in an address to the Educational Conference of the Academies and High Schools in Relations with the University of Chicago, Judd argued that high school teachers should cooperate with university faculty members to develop scientific studies of classroom activities. Claiming such cooperation would solve the problems found in high schools, Judd listed several problems that required scientific study. For example, he asked about the appropriate content of an introductory foreign language course. Should students imitate sounds or should the teacher concentrate on the formal structure of language? In the area of administration, he raised questions about the effects of different systems of assigning grades. Judd claimed his point in offering such a list was to show the connections between the scientific study of education and the practical work of teachers. For the cooperation to take place as Judd envisioned it, the teachers would have to approach their problems as scientists not as teachers. They should not try to improve their own instruction as much as they should seek evidence indicating the most efficient way to organize instruction. This meant that the teachers would conduct controlled experiments rather than seek to help every student.[47]

Judd made an impact in the field. According to Harold Rugg, two men served as bridges from psychology to education. One of them was Thorndike; the other was Charles Hubbard Judd. For almost twenty years, Rugg had a close association with the two psychologists. He had been in Judd's department from 1915 to 1920 at the University of Chicago. During the 1920s, Rugg was a professor at Teachers College with Thorndike.[48]

Rugg claimed that Thorndike and Judd shared three central beliefs. First, they believed that empirical studies that required statistical comparisons should be the basis of a science of education. Second, both scientists considered learning to be a mechanical process, and third, their conception of learning led them to reinforce the subject matter–oriented curriculum. Rugg claimed that, from 1900 to 1920, the prominence of these psychologists caused researchers to subject every aspect of education to quantitative measures. According to Rugg, educators considered statistics to be the route to educational salvation. They believed that better studies, better classification of students, better methods of grading, and better treatment of facts would lead to better schools.[49]

Although Thorndike and Judd shared similar conceptions of learning and used similar methods of research, they arrived at different conclusions. For example, Judd criticized Thorndike's conclusion that students could not transfer skills they had learned in one setting to another activity. Judd complained that Thorndike had arrived at incorrect conclusions because he misrepresented the doctrine of formal discipline, and he distorted his evidence.

In his text, *Psychology of High School Students,* Judd made two serious complaints about Thorndike's studies. First, Judd claimed that Thorndike portrayed the doctrine of formal discipline in exaggerated terms. To make this point, Judd quoted M. J. O'Shea who had been unable to find any educator who believed such things as studies in mathematics improved a person's ability to use reason. This issue was important because to Judd it seemed that everyone agreed that some sort of transfer took place in learning. That is, everyone believed that learning many things enabled people to do other things even when the new tasks required different information or skills; at least, they learned how to learn. The questions that remained were about the degree of transfer that was possible and the way it happened. Judd claimed that Thorndike had confused these issues by making the supporters of formal discipline appear more adamant than they were. Second, Judd showed that Thorndike misused his own data. In this regard, Judd quoted Thorndike's use of the responses that thirty-five girls gave in mental tests. In his book, *Principles of Teaching,* Thorndike compared the responses of the girls with their achievements in language study. His aim was to show that high achievement in the study of foreign languages did not improve abilities of observation or association. Judd went over Thorndike's tables showing that the differences among the students' performances were too scattered to prove any point about transfer.[50]

According to Judd, a student could transfer learning from one situation to another by grasping some generalization that applied to both situations. An example of such transfer took place in the study of algebra when a student learned to factor equations. Because the same method would not apply to all equations, the general principle was the process of determining which method worked in which case. Students did not learn this general principle directly. They could recognize this principle after they had factored several different equations.[51]

Although Judd criticized Thorndike's work, Thorndike overshadowed Judd's contributions to psychology. Thorndike's students carried on his work in the statistical analysis of educational problems. For example, Leonard Ayers conducted an extensive survey of the causes of student failure in several large cities. At the same time, George Strayer and Ellwood P. Cubberley applied the use of statistical methods to school administration. On the other hand, Judd's strengths were in program development and administration. From 1910 to 1930, Judd built the University of Chicago into a center for the quantitative study of education. He developed a psychological laboratory in which he and his students carried out investigations in particular learning problems.[52]

Because Judd believed that the science of education used statistical methods to study the efficiency of school courses and school organization, he used his position as head of the University of Chicago's Department of Education to carry out this function. As part of his responsibilities, Judd edited the journal *School Review,* which was sponsored by the university. Originally founded as a journal of secondary education, Judd used the journal to disseminate articles describing educational experiments carried out by many of his graduate students.[53]

When Judd created the laboratory to solve particular educational problems, the innovation attracted support from philanthropic organizations whose directors agreed that empirical studies could aid teachers in public schools. For example, the General Education Board appropriated funds to the Department of Education of the University of Chicago in 1915 to support studies in reading and writing. Such efforts seemed most important to Judd. Because he noted that schools in the United States depended almost entirely on textbooks for instruction, he argued that students had to master the ability to read in order to progress. Judd used the money to construct appropriate apparatus and to employ sufficient clerical and research assistants to conduct the studies. In making these studies, Judd depended on faculty members in his department such as William S. Gray, several graduate students, and members of the Chicago public schools. In their studies, the researchers analyzed various approaches to reading instruction, seeking to find the most effective method.[54]

Other teacher training institutions imitated the changes that Judd made. For example, in an effort to introduce prospective teachers to the concrete problems found in schools, Judd rearranged the curriculum in the university's department of education. He removed courses in the history and psychology of education from the curriculum and replaced them with courses entitled Introduction to Education and the Methods of Teaching. In 1918, Judd claimed that directors of most normal schools and colleges agreed that history of education was not a suitable introductory course. Following Judd's lead, most programs of teacher training changed psychology courses into discussions of how to use scientific methods to study educational problems. To aid these reforms, Judd published a textbook entitled *Introduction to the Scientific Study of Education* that he had developed for the introductory courses he instituted in Chicago. The text began with descriptions of the science of education and the problems that researchers should consider. For example, he suggested how to study student failure and how to improve student performance. Pointing out the intricacies involved in educational work, Judd concluded that schools were complex institutions and that good education was the result of constant study and expert supervision.[55]

For Judd, the scientific study of education was essential if school administrators were to make decisions that improved education. He complained that in many districts, lay school board members had control over the design of school buildings, the selection of texts, and the determination of teacher salaries and working conditions. The result was that they often ignored educational needs. Judd was careful to add that the problem was not the integrity of the school board members. The difficulties derived from the board members' unwillingness to make decisions based on expert knowledge. Although Judd considered a series of ways to organize boards of education, he concluded that the important factor was for school administrators to have the freedom to make decisions based on systematic scientific studies of educational procedures. To be worthy of such trust, the administrators had to make their decisions based on scientific studies.[56]

According to Thorndike's biographer, Geraldine Joncich, the appeals by Judd and Thorndike for cooperation among teachers and researchers in the study of problems of education appeared similar to calls for action research. By the end of the twentieth century, it was a common practice in graduate schools of education for teachers and administrators to conduct some sort of project in their own elementary or secondary schools. For example, they might compare two ways of administering a test or they might compare the benefits and dangers of two systems of grading pupils. The name "action research" referred to the fact that the teachers or administrators did the investigations as part of their jobs. Although they might publish their work later, they received university credit for it. According to Joncich, the trivial nature of most action research would scandalize a research scientist like Thorndike. Joncich added that the teachers or administrators contrived action research projects poorly using inadequate controls because they wanted to justify teaching or administrative practices already in use.[57]

How Did Bias Influence the Findings of Educational Psychologists?

When Clarence J. Karier considered the effect Thorndike had on schools, he claimed that Thorndike had brought about the classification of students into different ability groups. During World War I, Thorndike demonstrated to military leaders the benefits of using intelligence tests to determine proper assignments for different soldiers. After the war, Thorndike encouraged school administrators to apply the same technique to determine which students should enroll in which courses. Although such an arrangement promised to reveal an objective system of social organization, Karier argued that the tests had the effect of segregating children by race and social classes. According to Karier, the classification and separation of students did not disturb Thorndike because he had concluded that African American children were mentally inferior to white children. Thorndike believed a science of selective breeding or eugenics would provide the best service to humankind.[58]

Thorndike's biographer, Joncich, presented a more complicated view of Thorndike's participation with and endorsement of intelligence tests. For example, on the one hand, she noted that Thorndike considered the problems of identifying, defining, and measuring the individual differences in children's intellects to be critically important. On the other hand, she added that Thorndike repeatedly noted that intelligence was what intelligence tests measured. According to Joncich, in making this aphorism, Thorndike was not boasting about the value of intelligence tests. He was making a statement about the modest nature of the tests. There was no reason to think that the tests could predict people's abilities about anything beyond their future performance on intelligence tests. In making these observations, Joncich did not think Thorndike contradicted himself. She considered these apparent inconsistencies to be the result of Thorndike's attitude of scientific caution. [59]

For many years, Thorndike had argued that individuals had different capacities for learning, and he thought that part of the differences came from nature. For example, in his book *Education,* Thorndike offered three ways that nature influenced student intelligence. First, some differences were due to sex. He thought that, by nature, girls were more observant of small details than were boys. Girls were less likely to be colorblind and less interested in mechanical objects. Second, he argued that racial origins contributed to individual differences. He claimed that Jewish children could study academic courses that were too difficult for people who belonged to a tribe that he called Pygmies. Third,

Thorndike noted that the inherited tendencies from near relatives influenced children's abilities. The trick was for the school to provide the amount, the type, and the quality of work that best suited their native talents. As a result, Thorndike praised schools for accepting duties beyond instruction. He thought that gymnasiums, playgrounds, and study rooms open after school represented the willingness of educators to recognize that schools had to serve a variety of children. Most important, Thorndike praised the high school for widening the available courses beyond the academic programs that were popular in 1890. He was impressed that by 1910 the high schools offered vocational programs, domestic science, and several modern languages.[60]

If heredity played a role in determining school success, Thorndike thought it was reasonable to try to evaluate those abilities that instruction could not change. In the 1918 yearbook for the National Society for the Study of Education, Thorndike began his essay with the observation that whatever exists must exist in some amount. He added that knowing it thoroughly meant knowing its quantity as well as its quality. In his essay, Thorndike described the various achievement tests for things such as handwriting and arithmetic that researchers had devised. Although he praised the tests, he pointed to their limits. For example, he noted that a single test could not accurately indicate a student's achievement or a teacher's abilities. He added emphatically that achievement tests did not measure student abilities, and he noted that there were no convenient ways to sample that ability.[61]

Although Thorndike acknowledged the difficulties in testing intelligence in the 1918 essay, he had created several such tests by that time. In 1914, he began working for businesses such as the American Tobacco Company and Metropolitan to create tests that would select competent clerical workers. In making these tests, Thorndike isolated the skills required for the position. When a company wanted tests for a wide variety of tasks, he declined and asked the executives to be more specific about the jobs the applicants might perform. By 1916, he created tests for universities such as Cincinnati, Columbia, and the Massachusetts Institute of Technology to determine the fitness of candidates entering engineering programs. As a result, in 1917, Thorndike joined several other prominent psychologists on a committee dedicated to offer service to the U.S. government. Once World War I began, Thorndike joined the U.S. Army's Committee on Classification of Personnel where he created a series of aptitude tests to select recruits to serve in such positions as soldier or aviator.[62]

In 1922, Thorndike gave the National Society for the Study of Education an optimistic view of educational and psychological testing in schools that partially reversed his earlier cautious estimate. Noting in this essay that most elementary schools in the United States measured the children's abilities and achievements, Thorndike claimed that school administrators could use the tests to challenge the students to work to the extent of their abilities while protecting them from excessive demands. They could do this by finding the ratio between the students' capacities and their achievements. Whereas teachers could encourage students with high ability but low performance to improve, they could recognize the inabilities of children with low ability. As for those students who wanted to go to college, Thorndike thought they deserved some measures besides course grades. He noted that within the past three years, colleges had used tests to predict general capacities of students to handle facts and symbols. He thought such standardized testing reduced the problems presented by teachers who graded their students unfairly.[63]

In general, Judd agreed that the use of intelligence tests had led to improved school practices. For example, writing in 1934, Judd noted that American researchers had improved the intelligence tests that French psychologist Alfred Binet had developed in the nineteenth century. Judd added that the tests made it possible to determine what to expect from a particular child. In some schools, this led to placing children in different classes. In other schools, the tests indicated that certain children should receive different assignments.[64]

Although Karier claimed that school administrators used intelligence tests to segregate students based on race and social class, it was not clear that school officials relied on intelligence testing to segregate students who belonged to minority groups. For example, in a history of Los Angeles, California, schools, Judith Rosenberg Raftery noted that, in the 1920s, school officials created a Department of Psychology and Educational Research and hired experts to introduce intelligence testing in the schools. In 1920, the Los Angeles schools enrolled more than 50,000 students. Although school counselors administered tests to nearly the entire school population, many educators complained that the tests did not give accurate results. The problems were most acute when dealing with Mexican and black students. In these cases, language problems seemed to be the cause of low scores on various forms of the tests. Although Japanese students suffered from similar language difficulties, they tended to enjoy remarkable success in schools. The success of Japanese students may have been due to the extraordinary support for education the Japanese parents demonstrated or the success may have been a result of the rise in social class the Japanese families in Los Angeles enjoyed despite the racism they encountered.[65]

Although the Los Angeles schools segregated black high school students in the 1920s, they did not use intelligence test scores to justify those decisions. Raftery found ample evidence to show that officials ignored intelligence test results in making decisions to exclude black students from white classrooms. Sometimes, school staff members directed African American students to segregated classes. Other times, the school board redrew school attendance zones as neighborhoods changed to segregate buildings. In these instances, intelligence tests played no role.[66]

The evidence that Raftery drew from publications produced by the Los Angeles schools indicated that during the 1920s, teachers and supervisors were sensitive to the shortcomings of intelligence tests. The district undertook the most testing during the mid-1920s. At that time, teachers and principals controlled the placement of students. According to Raftery, they did not depend solely on the test results to make decisions about where to place students.[67]

If teachers and administrators in California resisted the use of intelligence testing to determine student placement, they had the support of experts as well. For example, in 1928, the National Society for the Study of Education devoted two volumes of its annual yearbook to the debate about the comparative influences of nature or nurture. When Thorndike reported that siblings shared similar levels of intelligence, he was careful to note that heredity did not cause all the similarities. In another essay, Joseph Peterson noted that, in Nashville schools, white children scored higher on mental tests than did Negro children. Nonetheless, Peterson added that white and black children from Chicago surpassed children from Nashville in their racial groups.[68]

Ten years later, Goodwin Watson referred to this yearbook and its articles to show that all students of the controversy about nature or nurture had to accept the view that environmental influences affected intelligence scores. Heredity could not receive all the praise or all the blame. The only question was how much influence a favorable environment could have.[69]

Although Karier have been correct in showing that the social biases of educational psychologists caused problems with intelligence testing, contemporary critics of Thorndike and Judd did not complain about their racial prejudices. For example, although Merle Curti accused Thorndike of supporting economic and political conservatism, he mentioned only briefly Thorndike's statements on racial differences.[70] Similarly, Harold Rugg criticized Thorndike and Judd for collecting facts while ignoring that education was an organism. He did not complain about implicit racism. Instead, Rugg railed against the tendency of Thorndike to treat education as a mechanism. Although Rugg described the various intelligence tests of his day, he did not complain about racial biases. His point was to show how educators could develop a critical spirit toward the practice of evaluation. Instead of examining parts of the school as the tests tried to do, Rugg called on teachers to be critical of the tendency to think about school improvement as something to do piecemeal. He thought educators should become artist-teachers who would bring together aesthetic knowledge with scientific understanding to solve the problems of humankind.[71]

In this case, Rugg may have pointed to the problem in the limits Thorndike and Judd placed on their research. This came out when Judd served on President Herbert Hoover's research committee on social trends published in 1933. Writing the essay on education, Judd claimed the changes in education since 1875 paralleled changes in the society. Rather than draw those parallels, Judd concentrated on such institutional practices as the ways the curriculums had broadened, the development of the junior high school, and advancements in higher education. The chapter ended that the most hopeful aspect was the adoption of scientific studies of education such as the use of school surveys to determine school offerings and the development of ability testing to diversify school programs.[72]

Although Judd described the increased enrollments of women, he did not write about educational opportunities of different ethnic and racial groups. Another member of the President's committee, T. J. Woofter, wrote about the status of racial and ethnic groups. According to Woofter, about a quarter million Negro children of elementary school age and three-quarters million Negro children of high school age did not attend school. He added that the schools for Negroes in the South were inadequate although they had improved in recent years. School terms were almost fifty days short of the typical nine months. School expenditures for Negro children in the South were about one-fourth the expenditure for white children. White teachers earned almost two-and-one-half times more than black teachers did. Woofter added that from 1910 to 1930 the most spectacular movement in the United States was the shift of hundreds of thousands of Negroes from the South to Northern cities. Unfortunately, the schools in those cities where Negroes had moved were often segregated. Woofter contended that the retardation caused by Southern education prevented racial integration.[73]

Although Woofter noted that African Americans faced serious educational difficulties, Judd did not acknowledge them. In fact, Judd did not acknowledge any social problem that related to school life. In writing a forward to the monograph containing the study of education for the president's committee, Judd argued that the aim of the research was to offer comprehensive surveys of the many changes that had taken place in society. He added that concentrating on a problem and offering solutions could draw attention away from changes going on in other areas of life. Thus, Judd claimed that the authors for the president's committee sought to present objective data about social changes that had taken place rather than answer questions of keen interest.[74]

When Judd contended that he could not consider social problems associated with education, he described his beliefs about research more than he reflected the aims of the Hoover committee on social trends. Two examples make this clear. First, in writing about the status of racial and ethnic groups, Woofter had noted that the education of African Americans reinforced the conditions of deprivation under which they suffered. Indeed, Judd could have noted that the school facilities for minority groups were inadequate. Second, another author who served on the president's committee, Robert Lynd, complained about the narrow focus of Judd's essay. Lynd's essay was entitled People as Consumers. When committee members exchanged drafts, Lynd asked Judd why consumer problems did not appear in Judd's description of home economics courses. Judd replied that he was concerned with home economics as an example of the introduction of practical courses in the curriculum. Social problems were outside his scope.[75]

Conclusion

The educational psychologists who sought to create a science of teaching differed from the educational philosophers who preceded them. Both groups followed the ideas of German scholars although they chose to borrow from different sets of intellectuals. Nonetheless, the late nineteenth century was a period wherein scientists on both sides of the Atlantic cooperated in their efforts to understand human nature and to offer practical suggestions to improve schools.

The faith that practical techniques could bring about moral progress was an attitude that came from Britain, characterized the Victorian era, and contributed to the rise of universities by introducing professionalism into the United States. One aspect of the movement for professionalism was the scientific movement in education that grew in a period of less than fifty years to dominate public schools and teacher-training institutions. An important element was the use of ability tests. Imported from France, the tests served a variety of institutions in the United States besides schools. Businesses and the U.S. Army employed psychologists to develop tests to select appropriate employees.

Although educational psychologists hoped that the study of education would lead to objective information about schools, questions surrounding the use of intelligence tests indicate that bias may have crept into those studies. Worse, because the educational psychologists followed a narrow focus, they tended to ignore social problems such as the segregation of students that their tests might have aggravated. Although it was not clear that the dangers the tests presented became rampart, the effect of educational psychology was to make schools similar.

Ironically, the development of educational psychology benefited from a Victorian faith in the practical applications of scientific discoveries. Eschewing a more sophisticated blending of science and philosophy, the educational psychologists ignored Dewey's efforts to create a model of educational research that originated with particular concerns of specific classrooms and asked everyone to consider how the proposed solutions suited the aims of education in a democracy. Instead, advocates of educational psychology, such as Thorndike and Judd, wanted teachers to help them with their experiments and to follow the specific and often narrow conclusions they revealed.

Educational psychologists claimed they wanted to protect educators from political influence. The way they would do this was to find the best way to organize schools, plan the curriculum, and conduct lessons. As a result, they sought to find the best pattern by which to codify schools. Although educational psychology may have protected educators from politics, the psychological studies introduced new pressures requiring conformity to bureaucratic decisions. According to some authors, two characteristics that lent to the growth of globalization were bureaucracy and concern for material possessions. As educational psychology enhanced those tendencies, it drifted toward globalization.

Endnotes

1. Ellen Condliffe Lagemann, "The Plural Worlds of Educational Research," *History of Education Quarterly* 29, no. 2 (Summer 1989): 185–214.
2. Alexis de Tocqueville, *Democracy in America,* trans. George Lawrence (New York: Harper & Row, 1966), 426–431.
3. Daniel Walker Howe, "American Victorianism as a Culture," *American Quarterly* 27, no. 5 (December 1975): 507–532.
4. Laurence Veysey, *The Emergence of the American University* (Chicago: University of Chicago Press, 1965), 121–179.
5. Ira Remsen, "Scientific Investigation and Progress," *Popular Science Monthly* 64 (February 1904): 291–303.
6. David Starr Jordan, "Comrades in Zeal," *Popular Science Monthly* 64 (February 1904): 304–315.
7. Burton J. Bledstein, *The Culture of Professionalism: The Middle Class and the Development of Higher Education in America* (New York: W. W. Norton & Co., 1978), 333–334.
8. David A. Hollinger, "Inquiry and Uplift," in *The Authority of Experts: Studies in History and Theory,* ed. Thomas L. Haskell (Bloomington: Indiana University Press, 1984), 142–156.
9. D. H. Myer, "American Intellectuals and the Victorian Crisis of Faith," *American Quarterly* 27, no. 5 (December 1975): 585–603.
10. Nicholas Murray Butler, "Status of Education at the Close of the Century," Meeting of the Department of Superintendence, *National Education Association's Journal of Proceedings and Addresses* 39 (February 1900): 188–196.
11. Geraldine Joncich, *The Sane Positivist: A Biography of Edward L. Thorndike* (Middletown, Conn.: Wesleyan University Press, 1968), 3–7.
12. Lagemann, "The Plural Worlds of Educational Research," 204–205.
13. Dorothy Ross, *G. Stanley Hall: The Psychologist as Prophet* (Chicago: University of Chicago Press, 1972), 3–105.
14. Ross, *G. Stanley Hall,* 112–119.
15. Charles E. Strickland and Charles Burgess, *Health, Growth, and Heredity: G. Stanley Hall on Natural Education* (New York: Teachers College Press, 1965), 12–13.
16. Granville Stanley Hall, "The Contents of Children's Minds," in *Readings in the History of Psychology,* ed. Wayne Dennis (New York: Appleton-Century-Crofts, Inc, 1948), 255–274.
17. Naomi Norsworthy, "Review of *Aspects of Child Life and Education,*" *The Journal of Philosophy, Psychology, and Scientific Methods* 5, no. 12 (4 June 1908): 326–331.
18. Hall, "The Contents of Children's Minds," 256–257.
19. Ross, *G. Stanley Hall,* 170–185, 279–293.
20. Ross, *G. Stanley Hall,* 186–198.
21. G. Stanley Hall, *Adolescence: Its Psychology and Its Relation to Physiology, Anthropology, Sociology, Sex, Crime, Religion, and Education,* vol. I (New York: D. Appleton and Co., 1907), v–xx.
22. H. Heath Baldwin, "Review of *Adolescence,*" in *The American Journal of Sociology* 10, no. 6 (May 1905): 824–836.
23. Edward L. Thorndike, "Review of *Adolescence: Its Psychology and Its Relation to Physiology, Anthropology, Sociology, Sex, Crime, Religion, and Education*" in *Science* 20, no. 500 (29 July 1904): 142–145.
24. Thorndike, "Review of *Adolescence,* 142–143.
25. Thorndike, "Review of *Adolescence,* 144.

26. G. Stanley Hall, *Youth: Its Education, Regime, and Hygiene* (1907; reprint, New York: Arno Press, 1972), 1–29.
27. Will S. Monroe, "Review of *Youth: Its Education, Regime, and Hygiene* in *The Journal of Philosophy, Psychology, and Scientific Methods* 4, no. 8 (11 April 1907): 218–219.
28. G. Stanley Hall, *Educational Problems,* vol. I (New York: D. Appleton and Co., 1911), v–xiii.
29. Charles De Garmo, "Review of *Educational Problems,*" in *Annals of the American Academy of Political and Social Science* 38, no. 2 (September 1911): 342–343.
30. Ross, *G. Stanley Hall,* 344–346.
31. Robert L. Church, "Educational Psychology and Social Reform in the Progressive Era," *History of Education Quarterly* 11, no. 4 (Winter 1971): 390–405.
32. Church, "Educational Psychology and Social Reform," 398–399.
33. Church, "Educational Psychology and Social Reform," 399–401.
34. Joncich, *The Sane Positivist,* 268–271.
35. Edward L. Thorndike, *Education: A First Book* (New York: The Macmillan Co., 1923), 112–115.
36. E. L. Thorndike and R. S. Woodworth, "The Influence of Improvement in One Mental Function upon the Efficiency of Other Functions," *Psychological Review* 3 (1901): 247–261.
37. Thorndike, *Education,* 115–116.
38. Edward l. Thorndike, *Educational Psychology: The Original Nature of Man,* vol. 1 (1913; reprint, New York: Teachers College, 1923), 1–4, 24.
39. Thorndike, *Educational Psychology,* vol. 1, 195–197.
40. Thorndike, *Educational Psychology,* vol. 2, 142–151.
41. Joncich, *The Sane Positivist,* 274–276.
42. R. G. Stauffer, "Thorndike's 'Reading as Reasoning': A Perspective," *Reading Research Quarterly* 6, no. 4 (Summer 1971): 443–448.
43. Edward l. Thorndike, "Reading as Reasoning: A Study of Mistakes in Paragraph Reading," *Reading Research Quarterly* 6, no. 4 (Summer 1971): 425–434.
44. Wayne Otto, "Thorndike's 'Reading as Reasoning': Influence and Impact," *Reading Research Quarterly* 6, no. 4 (Summer 1971): 435–442.
45. Harold Ordway Rugg, *Foundations for American Education* (Yonkers-on-Hudson, N.Y.: World Book Co., 1947), 124–125.
46. Lagemann, "The Plural Worlds of Educational Research," 200–201.
47. Charles H. Judd, "On the Scientific Study of High School Problems," *American Journal of Education* 91, no. 4 (1910; reprint, August 1983): 419–434.
48. Rugg, *Foundations for American Education,* 125.
49. Rugg, *Foundations for American Education,* 720–723.
50. Charles Hubbard Judd, *Psychology of High-School Subjects* (Boston: Ginn and Co., 1915), 392–413.
51. Judd, *Psychology of High-School Subjects,* 431.
52. Rugg, *Foundations for American Education,* 720–723.
53. Harold S. Wechsler, "The Primary Journal for Secondary Education, 1893–1938: Part I of a History of *School Review,*" *American Journal of Education* 88, no. 1 (November 1979): 83–106.
54. Charles Hubbard Judd, *Reading: Its Nature and Development* (Chicago: University of Chicago Press, 1918), 1–5, 177–187.
55. Charles Hubbard Judd, *Introduction to the Scientific Study of Education* (Boston: Ginn and Co., 1918), iii, 1–5.
56. Charles H. Judd, *Education and Social Progress* (New York: Harcourt, Brace, and Co., 1934), 139–151.
57. Joncich, *The Sane Positivist,* 558.
58. Clarence Karier, "Elite Views on American Education," *Journal of Contemporary History* 2, no. 3 (July 1967): 149–163.
59. Joncich, *The Sane Positivist,* 316, 418.
60. Thorndike, *Education,* 67–70, 273–274.
61. Edward L. Thorndike, "The Nature, Purposes, and General Methods of Measurements of Educational Products," in *The Measurement of Educational Products,* The Seventeenth Yearbook of the National Society for the Study of Education, ed. Guy Montrose Whipple (Bloomington, Ill.: Public School Publishing Co., 1918), 16–24.
62. Joncich, *The Sane Positivist,* 358–367.
63. E. L. Thorndike, "Measurement in Education," in *Intelligence Tests and Their Use,* Twenty-First Handbook of the National Society for the Study of Education, ed. Guy Montrose Whipple (Bloomington, Ill.: Public School Publishing Co., 1922), 1–9.
64. Judd, *Education and Social Progress,* 236–239.
65. Judith Rosenberg Raftery, *Land of Fair Promise: Politics and Reform in Los Angeles Schools, 1885–1941* (Stanford: Stanford University Press, 1992), 139–161.
66. Raftery, *Land of Fair Promise,* 153.
67. Raftery, *Land of Fair Promise,* 161.

68. Guy Montrose Whipple, *Nature and Nurture,* The Twenty-Seventh Yearbook of the National Society for the Society for the Study of Education (Bloomington, Ill.: Public School Publishing Co., 1928).
69. Goodwin Watson, "Testing Intelligence, Aptitudes, and Personality," in *The Scientific Movement in Education,* The Thirty-Seventh Yearbook of the National Society for the Study of Education, ed. Guy Montrose Whipple (Bloomington, Ill.: Public School Publishing Co. 1938), 357–373.
70. Joncich, *The Sane Positivist,* 376.
71. Rugg, *Foundations for American Education*, 723–807.
72. Charles H. Judd, "Education," Report of the President's Research Committee on Recent Social Trends, *Recent Social Trends* (New York: McGraw-Hill Co., 1933), 325–381.
73. T. J. Woofter, Jr., "The Status of Racial and Ethnic Groups," Report of the President's Research Committee on Recent Social Trends, *Recent Social Trends* (New York: McGraw-Hill Co., 1933), 553–601.
74. Charles H. Judd, *Problems of Education in the United States* (New York: McGraw-Hill Book Company, 1933), v–vii.
75. Lagemann, "The Plural Worlds of Educational Research," 209.

11

Using Committees to Reorganize Schools

Vocational school, early twentieth century

During the early years of the twentieth century, educators tried to change the organization of public elementary and secondary schools. Complaining that students had to pursue general education until they were nearly twenty years old, reformers launched several studies about economy in education. Although the reformers wanted to make school programs as short and as effective as possible, they went beyond such modest goals to broaden the curriculum, to allow for more diversification of studies, to increase the flexibility of schools, and to tie schools closer to what they considered the needs of the community.

In these efforts, the reformers reinforced the series of institutions that distinguished American schools. At its apex was the comprehensive high school. Known as democracy's high school, the comprehensive high school was supposed to allow every student to pursue his or her interests while developing skills and attitudes to advance the social order. As this chapter will show, the reformers sought to integrate the work of the philosophers of education discussed in Chapter 9 and the educational psychologists discussed in Chapter 10. Although such a synthesis may have been impossible, these reformers created a uniquely American institution called the comprehensive high school. As will be seen in Chapters 12 and 13, educators offered the comprehensive high school as the means to solve most social problems, including economic depression and international aggression.

Despite these efforts to reorganize schools, progressive educators such as Harold Rugg complained that liberal arts professors and subject-centered teachers prevented the reformers' ideas from entering the curriculum. According to Rugg, associations of liberal arts defenders secured over $500,000 from various philanthropies to justify their program of studies. To Rugg, the villains were the National Committee on Mathematical Requirements, the Classical Investigation, and the Modern Language Study that met from 1920 to 1925. Rugg argued that these organizations maintained traditional subject matters as the center of school curriculums throughout the 1920s.[1]

Edward A. Krug held a similar opinion. Whereas Krug attributed the continuance of the subject matter curriculum to the inertia of high schools, he added that professors of classical languages such as Latin and Greek as well as professors of mathematics resisted the changes that reformers wished to introduce to schools during the 1920s.[2]

Contrary to the complaints of Rugg and Krug, the committee reports made by associations of liberal arts teachers did not express reactionary responses to reform. Instead of defending traditional academic perspectives, the reports recommended that subject matters serve the same practical goals that reformers advocated for schools. Thus, the curriculum proposals written by subject matter teachers during the 1920s considered the subjects of history, mathematics, classical languages, and foreign languages as tools to solve practical concerns. This represented a considerable change in the conceptions of the subject matters because proposals written during the nineteenth century such as the reports of the Committee of Ten and the Committee of Fifteen portrayed academic subjects as offering aesthetic or intellectual understandings rather than providing means to advance social awareness.

In part, the change took place because the goal of social utility fit the twentieth century drive for economy. Another aspect might have been that reformers and subject matter specialists used the same method of expert deliberations to make their proposals. Although there may have been something in the method that implied the outcome, educators had followed a similar model of social reform before the turn of the century and arrived at views supporting academic subjects. For example, as discussed in Chapter 7, when the members of the National Education Association (NEA) decided in 1894 that they would profit from a study of each of the principal subjects found in programs of instruction in secondary schools, the organization had commissioned a Committee of Ten to select members of constituent conferences to report on various areas. The NEA repeated this procedure in 1895 when it created the Commission of Fifteen to study three aspects of elementary schools: the training of teachers, the correlation of studies, and the organization of city school systems. In both of those nineteenth-century studies, the NEA dedicated funds to pay the expenses. To the Committee of Ten, the NEA gave $2,500 to support the undertaking. To the Committee of Fifteen, the NEA appropriated $1,000 to cover expenses. Both of these committee reports urged teachers to preserve academic perspectives for the subject matters.[3]

The NEA studies during the nineteenth century were modest in comparison to the studies conducted by reformers and subject area teachers during the twentieth century. The efforts became more expansive because they enjoyed larger budgets as philanthropic organizations supported the committees of experts. This had not been possible during the nineteenth century. Although smaller foundations, such as the George Peabody Education Fund discussed in Chapter 6, had originated in the middle of the nineteenth century, these focused on narrow aims, such as the improvement of education in the South, and used relatively small amounts of money. Peabody had donated $1 million for this effort. On the other hand, in 1905, Andrew Carnegie established the Carnegie Foundation for the Advancement of Teaching, and in 1911, he created the Carnegie Corporation with donations that exceeded $350 million. John Rockefeller established the General Education Board in 1902 and the Rockefeller Foundation in 1913 as part of donations that exceeded $500 million.

How Did Educational Reformers Undertake the Process of Changing School Organization?

In 1905, an educational reformer, Paul Hanus, complained that the NEA's Committee of Ten and its Committee of Fifteen had limited effect because the committees had worked independently of each other. Further, Hanus noted that the strength of each of the reports might have corrected the deficiencies of the other. That is, although Hanus praised the Committee of Ten's report of 1894 because members based their decisions about the appropriate content of courses for secondary education on an overwhelming array of educational authority, he complained that the findings appeared separate from each other rather than organized around a rationale any program could follow. When Hanus considered the work of the Committee of Fifteen done in 1895, he complimented the report because it justified the selection of courses in the elementary schools, but he also complained that the principle justifying those courses came from one person's opinion. He noted that the report adopted the view of W. T. Harris that teachers should select each course of study according to its importance in correlating the individual to the civilization of his or her time. Thus, Hanus argued that the Committee of Ten should have interpreted the requirements for each course according to Harris's doctrine of correlation. In this way, the committee members could have blended the findings of educational authorities around Harris's organizing principle. This would have given Harris's principle more authority and it would have rendered the collection of studies more meaningful.[4]

Although Hanus went on to describe the contributions of other notable studies, he complained that they did not build on previous studies. Because educators wrote apart from each other, they could not integrate their different ideas around a sound guiding principle.[5] Educational reformers followed Hanus's suggestion. When they sought to reorganize education to achieve economy of time, they enlisted several experts from a variety of areas to form committees and make recommendations. In turn, these committee reports presented the resulting suggestions in ways that fulfilled the principle of social utility. This was the guiding principle they shared.

According to Harry B. Wilson, the movement for economy of time in education began in 1902 when William Rainey Harper, then president of the University of Chicago, addressed a meeting of the affiliated and cooperating schools of the university. Harper recommended that there be a reorganization of education. Because elementary schools extended to eighth grade at that time, Harper suggested connecting the work done in eighth grade to high school. Harper thought high schools, which went to twelfth grade, should cover the material from two years of college study. At the same time, he wanted elementary schools to complete the work they formerly did in seven years in six years. With these changes, Harper believed that he could remove two years from the chain of grades, thereby allowing students to graduate from college earlier and enter their occupations at younger ages. Harper noted that such an arrangement accorded with practices in European countries. As a result, he recommended that the conference establish three committees to study the problems of the elementary schools, the secondary schools, and the colleges. He offered $500 to each committee to support their investigations.[6]

Many educators agreed with the thrust of Harper's suggestions, although critics raised questions about the ways to achieve the economies. In subsequent discussions, F. Louis Soldan, superintendent of St. Louis Schools, quipped that education was changing from a preparation for life to becoming life itself, because the students had to pass through an ever-increasing chain of grades from elementary school through high school into college and on to the university. At the same time, Soldan warned that Harper's suggestion of reducing elementary schooling from eight to six grades and transferring work to different levels could cause students to leave schools earlier. Because elementary schools were close to students' homes and high schools were farther away in central locations, many students might choose to leave school at the end of the shortened elementary section. Thus, Soldan offered a compromise of reducing the elementary program to seven years. He recommended eliminating the tendencies of teachers to have students cover the same topics in different grades until the students had completely mastered these lessons. Further, he thought it would save time if administrators supervised the methods of teaching to ensure that teachers and students worked together in understanding the material and to ensure that the examinations of the students focused on essential aspects.[7]

As noted in Chapter 9, John Dewey was at the University of Chicago when this conference took place. He agreed with Harper to reduce elementary school programs from eight years to six years, but he voiced two fears. The first was that the move toward efficiency in teaching would cause instruction to become overly mechanical. Nonetheless, he thought a way to shorten elementary school programs was to have teachers concentrate on helping students acquire the tools of inquiry. The second was that moving vocational training to the beginning of university work would eliminate efforts to include cultural enrichment with professional studies. Although Dewey supported the proposal to expand the work of high schools, he worried that time was not the problem. For Dewey, the more serious problem was that high school teachers had no clear vision of what they should do.

He agreed that secondary education should introduce students to the world of work, but he wanted the schools to help students understand the worthwhile cultural aspects of their professions.[8]

As these initial discussions about the economy of time in education took place at the University of Chicago and appeared in the university's journal, *School Review*, philanthropic organizations began to support similar surveys. For example, the Russell Sage Foundation supported a study conducted by Leonard P. Ayers entitled *Laggards in Our Schools*. Ayers's study combined the results of several surveys from schools in most of the larger cities to determine why many children did not make normal progress through the grades, and why many students left before finishing elementary school. Since Ayers was a student of Thorndike, he reinforced the view that part of the problem derived from individual differences in the health and mental capacities of students. Although Ayers noted that children of Italian immigrants had more difficulties in schools than did children of German immigrants, he found school organization to be the greatest weakness. Consequently, he made two sets of recommendations. The first was legislative. This included asking state legislatures to provide for the adequate enforcement of compulsory attendance. The second was administrative. In this regard, Ayers recommended that schools maintain accurate records of student progress. Without such records, school administrators could not evaluate school practices or enable students to transfer to different schools without having to repeat work they had already completed. At the same time, Ayers suggested that programs of flexible grading could allow children to move ahead or stay behind in specific courses. When every child had to master the same assignments at the same rate with other students, teachers prevented children from moving to the next grade level although those children had difficulty in only one or two subjects.[9]

As studies like Ayers's confirmed the need for increased efficiency and flexibility in schooling, the NEA's Council of Education charged a committee chaired by James Baker, president of the University of Colorado, to consider the problem of economy of time in education. Although this committee did not make a report, Baker submitted the results of an opinion survey showing that many educators were concerned about the problem of economy of time. Consequently, NEA officials recommended that Baker head another Committee on the Economy of Time in Education (CETE). Baker charged various members of the committee with gathering the information pertaining to their sections. The NEA sent circular questionnaires to a large number of university and school administrators and supported the publication and distribution of conclusions.[10]

In 1913, Baker's committee delivered a formal statement of the problems. The committee's report claimed that the difficulty was that the period of formal education in the United States had grown too long. The members felt they could remove two years from the period of general education by selecting subject matters and type of instruction in accord with the ways those subjects helped students understand contemporary life. Although Baker and his colleagues claimed that college courses had to be revised, they were confident the changes would happen quickly because they quoted a report from the National Association of State Universities recommending university work begin after two years of college work and extend for two more years. Under this proposal, college education would provide general education and the university would offer specialized professional training. Considering all the adjustments, the committee members suggested that elementary schools enroll children from age six to twelve. The secondary education should have two divisions, one school that took up two years and another school that occupied four years. These secondary schools would enroll children from ages twelve to eighteen. Finally, college would take up two years, and university or graduate training would occupy four years. In this way, students could complete an entire set of courses arriving at a doctorate or professional degree by age twenty-four.[11]

According to the CETE report, students in the United States remained longer in general education preparing to enter specialized training than did students in European countries. French and English students began their specialized or technical training almost immediately after completing secondary school, whereas in the United States, the students finished secondary school, entered a four-year college, and then moved on to another four-year university program. The members of Baker's committee claimed that, at the least, the college years were unnecessary.[12]

In making its recommendations, CETE claimed the members followed two sets of principles. The first concerned educational principles that the members defined as the need for vocational education. The committee members agreed that university training should be an important stage of vocational education. Although the committee's statement acknowledged that vocational education was a factor in many secondary schools, the length of most educational programs prohibited professional university training. In addition, the committee noted considerable disagreement about the value of vocational training in elementary and secondary schools. Although some educators wanted to connect the studies of elementary and secondary schools to vocational training of some type, most educators thought vocational education should take place after school training. Students could learn industrial trades or business practices in the shop or office.[13]

The second set of principles was sociological, the view that the schools had to serve a democratic society. With the assistance of one of its members, Albion Small, the first professor of sociology in the United States, the members of the committee decided that academic subjects reinforced an aristocratic society. To the committee, an academic orientation was selfish and unsocial. In a democratic society, the students should learn skills and information that served the needs of the community. This would include learning to use the scientific method, developing the appreciations necessary for citizenship, and mastering the practical skills appropriate for vocations.[14]

To show the need for economy of time, the committee's report claimed that students in Germany, France, and England learned more in shorter periods than did students in the United States. To improve efficiency, Baker's committee recommended that elementary educators should emphasize the most important aspects of each subject. Thus, the aim of literature, history, and science was to inspire students to value their culture. Math was a tool for accuracy. The committee added that teachers in secondary schools should reduce the number of subjects and relate the courses that remained to contemporary social life. At the same time, students should have the opportunity to study subjects that had been adapted to their capacities and interests. Above all, the committee members recommended that students receive moral training preparing them for citizenship.[15]

Because the report of the CETE described the general condition of education, the NEA chose to set up a subcommittee chaired by Harry B. Wilson to propose the most economical ways of teaching in elementary schools. It did not create an analogous subcommittee for secondary schools because the organization could not afford a second study. Submitted in 1915, Wilson's report contended that the subcommittee members had been unwilling to agree to shorten the elementary school years. Nonetheless, members acknowledged that removing all content not related to modern life or unable to promote the students' growth would reduce the time needed to complete programs. Because the members could not agree how to make those distinctions, the committee used responses to surveys from fifty city school districts to determine what courses were held in most schools, what topics were covered, and how well those arrangements worked. The results showed that schools spent about 70 percent of class time on the traditional subjects of reading, language, penmanship, and arithmetic. Although students spent more time with music and drawing than with manual training or spelling, they stayed at recess for longer periods than they devoted to any subject except reading and arithmetic.[16]

In 1916, Wilson's subcommittee submitted another report about enhancing the economy of elementary school subjects. Although the author of each section was responsible for the evidence and the conclusions that appeared in his or her chapter, the authors agreed to achieve economy by ensuring that the students could apply what they learned in their lives outside school.[17]

An example of the type of study that appeared in Wilson's report was an effort to determine the minimum essentials in language and grammar that students would need in later life. In this chapter, W. W. Charters explained that his conclusions came from records of what students had not learned. Charters found several studies wherein teachers had collected lists of the errors that students made. He arranged these errors in order of frequency, with the most common error first and the least common last. After classifying the errors according to type, such as grammar, punctuation, or language, the teachers decided what facts the students had to learn to correct those faults. Charters concluded that such studies were easy to conduct. More important, this method provided a practical way to ensure that students learned skills or information that would be important to them.[18]

The model that Charters used became popular. For example, in 1918, the CETE published a report on the studies to determine what to teach in the different subjects in grades one through eight. In the various studies, the researchers found out what skills people needed to know to live and work as adults. For example, in a study of the essentials of arithmetic, the researcher gathered data from a standard cookbook, the payrolls of various factories, store advertisements, and a hardware catalogue. From these sources, the researcher determined the arithmetic processes that children would have to know in order to solve the problems that appeared in those sources.[19]

Two of the essays in the 1918 report of the CETE concerned courses in civics and history. For example, in determining the content for a course in civics, B. B. Bassett analyzed the platforms offered by various political parties during several different elections to reveal the political issues students should understand. In a similar way, Bassett sought to determine what historical information students should learn. In this case, he started with Albion Small's book, *General Sociology,* and listed the six main activities of humankind as Small described them. These included protection of health, promotion of wealth, and harmonizing human relations. Bassett went through twenty-two books to find information relating to these topics. After selecting the historical information in the texts, Bassett compiled charts indicating what historical period or event illustrated which topic. He claimed the teacher could arrange a course of study in this way to use history in ways that exposed the children to life in society.[20]

Because the CETE continued making studies about the minimum essentials for elementary schools, it created another subcommittee to describe the most economical methods of teaching the subjects. The members of the subcommittee agreed that the subjects had to have some direct usefulness in later life. In addition, the researchers agreed that they would use some variation of the scientific method to select the best teaching method. When the chair of the subcommittee, Ernest Horn, delivered the report in 1919, he claimed that it had been relatively easy to achieve economy in cases where the social utility of the subject was clear and when researchers could measure effective methods of teaching. Although agreement was more elusive when the relations between school subjects were complicated or the measurements of effective teaching were subtle, the researchers accomplished these ends by redefining those subject matters in simplistic ways.[21]

Handwriting was a subject in which the social utility was clear and the effectiveness of various methods of instruction was easy to determine. As a result, an essay in the report by Frank N. Freeman described findings from what he called scientific studies to determine how to teach the skill of handwriting. Freeman's scientific studies were controlled experiments that compared the results of different methods of instruction with two different groups of students. From these comparisons, he determined a set of twenty-eight rules that teachers should follow. These included having the students face the desks squarely, placing three-quarters of their forearms on the desks and tilting the paper to make a 30-degree angle with the edge of the desk. Freeman had found that the speed of handwriting should be about thirty letters per minute for children in third grade and increase to about seventy-three letters per minute at the end of grade eight. Above all, Freeman noted there had to be specific directed practice in writing, and he offered ways that teachers could keep accurate records of student achievement.[22]

When the Committee on the Economy of Time in Education made several studies and organized their findings around apparent social utility of the subject matter, they could do this when they used some form of activity analysis. In the case of Charters's study of essential language and grammar, he analyzed the mistakes children made with language and sought to correct them. With arithmetic, the researcher looked at cookbooks and advertisements to determine what type of arithmetic would be most valuable to the children. For the study of civics and history, researchers compiled inventories of important topics and lists of sources of information about such topics. Thus, the studies built on each other in ways that correlated to their organizing principles.

In their efforts to determine how to teach, the researchers made statistical evaluations of the comparative worth of different approaches. Thus, they used the most objective authority they could find to make their decisions rather than rely on one person's opinion. At the same time, the researchers reinforced the subject matter curriculum by seeking to find which aspect of the subject matters would be useful to the students in life outside school. The problem was they changed the nature of the subject matters from the ways that Harris and, to some extent, Dewey had held.

As described in Chapter 9, Harris believed that subject matters could inform the students about the ways of thinking found in the culture. When the students compared the different ways of knowing found in the culture, they came to understand the quality of reason.

Although Dewey considered subject matters to be tools, he wanted children to understand and to control experience. For Dewey, recognizing the differences among the subject matters was essential to grasping experience.

The researchers for the economy of time did not consider such abstract concerns. They took conventional views of math, history, or handwriting and found ways to teach them effectively. The researchers did not seek to find ways that information from one area could inform students about the nature of knowledge because, to them, such an aim seemed aristocratic and selfish.

How Did Efforts to Economize Instruction Change Secondary Education?

While the NEA continued studies of elementary education, similar controversies arose about secondary education. Although the 1894 report of the Committee of Ten recommended that all students pursue a course of study that prepared them for college, the report had allowed students to choose among four different programs. Thus, some choice appeared even though each of the four programs was overwhelmingly academic in nature. Further, Harvard College had adopted an elective system in 1884. As a result, in 1901, Paul Hanus conducted a study of students at the Harvard Seminary in Education to determine what they felt about the seminary's elective system. Hanus sent questionnaires to all the students who graduated from 1886 to 1900. Most of the students praised the opportunity to select their own courses, saying that they were able to study subjects that interested them and served them in life. Although a few students claimed the system allowed students to select easy courses, Hanus pointed out that almost no student admitted to have taken easier classes; they said their friends were guilty of shirking. Although Hanus claimed his study showed the wisdom of elective courses, he added that the students' responses indicated that a system of guidance in choosing the courses was necessary as well.[23]

In line with the desire to encourage increased flexibility of high school courses, the Secondary Department of the NEA accepted in 1910 resolutions requesting colleges to discontinue the entrance requirement of two foreign languages, later known as world languages, and to recognize as electives all the subjects that high schools taught well. To determine what work students should do in high school the NEA created a Committee on the Articulation of High School and College (CAHSC) chaired by Clarence D. Kingsley. At that time, Henry S. Pritchett, president of the Carnegie Foundation, expressed the view that students had to take too many subjects in the course of their education. Pritchett wanted to broaden high school curriculums, and he warned that colleges would have to accept more of these newer courses in vocational studies and civics. To Pritchett, this was reasonable because he thought that people in a democracy should develop their individual talents as well as a sense of the common culture.[24]

Following these suggestions, the CAHSC recommended in 1911 that high schools measure all work in units representing one year's work in some subject. Colleges could accept students who completed fifteen units of high school work. A part of those fifteen units could come from some sort of restricted elective courses. In addition, students in high school could select whether to study either foreign languages or mathematics. The report claimed that requiring students to take both sets of subjects caused excessive school failure. Further, the students could achieve intellectual power through other studies except physical training and chorus.[25]

After the CAHSC made its recommendations, several state boards of education and educational associations approved them. Because some elective courses could apply for college entrance, high schools had to form reasonable programs. To aid in the reorganization of high school subjects, the NEA created twelve committees to work on various subject fields in 1912–1913. The members of the CAHSC joined ten members who served at large to form the Commission on the Reorganization of Secondary Education (CRSE).[26]

When the CRSE released its final report in 1918, it arranged its recommendations in the form of twenty cardinal principles that expanded the two educational principles adopted by Committee on the Economy of Time in Education five years earlier. As noted previously, the Committee on the Economy of Time claimed that schools should change their organization to include vocational preparation and the need to advance democracy. Because this meant that schools had to impart skills appropriate for vocations, daily life, and citizenship, the CRSE's first principle was a statement of the need for comprehensive reorganization. In its second principle, the CRSE affirmed that schools should serve the democracy by enabling each person to develop his or her personality through activities designed for the well-being of society. The third principle accepted that the objectives of education should be determined by analyzing the activities of adults. Thus, the report determined that schools should meet seven objectives: health, command of fundamental processes, worthy home membership, vocation, citizenship, worthy use of leisure, and ethical character.[27]

When the CRSE considered the arrangement of elementary and secondary education, the committee members agreed with the CETE that eight years sufficed for elementary school. Districts should adopt a junior high school of two years and a senior high school of four years. The junior high should introduce students to different vocational programs available in the high school and offer the students a chance to become acquainted with the pattern of high schools where teachers formed departments and students took different classes with different teachers who specialized in those subjects.[28]

Although the CRSE did not issue a separate report on the junior high school, the National Society for the Study of Education (NSSE) had made the junior high school a subject of its fifteenth yearbook. Begun in 1914, the author of the NSSE study, Aubrey Augustus Douglass wrote from school reports he had obtained, questionnaires he sent to school officials, and letters he received from school administrators. Douglass noted that the idea was old; the members of the Committee of Ten had recommended in 1894 that the seventh and eighth grades of elementary schools form another secondary school. Despite the earlier recommendations, the first junior high schools did not appear until well into the twentieth century. Officials in Crawfordsville, Indiana, claimed to have opened a junior high school in 1907, and school administrators in Madison, Indiana, replied that they began one in 1909. Columbus, Ohio, opened a junior high school in 1909. Berkeley, California, followed in 1910, along with Concord, New Hampshire. In 1911, a junior high school opened in Los Angeles, California. Douglass found that the idea was popular. When he sent surveys in 1914 to 268 different cities, school officials in 189 districts reported having organized junior high schools, twenty were in the process, and twenty-nine thought they would begin shortly. According to Douglass, the most potent force in making the junior high popular was the work of the NEA committees studying the economy of time in education.[29]

Douglass found several reasons for schools to change the elementary school arrangement. One explanation was that it would shorten the time students had to stay in school, bringing U.S. schools in accord with practices in Europe. Another point of view was that adolescence began around age twelve or thirteen with the onset of puberty. Children in this age group required different treatment than did younger pupils. Nonetheless, Douglass had found disagreements about the proper curriculum for junior high schools. The most controversial were the diversification of subjects and the extent of vocational education.[30]

In part, vocational education was controversial for practical reasons. Many secondary schools offered some form of vocational preparation at the beginning of the twentieth century. The problem was that many high schools had enrollments of less than thirty students and one teacher. Thus, there was little choice among vocational programs and few opportunities for teachers to specialize in subject areas. Nonetheless, as the twentieth century progressed, the number of students attending high schools grew rapidly. Some of these high schools were strictly academic, and other high schools were business schools. A third group of high schools offered some sort of training in a trade. In addition, a considerable number of high schools had become merged or cosmopolitan schools. That is, they offered academic and vocational courses in the same building.[31]

The CRSE took a side in this controversy. The sixteenth principle of the CRSE report stated that the comprehensive high school would be the standard secondary school. Furthermore, it held that junior high schools would be of the comprehensive type as well. At least, this would be the case in those cities with sufficient numbers of students to warrant such arrangements. The reason the report made this choice was that the members felt the comprehensive high school with differentiated curriculums was uniquely suited to prepare students for life in a democracy. On the one hand, students could pursue their specific interests or abilities within various specialized programs. On the other hand, the different types of students could learn to work together with students with a variety of talents in group assemblies or organizations. Furthermore, when one school offered a variety of programs, students could change the emphasis of their studies without applying to a different school.[32]

The rationale of the CRSE held that there had to be system of guidance to help young people take advantage of the different options the schools provided if the high schools were going to be comprehensive. Thus, the CRSE's committee on vocational guidance defined vocational guidance as a continual process beginning in elementary schools that enabled children to choose a vocation, to prepare for it, and to advance within it. The committee's report emphasized there were no systems of analysis that schools could use to classify children and decide which students should prepare for particular occupations. According to the committee on vocational guidance, schools teach children to adjust to the needs of businesses and of society. At the same time, however, schools should help students learn how to change business or institutions that harmed people. In this way, thoughtful educators could help the pupils and the society.[33]

Because vocational guidance was a new area, the CRSE's committee could not recommend reorganization. Instead, the report offered descriptions of how some school districts had implemented vocational guidance in hopes that other educators could adapt the methods to their situations. These options included appointing a school supervisor who worked with children already employed in some seasonal, monotonous work that appeared to have no future. In some cases, continuation classes after work hours would direct these children to better employment opportunities. In other cases, an employment supervisor could offer the assistance. Above all, schools had to provide employment information during specific courses labeled "occupations." In addition, the report added that some schools had established school placement bureaus.[34]

The report of the CRSE's committee on business education illustrated the view of the commission's members on the ways that vocational studies could be included in schools. The report noted that public high schools began offering commercial education around 1880, and such courses became popular. In fact, since 1914, the enrollments in business courses had increased more rapidly than had the enrollments in high schools generally. Although the committee's report acknowledged that there were several different arrangements of commercial education, the members complained that the curriculums were loosely grouped series of electives with no unity to the selections. For example, because most people thought of commercial education as programs for women, the classes had concentrated on stenography and bookkeeping. The committee claimed this was misleading. They recommended that business programs address the broader tasks of training for service in the community, participation in social life, and knowledge of business as a whole. Thus, the committee wanted programs to offer courses that could enable students to enter sympathetically into life as well as discharge their vocational duties.[35]

Because the initial report of the CAHSC had noted that requirements for students to study ancient languages, also known as classical languages, and mathematics had caused excessive school failure, the CRSE created a Committee on the Problem of Mathematics. Chaired by William Heard Kilpatrick, whose ideas appear in Chapter 12, the committee on mathematics noted five reasons to reconsider the role of mathematics in secondary education. These included the need for each subject to justify itself, the unwillingness to accept mental discipline as a rationale, the acceptance of diversified curriculums, the call for social utility, and questions of effective presentation of the subject matter. In making suggestions for the reorganization of mathematics, Kilpatrick's committee recommended that the subject serve instrumental values. This meant that students should learn aspects of mathematics in the order and in the ways that they could use them while executing projects in areas of interest to them.[36]

Because the committee decided that the use of mathematics determined its form of instruction, the report noted that different groups of students required distinct types of mathematical knowledge. For example, general readers needed to have the skills in arithmetic to proceed through the day and the understandings of mathematical notions that would advance their thinking. Thus, they might learn arithmetic along with some algebra and the use of graphs. Kilpatrick's report added that recent surveys indicated mechanics and craftspeople needed practical understandings such as found in arithmetic and simple geometry used to measure angles and work with circles. Although students preparing for work as engineers needed sophisticated types of mathematics, surveys had not formulated what those needs were. As a result, the committee recommended that school people conduct surveys to learn what engineers needed to know and evaluate secondary school courses to determine if the content was appropriate. Mathematical specialists required the most knowledge. Although the committee on mathematics wanted these students to enroll in introductory courses with other less-gifted students, the report called for developing ways to select the students who would move on and to provide a means of organizing advanced classes so that they met students' interests.[37]

In an effort to meet the need for citizenship training, the CRSE created a new school subject called the social studies by joining courses such as history, geography, and civics already present in most schools and having instruction in these classes focus on the organization and development of human society. Compiled by Arthur William Dunn, the report of the CRSE's committee on the social studies recommended sequences of the social studies courses with a culminating class covering the social, economic, and political problems of democracy. The aim of such studies was to teach the students to appreciate the laws and nature of social life, to develop a sense of responsibility in individuals as members of social groups, and to acquire the intelligence and the will to participate in the promotion of the social well-being.[38]

Although the social studies report noted that the social studies should begin with an understanding of the ideals of the students' nation, the report qualified the aim of patriotism by adding that these nationalistic feelings were to be the basis of a sense of membership in the world community. Thus, the students should learn to promote the well-being of the human race. Although the social studies could advance society by fostering high national ideals, it would aid the students by encouraging intelligent loyalty to those ideals.[39]

In describing the point of view of the committee, the report on social studies quoted John Dewey to the effect that the best way to provide for the future of the students was to attend to their needs for growth in the present. As an example of a school that followed this principle, the committee's report quoted J. L. Meriam in whose elementary school at the University of Missouri the children would study present-day difficulties and then undertake historical research to understand how those problems came to be. For example, in sixth grade, the children spent six weeks learning about such different forms of transportation as railways, steamships, and public highways. In seventh grade, they considered the problems of transportation from a historical perspective. Thus, Meriam could assert that although there were no history courses in his school, the children learned a great deal of history. He added there were no geography courses, but the students mastered a considerable amount of geography.[40]

The emphasis on practical studies seemed to exclude classical academic studies such as Latin from the curriculum. Although Kingsley and the CAHSC had suggested that some courses such as social studies should replace Latin and algebra for college entrance requirements because many students could not pass these subjects, the CRSE included committees on ancient languages and on modern foreign languages. According to Edward Krug, neither of these areas appeared in the final report. Krug added that the committee on ancient languages had submitted a preliminary report that appeared among those the CRSE released. The CRSE did not accept the final report that the committee on ancient languages submitted. Thus, the CRSE's final report emphasized the need for students to master English.[41]

How Did Mathematics Teachers React to the Reform Efforts?

The movement for economy of time in education encouraged other organizations to criticize traditional subject matters. For example, at a meeting of the Rockefeller Foundation's General Education Board in 1915, Charles W. Eliot presented his ideas on the changes needed in secondary education. Eliot took a different position in this paper than he had as chair of the NEA's Committee of Ten in 1894 when he asserted that high schools should offer academic rather than vocational studies. In 1915, he praised new schools for the mechanical arts, trade schools, and such institutions as the Tuskegee Institute. Eliot argued that students learned and understood subjects better when they practiced some sorts of practical applications.[42]

Following Eliot's paper, Abraham Flexner submitted in 1916 a paper for discussion to the General Education Board. At that time, Flexner was the board's secretary, and in 1910, he had completed a study of 115 medical colleges that led to substantial changes in the training of physicians. In this paper, entitled "A Modern School," Flexner expressed the view that educational practices should serve practical ends.

In his essay, Flexner claimed that results from college entrance exams showed that students had not mastered Latin, algebra, or geometry. Thus, he claimed it was not worthwhile to ask if knowledge of Latin or algebra was valuable. The students did not achieve it. Flexner suggested that researchers should consider what students could learn before they reached the age of twenty. Flexner divided the appropriate studies into two divisions. In the first category, he placed what he called the fundamental tools of knowledge. These included reading, writing, and arithmetic. In the second category, he listed four fields that facilitated the students' abilities to think: science, industry, aesthetics, and civics. Under science, he claimed that schools could easily construct activities about acquiring food, building shelter, or making clothes to teach scientific principles in interesting and appropriate ways. Under aesthetics, he placed literature, art, and music. He discouraged teaching classics but emphasized developing the students' interests and tastes. Although Flexner criticized the teaching of Latin, he acknowledged that students might acquire a modern foreign language in school to aid in travel, trade, and enjoyment. In civics, the students should learn those things about history that enabled them to understand present-day conditions.[43]

Harris Hancock, a mathematician, complained that Flexner quoted few figures from the College Entrance Examination Board to show that students failed to learn Latin and algebra. Showing results from those tests, Hancock pointed out that candidates fared better in Latin than any other subject. Further, Hancock complained that psychologists such as Edward L. Thorndike misused statistics to arrive at misleading statements when they decided that the study of mathematics did not improve students' ability to reason. Worse, Hancock added, teacher-training institutions accepted Thorndike's misunderstandings as truths with the result that the teaching of mathematics suffered. He claimed it was time that something was done.[44]

Mathematicians in many countries proposed some form of mathematics reform. For example, in 1910, E. W. Hobson noted in his address to the Mathematical and Physical

Section of the British Association for the Advancement of Science that there was a new movement among British schoolteachers. They began instruction in mathematics with concrete examples and moved gradually to abstract principles. Although Hobson thought that such pedagogy made the studies of more use to physicists and to engineers, he worried about an overly practical bias to the subjects. Noting that all mathematics had practical and theoretical sides, he recommended that in the earliest grades the instruction could be almost entirely concrete. As the students advanced through the grades, they could rely increasingly on logical deductions. He warned that teachers should not forget what was essential to help students grasp the principles of mathematics and that these essentials were abstract.[45]

Further, the Mathematical Association of America (MAA) credited E. H. Moore for introducing the association to the reform movement in his presidential address of 1902. The hope that a competent and complete study could vindicate the value of mathematics instructions in general education led the MAA to create in 1916 the National Committee on Mathematical Requirements. Ironically, the efforts of the national committee were unavailing until the philanthropic organizations distributed criticisms of the subject matters. In 1920, after publishing Eliot's and Flexner's criticisms, the General Education Board offered the MAA a grant to conduct studies that validated the need to include their areas in elementary and secondary schools. With these funds, the MAA committee established a central office, hired full-time assistants, and began an extensive nationwide survey.[46]

The wider study was necessary because the initial efforts met serious criticism. For example, in 1917, the Chicago Mathematics Club published the results of a survey completed in cooperation with the MAA. In this effort, the Chicago group sent letters to prominent doctors, lawyers, merchants, and bankers in the city, asking their opinions about the value of teaching mathematics. Although the members of the Chicago club were prominent educational administrators, they did not sample the views of teachers. The results showed that most respondents thought that geometry and algebra should be required studies in all secondary schools.[47]

Shortly after the Chicago report appeared in the journal *School and Society,* David Snedden congratulated the administrators for examining the reasons why some subjects appeared in curriculums. Complaining that the report was no more than a collection of opinions, Snedden suggested that the committee recognize that they surveyed people who preferred algebra to useful subjects. Snedden did not think everyone had to study algebra. For example, he thought that girls, most of whom would leave school at sixteen years of age, should not have to take the course.[48]

Published in 1923, the report of the National Committee on Mathematical Requirements contradicted Snedden. Most important, it was extensive. Entitled *The Reorganization of Mathematics in Secondary Education,* the report totaled over 650 pages. It described suggestions for the curriculum in grades seven through twelve, offered suggestions for college entrance requirements, and explained the mathematical concepts important to each area. In addition, the report described eight different investigations that subcommittees had performed. These included considerations of the disciplinary value of mathematics, the correlation between grades and mathematical studies, and the mathematics curriculums in foreign countries.

Most relevant to this discussion, the report embraced the progressive and practical considerations that critics had pushed forward. For example, according to *The Reorganization of Mathematics in Secondary Education,* there were two aims of mathematical instruction. The first was to develop the powers of understanding and analyzing relations of quantity and space in the students. Such powers would give insight and control over the environment and foster an appreciation of the progress of civilization. The second aim was to develop in the students habits of thought to make effective use of the analysis of space and quantity. Thus, instruction should reinforce the development of these powers rather than acquiring a certain facility with facts. In making these statements, the report warned against teachers using drill and repetition as the means of instruction. It quoted John Dewey's book *How We Think* to illustrate that the logical organization of subject matter was the goal of instruction, not its inception.[49]

The report noted that most educational authors divided educational aims into three categories. These included practical or utilitarian aims, disciplinary aims, and cultural aims. Although the authors accepted the divisions as a convenient way to consider objectives, they noted that teachers could not achieve such aims separately. For example, a disciplinary aim could be practical in a broad sense and therefore be a cultural aim as well.[50]

The Reorganization of Mathematics in Secondary Education acknowledged many practical aims of mathematics. Undisputed was the value of understanding the fundamental processes of arithmetic, such as addition or multiplication. Of equal importance was an understanding of algebra because the simple formulas clarified the quantitative relations found in everyday life. Finally, graphs and geometric forms appeared in most industrial and political settings.[51]

As to the question of the disciplinary aims of mathematical instruction, *The Reorganization of Mathematics in Secondary Education* avoided the controversies about transfer of training described in Chapter 10 by describing which skills students learned in mathematics and how they could use them in life. Instead of considering general qualities of clear thinking, the report noted that people needed quantitative and spatial thinking in life. Because the skills learned in mathematic classes enhanced those abilities, the question of transfer to less mathematical situations was not relevant. Thus, the students should learn to use concepts relating to quantity and to approach situations thoughtfully. Although the report called such an approach the scientific method, it used terms similar to those favored by more progressive educators. For example, the students should learn to break complex situations into simpler parts. They should recognize the logical relations among interdependent factors, and they should form generalizations that had specific applications. Although these mental habits were valuable in life, they were essential to mathematical situations; thus, the question of transfer was unimportant.[52]

Under the category of cultural aims, the report listed aesthetic aims such as developing an appreciation of beauty, recognizing the ideal of perfection, and understanding the power of mathematics. Although the students might not apprehend these aims until late in their studies, the authors thought they should be present in the early courses as well as the later ones.[53]

In describing the appropriate organization of mathematics courses, the authors of *The Reorganization of Mathematics in Secondary Education* noted that many teachers had moved away from subject-oriented classes. Instead of separating arithmetic, geometry, and algebra, these instructors offered general courses wherein students could see clear interrelations among the methods. Although the committee members could not find any substantial agreement among teachers, they noted with approval that many school districts had initiated experimental programs, especially at the junior high school level. With this new two-year secondary school, teachers could tailor the instruction to the mental traits peculiar to the ages of the students. In seeking these ends, the report urged teachers to encourage the students' inquisitiveness, to build on their desires to experiment, and to foster their wish to know why and how something happened. The best examples of such changes took place at the Lincoln School, which was founded by the General Education Board that John D. Rockefeller endowed, and in the University of Minnesota's High School. In these junior high school curriculums, the committee members found three important features. They correlated mathematical studies with the children's life outside school, they related the studies to human activities, and they gave students the means to control the numerical and spatial relations of human life. In the Lincoln School and the University of Minnesota High School, the teachers and students organized their curriculums together and published the lessons in mimeograph form; major publishers then produced texts from those sheets.[54]

At this point, readers should note that the recommendations found in *The Reorganization of Mathematics in Secondary Education* described progressive models as acceptable. Although the MAA's committee offered its suggestions in a tone of scientific caution, these reports did not seek to prevent progressive ideas from entering the curriculum as Rugg and Krug contended. To the committee members, the junior high school offered the opportunity to reasonably diversify the curriculum. In addition, the report asked teachers to concentrate more on helping the students appreciate the ways of thinking found in the various fields of mathematics and the ways mathematics made sense of human life.

One example might clarify the differences between these proposals and the more idealistic views that W. T. Harris expressed when he wrote the report for the Committee of Fifteen in 1895. Although Harris pointed out that arithmetic was the means to measure and to record such things as order of succession, dates, and extent of influence, he believed there was a psychological side of mathematics that was more important than this practical side. According to Harris, the ways of thinking found in arithmetic differed from the method found in algebra or in geometry. In arithmetic, people depended on counting whereas, in algebra, people arrived at answers indirectly. To keep these spheres separate, Harris argued that teachers should not dwell on the concrete applications that required counting. Instead, after sixth grade, the students should begin studying simple but more theoretical formulations that would prepare them to undertake algebra in the ninth grade. Thus, Harris recommended that instruction be academic, not practical; the teacher should teach children to use letters for unknown quantities and to exhibit the general form of a solution so that they would be able to move into analytical geometry, differential calculus, and mechanics.[55]

How Did Teachers of Ancient and Foreign Languages React to Reform Efforts?

Teachers of Latin faced the same criticisms that mathematics teachers endured. According to W. L. Carr, the *Atlantic Monthly* carried an article in March 1917 by Abraham Flexner criticizing Latin instruction under the title "Education as Mental Discipline." In the April 1917 issue, Charles W. Eliot published his article, "The Case against Compulsory Latin." Although critics labeled these articles as attacks against humanism, the General Education Board funded two more papers by Flexner and Eliot. More important, the Board accepted Flexner's *A Modern School* quoted above as the blueprint for the science-centered, experimental, progressive Lincoln School that it founded in 1917.[56]

When Carr described these events, he added that Andrew West, a dean at Princeton University and president of the newly created American Classical League (ACL), challenged the General Education Board to support a Latin and Greek–centered school. Although the Board refused to provide funds for such a school, its members voted in 1920 to finance a study of the status of Latin and Greek in secondary schools in the United States.[57]

The Classical Investigation was an extensive effort. Arranged by a special committee of the ACL, the investigation was to have three parts. The first step was to survey the present situation in schools and colleges. The second was to analyze the information accumulated by the survey. Finally, the committee wanted to prepare a plan to teach the classics. To conduct this process, the special committee appointed an advisory committee of fifteen members. Headed by Andrew West, the advisory committee installed its central office at his university, Princeton. Auxiliary offices opened in Oberlin, Ohio; in Rochester, New York; and in Springfield, Illinois. Fifty-five persons joined eight regional committees that covered separate parts of the United States including the New England states, the South, and the Rockies. In addition, the investigation sought the collaboration of forty-eight professors of education and psychology. These included such critics as Edward L. Thorndike, W. W. Charters, Charles Judd, William C. Bagley, and Franklin Bobbitt. Nearly 9,000 teachers volunteered to assist in the experimental work. They came from over 1,300 schools and tested over 150,000 pupils. The total number of tests exceeded 750,000.[58]

According to Edward Krug, the teachers of classical and modern foreign languages endured awkward positions. The study of German dropped from about 25 percent of the high school enrollment in 1915, before World War I, to less than 1 percent in 1922, after the war. In other foreign language classes, enrollments dropped from about 84 percent in 1910 to about 55 percent in 1922, but the total number of students in language classes increased because the number of students in high schools increased.[59]

When the American Classical League (ACL) compiled the enrollments in ancient and foreign languages for the Classical Investigation, the members did not think they were in an awkward position. They claimed that the declines were reasonable. According to the ACL, enrollments in Latin in public high schools had declined from about 40 percent of the pupils in 1914–1915 to nearly 30 percent in 1921–1922. The loss in private school enrollments had been about 2 percent with enrollments remaining over 50 percent. To the members of the ACL, these declines were caused by the increased enrollments of students who had few academic interests and preferred agricultural, technical, or vocational courses. At the same time, the ACL members were pleased that enrollments in Latin totaled about 940,000 students in 1923–1924, which exceeded the enrollments in other foreign languages at 926,000. A source of dismay was that only 11,000 students enrolled in Greek and of these about 8,000 were in private schools.[60]

The ACL concluded that the problem was not declining numbers of students enrolled in Latin. It was the need to obtain enough qualified teachers for the high school students.

High schools serving communities of less than 2,500 citizens used teachers who lacked college training and who had not studied the language adequately. According to the ACL report, about 75 percent of the public high schools fell into this category. In addition, all types of high schools faced a serious shortage of teachers of Greek. Yet the report added that adequate instruction in classical languages required appropriately trained teachers.[61]

As to whether high school students could learn Latin, the ACL report acknowledged that performance on tests from the College Entrance Examination Board was not as high as it could have been had all students received proper instruction. Nonetheless, the report added that the scores of students in Latin for the years from 1914 to 1923 were better than the scores in most other secondary school subjects.[62]

When the authors of the Classical Investigation turned to the questions of the objectives of Latin teaching, they noted that most students enrolled for one or two years. Thus, the goals did not require extended study. To determine what those objectives should be, the investigators compiled a tentative list from literature available on the subject. To test the validity of the various objectives, the investigators took two directions. First, they set up tests to determine whether the students could achieve the objectives under present conditions. Second, they sampled expert opinion in a variety of ways. The researchers asked 1,150 Latin teachers to fill out questionnaires, and they sent scorecards to 300 teachers in various parts of the country asking them to note whether and how well they had achieved the objectives during the year. To verify their findings, the authors held a conference with nearly seventy professors of education and psychology to discuss the results.[63]

The report of the Classical Investigation divided the objectives of Latin study into three categories that embraced the practical and progressive ideals of the critics. The first category was instrumental objectives. Although the first two of these objectives were the ability to read Latin and the ability to understand Latin phrases that appeared in English, the other seven aims under this heading included such everyday aims as increased ability to read English, increased ability to speak and write in English, and increased knowledge of the principles of English grammar. In the second category, the investigators placed four disciplinary objectives that referred to developing habits of sustained attention and orderly procedure as well as developing habits of reflective thinking and the use of logical analysis. The third category included cultural objectives such as the development of a historical perspective, recognition of the influence of Roman civilization on contemporary life, and appreciation of the elements of literary technique.[64]

The objectives included the development of rational or scientific thinking as the reformers wished. For example, the act of reading Latin with understanding was one that required the development of thinking skills, because the system of word order differed greatly from the system found in English. Although many teachers used what the authors called an analytic method that consisted of a student finding the verb and fitting the rest of the sentence to it, the report recommended having the pupils grasp the meaning of groups of Latin words in a sentence, placing those together, and translating the sentence.[65]

In addition, the Classical Investigation met the aims of social utility. For example, the report recommended collateral reading in English as a part of regular coursework. In this way, the students could develop a wider understanding of aspects of Roman life. They could recognize the unique patterns of Roman thought, and they could appreciate the historical effects of Roman civilization. In addition, the report urged teachers to associate Latin words with English derivatives and to determine the meanings of Latin words by looking for English cognates, because such methods taught the students about their culture and increased their abilities to solve problems.[66]

Concerning the social utility of Latin, the Classical Investigation reported the results of surveys in Britain, France, and Germany. Making comments regarding Germany shortly after World War I, the report described debates about changing school programs. Before the war broke out, German critics of classical training urged the end of Latin and Greek training in the gymnasiums, which were classical secondary schools. These critics claimed that German children should prepare for life and learn technical skills to advance the country. On the other hand, the supporters of classical studies argued that reading classical authors gave students the chance to develop spiritual values not associated with material gain. Writing in 1925, the authors of the Classical Investigation noted that many states in Germany had adopted more flexible school plans than existed before the war. The cosmopolitan school was a popular model in Germany. It combined classical studies with a variety of other programs to encourage students to prepare for life and to acquire spiritual values. These cosmopolitan schools differed from the comprehensive high school found in the United States because the German model rarely included technical or vocational courses.[67]

Writing in 1965, W. L. Carr claimed that the Classical Investigation had its most impressive impact on textbook publishers. Titles such as *Latin for Today* and *Our Latin Heritage* replaced titles such as *Elementary Latin* after the ACL established the American Classical League Service Bureau to disseminate the findings of the investigation. Textbook authors and publishers cooperated with the bureau to produce new texts and to revise old ones. Carr concluded that the investigation sought to make Latin a living language that had social utility, and this derived from its objective to teach students to read Latin.[68]

The shift from learning to write in Latin to learning to read Latin was important. In 1894, the Committee of Ten recommended that all students learn to write as well as read because such training advanced their understanding of the language. The members of the Committee of Ten's conference on Latin held that writing was the reverse of reading, and they wanted teachers to ask students to write sentences similar to those found in the Latin texts. In fairness, the conference members wanted teachers to use books that were easy for the students to read, such as those works by Eutropius or Nepos that were popular at the time among German and French school teachers. Nonetheless, the requirement to write correct Latin sentences prevented the students from investigating more cultural and literary aspects of the works. For example, the Committee of Ten did not recommend what the Classical Investigation called collateral reading in English. Consequently, Latin could not serve the Committee of Ten as a course in comparative cultures. It was a course in the classics.[69]

As the Classical Investigation was underway, teachers of modern foreign languages carried out an investigation similar to those conducted by the teachers of mathematics and the instructors of ancient languages. From 1924 to 1927, the Carnegie Corporation supported a study of the teaching of modern foreign languages in the United States. Cooperating with the Canadian Committee on Modern Foreign Languages, the members of the study surveyed the work done in French, German, and Spanish.[70]

The investigators with the Modern Foreign Language Study (MFLS) collaborated extensively with the researchers for the Classical Investigation and organized both projects in similar ways. The MFLS was extensive. Before it ended, the study published twelve volumes describing the work. For example, Ben D. Wood, a student of Edward L. Thorndike, constructed standardized tests to measure achievement. At the same time, the study gathered enrollment data, surveyed the opinions of practicing teachers, and collected and analyzed course outlines and syllabi. The study sponsored investigations into the processes of learning to read and whether or how learning a foreign language improved students' use of English. In addition, the study prompted analyses of Spanish and French textbooks to determine their cultural content.[71]

In a short period, expectations for the instruction of modern foreign languages had changed dramatically. For example, in 1898, the Modern Language Association's (MLA) Committee of Twelve had determined that the primary objective in the study of a modern foreign language was reading ability. They were less concerned with speaking ability. Further, they thought students should learn grammar, translation, and composition to help them achieve fluency in reading. Once students could read in a foreign language, the Committee of Twelve's report expressed the hope that the students could partake in the cultural life of other peoples. On the other hand, in 1929, when the authors of the MFLS surveyed articles written by such advocates of economy as Franklin Bobbitt, Alexander Inglis, and David Snedden, they found that these reformers held to a different set of objectives. These advocates thought students of modern foreign languages should develop the ability to speak a simple form of the foreign language without great fluency, they should be able to read with moderate ease, and they should hold an improved attitude toward the foreign language speakers. At the same time, these advocates of economy hoped that foreign language study would improve the students' English language skills.[72]

Following the procedures of the Classical Investigation, the authors of the MFLS set out to determine what the objectives should be. They began by setting up a tentative list of immediate and ultimate objectives, both of which placed reading ability first and speaking ability second. The list of ultimate objectives expanded to include increased proficiency in English, enhanced knowledge of history and culture of foreign lands, and expanded understanding of the ideals of immigrants to the United States. The next step was to determine whether and how students could attain these goals. After several extensive series of tests, the MFLS acknowledged that there was no certain information about what students could achieve. The one finding was that the lower 50 percent of the modern foreign language students learned very little grammar, vocabulary, or pronunciation.[73]

The MFLS concluded that one way to reduce the problem of many students not profiting from foreign language study was for teachers to concentrate on those goals they could achieve. These objectives seemed to be in the reading of the foreign language. Thus, the MFLS concluded that the important goal should be the development of the ability to read books, newspapers, and magazines that catered to the students' interests. Either from this activity or in addition to it, students should learn more about foreign countries and the derivations of English words. Although these objectives expanded at each grade level, they remained relatively consistent and in the same order.[74]

The conclusion of the MFLS to concentrate on reading was similar to what the Committee of Ten in 1894 and the MLA's Committee of Twelve in 1898 had decided about foreign languages, but the MFLS added considerable concern that the texts the students read describe cultural practices in the foreign countries and in the United States. In this regard, the MFLS adopted the aim of social utility that the reformers wanted. Because the MFLS concluded there was little vocational need for foreign language, the studies could not adopt such a thrust. At the best, foreign language study would reinforce citizenship in a broad sense.

How Popular Was the Drive to Organize Schools around the Ideal of Social Utility?

When the movement for the economy of time brought about the creation of the comprehensive high school, it made the abiding American contribution to education. According to Burton Clark, the system in the United States was the only one that moved toward universal participation in the early years of twentieth century. European secondary schools remained elite and diversified whereas American secondary schools blended smoothly with the elementary schools, forcing all schools to cover all subjects. Although Japan began to imitate this system after World War II, European countries waited until the 1960s to adopt such models because it seemed to retard intellectual development.[75]

According to James Conant, president of Harvard University, the comprehensive high school was the only model of secondary education that fit the public devotion to the ideals of equality of opportunity and status. Conant had been a member of the NEA's Educational Policy Commission (EPC) in 1944 when the commission had published the report, *Education for All American Youth*. In 1951, when the EPC published a revision, *Education for All American Youth: A Further Look*, Conant was chairperson of the commission. Since these reports from the EPC reproduced the plans for the comprehensive high school found in the CRSE's cardinal principles report, Conant restated them in 1959 when he made his study of high schools entitled *The American High School Today*.[76]

Although the members of the EPC and educators such as James Conant held that the comprehensive high school was the best model for a democracy, they resisted the temptation to impose such a system on every school district. Instead, they repeated the same message because each school district could set its own curriculum policies even though there were some pressures toward uniformity, such as college entrance requirements. As this chapter has shown, organizations such as the NEA, the MAA, and the ACL sought to give school districts intelligent guidance in framing the curriculum.

A strategy of persuasion was reasonable. Because most educators feared central control of schools, the reformers followed a model of expert studies because it promised to integrate practical suggestions with general aims and objectives while still allowing for popular choice. Herbert Hoover made the idea popular. A study began when a core group of experts defined a problem, called a conference to interest the public in the ideas, and conducted a survey to reveal the nature of the difficulties and propose solutions. Finally, the experts expected intelligent public officials to adopt the recommendations and fit them to local circumstances. Although the model did not impose any particular outcome, it required that decisions be in accord with popular tastes because the findings of the experts did not carry any authority beyond that which any experts would have. The model called for the public to accept the findings through some sort of consensus and to take steps to influence school policies.[77]

The problem was that administrators in many school districts could not choose the best system of education. For example, in 1927, George Counts analyzed responses to questionnaires he had sent to 900 cities in the United States. Counting the numbers of courses that were added or dropped during the previous five years, Counts noted that established courses remained in place unless they suffered from popular resentment, as German studies did after World War I or died of old age as did the study of Greek. He noted that as long as numerous teachers were engaged in a school subject, it would remain in the curriculum whether it was reasonable or not. Further, when adding a course, most schools imitated a neighboring district, and they considered what the costs might be of making the addition. Concerns for training teachers, buying equipment, or providing space seemed crucial in such decisions. The school administrators did not refer to scientific studies to make decisions about the curriculum. Thus, Counts noted that most high schools offered an accumulation of courses rather than a well-organized plan of studies.[78]

Despite these problems, most public school districts adopted the idea of a unified system leading to a comprehensive high school for all students. With the exception of many Catholic schools, most elementary schools in the United States restricted themselves to six grades. After a period of slow growth in the 1930s and 1940s, junior high schools became popular, although the number and spread of grades varied by convenience. For example, some junior highs included grades seven and eight while other junior highs had grades seven, eight, and nine. In 1973, the National Middle School Association formed with the intent of changing junior high schools from miniature high schools into institutions designed to meet the developmental needs of adolescents through such techniques as interdisciplinary courses, individualized instruction, team teaching, and flexible scheduling. Although many junior highs adopted the name of middle schools, fewer took on the characteristics.[79]

As noted above, the CRSE created the social studies to replace courses in classical languages and mathematics. This was part of the drive to social utility because the social studies would teach citizenship skills. The innovation was surprisingly successful. When C. O. Davis sent questionnaires to 1,180 schools distributed over the eighteen states comprising the North Central Association in 1920 asking about the extent to which those schools taught civics. Of the schools sampled, 1,148 had courses in civics in the high school. Nearly a thousand of those schools taught the course apart from history. Usually, high school seniors studied civics following the recommendations of the CRSE for a course in problems of democracy.[80]

In part, the rapid acceptance of social studies was due to the influence of the federal government during World War I. In 1917, as part of the effort for Americanization, the U.S. Food Administration and the U.S. Bureau of Education enlisted Charles H. Judd and Leon C. Marshall to direct various teachers and social science experts in the composition of a series entitled *Lessons in Community and National Life*. According to Earle Rugg, the important feature of these lessons was that they discussed given problems for several pages and included historical and geographical information to make the issues clear to the readers. One such lesson described the concentration and integration of modern businesses and focused on three industries, steel, railroads, and meatpacking, to explain how this happened. In a short period, several authors wrote texts using the same approach thereby encouraging schools to adopt courses in community civics.[81]

Many things caused educators to change the emphasis of subject areas from aesthetic concerns to practical orientations. As mentioned in Chapter 10, the basis for the shift may have been the Victorian faith in technology. During the period between 1912 and 1917, popular attitudes changed markedly. According to Henry F. May, the opening of the twentieth century marked the end of American innocence because Americans turned away from the nineteenth century search for philosophical truths. Instead, they retained the belief that they could create a bright future through a concern with facts and accomplishments. After 1917, Americans lost faith in technical gains, May added, because the rise of such evils as racial violence made such optimism appear unreasonable.[82]

In the face of publicly shared realism, educators may have decided that social utility was a publicly acceptable goal around which they could shape a comprehensive plan for education. If this was the case, the educators may have created a system of education that reinforced people's materialistic desires at the expense of their aesthetic appreciations.

Conclusion

As the twentieth century opened, educators expressed concern that students had to pursue general education until they were nearly twenty years old. The problem was that students could not begin professional or vocational education until they entered a university. To solve this difficulty, the National Education Association conducted several studies about economy in education. Because such studies appeared to denigrate the studies of ancient and foreign languages and mathematics, academic groups in those areas conducted competing studies. Ironically, the findings of all these studies moved schools toward broader curriculum options that related school studies to community needs.

The movement for the economy of time in education sought to integrate the findings of educational psychologists with the ideas of educational philosophers; this effort failed. Nonetheless, the movement brought about lasting changes in the organization of elementary and secondary schools in the United States and in other countries around the world.

In the face of such confusion, educational reformers such as the members of CRSE and members of professional associations such as the MAA and the ACL offered suggestions to organize curriculum without trespassing on the principle of local control of schools. In this effort, the progressives and the subject matter specialists shared the same aims. They did not resist each other as much as some commentators claimed. Nonetheless, it is not clear the changes reflected progress. For example, the reforms turned the curriculum away from theoretical understandings and toward practical concerns. Although this made education accessible to more people, making courses demonstrate their social usefulness was a less sophisticated aim than Harris's desire to introduce students to the different ways of knowing that had developed over centuries. As a result, educational reforms coincided with an increased concern for material prosperity that some authors suggest was an aspect of globalization.

Endnotes

1. Harold Rugg, *Foundations for American Education* (Yonkers-on-Hudson, N.Y.: World Book Co., 1947), 606–607.
2. Edward A. Krug, *The Shaping of the American High School, 1880–1920*, vol. 1 (Madison: University of Wisconsin Press, 1969), 341–353; Edward A. Krug, *The Shaping of the American High School, 1920–1941*, vol. 2 (Madison: University of Wisconsin Press, 1972), 66.
3. National Education Association, *Report of the Committee of Ten on Secondary School Studies with the Reports of the Conferences Arranged By the Committee* (New York: American Book Co., 1894), 3–4; National Educational Association, *Report of the Committee of Fifteen on Elementary Education with the Reports of the Subcommittees: on the Training of Teachers; on the Correlation of Studies in Elementary Education; on the Organization of City School Systems* (New York: American Book Co., 1895), 8.
4. Paul Hanus, *A Modern School* (New York: Macmillan Co., 1913), 224–230.
5. Hanus, *A Modern School,* 231–247.
6. Harry B. Wilson, *The Minimum Essential in Elementary School Subjects,* Fourteenth Yearbook of the National Society for the Study of Education (Bloomington, Ill.: Public School Publishing Co., 1919), 9; Editorial, "The High School of the Future," *School Review* 11, no. 1 (January 1903): 1–3.
7. F. Louis Soldan, "Shortening the Years of Elementary Schooling," *The School Review* 11, no. 1 (January 1903): 4–17.
8. John Dewey, "Discussion: Shortening the Years of Elementary Schooling," *The School Review* 11, no. 1 (January 1903): 17–20.
9. Leonard P. Ayers, *Laggards in Our Schools: A Study of Retardation and Elimination in City School Systems* (New York: Charities Commission, 1909), 1–7, 185–200.
10. James Baker, *Report of the Committee of the National Education Association's Council of Education on Economy of Time in Education,* U.S. Bureau of Education Bulletin no. 38 (Washington, D.C.: Government Printing Office, 1913), 5–7, 60–86.
11. Baker, *Report of the Committee on Economy of Time in Education,* 7–10.
12. Baker, *Report of the Committee on Economy of Time in Education,* 9.
13. Baker, *Report of the Committee on Economy of Time in Education,* 10–13.
14. Baker, *Report of the Committee on Economy of Time in Education,* 13–14.
15. Baker, *Report of the Committee on Economy of Time in Education,* 14–17.
16. Wilson, *The Minimum Essential in Elementary School Subjects,* 9–27.
17. Harry B. Wilson, ed., *Second Report of the Committee on Minimal Essentials in the Elementary School,* The Sixteenth Yearbook for the Study of Education (Bloomington, Ill.: Public School Company, 1917), 9–16.
18. W. W. Charters, "Minimum Essentials in Elementary Language and Grammar," in *Second Report of the Committee on Minimal Essentials in the Elementary School,* The Sixteenth Yearbook for the Study of Education, ed. Harry B. Wilson (Bloomington, Ill.: Public School Company, 1917), 85–110.
19. H. B. Wilson, "Introduction," *Third Report of the Committee on Economy of Time in Education,* The Seventeenth Yearbook of The National Society for the Study of Education, ed. H. B. Wilson (Bloomington, Ill.: Public School Publishing Co., 1918), iii–ix.
20. H. B. Wilson, ed., *Third Report of the Committee on Economy of Time in Education,* The Seventeenth Yearbook of the National Society for the Study of Education (Bloomington, Ill.: Public School Publishing Co., 1918), 63–89.
21. Ernest Horn, *Fourth Report of the Committee on Economy of Time in Education,* The Eighteenth Yearbook of the National Society for the Study of Education, ed. Guy Montrose Whipple (Bloomington, Ill.: Public School Publishing Co., 1919), 8–10.
22. Frank N. Freeman, "Principles of Method in Teaching Writing as Derived from Scientific Investigation," in *Fourth Report of the Committee on Economy of Time in Education,* The Eighteenth Yearbook of the National Society for the Study of Education, ed. Ernest Horn (Bloomington, Ill.: Public School Publishing Co., 1919), 11–25.
23. Hanus, *A Modern School,* 287–306.
24. Clarence D. Kingsley, *College Entrance Requirements,* U.S. Bureau of Education Bulletin no. 7 (Washington, D.C.: Government Printing Office, 1913), 97–103.
25. Kingsley, *College Entrance Requirements,* 5–11, 103.
26. Clarence D. Kingsley, "Origins of the Commission," in *Preliminary Statements by the Chairmen of the Committees of the Commission of the*

National Education Association on the Reorganization of Secondary Education, U.S. Bureau of Education Bulletin no. 41 (Washington, D.C.: Government Printing Office, 1913), 7–9.

27. Clarence D. Kingsley, *Cardinal Principles of Secondary Education: A Report of the Commission on the Reorganization of Secondary Education,* U.S. Bureau of Education Bulletin no. 35 (Washington, D.C.: Government Printing Office, 1918), 5–11.
28. Kingsley, *Cardinal Principles of Secondary Education,* 17–19.
29. Aubrey Augustus Douglass, *The Junior High School,* The Fifteenth Yearbook of the National Society for the Study of Education (Bloomington, Ill.: Public School Publishing Co., 1917), 9–27.
30. Douglass, *The Junior High School,* 28–64.
31. Edward A. Krug, *The Shaping of the American High School, 1880–1920,* vol. 1, 178–183.
32. Kingsley, *Cardinal Principles of Secondary Education,* 24–27.
33. National Education Association, *Vocational Guidance in Secondary Education,* A Report of the Commission on the Reorganization of Secondary Education Appointed by the National Education Association, U.S. Department of the Interior, Bureau of Education, Bulletin no. 19 (Washington, D.C.: Government Printing Office, 1918), 9–10.
34. NEA, *Vocational Guidance in Secondary Education*, 10–15.
35. National Education Association, *Business Education in Secondary Schools,* A Report of the Commission on the Reorganization of Secondary Education, U.S. Department of the Interior, Bureau of Education, Bulletin no. 55 (Washington, D.C.: Government Printing Office, 1919), 11–15, 20.
36. National Education Association, *The Problem of Mathematics in Secondary Education,* A Report of the Commission on the Reorganization of Secondary Education, U.S. Department of the Interior, Bureau of Education, Bulletin no. 1 (Washington, D.C.: Government Printing Office, 1920), 9–14.
37. National Education Association, *The Problem of Mathematics in Secondary Education,* 14–21.
38. Arthur William Dunn, *The Social Studies in Secondary Education*, Report of the Committee on Social Studies of the Commission on the Reorganization of Secondary Education of the National Educational Association, U.S. Department of the Interior, Bureau of Education, no. 28 (Washington, D.C.: Government Printing Office, 1916), 9–12.
39. Dunn, *The Social Studies in Secondary Education,* 9–10.
40. Dunn, *The Social Studies in Secondary Education,* 10–11, 49–50.
41. Krug, *The Shaping of the American High School, 1880–1920*, 339–344.
42. Charles W. Eliot, *Changes Needed in American Secondary Education* (New York: General Education Board, 1921).
43. Abraham Flexner, *A Modern School* (New York: General Education Board, 1916).
44. Harris Hancock, "Remarks on Certain Attacks that Have Been Made Upon the Teaching of Mathematics with Counter Criticisms," *School and Society* 6, no. 143 (22 September 1917): 339–344.
45. E. W. Hobson, "Address to the Mathematical and Physical Section of the British Association for the Advancement of Science," *Science* 32, no. 821 (23 September 1910): 385–403.
46. National Committee on Mathematical Requirements, *The Reorganization of Mathematics in Secondary Education* (Oberlin, OH: Mathematical Association of America, 1923), vii–x.
47. Alfred Davis et al., "The Status of Mathematics in Secondary Schools," *School and Society* 6, no. 151 (17 November 1917): 576–582.
48. David Snedden, "Mathematics in Secondary Schools," *School and Society* 6, no. 153 (1 December 1917): 651–652.
49. National Committee on Mathematical Requirements, *The Reorganization of Mathematics in Secondary Education,* 10–12.
50. National Committee on Mathematical Requirements, *The Reorganization of Mathematics in Secondary Education,* 6.
51. National Committee on Mathematical Requirements, *The Reorganization of Mathematics in Secondary Education,* 6–8.
52. National Committee on Mathematical Requirements, *The Reorganization of Mathematics in Secondary Education,* 8–9.
53. National Committee on Mathematical Requirements, *The Reorganization of Mathematics in Secondary Education*, 9–10.
54. National Committee on Mathematical Requirements, *The Reorganization of Mathematics in Secondary Education,* 19–20, 234–237, 262–263.
55. National Education Association, *Report of the Committee of Fifteen on Elementary Education,* 52–58.
56. W. L. Carr, "The Classical Investigation Forty Years After," *The Classical Journal* 60, no. 4 (January 1965): 151–154.
57. Carr, "The Classical Investigation Forty Years After," 151.

58. The American Classical League, *The Classical Investigation Conducted by the Advisory Committee of the American Classical League,* Part One (Princeton: Princeton University Press, 1924), 1–15.
59. Krug, *The Shaping of the American High School, 1880–1920,* 341–342.
60. The American Classical League, *The Classical Investigation,* Part One, 18–19, 269, 276.
61. The American Classical League, *The Classical Investigation,* Part One, 22–23.
62. The American Classical League, *The Classical Investigation,* Part One, 249–250.
63. The American Classical League, *The Classical Investigation,* Part One, 35–37.
64. The American Classical League, *The Classical Investigation,* Part One, 34–35.
65. The American Classical League, *The Classical Investigation,* Part One, 188–204.
66. The American Classical League, *The Classical Investigation,* Part One, 204–210.
67. The American Classical League, *The Classical Investigation,* Part Three (Princeton: Princeton University Press, 1925), 190–199.
68. Carr, "The Classical Investigation Forty Years After," 153.
69. National Education Association, *Report of the Committee of Ten on Secondary School Studies,* 60–75.
70. Algernon Coleman, *The Teaching of Modern Foreign Languages in the United States: A Report Prepared by the Modern Foreign Language Study* (New York: Macmillan Co., 1930), v–6.
71. Coleman, *The Teaching of Modern Foreign Languages,* 1–2.
72. Coleman, *The Teaching of Modern Foreign Languages,* 7–8.
73. Coleman, *The Teaching of Modern Foreign Languages,* 9–18, 50–53.
74. Coleman, *The Teaching of Modern Foreign Languages,* 104–110.
75. Burton R. Clark, "Conclusions," in *The School and the University in International Perspective,* ed. Burton R. Clark (Berkeley: University of California Press, 1984), 290–323.
76. James Bryant Conant, *The American High School Today: A First Report to Interested Citizens* (New York: McGraw-Hill, 1959); Educational Policies Commission, *Education for All American Youth* (Washington, D.C.: National Education Association, 1944); Educational Policies Commission, *Education for All American Youth: A Further Look* (Washington, D.C.: National Education Association, 1952).
77. For example, see Barry D. Karl, "Presidential Planning and Social Science Research: Mr. Hoover's Experts," in *Perspectives in American History,* ed. Donald Fleming and Bernard Bailyn (Cambridge, Mass.: Charles Warren Center, 1969), 347–412.
78. George S. Counts, "Current Practices in Curriculum-Making in Public High Schools," in *Foundations and Technique of Curriculum-Construction,* The Twenty-Sixth Yearbook of the National Society for the Study of Education, ed. Harold Rugg (Bloomington, Ill.: Public School Publishing Co., 1926), 135–162.
79. Daniel Perlstein, "Junior High Schools," in *Historical Dictionary of American Education,* ed. Richard Altenbaugh (Westport, Conn.: Greenwood Press, 1999), 197–199; Vincent A. Anfara, Jr., ed., *The Handbook of Research in Middle Level Education* (Greenwich, Conn.: Information Age Publishing, 2001).
80. C. O. Davis, "Training for Citizenship in the North Central Association Secondary Schools," *The School Review* 28, no. 4 (April 1920): 263–282.
81. Earle Rugg, "How the Current Courses in History, Geography, and Civics Came to Be What They Are," in *The Social Studies in the Elementary and Secondary School,* The Twenty-Second Yearbook of the National Society for the Study of Education, ed. Guy Montrose Whipple (Bloomington, Ill.: Public School Publishing Co., 1923), 48–75.
82. Henry F. May, *The End of American Innocence: A Study of the First Years of Our Time, 1912–1917* (1959; reprint, Chicago: Quadrangle Books, 1964), 9–18, 393–398.

12

Building Curriculums on Student Interest

Children participating in activity movement, 1930

As the movement for economy of time in education was underway, another effort moved ahead. Begun as the project method, this movement tried to link the movements of philosophy of education, educational psychology, and administrative consolidation. Although the advocates changed their ideas to the wider term *activity movement,* the new phrase could not unite the diverse strands of educational thought because the various participants held significantly different opinions.

Whereas the leaders of the movement for economy of time discussed administrative matters, the educators in the activity movement focused on pedagogy. Nonetheless, the participants in both movements wanted schools to advance the democratic nature of the society. In addition, both groups of reformers believed the idea of making schools democratic meant that science could reveal the best way to enable children to acquire essential skills and that knowledge should be socially useful.

The members of the activity movement had a different conception of science than did the educators concerned with the economy of time. For example, educators who attended to student activity wanted psychological studies to suggest how to align the subject matters with the ways children learned. On the other hand, educators concerned with economy of time wanted scientific studies to reveal the most efficient ways to conduct classroom lessons.

In addition, the members of the activity movement and advocates for economy of time disagreed about the ways that school subjects should serve the children in adult life. Whereas the reformers in the activity movement thought about social utility as something related to the children's interests, the educators in the movement for economy of time considered the measure of social utility of school subjects to be the extent to which the students learned the skills and information they would need as adults in society. The members of the activity movement hoped that children would develop the attitudes and habits useful to adults if they did what they wanted to do. Consequently, these educators sought to redefine the nature of the subject matters. They introduced such curriculum models as the project method that allowed children to shape the curriculums. In contrast, reformers who sought economy of time championed efforts to reorganize the schools with such arrangements as the junior high school and the comprehensive high school that would offer well-planned vocational studies.

As noted in Chapter 11, the movement of the economy of time influenced secondary education because it maintained the subject matters arranged in practical ways. On the other hand, the advocates of the activity movement ignored the lines among subject matters to offer the students ways to learn the attitudes appropriate for life in a democracy. Consequently, elementary school teachers found the activity movement attractive.

By 1934, many educators used the term *activity* to describe an approach to the curriculum. Consequently, the National Society for the Study of Education (NSSE) devoted the second half of its yearbook to the activity movement. Writing the introduction for the NSSE yearbook, Lois Coffet Mossman noted that educational indexes had not carried the term *activity* until 1929. Nonetheless, Mossman thought the idea was more than five years old. She added that educators who thought in similar ways before 1929 had used the phrase *project method* to make the same points. According to Mossman, the rationale behind the term *activity* was to include in the curriculum attention to the children's natures, recognition of their tendencies to action, and awareness of their games.[1]

The NSSE committee assigned William Heard Kilpatrick and three colleagues to write a definition of the term *activity movement.* Kilpatrick pointed out that the term *activity movement* did not describe progressive education because there were many educators who claimed to be progressives but did not identify with the effort. In general, Kilpatrick found the activity movement was a reaction by elementary school teachers against the practice of planning lessons in advance from textbooks. To move beyond this general observation, Kilpatrick and his colleagues analyzed forty-two definitions constructed by experts, considered twenty-five published curriculum guides, and surveyed fifteen books on the subject. Tabulating the results, Kilpatrick and his colleagues concluded that the movement sought to allow children to proceed in school in ways similar to the ways they would learn at home. Consequently, the children undertook experiences. Although Kilpatrick and his colleagues agreed that an essential aspect of the movement was that the teacher did not assign lessons, they found some disagreement about the appropriate role of the teacher. Some definitions suggested the teacher should construct general plans in advance; other definitions wanted the students to have the responsibility of selecting and planning the lessons. Further, there was disagreement questioning if students should learn facts and skills in the projects. Whereas some authorities wanted drill and memorization to supplement the activities, other authorities opposed such adult imposition. Finally, the activity movement might weaken traditional subject matter distinctions. Some educators thought the projects should be independent of subject matters distinctions. Other educators wanted the projects to draw on information from a variety of subjects as they proceeded. In all, Kilpatrick noted that the activity movement was not a philosophical position. Although he thought the activity movement derived from the democratic regard of the individual students, he found it to be a method of teaching rather than a complete theory of education.[2]

What Was the Project Method?

The project began as a method of teaching rather than as a theory of education. According to several commentators, the project method was a part of vocational education. For example, Herbert M. Kliebard asserted that one of the first efforts to use projects took place in 1908 when Rufus W. Stimson implemented the home project plan to help boys studying vocational agriculture apply the teachings of the school to the home.[3]

Stimson was the director of Smith's Agricultural School in Northampton, Massachusetts. In this position, he developed a wide range of farming projects that included building a concrete walkway, planting new types of fruit trees, or determining the best feed for milk cows. In these projects, the students surveyed the conditions, determined the cost of the innovations, and decided whether the cost of the new procedure was justified by the resulting improvements. Cost was the primary factor because Stimson sought to teach the students ways to maximize farm profits.[4]

The idea fit academics. In 1915, John F. Woodhull argued that science teachers should imitate teachers of agriculture and use projects to make the subject more practical. Woodhull claimed that, in 1912, the Massachusetts Board of Education praised the use of projects, and, in 1914, the U.S. Congress appropriated $5 million annually to include projects in the study of agriculture as part of the Smith-Lever bill. According to Woodhull, projects became popular because they offered an antidote to the tendency of having students memorize facts. Woodhull added that projects taught the students to arrange facts in a direction, to take the first steps in finding the solution for a problem, and to acquire the habit of having one experience lead to another. The projects did not have to be elaborate. For example, Woodhull described, as a project, an experience that a young man had when he tried to determine why certain trees had drowned when he blocked a small stream to make a skating pond. From this investigation, he went on to determine how to care for potted plants. Woodhull concluded that the projects offered ways for the daily life of the community to energize the schoolroom.[5]

As educators claimed that projects could make schools more educative, the term *projects* lost its meaning. At least, this was the complaint that David Snedden made in 1916. According to Snedden, educators had been using the term *project* to describe a unit of educative work that culminated in a concrete achievement. Thus, they came to describe as projects such activities as baking bread, making a shirtwaist, or installing an electric bell as projects, provided students undertook the tasks in order to acquire knowledge. To Snedden, such an open definition caused four problems. First, it did not show the unity the undertakings needed. Second, it did not indicate that the student had to conceive the outcome and be interested in it. Third, it did not suggest that the standards of achievement had to be objective. Finally, it did not show that the student had to apply the knowledge previously gained and learn new things. Because educators were applying the term to vocational and academic areas, Snedden recommended that teachers think of different categories of projects such as *observation projects* or *execution projects.* With such categorical names, Snedden suggested that teachers assign different types of projects to different grade levels by matching the skills the project required with the abilities the children had developed.[6]

Charles A. McMurry offered a more academic definition of the term *project* in 1920. He contended that projects offered teachers the opportunity to reorganize the materials of the elementary school around practical life centers. His hope was that these smaller projects would grow into the larger project important to community life. To McMurry the benefit of incorporating projects in schools was that the projects were always objective. Because they referred to some concrete thing or event, the children had to use information that was objective; it could not be abstract. Most important, the children undertook these on their own and often found them fascinating.[7]

When McMurry offered examples of appropriate projects, he began with the popular idea of growing a school garden. He listed twenty-three tasks the students had to perform to make a garden. These included planning the garden, laying out the plots, planting the seeds, studying the soil, and using legumes as fertilizers. These steps appeared in an order, and they moved into broader areas such as soil study and fertilization that had applications to the community. According to McMurry, teachers in academic areas should apply this principle of organization. He called it a unit. For example, McMurry offered the example of a project that began with the story of two men who left Chicago in 1848 to search for gold in California. After the students discovered the difficulties the men encountered in the overland journey, they set out to find what other prospectors encountered. This moved into a study of the settlement in California. Thus, the unit began with the personal story of two men and broadened into a wider story of the great migration in the same way the garden project had begun with planning the garden and moved into soil study. In addition to covering the nineteenth-century westward movement, the unit could look back to consider migrations from European countries to the New World. According to McMurry, although such units organized the information and made it interesting, they required that students and teachers have large blocks of time in which to work and a rich supply of materials to help them.[8]

Although McMurry did not specifically claim that the project method carried moral lessons, he suggested that this was the case because those projects took advantage of what McMurry considered the important principles of human learning. First, the large teaching units involved large amounts of logically organized material that forced the students to follow what McMurry called inductive–deductive thought movements. That is, the students began with particular ideas, such as the prospectors' trip across the country, and moved into larger areas, such as the westward movement. Second, in making the connections among the parts of a unit, the students applied knowledge gained previously to new problems. McMurry called this the quality of apperception. Finally, the students engaged in self-activity. Since they were interested in the topics of the unit, they brought all their powers into the effort. Thus, McMurry concluded that students developed longer-lasting interests that stamped their characters, giving them strength and unity of life.[9]

Whereas advocates such as Woodhull, Snedden, and McMurry took an idea from vocational agriculture to reorganize academic subjects, Arthur E. Morgan turned the notion of projects back to their vocational meaning. He retained the idea that projects helped children develop practical, intellectual, and moral abilities. Morgan was an engineer not an educator. In 1916, he founded Moraine Park School in Dayton, Ohio, with the hope that in his school, students would undertake business enterprises. The school organization imitated an industrial plant. The students engaging in a variety of activities wherein they had to analyze the cost and value of production, maintain budgets, and develop the moral standards required by proper manufacturing. On the side, the students would take classes in the academic subjects they needed for college. Examples of the business enterprises that the students formed included a bank for student funds, a print shop for school publications, and a photography shop to maintain a pictorial record of school activities. In Moraine Park, the student government imitated the newly formed city manager system adopted by Dayton. This meant a board of three student commissioners made policies, a student-elected mayor appointed another student as manager to oversee daily activities, and the manager appointed students to a department of safety to enforce regulations.[10]

To find a headmaster for the school, Morgan sent a flyer around the country to people he thought could help him. Several of these flyers went to Teachers College at Columbia University where William Heard Kilpatrick received a copy. He expressed interest in the proposal and recommended one of his students, Laura Gillmore, to be a teacher of young children at the school. He also invited Morgan and his headmaster to participate in a seminar with other educators discussing innovative school plans such as the Fairhope Organic School, the Horace Mann School, and the Gary, Indiana Schools.[11]

Because of his work with Kilpatrick, Morgan became an early participant in the founding of the PEA and he served three terms as the first president of the Progressive Education Association (PEA). Despite his prominence among educational reformers, his idea of the project did not spread beyond his personal scope. As an important engineer for the construction of dams, Morgan used the Moraine school model when he had long-lasting jobs in the Miami Valley or in the Tennessee Valley Authority (TVA), where he served as chief engineer until 1936. He built camps for the workers with homes and schools. For teachers in those schools, he hired people who were familiar with his idea of the project method. When Morgan became president of Antioch College, he changed the traditional liberal arts college into a progressive model requiring all students to undertake the same type of business experiences that he had created at Moraine Park School.[12]

During his life, Morgan enjoyed or endured extensive public attention. For example, amidst considerable publicity, U.S. President Franklin Roosevelt fired Morgan from the TVA. Perhaps because of his controversial stature, few schools or colleges adopted his version of the project method or the similar work experience Morgan adapted to Antioch College. According to Lawrence A. Cremin, the person who brought the project method to national attention was William Heard Kilpatrick. After his article entitled the "Project Method" appeared in the *Teachers College Record* in 1918, over 60,000 reprints circulated in the next twenty-five years. Promoted to senior chair of philosophy of education at Teachers College in 1918, Kilpatrick taught more than 35,000 teachers from every state in the union over the course of his career at a time when a substantial number of educational leaders came from Teachers College. Thus, Kilpatrick was able to spread his ideas widely. Cremin added that the important element in Kilpatrick's proposal was that he had based his idea of the project method on Dewey's view of the school as a refined social environment. As a result, Kilpatrick thought that he found a way to bring philosophical ideas into school practices.[13]

As a young man, Kilpatrick had taught mathematics in an elementary and high school in Blakely, Georgia, for four years after graduating from Mercer University, a Southern Baptist denominational institution. In 1897, Kilpatrick returned to Mercer to teach mathematics. By 1906, Kilpatrick lost interest in the subject of mathematics. To Kilpatrick, the subject seemed to be a closed system separate from the problems of instruction. He complained that an hour of original thinking in mathematics for a teacher could take students a year to understand. Thus, teachers could not share investigations in their subjects with their classes. To help him understand his students, Kilpatrick wanted to move into the study of education and psychology. Events helped him make the shift. In 1906, the trustees of Mercer fired Kilpatrick when he admitted to skepticism about the divinity of Jesus. Kilpatrick moved to New York City, entered Teachers College, and met John Dewey.[14]

The article, "The Project Method," defined Kilpatrick's orientation. Explaining why the term was important, Kilpatrick noted that the term offered a way to integrate three aspects of education: the importance of action, the laws of learning, and the essential elements of ethical conduct. Defining a project as a wholehearted, purposeful activity carried out in a social setting, Kilpatrick used the example of a girl making a dress to illustrate the way dressmaking integrated these factors. In this case, he argued that because the girl had the desire to sew the dress she undertook the activity in a wholehearted manner. As a result, each of the actions was a part of the plan the girl created, and the process took place in a social setting because the girl intended to wear the dress to some events.[15]

To explain why these elements had to be present, Kilpatrick noted that the typical unit of a worthy life was a purposeful act. People who framed purposes for themselves mastered their own fates rather than accept chance events. More important, he added, purposeful acts utilized the laws of learning. In this regard, Kilpatrick showed how the project method fulfilled the three laws of learning found in Edward L. Thorndike's *Educational Psychology:* any action was a response to a situation, the response came from some connection between the situation and the response, and a pleasurable result strengthened the bond. To this set of laws, known as *connectionism,* Thorndike had added the assertion that, when the children performed actions in which they were interested, they cemented the bonds in place. Thus, Kilpatrick used these assertions to claim that people learned best when they tried to achieve things they wanted to do. Because they thought the situations were important, they made strong connections between the stimuli and their responses. When the situations arose again, they were likely to make the responses that led to favorable results.[16]

To make the case clear, Kilpatrick gave an example of two boys who set about making kites. One of the boys was doing the work because an authority figure told him to do it. The other boy wanted to build and fly his own kite. According to Kilpatrick, the child working under compulsion had little interest in the steps he went through or in the ways that he solved the problems that arose. This child wanted to finish and forget the task as soon as possible. On the other hand, the child who began to build the kite wholeheartedly approached everything from the standpoint of interest. All the steps were part of his purpose. Because each part led to the desired result, the child remembered what he had learned long after the kite was thrown away.[17]

Because examinations made students learn for reasons of compulsion, Kilpatrick believed that most school activities caused students to want to forget what they had learned rather than to internalize the lessons to the point where they could apply those skills in new and different situations. Nonetheless, Kilpatrick warned that teachers should not allow children to do whatever they wanted. According to Kilpatrick, social demands were in accord with students' interests because the fabric of institutional life had grown out of human interests. To Kilpatrick, this meant the children already possessed the interests that had caused the human race to flourish. Thus, he declared that teachers should lead the students from their present interests into the wider claims of social life.[18]

Moral education required three parts. Kilpatrick stated that the students had to master a body of information, develop the skills to judge a moral situation, and forge the appropriate bonds or connections between the situation and the proper responses. He thought these conditions were present in the projects because the projects took place in a social setting. Working under the direction of a teacher within what Kilpatrick called an embryonic community, the children developed proper sets of responses. For Kilpatrick, the teacher did not have to act as an authority figure because the other children would be severe taskmasters. The pressure of other children for conformity dissolved an individual pupil's opposition, allowing the students and teacher to work together in ways that encouraged the children to acquire the ideals needed for approved social life.[19]

Kilpatrick faced the problem of explaining how children could develop new or wider interests if the motive for learning came from their interests. In part, Kilpatrick decided that the answer was that children's interests matured as they grew. Another part of the answer was that teachers could build up children's spans of interests by showing how things were related to those interests the children had already. This led to another problem. If interest could infect an activity that was foreign to the child, coercion might be a reasonable teaching practice. Although Kilpatrick acknowledged such a possibility, he thought the evils of compulsion outweighed any benefits it could bring.[20]

Kilpatrick divided projects into four types. Numbering the projects one through four, Kilpatrick thought the differences lay in the purposes behind them. One was a plan to do something such as build a boat or produce a play. Another was to enjoy something such as a symphony. A third was to solve a problem such as determining why New York City grew faster than Philadelphia. The last type was to achieve some level of skill such as passing an achievement test in reading or handwriting.[21]

According to Kilpatrick, the problem project was the best-known type because of the work of John Dewey as described in Chapter 9 Kilpatrick argued that when students learned to solve problems, they learned to follow the steps of thinking that Dewey described: purposing, planning, executing, and judging. Kilpatrick did not make these steps central to all projects, though. For example, students could not use Dewey's four steps of problem solving when they set out to master some skill, which was the last type of project. Although an educational psychologist might follow these steps to determine how children could learn the skills quickly, the students would follow the psychologist's instructions.[22]

In his article, Kilpatrick acknowledged that the term *project method* had become popular before he decided to use it. As noted above, colleagues of Kilpatrick such as Woodhull and Snedden had published articles recommending the use of projects before Kilpatrick did. Nonetheless, Samuel Tenenbaum, Kilpatrick's biographer, believed that no one had used the term *project method* with the philosophical emphasis on the purposeful act in the way Kilpatrick did. For this reason, Tenenbaum contended that Kilpatrick's work was original.[23]

As noted above, Kilpatrick thought the important aspect of his use of the term *project method* was that it allowed him to fuse Dewey's ideas of problem solving with Thorndike's ideas of connectionism. Although such a fusion enhanced the popularity of Kilpatrick's approach, Kilpatrick had considerable difficulty when he tried to explain how children set purposes for themselves from the mechanical stimulus–response connections that Thorndike defined.[24]

The difficulties were so severe that one critic, Boyd Bode, complained that Kilpatrick's formulation of the project method did not offer any way to think more clearly about the ways to make schools more democratic. This was a serious charge made more so because Bode shared Kilpatrick's perspectives. Although separated by half a continent, both Kilpatrick and Bode followed the ideas of Dewey. Kilpatrick taught at Columbia University in New York City whereas Bode held classes in The Ohio State University in Columbus, Ohio. According to Cremin, between the years 1921 and 1944, Bode made The Ohio State University a center for graduate studies in education that rivaled New York in quality and in importance. To Cremin's eyes, though, Bode's work closely resembled the spirit of Dewey whereas Kilpatrick tried to turn Dewey's ideas into practical suggestions and thereby changed the meanings.[25]

What Was Wrong with the Project Method?

Bode's complaints took two directions. First, Bode suggested that Thorndike's laws of learning contradicted a democratic theory of education because they ignored the role of intelligence. In addition, Bode warned Kilpatrick that the project method had not changed the typical arrangement of classroom activities.

According to Bode, America's contribution to the world was a tradition of democracy. Although the country's founders thought of democracy as a political ideal reserved for white men, the notion had broadened and deepened into a hope for the world. Nonetheless, Bode warned against narrow conceptions of democracy. He preferred to think about democracy as a state of mind. Since democracy meant that every individual had the fullest opportunity to express his or her native capacities, Bode defined democracy as a form of social organization in which the members cooperated with each other and with other groups to pursue shared interests. Thus, for Bode, democracy was never finished. It was a process of continual readjustment in the direction of more extensive mutual recognition of different people's interests.[26]

The problem Bode found in Thorndike was that the so-called laws of learning simplified mental processes to the point that Thorndike ignored thinking. To explain this point, Bode recalled Thorndike's example of an animal running when a tiger appeared. According to Thorndike, the situation, seeing the tiger, brought out the response, running, that satisfied the animal because it saved the animal's life. Thorndike added that if the animal behaved differently in another but similar situation, this happened because the situation appeared different for some reason. Thus, Bode complained that Thorndike's formulation gave no role to foresight or intelligence. Different responses came about because the situations had changed in some ways. Bode added that, when Thorndike applied his model to thinking, he avoided any explanation of how people thought or how people could expand their native capacities. As a result, Bode contended that Thorndike's view of learning was not appropriate for a curriculum dedicated to democracy.[27]

When Bode turned to the project method, he acknowledged that Kilpatrick had expanded the concept beyond the limits other educators had used because those educators considered projects in limited ways. For example, Snedden had considered a project to be a specific task such as building a chicken coop. Bode pointed out that such an activity could not substitute for a complete and well-organized course in mathematics even though children may learn a great deal of arithmetic from such a practical activity. Bode thought McMurry's definition of a project was equally limited. McMurry had considered a project to be an arrangement of any subject matter into central teaching units that brought together large amounts of information, illustrated a real-life setting, and developed ideas that could be used elsewhere. The problem was that McMurry had failed to offer any guiding purpose to select the activities. That is, Bode did not find any indication why a unit should concentrate on one thing rather than another. McMurry selected the curriculum at random or by authority. Neither method would enhance democracy.[28]

When Bode considered the ways that Kilpatrick considered the project method, he found a different way of thinking. It appeared to Bode that Kilpatrick identified the project method with student interest. The organizing principle for Kilpatrick was in the students' attitudes toward their work. On the other hand, McMurry followed a more traditional orientation because the organization was a logical arrangement of the subject matter. As a result, Bode acknowledged that Kilpatrick's idea seemed revolutionary. The teacher was not a dominating force, and the pupils could construct their own curriculums. Nonetheless, Bode found that Kilpatrick violated his own principles. He did not want children to do what they wanted because there were certain essentials such as the skills of reading and writing that were so important the students had to stop everything and learn them. Thus, Bode accused Kilpatrick of reinforcing conventional attitudes toward classroom instruction by oscillating between extremes. Although Kilpatrick urged teachers to interest the students in school activities, he allowed that teachers could impose assignments when their devices failed.[29]

The problem of teacher guidance was difficult. Most school people avoided the problems by dividing the school day between curricular studies and extracurricular activities. As a result, the teachers oscillated between extremes of being in charge at one time and invisible the next. In fact, by 1937, extracurricular activities had become widely used in elementary and secondary schools.

One reason extracurricular activities were popular was that teachers believed such activities outside class would reinforce democratic values. For example, as described in Chapter 11, the NEA's Commission on the Reorganization of Secondary Education in 1918 recommended that all secondary schools include a wide range of courses offering academic studies and vocational preparation because such a comprehensive high school allowed students opportunities to pursue extracurricular activities that taught them about democracy. For example, students with different vocational goals attended school assemblies or joined school organizations, such as arts and crafts clubs, literary and debating societies, and music organizations. Thus, they learned that their common interests were more important than the different talents that separated them.[30]

By 1926, Leonard V. Koos noted that high schools sponsored a wide range of organizations such as current events clubs, buildings and grounds committees, seasonal games clubs, poetry clubs, zoology clubs, food canning clubs, stenographic clubs, city history clubs, and operetta clubs. By a wide margin, the most popular extracurricular functions were those designed to serve civic or social interests, such as building and grounds committees, and physical and athletic interests, such as seasonal games clubs. Among the least popular were those activities designed to serve academic interests, such as city history clubs. Koos noted that extracurricular activities were common among secondary schools but not in elementary schools.[31]

An extracurricular activity in secondary schools that aided students in learning about democracy was student participation in school government. When Earle Rugg described the opinions he found in available literature and in responses to questionnaires he sent to 167 high school principals and to 200 high school students, he concluded that there was wide agreement that students should participate in school governance, especially concerning questions of discipline. According to Rugg, most people believed that the students learned about citizenship through student government. In addition, people felt the students would obey the rules they had helped to form.[32]

Despite the benefits of extracurricular activities, there were problems. For example, in 1926, Paul W. Terry sent questionnaires to teachers in eight secondary schools in Seattle, Washington asking about their views toward extracurricular activities. Terry received 314 replies, which accounted for almost all the teachers in those schools. Although Terry found that the great majority of teachers approved of the extracurricular activities, he noted that what he called a "significant minority" of teachers considered the clubs disorganized and feared the clubs allowed students to behave badly. Nonetheless, most of the teachers who served as advisors felt that they had adequate training or expertise to help their students' clubs. A bigger problem was the extent of the workload for which the teachers did not receive reduced teaching assignments or extra pay. Although most teachers considered it part of their job to help with extracurricular activities, they did not extend equal efforts. An advisor of a poetry club had light duties whereas the advisor for an operetta club worked long hours to mount a show.[33]

Within a decade, elementary schools adopted extracurricular activities. In a study conducted in 1934, Henry J. Otto and Shirley A. Hamrin sent twenty-four page questionnaires to 200 principals of elementary schools scattered throughout the United States. In addition, they asked those principals to give eleven-page forms to each teacher in their buildings and three-page forms to each club sponsor. They found that elementary schools sponsored such extracurricular activities as trips outside school, school assemblies, school newspapers, athletics, and student councils. Although most of the teachers and principals responded that they viewed such extracurricular activities as beneficial, many teachers only offered them to students at odd moments as rewards. Some teachers considered these activities as essential but divorced from academic studies. The authors were saddened to find that few teachers considered the school newspaper, a corner sand table, or auditorium programs as vehicles to make school lessons practical and meaningful.[34]

To prove that student interest could organize an entire school program, Ellsworth Collings, a graduate student of Kilpatrick's, set up an experiment in 1921 in McDonald County, Missouri, where he was the superintendent of schools. For this experiment, Collings chose three rural elementary schools. One of them, with an enrollment of forty-one students, served as the experimental school. Collings claimed that teachers in this building followed the project method. The other schools, with a combined enrollment of sixty students, became the controls because the teachers followed a more traditional program. In all schools, the students ranged from about six years to sixteen years of age.[35]

In the experimental school, Collings found the students achieved more when compared to the students in the control schools. The students in the experimental school exceeded the national standards as well. Collings claimed that he administered and scored the various tests of achievement himself. In addition to improved academic achievement, Collings found that the children in the experimental school had better attitudes in school and demonstrated better behavior outside school than did the children in the control schools. Their parents tended to give greater support to the school and more of the students from the experimental school went on to high school. Collings determined these changes by looking at records teachers kept, attendance reports, records of corporal punishments, parents' voting records, and high school enrollment forms. At the end, he claimed the experiment proved that the project method worked.[36]

When Collings had to defend his thesis at Columbia, several professors on his committee did not want to accept the thesis. According to one of Kilpatrick's biographers, Samuel Tenenbaum, the problem was that the dissenting professors were conservative by nature and resisted the innovations represented by the project method. Although the controversy disheartened Kilpatrick, he convinced the other professors to allow Collings to make minor revisions in his doctoral dissertation and to pass. Claiming Kilpatrick was correct, Tenenbaum added that Collings' dissertation became a 350-page book, translated into different languages, and served as a model for the reorganization of schools in the Soviet Union.[37]

Tenenbaum may have been mistaken. In 1996, Michael Knoll claimed that Collings had faked his dissertation. Although Knoll acknowledged that Collings presented more than seventy tables and charts, he added that Collings did not provide enough information for subsequent researchers to verify his interpretations. When Collings offered results of comparisons, he gave only averages with differences and increases. More important perhaps, Knoll accused Collings of exaggerating the differences among the schools. Evidently, the experimental school was a newly constructed building and better equipped than the other older buildings. Further, Knoll contended that all the schools followed the Missouri State Course of Study.[38]

Knoll focused on an influential example from Collings's book. This was the typhoid experiment. According to Collings, one day, a student in the experimental school asked the teacher why another student missed several days of school. The teacher and the other students observed that the family had suffered with typhoid. Because no other family seemed to contract the disease to the same extent, the children wanted to find out what was wrong on the sick student's farm. The students obtained permission from the family to investigate. They visited to observe the conditions, returned to the classroom to read references books, and verified their observations. They decided the cause of the disease was flies, and they set about finding in reference books ways that the farmer could combat the infestations. Collings concluded that the pupils and the farmer worked together implementing the suggestions, with the happy result that typhoid left the farm.[39]

According to Knoll, the typhoid project was important in Europe. During the 1960s, teachers in Germany pointed to Collings's description of the typhoid project as a model of social education and a measure for correct student participation. Yet, Knoll added that the lesson did not take place as Collings described it. Knoll found that Collings had described the lesson of the typhoid investigation in an article published earlier in the *Missouri School Journal.* In the journal article, Collings told how a teacher led the students in grades six through eight to study infectious diseases. In the journal article, Collings described how the teacher prepared the students and led the pupils through the steps of investigating typhoid on a farm. Assuming the first account was the more truthful, Knoll thought this assignment was more correctly a teacher-directed activity with a tangible object at the end instead of a spontaneous project or wholehearted activity as Collings asserted in his book.[40]

Whereas Knoll contended that the possibility of Collings faking his dissertation threatened the worth of the project method, Harold Alberty claimed in 1962 that thirty years of careful studies had confirmed Collings's conclusion that the project method produced results superior to those derived from traditional models of schooling.[41] Whether Collings's work was true or false, it was an example of Kilpatrick's view that children learned socially useful information and skills through the project method because their interests followed the directions people had followed to establish civilization. According to Collings, the typhoid experiment demonstrated that children were interested in things that concerned adults.

How Did the Project Method Influence Other Educators across the Globe?

The practical orientation that Collings had found within the project method influenced a wide variety of educators. Most interesting, the project method could justify changing such aesthetic activities as art instruction from appreciation of beauty to experiences with social utility. For example, in 1928, Harold Rugg and Ann Schumaker of the Lincoln School at Teachers College suggested that what they called child-centered schools should develop the creative impulses in children. According to Rugg and Shumaker, the child-centered school was a product of a revolution in education led by such thinkers as John Dewey and William Heard Kilpatrick. The new schools were to be places where children experienced rather than places where unwilling children recited lessons. Noting that a parallel movement took place in Europe, Rugg and Shumaker listed the articles of faith they found on what they called the frontier of educational thinking. First, the children's freedom was essential. Joined to freedom was the view that students should share in their own government. Third, the school should be a place for activity. Fourth, the curriculum should be organized to support the children's interests. Fifth, the new school should encourage the children's creative spirit. Sixth, the children should become distinct personalities who learn to cooperate in successful social living. In traditional classrooms, the children conformed to rigid discipline, worked side by side, and competed with each other to form a dangerous type of individualism. One benefit that Rugg and Shumaker found in the child-centered school was that art played an important role in the development of self-expression. Dramatics taught children to work together for a common goal. Dance provided the physical outlets offered by athletics without the competition and provided each child the opportunity to acquire grace and physical poise. Thus, instead of offering extracurricular activities at the end of the day as unrelated recreation, the students in the new school undertook these formerly aesthetic activities together in groups as part of daily school life to learn social skills.[42]

Because Rugg and Shumaker considered the aim of art instruction to be self-expression, they dismissed art presented as information, principles, design, or respect for classics. To them, art came from the artist's desire to translate an inner image into an outward form. Because Rugg and Shumaker claimed artists wanted to leave personal impressions on material, they criticized the work of artists such as Arthur Wesley Dow who published texts that organized art instruction in public schools around the principles of design. Rugg and Shumaker complained that Dow's approach to art was intellectual and did not aid self-expression. They claimed that when creative artists entered classrooms in Lincoln School, they changed art instruction into opportunities to help the children use artistic techniques to express their feelings.[43]

Although Rugg accused Arthur Wesley Dow of being traditional, Dow thought of his work as revolutionary. Complaining that most art instruction, such as drawing, served a practical function, Dow thought the true purpose of art instruction was to foster appreciation. Dow believed that a few gifted students could create art, yet he wanted every student to learn to desire finer form and more harmony of tone and color in surroundings and in things in daily use. Dow added that academic art instruction had not taught such general appreciation. By asking the students to analyze academic styles and thereby learn to draw, academic instruction had placed the principles of design under a less important category of decoration.[44]

After studying five years in French schools, Dow became dissatisfied with the then traditional method of having students imitate the paintings of great masters. As a result, in the 1880s, he began to work on a series of exercises that taught students to understand what he called the essence of beauty. The result was a method in which he taught students to apply the principles of composition through line, mass, and color to a wide variety of art forms. Instead of focusing on great European masters, he spent considerable time teaching about art from Japan, India, and Egypt. In one sense, he hoped that this understanding would increase the creative power of the students whether they were painters, sculptors, or designers. For most children, he arranged series of lessons that extended from kindergarten to high school to teach them to learn how to judge the quality of form, tone, and color of many objects from paintings to clothes to teacups.[45]

Other nineteenth-century educators wanted art to emphasize moral lessons. For example, writing in 1898, William Torrey Harris, whose ideas appear in Chapter 9, contended that different art forms tended to reveal human nature in such ways that people came to know the springs of action of their fellow beings. Thus, for Harris, art made external the passions and feelings of the artist. Nonetheless, Harris did not consider this process of drawing out feelings to be self-expression; it was a revelation of the human spirit. Consequently, for Harris, the aim of art instruction was to seek wider moral insights into particular human experiences.[46]

Although Rugg and Shumaker wanted art instruction to play a central role in their school, they made art less significant by turning it into a tool for the development of self-expression. For them, art would enhance student growth by giving the children the confidence and ability to express their best selves in many mediums. These were traits necessary for life in a democracy. As a result, they denied Arthur Wesley Dow's contention that beauty was an objective condition brought about by the proper use of artistic techniques. In addition, Rugg and Shumaker dismissed Harris's notion that art was part of the pursuit of universal values. Instead of Dow's and Harris's broad humanistic aims, Rugg and Shumaker held narrower socially useful aims.

In other countries, the fact that the project method served practical aims made it popular among officials who wanted schools to reform society by teaching the children useful skills and attitudes. For example, in Russia, after the revolution in October 1917 that empowered the Bolsheviks, officials in the Commissariat of Enlightenment (Narkompros) tried to use Kilpatrick's ideas to reshape human behavior. According to Larry E. Holmes, when educators in the Russian areas of the Union of Soviet Socialist Republics read Kilpatrick's article on the project method, they believed they had found a way to use schools to create the new human beings required by the recent revolution. Following their understanding of the project method, officials in the Narkompros created what they called the "complex method," so named because, instead of subjects, teachers focused on themes arranged under categories of nature, labor, and society. The students would work with different topics on different days in ways that would relate to the themes for a particular week. In turn, the weekly themes were part of overarching themes for the month. This pattern went on among grade levels as well. That is, teachers arranged topics and themes successively for the various grade levels so that students in elementary schools were to work on topics that were familiar and concrete whereas secondary students would focus on topics that were general and abstract.[47]

When Holmes looked for examples of schoolwork that fit the complex method, he found that younger children worked on themes that centered on such things as the importance of hygiene and the value of education. They decorated their classrooms, creating arrangements such as a living corner where they placed collections of plants and animals they had gathered during nature walks. In celebrating a seasonal theme, older children conducted interviews with people who had participated in the October Revolution. The students and teachers prepared dramatizations depicting the changes that had taken place in everyday life because of the revolution, and they made posters celebrating their villages and their schools.[48]

Although the pedagogical section of Narkompros issued plans for teachers to lead the students through cycles of themes and topics, things did not go smoothly. One problem was that teachers lacked the training to present material that came from several different subjects. Another difficulty was teachers did not have materials to follow these schemes. Nonetheless, the officials in the Narkompros sought to avoid grades, examinations, and textbooks. In another proposal, some Narkompros officials recommended that schools adopt the Dalton Plan, a method for individualized learning developed at a Massachusetts high school in 1919 by Helen Parkhurst for students with handicaps. Although the teachers were to serve as guides under the Dalton Plan, the curriculum remained subject matter oriented. In this model, the students could work at their own pace, with other students, and plan their own schedules. Because the original Dalton Plan tended toward individualism, Soviet officials sought to modify it by requiring that students work in groups.[49]

According to Holmes, by 1925, it appeared that the effort to implement the complex method in the Soviet schools had not succeeded. In many schools, the teachers had manipulated the themes and topics in ways that reconstructed the subject matter divisions. As a result, traditional subjects continued to dominate the classrooms, and teachers tended to dictate information for the students to memorize. Although mathematics, science, and the Russian language remained fixed in classrooms, the schools had ended instruction in classical languages and religion.[50]

In 1928, Lucy L. W. Wilson visited Russia to learn about the schools. She came away impressed at the progress made by Soviet educators to overcome enormous problems. The People's Commissariat of Education passed policies in 1918 making education free, obligatory, and universal. For children of three to seven years of age, there were to be preschools. Elementary schools were to include children of eight to twelve years, and students of thirteen to sixteen were to attend secondary schools. Unfortunately, many children did not attend school in 1925. The available schools were poorly equipped. Wilson found that when towns and cities began elementary schools, these were usually in the former home of a wealthy family or the hut of a peasant. As a result, the buildings were ill adapted to school work. In addition, she noted that although schools were supposed to be free, most students paid some tuition.[51]

In 1928, John Dewey traveled to the Soviet Union and wrote a series of articles describing his observations. Finding that the Soviet schools sought to connect the students to the society, Dewey exclaimed that this was the first time in history that a society had recognized a well-known principle to this extent. This happened, he added, because the Soviet leaders placed economic and industrial life in the center of schoolwork without making it vocational in nature. That is, everything in schools helped the students develop the capacities to carry on socially useful work in cooperative ways. Dewey thought there were two reasons why this happened in the Soviet Union. One was that the progressive educational movement had become highly developed in the United States and Soviet educators were willing to borrow those ideas. The other reason was that the revolution brought about the notion that all work should advance socialist society. Thus, the schools prepared the students to share in the ideology of the workers.[52]

Dewey noted that with the complex method, teachers organized school studies around the history of labor. He found that instead of making special studies of subjects, teachers showed children the work that people did in the local area. This required that teachers become students because they had to find ways to make connections between the subjects they had taught, local conditions, and the economic plans of the central government. Although many commentators thought the complex system was similar to the project method, Dewey disagreed for two reasons. First, the complex system revolved around a centrally unified intellectual scheme. For the Soviet educator, a project was the means to relate some complex of subject matter to socially useful work. Thus, the projects were about such things as sanitation, hygiene, or illiteracy campaigns. Finally, the projects provided the discipline for the students rather then their own interests. That is, the students worked within groups set up to accomplish specific tasks. It appeared to Dewey that the groups provided the necessary direction for each student.[53]

In closing his observation of Soviet schools, Dewey noted that he understood why critics complained about the Americanization of Russian schools. The Soviet educators had taken American progressive ideas and incorporated them into the schools. He concluded that Americans could learn from these efforts.[54]

One year after Dewey made his visit, Kilpatrick went to see the schools in Russia. Because translations of his books were texts for teacher-training institutions, he was a celebrity. Kilpatrick and a translator visited a variety of schools where he found the complex method in use. To Kilpatrick, the complex method differed from his project method in that a central office assigned the topics to every school and every grade in the land. Once the class began a topic, though, the teachers had wide latitude and could rely on student planning to investigate the topics. Kilpatrick was impressed with the amount of freedom the students had when he compared the notebooks of several students. In addition, he approved that teachers did not impart directly the skills of reading, writing, and arithmetic. The students acquired these abilities through their work with the topics. In general, the topics covered practical concerns such as how to increase agricultural yields or how to train pigeons to carry messages. As a result, Kilpatrick claimed that this was the first school system designed to reinforce the social and political program of the state.[55]

At the same time that Kilpatrick praised the Soviet schools, he found reasons to dislike their program. For example, he found widespread indoctrination and propaganda. Posters in classrooms reminded children to subscribe to government loans and other pictures portrayed priests as drunken womanizers. He was disappointed to find that no student could question any fundamental assumption of the government. As a result, he wondered whether the students could learn to think for themselves.[56]

After Dewey's and Kilpatrick's visits, statistical reports suggested that the schools failed to educate the children. Although urban schools in the Russian Republic retained about nine out of ten students, the failure rate in rural schools was high. Almost half the students who entered first grade in rural schools from 1924 to 1928 failed to move to the third grade. The same failure rate took place at the secondary level. From 1925 to 1928, one-third of fifth graders did not enter the seventh grade.[57]

Although schools may not have enjoyed success, some commentators argued that Soviet authorities brought culture to the masses through the publication of books, pamphlets, and magazines. Writing in 1926, Scott Nearing claimed that the number of books published in the Soviet Union rose from about 18,000 in 1923 to more than 25,000 in 1925. The size of the books increased at the same time. More important, the state built up machinery for distribution by opening bookstalls and reading quarters in all parts of the country. Nearing was impressed to find that Soviet newspapers had fewer sensational stories and more serious reporting than many of the papers published in the United States.[58]

Conditions in the Soviet Union improved quickly. In 1927, Lucy L. W. Wilson reported that in a period of two years the quality of the students and teachers that she met improved considerably. In 1925, she thought that many of the students did not belong in any school. At the same time, she did not see many peasant children in schools. Two years later, in 1927, she was much impressed with the quality of the teachers and the students that she met. In addition, in 1927, she met children of peasant families in schools, and she found them to be alert and intelligent.[59]

Wilson's optimistic observations came shortly before the Soviet system of education underwent a drastic change. In 1931, the Central Committee, the highest organ of the Communist Party at that time, issued policies stating that the central task of schools was to expand knowledge and skills. The Party's statements ordered teachers not to work for social transformation. Such efforts prevented students from learning important subject matter. Although this policy reversed the aims of such efforts as the complex method, the change did not derive from educational concerns. According to Larry Holmes, the changes came because, after Joseph Stalin became secretary-general of the Communist party in 1922, he and his followers consolidated their hold on all aspects of society. The edict had little to do with school performance, Holmes added. The Party wanted the schools to reflect Stalin's authoritarian government.[60]

Although Holmes claimed the changes in favor of authoritarianism in the Soviet Union came from shifts in governmental policy, he did not think they came unilaterally from the Communist Party. Although some of the officials in Narkompros had humane ideas for schools and for society when they proposed the complex method, some elements in Narkompros had favored authoritarian rule. In addition, many teachers had resisted the progressive innovations that the pedagogical unit recommended. Thus, Holmes concluded that the Party was able to capitalize on the complaints of teachers and disgruntled officials to reject the hope of constructing a humane social order through education.[61]

Whereas the project method became popular in Russia, the activity school spread through Europe. For example, by 1920, the term *activity school* was common in France. According to Adolph Ferrière, a professor of education in Switzerland, the idea derived in part from the ideas of the American psychologist, G. Stanley Hall. In addition, Ferrière acknowledged the contributions of Rousseau and Pestalozzi whose works inspired such educational reforms in the United States as the object method. To Ferrière, the activity school was not a reform. He claimed the activity school was a transformation that released a new spirit. Instead of conducting school along lines of routine, teachers designed lessons on scientific studies that included concerns for student interest and bodily health.[62]

An expression of the interest in the activity school came in 1921 when representatives from several European countries met in Calais, France, to form the Ligue Internationale pour l'Education Nouvelle. The goal of this international league for new education was to form schools wherein children could increase their spiritual energy and enhance their individuality by pursuing their interests. The children were to work in groups with the aid of their teachers. Discipline was to come from the students rather than the teachers. Cooperation should replace competition and coeducation would allow boys and girls to have salutary effects on each other. Ferrière noted that despite the progress the league achieved in a short time, the activity school was limited to elementary levels. It had not reached into the secondary schools when he wrote in 1927. To advance their aims, members of the league took on several American progressives as educational patrons. These included John Dewey and Carlton Washburne, superintendent of the Winnetka, Illinois schools.[63]

Washburne had instituted a two-part program in Winnetka in 1919. During the morning, the children studied individually what he called the common essentials, or academic skills. In the afternoons, the children worked on projects. In 1926, Washburne took a leave from the Winnetka schools to visit experimental schools in Europe accompanied by his wife and two teachers from Winnetka. Washburne's group visited twelve different schools in such countries as Czechoslovakia, Belgium, Holland, France, and Switzerland. Each of the schools was unique. For example, in the Girl's Secondary School in Streatham Hill, England, Washburne found the Dalton Plan. According to Washburne, the founder of the Girl's Secondary School, Rosa Bassett, visited Dalton, Massachusetts, where she learned about the plan that allowed students to work independently. Although few people in the United States knew about the Dalton Plan, Bassett made the plan famous in Europe. In Bassett's school, the activities changed regularly. Some students worked through a series of mimeographed, programmed lessons while other students studied together in classes. In Switzerland, Washburne visited a boarding school where the students chose the master under whom they would live and study. The result was the formation of house groups wherein the teacher and students worked together. Although Washburne did not find a scientific organization in any of these schools, he thought the teachers encouraged the fullest development of each individual child. He recommended that teachers in American schools adopt the same aim.[64]

Although Washburne praised the activity schools in Europe, critics such as Michael J. Demiashkevich complained that the new education in Europe was a one-sided affair solely concerned with directing children's actions. After his survey of activity schools in France and Germany, Demiashkevich claimed the reformers ignored history or philosophy because they thought only about the children and the things the children could do physically. Demiashkevich found this to be the case even when the educators wanted to bring about massive changes in the social order.[65]

Demiashkevich found that the new educators in Europe wanted to eliminate attention to subject matters. The educators in the activity schools thought the children should undergo experiences. They believed the students would learn academic skills as they solved various problems. Demiashkevich complained that, in expressing this view, teachers made a false synthesis because they were mentally lazy. Rather than teach complicated subject matters, the teachers in the activity schools trusted the children would learn on their own.[66]

According to Demiashkevich, a particularly dangerous tendency among teachers in activity schools in Europe was a campaign against books. He found the reactions against books to be so violent that the ideal appeared to be a bookless school even though the activity school held democracy as a goal and the printing press brought about the age of democracy. Demiashkevich suggested that the fear of books derived from what he called the myth of child passivity. When activists contended that bookishness was a substitute for living, Demiashkevich countered that reading a book and thinking was an intense and important activity that built experience. To Demiashkevich, reading was an essential aspect of the ability to solve problems. It introduced new ideas, taught logic, and offered a command of facts. The problem with the old schools was not that they were bookish, he concluded. It was that they were bookish in the wrong ways. The solution for Demiashkevich was for educators to return to a form of idealism roughly similar to the ideals of W. T. Harris, wherein educators reintroduced concern for a higher social morality.[67]

How Did Educators Build Curriculums on Students' Interests in the United States?

An extensive and intelligent effort to advance the ideals of the activity movement was the Progressive Education Association's (PEA) Eight-Year Study. It began in 1930 when about 200 members of the PEA met in Washington, D.C., to discuss ways to bring about changes in secondary school programs. Although the members felt they had succeeded in opening elementary schools to student freedom, they feared that college entrance requirements forced secondary schools to emphasize subject matters. Seeking to change secondary schools, the PEA secured agreement from 200 colleges to admit students who graduated from high schools in which faculty members had created their own curriculums in line with their understandings of the needs of youth. At the same time, the PEA set up committees to help participating high schools construct curriculums that met the needs of youth, and the organization established studies to determine how adolescents developed. When the study of adolescents determined that young people needed to know about many types of human relations, the PEA created a commission on human relations to help young people realize how human relations governed the ways they felt about themselves. In addition, the PEA hired a staff to evaluate how well the graduates of the experimental high schools did when they entered college compared to similar graduates from traditional high school. According to Lawrence Cremin, the study was the PEA's abiding contribution to American education. It was an enormous undertaking.[68]

To conduct the study, the PEA charged various commissions and committees with different aspects of the undertaking. Support for the endeavor came from contributions from the Carnegie Foundation and the General Education Board. For the first year, donations totaled $800. From 1932 to 1936, the PEA garnered about $70,000 to support its activities. At this point, the first group of high school students entered college. From 1936 to 1940 when the study ended, contributions totaled more than $1.5 million. With these funds, the PEA expanded the evaluation staff, increased the number of curriculum consultants, and conducted workshops with faculty in the participating high schools. Thus, the greatest efforts to change high school programs came after the first group had left high school, although the PEA followed the progress of this first group of students most carefully.[69]

The PEA called the high schools that agreed to join the study the *thirty schools* although the actual number was greater. Another name for the participating high schools was the *unshackled schools* because they did not have to meet college entrance requirements and the coordinating committee was careful not to impose a curriculum model on any of the high schools. At most, the schools had to agree to two principles: life in the school would conform to available knowledge about the ways human beings grow and develop and the school should rediscover its reason for existence. In 1937, when more than half the study had passed, the participating high schools decided they should help the students appreciate the ideal of democracy that was basic to the American heritage. Once the school people accepted the democratic ideal as the overarching philosophy of education, the ideal permeated the reports of what their schools had tried to do.[70]

To evaluate the success in college, the College Follow-Up staff statistically matched about 1,500 graduates of participating schools with students from other high schools who were attending the same university and were similar in age, sex, race, home community, and social or economic class. The results were favorable. The students from the participating high schools earned slightly higher grade point averages than did the other students. More important to the PEA, the students from the participating high school were more intellectually curious, more objective in their thinking, and more resourceful. Because the students who had attended the most progressive high schools outperformed everybody else, the College Follow-Up staff proclaimed that students profited most from the more experimental schools.[71]

One of the most experimental high schools was The Ohio State University School. In this laboratory school, subject matters had little separate identity. Students enrolled in core courses wherein different students worked on problems or projects that called on aspects of several subject matters. The students chose these problems, they worked cooperatively on the projects, and they pursued them by using the scientific method. That is, they recognized a problem, surveyed the conditions, made a hypothesis, conducted some sort of experiment, and derived a conclusion. The entire school, the administrators, teachers, and parents, worked together in what they described as democratic relationships. To facilitate such cooperation, the school held frequent conferences and the teachers served on several committees that shared the responsibilities of administration. Teachers evaluated students in a system of cumulative folders that contained records of accomplishments, notes of performance on tests, and anecdotes from parents and teachers.[72]

In 1938, while the Eight-Year Study was in progress, the students of the Ohio State University School wrote and published a description of their time together. Complete with photographs, *Were We Guinea Pigs?* described how they decided what they wanted to do and how they set about the tasks. The first effort was to design their classroom. This required studies of home economics to select appropriate furniture, of architecture to determine layout, and of science and literature to create a library. Forming committees, the students approached each of these tasks using a version of the scientific method. They surveyed the conditions, made some suggestions, tried an approach, and determined the results. In writing the book, the students approached the task democratically. They formed committees and divided the responsibilities.[73]

While the PEA's Eight-Year Study was underway, the president of the PEA, Willard W. Beatty, became the U.S. director of Indian education. On February 10, 1936, *Time,* a weekly newsmagazine, reported that Beatty would dispense the faith of progressive educators to Amerindian students. Claiming that previous efforts to teach Native Americans to adjust to mainstream society had failed, the article in *Time* wrote that Beatty would teach the Native Americans about their own cultures, arts, and languages.[74]

The article in *Time* exaggerated the effects that Beatty would have and it misrepresented the administrations that preceded Beatty at the U.S. Bureau of Indian Affairs.

Changes had begun in 1928, when Lewis Meriam led a research team from the Brookings Institution to make a comprehensive study of Indian affairs. W. Carson Ryan, Jr., who compiled and wrote the education section of Meriam's report, was a professor of education at Swarthmore, a participant in the Eight-Year Study, and from 1937 to 1939, the president of the PEA. Meriam's report made such extensive criticisms of the Bureau of Indian Affairs that when Herbert Hoover took office as president in 1929, he appointed Charles James Rhoads to be U.S. Commissioner of Indian Affairs, with the understanding that he would enact the changes the Meriam report had recommended. Rhoads appointed Ryan to be director of Indian education.[75]

When Ryan wrote the education section of Meriam's report, he complained that the Indian Service had imposed in 1915 a uniform academic curriculum for all schools. Although the curriculum had many noteworthy objectives, most of the schools lacked the necessary facilities, such as libraries, to achieve them. Thus, he recommended that the Indian Service adopt progressive practices. This meant the teachers should work closely with parents to develop curriculums appropriate for Native American children.[76]

When Franklin Roosevelt became president in 1933, he appointed Harold L. Ickes to be U.S. Secretary of the Interior and Ickes picked an outspoken activist for Native Americans, John Collier, to become U.S. Commissioner of Education. Collier began a campaign for the Indian Reorganization Act, called the Indian New Deal. This legislation ended the system of land allotments in which individual Native Americans could own parts of reservations and it gave Native Americans the freedom to organize into self-governing bodies.[77]

As part of the Indian New Deal, Collier and Ryan carried out the educational programs that *Time* claimed Beatty would introduce. Unfortunately, Ryan ran into controversies when he tried to implement the recommendations of the Meriam report. For example, Ryan established schools designed to appear as hogans, traditional Navajo structures, on the 24,000-square-mile Navajo reservation that straddled Arizona, New Mexico, and Utah. This was part of an effort to reduce the dependence on the boarding schools that the Meriam report had criticized for overcrowding, providing inadequate food, and assigning children to dangerous labor. Costing about $1.5 million, the day schools, of which the hogan schools were part, had classrooms, showers, kitchens, and mechanical shops to teach skills needed on the reservation. In 1934, when Ryan selected fifty young Navajo teachers to teach in the hogan schools, some Native Americans complained so furiously that Ryan relented and announced that trained teachers would take their places. In addition, these Native Americans asked Ryan to offer more boarding schools so that children could obtain the skills needed to leave the reservation.[78]

When Beatty became director of Indian education, he did not change the direction of the U.S. Bureau of Indian Affairs as much as he became Collier's close friend. In his memoirs, Collier praised Beatty, explaining that Beatty developed theories of education out of his experience in the office. Collier cited as exemplary the work of Pedro T. Orata at Little Wound Day School on the Pine Ridge Indian Reservation in South Dakota from 1936 to 1937.[79] Despite Collier's praise, Orata did not bring anything unique to his school. Before coming to Pine Ridge, Orata had worked at The Ohio State University School. When Orata moved to South Dakota, he applied the progressive ideas that he had seen in Ohio. For example, Orata and his staff of six teachers tried to share every decision as they taught 140 students who attended grades one through nine. As had been the case in The

Ohio State University School, the children shaped the curriculum. For example, they planned a carnival for Thanksgiving. Taking up most of November, the students formed committees, divided responsibilities, and used academic skills to perform their tasks. The students wrote invitations, searched through magazines and books to find the proper ways to prepare and serve food, and used arithmetic to measure proportions. As the year progressed, the lessons moved into areas of personal hygiene when a dentist visited the school. Questions of health moved into lessons about sanitation and proper construction of outhouses.[80]

How Did Encouraging Students to Pursue Their Interests Encourage Conformity?

Although Orata may have had a successful year in South Dakota, he did not reinforce Native American cultures in his school. He taught the children to use democratic, scientific thinking as The Ohio State University School had taught the children in Columbus. Evidence of the progressive direction of Orata's school came in 1955 when George A. Dale conducted a survey to determine the effectiveness of the vocational educational program at Pine Ridge. Dale found that the day schools had followed Orata's example of adapting the curriculum to the students' needs, and there was evidence that the Indian students learned more on the reservation school than they would have in a public school. Dale's study showed that about half the students who had graduated from schools on Pine Ridge from 1937 to 1947 left the reservation. Further, the Native Americans who lived off the reservation enjoyed a higher standard of living than did those who remained.[81]

After World War II, Collier and Beatty left the Department of the Interior and, amidst a flurry of departmental controversy, the new Secretary of the Interior, Oscar Chapman, characterized reservations as prisons. Consequently, Chapman thought Indian education should help Native Americans move into the more prosperous cities. As a result, Dale's study took place at a time when the Bureau of Indian Affairs had moved away from Collier's aim of reinforcing traditional Native American culture. Although Collier, Ryan, Beatty, and Orata disapproved of the shift, the progressive practices of Orata's school had pointed in a similar direction because they prepared children for life in a democratic, scientific society.[82]

The activity movement grew out of an effort to enlist the interests of children in furthering school studies. It sought to make school lessons practical. Since the project method began in vocational education, it illustrated how the students' interests coincided with practical applications. In a short period, the activity movement grew into an effort of encouraging moral and intellectual development in the hope that students would learn things that would help them become contributing citizens. This practical aim continued even when reformers wrote about changes in the instruction of art.

The general idea behind the activity movement was that children would become full human beings when they did what they wanted, because their desires followed the development of human civilization. According to Clyde Hissong, the reformers displayed an excessive faith in human nature when they trusted that the interests of the children would lead to an organized curriculum. When Hissong surveyed different schools that followed the movement, he found that those reformers depended on improvisation rather than planning, taking snippets of subject matter almost at random. To Hissong, a better approach would have been to work out a consistent system wherein the children experienced a progressive development of subject matter to meet the needs of varied circumstances and of different people.[83]

Some experimental schools sought to build curriculums in ways that gradually introduced the children to the communities in which they lived. An early model was Junius Lathrop Meriam's University Elementary School of the University of Missouri. In 1918, Meriam began his experiment to make the school function as an agency for social and industrial improvement. To accomplish this end, he focused on the curriculum. His aim was to adapt the subject matters found in academic subjects in ways that corresponded to what he called the subject matter found in real life. Meriam believed that the subject matter in textbooks came from people's efforts to control situations. For example, he contended that the multiplication of numbers came from people looking for ways to determine a total amount when quantities repeated themselves. Because most textbooks presented materials unrelated to children's activities, Meriam outlined a course of study matched to experiences children would probably have in the community.[84]

In constructing the curriculum, Meriam's aim was to help children improve their performance of things they did normally. Thus, he organized the curriculum around what he called observation, play, stories, and handiwork. Although these names did not seem to designate academic subjects, Meriam thought they reflected actions the children performed that could include academic skills. For example, under observation, the children acquired the ability to read and write as well as to use numbers by observing their environment. The topics within observation included people, animals, and earth for the early grades. As the children grew, the observations spread into industries, occupations, and leisure activities. Although each subject had some arrangement of topics that moved from concrete to abstract and from things near the children to things far way, Meriam allowed teachers to rearrange the topics and the subjects during the daily schedule provided they followed general allotments of time. In that way, teachers and children could follow their interests and they could cover all the areas.[85]

Because Meriam sought to prepare children for the community, his model prepared children for the world. To the teachers in The Ohio State University School, Meriam's model was overly static. They sought to prepare children for a society that was constantly changing. Thus, at Ohio State, the activities taught the students to approach problems rationally, to apply the scientific method, and to cooperate with other people in achieving common goals. Most important, the students learned these lessons while they pursued interests such as decorating their classrooms. Thus, the unifying idea for the Ohio State University School was an approach to life rather than a set of subjects. Pedro Orata took this model to the Native American school in South Dakota. As the instructors at the Ohio State school had allowed the students to decorate their room, Orata and his faculty helped the students to plan a Thanksgiving carnival.

Neither Meriam nor the instructors at The Ohio State University School ignored academic subject matter. They found the subject matter within the activities the students pursued. Comparisons of the students' performances in colleges showed that they performed well in classes and had more appreciation for the complexities of life than did students who followed other sorts of curriculums.

Conclusion

Reformers claimed the activity curriculums reinforced the ideal of democracy. In making such an affirmation, they meant that the curriculums served the unique talents and interests of the children. At the same time, the reformers claimed their students learned to think independently, which was another aspect of democracy.

The experience in the Soviet Union and Orata's experience in a Native American school showed that the model did not allow traditional societies to retain their unique values. In both cases, the overwhelming lesson for the children was to approach life democratically and scientifically rather than in some way appropriate to peasant or indigenous societies. Thus, when officials in the Soviet Union wanted to revert to autocratic rule, they had to change the system of instruction. Although the children in Orata's school may have read Native American stories, they learned to work cooperatively rather than in some traditional Native American manner.

The project method changed schools in mainstream American society as well. Although many American progressives disparaged the blatant vocational preparation found among the reformers seeking economy of time in schools, educational reformers sought to teach the children things they would find socially useful. Thus, educators who emphasized art and creative activities claimed those studies were practical. The argument was that the study of art would enable children to learn how to express themselves. Therefore, the members of the activity movement wanted students to express themselves, not acquire competence as artists or use the art as a means to search for universal values. In taking such a position, the reformers substituted a narrow realism for the abstract idealism of nineteenth century educators.

Although the activity method sought to bring freedom to classrooms, it encouraged a democratic, scientifically organized atmosphere. Originating in elementary school classrooms, the PEA succeeded in showing how the model could apply to secondary schools and to underdeveloped societies. Not surprisingly, when versions of the activity method spread around the world, teachers reinforced the American conception of democracy based on some form of scientifically based thinking. As noted earlier, some authors contend that the increasing dominance of such a progressive model of thought is one element of globalization.

Endnotes

1. Lois Coffey Mossman, "Statement of the Problem," in *The Activity Movement,* The Thirty-Third Yearbook of the National Society for the Study of Education, Part 2, ed. Guy Montrose Whipple (Bloomington, Ill.: Public School Publishing Co., 1934), 1–8.
2. William Heard Kilpatrick, "Definition of the Activity Movement," in *The Activity Movement,* The Thirty-Third Yearbook of the National Society for the Study of Education, Part 2, ed. Guy Montrose Whipple (Bloomington, Ill.: Public School Publishing Co., 1934), 45–64.
3. Herbert M. Kliebard, *Struggle for the American Curriculum, 1893–1958* (New York: Routledge, 1986), 154–155.
4. R. W. Stimson, *The Massachusetts Home-Project Plan of Vocational Agricultural Education,* U.S. Bureau of Education Bulletin no. 8 (Washington, D.C.: Government Printing Office, 1914).

5. John F. Woodhull, *The Teaching of Science* (New York: Macmillan Co., 1918), 207–209, 214–217, 226–227.
6. David Snedden, "The Project as a Teaching Unit," *School and Society* 4, no. 90 (16 September 1916): 419–423.
7. Charles A. McMurry, *Teaching by Projects: A Basis for Purposeful Study* (New York: MacMillan Co., 1920), 1–17.
8. McMurry, *Teaching by Projects,* 18–21, 29–37.
9. McMurry, *Teaching by Projects,* 84–97.
10. Pupils of the School, *After a Year: Moraine Park School, Dayton, Ohio, 1917–1918,* Arthur E. Morgan Papers, Moraine Park Series, Antiochiana, Antioch College Library, OH.
11. Roy Talbert, Jr., *Beyond Pragmatism: The Story of Arthur Morgan,* Master's Thesis, Vanderbilt University [1971] Antiochiana Archives, OH, 93.
12. Roy Talbert, Jr., *FDR's Utopian: Arthur Morgan of the TVA* (Jackson: University Press of Mississippi, 1987).
13. Lawrence A. Cremin, *The Transformation of the School: Progressivism in American Education, 1876–1957* (New York: Alfred A. Knopf, 1964), 215–220.
14. Samuel Tenenbaum, *William Heard Kilpatrick: Trail Blazer in Education* (New York: Harper & Brothers, 1951), 19, 34–36, 42–43, 52–60.
15. William Heard Kilpatrick, *The Project Method: The Use of the Purposeful Act in the Educative Process.* Reprinted from *Teacher College Record* 19, no. 4 (1918; reprint, New York: Teacher College, 1922), 1–5.
16. Kilpatrick, *The Project Method,* 5–9.
17. Kilpatrick, *The Project Method,* 9–11.
18. Kilpatrick, *The Project Method,* 11–13.
19. Kilpatrick, *The Project Method,* 13–14.
20. Kilpatrick, *The Project Method,* 15–16.
21. Kilpatrick, *The Project Method,* 16.
22. Kilpatrick, *The Project Method,* 16–18.
23. Tenenbaum, *William Heard Kilpatrick,* 140.
24. John A. Beineke, *And There Were Giants in the Land: The Life of William Heard Kilpatrick* (New York: Peter Lang, 1998), 107–109.
25. Cremin, *The Transformation of the School,* 220–222.
26. Boyd H. Bode, *Modern Educational Theories* (New York: Macmillan Co., 1927), 3–15.
27. Bode, *Modern Educational Theories,* 189–191.
28. Bode, *Modern Educational Theories,* 141–157.
29. Bode, *Modern Educational Theories,* 157–165.
30. Clarence D. Kingsley, *Cardinal Principles of Secondary Education: A Report of the Commission on the Reorganization of Secondary Education,* U.S. Bureau of Education Bulletin no. 35 (Washington, D.C.: Government Printing Office, 1918), 25–26.
31. Leonard Koos, "Analysis of the General Literature on Extra-Curricular Activities," in *Extra-Curricular Activities,* The Twenty-Fifth Yearbook of the National Society for the Study of Education, ed. Guy Montrose Whipple (Bloomington, Ill.: Public School Publishing Co., 1926), 9–22.
32. Earle Rugg, "Special Types of Activities: Student Participation in School Government," in *Extra-Curricular Activities,* The Twenty-Fifth Yearbook of the National Society for the Study of Education, ed. Guy Montrose Whipple (Bloomington, Ill.: Public School Publishing Co., 1926), 127–140.
33. Paul W. Terry, "Cooperation of Teacher Advisors," in *Extra-Curricular Activities,* The Twenty-Fifth Yearbook of the National Society for the Study of Education, ed. Guy Montrose Whipple (Bloomington, Ill.: Public School Publishing Co., 1926), 101–110.
34. Henry J. Otto and Shirley A. Hamrin, *Co-Curricular Activities in Elementary Schools* (New York: D. Appleton-Century Co., 1937), 386–396.
35. Ellsworth Collings, *An Experiment with a Project Curriculum* (New York: Macmillan Co., 1925), 5–7.
36. Collings, *An Experiment with the Project Curriculum,* 6–7, 236, 260–261.
37. Samuel Tenenbaum, *William Heard Kilpatrick,* 224–225.
38. Michael Knoll, "Faking a Dissertation: Ellsworth Collings, William Heard Kilpatrick, and the Project Curriculum," *Journal of Curriculum Studies* 28, no. 2 (1996): 193–222.
39. Collings, *An Experiment with the Project Curriculum,* 54–69.
40. Knoll, "Faking a Dissertation," 199–200.
41. Harold B. Alberty and Elsie J. Alberty, *Reorganizing the High School Curriculum,* 3rd ed. (New York: Macmillan Co., 1962), 310.
42. Harold Rugg and Ann Shumaker, *The Child Centered School: An Appraisal of the New Education* (New York: World Book Co., 1928), 34–67.
43. Rugg and Shumaker, *The Child Centered School,* 216–232.
44. Arthur Wesley Dow, *Theory and Practice of Teaching Art* (New York: Teachers College, 1912), 1–4.
45. Arthur Wesley Dow, *Composition: A Series of Exercises in Art Structure for the Use of Students and Teachers* (1899; reprint, New York: Doubleday, Doran, & Co., 1929), 3–5.
46. W. T. Harris, *Psychologic Foundations of Education: An Attempt to show the Genesis of the Higher Faculties of the Mind* (New York: D. Appleton and Co., 1899), 351–375.

47. Larry E. Holmes, *The Kremlin and the Schoolhouse: Reforming Education in Soviet Russia, 1917–1931* (Bloomington: Indiana University Press, 1991), 3, 32–33.
48. Holmes, *The Kremlin and the Schoolhouse,* 33–34.
49. Holmes, *The Kremlin and the Schoolhouse,* 34–35.
50. Holmes, *The Kremlin and the Schoolhouse,* 39–41.
51. Lucy L. W. Wilson, *The New Schools of New Russia* (New York: Vanguard Press, 1928), 44–45, 159–167.
52. John Dewey, *Impressions of Soviet Russia and the Revolutionary World Mexico-China-Turkey* (New York: Teachers College, 1929), 88–92.
53. Dewey, *Impressions of Soviet Russia,* 92–98.
54. Dewey, *Impressions of Soviet Russia,* 99–100.
55. Tenenbaum, *William Heard Kilpatrick,* 264–266.
56. Tenenbaum, *William Heard Kilpatrick,* 266–267.
57. Holmes, *The Kremlin and the Schoolhouse,* 93–95.
58. Scott Nearing, *Education in Soviet Russia* (New York: International Publishers, 1926), 154–155.
59. Wilson, *The New Schools of New Russia,* 163–164.
60. Oskar Anweiler, "Origin and Development of Progressive Education in Eastern Europe," in *Progressive Education across the Continents: A Handbook,* ed. Hermann Röhrs and Volker Lenhart (New York: Peter Lang, 1995), 121–130.
61. Holmes, *The Kremlin and the Schoolhouse,* 142–143.
62. Adolph Ferrière, *The Activity School,* trans. F. Dean Moore and F. C. Wooton (New York: John Day Co., 1927), 3–14.
63. Ferrière, *The Activity School,* 240–255.
64. Carlton Washburne and Myron M. Stearns, *New Schools in the Old World* (New York: The John Day Co., 1926), vi–xiv, 14–26, 102–109, 171–174.
65. Michael J. Demiashkevich, *The Activity School: New Tendencies in Educational Method Critically Examined* (New York: J. J. Little and Ives Co., 1926), 143–150.
66. Demiashkevich, *The Activity School,* 103–105.
67. Demiashkevich, *The Activity School,* 131–150.
68. Wilford M. Aikin, *The Story of the Eight-Year Study with Conclusions and Recommendations* (New York: Harper and Brothers, 1942), 1–12; Lawrence Cremin, *Transformation of the School: Progressivism in American Education* (New York: Alfred A. Knopf, 1964), 251.
69. Cremin, *Transformation of the Schools,* 256–258.
70. Aikin, *The Story of the Eight-Year Study,* 16–31.
71. Dean Chamberlin et al., *Did They Succeed in College? The Follow-Up Study of the Graduates of the Graduates of the Thirty Schools* (New York: Harper and Brothers, 1942), 1–21, 206–209.
72. *Thirty Schools Tell Their Stories* (New York: Harper and Brothers, 1943), 718–745.
73. Ohio State University, University School, *Were We Guinea Pigs? By the Class of 1938, University High School, The Ohio State University* (New York: H. Holt and Co., 1938), 3, 29–54, 295–299.
74. "Beatty to Indians," *Time,* 10 February 1936, 36–37.
75. Brookings Institution. Institute for Government Research, *The Problem of Indian Administration: Report of a Survey Made at the Request of Honorable Hubert Work, Secretary of the Interior* (Baltimore: The Johns Hopkins Press, 1928), 3–13; Francis Paul Prucha, *The Great Father: The United States Government and the American Indians,* vol. 2 (Lincoln: University of Nebraska Press, 1984), 921–939.
76. Brookings Institution, *The Problem of Indian Administration,* 32–37, 370–374.
77. Kenneth R. Philp, *John Collier's Crusade for Indian Reform, 1920–1954* (Tucson: University of Arizona Press, 1977), 96–141.
78. Donald L. Parman, *The Navajos and the New Deal* (New Haven: Yale University, 1976), 193–200; see also Phelps-Stokes Fund, *The Navajo Indian Problem* (New York: Phelps-Stokes Fund, 1939).
79. John Collier, *From Every Zenith: A Memoir and Some Essays on Life and Thought* (Denver: Sage Books, 1963), 195–198.
80. Pedro T. Orata, *Fundamental Education in an Amerindian Community* (Lawrence, Kans. Printing Department, Haskell Institute, 1953), 2–31, 87–88.
81. George A. Dale, *Education for Better Living* (Lawrence, Kans.: U.S. Department of the Interior, 1955), 11–26.
82. Philp, *John Collier's Crusade for Indian Reform,* 225.
83. Clyde Hissong, *The Activity Movement* (Baltimore: Warwick and York, 1932), 98–118.
84. Junius L. Meriam, *Child Life and the Curriculum,* Yonkers-on-Hudson, NY: World Book Co., 1920), 480–485.
85. Meriam, *Child Life and the Curriculum,* 382–414.

13

Independent Educational Commissions to Spread Democracy

Civilian Conservation Corps Poster

As noted in the introduction, Henry R. Luce claimed the twentieth century was the American Century. In the February 1941 issue of *Life,* Luce pointed out to his readers that such prominence entailed responsibilities. Asserting that Americans had to decide to take a part in the war going on in Europe, he called on his readers to overcome the view that such conflicts fell outside their interests. According to Luce, Americans had the obligation to share their conception of democracy with the other countries of the world and to employ their industrial wealth and their technical skills in this endeavor.[1]

Although people in the United States entered World War II reluctantly, they endeavored to protect the peace after the conflict ended. An important part of the efforts to build a new world order was the attempt to share the democratic forms of education they created in the United States. To accomplish this goal, educators formed independent commissions similar to those created by U.S. President Franklin Roosevelt. In education, these commissions recommended that all school districts adopt a unified system of elementary and middle schools leading to a comprehensive high school. This was the model described in Chapter 11. After World War II, the commissions recommended that the forces of occupation impose such models on the defeated dictatorships. Although this recommendation implied that one country should impose democracy on another, the hope behind independent commissions derived from the view that democratic methods could solve the social ills presented by the Great Depression.

A downturn in economic production accompanied by severe unemployment and acute deflation beset the industrialized Western world from 1929 to about 1938. In the United States, people disagreed about the appropriate way to alleviate the Panic of 1929 and the Great Depression. Whereas some people wanted the federal government to provide economic stability, other groups feared that central economic planning would restrict opportunities for people to use their personal initiative. According to David M. Kennedy, when President Franklin Roosevelt began the New Deal, he tried to meet these contradictory expectations and cope with the problems of the Depression. In a period of five years, from 1933 to 1938, Roosevelt enlarged the nation-state to enable the federal government to provide a structure offering security to a wide range of people, including capitalists, consumers, farmers, and homeowners. Kennedy added that the federal framework that Roosevelt created did not impose rigid strictures to limit business or industry. Further, with few exceptions, Roosevelt did not purchase the security with federal dollars. He offered reforms that enabled free markets to work properly.[2]

To explain how Roosevelt was able to straddle contradictory tendencies, Kennedy cited the example of the Securities and Exchange Commission (SEC). Although the SEC required considerable legislative activity, this independent commission created the complicated regulations to make reliable information about stocks and bonds available to the public. In this way, the SEC prevented wealthy business leaders from taking unfair advantage of their positions to cheat ordinary investors. Cited by the Hoover Commission's study of the executive branch as an outstanding example of a successful independent commission, the SEC was composed of wealthy businesspeople similar to the people the commission restrained. Although critics complained that, in creating the SEC, Roosevelt had asked the foxes to watch the chickens, this was not the case. The businesspeople knew how markets functioned and could protect them.[3]

Although Kennedy believed Roosevelt's approach was beneficial, Ellis W. Hawley complained that Roosevelt's solution was politically sound but ultimately unsatisfactory. According to Hawley, the New Deal reflected two contradictory economic ideals common to Western civilization. On the one hand, industrial development freed people from traditional codes and behaviors. On the other hand, monopolies grew and dominated industrial societies. Hawley added that the New Deal had components that advanced individual freedoms and other parts that controlled people. Whereas the New Deal's antitrust actions encouraged the liberation of people from monopolistic control, the New Deal offered economic planning that restrained individual freedoms. Within the New Deal, there were factions of officials who supported each of these alternatives. Although the balances among these groups switched from time to time, Hawley claimed that neither side was victorious. To Hawley, the decision to straddle contradictory views enabled Roosevelt to retain control over conflicting interests. Unfortunately, it failed to solve the problems of monopoly that critics had claimed was the cause of the depression.[4]

Whether Roosevelt's actions were beneficial or not, they were instructive to educators. Faced with declining financial support for schools, educators created independent commissions to consider policies and provide direction for educational reform. To include as many perspectives as possible, educators that were included on the commission were chosen to represent different types of educational thought. Unfortunately, since the commission members had distinct perspectives, the proposals they made seemed to contradict each other. As a result, long-standing questions about education went unanswered.

An example of a nationally prominent but independent commission was the Educational Policies Commission (EPC). Created by the National Educational Association and the Department of Superintendence, the EPC commanded attention in two ways. First, the policy planners warned local school officials that if they ignored the planners' recommendations, the federal government might close local schools and substitute nationally organized ones. Second, the members of the national educational organizations participated in the educational missions to countries defeated in World War II, mainly Japan and Germany. The suggestions these educational missions made were the views that came from the independent commissions such as the EPC. In turn, the Allied forces of occupation imposed these recommendations on the defeated countries.

What Were the Effects of Federally Sponsored Educational Programs?

In March 1933, shortly after his first inauguration, Roosevelt sent legislation to the U.S. Congress proposing the creation of the Civilian Conservation Corps (CCC). Approved within two weeks, applications swamped the program in less than ten days. Although the original legislation did not propose the CCC as an educational venture, it became one within a month. In May 1933, the War Department issued an order indicating that the U.S. Army would offer classes in general and vocational education. A few weeks later, another order called for the establishment of libraries in the CCC camps.[5]

According to Kenneth Holland and Frank Ernest Hill, the CCC was wildly popular although it was unprecedented in American history. By July 1933, three months after the first enrollee entered the CCC, more than 300,000 enrollees were scattered across the country in about 1,500 camps. Some countries in Europe had begun youth camps earlier, but none of them involved as many people in as many places. When the CCC began, the program offered jobs to unmarried young men aged 18 to 25. Although the CCC allowed some older men to enroll as time passed, Holland and Hill noted that although most of the enrollees were white, about 9 percent of the enrollees were Negro and there were reasonable percentages of Mexicans, Chinese, Japanese, Filipinos, and American Indians. In all cases, the rationale was to put the young men to work conserving the soil and the forests. This made sense for two reasons. First, erosion had ruined over 200 million acres. For example, in the Southwest, the excessive cultivation of wheat had depleted the topsoil. When a drought struck, the wind picked up the dirt, caused dust storms, and created a dust bowl. Second, experts claimed that there were almost 14 million unemployed people in March 1933, and many young men drifted about the country looking for work. Thus, the program promised to send the young men to outdoor military-style camps, give them vigorous work, and meet the conservation needs of the country. Education was a late addition to CCC camp life because people thought that the fresh air, physical labor, and rural settings would reform the morals of the formerly transient young men.[6]

The camps were in uninhabited parts of the country. In 1935, when Frank Ernest Hill surveyed the educational programs in the CCC camps, he noted that there were about 1,700 camps with about 370,000 enrollees who had agreed to spend two years in the CCC. More than three-quarters of these camps were in isolated parts of national forests or parks. Usually, the camps did not appear on maps and travel to them was difficult.[7]

According to Hill, the camps made educational history because officers in the U.S. Army worked with former educators to form curriculums and methods of instruction that appealed to young men who disliked schools. Most of the subject matter taught in the CCC came from schools. The unique twist the CCC offered was to present the material in practical situations, such as building bridges or houses, and to have the enrollees work on the projects in groups. To accommodate the practical nature of the activities, the CCC employed teachers who had practical experience in the jobs the enrollees were to perform. Hill concluded that programs of adult education could imitate the model of the CCC.[8]

Although education was a late addition to CCC camp life, by 1939, guidance, job training, and evening classes became part of the CCC. In a survey of ten camps, investigators found three types of training: general explanations of the projects underway, individual skill training such as truck driving related to the projects, and evening classes. The CCC did not take early advantage of the opportunities to advance the recruits' education because camps did not provide facilities for evening classes until 1935. When the camps built schoolrooms, they were usually unpleasant places furnished with old chairs and tables, a blackboard, and a few maps. Usually, instruction was rudimentary; it focused on reducing illiteracy and offering simple vocational training. By 1937, possibilities broadened when the War Department set up traveling libraries each containing about 100 books that moved around through the camps.[9]

When G. Wayne Cruey conducted an investigation of the CCC for Bowling Green University, he found that the camps served a type of young man whom schools seldom reached. At the same time, he found the classroom and study facilities to be inadequate. Although some advisors and instructors had adequate training, others did not. Cruey decided all the teachers would profit from in-service training. According to Cruey, the library resources were inadequate to help the young men advance their vocational skills or pursue intelligent leisure.[10]

Because planners had designed the CCC for young men, the Roosevelt administration created the Federal Emergency Relief Administration (FERA) in May 1933 to help unemployed adults. FERA did not give money directly to people. At first, it assigned them to manual labor on some sort of public project. When relief administrators realized that many teachers and white-collar workers had lost their jobs, the administrators dispersed monies to rural districts to utilize the trained teachers and other literate adults to staff the elementary and secondary schools and to begin programs of adult literacy. By September 1933, FERA created a Division of Education Projects and appointed a member from the U.S. Office of Education and a member of the Federal Board of Vocational Education to supervise the educational programs. The result was that federal aid spread to urban schools, supported vocational training for individuals with handicaps, started a variety of vocational retraining programs, and staffed nursery schools to care for children of parents who were on relief. Consequently, by May 1935, when the Works Progress Administration (WPA) was established, many federal educational programs were underway.[11]

Under the WPA, educational activities fell into three main categories: adult literacy and naturalization programs, general adult and vocational education, and nursery school and parent training. In addition, there were a variety of miscellaneous programs, such as initiating correspondence schools in states where the population was spread over wide areas, supporting the education of African Americans in the rural South, and creating a variety of training projects to prepare teachers for elementary and secondary schools.[12]

When Roosevelt directed nearly $50 million of relief funds to create the National Youth Administration (NYA) in June 1935, he increased the educational programs under the WPA. To justify his action, Roosevelt expressed the fear that the unemployment crisis might produce a generation of unskilled, uneducated, demoralized people. Consequently, he called on educators, employers, and labor leaders to cooperate with the NYA leadership in providing opportunities for young men and women to advance in schools, to learn various trades, and to hold appropriate jobs. The program paid high school and college students to perform work planned by their schools. The NYA offered part-time work to students whose families were on relief in hopes that they would be able to remain in school. In addition, the NYA organized vocational training programs.[13]

Various advocates such as Eleanor Roosevelt, Harry Hopkins, and officials in the U.S. Office of Education called for comprehensive efforts to help young people. According to Betty and Ernest K. Lindley, the NYA was Roosevelt's response. Thus, when the U.S. Congress appropriated almost $5 billion for work relief, Roosevelt took the opportunity to create the NYA. Although officials in the U.S. Office of Education argued strongly that they should administer the program, Roosevelt appointed an official from the WPA to be executive director, and he created two advisory committees made up of representatives from a wide range of interests such as business, education, religious groups, and labor.[14]

The NYA recruited unmarried people between the ages of 18 and 24 years. Sample studies in several states revealed that NYA projects employed equal numbers of young men and women. Further, the distribution of white, African American, Native American, and other minority project workers reflected the proportions found in the general population. The workers had various amounts of education before they entered the programs. For example, the programs in Southern states tended to have young people with less education than did programs in the North. Nonetheless, the general pattern was that about 50 percent of the NYA recruits had left school after finishing the eighth grade and less than three percent had attended college. When asked why they left school, about 47 percent of the NYA recruits responded that they had left school to look for work whereas 25 percent indicated they had no interest in school.[15]

After many educators complained the federal government had usurped the job of schools, Roosevelt commissioned in 1937 the President's Advisory Committee on Education to evaluate the relation of federal efforts to advance education to the responsibilities of state agencies. The advisory committee's report about the educational activities of the WPA noted that in most states, the federal education projects operated independently of the public schools, although state education officers were supposed to supervise the projects. The report could not explain why such problems occurred, but it noted that the fault could fall on both sides. Public school officials may have feared federal aid whereas federal officials may have considered their projects as relief efforts, not educational ones. As for the effects of the educational activities of the WPA, the advisory committee's report claimed that the WPA had expanded the fields of adult and nursery school education. It had introduced practical programs to help with family living, provided instruction in such public affairs as voting and governmental procedures, and taught people to engage in healthful leisure-time pursuits. Most important, the report noted that the WPA concentrated its efforts on people who were underprivileged and would not otherwise have enjoyed an education.[16]

At the same time, Roosevelt commissioned a study of the NYA. According to the advisory committee's report, the NYA provided thousands of college students and boys and girls in high school the opportunities to receive valuable educations for less than the cost of one battleship. At the same time, the report added that the NYA revealed the challenges that public schools faced. The first problem was that the various states supported schools unequally. The inequality of educational opportunity derived from the difference in the wealth of the states. For example, the Northeast region had 42 percent of the national income and had to care for about 8.5 million children between the ages of 5 and 17 years whereas the Southeastern region had about 2 percent of the national income but had to care for over 4 million children. The report concluded that federal aid to disadvantaged areas was the only way to reduce such inequality. The second challenge the NYA offered public schools was that the NYA offered useful programs to the students not available in schools. The report quoted young people who had dropped out of school because the schools required them to study foreign languages. The recruits claimed that they loved the NYA because they learned trades such as automotive repair.[17]

Public school educators took the view that they should receive the federal monies, claiming that, without federal aid to education, schools could not improve during the Great Depression. In 1936, Paul Mort conducted an extensive study of the relative ability of states to support education. Financed by grants from the General Education Board, the WPA, and the Columbia University Council for Research, Mort's study found that state support for education varied from as little as $25 per pupil per year to as much as $130 per pupil per year. Because the differences derived from variations in the wealth of the states, the best way to equalize educational opportunities among states was to use federal taxes to support state schools. In addition to reducing inequalities, federal aid to local schools would reduce excessive pressures on local property taxes, thereby making the total system of taxation more efficient.[18]

In making these arguments, educators convinced several officials in the federal government to agree that federal aid to education was essential. For example, Roosevelt requested in 1937 that his advisory committee on education evaluate the possibilities of federal aid to education. The advisory committee enlisted Paul R. Mort to repeat the work he had done a year earlier. Mort also arrived at the conclusion that local funds did not provide adequate support for public education in many states, that the states' inabilities to support schools hampered the development of public school systems, and that in all states the property tax was overburdened to pay for local education. Thus, he offered several recommendations on how the federal government could provide support for local schools.[19]

The question of federal aid to education differed in outlying areas or territories. Although the problems in Alaska, Hawaii, Puerto Rico, the Virgin Islands, Guam, and America Samoa differed from each other and from the difficulties found in the continental states, these areas had direct relations to the federal government. In 1939, federal statutes designated Puerto Rico, the Virgin Islands, Guam, and America Samoa as outlying possessions whereas Alaska and Hawaii were territories. In the outlying possessions, the federal government selected the administrative personnel who hired the teachers and staff. In the territories, public education functioned as in the states with little federal supervision. Despite the unique relationships to the federal government, none of these outlying areas received adequate aid to support public schools adapted to their needs. As a result, a study commissioned by the President's Advisory Committee on Education recommended that all these outlying areas and territories receive federal aid on the same basis as states.[20]

The advisory committee on education transmitted Mort's report and the other reports about federal aid to education to the president in 1938. In turn, Roosevelt sent them to the U.S. Congress. The NEA held a legislative conference attended by members of the president's advisory committee to draft legislation to provide federal aid to education. Although educators supported the legislation, the U.S. Congress adjourned without taking action. When Congress reconvened in 1939, efforts began again. Although the Senate Committee on Education and Labor made a favorable report on the bill, the House did not hold hearings on the proposed legislation.[21]

At least one group of educators, the Educational Policies Commission (EPC), argued that the federal government could afford to extend financial support to public schools if it disbanded supposedly emergency programs such as the CCC and the NYA. In 1941, before the United States entered World War II, the members of the EPC claimed that programs such as the CCC and the NYA trespassed on the proper domains of public schools. The members of the EPC believed it was appropriate for the federal government to provide work for young people, but they claimed that the training for the work should come from the schools. Thus, the report of the EPC called on the federal government to disband the CCC and the NYA and to make assurances that state and local educational agencies would direct long-term educational programs for youth.[22]

The controversies about federal aid to education and the control of federal education activities ended when World War II brought about the end of the New Deal's domestic programs. According to Edward Krug, the war effort absorbed the federal monies.[23]

What Were the Effects of Independent Educational Commissions?

When Roosevelt created programs to reduce the problems of the depression, he placed representatives of differing viewpoints on the same commission, and he made these commissions operate independently. When educators felt excluded from economic recovery efforts, they formed independent commissions that were to unite the various factions within their field. An important example of such an independent educational commission was the Educational Policies Commission (EPC) that proposed policies from its inception in 1936 to its end in 1968.

The EPC derived from efforts to protect schools from financial reverses during the depression. In 1933, the National Education Association (NEA) and the Department of Superintendence, later named the American Association of School Administrators, created the Joint Commission on the Emergency in Education as the first policy-planning group that could secure stable financial support for schools. Until 1935, this group focused on policies related to school finance. The commission held regional conferences and distributed newsletters to help local school people avoid difficulties. Because the commission had a narrow focus, the members thought the NEA and the Department of Superintendence should create another commission to consider wider difficulties.[24]

To form the more permanent commission, the executive committees of the NEA and the Department of Superintendence agreed in December 1935 to appoint sixteen educators to make up the EPC. To ensure the independence of the EPC, the NEA requested around $50,000 from the General Education Board to support its activities. Once the NEA received the money, the NEA set up a central office for the EPC in Washington, D.C., and placed the funds at the organization's disposal. Another way the EPC protected the independence of its members was that it did not join with any research or deliberative bodies. Instead, the EPC depended on its membership of what it called forward-looking educators who considered available data and constructed policies or plans of action.[25]

When John A. Sexton announced the formation of the EPC to the Department of Superintendence, he claimed that public schools in many parts of the country were continuing to suffer the ills of the depression even though other institutions appeared to be recovering. Claiming that schools would not benefit until they adopted a program of education compatible with national needs, Sexton asserted that the EPC would formulate a statement of purposes that would make schools appear more deserving of aid. He added that the EPC would confront two issues immediately. One was the need for federal aid to public schools. The other was the threat presented to public schools by the newly created federal agencies aimed at helping young men and women. He added that these agencies were taking students from schools and colleges and enrolling them in new institutions. In such a fight, Sexton concluded, the EPC would serve as a unifying agency around which the different types of educators could rally.[26]

If the EPC was to serve as a unifying agency, the representatives should have formed some sort of unified view of what constituted a good education. This was not what they did. According to Frederick M. Hunter, a founding member of the commission, the membership included the U.S. Commissioner of Education, officials from the American Council on

Education, the NEA, the Department of Superintendence, and thirteen people selected from the profession based on their ability to contribute to the solution of educational problems. At the first meeting, the commission members made a list of fifty-six different problems confronting American schools. The committee decided to make a report on each topic that drew from a wide range of opinion and that offered a practical recommendation school people could follow in ameliorating the difficulty.[27]

Not only did the membership of the committee include teachers, administrators, educational theorists, and politicians, they selected problems in an open fashion. To explain the principles that would guide the work of the members of the EPC, the chairperson, Alexander J. Stoddard, described the principles on which they agreed to build programs. First, the schools cooperated with other social agencies. Second, educational policies had to be consistent with democratic values. Third, the policies derived from studies using the scientific method. Fourth, the members of the EPC agreed to try to persuade people to accept the correctness of their policies rather than force them to adopt those suggestions. Fifth, social issues and needs must dictate policies. Sixth, policies must be flexible and open to change. Seventh, policies must be broad in scope. Eighth, policy had to influence school practices.[28] Because these principles represented the ground rules for debate rather than a coherent pattern to organize policies, the first two reports resulted in contradictory views of the proper curriculum.

The first report from the EPC appeared in 1937. Charles Beard wrote the draft of the report and the members of the EPC made some revisions. The EPC report, *The Unique Function of Education in American Democracy,* repeated the structure and the ideas of *A Charter for the Social Studies* that Beard had written in 1932 for the American Historical Association's Commission on the Social Studies in the Schools.

In *A Charter,* Beard described the attitude of scientific detachment that scholars cultivated. He pointed out that schools could not synthesize disciplines such as sociology and history because the practitioners of each science held different points of view as they gathered the material they studied. Beard pointed out that society was rapidly changing, that the spread of industrialism caused the need for increased planning and intelligent cooperation, and that the students had to develop the qualities of mind that enabled them to become active participants in the democratic society. Above all, in order for schools to contribute to the social order, teachers should act as intellectuals with academic freedom.[29]

For the EPC, Beard repeated many of these same ideas. The scientific method practiced by social scientists offered methods needed to direct an increasingly complex society. Educational and social planning had become nationwide and schools needed to ensure that society retained its democratic ethos in the midst of social change. To preserve democracy, schools had to avoid separating studies into practical and theoretical fields. Unless humanized with the accumulated wisdom of humankind, students could employ technical knowledge in ways that destroyed civilization. Instead of having overly practical aims, schools should transport into the present the ethical views developed by scholars in the past.[30]

The next year, 1938, when the EPC published its second statement, *The Purposes of Education in American Democracy,* the organization contradicted the principles found in the first EPC report. Whereas Beard's volume described the educational conditions needed for intellectual activity to direct social change, the second statement compared schools to corporations and taxpayers to stockholders who deserved statements about the practical value of their investments. Thus, for example, the second volume called for changes in the presentation of subject matters. English courses should not emphasize grammar or classical literature as much as they should encourage students to read for pleasure. Instruction in mathematics should be restricted to practical arithmetic. Foreign languages were unnecessary, and social studies should teach about contemporary problems. Most important, the measurement of student outcomes must relate to such practical goals as whether the students spent money wisely or lived in accordance with the rules of good health. These recommendations contradicted Beard's notion that traditional subjects carried ethical orientations students had to acquire.[31]

Whereas the EPC concerned itself with the ways that schools could reduce domestic problems, other educators discussed the role of education in advancing international understanding. For example, in 1937, Isaac Leon Kandel chaired the Committee on International Understanding for the National Society for the Study of Education. Publishing their views in the NSSE yearbook, the editors of the yearbook warned school administrators not to encourage overly patriotic feelings among the students. The committee members took the position that the curriculum should impart ways to thinking that opened students to the possibilities of international cooperation. The editors complained about the feelings of isolationism they believed was popular in the United States. Although they disparaged the supernationalism of Italy and Germany, they believed that proper feelings of nationalism recognized the similarities among different peoples, the ways that different countries were interdependent, and the common efforts of different societies as they advanced through civilization. It was this more healthy view of nationalism the editors wanted the school people to convey.[32]

The 1937 NSSE yearbook suggested that promotion of internationalism did not require the introduction of new subjects into the curriculum. The traditional academic subjects were well suited to promote international understanding when they showed how the different ways of thinking had advanced civilization. Thus, for example, W. L. Carr argued that the study of classical languages, Greek and Latin, introduced students to the roots of modern civilization that all Western countries shared. Robert Herndon Fife suggested that the study of modern foreign languages introduced students to the soul of another culture when the students learned to read with ease in that language. David Eugene Smith contended that mathematics was the basis of all sciences because it provided objective ways to determine the truth of any proposition. As a result, he thought the study of mathematics encouraged students to develop sane and rational approaches to life. Henry Neumann wrote that the teaching of literature, even in elementary schools, could widen children's sympathetic understandings of other people.[33]

Although Kandel and his colleagues thought that schools should retain traditional academic courses, this changed after the United States entered World War II in 1941 because groups such as the EPC called for curriculums to emphasize practical applications. For example, in 1943, the EPC distributed statements about what schools should teach in order to help the war effort. Anticipating an Allied victory, the members of the EPC recommended that teachers prepare elementary school students for adult life in peaceful and democratic society. This meant that they should learn fundamental academic skills, avoid developing pathological hatred of the enemy, and develop citizenship skills by working with the Red Cross or planting victory gardens. The EPC suggested that teachers consider high school students to be reservists in preparation for the military or war industries. Thus, the EPC report recommended that all high school studies become opportunities to teach the vocational skills for such occupations. Thus, formerly academic subjects such as mathematics and science should serve wartime uses. The report discouraged teaching foreign languages to most students. Instead, the EPC recommended that only a few students should study foreign languages in order to become proficient in the languages involved in the war such as German, French, Russian, Japanese, and Italian. For arts classes such as music, the EPC suggested that these formerly aesthetic endeavors should aid the war effort by teaching children to participate in parades and ceremonies to send off military personnel.[34]

By 1944, with the Allied invasion of Northern France, the EPC decided that it was time to plan for postwar education. According to the EPC report, *Education for All American Youth,* the biggest danger facing educators was the possibility that the federal government would impose a federal system of education to replace state and local control of education. The report warned that the returning soldiers and workers in war-related industries were young and needed training to enter civilian pursuits. One problem was that state and local boards of education had lacked sufficient funds during the Depression and the war to build and equip schools to meet the needs of these young people. Worse, the federal government had denied the schools the federal aid they needed to improve. A second problem was that secondary school teachers focused on academic subjects and refused to tailor the instruction to the individual needs of the youth. As a result, the federal government had created agencies such as the NYA to provide vocational guidance and training.[35]

To solve the conflict between the academic orientations of schools and the vocational needs of youth, the EPC suggested that all high schools should meet the ten imperative needs of youth while attending to differences among the individual students. These needs were as follows: acquire salable skills, develop good health, understand the rights and duties of citizens in a democracy, appreciate the importance of family life, know how to purchase goods intelligently, recognize the role of science in the modern world, expand their capacities to appreciate art, discover how to use leisure time effectively, grow in insight into ethical concerns, and learn to think rationally.[36]

Although the EPC recommended a different form of organization for rural schools than urban ones, the differences were in degree, not kind. That is, in both cases, schools divided secondary education into a junior high school or lower secondary school and a high school or upper secondary school. The curriculum fell into six parts that included opportunities for the students to pursue their interests through individual activities, vocational training or college preparation, a course in science to learn principles, a common learning course that blended social studies, literature, and art, and health and physical education.[37]

In 1945, the National Society for the Study of Education (NSSE) divided its yearbook into two parts, both dealing with aspects of the postwar demands on the schools. The first part considered the ways to plan and provide extensions in the educational programs. The second part dealt with the ways to organize school districts and states to promote the improvement of educational services.

The NSSE reinforced the policies the EPC advocated. For example, Hilda Taba mapped out a process for determining the curriculum to enable schools to meet all the needs of a variety of people living in changing circumstances. Noting that there was no agreement on the question of the best curriculum, Taba concluded that curriculum planners should begin with materials from three sources: studies of society to determine what people need to know to function as members, studies of individual learners showing how learning takes place, and studies of subject matter content showing concepts people should master. Using this information, the planners should decide what behaviors the students should acquire and what experiences would enable the students to change their behaviors. These experiences had to lead to the behavior that was to change. They should open into a variety of things to learn. They should fit the needs and interests of the students, and they should serve the society.[38]

Taba's model reinforced the EPC's efforts to change the classical curriculum and aesthetic activities into practical activities. The second part of the yearbook used discussions about the organization of school districts to repeat the longstanding plea of the EPC for adequate funding and the desire to open schools to all types of people. In describing the structural reorganization of schools, the NSSE yearbook of 1945 noted that educational facilities should expand to serve youth and adults. All children with handicaps should receive appropriate services. Local and state boards of education should have clear working relations with federal officials. In making these reforms, school people should begin with studies of the costs of an adequate program and determine available financial support from local, state, and federal sources.[39]

The EPC repeated its calls for expanded education related to the needs and interests of children after it distributed *Education for All American Youth.* For example, in 1945, the EPC published *Education for Young Children.* The commission called for increased services for children two to four years old because children had to acquire seven disciplines in order for the democracy to be fully functioning. The report listed these disciplines as follows: respect for other people, willingness to cooperate with other people, appreciation of deferred benefits, acceptance of the rules of fair play, admiration for the scientific method, development of self-reliance, and valuing individual freedom. Services such as regular health clinics for prenatal and postnatal care could protect children's health, and other services as supervised playgroups could enable young children to learn to work with other people. Nursery schools could carry on these lessons. The EPC report suggested attaching nursery schools to secondary schools so pupils in home economics could learn from working with children as young as two years old.[40]

In line with the desire to increase educators' attention to ways they could enhance the values of democracy, the EPC issued a report about elementary schools in 1948. Entitled *Education for All American Children,* the commission's report called for schools to begin planning the curriculum by making an inventory of the activities of adults in the community. The teacher should determine the psychological makeup of the children and ascertain their interests. The goals of instruction should come from commonly accepted values such as the desirability of cooperation. Finally, the experiences the children would undertake in the school should begin with things close to their homes. Gradually, those experiences would expand into the community, the state, the nation, and the world. In addition, the EPC recommended combining lessons around practical activities. For example, it praised a school district wherein children took part in a community chest drive. As the children discussed their success in gathering charitable donations, they used percentages to determine how they were approaching their goals and considered the needs of the community as they thought about the ways the money would be spent. The EPC report concluded that the appropriate curriculum aimed at helping children developing democratic values because the teachers planned a variety of various projects or activities that built on the interests of the children and taught them to cooperate with each other.[41]

When educators sought to advance the reconstruction that had resulted from World War II, they recommended that the defeated countries adopt the EPC's idea of the one track of elementary and junior high schools leading into a comprehensive high school because they thought such a model would introduce democracy into those societies. This was the case in Japan.

How Did U.S. Educators Influence Schools in Japan?

The Pacific War ended on August 14, 1945, and the Japanese signed an official surrender on September 2, 1945. Before the Allied occupation began, the Japanese Ministry of Education issued directives eliminating militarism and encouraging democracy in the schools. On September 22, 1945, a military government took office in Japan with U.S. General Douglas MacArthur holding the position of Supreme Commander for Allied Powers (SCAP). In a short time, the designation SCAP referred to American military and civilian personnel in charge of the occupation. Thus, SCAP meant MacArthur's organization, and it dominated the proceedings even though the Far Eastern Commission and an Allied Council that included the Soviet Union, China, and the British Commonwealth countries were supposed to share the administration of the occupation. The SCAP sent directives to a staff section called Civil Information and Education (CIE) that relayed the orders to the Japanese officials. In each of Japan's forty-six prefectures, or administrative sections roughly comparable to states, an American military team exercised surveillance over the local officials to ensure they carried out SCAP directives. As soon as possible, an American teacher joined each team to assist and to inspect schools.[42]

The first efforts to change the Japanese system of education took three general directions. First, the CIE prohibited any militaristic ideas in schools and replaced Japanese authoritarianism with democratic ideals. Second, the CIE set up measures to evaluate the ideas of Japanese teachers to remove any teachers who sympathized with the former government and Japan's war effort. Third, the CIE forbade the Japanese schools to advance any Japanese religion such as Shinto doctrines. To enforce the third directive, officials had to read the available textbooks and remove any offending sections. In this effort, censors destroyed some books and mutilated others.[43]

In January 1946, SCAP requested that the U.S. War Department send a team of twenty-seven qualified educators to visit Japan for one month and make suggestions about the needed changes in the schools. According to Victor Kobayashi, the War Department selected the members of what became the U.S. Education Mission to Japan deliberately to ensure that they represented the various views found in the United States. For example, some members, such as T. V. Smith and George Counts, held to ideals related to the project method and the activity movement. Two members, Monsignor Frederick G. Hochwalt and Roy Deferrari were Catholic educators. Other members, such as Isaac Leon Kandel, wanted school curriculums to follow traditional academic lines.[44]

Because the members of the U.S. Educational Mission did not claim to be experts on Japan, they tried to learn a great deal in a short time. Before departing, they attended conferences designed to teach them about Japan and what awaited them. During the trip, the group stayed in Hawaii and in Guam where the members held interim conferences. For the first ten days, the members visited schools, interviewed Japanese educators, and visited cultural sites in Kyoto and Nara.[45]

Claiming that the former Japanese system of education reinforced authoritarianism, the members of the mission recommended that the aims of education start with concern for the individual in ways that corresponded with the Charter for the United Nations Organization and UNESCO. Thus, for the curriculum, the U.S. Educational Mission's report urged that instructional planning begin with the interests of the students. With this beginning, teachers could cooperate with central education officers to select texts and plan assignments. The report complained that, at the time of the mission's visit, a central department of education in Japan selected and bought the texts for all the schools. They recommended that representative groups of teachers from the different areas make decisions about textbooks.[46]

The members of the educational mission noted that before the war the students took courses in ethics that taught obedience. Although the occupation forces had removed these courses before they arrived, members of the mission agreed that children had to learn to act in ethically correct ways. The problem was that the mission wanted the children to learn ethics that served democracy rather than authoritarianism. Such instruction could appear when teachers modeled the ethics and the students cooperated in their lessons, the report added. Nevertheless, the members acknowledged the separate classes on morals could appear in the schools provided the aim was to change Japanese manners in directions that respected equality, provided for cooperation, and encouraged children to value work.[47]

When Isaac Leon Kandel looked back on his work with the U.S. Education Mission to Japan, he worried that the recommendations ignored all possible connections to Japanese tradition. Instead of building on the Imperial system, the commission report substituted an American style system with local school boards, freedom for teachers, extensive educational opportunities for different types of people, and the education of boys and girls together.[48]

Although there was truth to Kandel's view, he ignored the tradition of democratic education that had begun in 1868 when the Meiji Restoration caused the Japanese to examine Western thought. In the 1870s, scholars left Japan to enroll in American universities where they learned about William James and G. Stanley Hall. As a result, such progressive innovations as a child study movement began in Japan in 1902. As the twentieth century opened, Japanese scholars translated and published in Japan the works of John Dewey. In return, Dewey visited Japan in 1919 where he lectured at the Tokyo Imperial University and visited progressive Japanese schools. The lectures that Dewey gave in Japan appeared in the United States as *Reconstruction in Philosophy.* Other progressive American educators such as Carlton Washburne and William Heard Kilpatrick visited Japan in the 1920s and 1930s. At the same time, teacher-training institutions opened in Japan to spread the new education.[49]

In fairness to Kandel, although many Japanese teachers had adopted the progressive models of teaching such as the project method or the Dalton plan or the Winnetka plan before the war, they had retained an authoritarian tradition. According to Kobayashi, this happened because the Japanese meshed the progressive techniques of teaching with nationalistic aims. For example, while progressive teachers in America wanted to plan lessons that taught children how to solve their own problems while focusing on the children's interests, Japanese teachers did not have a similar interest in the students' individual talents. Japanese teachers allowed the children to bring their interests from their homes into the school; however, Japanese teachers saw these experiences as opportunities to build national loyalty among the children. Thus, although Japanese progressive teachers knew the technical innovations, they disregarded the theoretical bases of those suggestions. Kobayashi suggested that, before the war, the Japanese teachers turned the progressive tools into ways to exalt the Japanese national spirit.[50]

The aim of the educational mission to Japan was to break the authoritarian tradition and replace it with a democratic one. For example, in an address to the National Catholic Educational Association in 1946, one of the members of the U.S. Educational Mission, the Very Reverend Monsignor Frederick G. Hochwalt said that the mission was concerned about three major issues. The first was the central control exercised by the Japanese ministry because this reinforced the traditional authoritarian style that permeated school relationships. He complained that children had to bow to many people and to portraits to show their submissiveness. The second issue was the excessive control of students. He noted that schools had been divided into groups of thirty students who were watched by a coach teacher who punished any student who strayed from the approved pattern of political thought. Finally, girls could not study academic subjects. They learned those skills needed by wives and mothers. He concluded the U.S. mission tried to establish local control of schools, reduce authoritarian discipline, and provide equal opportunities for boys and girls.[51]

As Hochwalt described, the members of the U.S. mission recommended that Japan adopt a decentralized system similar to those found in the United States. First, the arrangement of grades was to follow a 6-3-3 plan with a six-year elementary school, a three-year lower secondary school, and a three-year upper secondary school. In addition to academic courses, the curriculum would include health and physical education as well as vocational studies. Second, administrative control and financial support had to be decentralized. Before the war, a central ministry had controlled education throughout the country. The U.S. mission recommended that each prefecture appoint an educational leader who established and maintained standards for the schools, certified teachers, approved textbooks, arranged in-service training of teachers, and examined and certified teachers. At the same time, the mission recommended that each city or other subdivision of the prefectures set up an agency with elected members to appoint a qualified educator as head of the schools. Finally, in order to have the schools enroll students without tuition and to provide trained teachers with small classes in well-equipped facilities, the schools required stable financial support. The mission recommended that such funds come from the national government, the prefectures, and local sources.[52]

In making their recommendations, the members of the U.S. mission adapted to Japan the system they wanted to have in the United States. First, the arrangement of school grades followed the recommendations found in the EPC reports. Second, the arrangement of responsibilities of prefecture officials and the local district agencies were the duties the

EPC recommended for state superintendents, school boards, and district superintendents to undertake in the United States. Finally, the Japanese system was to diversify taxation in the ways that the EPC had recommended when it unsuccessfully called for federal aid to schools.

A report from the Japanese Ministry of Education labeled the recommendations of the U.S. mission as drastic. Nevertheless, most of the mission's reforms appeared in the Fundamental Education Law approved in 1947 by the National Diet, Japan's legislature, making democracy the aim of education. The law called for equal opportunity of education, made education for boys and girls together free and compulsory, and established the 6-3-3 model of elementary and secondary schools with a four-year college program to follow. Although the upper secondary schools introduced vocational training and guidance to the schools, few students enrolled in these courses. The ministry blamed low enrollments on popular prejudices against vocational education, a lack of trained teachers, and poor facilities.[53]

Before the war, Japanese schools had a system with five separate educational tracks. The students' scores on examinations determined which track students could follow. For example, they might pass from elementary school into an academic middle school or a vocational program. Because these examinations were difficult, few students qualified to move into high school. The U.S. educational mission recommended a single track with students attending the same schools, the elimination of the qualifying examinations, and schools open to all students. The Japanese accepted these suggestions, adopting a comprehensive upper secondary school with a design similar to the comprehensive high school found in the EPC reports that offered academic and vocational subjects.[54]

To make these changes, the report from the Japanese Ministry of Education claimed that the ministry created a committee charged with revising the curriculum. Although the hope was to publish the curriculum plans as general principles that classroom teachers could modify, the ministry found that most teachers lacked the training to make changes. In addition, the agencies in the prefectures and in the subdivisions could not offer assistance. Therefore, the ministry compiled courses of studies for the various grades of elementary and secondary schools.[55]

To reform teaching methods, the ministry adopted what it called the methods of the United States. This included using the unit approach, applying the problem project approach when possible, and offering opportunities for the students to be active. To ensure lessons moved appropriately, the ministry called for the establishment of definite objectives for instruction and the opportunities for students to use libraries and audio visual aids.[56]

According to Ronald S. Anderson, during the month the U.S. Educational Mission made its inspection, the members had the cooperation of the Japanese Education Committee (JEC). When the mission left, the Japanese government raised the JEC to a cabinet-level position directly responsible to the Prime Minister and renamed it the Japanese Education Reform Committee (JERC). In forming the Fundamental Education Law, representatives from the JERC, members of the Japanese ministry of education, and agents of the CIE of the U.S. occupation forces met to discuss the various points. Because few Americans spoke Japanese, these meetings proceeded slowly. Nonetheless, Anderson claimed that the law was the product of compromise that included sensitivity to Japanese traditions. Thus, although it removed excessive nationalism, it did not bring democracy to all aspects of education. For example, the law called for citizens to elect school boards in prefectures and in cities. The duties of these boards would be similar to those in the United States. Prefectures would certify teachers as did state departments of education in the United States. City boards would hire them. Because the Japanese had no experience with volunteer citizen participation on boards of education, the law proposed a compromise allowing professionals to participate in school administration. This meant that teachers could serve on the school boards. Districts paid board members for their efforts. Although U.S. consultants worried that teachers sitting on the boards would be their own bosses and set their own salaries, a bigger problem was that local boards could not raise taxes to pay for schools. As a result, most financial support came from the central ministry. This reasserted the problem of central national control.[57]

In 1950, General MacArthur invited another educational mission to evaluate the progress in the reform of Japan's educational system. The members of this second mission concluded that Japan had adopted the plan for a six-year elementary school, a three-year lower secondary school, and a three-year higher secondary school that the first educational mission had recommended. Although the members of the second mission noted the schools were more democratic, they feared that Japan faced serious financial problems. School buildings were inadequate. Teachers' salaries were low. Furthermore, the opportunities for children with handicaps remained inadequate. Thus, the report called for more financial support to complete the reforms.[58]

Despite the enthusiasm of the second educational mission, some of the recommendations of the first mission were extreme and impossible. For example, the U.S. report devoted its second chapter to recommending a change in the written form of the Japanese language, *kanji.* The members of the mission complained that the traditional patterns were so complex that few students could master them. As a result, the children left school without being able to read. The mission's answer was to abandon the ideographic forms that abstractly represented the thing or the concept and adopt the Roman alphabet that used letters to represent sounds, because the Roman form, called *romaji,* would make reading Japanese simpler and increase student achievement. A member of the U.S. Navy who served as language simplification officer for the CIE, Robert King Hall, devoted over one hundred pages of his book, *Education for a New Japan,* to similar arguments for a change in the Japanese language.[59]

According to Toshio Nishi, the CIE, a U.S. organization, tried to force the Japanese government to adopt roman letters for the written form of the Japanese language. By 1950, though, the CIE recognized that it would be impossible to make the change. As a result, members of the CIE contented themselves with the explosive popularity of English courses that had proliferated throughout the schools. Before the war, the Japanese government had prohibited teaching English. After the war, the Japanese Broadcasting Corporation began teaching Japanese people to speak English with fifteen-minute daily segments that attracted large audiences.[60]

How Did U.S. Educators Influence Schools in Germany?

During the occupation, the United States influence in Japan was stronger than it was in Germany and the other Axis countries. Although other nations such as Britain and the

Soviet Union requested to share in the administration of the Japanese occupation, General MacArthur received orders from President Harry S Truman and the U.S. Joint Chiefs of Staff that he interpreted in ways that gave him complete control. As a result, he made the decisions to do such things as invite the U.S. Educational Mission. Conditions differed in Europe. For one thing, other Allied powers, including Britain, France, and the Soviet Union, had participated directly in the fighting in Europe whereas MacArthur could claim the U.S. had fought alone in the Pacific. For another thing, according to Isaac Kandel, educational reform in Germany was difficult because, after the war, America, the Soviet Union, Britain, and France divided the country into four parts and exposed it to four different types of educational ideas.[61]

Another problem was that although the U.S. government wanted Germany and the other Axis powers to adopt democracy as a way of thinking and living after the war, officials did not construct the plans they were to follow, because Roosevelt refused to prepare for an occupation while the war proceeded. As a result, different governmental agencies adopted contradictory views as to how reeducation should take place, and German officials took advantage of the disagreements to resist incorporating the changes.[62]

In 1943, while the war was underway, the Allies agreed that when the war ended, Germans would have to learn to be democratic. For example, when the members of Britain's Royal Institute of International Affairs, Chatham House, held a study group, the participants agreed that the German people would have to reject racial pride and aggressiveness in the service of the state that Nazism had spread through the country. Although these intellectuals thought maintaining peace was an educational problem, they doubted that schools could perform the function. They wanted to open schools to democratic materials and to remove Nazis from teaching positions while recognizing that no one could force a democratic ethos on people. They held that democratically inclined leaders would have to change the German political system and thereby change the political environment.[63]

In Germany after the war, the attitude among occupation forces was that the extent of their responsibility was to open the German schools that had closed due to the fighting. For example, in 1945, the U.S. chief education officer, John Taylor, announced that each *Land,* or state, in Germany would have to initiate its own plans to solve its own problems. When Taylor received reports of the U.S. Educational Mission to Japan, he did not feel that such a mission would help in Germany. He believed that the Education and Religious Affairs branch had begun a program that appeared to be positive. After other U.S. officials pressured Taylor, he approved the formation of an educational mission to Germany.[64]

The U.S. Educational Mission to Germany consisted of ten men and women including Reinhold Niebuhr, professor of theology, and George Zook, president of the American Council on Education and former U.S. Commissioner of Education. One member, T. V. Smith, had served on the educational mission to Japan and another member, Reverend Felix Newton Pitt, represented Catholic educators. After a month-long investigation in Germany, the commission issued its report in October 1946.[65]

The U.S. mission noted that Germany had compulsory education and that almost all children attended school. At the elementary level, as many as eighty children sat in the same class. After fourth grade, about 10 percent of the students went on to a secondary school. The highest type was the gymnasium or classical high school. Most children remained in elementary school until eighth grade, after which they went into an apprenticeship or part-time vocational school. The remainder of the children, who were from middle-class homes, passed from elementary school to a middle school that prepared them for work in business or government service. Not only did attendance in these various schools follow lines of social class distinctions, but the different institutions were separate from each other.[66]

The U.S. education mission report stated that the most important change was to replace the diversified German system with a comprehensive system open to all students. In such a comprehensive system, boys and girls would attend elementary schools for six years. Because the instruction in these schools would be the same for all students, the traditional distinctions among German elementary schools would not apply to the quality of instruction although there could be distinctions among levels. At the secondary level, the same school offered both academic education and vocational training. In such a comprehensive high school, different types of students could participate in a common school life, cooperate on projects of mutual interest, and develop feelings of unity.[67]

In addition, the mission's report recommended reorganizing the curriculum to provide experience in democratic living. For example, cooperative class projects, student clubs, and community service had to be developed. Although instruction in German language, literature, and mathematics could continue, the report urged blending those academic subjects with the social sciences. Similarly, the report suggested that vocational education provide equal attention to developing citizenship skills and training in specific trades.[68]

Although the educational mission's recommendations for Germany were similar to those directed to Japan, the recommendations differed from a report the U.S. State Department had issued when the mission departed for Germany. Entitled "Long-Range Policy Statement for German Reeducation," the statement from the U.S. State Department asserted that the German people had to direct the reconstruction of their cultural life. Thus, whereas the U.S. Educational Mission took the view that Germans had to redesign their schools along the lines of existing American institutions, the U.S. State Department took the position that Germans should direct their own affairs.[69]

Another glaring contradiction appeared when the assistant secretary of state for public affairs, William Benton, wrote the letter of transmittal to the secretary of state for the report of the U.S. Educational Mission to Germany. After describing the report's recommendation to impose a uniform system of education with a comprehensive high school that included vocational and academic courses, Benton added that he disagreed with the mission's view that democratic education required the integration of vocational and academic education under one roof. Further, in regard to the mission's recommendations of integrating practical and academic studies around the ideal of citizenship training, Benton warned that, although there should be equal opportunity for students to pursue academic educations, vocational courses should not overshadow or dilute the program of liberal courses.[70]

In the United States, educators questioned Benton's qualifications for making any evaluation of the mission's report. For example, angered by Benton's letter, Willard B. Spalding, superintendent of schools for Portland, Oregon, distributed a statement in which he complained that Benton had been an advertising executive. As a result, in Spalding's view, Benton lacked the training that would qualify him to question the collective judgment of the U.S. Educational Mission.[71]

Despite the conflicts, John Taylor, the U.S chief education officer followed the educational mission's recommendations. Sending a message to the ministries of education in Bavaria, Greater Hesse, and Württemberg-Baden, Taylor stated that the goal of the U.S. occupation was to democratize Germany. Taylor's plan called for elementary schools to enroll all children for six years. There would be no differences in the type of education offered in different elementary schools. Although secondary schools would have branches that distinguished among students' interests and vocational interests, all students took a core of general education classes. Allowing some students to pursue only academic courses, Taylor's plan forbade the traditional gymnasium to have students concentrate on classical languages. In reply to Taylor, the Bavarian minister of education, Alois Hundhammer, launched a public campaign in which he revealed the criticisms that U.S. officials directed at the U.S. mission's report. As a result, Hundhammer claimed some members of the occupation forces disagreed about the plans. To the Bavarian public, he complained the American model would destroy the system of education and especially the ideal of liberal education Germany had advanced. Although the dispute in Bavaria continued at a deadlock, economic issues about tuition, teacher pay, and textbooks overshadowed the larger curriculum matters.[72]

By 1948, American authorities realized that there would be a West German State. As a result, policies of the occupation changed from trying to structure a program of reeducation to seeking some form of reorientation that enlisted the German authorities in programs to strengthen democratic sentiments among the citizenry. In 1949, the United States, Britain, and France consolidated their zones of occupation in Germany, forming West Germany, and the Soviet Union formed East Germany. In 1990, these divisions ended as East Germany joined West Germany to make a united country, the Federal Republic of Germany.[73]

Although the Japanese people had appeared more willing to accept educational ideas from the United States during the occupation than did the Germans, the countries were equally unwilling to retain the ideas of a so-called democratic education. In Japan, some things changed while other things did not. On the one hand, in Japan, coeducation was the most widely accepted radical suggestion and by the 1970s the percentage of female middle school students advancing to high schools equaled the percentage of male students. On the other hand, once the occupation ended in 1952, Japanese schools reverted to multitrack, competitive institutions. Because SCAP had tried to move school administration away from the national ministry and toward the local level, some prefectures had been able to resist the idea of comprehensive high schools. In 1958, the Central Council on Education recommended adding two other tracks offering vocational and technical training to the overall 6-3-3 plan that the U.S. mission had recommended. By 1960, about 30 percent of high school students attended private, secular academic college preparatory schools. Such tracking moved in the public schools so that, by the 1970s, about a third of high schools offered only academic courses and another third of the high schools were strictly vocational schools. Further, in most Japanese cities, the students in middle schools who wished to continue their education had to pass competitive examinations that determined which type of high school they could enter. Despite the increasing specialization of public high schools, by 1970, about 40 percent of the students at the prestigious Tokyo University came from private academies.[74]

What Did Critics Think of the Influences of Independent Agencies on Education Around the World?

Trying to spread democracy, many American educators recommended models of education that favored a unified system of education leading to a comprehensive high school with academic programs, vocational training, and some sort of common or social learning. These were the ideas the U.S. forces of occupation imposed on the defeated countries of Japan and Germany. The educational proposals had appeared in various EPC documents.

Despite the popularity of the EPC's recommendations, many intellectuals disagreed with the EPC's contention that a country had to have a unified system of education including a comprehensive high school to prepare children for a democratic society. For example, a member of the U.S. Mission to Japan, Isaac Leon Kandel, complained that the emphasis the EPC placed on curriculum reorganization was misdirected. To Kandel, it was useless to adapt the curriculum to the needs and interests of the students and to rearrange the courses accommodating vocational and academic studies. He considered the training of the teachers to be more important than program changes, although he had found that few experts considered the problems of teacher education. According to Kandel, teachers should learn child psychology, they should possess knowledge of the subject matter, and they should have a thorough grounding in liberal or general education at the university level. The reason he found these elements important was that he believed the success of any educational program depended on the quality of the teachers' minds. Kandel found it contradictory that, on the one hand, the EPC asserted that teachers needed liberal education and strong preparation in their subject matters, yet on the other hand, the EPC removed the intellectual aspects of academic subjects in the curriculums for the students in *Education for All American Youth.* He wondered where the teachers would learn the theoretical aspects of subject matters if they graduated from high schools studying only the practical applications of academic subjects.[75]

In a similar manner, Arthur E. Bestor complained the EPC claim that schools should meet the needs of students and build curriculums on their interests was shallow. Those reports considered the purpose of education to be helping children solve children's problems. Bestor argued that schools should teach children to think in the disciplined ways found in the academic subject matters. In this way, children could prepare to solve the problems that adults face. Further, Bestor thought that the EPC list of needs implied that there were no agencies in society that could meet some of the needs better. For example, one of the needs was to help children maintain good health. Bestor asked if physicians and hospitals could do a better job in this regard than the schools.[76]

Bestor argued that the problem was that the members of the EPC distrusted intellectual subjects such as history or mathematics, and they protected their anti-intellectual prejudice by forming an interlocking directorate. When professors of education formed alliances with administrators and teachers of elementary and secondary schools, they protected their positions of power and influence by monopolizing discussions about education. Once the educators created commissions, they asserted that they alone had the expertise to solve problems of school reform. Bestor claimed that, in this way, educators prevented anyone outside the field from criticizing any ideas that these groups had accepted.[77]

Bestor's complaint about an interlocking directorate was reasonable. The EPC was not the only independent commission to influence education around the world. Another prominent agency was the United Nations Educational, Scientific, and Cultural Organization (UNESCO) that involved many educators and authors who had been part of the Progressive Education Association such as Julian Huxley, W. Carson Ryan, Jr., and Willard W. Beatty.

When the EPC published *Education for All American Children,* it called for international organizations to furnish leadership in developing techniques to promote interaction among schools and their communities. The EPC recommended that educators turn to the then newly formed, independent agency UNESCO because the members of the EPC believed that UNESCO would foster relationships between schools and the world community.[78]

After representatives from fifty countries met in San Francisco to sign the Charter of the United Nations, the U.S. delegate suggested forming a special organization to advance education. Various American educational organizations such as the NEA and the National Federation of Teachers supported this idea. Although the UN delegates agreed to form such an agency, they did not decide what it should do or how it should go about its work until later.[79]

When the delegates met in London in 1946, they created a specialized agency, UNESCO. An important aim of the organization was to build a climate of public opinion that would prevent Nazism from reappearing. Thus, considerable attention was devoted to establishing organizations such as worldwide radio networks that would provide means for different peoples to communicate. In order to advance such a climate of opinion, delegates argued that an effort to eradicate illiteracy was important. Interestingly, although Julian Huxley proposed an overarching philosophy of scientific humanism for UNESCO, delegates from the United States resisted. Thus, although UNESCO became an independent agency with a substantial budget dedicated to education, it lacked an integrating philosophy in the same way the EPC had lacked a comprehensive view of education.[80]

In an effort to create a UNESCO educational program, the UN delegates chose the name *fundamental education* to describe methods of adult literacy programs because it implied a type of training to which people could add something else. Although other terms, such as popular education or mass education, had the same connotation, they implied a focus on children or the use of methods of instruction that ignored individual differences. UNESCO called together a commission made up of fifteen world authorities to consider the issues. The discussions revealed that fundamental education was for people considered backward because of illiteracy or because of the failure to know a second language required by schools and other institutions. It was for children and for adults, and it was to blend some mastery of science and technology with the benefits found in traditional ways of life.[81]

Among the several progressive educators who joined UNESCO was Pedro T. Orata who moved to Paris in 1948 to serve as program specialist in the department that focused on fundamental education. In advancing fundamental education, Orata applied a model of curriculum that he had learned while he worked at The Ohio State University School as part of the Eight-Year Study. As described in Chapter 12, Orata had transplanted this curriculum idea to Little Wound Day School on the Pine Ridge Indian Reservation in South Dakota in 1936. To Orata, this model, which he came to call "fundamental education," enhanced democracy because people learned to follow Dewey's five steps of thinking by studying the situation, formulating problems, planning their solution, enacting their plans, and evaluating the results.

UNESCO's definition of fundamental education suited Orata. He claimed that fundamental education was the view that education should enhance health, improve family solidarity, provide vocational training, and teach people to live in harmony. To help people in underdeveloped countries achieve these ends, fundamental education combined instruction in literacy with citizenship training and community development. Orata believed that literacy was the means to improve the standard of living in the community. By helping impoverished minority groups become more self-sufficient, fundamental education reduced the problems of prejudice and neglect. Finally, fundamental education enhanced the meaning of democracy by enabling minority groups to participate more fully in the life of the community.[82]

UNESCO spread fundamental education. For example, Orata helped to create a project of fundamental education in Viani, Columbia. Located in the Andes Mountains, Viani was an agricultural community dependent on coffee, corn, yucca, anise, bananas, and sugar cane. Unfortunately, the exhausted soil in Viani was eroding. UNESCO sent a soil conservationist to Viani who began a program of fundamental education to teach farmers steps they could make to save their lands. The conservationist held seminars with schoolteachers to show them how soil conservation could become a core topic within school curriculums. Finally, the UNESCO expert organized young people who did not attend school to show them how to approach the problems of soil conservation scientifically.[83]

According to Orata, fundamental education changed the definition of adult literacy because it could teach adults to read meaningfully and thoughtfully. For example, he argued that in order for adults to understand the implications behind what they read, they must learn to read materials related to their daily occupations. In this way, they could learn how to find information from reliable sources. They would learn to be critical because they could tell whether or when the information was reasonable. Although Orata acknowledged that fundamental education was a slow means of encouraging literacy, he believed that it was most effective.[84]

The strength of fundamental education was that it served community development by enhancing adult literacy. Ironically, this strength led to its downfall. According to Phillip Jones, UNESCO introduced other programs of literacy to replace fundamental education because of interagency competition. By 1955, other agencies within the UN system, such as the UN Bureau of Social Affairs, claimed that development policy should come under their control as community development. In response to such complaints, Jones claimed that UNESCO replaced fundamental education with weaker notions of universal literacy.[85]

Although fundamental education may have been a strong model of adult literacy, critics such as Paulo Freire argued that fundamental education was not democratic. Freire contended that many such efforts to modernize developing countries represented cultural invasion. To correct this problem, Freire developed an approach to adult literacy that he called problem-posing education when he worked for UNESCO in Chile from 1964 to

1969. Freire's model depended on the adults and the teacher engaging in dialogues to critically examine their situations.[86]

According to Freire, the problem-solving approach that Dewey and Orata favored was authoritarian because the teacher had the answer and the students had to discover it. Freire believed that problem-posing education called for teachers and the students to work together to understand what he called a limit situation. In this way, the problem of authoritarianism disappeared, he thought, because teachers and students learned from each other.[87]

Although Freire hoped to make the aims of progressive education personally liberating, his ideas of literacy teams became as authoritarian as the curriculum ideas he opposed. For example, in 1974, Peter Berger complained that teachers who followed Freire's ideas tended to impose their views on the peasants they taught. This arose because Freire characterized the peasants as lacking the powers of reason that would enable them to understand their situations. As a result, teachers manipulated the peasants to perform actions the teachers thought reasonable to improve living conditions in the area.[88]

Conclusion

During the Great Depression and the postwar years, educators formed independent commissions in ways that imitated the approach that U.S. President Franklin Roosevelt took to cope with domestic and international problems. Although not directly involved with educational organizations, these commissions, such as the EPC, sought to gather information from a wide variety of sources and to recommend practical policies school people could adopt. The commission members began by working on issues of finance to provide stable support for schools. They moved into questions about the legitimate authority of state and local school boards. In addition, they made several statements about the proper organization of schools. Because these commissions included representatives with different perspectives, the conclusions satisfied the various interest groups involved. Unfortunately, they did not solve the contradictions that had caused the groups to hold the different opinions in the first place. For example, the idea that schools in a democratic society had to form a system that led to a comprehensive high school was to support democracy for three reasons. First, students could pursue their interests when they worked in ways that enabled them to develop their unique talents, and the students could develop common understandings when the students met their common imperative needs. Second, academic courses remained intact for college-bound youth, but youth with no desire to go to college would learn intellectual materials that were applicable to everyday life and work. Third, because the local communities controlled the schools instead of the federal government, a wide range of community groups and citizens participated in shaping and supporting the schools. The problem was that this model did not solve the contradiction between vocational courses and academic offerings. In fact, critics complained that the members of the EPC discredited the benefits that academic subjects could provide. Nonetheless, many educators joined to protect their conclusions. Furthermore, when educators served on educational missions with the U.S. forces of occupation, they tried to impose these ideas on the defeated countries of Japan and Germany. Another independent agency, UNESCO, sought to apply ideas from the Progressive Education Association to the problems of adult literacy. The aim of fundamental education was to teach individuals that they could find answers to their practical problems in books. Because there were ready-made answers to problems such as soil erosion or waste disposal, critics complained that fundamental education represented an effort to dominate the developing nations. Unfortunately, the plan to create a liberating, problem-posing education imposed a similar scientifically "democratic" way of thinking that turned out to be as authoritarian as the method it replaced.

Although American educators could not force the defeated countries to accept the comprehensive high school after World War II, they moved those countries to adopt some version of the progressive bias favoring the practical application of subject matters. These policies derived from several independent educational commissions. The faith in such commissions was that they represented democratic methods because the members represented groups with distinctive orientations and no government agency controlled the commissions. The commissions may have been independent, but they adopted similar programs that disparaged academic subjects as aristocratic. Nonetheless, these commissions fulfilled Henry Luce's recommendation that Americans accept the responsibilities of being world leaders and share their conception of democracy with the other countries in the world.

Endnotes

1. Henry R. Luce, "The American Century," *Life* (17 February 1941): 61–65.
2. David M. Kennedy, *Freedom from Fear: The American People in Depression and War, 1929–1945* (New York: Oxford University Press, 1999), 363–365.
3. Kennedy, *Freedom from Fear,* 365–380.
4. Ellis W. Hawley, *The New Deal and the Problem of Monopoly: A Study in Economic Ambivalence* (Princeton, N.J.: Princeton University Press, 1966), 3–16, 489–490.
5. Lawrence Cremin, *Transformation of the School: Progressivism in American Education, 1876–1957* (New York: Alfred A. Knopf, 1964), 318–320.
6. Kenneth Holland and Frank Ernest Hill, *Youth in the CCC* (Washington, D.C.: American Council on Education, 1942), 7–28.
7. Frank Ernest Hill, *The School in the Camps: The Educational Program of the Civilian Conservation Corps* (New York: American Association for Adult Education, 1935), 1–3.
8. Hill, *The School in the Camps,* 65–84.
9. Holland and Hill, *Youth in the CCC,* 148–165.
10. G. Wayne Cruey, *The Educational Program of the CCC: Its Provision for Leisure Time and Vocational Guidance* (Master's Thesis, Bowling Green University, 1938), 75–82.
11. Doak Campbell, Frederick H. Bair, and Oswald L. Harvey, *Educational Activities of the Works Progress Administration* (Washington, D.C.: U.S. Government Printing Office, 1939), 1–10.
12. Campbell, Bair, and Harvey, *Educational Activities of the Works Progress Administration,* 63–139.
13. Betty and Ernest K. Lindley, *A New Deal for Youth: The Story of the National Youth Administration* (New York: Viking Press, 1938), 3–4.
14. Lindley and Lindley, *A New Deal for Youth,* 12–16.
15. Lindley and Lindley, *A New Deal for Youth,* 16–19.
16. Campbell, Bair, and Harvey, *Educational Activities of the Works Progress Administration,* 141–157.
17. Lindley and Lindley, *A New Deal for Youth,* 184–218.
18. Paul R. Mort, *Federal Support for Public Education* (New York: Columbia University Bureau of Publications, 1936), 1–43.
19. Paul R. Mort, Eugene S. Lawler, and Associates, *Principles and Methods of Distributing Federal Aid for Education* (Washington, D.C.: U.S. Government Printing Office, 1939), 1–18.
20. Lloyd E. Blauch and Charles F. Reid, *Public Education in the Territories and Outlying Possessions* (Washington, D.C.: U.S. Government Printing Office, 1939), 10, 229–239.

21. Educational Policies Commission, *Federal Activities in Education* (Washington, D.C.: NEA, 1939), 132–134.
22. Educational Policies Commission, *The Civilian Conservation Corps, The National Youth Administration, and the Public Schools* (Washington, D.C.: NEA, 1941), 3–7, 73–79.
23. Edward A. Krug, *The Shaping of the American High School Volume 2, 1920–1941* (Madison: University of Wisconsin Press, 1972), 321–327.
24. Walter Stille, *The Educational Policies Commission, A Leadership Organ in American Education* (Ph.D. diss., George Peabody College for Teachers, 1958), 10–11.
25. Stille, *The Educational Policies Commission,* 13–16.
26. John A. Sexton, "The Educational Policies Commission," in *Proceedings of the Seventy-Fourth Annual Meeting of the National Education Association* (Washington, D.C.: NEA, 1936), 463–467.
27. Educational Policies Committee, *Planning Educational Progress, We Chart Our Future Policies* (Washington, D.C.; NEA, 1936), 13–21; Stille, *The Educational Policies Commission,* 16–18.
28. Educational Policies Committee, *Planning Educational Progress,* 5–11.
29. American Historical Association, Commission on the Social Studies in the Schools, *A Charter for the Social Studies* (New York: Charles Scribner's Sons, 1932).
30. Educational Policies Commission, *The Unique Function of Education in American Democracy* (Washington, D.C.: NEA, 1937).
31. Educational Policies Commission, *The Purposes of Education in American Democracy* (Washington, D.C.: NEA, 1938).
32. I. L. Kandel and Guy Montrose Whipple, eds., *International Understanding through the Public-School Curriculum,* Thirty-Sixth Yearbook of the National Society for the Study of Education (Bloomington, Ill.: Public School Publishing Co., 1937), ix–xii, 38–39.
33. Kandel and Whipple, eds., *International Understanding through the Public-School Curriculum,* 35–44, 45–54, 71–78, 193–200, 207–214.
34. Educational Policies Commission, *What the Schools Should Teach in Wartime* (Washington, D.C.: NEA, 1943).
35. Educational Policies Commission, *Education for All American Youth* (Washington, D.C.: NEA, 1944), 1–10.
36. Educational Policies Commission, *Education for All American Youth,* 15–17, 225–226.
37. Educational Policies Commission, *Education for All American Youth,* 34–35, 240–245.
38. Hilda Taba, "General Techniques of Curriculum Planning," in *American Education in the Postwar Period: Curriculum Reconstruction,* Forty-Fourth Yearbook of the National Society for the Study of Education, Part One, ed. Nelson B. Henry (Chicago: University of Chicago Press, 1945), 80–114.
39. The Committee, "A Program for Reconstruction," *American Education in the Postwar Period: Structural Reorganization,* Forty-Fourth Yearbook of the National Society for the Study of Education, Part One, ed. Nelson B. Henry (Chicago: University of Chicago Press, 1945), 295–320.
40. Educational Policies Commission, *Education for Young Children* (Washington, D.C.: NEA, 1945), 3–24.
41. Educational Policies Commission, *Education for All American Children* (Washington, D.C.: NEA, 1948), 99–156.
42. Ronald S. Anderson, *Japan: Three Epochs of Modern Education,* U.S. Department of Health, Education, and Welfare Bulletin 11 (Washington, D.C.: U.S. Government Printing Office, 1959), 18–21.
43. Anderson, *Japan,* 20–23.
44. Victor Kobayashi, *John Dewey in Japanese Educational Thought* (Ann Arbor: University of Michigan, 1964), 120–122.
45. U.S. Education Mission, *Report of the U.S. Education Mission to Japan* (Washington, D.C.: U.S. Government Printing Office, 1946), 1–2.
46. U.S. Education Mission, *Report,* 7–14.
47. U.S. Education Mission, *Report,* 12–13.
48. I. L. Kandel, *The New Era in Education: A Comparative Study* (New York: Houghton Mifflin Co., 1955), 10–11.
49. Kobayashi, *John Dewey,* 37–71.
50. Kobayashi, *John Dewey,* 110–111.
51. Very Rev. Msgr. Frederick G. Hochwalt, "The United States Educational Mission to Japan," *National Catholic Educational Association Bulletin,* 43, no. 1 (August 1946), 375–386.
52. U.S. Education Mission, *Report,* 24–31.
53. Japanese Ministry of Education. *Progress of Educational Reform in Japan* (Typescript, 1950), 1–12, 28–29.
54. Anderson, *Japan,* 36–50.
55. Ministry of Education, *Progress of Educational Reform,* 14–15.
56. Ministry of Education, *Progress of Educational Reform,* 16–17.
57. Anderson, *Japan,* 20–24, 78–81.

58. Second U.S. Education Mission, *Report of the Second U.S. Education Mission to Japan* (Washington, D.C.: U.S. Government Printing Office, 1950).
59. U.S. Education Mission, *Report,* 20–23; Robert King Hall, *Education For a New Japan* (New Haven: Yale University Press, 1949), 293–401.
60. Toshio Nishi, *Unconditional Surrender: Education and Politics in Occupied Japan, 1945–1952* (Stanford, Cal.: Hoover Institution Press, 1982), 199–209.
61. Nishi, *Unconditional Surrender,* 34–38; Kandel, *The New Era in Education,* 10–11.
62. James F. Tent, *Mission on the Rhine: Reeducation and Denazification in American-Occupied Germany* (Chicago: University of Chicago Press, 1982), 13–14.
63. Richard L. Merritt, *Democracy Imposed: U.S. Occupation Policy and the German Public, 1945–1949* (New Haven: Yale University Press, 1995), 32–35.
64. Tent, *Mission on the Rhine,* 110–114.
65. United States Education Mission to Germany, *Report of the United States Education Mission to Germany* (Washington D.C.: U.S. Government Printing Office, 1946), xiii–xiv.
66. *Report of the United States Education Mission to Germany,* 17–19.
67. *Report of the United States Education Mission to Germany,* 22.
68. *Report of the United States Education Mission to Germany,* 23.
69. Tent, *Mission on the Rhine,* 188.
70. William Benton, "Letter of Transmittal," *Report of the United States Education Mission to Germany* (Washington, D.C.: U.S. Government Printing Office, 1946), vi.
71. Tent, *Mission on the Rhine,* 119.
72. Tent, *Mission on the Rhine,* 126–127, 129–163.
73. Merritt, *Democracy Imposed,* 273–278.
74. Byron K. Marshall, *Learning to Be Modern: Japanese Political Discourse on Education* (Boulder: Westview Press, 1994), 195–205.
75. I. L. Kandel, *The Impact of the War upon American Education* (Chapel Hill: University of North Carolina Press, 1948), 101–122.
76. Arthur E. Bestor, *Educational Wastelands: The Retreat from Learning in our Public Schools* (Urbana: University of Illinois, 1953), 74–75.
77. Bestor, *Educational Wastelands,* 109–111.
78. Educational Policies Commission, *Education for All American Children,* 278.
79. Walter H. C. Laves and Charles A. Thomson, *UNESCO: Purpose, Progress, and Prospects* (Bloomington: Indiana University Press, 1957), 3–24.
80. George N. Schuster, *UNESCO: Assessment and Promise* (New York: Harper & Row, 1963), 3–9.
81. Special Committee to the Preparatory Commission of UNESCO, *Fundamental Education: Common Ground for All Peoples* (New York: Macmillan Co., 1947), 215–221.
82. Pedro T. Orata, *Educational Trends Abroad* (Manila, Philippines: University Publishing, 1954), 1–3.
83. Orata, *Educational Trends Abroad,* 4–5.
84. Pedro T. Orata, *Education for Better Living* (Manila, Philippines: University Publishing, 1953), 118–120.
85. Phillip W. Jones, "UNESCO and the Politics of Global Literacy," *Comparative Education Review* 34, no. 1 (February 1990): 41–60.
86. Richard Shaull, "Forward," *Pedagogy of the Oppressed,* trans. Myra Bergman Ramos (New York: Herder and Herder, 1997), 12–14.
87. Paulo Freire, *Pedagogy of the Oppressed,* trans. Myra Bergman Ramos (New York: Herder and Herder, 1997), 62–72.
88. Peter L. Berger, *Pyramids of Sacrifice: Political Ethics and Social Change* (New York: Basic Books, 1974), 111–120.

14

International Conditions Influence the American Curriculum

Southern School integration, Little Rock, Arkansas, 1957

Before World War II, American educators sought to spread uniquely American ideas of education such as the comprehensive high school explained in Chapter 11 and the activity movement described in Chapter 12. Immediately after the war, as noted in Chapter 13, independent commissions of educators tried to introduce these ideas to the defeated countries and to developing nations. With the rise of the Cold War, the process reversed direction. Instead of Americans exporting their ideas, educators in the United States found themselves changing school programs in response to shifts in foreign affairs.

In the United States, the Cold War caused American educators to undertake three important changes in schools. The first change was an effort to use the schools to teach children to distrust communism. Because the Cold War was an ideological conflict, educators tried to help children to appreciate democratic traditions and to disparage communism. The second reform was to reintroduce strictly academic programs and to remove the social utility previously recommended for courses in mathematics, science, and foreign languages. By 1957, when the Soviet Union sent a satellite into space, the federal government offered extensive financial aid to schools to train scientists and technicians who could build the weapons needed in armed conflict. The third change was the movement to end racial discrimination and segregation in schools. The federal government sought to advance civil rights during the 1950s because officials recognized that communist agents pointed to racial discrimination and prejudice to show the rest of the world that the United States could not live up to its ideal of democracy. When federal agencies moved slowly, a public campaign to end racial segregation overtook official efforts and pushed the federal government to speed up racial integration. As a result, the U.S. Congress passed and President Lyndon B. Johnson signed the U.S. Civil Rights Act of 1964 requiring racial integration and the U.S. Elementary and Secondary Education Act in 1965 offering funds to educate children from low-income homes.

The Cold War resulted from the inability of the United States and the Soviet Union to cooperate to keep the peace. It began with the defeat of Germany and Japan in 1945. The alliance among the United States, Britain, and the Soviet Union turned into a struggle to control Eastern Europe. When the U.S. provided aid to Western European countries through the Marshall Plan in 1948, the Soviet Union and other Eastern European countries refused to participate, revealing the split that defined the Cold War. Although the United States and the Soviet Union participated in various conflicts among nations around the globe such as the fighting between North and South Korea in 1950, they avoided direct armed conflict in their efforts to influence other countries. Katherine A. S. Sibley credited Walter Lippmann, a journalist, with coining the term "Cold War" to describe the belief that diplomats from the two powers could not settle the issues separating them. Although tensions declined during the 1970s, the Cold War did not end until the Soviet Union broke apart into fifteen newly independent nations in 1991.[1]

As these two countries competed for the support of other countries, U.S. officials sponsored contradictory educational programs in the United States. For example, on the one hand, federal officials sought to use the schools to achieve military superiority by creating programs to develop elite scientists. On the other hand, federal officials wanted to end racial discrimination and realize democratic ideals by requiring schools to provide equal conditions for all students. Rather than resolve contradictions caused by encouraging elitism and equality at the same time, officials increased their support of the various programs over the years. In part, this happened because the officials were more concerned with other issues such as relieving international tensions than with education, and they may have hoped that educators could blend elitism and equality by themselves. By the time the war in Vietnam ended in 1975, officials withdrew support from the educational efforts to increase patriotism, to improve academic programs in science and mathematics, and to integrate schools racially.

How Did Educators Seek to Reinforce Patriotism?

During the Cold War, the U.S. government sought to defeat communism. To aid in the effort, educators sought to meet the needs of youth in ways that helped students develop loyalty to their country and recognize the benefits of democracy. Consequently, the materials used in school courses and the attitudes of teachers became aspects of a patriotic education. Whereas teachers could discuss communism, members of the Communist Party could not become teachers. Because educators reaffirmed their belief that students should pursue their interests and learn to work cooperatively, organizations such as the NEA's Educational Policies Commission (EPC) recommended paradoxical combinations of censorship and teacher loyalty oaths with the recognition that everyone had the right to exercise academic freedom.

In part, the paradox developed because the EPC revised its recommendations repeatedly to reflect the changing world situation. For example, before World War II, the EPC called for open discussion of unfolding events. During the war, the EPC recommended that instruction about different nations could enhance international understanding and bring about world peace. Facing the Cold War, the EPC urged schools to withstand the threat of communist conspiracies. The following paragraphs illustrate these changes.

In 1939, as the war in Europe was escalating, the EPC recommended that schoolteachers help students distinguish between rumor and fact. This meant that the teachers had the responsibility to explain how reporters gathered news, to offer some insight into ways of distinguishing reliable information, and to enable students to recognize propaganda. At the same time, the EPC warned that foreign policy should not overshadow domestic problems because problems of poverty, unemployment, and inefficient government remained the greatest menace to American democracy.[2]

The Allied forces began to enjoy success in Africa, in the Pacific, and on the eastern front in 1943. Assuming that the Allies would be victorious, the EPC hoped that the allied countries would remain together as a United Nations to build a lasting peace. The EPC added that educators could assist in this effort by informing students about the necessity of cooperating with an international organization as it sought to build a lasting peace. Not only would this mean that teachers should demonstrate the mutual connections among the events in all countries, but such an organization should monitor the instruction in different countries to determine if any systems encouraged militarism and aggression. Finally, the EPC noted that educators in the various democratic countries had to offer school programs that could solve the economic and social problems the people faced or conflicts would reappear.[3]

Other educational organizations joined the EPC in suggesting ways that schools could foster international understanding. For example, in the 1945 yearbook for the National Society for the Study of Education, Howard E. Wilson recommended that schools expand the curriculum in two directions. First, Wilson wanted the curriculum to discuss the many different countries that had contributed to life in the United States. Second, he thought the curriculum should include opportunities for students to learn about many parts of the world, especially those areas rarely considered, such as Latin American, Asia, and the Soviet Union. To encourage teachers to learn about educational movements in different countries, Wilson endorsed the EPC's suggestion of forming an international organization that could facilitate cooperation among educators from different nations.[4]

The NEA asked its Committee on International Relations to consider ways that schools could enable youth to understand complex problems of international relations. Releasing its report in 1948, the committee noted that World War II had made Americans realize that events in nations around the world affected their lives. Because there were parts of the world and the United States where freedom, individual dignity, and restraint of authority did not exist, Americans had to defend their freedoms. On the international scene, this meant that Americans had to support the United Nations in its efforts to construct a world order based on law. Teachers faced the responsibility of imparting an understanding of the problems that surrounded young people growing up in the midst of international crises. To the NEA's committee, the hope for lasting peace came from schools that taught students how people in other lands lived and imparted to them a sense of the common humanity all people shared. The committee's report added that teachers could use such lessons to encourage students to desire world peace and to be concerned for people's well-being. According to the report, children could learn the human relations skills necessary for cooperative living by working together on various classroom projects, and they could experience the difficulties involved in resolving international tensions by participating in a model United Nations assembly.[5]

The newly created United Nations could have facilitated cooperation among teachers, and it could have provided a means to determine if different countries were pursing democratic educational goals. By 1949, however, the EPC admitted that the United Nations could not bring the Soviet Union and the United States together. Because the EPC thought there would be no peaceful solution to the conflict between those countries, the members of the commission outlined a strategy for American educators to follow in resisting communism. The steps included teaching accurate objective information about the principles of communism to young people. At the same time, the EPC noted that advocacy of communism would not be tolerated in American schools. Instead, teachers should advance the principles of the American way of life.[6]

Although the EPC did not explain where objective information ended and advocacy began, the report added that school districts should not employ members of the Communist Party as teachers. The members of the EPC justified this exclusion by noting that teachers had to think for themselves, and members of the Communist Party surrendered that obligation when they joined a movement characterized by deceit. At the same time, though, the EPC report warned against investigations seeking disloyal citizens because censors might attack people or burn books that expressed unique ideas.[7]

When the EPC warned against investigations, the United States was in the midst of anticommunist drives. From 1947 to 1954, the U.S. House Un-American Activities Committee and officials such as such as J. Edgar Hoover, director of the Federal Bureau of Investigation, mounted efforts to find potentially subversive people. For example, these officials screened over 20,000 government employees, causing about 400 people to lose their jobs. In 1950, U.S. Senator Joseph McCarthy from Wisconsin took the opportunity of a speech to a Republican club in West Virginia to accuse 250 government officials of being communists. When a senate committee called on McCarthy to testify, he could not support his charges. Thus, the committee called McCarthy's assertion a fraud and a hoax. In the midst of such controversies, the EPC reports avoided any mention of how school districts could determine whether teachers were communists. Many school districts adopted the simple method of requiring teachers to sign oaths professing loyalty to the U.S. government.[8]

In addition to teachers' loyalty, educators thought they could arrange academic subjects in ways that protected democracy. They organized the schools to allow students to pursue specific vocational interests and to provide opportunities for students to learn to function cooperatively. Thus, organizations such as the EPC repeated their recommendations that U.S. school districts adopt some form of the comprehensive high school. These were the same recommendations the CRSE made in 1918, the EPC made in 1944, and the U.S. forces of occupation made to officials in Japan and Germany after the war.

In 1952, the EPC published a revised edition of *Education for All American Youth.* As the title implied, the EPC wanted to design a program that could benefit every adolescent in the United States. The image the EPC conveyed was that students who were academically talented would attend the same building with young people who had no interest or talent for intellectual activities. Despite the differences among the students, the EPC believed that communities could arrange programs to enable all students to benefit from the time they spent together. Since they had made these recommendations in 1944, the EPC members praised in this revised version of their report the many communities around the nation that developed high school programs combining vocational training and academic preparation with guidance programs to meet the students' needs and to prepare them for life in a democracy. Although the EPC claimed that some communities had begun to change, the report lamented that the reforms had only achieved half the desired results because approximately 50 percent of American youth had dropped out of high school or did not receive the education they needed.[9]

According to the 1952 EPC report, officials in many different school districts in the United States had to accept the responsibility to adapt schools to the abilities and interests of different students. To overcome inertia, the EPC report recommended that educational and civic leaders in each community contact leaders in other communities and exchange information on how to make secondary schools appropriate for all youth.[10]

Because the Cold War was under way, the members of the EPC maintained the recommendations in 1952 that they had made during World War II. For example, the report predicted that international discord would continue for many years. Because young men would have to continue serving in the military during the Cold War, the EPC recommended that academic subjects impart the general skills and information that soldiers needed. This included training in mathematics, science, communication, and ethical behavior. Health was important because medical examiners had rejected a higher rate of candidates for military service during World War II than they had for World War I. The EPC claimed that improved medical and educational programs could correct many of the problems that had led to rejections.[11]

The EPC thought young women would play important roles in national defense, filling such roles as nurses, teachers, and social service workers. The needs in these areas should increase during a national emergency, the EPC predicted. Thus, the EPC report recommended that schools offer guidance activities to help young women learn those vocational skills as well as develop homemaking abilities. In addition, high schools should help those young women with academic abilities to attend college to train for professional positions.[12]

As in the 1944 edition of *Education for All American Youth,* the EPC's postwar version expected schools to meet the ten imperative needs of youth such as the need to develop salable skills and the need to understand the rights and duties of a citizen. To help students develop salable skills, the schools provided vocational preparation that included academic studies. To help students understand the rights and duties of a citizen, the schools offered a course on common learnings wherein students considered the social, economic, political, and cultural aspects of their communities. In addition, the students learned about health and engaged in activities to promote physical fitness. At the same time, they had opportunities to work with teachers to pursue their own interests.[13]

Since the members of the EPC believed that students had to learn about the scientific method, they recommended that students in elementary schools should perform simple experiments and explore their own natural surroundings. For tenth-grade students, the EPC recommended a course entitled "The Scientific View of the World and of Man" that would teach about scientists such as Pasteur and Mendel. In this one-year course, they would learn how science shaped the modern world and recognize science as the instrument of social progress.[14]

When the EPC had made the same recommendation about science in 1944, Franklin Bobbitt complained that the EPC did not place any specific sciences among their recommended courses. There were no classes in geology or chemistry, he claimed, unless a student wanted to pursue these subjects as part of vocational training or as special interests. Bobbitt concluded that a general introduction to science did not offer the students the chance to learn about science. It was a study of science with the science left out.[15]

In fairness to the EPC report, the commission members thought the aim of the course, "The Scientific View of the World and of Man," was to teach, in general terms, the influence science had on society. The more interested and talented students could work in small groups with other talented children to learn the science needed to enroll in academically challenging university programs. A general course to teach about science was important because young people with different abilities had to study some classes together in order for them to learn to work with different types of people. In other classes, students with special talents who were interested in careers in science could work with teachers who could arrange tasks to challenge their abilities. Under such an approach, all the students came to understand democracy and to develop their special skills.[16]

Although the members of the EPC thought that had found a way to produce the elite scientists necessary for social progress while enabling all students to recognize how science shaped society, critics claimed that the comprehensive high school was not a democratic institution. According to Joel Spring, it was a sorting machine designed to advance the industrial society. Spring argued that school people determined the students' abilities and interests. The teachers directed the students into programs that led to specific slots in the work force, in management, or in research. Thus, Spring contended that the aim of the comprehensive high school was to train children to become willing workers and obedient citizens.[17]

How Did the Cold War Influence the Teaching of Mathematics and Science?

Despite the possibility that the special programs for gifted youth reinforced elitism, federal officials recommended that the government create opportunities for elementary and secondary students to study specialized courses in science and mathematics when World War II ended. For example, because technical discoveries such as radar and the V-2 rocket had influenced military affairs, President Franklin Roosevelt asked Vannevar Bush, the director of the Office of Scientific Research and Development, in 1944 to suggest ways that the federal government could discover and develop those American young people with scientific talent. To answer the question, Bush convened a committee of experts to make suggestions, from which Bush wrote a report.[18]

Entitled *Science: The Endless Frontier,* Bush's report claimed that the security of the nation depended on the extent of scientific progress. He added that there was only a small group of men and women who possessed the necessary information and skills needed to develop such knowledge. Because the training for a career as a research scientist was long and expensive, many people with the talent could not pursue it. Another problem was that military officials had classified as secret many findings developed to aid the war effort. If many scientists could have this information, scientific progress might ensue. As a result, Bush recommended that the federal government establish an agency that would have two functions. First, it should provide scholarships for talented students to enter scientific training programs in colleges and universities. Second, the agency should create a board that would review existing research projects and release as much information as possible to advance scientific investigations.[19]

From 1945 to 1950, several members of Congress proposed legislation to enact Bush's proposal. Finally, in 1950, Congress approved and President Truman created the National Science Foundation (NSF). Although the enabling act described the functions of the NSF as promoting scientific research, it added that the NSF should promote education in the sciences. Although Bush had suggested that the NSF should furnish scholarships to talented graduate students at major universities, the NSF interpreted this aim to mean that it should support teacher education, provide for the creation of precollege instructional materials, and cooperate in improving elementary and secondary school systems.[20]

In 1953, the NSF informed colleges and universities that it had about $160,000 to support experimental programs in science education. During the summer, NSF organized four science teacher institutes. The summer of 1954 represented a small beginning. By 1965, the NSF spent over $165 million to support institutes for secondary science teachers. The reason for the growth was that many high school science teachers had not studied their subjects in college. For example, the American Association for the Advancement of Science (AAAS) recommended that science and mathematics teachers complete eighteen semester hours in their subjects as part of their undergraduate programs. When the AAAS compiled a study in 1963, the researchers found that as many as two-thirds of the teachers did not fulfill this requirement.[21]

The first efforts of the NSF to support curriculum reform began in 1954 as well. These expanded rapidly so that by 1966 the NSF supported publication of almost 280 texts and produced films on more than 500 scientific topics for high school and elementary students.[22] The NSF programs grew because the tensions in the Cold War increased. On October 4, 1957, the Soviet Union launched the first space satellite. Popular magazines warned that the United States had lost the technological supremacy needed to survive. President Dwight D. Eisenhower did not want to stimulate the accumulation of weapons. When he told the NEA that schools provided for the national defense, other commentators repeated the message that the Cold War was no longer an arms race. It was a brains race. As result, in 1958, the U.S. Congress approved and Eisenhower signed the National Defense Education Act (NDEA) that appropriated about $1 billion to various aspects of education if the states matched the federal funds with monies of their own.[23]

Although supporters of the legislation contended the NDEA would improve science and mathematics instruction, critics complained that the bill lacked a focus. They characterized the NDEA as a hodgepodge that offered something to everyone. For example, the NDEA was broken into parts or titles that designated funds to certain areas. One aspect provided loans for college and university students while Title III offered support to strengthen teaching in mathematics, science, and modern foreign languages in elementary and secondary schools. Although Title III offered to pay for state departments of education to improve the supervision of teachers, almost all the money in this title went toward purchasing equipment such as language laboratories or planetariums and remodeling buildings. Another aspect offered scholarships to universities, and a different title provided for guidance and testing services. A part of NDEA paid for teachers or professionals to study foreign languages and another part supported technical training for workers to enter a scientific field below the level of university research. The last title of the NDEA was for state educational agencies to develop their abilities to gather statistical information about the schools under their direction.[24]

If the NDEA offered something for everyone, it was because Eisenhower did not want to change elementary and secondary schools. In this regard, he took advice from James Conant, who was chairperson of the EPC in 1952 when the commission published *Education for all American Youth, A Further Look.* Conant claimed that American high schools were working well. Although Conant approved of the model of the comprehensive high school that the EPC had outlined, he noted that some programs required more financial assistance to function appropriately. According to Barbara Clowse, when Conant sent a telegram to Eisenhower containing these remarks, Eisenhower adopted them verbatim in a public speech he gave in Oklahoma City.[25]

In his speech in Oklahoma, Eisenhower claimed that the Soviet Union had a greater number of scientists than did the United States. Although he acknowledged that the United States needed more scientists, it also needed people who could approach social problems with wisdom and courage. Eisenhower acknowledged that the country needed people like Einstein to push the frontiers of science. He added that it needed people like Emerson as well to provide insight into human affairs. This was the view that Conant took and it was the reason why he thought the comprehensive high school was essential. The comprehensive high school could bring forth both types of leadership.[26]

In his special message to the U.S. Congress on January 27, 1958, Eisenhower assured his listeners that the basic structure of American education was sound. He had no desire to take control of schools from local communities, school boards, teachers, and state boards of education. The role of the federal government should be to assist the elementary and secondary schools in carrying out their roles. He acknowledged the efforts of the NSF, adding that NSF worked through scientific organizations, colleges, and universities to modify science education. Eisenhower said that he wanted Congress to approve additional programs administered by the U.S. Department of Health, Education, and Welfare (HEW) to strengthen general education.[27]

In 1959, Conant published *The American High School Today,* in which he advanced the views that Eisenhower had used. This was the report of a study that Conant had undertaken to determine if a community could maintain a true comprehensive high school. Although Conant noted that there were many variations of the model, he decided that those different arrangements did not depart radically from the ideal. Conant disagreed with the critics who complained that the comprehensive high school was in chaos and not a model. To Conant, the differences between rural high schools and those found in urban areas arose because communities differed. Although Conant was careful not to disparage single-purpose schools, such as specific vocational schools, he thought the members of all communities should improve their comprehensive high schools by displaying sufficient interest and supporting their school boards.[28]

Although the NDEA did not give HEW the authority to control school districts, it required school administrators to keep records of what they had requested, what they had received, and what they had spent. At first, administrators complained about excessive record keeping, but they adjusted to these accounting problems as the programs progressed.[29]

The NDEA did not require records to show evidence of the benefits federal aid produced. The reports from school officials showed that they used Title III funds to remodel and equip classrooms for improved instruction and to raise the number and quality of classes in science, mathematics, and modern foreign languages. For example, in 1962, schools remodeled more than 3,000 classrooms or laboratories. Several state agencies reported that schools changed science classes from the lecture method of teaching to student investigations in science with the new facilities. Such shifts implied improved quality of instruction.[30]

Since reports indicated that the NDEA had improved the instruction in science, mathematics, and foreign languages, the U.S. Congress amended the NDEA in 1964 to include support for history, civics, geography, English, and reading. In the next two years, Congress added support for courses in economics and in industrial arts. Thus, although the drive to improve national defense through science and mathematics dissipated, the U.S. Congress retained the idea that federal aid to education was necessary. As a result, Congress expanded the aid and came to recognize shortcomings in the administration of such aid. For example, in making a study of eighteen states a research team found that most states collected only subjective and informal information to demonstrate the effectiveness of the NDEA expenditures. Enrollments in certain subjects offered the most objective evidence of improvements.[31]

When the Modern Language Association (MLA) published its study of modern foreign languages in American schools, it noted that the NDEA had accelerated instruction in world languages. Before the act, three states had foreign language education supervisors. By 1965, thirty-eight states added such positions to their state departments. Most important, following the recommendations of James Conant, most school districts had added courses enabling students to continue studying a language other than English for more than two years. Elementary school programs had increased to over one million students and secondary enrollments rose to almost 2.5 million students. This represented about 25 percent of the high school population. In addition, the teaching methods turned from writing to speaking and hearing the languages. More schools used laboratories to advance speaking and hearing the language. Many schools tried to use media such as television and they adopted various programmed instructional devices to foster the teaching of foreign languages. The MLA report indicated that the areas that did not advance under the NDEA were linguistics and literary research. Although the MLA report noted that officials did not evaluate NDEA-supported programs, the report characterized the lack of different forms of evaluation as missed opportunities for foreign language professionals. For example, such studies could show the comparative worth of different approaches to instruction in world languages and indicate fruitful directions for the future.[32]

How Did the Cold War Influence Changes in Curriculum Theory?

Title IX of the NDEA established the National Science Service within the NSF, which took over the NSF's responsibilities to disseminate scientific and technical information. In the main, however, the NSF supported different activities than did the NDEA.[33]

The NSF was an independent agency. On the other hand, HEW was one of the nine departments of Eisenhower's administration whose chief administrators held positions on the president's cabinet of advisors. Because a director and a national science board controlled NSF, they could select the projects that they would support. This freedom was not available to HEW. Working with scientists and university faculty, the NSF took a more intellectual approach with its grants than could the HEW in administering the NDEA. Although the NSF supported teacher training at first, it moved into curriculum design.[34] In this effort, the NSF supported projects that made two major changes in curriculum theory. The first was that the curriculum project leaders came to think about the organization of the disciplines or subject matters rather than search for effective methods to teach the information. The second was that the NSF projects encouraged psychologists to follow the ideas of Jean Piaget who argued that children had ways of thinking that corresponded to the organization of the subjects. Jerome Bruner wrote about both of these ideas in a record he kept of a conference sponsored by NSF held at Woods Hole, Massachusetts in 1959.

Entitled *The Process of Education,* Bruner listed the several projects that the NSF had funded before the conference began. These included the Physical Science Study Committee that produced a series of films on physics and the School Mathematics Study Group that produced a series of textbooks designed to help children think more abstractly about mathematics. According to Bruner, what tied these projects together was that they conceived of each subject as having a structure. To Bruner, the structure was the set of fundamental assumptions that specialists used when they thought about their work. Because the assumptions were fundamental, they provided patterns of organization that held together a wide range of observations. Bruner added that when students learned the structure of a discipline such as mathematics, they could perform a wide range of new operations even though they did not understand why the answers were correct.[35]

The idea that a discipline had a structure was the first principle the scientists advanced. Such a conception of knowledge changed curriculum because it implied that subjects such as history, mathematics, and language did not evolve simply to solve human problems. They represented unique ways of thinking. Although the subjects might help solve practical problems, they had integrity in themselves. Furthermore, the formal relation of ideas interested scholars because those relationships made clear new ways of thinking. The trick in teaching was to have students find similar interests. For Bruner and his colleagues, the answer was that students could develop interest in the subject matter if they began to discover the structure of the subject themselves. As a result, the scholars produced textbooks, films, and teaching aides designed to help students discover the fundamental ideas in a discipline and realize why those ideas were basic.

The idea that each discipline or subject matter had its own structure led to the notion that children thought in ways that were roughly similar to the ways that the subjects were organized. To explain this idea, Bruner quoted the ideas of Piaget who claimed that children followed patterns of learning. That is, Piaget characterized the thinking of young children as corresponding to particular stages. Within each stage, the children could think in some ways but not in others. For example, a child of six or seven could recognize that the angle in which a ball approached a wall equaled the angle at which it bounced off the wall. As children approached the age of ten years, they could master increasingly complicated sets of such operations. What they could not do was move beyond the present reality of balls and walls to consider abstract or hypothetical events. To accomplish this feat, the children needed to think in different ways.[36]

Bruner arrived at a design for the curriculum by combining the idea that subject matters had their own structures with the view that children moved through stages of development. Bruner decided that children could learn any subject provided the children approached those aspects of the subject matter that corresponded to their stages of development. For example, if subject matter specialists decided that the essential concepts for the study of science included number, measure, and probability, children should learn these concepts in honest but simple forms in the lowest grades. As the children advanced through the grades, they could meet these concepts in increasingly complicated settings that matched the children's stage of reasoning. Thus, Bruner thought specialists should arrange the curriculum in a spiral twirling around the few fundamental ideas that provided the structure for the discipline and which reached up into information that is more complicated.[37]

Because Bruner was a psychologist, he was interested in how these views about curriculum related to theories about learning. He noted that in the late nineteenth century, psychologists abandoned the notion of general understanding and concentrated on studying the ways people acquired specific skills. The earlier notion depended on some understanding of formal discipline. Studies in the early twentieth century focused on whether or how a student could transfer training acquired in classrooms to other situations. Although those studies showed that the original theory misstated the role of faculties such as memory or judgment, Bruner added that the more recent work suggested that children could apply knowledge mastered in one context to another if they learned how to learn.[38]

According to Lee Shulman, *The Process of Education* was a landmark. Schulman credited Bruner with capturing the essence of the new psychology and the discovery method. At the same time, though, Shulman pointed out that Bruner did not invent those ideas. He pulled them together into a coherent whole. Although Bruner had based his curriculum on Piaget's psychology, he changed the arguments. Piaget had coined the notion of stages of reasoning to explain why teachers should not rush children into the study of academic subjects. Bruner took these ideas and flipped them into a plan to accelerate such teaching. Bruner did this, Shulman added, by reducing subject matters to a few simple ideas, and he believed teachers could present these ideas in a variety of ways. Shulman argued that Bruner would alter the setting or the presentation of the ideas as the curriculum spiraled upward. Thus, if a child needed one form of presentation to discover an idea, Bruner would put things in that form. If they could handle a more advanced form, Bruner would use it. For Bruner, the ideas did not change; the thing that changed was the form the ideas took.[39]

Although Bruner's ideas were controversial, specialists in a wide range of academic subjects formed groups to advance similar ideas. For example, in 1958, the NSF sponsored a conference of mathematicians about the training of research specialists. Instead of considering university graduate training, the participants approved a motion asking the American Mathematical Society and the Mathematical Association of America to meet with the National Council of Teachers of Mathematics to form a committee to direct reform of secondary school mathematics. When Edward G. Begle accepted the responsibility of directing the committee called the School Mathematics Study Group (SMSG), the NSF agreed to supply $100,000 to begin work on designing textbooks that would teach high school students to understand the basis of modern mathematics.[40]

When Begle explained what his group wanted to accomplish, he noted that mathematics had changed in the late nineteenth century. Instead of relying on intense and ingenious computations to solve problems, mathematicians began to pay careful attention to the structure of mathematics itself. They found that by attending to basic concepts, they could solve many difficult problems. By World War I, this approach to modern mathematics penetrated graduate training, and, by World War II, it influenced undergraduate college studies. Begle added that the hope of SMSG was to bring this approach to secondary schools and replace excessive dependence on drill and computation. Although the SMSG focused the first texts on college preparatory students in high schools, they turned to producing materials for junior high school students with a wider range of abilities. As a result, within ten years, the SMSG produced a textbook for each grade level from preschool through grade twelve. They modified texts for use with disadvantaged children from low-income homes, and they translated texts into Spanish for schools in Puerto Rico.[41]

The SMSG began a longitudinal study of mathematics achievement in 1962 that involved over 100,000 students in grades four, seven, and ten. Comparing groups of students using several different texts including the SMSG texts, the study showed that the SMSG texts were most influential in the lower grades. The older students did not profit from the SMSG texts to the extent that the younger students did. Beyond this simple finding, the results were complicated. For example, some textbook approaches were more successful than the SMSG in teaching computational skills. Because the various texts presented topics in different sequences, the timing of the presentation affected the students' achievement scores. Nonetheless, Begle was satisfied that the study showed SMSG texts to be successful.[42]

The efforts of the SMSG influenced mathematics instruction in Europe. According to Bob Moon, the ideas from the SMSG did not simply cross the Atlantic. He argued that groups such as the Organization for European Economic Cooperation (OEEC) had called for a conference in 1958 to consider mathematics education. The Mathematical Association of America aided in this work with a grant from NSF. Other groups such as UNESCO had studied mathematics education in the primary grades. Consequently, the OEEC funded a conference on mathematics education in the Cercle Cultural de Royaumont in Asnières-sur-Oise, France. Members of the SMSG, including Begle, addressed this meeting and described the ways they were designing textbooks.[43]

There was an interesting controversy about what happened to the new mathematics. The question turned on three points. One was whether elementary and secondary schoolteachers resisted new mathematics. Another was whether the scholars failed to produce a reliable approach to teaching mathematical concepts. A third was whether federal officials turned to other programs before the new programs could develop.

Historians such as Marvin Lazerson and his colleagues took the first approach. They contended that the problem was that mathematicians such as Begle did not realize how difficult it was to change teaching practices. The SMSG offered little teacher training. After a short time, enthusiasm for the new approach dwindled and disappeared.[44]

Another author, Bob Moon, took the second view. He claimed that the new math did not accomplish what it promised. As a result, educators in several European countries tried to reform school curriculums around the structure of the disciplines for ten years until 1969. Unfortunately, these educators encountered several problems, and authorities confirmed the reality of those difficulties. In 1969, Begle attended a conference of mathematics educators in Lyon, France, at which he told his audience that the results of studies of the SMSG had not clearly shown the superiority of the SMSG approach. Begle concluded that researchers should conduct more studies before extensive progress could take place. Such disheartening news caused schoolteachers to lose interest in the conferences about subject matter–based curriculum reform. In the years prior to 1980, fewer teachers and more university professors attended the conferences.[45]

The third view was that despite the promise of the innovations, agencies such as the NSF did not provide the money needed for extensive research. According to Robert W. Hayden, the problems of the late 1960s, such as the Vietnam War and efforts to eradicate poverty, overtook the desire to achieve technological supremacy in the world. As a result, the publicity and the grants turned to other topics. At the same time, university mathematicians returned to their classrooms and their research. Hayden concluded that the so-called failure of new math appeared greater than it was because federal officials stopped supporting it.[46]

In the late 1960s, federal support moved from improving science education toward efforts to reduce racial segregation and the problems of poverty. Research to find ways to help children from low-income families succeed in schools could have followed Bruner's line of reasoning. Most of it did not. Instead, most of the studies employed far simpler models of enrichment or basic skills remediation to prevent school failure of children from low-income families.

How Did World War II and the Cold War Influence the Civil Rights Movement?

As the Allied troops moved through Europe during World War II, they found evidence that Nazi officials had killed over six million human beings, mostly Jews whom the Nazis believed belonged to an inferior race. In reaction to the horror of such brutality, the newly created United Nations formed a Genocide Convention in 1948, coining the word *genocide* to describe the Nazi attempt to destroy a whole people based on race. In turn, UNESCO issued in 1950 a statement on race, hoping to end the myth that race determined mental aptitude, temperament, or social habits.[47]

UNESCO's statement consisted of twenty-one paragraphs comparing the ways anthropologists used the concept of race and the ways most people used it. For example, when people used the term *race,* they implied that human beings inherited qualities such as intelligence or personality through heredity. The UNESCO statement asserted that this was a myth because there was no evidence supporting the conclusion that there were inborn differences among human groups. Worse, people ignored the horrible effects such myths had caused during World War II by preventing the members of some so-called races from interacting with the rest of society. According to the UNESCO statement, such segregation prevented millions of human beings from developing normally.[48]

Before disseminating the statement of race, UNESCO submitted it for approval to a group of internationally prominent scientists from such areas as biochemistry, embryology, anthropology, and genetics. The hope was that the scientists' endorsement would lend weight to the statement, remove the basis of race prejudice, and encourage people to recognize the artificial barriers that separated groups from each other.[49]

The United Nations and UNESCO were not the first organizations that sought to discredit the concept of race. In the United States, arguments against racial distinctions became part of a movement against racism in the early years of the twentieth century. For example, in 1909, when white people rampaged through the black sections of Springfield, Illinois, Oswald Garrison Villard, grandson of abolitionist William Lloyd Garrison and president of the *New York Evening Post,* decided to hold the National Negro Conference in New York City. Attended by liberal newspaper editors and other popular leaders, the two-day meeting consisted of a variety of lectures. Leading scientists contradicted claims of Negro inferiority, and economists showed that Negro poverty derived from social situations, not from physical inabilities. W. E. B. Du Bois pointed out that Negroes lived within a new slavery because they were unable to vote in public elections, limited to vocational education, and denied civil liberties.[50]

In calling for an end to racism, the conference illuminated the divisions among white humanitarians and African American leaders. According to Charles Flint Kellogg, before the American Civil War, the activists seeking the abolition of slavery cooperated with liberals who wanted to emancipate women. By 1909, white suffragists felt such distance from the concerns of African Americans that they forbade Negro women from speaking at meetings organized to advance women's right to vote. Further, Booker T. Washington, a black educator, and his African American supporters rejected the aims of the National Negro Conference. They claimed African Americans needed to learn vocational skills more than they needed to cast ballots in elections.[51]

Despite the problems, Villard and other leaders of the conference created a Committee of Forty to form a new organization that would work to improve race relations. The members officially chartered the National Association for the Advancement of Colored People (NAACP) in 1911. In addition, they appointed Du Bois as director of publicity. In turn, he began publication of the official magazine for the NAACP, named *The Crisis.*[52]

From 1935 to 1938, the NAACP devoted considerable attention to lobbying the U.S. government to adopt legislation prohibiting lynching. To some extent, the NAACP lobbied for federal aid to African American schools and protested against the segregation of schools. These problems of discrimination increased in Northern cities as large numbers of African Americans moved from the rural South to the urban areas of the North and the West. At the time, school segregation was not an important concern for the organization. Nevertheless, the NAACP campaign against lynching brought Southern racial discrimination to the public's notice. It did not lead to the federal legislation the organization sought.[53]

A second means by which Americans came to recognize the evils of race prejudice was from popular fiction. During the Great Depression, the Communist Party supported several major American authors who pointed to the social problems caused by racial discrimination. For example, in 1937, Richard Wright became the Harlem editor of the communist newspaper *Daily Worker.* He gained wide public attention a year later with his book *Uncle Tom's Children.* In 1940, he published his best-selling *Native Son,* describing how racism drove the main character, an impoverished young black man, to his destruction. Five years later, in his autobiography, *Black Boy,* Wright wrote about the extreme poverty of his childhood home, the violence and prejudice that surrounded him in the South, and the way that literature offered him an escape.

A third important force making Americans aware of the contradictions within racism was the research sponsored by organized philanthropies. Although philanthropic organizations such as the Phelps-Stokes Fund and the General Education Board devoted considerable attention to the problems in the South, the Carnegie Foundation had distributed funds unsystematically. To organize a system for its contributions, the president of the Carnegie Foundation, Frederick Keppel, decided in 1938 that the corporation should sponsor a study of black Americans. Keppel chose to ask a Swedish economist, Gunnar Myrdal, to conduct the study and provided a staff of American social scientists with whom Myrdal would work.[54]

Writing the foreword to Myrdal's *An American Dilemma,* Keppel explained that he thought a study about the Negro in America was important to the nation, but he added that such work was too broad for a single university to undertake. Thus, it seemed reasonable to him that a private philanthropy should support it. In addition, such a study could help the Carnegie Foundation decide how to undertake future programs. Although Keppel knew many competent American social scientists with the skills to conduct such a study, he added that he chose a foreign social scientist because he doubted that an American could avoid the emotions surrounding the status of African Americans and approach the study objectively.[55]

When Myrdal began his work, he found that most studies of the Negro focused on aspects of the African Americans such as their education, their patterns of interactions, or their lifestyles. Myrdal decided not to pursue such a course because he determined that Negroes did not differ considerably from white people in basic human traits. Because white people held the economic, social, and political power enabling them to determine what happened to African Americans, Myrdal thought the difficulties arose from a white problem. On the one hand, white Americans professed a creed that valued freedom and equality. On the other hand, they restricted and hurt African Americans. To Myrdal, this contradiction went to the heart of the American civilization, infecting all human relations; it was not an isolated or separate difficulty. Calling the condition a dilemma, Myrdal found the contradiction to be irresolvable because white Americans refused to acknowledge that their actions were immoral. Nonetheless, Myrdal warned that Americans faced severe dangers. He quoted John Dewey to show that the attitudes of white Americans welcomed and supported totalitarianism.[56]

Although some academics, such as Robert Merton, complained that *An American Dilemma* was not helpful to social scientists, most reviewers praised the work. Surprisingly, the Carnegie Foundation did not celebrate its publication despite the overwhelming success of the book. Instead, Carnegie's officials discouraged funding any further studies of race relations.[57]

Whereas private philanthropies withdrew from studies of racism, President Harry S Truman created the President's Commission on Civil Rights in 1946. In his executive order establishing the commission, Truman wrote that he wanted to protect the liberties guaranteed by the Constitution. He added that the danger came from such incidents as in Monroe, Georgia, where a mob dragged two African American men, one of whom was a newly returned war veteran, and their wives from a car and shot them. Not only did officials fail to prosecute, they engaged in similar actions. The mayor of a southern city and a city marshal removed an African American soldier from a bus and beat him so badly that the soldier lost the sight in one eye. Consequently, Truman asked his commission to recommend what the federal government could do to grant everyone in the United States the freedom from fear.[58]

Submitting its report in 1947, when the Cold War between the United States and the Soviet Union was beginning, this commission agreed with Myrdal that racial discrimination was a moral problem. It resulted from white people who violated their own beliefs in freedom and equality. To reduce racial discrimination, the members of the commission recommended such measures as the elimination of racial segregation, the enactment of fair employment practices, and the end of restrictive covenants in housing deeds. To explain why the federal government should take these steps, the commission's report warned that foreign diplomats reported communist agents using examples of mob violence, lynching, and discrimination to prove American democracy to be a fraud. If the United States wanted other nations to stand with it in defense of freedom, the government had to find effective means of ending racial discrimination.[59]

In addition to providing reasons for ending segregation and discrimination, the president's commission suggested there was no need to ask the U.S. Congress to create new legislation to reduce racial discrimination. Instead, the commission's report noted that the U.S. Supreme Court could rule racial segregation to be illegal. According to Kevin J. McMahon, Truman accepted this advice. As soon as the commission released its report, the U.S. Solicitor General's Office submitted briefs seeking to persuade the U.S. Supreme Court to outlaw covenants in real estate deeds that would prevent white people from selling their homes to black families.[60]

Politics may have forced Truman to support civil rights more than he wished. According to Simon Topping, although black voters had backed Roosevelt, they were becoming dissatisfied with the Democratic Party because the Democrats who controlled Southern politics prevented the U.S. Congress from passing civil rights legislation. Truman needed the votes of African Americans to defeat Thomas Dewey in the 1948 election. Topping argued that Truman triumphed because African American voters turned out in strength to vote for him.[61]

Politics may have dictated Truman's stance on civil rights, but his Department of Justice continued to help the NAACP's legal campaign against segregation after the election. For example, in 1950, the Justice Department encouraged the U.S. Supreme Court justices to side with the NAACP in *Sweatt v. Painter* and in *McLaurin v. Oklahoma.* These cases concerned the racial desegregation of graduate university programs.[62]

The legal campaign of the NAACP had begun in the 1930s when Walter White and other NAACP officials decided to appeal to the courts to end racial discrimination. In 1896, in a case named *Plessy v. Ferguson,* the U.S. Supreme Court had agreed that railroad companies could require African Americans to ride in separate cars provided the separate accommodations were equal. Nathan Ross Margold had suggested that the NAACP attack the *Plessy* doctrine of separate but equal in various state courts on the grounds that the state governments did not provide equal funds to the Negro and the white schools. Margold did not think the NAACP should try to prove that the *Plessy* decision was wrong. He thought the more effective legal campaign was to contend that state governments had not abided by the decision.[63]

Charles Hamilton Houston undertook the task and, as dean of the Howard University Law School, trained such prominent civil rights lawyers as Thurgood Marshall, who carried on the campaign after Houston's death in 1950. Houston and Marshall began their campaign with cases arguing that African American teachers should receive the same pay given to white teachers. These cases occupied their attention from 1935 to the mid-1940s. In 1946, the NAACP stopped arguing teacher salary cases because Southern school districts revised their systems of determining salaries. Instead of using racial criteria, the districts formulated merit pay schedules. Because these salary scales depended on individual evaluations, the courts had to approve them even though black teachers usually fell into the lowest categories.[64]

The National Teachers Exam (NTE), later named Praxis, played an unfortunate role in the teacher pay disputes. In 1939, Ben D. Wood, a student of Edward Lee Thorndike, secured a grant from the Carnegie Foundation to enable his newly formed National Committee on Teacher Examinations to create an instrument that would measure the mental ability of teachers, their knowledge of liberal arts subjects, and their understanding of professional information. According to Scott Baker, this test promised to be an objective method that school superintendents could use to hire as teachers the most promising applicants. Baker added that Wood offered a different rationale to educators in Southern states. Taking advantage of the fact that African Americans scored lower on the tests than did whites, Wood suggested that states could use the test to maintain the lower salaries Southern states paid to African American teachers. In this way, the states could pay white teachers more while maintaining low school budgets. Because the NAACP was challenging separate pay scales in courts, South Carolina adopted a statewide salary system based on NTE scores. The test preserved the inequalities. Although about 90 percent of the white applicants taking the tests received the highest rating, less than 30 percent of the African American applicants scored as high. Because machines graded the tests, no one could argue that malicious graders changed the results.[65]

The NAACP's failures in cases of teacher salaries may have been fortuitous because, in 1946, the NAACP staff decided not to pursue cases that would lead to the equalization of facilities. Such suits implied that the NAACP accepted some forms of segregation. The

NAACP decided to prove that *Plessey* was wrong. Thus, the NAACP decided inequality was relevant if it was evidence to show that practices of racial segregation contradicted the U.S. Constitution. It was on these grounds that the NAACP built the cases making up the *Brown* decision.[66]

On May 17, 1954, the U.S. Supreme Court released its decision in the case called *Brown v. Board of Education of Topeka, Kansas.* The name was deceiving because the litigation involved four class action lawsuits. In addition to Kansas, the case included Clarendon County, South Carolina; Prince Edward County, Virginia; and New Castle County, Delaware. In writing for the court, Chief Justice Earl Warren noted that in an earlier case, *Sweat v. Painter,* the justices had decided that separate facilities for law students placed the segregated students at a disadvantage. Further, Warren quoted a lower court decision that held segregation with sanction of law retarded the educational and mental development of African American youth, and he noted that modern authorities supported this finding. Thus, Warren concluded that separate was inherently unequal.[67]

The NAACP lawyers had prepared to use social scientists in the trials that took place in the lower courts before *Brown* reached the U.S. Supreme Court. According to John P. Jackson, the lawyers wanted to prove that state-sponsored segregation caused feelings of inferiority among black youth. Because there were no studies of state-sponsored segregation, they looked at studies of segregation in general arguing that the state should not sponsor any practice that caused harm. For example, in a courtroom trial in Delaware, Frederic Wertham described psychiatric examinations he had made that showed that African Americans suffered from feelings of racial inferiority. The attorneys for the schools pointed out that Wertham could not show that segregated schools had caused the problems. Wertham agreed but added that many places and people indoctrinated the children with racial hatred. When the children went to school, they noted that the state required them to attend segregated facilities, and they believed it was because they were inferior.[68]

Although there were many social scientists who testified for the NAACP, Kenneth Clark received the most attention and the most criticism. As Jackson told the story, Clark and his wife, Mamie Phipps Clark, had conducted research in which they applied to young children techniques from studies of self-hatred. One set of studies involved using two sets of dolls; one doll was black and another doll was white. When the Clarks asked African American children which doll they preferred, the children tended to indicate the white doll. In another set of tests, the Clarks asked the children to color pictures to match, first, the color they were, and second, the color they wanted to be. The Clarks interpreted the results to indicate self-hatred.[69]

In 1963, critics of racial desegregation sought to reverse the *Brown* decision in the case *Stell v. Savannah.* According to Jackson, the segregationist arguments followed two directions. The first direction was to argue that school segregation was reasonable because the results of intelligence tests showed that average scores of African Americans fell below the average scores of whites. The second direction was to claim that social scientists such as Kenneth Clark misled the court. According to the segregationists, studies such as Clark's involved small groups of children with the children responding in ambiguous ways that experts could manipulate. They added that the testimony Clark gave in court did not match the content of his articles. Although the U.S. district court justice agreed with the segregationists, the justices in the court of appeals refused to consider whether racial segregation was reasonable. The only fact the justices in the court of appeals wanted to know was if any school officials had assigned children to school buildings based on their race. To these justices, since the *Brown* decision had determined that segregation by force of law was illegal, they did not have to reconsider that decision to dismiss the segregationists' pleas. The U.S. Supreme Court affirmed its decision in *Brown* by refusing to hear *Stell v. Savannah.*[70]

How Did Attorneys and Government Officials Expand the Meanings of the Brown *Decision?*

Although the Supreme Court's decision in *Brown* was short and the prose was clear, questions arose about what it meant. For example, the decision did not indicate what schools had to do to end discrimination or when school officials had to finish the process of racial integration. The answers to these questions came from two sources. The first source was the subsequent decisions of federal judges that expanded the meaning of the original decision. This happened because the American system of jurisprudence follows a tradition of common law in which decisions from cases accumulate to form precedents and justices refer to them in making subsequent decisions. The second source was legislation from the U.S. Congress. The following section will explain each of these directions.

According to Mark Tushnet and Katya Lezin, the justices had not answered many questions in *Brown* because they wanted to present a unanimous opinion. They left questions unanswered on which they could not agree. Thus, they trusted that subsequent decisions by lower courts would illuminate the direction events should take.[71]

After winning the *Brown* decision, the NAACP lawyers went on to win case after case. With each victory, they expanded the definition of racial desegregation. For example, in 1955, in *Brown II,* the Supreme Court confronted the question of when desegregation should occur. Leaving those decisions to lower courts, the Supreme Court asked justices to order prompt and reasonable starts so that desegregation could proceed with all deliberate speed. In 1964, with *Griffen v. School Board of Prince Edwards County,* the court prohibited a community from closing public schools in efforts to avoid racial integration. In 1968, in *Green v. County School Board of New Kent County,* the court decided that school districts had to do more than to offer children the freedom to enroll wherever they wished if few children took advantage of the opportunities. Attendance policies had to remove all racial discrimination and statistical evidence had to verify the extent of the desegregation. In *Alexander v. Holmes County Board of Education,* in 1969, the court refused to allow school districts found guilty of segregation to wait until every possible appeal ended before they acted. These school districts had to implement desegregation while the appeals process unfolded. Finally, in *Swann v. Charlotte Mecklenburg Board of Education,* the court decided in 1971 that a school district would have to transport children to distant schools if necessary to bring about racial desegregation.[72]

The NAACP's campaign of litigation was a slow process because it expanded school desegregation one school district at a time. As a result, Martin Luther King, Jr. complained that in 1963 only 9 percent of the African American students in the South attended racially integrated schools. He added that the U.S. Supreme Court's decision on school desegregation placed the burden on individual African Americans to bring legal actions to obtain their rights. King added this meant the most impoverished Americans had to face financially equipped adversaries in proceedings that cost tens of thousands of dollars. Because King believed that no voluntary organization had the necessary resources, he concluded the federal government had to help.[73]

When the U.S. Congress adopted the Civil Rights Act of 1964, it created another source to expand the meaning of racial desegregation. A variety of demonstrations took place around the South and culminated with the March on Washington in August 1963. The March changed popular attitudes about racial segregation, thereby encouraging the federal government to take a more active part in the process of school desegregation. It was impressive. As King noted, over 250,000 people came to the city for a period of three days to listen to speakers who called on them to advance civil rights. The cooperation of the white churches amazed King. During the bus boycott in Montgomery, Alabama in 1955, white religious leaders had not shown public support even if they were sympathetic. In 1963, King thought that the March had brought the three main religious faiths, Catholic, Protestant, and Jewish, closer together than had any other peacetime event. Since millions of people saw the event on television, King was convinced that the stereotype of the Negro had suffered a blow and race relations would improve.[74]

As King pointed out, millions of Americans watched the March on Washington on their television sets. Several other televised events had broadcast activists' efforts to advance civil rights. Since President John F. Kennedy took office in 1961, Americans had watched television portrayals of mob violence opposing racial integration. For example, when an African American, James Meredith, sought admission to the University of Mississippi in the fall of 1962, viewers watched as white demonstrators gathered to protest Meredith's entrance. Televisions carried pictures of the governor of Alabama, George Wallace, standing in front of the University of Alabama to prevent two black students from registering for classes. An extremely jarring set of images came from Birmingham, Alabama in April 1963 when police beat middle-aged women, dogs attacked young people, and high-pressure fire hoses sent people rolling down streets. When white segregationists realized that television cameras displayed these images across the nation, they attacked reporters and camera operators. As a result, newspaper and television coverage became more critical of segregationists. According to Robert D. Loevy, these continual reports of racial oppression caused President Kennedy to act in ways that favored civil rights legislation.[75]

Kennedy sent a draft of a civil rights bill to the U.S. Congress in June 1963. As had been the case with earlier civil rights legislation, conservative Southerners resisted. Calling the filibuster led by Southern legislators the longest debate in history, Charles Whalen, a former U.S. representative from Ohio, and his wife, Barbara, claimed it lasted thirteen weeks and filled records with more than four million words.[76]

Kennedy did not live through the filibuster. On November 22, 1963, as Kennedy rode in an open limousine through Dallas, Texas, two bullets struck and killed him. Lyndon Baines Johnson, the vice-president, took the oath of office that afternoon, and five days later, Johnson delivered his first speech as president. Taking the theme "Let us continue," Johnson affirmed his determination to honor Kennedy by signing the civil rights legislation that Kennedy had wanted. Nick Kotz contended that Johnson was the first president from the South to express a commitment to eliminate every vestige of discrimination based on race and color. Kotz added that Johnson's pledge caused civil rights leaders such as Martin Luther King, Jr. to respond enthusiastically.[77]

One aspect of the Civil Rights Act escaped critics' attention. Title VI promised that no person could suffer discrimination in any program receiving federal financial assistance. During the congressional debates, advocates for the legislation explained that the aim of Title VI was to ensure that various institutions followed the U.S. Supreme Court decisions. Such a requirement may have seemed innocuous in 1964 when districts could not close public schools to avoid racial desegregation. The requirements grew as the NAACP forced the court to expand the meaning of its original decision. As a result, by 1968, in *Green v. County School Board of New Kent County,* the court required school districts to undertake complete racial desegregation.[78]

Although the legislation delegated the authority to define and end discrimination to the U.S. Department of Health, Education, and Welfare (HEW), the agency could not act on its own. Before any guidelines could take effect, the president had to approve them. Because the HEW staff had nothing to guide them, they drafted standards that followed the Supreme Court decisions and mailed them to schools throughout the South.[79]

According to Gary Orfield, HEW administered a social revolution during the summer of 1965. The racial integration of Southern schools increased more than 100 percent. Most school districts ended total segregation of faculty members. Furthermore, student integration increased from 6 percent to 16 percent. Orfield added that this was an exceptional change to take place in one year. He argued that it happened because, for this short period, the public was overwhelmingly committed, a presidential election made the votes of African Americans appear to be important, and the president was willing to risk alienating people who opposed these plans.[80]

In 1965, with the adoption of the Elementary and Secondary Education Act (ESEA), the threat of terminating federal funds became significant. ESEA directed nearly one billion dollars of federal aid to local schools for the education of children called culturally deprived. During the 1964 presidential campaign, Johnson had promised that he would take steps to end poverty. Neither supporters nor critics pointed out during the congressional debates that ESEA offered a means to make Title VI meaningful. Once the president had signed the bill, the director of HEW, Francis Keppel, pointed out that ESEA could turn Title VI into a means to encourage further progress in racial desegregation of schools. Those districts that strove to abide by Title VI would qualify for the new monies.[81]

The thrust of curriculum reform under ESEA was to enable children from low-income homes to enjoy increased academic success. During the 1950s, most educators believed that the migration of African Americans from the rural South caused these problems. As a result, the superintendents and board members of the largest cities formed the Great Cities Program for School Improvement. Believing that racial integration would not help the so-called culturally deprived black youth, the schools in these cities created more than forty different programs, such as Higher Horizons in New York City, seeking to help these children learn to learn.[82]

Writing in 1962, Deborah Partridge Wolfe defined culturally deprived children as those who were born into a narrow level of society from which they could not move. Unable to participate in the wider culture, these children suffered from deprivation that was physical and intellectual. Wolfe contended that rural African Americans developed weak or deformed bodies because they lacked milk, fruits, and vegetables to eat. She added that Negroes living in rural and in urban areas suffered from poor linguistic development that retarded their intellectual growth. Consequently, she urged schools to emphasize health needs, to widen the recreational activities of the children offering them chances to create and appreciate beauty, and to provide improved personal and vocational guidance. To prove that a city school district could meet such objectives, Wolfe quoted the director of New York City's Higher Horizons program who claimed the students displayed more interest in school because of the interventions.[83]

With the approval of ESEA, the U.S. Office of Education (USOE) and a variety of other governmental agencies distributed information similar to that of Wolfe to introduce educators to the ideas of education of disadvantaged children. The USOE's Educational Research and Information Center (ERIC) abstracted and put on microfilm over 1,700 documents on the education of the disadvantaged.[84]

As the USOE drafted the guidelines for implementation, officials faced the problem that the ESEA funds could cause racial segregation. Because the money was for disadvantaged children, school districts could place African American students in the same classrooms but separate from white children, claiming that such segregation enabled teachers to give the black children the appropriate aid. For the first year, the USOE did not address this problem. During the second year, federal officials sent school administrators warnings that they could not receive federal funds unless they moved toward racial desegregation and the assurances that the money would follow the disadvantaged children into the desegregated classrooms.[85]

While the Congress drafted the ESEA, Senator Robert F. Kennedy, brother of the former president, urged that an amendment be added to require school districts accepting the federal funds to institute objective measures annually to demonstrate the effectiveness of the provisions in meeting children's needs. According to Stephen K. Bailey and Edith K. Mosher, this requirement was an unprecedented mandate. Nonetheless, they added that the USOE tried to comply. The reports that came back to the USOE were not objective, though. At best, they were anecdotal reports that described children being pleased that they received tutorial help or that the children enjoyed trips to the zoo paid for by the ESEA funds. Despite the impressionistic tone of the reports, it was clear to Bailey and Mosher that schools offered more attention to disadvantaged children and that school dropouts could take advantage of more programs, even though school officials did not measure the impact of these interventions on educational achievement.[86]

In bringing about school desegregation, Title VI was the important aspect of the Civil Rights Act, yet it did not work by itself. The act had two other provisions contained in Title IV that complimented the requirement in Title VI. One part of Title IV authorized the U.S. Department of Justice to initiate lawsuits against school districts that refused to undergo racial desegregation. Thus, the federal government could move against a school district that decided to go without federal funds and remain segregated. Another part of Title IV offered federal support for technical assistance in human relations instruction or in methods of teaching disadvantaged children to school districts undergoing racial desegregation. In addition, Title IV offered to pay consultants to advise school officials in ways to involve community members in school desegregation plans. Although Congress initially appropriated $4.6 million for Title IV programs, the appropriations grew to over $19 million by 1971.[87]

The aim of Title IV was to recruit local educational professionals to act as consultants to school districts undergoing school desegregation. The U.S. Office of Education established guidelines and monitored the ways that state and local education agencies used Title IV funds. Because state and local educational agencies had ties to colleges and universities, they should have been able to recruit professors to act as consultants and obtain Title IV grants to support them. When the U.S. Commission on Civil Rights evaluated the influence of Title IV, the report claimed that Title IV programs were weak and ineffectual. The commission blamed the failure on the local connections that should have made Title IV a success. That is, local authorities and experts were unwilling to take bold steps to advance the controversial programs of school desegregation on fears that they would harm their local reputations.[88]

Conclusion

The Cold War inspired three types of school reforms. The first was to encourage appreciation for democracy among the students. Besides requiring teachers to be patriotic and to express faith in American traditions, educators believed that organizational arrangements such as the comprehensive high school would advance democracy by allowing students to develop their talents while they learned to work with other people with different interests. The second reform was to change the curriculum to produce elite scientists who could improve military defenses. Some educators thought the comprehensive high school would meet his need because it allowed talented students to pursue challenging studies with knowledgeable teachers. Other educators believed the curriculum should change to reveal the structure of the subject matters to the students. The third reform was to end the racial discrimination found in schools so that people in foreign countries could see that Americans lived up to their ideals. This required that schools racially desegregate. The link between poverty and segregation encouraged the federal government to pass the ESEA, offering financial support to help schools break the cycle of poverty.

Although these programs did not compete openly, they moved in different directions. For example, when the EPC forbade teachers to belong to the Communist Party or to suggest the superiority of communism, the warning limited teachers' abilities to present objective information about world conflicts. Similarly, the comprehensive high school could not train elite scientists and advance democracy. Placing children in different tracks reinforced distinctions based on occupations. Finally, efforts to enable low-income children to succeed in schools distracted school people from arranging the curriculum around the structure of the subject matters to prepare college-bound youth for advanced studies in science or math.

Officials did not seek to resolve these contradictions. Instead, as time passed federal interest in anticommunism declined as did support for math and science programs. The decision to end these programs appeared to be similar to the reason for starting them. Their value came from their promise to strengthen the United States in the Cold War. As a result, although the reforms aimed at changing schools within the United States, the motive appeared to be that those changes would enable federal officials to maintain and spread American ideals elsewhere. This was also the case with efforts to end racial discrimination, which continued for some years beyond the other efforts described in this chapter.

Endnotes

1. Katherine A. S. Sibley, *The Cold War* (Westport, Conn.: Greenwood Press, 1998), 3–33.
2. Educational Policies Commission, *American Education and the War in Europe* (Washington, D.C.: NEA, 1939), 1–10.
3. Educational Policies Commission, *Education and the People's Peace* (Washington, D.C.: NEA, 1943), 5–14, 52–56.
4. Howard Wilson, "Postwar Education for International Understanding," in *American Education in the Postwar Period: Part one, Curriculum Reconstruction,* Forty-Fourth Yearbook of the National Society for the Study of Education, ed. Nelson B. Henry (Chicago: University of Chicago Press, 1945), 246–266.
5. National Education Association, Committee on International Relations, *Education for International Understanding in American Schools: Suggestions and Recommendations* (Washington, D.C.: National Education Association, 1948), 1–14, 109–118, 187–191.
6. Educational Policies Commission, *American Education and International Tensions* (Washington, D.C.: NEA, 1949), 1–4, 35–38.
7. Educational Policies Commission, *American Education and International Tensions,* 38–40.
8. Sibley, *The Cold War,* 37–42.
9. Educational Policies Commission, *Education for All American Youth: A Further Look* (Washington, D.C.: NEA, 1952), 1–11.
10. Educational Policies Commission, *Education for All American Youth: A Further Look,* 10–11.
11. Educational Policies Commission, *Education for All American Youth: A Further Look,* 11–16.
12. Educational Policies Commission, *Education for All American Youth: A Further Look,* 16–17.
13. Educational Policies Commission, *Education for All American Youth: A Further Look,* 216, 230–238.
14. Educational Policies Commission, *Education for All American Youth: A Further Look,* 129–132.
15. Franklin Bobbitt, "The Educational Policies Commission Banishes Science," *Scientific Monthly* 63, no. 2 (August 1946): 117–124.
16. Educational Policies Commission, *Education for All American Youth: A Further Look,* 279–280.
17. Joel Spring, *The Sorting Machine: National Educational Policy Since 1945* (New York: David McKay Co., 1976), 1–3.
18. Vannevar Bush, *Science: The Endless Frontier* (1945; reprint, Washington, D.C.: National Science Foundation, 1960), 1–4.
19. Bush, *Science: The Endless Frontier,* 5–9.
20. Dorothy Schaffter, *The National Science Foundation* (New York: Frederick A. Praeger, Publisher, 1969), 95–100.
21. Hillier Krieghbaum, *An Investment in Knowledge: The First Dozen Years of the National Science Foundation's Summer Institutes Programs to Improve Secondary School Science and Mathematics Teaching* (New York: New York University Press, 1969), 3–14, 123–129.
22. Schaffter, *The National Science Foundation,* 104–105.
23. Barbara Barksdale Clowse, *Brainpower for the Cold War: The Sputnik Crisis and National Defense Education Act of 1958* (Westport, Conn.: Greenwood Press, 1981), 17–27.
24. Clowse, *Brainpower for the Cold War,* 144: Sidney C. Sufrin, *Administering the National Defense Education Act* (Syracuse, N.Y.: Syracuse University Press, 1963), 16–27.
25. Clowse, *Brainpower for the Cold War,* 56–57.
26. Dwight D. Eisenhower, "Radio and Television Address to the American People on Our Future Security, 13 November 1957," *Public Papers of the Presidents of the United States: Dwight D. Eisenhower, 1957* (Washington, D.C.: U.S. Government Printing Office, 1958), 807–817; James Bryant Conant, *The American High School Today: A First Report to Interested Citizens* (New York: McGraw-Hill Co., 1959), 95–96.
27. Dwight D. Eisenhower, "Special Message to the Congress on Education, 27 January 1958," *Public Papers of the Presidents of the United States: Dwight D. Eisenhower, 1958* (Washington, D.C.: U.S. Government Printing Office, 1959), 127–132.
28. Conant, *The American High School Today,* 1–9, 41–76.
29. Clowse, *Brainpower for the Cold War,* 139–151.
30. U.S. Department of Health, Education, and Welfare, *Report on the National Defense Education Act Fiscal Years 1961 and 1962* (Washington, D.C.: U.S. Government Printing Office, 1963).
31. U.S. Department of Health, Education, and Welfare, *NDEA Title III Fiscal Years 1959–1967: A Management View* (Washington, D.C.: U.S. Government Printing Office, 1969), 3–8, 30–31.
32. John S. Diekhoff, *NDEA and Modern Foreign Languages* (New York: Modern Foreign Language Association, 1965), 1–9, 35–50.
33. Schaffter, *The National Science Foundation,* 127, 161; Clowse, *Brainpower for the Cold War,* 4.

34. Schaffter, *The National Science Foundation,* 22–33; Clowse, *Brainpower for the Cold War,* 136–137.
35. Jerome Bruner, *The Process of Education* (Cambridge, Mass.: Harvard University Press, 1960), 2–8.
36. Bruner, *The Process of Education,* 31–38.
37. Bruner, *The Process of Education,* 33, 38–54.
38. Bruner, *The Process of Education,* 5–6.
39. Lee S. Shulman, "Psychology and Mathematics Education," in *Mathematics Education,* The Sixty-Ninth Yearbook of the National Society for the Study of Education, ed. Edward G. Begle (Chicago: University of Chicago Press, 1970), 23–73.
40. William Wooton, *SMSG: The Making of a Curriculum* (New Haven: Yale University Press, 1965), 8–16.
41. Edward G. Begle, "SMSG: Where We Are Today," *Confronting Curriculum Reform,* ed. Elliot W. Eisner (Boston: Little, Brown and Co., 1971), 68–82.
42. Edward G. Begle and James W. Wilson, "Evaluation of Mathematics Programs," *Mathematics Education,* the Sixty-Ninth Yearbook of the National Society for the Study of Education, ed. Edward G. Begle (Chicago: University of Chicago Press, 1970), 367–404.
43. Bob Moon, *The 'New Maths' Curriculum Controversy: An International Story* (London: Falmer Press, 1986), 43–52.
44. Marvin Lazerson, Judith Block McLaughlin, and Bruce McPherson, "New Curriculum, Old Issues," *Teachers College Record* 86, no. 2 (Winter 1984): 299–319.
45. Moon, *The 'New Maths,'* 57–58.
46. Robert W. Hayden, "A History of the 'New Mathematics' in the United States" (Ph.D. diss., Iowa State University, 1981), 240–244.
47. Clark M. Eichelberger, *UN: The First Twenty-Five Years* (New York: Harper & Row, 1970), 78.
48. Ashley Montagu, *Statement on Race* (New York: Henry Schuman, 1951), 3–20.
49. Montagu, *Statement on Race,* 18–19.
50. Charles Flint Kellogg, *NAACP: A History of the National Association for the Advancement of Colored People,* vol. 1 (Baltimore, Johns Hopkins Press, 1967), 9–22.
51. Kellogg, *NAACP*, 23–28.
52. Kellogg, *NAACP*, 28–52.
53. Walter A. Jackson, *Gunnar Myrdal and America's Conscience: Social Engineering and Racial Liberalism, 1938–1987* (Chapel Hill: University of North Carolina Press, 1990), 6–7.
54. Jackson, *Gunnar Myrdal and America's Conscience,* 25–27.
55. F. P. Keppel, foreword to *An American Dilemma,* vol. 1, by Gunnar Myrdal (New York: Harper & Row, 1944; reprint, New York: McGraw-Hill Co., 1964).
56. Gunnar Myrdal, *An American Dilemma,* vol. 1 (New York: Harper & Row, 1944; reprint, New York: McGraw-Hill Co., 1964), lxix–lxxix.
57. Stephen Graubard, "An American Dilemma Revisited," in *An American Dilemma Revisited,* ed. Obie Clayton, Jr. (New York: Russell Sage Foundation, 1996), 1–24.
58. David McCullough, *Truman* (New York: Simon & Schuster, 1992), 588–589.
59. President's Committee on Civil Rights, To Secure These Rights (New York: Simon and Schuster, 1947), 4, 146–148.
60. Kevin J. McMahon, *Reconsidering Roosevelt on Race: How the Presidency Paved the Road to Brown* (Chicago: University of Chicago Press, 2004), 187–189.
61. Simon Topping, " 'Never Argue with the Gallup Poll': Thomas Dewey, Civil Rights and the Election of 1948," *Journal of American Studies* 38, no. 2 (2004), 179–198.
62. McMahon, *Reconsidering Roosevelt,* 192–193.
63. Lawrence A. Cremin, *American Education: The Metropolitan Experience, 1876–1980* (New York: Harper & Row, 1988), 196–200.
64. Mark V. Tushnet, *Making Civil Rights Law: Thurgood Marshall and the Supreme Court, 1936–1961* (New York: Oxford University Press, 1994), 116–121; Scott Baker, "Testing Equality: The National Teacher Examination and the NAACP's Legal Campaign to Equalize Teacher's Salaries in the South, 1936–63," *History of Education Quarterly* 35, no.1 (1995): 49–64.
65. Baker, "Testing Equality," 49–64.
66. Tushnet, *Making Civil Rights Law,* 147–149.
67. Richard Kluger, *Simple Justice: The History of Brown v. Board of Education and Black America's Struggle for Equality* (New York: Vintage Books, 1975), 780–782.
68. John P. Jackson, *Social Scientists for Social Justice: Making the Case against Segregation* (New York: New York University Press, 2001), 125–131.
69. Jackson, *Social Scientists,* 139–145.
70. John P. Jackson, Jr., *Science for Segregation: Race Laws and the Case against Brown v. Board of Education* (New York: New York University Press, 2005), 131–147.

71. Mark Tushnet and Katya Lezin, "What Really Happened in *Brown v. Board of Education,*" *Columbia Law Review* 91 (December 1991): 1867–1930.
72. Rosemary C. Salomone, *Equal Education under Law: Legal Rights and Federal Policy in Post-Brown Era* (New York: St. Martin's Press, 1986), 45–48.
73. Martin Luther King, Jr., *Why We Can't Wait* (New York: New American Library, 1963), 142–143.
74. King, *Why We Can't Wait,* 123–124.
75. Robert D. Loevy, "Introduction," in *The Civil Rights Act of 1964: The Passage of the Law that Ended Racial Segregation,* ed. Robert D. Loevy (New York: State University of New York Press, 1997), 1–48.
76. Charles and Barbara Whalen, *The Longest Debate: A Legislative History of the 1964 Civil Rights Act* (Cabin John, Md.: Seven Locks Press, 1985), 192–193.
77. Nick Kotz, *Judgment Days: Lyndon Baines Johnson, Martin Luther King, Jr., and the Laws that Changed America* (Boston: Houghton Mifflin Co., 2005), 32–33.
78. Gary Orfield, *The Reconstruction of Southern Education: The Schools and the 1964 Civil Rights Act* (New York: Wiley-Interscience, 1969), 36–45.
79. Orfield, *The Reconstruction of Southern Education,* 98–99.
80. Orfield, *The Reconstruction of Southern Education,* 147–150.
81. Stephen K. Bailey and Edith K. Mosher, *ESEA: The Office of Education Administers a Law* (New York: Syracuse University Press, 1968), 39–41; Orfield, *The Reconstruction of Southern Education,* 94.
82. Bailey and Mosher, *ESEA,* 8–9.
83. Deborah Partridge Wolfe, "Curriculum Adaptations for the Culturally Deprived," *Journal of Negro Education* 31, no. 2 (Spring 1962): 139– 151.
84. Bailey and Mosher, *ESEA,* 128–133.
85. Bailey and Mosher, *ESEA,* 149–150.
86. Bailey and Mosher, *ESEA,* 50–51, 162–167.
87. U.S. Commission on Civil Rights, *Title IV and School Desegregation: A Study of Neglected Federal Program* (Washington, D.C.: U.S. Government Printing Office, 1973), 1–3.
88. U.S. Commission on Civil Rights, *Title IV and School Desegregation,* 43–44.

15

Pluralism, Effective Education, and Choice

U.S. president Ronald Reagan, 1980s

Until 1969, the Cold War inspired educational changes designed to help Americans fulfill their ideals and to preserve world peace. In a short period, the national mood changed and people turned away from concerns for civil rights and away from the belief that the United States should act as guardian of world peace. According to many commentators, people lost the desire to carry out the reforms because of urban riots and the fighting in

Vietnam. The result was that the racial desegregation of schools slowed, and political leaders recommended that teachers pay increased attention to basic academic instruction. Although politicians wanted the schools to maintain the supremacy of the United States throughout the 1970s and the 1980s, they did not want the schools to produce able scientists as much as they sought competent workers and soldiers.

As had been the case during the late 1940s and 1950s, officials continued to point to foreign affairs to justify curriculum reforms. The direction of the reforms changed, however. Instead of forcing racial integration, officials called for more local control of schools. Instead of suggesting students should pursue interesting activities or master the structure of the subject matters, models of curriculum reform required that teachers challenge the students with more homework and that administrators make school days longer. Finally, during the 1990s, political leaders and educators rejected the model of the comprehensive high school as an instrument of democracy. Instead, they sought mechanisms that enabled parents to select the children's school such as smaller schools and market systems. The result was that, as parents exercised choices, they exacerbated the racial and ethnic segregation of schools making it difficult for schools to reinforce the ethic of democracy.

Explaining the policy shifts, John A. Andrew III suggested that the turn began in 1966. According to Jackson, from 1964 to 1966, President Lyndon Johnson pushed through the U.S. Congress a burst of legislation that approached the level of reforms undertaken during the New Deal of the 1930s. Designed to usher in the Great Society, Johnson's domestic reforms enhanced school desegregation through the Civil Rights Act and the Elementary and Secondary Education Act. After 1966, the coalition supporting civil rights fell apart. Andrew claimed that some black leaders called for separatism, and riots broke out in cities such as Los Angeles and Detroit. White people felt alienated from the war on poverty.[1]

The shift of public opinion was rapid and dramatic. For example, according to James L. Sundquist, in 1965, public opinion polls measured 90 percent approval for voting rights bills and over 70 percent approval of antipoverty legislation. One year later, in October 1966, the president lost a civil rights bill that offered fair housing provisions, and public opinion polls showed that the level of voter approval for the president himself had dropped by 20 percentage points to 44 percent. In legislative elections that year, Johnson's party, the Democratic Party, lost forty-seven representatives in the U.S. Congress and three senate positions. Although Gerald Ford, then House Minority Leader, claimed the Republican victory showed that American voters did not want antipoverty programs to continue, Sundquist disagreed. He pointed to three reasons for voter dissatisfaction. First, people had not expected U.S. involvement in Vietnam to grow as fast as it did. Second, consumer prices had risen 4 percent in one year. Third, riots had broken out in thirty-eight U.S. cities during the summer. A notable example was the riot in the Watts section of Los Angeles in August 1965.[2]

In addition to these problems, Sundquist suggested that Johnson's difficulties derived from a natural cycle of political change. According to Sundquist, in recent years, political parties alternated control about every twenty-five years, and these changes resulted from concerns about the speed of social change. Although the parties moved in the same directions, they did so at different rates. Under Eisenhower, the peak of Republican power had come in 1952. As measured by the tempo of social change, Eisenhower's administration had been a conservative period. When Johnson took office, he sped up the process by taking an activist stance. Sundquist concluded that because Johnson did not alter the direction of social change, the public reacted against the rate of change. As Johnson encouraged more legislation, the public reacted to the speed of change rather than the direction he took.[3]

Some commentators began to refer to Vietnam as the tragedy of the Johnson administration. H. W. Brands referred to the war as part of the U.S. Cold War strategy of preventing changes in the political regimes of other countries. According to Brands, the difference in Vietnam was that Johnson would not recognize the limits within which he could work once he became interested in the situation. Brands claimed that Johnson became obsessed with Vietnam to the point that he ignored other aspects of his policies in which he could enjoy success.[4]

The urban riots threatened Johnson's domestic programs. Beginning in 1965, those disturbances caused many people to wonder why civil disorder broke out when the U.S. government was trying to remediate the difficulties facing low-income families in cities. To answer such questions, Johnson established a National Advisory Commission on Civil Disorders in July 1967. Headed by Otto Kerner, governor of Illinois, the commission included representatives of businesses, labor unions, and the NAACP.[5]

Charged with answering questions about what happened, why it happened, and what could prevent future occurrences, the commission contended that there was no single pattern to the disorders. Although typical rioters were African American adolescents or young adults acting against symbols of white authority, black civilians suffered the overwhelming majority of deaths and injuries. Losses to property were high. The commission estimated that the disturbance in Detroit destroyed about $5 million worth of property and Newark suffered about $10 million loss. Usually, there was a precipitating incident before the violence began. More important, the cities had undergone a longstanding atmosphere of tension even when officials instituted systems for citizens to resolve grievances.[6]

Because there was no simple cause for the riots, the commission concluded that the riots were an expression of frustration at the fact that the United States was becoming two societies—one black, one white, separate and unequal. The remedy was to fulfill the promises of democracy for all citizens whether they were urban or rural, white or black, Hispanic or Native American. This meant that various levels of government should mount more programs to combat poverty and discrimination.[7]

Although Johnson accepted the verdict of his commission, Michael Harrington complained that Johnson would not recognize the extent to which his commitment to Vietnam hindered him from implementing the commission's recommendations. According to Harrington, when Sargent Shriver launched innovations through the U.S. Office of Economic Opportunity (OEO) in 1966, he presented Johnson with a proposed budget that would have allowed a fair test of initiatives such as community action programs. Harrington estimated the OEO needed about $40 billion for the first year. Johnson rejected Shriver's request and allocated about $800 million. Harrington claimed that Johnson promised Shriver the additional money in 1967 because he believed the Vietnam War would be over and the administration could transfer funds from the military to domestic affairs.[8]

To some extent, Jeffrey W. Helsing offered a similar explanation of difficulties within the Johnson administration. Helsing noted that Johnson tried to achieve the goals of the Great Society goals while spending increasing sums of money and dispatching more U.S. forces to stop the North Vietnamese army from capturing South Vietnam. Although Helsing contended that the resulting inflation harmed the economy, he found that Johnson could not or would not let information about military actions flow freely among his advisors. Helsing concluded that Johnson's deceptions prevented program analysts and public officials from making intelligent plans.[9]

How Did the Process of Racial Desegregation Slow or Reverse?

In fairness, Johnson's problems stretched beyond his administrative practices. In the case of the racial desegregation of schools, public sentiment turned quickly against racial desegregation when federal efforts expanded into Northern cities. For example, in 1965, the HEW decided to act on a complaint alleging that the Chicago, Illinois, school board had enacted policies to segregate the schools. This was the first time that federal officials had decided to move against Northern cities. The ensuing controversy was intense. In fact, the mayor, Richard Daley, a strong Democratic Party supporter, complained to Johnson. Although Johnson did not order HEW to withdraw its ultimatum, he wanted the controversy to end. When HEW softened its requirements considerably, Chicago officials accepted the apparent compromise.[10]

Even in his own home area of East Texas, Johnson faced problems bringing about racial desegregation of schools. In 1965, HEW found that many Southern school districts desegregated building faculties by firing black teachers and hiring white teachers. Although Johnson ordered HEW to prevent Southern schools from discriminating against black teachers, they lacked the personnel to conduct investigations and order reversals. As a result, districts in East Texas removed experienced, trained black teachers from schools with black pupils, replacing them with unqualified white teachers through 1968.[11]

The war in Vietnam blunted the civil rights movement by causing civil rights activists to change their focus. For example, on April 4, 1967, Martin Luther King, Jr. made a public address opposing U.S. involvement in the war. Almost immediately, on April 12, 1967, the NAACP adopted a resolution warning that the effort to merge the civil rights movement with the peace movement would dilute the fight for racial justice. The NAACP turned out to be correct. Although King sought to include all poor people in a coalition seeking an end to poverty, he was unable to recruit the groups he needed to form a multiracial populist movement.[12]

Among the groups that resisted the effort to join in a coalition of poor people striving for economic justice were black separatists. This included religious organizations such as the Black Muslims, whose prominent speakers included Malcolm X. Another separatist group was the Student Nonviolent Coordinating Committee (SNCC). Although SNCC began as an integrated civil rights organization that had been most active in voter registration efforts in the South, SNCC expelled white volunteers in efforts to become a black organization in 1966. The following year, former SNCC members Stokely Carmichael and

Charles Hamilton described the need for "Black Power." They claimed that African Americans had to control their own institutions if they were going to improve their lives. Thus, Carmichael and Hamilton urged black parents to run black schools. Those parents should select the teachers, oversee the administrators, and select the curriculum.[13]

After Richard M. Nixon became president in 1969, he announced that HEW would no longer withhold federal funds because of racial segregation. Federal officials would rely on litigation to bring a school district into compliance with the U.S. Civil Rights Act. According to George R. Metcalf, this was one of Nixon's many efforts to end the racial desegregation of schools. Writing about the effect Nixon had on school desegregation, Metcalf complained that Nixon was a malevolent catalyst determined to slow down integration. Nixon hindered the enforcement of Title VI of the 1964 Civil Rights Act, and his opposition to busing so aroused the nation that public opinion turned strongly against the racial integration of schools. Although Metcalf added that the members of the U.S. Congress adopted Nixon's opinions, Metcalf blamed the four justices that Nixon appointed to the U.S. Supreme Court for blocking the cause of racial desegregation by reversing lower-court decisions to integrate the city schools of Detroit with the surrounding suburbs.[14]

If Nixon was a malevolent catalyst bringing back the segregation of schools, he did not act alone. In fact, according to Sundquist, there had been a reservoir of distrust about the Great Society and racial integration even when those programs enjoyed high levels of public approval. For example, in 1964, when the public generally accepted civil rights legislation, George Wallace, the segregationist governor from Alabama, entered presidential primaries in Northern states, taking entire precincts of working-class Democratic voters away from Johnson.[15]

Whereas voters may have objected to the social changes, the U.S. Supreme Court focused on culpability. Although Metcalf asserted that Nixon's appointees to the court blocked racial desegregation, the court's decisions in every case had affirmed that the illegal act was for an official to use the students' race in deciding which schools they should attend. NAACP lawyers broadened the definition of desegregation, but the Supreme court had never decided that the fact of segregation was illegal. Because Southern state constitutions required or allowed segregation, courts could easily decide that such segregation was illegal. In the North, NAACP lawyers could not easily fix the blame for segregation and they had difficulty deciding what should be the extent of the remedy.

In Southern cities, conditions made solutions simple. For example, in the 1971 decision, *Swann v. Charlotte-Mecklenburg,* the school district comprised the entire 530-square-mile county of Mecklenburg that included the city of Charlotte, North Carolina, six smaller municipalities, and suburban and rural communities. Although some areas had white populations and other areas had black residents, they belonged to the same school district. When the court required the school board to find a way to integrate the schools, they could include all the schools from the different cities and suburban communities. The busing plan was a simple exchange of some children in white elementary schools with children in black elementary schools. Because the planners paired the schools, children stayed with their friends from their neighborhoods although traveling as groups to schools in other areas. Most junior and senior high schools drew from large enough attendance zones that busing was unnecessary.[16]

In 1972, the NAACP turned its focus on Northern schools where state laws had not required racial segregation, and in some cases, had forbidden creating dual segregated systems. In these cases, the NAACP lawyers called attention to the actions of school boards and officials in state departments of education. In *Keyes v. School District No. 1, Denver, Colorado,* the NAACP lawyers showed that the members of the school board had mandated segregation by building schools in neighborhoods where the residents were of the same race. When housing patterns changed, the board manipulated attendance zones to maintain racially separate schools. Further, to keep some schools as black schools and other schools as white schools, the central office assigned teachers of one race to specific buildings.[17]

Although the victory in *Keyes* provided the NAACP lawyers with the strategies to proceed against school districts in Northern cities, the decision did not suggest that courts could order racial integration beyond specific school districts. This represented a problem because, in Northern and Western metropolitan areas, racial segregation followed city and suburban lines. African American children tended to live in cities whereas white students lived in the suburbs. In these areas, each city and every suburb was a separate school district with its own school board and administrative structure.

In Detroit, Michigan, the city school district remained apart from the suburban communities. Further, the populations were racially distinct because the population had shifted. In the city, the population reached its highest point in 1950 when it held about 61 percent of the population for the metropolitan area. From that point until 1970, the city's population declined by about 170,000 people each decade. Since 1940, the eighty-five contiguous suburban communities in the metropolitan area had grown by almost 2 million people. More important, the city's racial percentages had changed as older white families without children left the city and younger black families with children moved into their homes. As a result, black students represented about 64 percent of the total enrollment in Detroit schools whereas the suburban schools had white student populations. Thus, when the U.S. district judge found the Detroit school board guilty of enacting policies that segregated school buildings, he asked for the desegregation plan to include the suburban communities. The judge argued that if segregation caused harm, the remedy should remove segregation no matter who caused it.[18]

In a sense, the U.S. Supreme Court had forecast the solution to the problem of segregation between suburban and urban areas when it ruled in *Swann* that school districts should transport the students to different schools if necessary. Although the *Swann* decision did not speak to questions involving separate school districts, it suggested that school officials could move children to bring about racial integration. Thus, in the case *Milliken v. Bradley,* the NAACP lawyers argued before the Supreme Court in 1974 that an effective desegregation plan had to involve city and suburban schools because any plan that involved only city schools would not include enough white students to make the desegregation reasonable. Because most of the students in city schools were black, the NAACP sought to reach beyond the city lines to include students from fifty-three surrounding suburban communities. Five Supreme Court justices, a majority, disagreed, because there was no evidence that suburban communities had participated in practices that resulted in segregation. They added that there was no evidence that state officials had drawn city and suburban boundary lines to form racially homogeneous areas. Consequently, the Supreme Court justices restricted the desegregation plan to Detroit city schools.[19]

The decision in *Milliken v. Bradley* affirmed the original *Brown* decision by holding that segregation by force of law caused harm. The fact of segregation was not important.

According to Gary Orfield, the decision stopped a popular movement for a constitutional amendment to prohibit busing for racial balance. Although newspapers announced that suburbs were beyond the reach of any court order to integrate schools, *Milliken v. Bradley* did not prohibit the creation of metropolitan plans for racial desegregation. For example, in 1975, one year after *Milliken v. Bradley,* the U.S. Supreme Court approved a plan to integrate schools in Louisville, Kentucky, with suburban schools outside the city. One reason for the different decision was that Jefferson County school officials had drawn district lines between Louisville and its suburb to segregate students. Another reason was that a metropolitan plan in Kentucky was simple because the Louisville schools would merge with one other district. The proposed plan for Detroit, Michigan, would have been complex because it involved over fifty different administrative units. Nonetheless, the drive for metropolitan desegregation and meaningful integration slowed dramatically. Before the court decided *Milliken v. Bradley,* the NAACP had begun efforts to desegregate several other cities with their surrounding suburbs. Once the court announced its decision in *Milliken v. Bradley,* the NAACP ended those efforts.[20]

How Did Social Conceptions Influence the Racial Segregation of Schools?

Although Presidents Nixon and Reagan argued strongly against busing, it was not clear that the public disliked the idea of forced racial desegregation. According to Gary Orfield and his colleagues at Harvard University, the public was growing used to desegregation despite official efforts to dismantle it. They based their conclusion on several facts. The rate of desegregation remained strong throughout the first part of the 1980s. Further, public school enrollments rose by more than 7 percent, segregation levels declined slightly, and private school enrollments dropped by almost 9 percent. Although these facts suggested that racial desegregation was acceptable social policy, the Supreme Court issued a series of rulings from 1986 to 1991 that allowed school districts to end desegregation plans if justices could declare the school district unitary. A system was unitary when desegregation plans had been in effect long enough to alleviate any harm caused by the official acts of segregation. School officials turned to federal courts seeking release from desegregation orders. As a result, Gary Orfield and his colleagues found the proportion of black students in schools whose enrollments were more than half minority had increased from 1986 to 1991 to the level it had been before the 1971 decision in *Swann.* At the same time, Latino students endured more segregation because they were more likely to be in predominantly minority schools than were black students. By 2000, the courts had allowed schools in many states to return to some form of neighborhood schools.[21]

A group of researchers in the Lewis Mumford Center confirmed Gary Orfield's view. They found that the effort to end racial segregation in schools had been successful until the 1989–1990 school year because measures of segregation showed schools more racially integrated than neighborhoods. In 2000, the measures reversed, showing schools more segregated than neighborhoods. This meant school segregation had resulted from changes in policies, not from changes in residential patterns. In addition, Mumford researchers contended that school administrators in the fifty largest metropolitan areas had chosen to enact policies that reasserted segregation once the federal courts allowed them to do so.[22]

In the main, there had been three arguments against the racial desegregation of schools. The first was that people would not accept it and violence would result. The second was that school integration would cause white parents to leave the schools, making desegregation much more difficult. The third was that the policies would make school life more difficult for African Americans and harm their academic progress. At best, each of these views was partly true because they shared the assumption that people preferred racially homogeneous situations. The complaints overlooked the point that school officials could change conditions to encourage interracial contact.

The first complaint derived from early experiences in the South and in cities such as Boston where mobs tried to upset the process of school desegregation. These were short-lived because authorities learned to control the process. For example, in 1976, the U.S. Commission on Civil Rights published the results of its nationwide survey about school busing for racial balance. The commission noted that Presidents Nixon and Ford had opposed efforts to transport students. In addition, violent opposition in Pontiac, Michigan; Boston, Massachusetts; and Louisville, Kentucky, received national media attention. After holding hearings and surveying the experiences in twenty-nine cities that underwent school desegregation, the commission members decided these exceptional cases did not tell the story of busing. Instead, the commission members concluded confidently that busing for racial balance was successful, providing the planners organized the programs correctly. In each city where city leaders had given their cooperation, the busing programs unfolded smoothly. This meant the superintendent and the school board had to support the plan. The religious leaders in the community had to marshal support. Elected officials had to approve the necessity of school desegregation and the police had to follow the lead of the politicians. When these things happened, as they did in most cities, school doors opened, buses rolled, and there was no violence or any threat of it.[23]

It was interesting to note that the urban riots of the 1960s did not occur again, although the causes as described in 1967 by the National Advisory Commission on Civil Disorders remained throughout the 1980s. According to Michael Katz, the authorities in the cities learned to control aggression to such an extent that the possibility of mass violence disappeared.[24]

The second complaint about white flight represented the peaceful resistance that white people showed to racial desegregation. According to this argument, white people left cities when school desegregation plans began. Although white flight may have happened, critics exaggerated the extent to which school busing caused people to leave the cities. As the Supreme Court justices noted in *Milliken v. Bradley,* the population of cities in the United States underwent significant changes in the last part of the twentieth century. Historians agreed with their analyses. For example, in writing a history of the growth of suburban communities entitled *Crabgrass Frontiers,* Kenneth Jackson listed four conditions that encouraged Americans to abandon cities and escape into the suburbs. First, although most Americans had moved to the cities in search of better jobs and easier lives, they distrusted city life and idealized country living. Second, racial conflicts including the threat of school desegregation encouraged middle-class Americans to seek suburban advantages.

Third, the cost of housing in the suburbs was low because land was cheap, construction techniques were efficient, and federal mortgage insurance combined with income tax deductions for mortgage interest were readily available. Finally, federal highway programs made transportation to work and home easy. As a result, it was more practical to own a home in the suburbs than to rent an apartment in the city.[25]

Whereas school desegregation may have influenced suburban sprawl, the spread of suburban developments would have happened without desegregation. At the least, the end of most programs of school desegregation by 2000 did not alter suburban sprawl. The population shifts continued to the extent that chains of cities extending from Boston to Washington, D.C., or from Pittsburgh to Chicago appeared to meld together to form large urban areas dotted with parks and recreation areas. Although minority groups moved to the suburbs, the process repeated the patterns of segregation found between cities and suburbs. For example, according to a study of the 330 metropolitan areas in the United States conducted by the Mumford Center in 2002, about 18 percent of the suburban population was minority in 1990, increasing to 27 percent in 2000. Blacks represented about 9 percent of the total suburban population, Hispanics represented about 12 percent, and Asians represented about 5 percent. Not only were whites the largest group, but the various minority groups tended to live in ethnic enclaves within the suburbs. Thus, the extent of segregation remained unchanged, and the population shifts transferred the problems of racial segregation of schools from the cities to the suburbs.[26]

By 2002, social research institutions such as the Brookings Institution claimed that major governmental policies exacerbated the segregated growth patterns of metropolitan areas in ways that hurt the lower social classes. According to Myron Orfield, because Americans moved a great deal, communities changed rapidly. Across the United States, he found a recurring pattern. As gradually increasing African American and Latino middle classes moved into suburban communities, white middle-class people perceived the area as minority and avoided it. Because there were insufficient numbers of African American and Latino middle-class people to buy the homes, low-income families began to move into the area. In a short time, the middle class moved out and the poverty level rose in the community, overloading the schools and other social services. At the same time, the tax base fell. Because the nonwhite population in the United States has grown steadily since 1940, all major metropolitan areas suffered from this syndrome. Nevertheless, Myron Orfield argued each city and its suburbs could have cooperated by sharing the tax base, enacting housing codes to preserve open lands, and constructing coalitions to provide adequate social services such as schools because the cities and the suburbs shared the same problems. This did not happen. Myron Orfield found that the thousands of little communities competed fiercely with each other, causing the problems to worsen. He thought this was wrongheaded because the simple solution was to expand regional governments and seek mutually beneficial solutions.[27]

Despite the promises of regional government, such cooperation could not solve some of the educational problems. For example, in 2003, John Ogbu published the results of a study he conducted with Astrid Davis of Shaker Heights, Ohio, a suburb of Cleveland. Although the median annual family income was $66,000, the range of incomes extended from below the poverty level to over $1 million. African Americans represented about 33 percent of the population and white families constituted the remainder. The school district held a high reputation and enjoyed the highest rate of school taxes in the state, yet there was a wide gap in achievement between the black students and the white students. Ogbu and Davis concluded the problem was the black students did not believe the school could help them succeed in life. As a result, they disengaged from the class work, formed their own standards of behavior, and exerted pressure on any black students who sought to excel academically. They ridiculed the striving students for acting white.[28]

Although white and black people seemed to choose segregation when they could, it was not clear that they opposed racial integration. In a long-term statistical survey of school desegregation, Charles T. Clotfelter found that the exodus of white students from most city schools had been at the same steady rate before the implementation of a desegregation plan and afterwards. When a desegregation plan began, the loss of white students jumped about 2 to 4 percent; however, Clotfelter noted that this increase was short-term and returned to the normal rate quickly. These tendencies were clearest when suburban and urban school districts were close together, as in Detroit. They were less marked in large counties that underwent desegregation such as Charlotte-Mecklenburg. From this evidence, Clotfelter concluded that white people chose to send their children to schools with white children when such a choice was easy. He tested this assumption by considering the effect that private schools had on segregation. Although he found that some white students had escaped desegregation of public schools by attending private academies or religious schools, the extent these schools contributed to racial segregation was minimal. Further, most of the private or religious schools in a city underwent racial desegregation shortly after the public schools desegregated.[29]

The last important argument against racial desegregation was that school desegregation harmed African American children. Clotfelter presented a summary of the evidence about this possibility. He found that there was no support for such claims although racial integration had not performed miracles. For example, Clotfelter acknowledged that it was not clear that integration raised the academic achievement of African American children despite the many studies that had sought such evidence. Further, it appeared that racial integration had no influence on African American self-esteem. As noted in Chapter 14, during the trials in the *Brown* case, social scientists contended that segregation hurt African American children's self-image. Clotfelter found that subsequent studies showed that black children did not suffer from low self-esteem. On the other hand, studies of interracial friendships showed that black and white people who attended integrated schools tended to have more interracial friendships later in life than did people who attended segregated schools. Finally, African Americans who graduated from integrated schools were more likely to hold white collar or professional positions than were black people who attended segregated facilities.[30]

The movement for the racial desegregation of schools influenced other aspects of education because advocates for other minorities tried to follow the same pattern of reform that the NAACP had followed. That is, although local and state agencies controlled public schools, advocates complained to the federal government that those officials had ignored the educational need of their constituents. Advocates for children with exceptionalities were among the most successful of these petitioners. The Council for Exceptional Children (CEC) hired lawyers who had worked for the NAACP and they argued their cases in federal courts. They took their few victories to the U.S. Congress and lobbied for legislation that would force public schools to adopt the practices the court cases had approved. In addition, the CEC and other advocacy groups sought financial support for the education of children with exceptionalities. In 1966, the CEC succeeded in having such provisions included in the renewal of the ESEA. That legislation established a bureau within the U.S. Office of Education to direct congressional committees to important advocacy groups. Thus, the CEC gained direct and frequent access to legislators. The result was that the U.S. Congress approved and President Gerald Ford signed in 1974 Public Law 94-142, The Education of All Handicapped Children Act. This federal law required schools to provide a free appropriate education for children with exceptionalities. The schools had to inform parents of this opportunity and offer expert evaluations of the child's condition. Finally, the school had to hold a hearing with the teachers, the experts, and the parents to decide what the long-term goals and short-term objectives should be and enter them on an individual educational plan.[31]

The members of the CEC called their campaign a quiet revolution because they met little resistance. Other advocacy groups were less successful although they followed the same procedures. For example, advocates for children of linguistic minorities persuaded Congress to add Title VII, the Bilingual Education Act, to the 1967 renewal of ESEA. With this title, the U.S. Congress added support programs for children with limited English-speaking abilities. By 1977, though, researchers contended the programs were ineffective, and critics such as Senator H. I. Hayakawa complained that bilingual education threatened to separate Americans into several different linguistic groups. In the face of such opposition, the advocates of bilingual education lost many of their initial gains.[32]

How Successful Was the Education of Children from Low-Income Families of Minority Groups?

The education of children with exceptionalities escaped the extensive criticism that bilingual education and the education of children from low-income families suffered. Part of the reason may have been that special educators did not have to face the problems of prejudice that different racial, linguistic, and socioeconomic groups confronted because any family could have a child with special needs. Another part of the reason was that PL 94-142 had not specified any approach or any goal. Instead of promising increased cognitive development, the advocates for children with exceptionalities asked that schools follow a set of steps. These began with identifying children with exceptionalities and testing them to determine the nature and extent of the difficulties. In setting the goals for remediation, the schools had to involve teachers, experts, and parents. In addition, the schools had to provide regular evaluation to ensure the children progressed. Whereas the IEP required that teachers measure the growth of a child, the pattern of growth could differ for each child. Therefore, it was impossible to aggregate those increases in ways that gave a simple measure determining whether the attention was worthwhile. On the other hand, bilingual education and Project Head Start had started with promises to improve the intelligence and academic performance of children from low-income families. Thus, researchers could compare the performance of children from a program to the success of children who did not enter such program. The example of Head Start illustrated this tendency.

Project Head Start developed out of the Economic Opportunity Act of 1964 in which Congress and President Johnson sought to provide education and job training as part of the effort to eliminate poverty. This legislation established within the OEO such innovations as the Community Action Program (CAP); the Jobs Corps; VISTA, a domestic version of the Peace Corps; and a program of loans to small businesses and farms. According to Edward Zigler, who had helped shape Head Start, Congress allocated $300 million to the CAP, but city administrations had requested only $26 million. Thus, in 1965, Shriver, the director of the OEO, decided to spend the money on children. The result was Head Start.[33]

The idea of a program for preschool-age children was popular among politicians. Because Shriver wanted a comprehensive program, Head Start sought to improve children's health through physical examinations, inoculations, and nutrition assessments as well as establish patterns of success for the children and their parents. The idea of including parents in Head Start represented an effort to help the entire family as well as the children. With such aims, the OEO undertook to start an eight-week summer program for 100,000 children and promised to expand it to include 500,000 in the autumn. Zigler acknowledged that this was a rushed start, but he added that anything else would have doomed Head Start because the next year the Vietnam War absorbed available funds. The lavish beginning established Head Start as an important program.[34]

Project Head Start differed from nursery schools or kindergartens of the day. According to Sar A. Levitan, more than 25 percent of the children came from families receiving welfare or without a father. Because the planners considered these families as deprived, they wanted to prepare the children for school by improving their health and changing their self-images. The program wanted each center to maintain a ratio of one professional teacher for fifteen children. In addition, those teachers had an untrained assistant and a volunteer, both of whom were usually mothers of participating children that brought the teacher–student ratio down to one to five. Because almost a third of the children's parents required adult literacy training, many centers offered a range of courses for them.[35]

Although most Head Start centers enrolled at least some children from more affluent homes, hoping the more advantaged children could enrich the classroom experiences for the other students, several projects in the South opened centers exclusively for African American children. According to Levitan, the Southern districts used several strategies to avoid civil rights guidelines, such as using only black schools, aggressively recruiting black rather than white children, and selecting only African American staff. Other areas had similar problems because in 1966 about a third of all Head Start centers served one race. In part, this represented the segregated nature of the communities. In general, the OEO did not enforce racial integration guidelines. In 1965, out of 2,500 different programs, the OEO closed 60 for discrimination.[36]

Although the Head Start program began with high hopes, the first evaluation was disastrous. In 1969, the Westinghouse Learning Corporation worked with Ohio University to compare the success of about 2,000 children who had attended Head Start with about the same number of similar children who had not been part of Head Start. The study concluded that Head Start had not helped the children advance cognitively or affectively. Although other researchers complained that the study had made several errors, the director defended his work. President Nixon seemed unimpressed by the controversy. He established the Office of Child Development (OCD) within HEW, placed Head Start under OCD, announced his intention to expand Head Start to include younger children, and created Follow Through to help the Head Start children pass through elementary school.[37]

In maintaining Head Start, Nixon acted in accord with prevailing opinions to translate the reports of failure into calls for increased efforts. For example, when James Miller considered the results of the Westinghouse report, he consulted data the OEO offered about the professional preparation of the preschool teachers. He noted that the teachers who staffed the preprimary programs had little formal education and little experience with primary-age children from disadvantaged environments. According to Miller, most teachers in the field of early childhood education lacked reasonable preparation. Miller proposed developing in-service training systems to help practicing preschool teachers improve their abilities. In addition, he recommended the creation of a National Institute on Early Childhood Education that could conduct research, collect information, and disseminate data through regional teacher demonstration centers. Although he approved of a drive for the certification of preschool teachers, he cautioned that the requirements be more practical than a list of academic courses from universities.[38]

Despite Miller's cautions, when the federal government claimed that Project Head Start would improve the lives of children, many state officials considered improving early childhood education in their areas. These efforts increased even after the dismal reports about the failure of Head Start to improve the children's cognitive abilities. For example, a third of the state departments of education commissioned studies on how to establish certification standards for early childhood teachers, and Iowa, Vermont, and Oklahoma adopted certification requirements. In addition, public pressure grew to establish statewide kindergarten programs.[39]

With the inauguration of Head Start, national early childhood organizations flourished. The National Association of Nursery Education (NANE) began in 1929 with a handful of members. In the 1950s, NANE formed affiliations with existing local, regional, and state organizations and it grew to enroll 5,000 members. In 1964, NANE became the National Association for the Education of Young Children (NAEYC). When people raised questions about the quality of the teachers in the Head Start programs, NAEYC supported the development of the Child Development Associate Program (CDA) to offer training toward a credential in preschool teaching. By 1994, teachers of Head Start programs with more than twenty children were required to have a CDA credential or an associate's degree in early childhood education.[40]

Although the failures of programs such as Head Start inspired increased efforts, early child development programs did not expand in unlimited ways. For example, in 1971, President Nixon refused to sign a Comprehensive Child Development Act that would have provided federally funded childcare and education as well as established a framework for child development services. Nixon complained that the bill would put federal resources on the side of communal approaches to childrearing as opposed to the traditional, family-centered approach.[41]

Despite Nixon's criticism, it was not clear that Head Start was a communal approach to childcare. For example, in 1978, President Carter tried to place Head Start programs under the newly formed Department of Education. Black civil rights leaders protested that Head Start should remain a community action program within the Office of Economic Opportunity rather than part of the education bureaucracy subject to state departments of education. According to former Head Start founder Edward Zigler, this reaction derived from the general distrust black activists held for public school officials. They complained that the only way to overcome the alienation poor parents felt toward schools was to maintain Head Start apart. In this way, Head Start could help parents and their children improve their attitudes about education.[42]

Head Start was not the only disappointment in the war on poverty. According to Henry Levin, during the 1960s and 1970s, most experts believed that education could end poverty. Further, such a view fit the American ethos by offering poor people an equal opportunity to become rich with the proper training. The prevailing view was that poor people shared some sort of culture of poverty or deprivation that prevented them from taking advantage of the opportunities schools provided. Thus, the hope was that compensatory education could teach children to hold attitudes that would be more positive. By Levin's count, the federal government started at least thirty different programs from 1965 to 1974 that followed this model. These included Head Start, the ESEA programs such as bilingual education, and the Job Corps. In each case, Levin found that they failed to reach their goals. He concluded that the overwhelming characteristic of the efforts to break poverty through compensatory education was their uniform failure.[43]

Although the failure of compensatory education should have indicated the inadequacy of the conception of cultural deprivation, researchers continued to look to the children's backgrounds to explain the failure of compensatory education. Although the resulting interpretations took different directions, they blamed the poor people for the school failure they endured. For example, on the one hand, Arthur Jensen contended that poor people suffered economically because they had inherited lower capacities for intelligence, and these genetic imbalances prevented their children from benefiting from educational programs.[44] On the other hand, John U. Ogbu contended that programs failed because subordinate minorities, such as black people and Mexican Americans, had adopted the cultural perspective that they could not succeed through traditional ways.[45] Thus, while Jensen believed poor people had some genetic difficulties, Ogbu argued that the social and economic domination of poor people caused them to adopt attitudes that prevented them from enjoying school success.

The war on poverty ended in 1980 with the election of Ronald Reagan as president. Once in office, the Reagan administration reduced social spending, especially the antipoverty measures that had survived from Johnson's efforts. To justify his actions, Reagan repeated the ideas that a free market would improve social conditions. According to Martin Carnoy, the image of granting equal results for equal efforts appealed to white middle-class voters, and Reagan intensified these feelings by claiming people abused welfare to avoid working. Although African Americans had made gains in income since 1964, Reagan's policies reversed the trend. Seeking to control inflation by holding down wages, Reagan worsened the conditions of low-income minority groups.[46]

How Did the Conservative Reaction Redirect Educational Reform?

With the end of the war on poverty, school reform took two different directions. The first was to call for state and local authorities to adopt policies that would reinforce basic academic instruction in public schools. The second was to increase the opportunities for parents to choose the schools their children would attend. These efforts represented a more conservative approach to education. Unfortunately, they did not prove any more successful than the more liberal approaches of compensatory education.

Although Reagan had blamed the antipoverty programs for causing economic problems, inflation and unemployment did not decline when he cut those expenditures. As a result, conservatives sought another solution. They decided the problems derived from inadequate instruction in public schools. In 1983, the National Commission on Excellence in Education (NCEE) issued its report. Entitled *A Nation at Risk,* this report argued that educators jeopardized the economic prosperity of the nation by forgetting the basic purposes of schools. Noting that the world had become a global village, the NCEE report claimed that learning was indispensable in the information age. The problems were deceptive. Although the average adult was better educated than was the average adult a generation ago, the average graduate of high school or college was less knowledgeable than were the graduates a generation ago. For the NCEE, the answer was to demand that students learn more in English, mathematics, science, social studies, and computer science. College-bound students needed two years of foreign language study. Such improvement would come through more rigorous testing, more homework, more and longer school days, and highly trained teachers. The result would be increased productivity of American factories and businesses.[47]

Although only one member of the NCEE was a business leader, the Committee for Economic Development, an organization of businesses, issued a call for corporations to cooperate with public schools to improve curriculum and broaden educational opportunities within communities. Other organizations of businesses, such as the Business Roundtable, called on major corporations to help improve American education. According to a survey conducted by the Conference Board in 1993, the result of these calls was that various businesses worked together in four different waves. First, they sought to strengthen programs in early childhood and in science and mathematics. Second, they sought to apply popular management techniques such as creating mission statements, organization plans, and engaging all stakeholders. Third, they encouraged the adoption of research programs and providing options for students to use state funds to attend private schools. Fourth, they sought to change the systems by providing ways that university graduates from liberal arts programs and adults experienced in certain areas could become teachers.[48]

Twenty years later, most analysts acknowledged disappointing results for these reform efforts. According to Maris A. Vinovskis, almost every state increased the number of courses students had to take to graduate from high school. School districts reduced the size of classes in the early grades. Supervisors evaluated teachers and students more frequently and more effectively. Nonetheless, there was no evidence that the students learned more. Vinovskis claimed the flaw derived from the assumption within the report that the solution to the problems was for teachers to demand more effort from the students. Therefore, the federal government did not invest any funds in educational research to determine how to help students and teachers improve. The result was that the simplistic suggestions proved inadequate.[49]

To some extent, the U.S. Congress sought to redress the problem of inadequate research when it reauthorized the Elementary and Secondary Education Act in 2001. Renaming the bill No Child Left Behind (NCLB), the legislation referred several times to the need to base school policies on scientifically based research. Although the legislation cited as best such experiments as comparing the results of practices with randomly selected groups of students, some educational researchers complained that this model excluded other equally legitimate ways of knowing, such as practice-oriented models. After considerable debate among researchers about what constituted scientifically based research, the U.S. Congress approved legislation widening the framework for research designs that qualified for federal support.[50]

The hope behind the call to use scientifically based research to form school policies was that objective studies would furnish practical suggestions for teachers in the same way that drug trials inform physicians how to treat various illnesses. The problem was that education was more complex than such a medical model implied. For example, Monika Williams Shealey complained that the focus on systematic, empirical studies would eliminate the multicultural aspects of research that could be most beneficial for urban schools. According to Shealey, urban researchers relied heavily on such qualitative techniques as interviews and observations to reveal complex patterns of cultural change. Although teachers had to understand these patterns to succeed, they did not arise from studies that utilized mathematical comparisons. Because she feared the federal funding to support such research would disappear if the bias for scientifically based research continued, she warned that the result would be the disappearance of fruitful approaches to urban education.[51]

Whether the limited nature of acceptable research caused problems or not, the Civil Rights Project at Harvard University found in June 2006 the studies revealed that NCLB did not narrow racial gaps in school achievement. Comparing state assessment measures with findings from the National Assessment of Education Progress, the Harvard researchers found that the NCLB rules on accountability, such as the threat of removing federal support when a school did not demonstrate adequate yearly progress, had little or no impact on achievement among students from minority groups or families suffering from poverty. In fact, the Harvard report contended that when school officials applied more pressure on minority students, the gap between these students and their white peers increased.[52]

What Happened When Reformers Tried to Introduce Free Market Systems to Education?

With the apparent failure of calls for more homework and increased testing, reformers sought to use the free market ideology to improve schools. According to Henry Levin, private providers began to compete with public school officials using a surprising number of different arrangements such as vouchers, charter schools, or tuition tax credits. Private schools had preceded public schools in the history of schooling in the United States, and Levin added that economists had long advanced the supposed benefits of privatization. For example, in 1776, Adam Smith recommended that a community should engage a schoolmaster and pay a portion of his salary. The parents should pay the rest to ensure that the teacher satisfied their desire to train their children. Most important, Levin noted that the shift to some form of private education was a worldwide phenomenon, although different countries adopted private schools in different ways.[53]

Martin Carnoy credited Milton Friedman for conceiving the idea of vouchers in 1955. Friedman recommended that the government offer each child an entitlement to pay at least some of the expenses to attend any school, public or private. Carnoy added that supporters made two related promises. The first was that vouchers would enable parents to choose the schools their children attended and the resulting competition would cause all schools to improve. The second was that governmental costs for education would decline when schools increased their efficiency. To determine whether these arguments were reasonable, Carnoy studied the experiences in Chile and Sweden because these programs had been in operation long enough to offer such evidence. Chile had adopted vouchers in 1981 and Sweden implemented them in 1992.[54]

Carnoy found that the effects of vouchers depended on how people viewed public education before the voucher system began. In Chile, private schools enjoyed a higher status than public schools. As a result, Chileans used vouchers to leave public schools. In Sweden, public schools enjoyed strong public support. The vouchers did not cause Swedes to leave those schools. More important, there was no persuasive evidence that students learned more in private schools, and there was little evidence that private schools were more efficient. The vouchers did exacerbate school segregation because low-income families lived farther away from the private schools than did the families with more wealth.[55]

One problem that prevented the rapid growth of voucher plans was whether such programs would violate the principle of separation of church and state. In *Zelman v. Simmons-Harris,* the Supreme Court decided in 2002 that state governments could extend vouchers for students to attend religious schools. This case concerned a program in Cleveland, Ohio, where a state scholarship fund provided tuition aid for students from city schools to attend private schools. About 82 percent of the private schools that participated had a religious affiliation. Although nearly 96 percent of the children in the program chose to attend religious schools, the justices decided that the vouchers did not represent state aid to religion because the children had chosen the private schools. The government had not directed them to any religious institution.[56]

The idea of vouchers expanded quickly. As a result, middle-class parents sought to use them although state legislatures directed them to low-income families. For example, in Ohio, the Educational Scholarship Program offered choice grants of about $4,250 to $5,000 to children attending schools that the Ohio Department of Education (ODE) listed as on academic emergency or academic watch. These categories were the two lowest ratings out of five that the ODE made of the state's school districts using twenty-five performance indicators such as student achievement levels, Ohio Graduation Test scores, and graduation rates. Because the schools that fell into these categories tended to be urban schools with students from families living in poverty, the aim was to offer the children from low-income families the option to attend a private school instead of their failing public school. In some cases, though, the aid went to affluent parents. For example, in June 2006, after the ODE offered the grants, more than 100 families living in well-to-do suburbs withdrew their children from private Catholic schools at the very end of the term and enrolled them in an underperforming public school. If the children attended one day in the public school, they could receive a state scholarship to return to the Catholic school from which they had withdrawn.[57]

Charter schools represented another option to introduce some sort of free market system into education. The idea grew rapidly. According to Pearl Rock Kane and Christopher J. Lauricella, the first person to mention charter schools was Ray Budde. In 1988, Budde envisioned teachers taking charters from school districts, setting up schools, and experimenting with new ideas of curriculum. To some extent, the Minnesota legislature changed the concept when it approved in 1991 the idea that parents and teachers could create schools to compete with the public schools. Under this framework, the charters did not exist within the school districts. They were independent of them. From this first charter school legislation, the plans proliferated. By 2001, thirty-six states and the District of Columbia had passed some form of charter school legislation. These laws differed considerably from each other. Some states retained careful control over the charter schools whereas other states allowed the charter schools to grow almost as they wished.[58]

The extent to which charter schools maintained segregation was controversial. In 1997, the U.S. Department of Education claimed that charter schools attracted students that matched the social composition of the states. A few years later, in 2003, Erica Frankenberg and Chungmei Lee analyzed the national data on charter schools. They noted that although some charter schools were diverse, many individual charter school buildings were more segregated than the public schools, and many white students went to all-white charter schools. The problem was not a lack of minority students because, in some states, more minority students enrolled in charter schools than in public schools. It appeared to the authors that charter schools encouraged segregation through such methods as choosing to open a school in a segregated neighborhood or recruiting students in limited ways.[59]

Charter schools offered an opportunity for entrepreneurs to build schools and to operate them for profits. The largest company that took advantage of this opening was Edison Schools. Created in 1989 by Chris Whittle, Edison Schools built on the hope that private enterprise and competition could make schools more responsive to people's needs. By 2005, Edison Schools enrolled about 70,000 children in nineteen states, in the District of Columbia, and in Great Britain. In addition, Edison Schools provided such services as tutoring and summer help to about 200,000 more students. According to Whittle, Edison Schools was still too small. He argued that many educational problems resisted solution because the school districts lacked the size to tackle them effectively. Whittle argued that large size brought more than efficiency. It offered the capability of designing buildings, creating curriculums, and organizing teaching. Most important, the large budgets brought about by enormous size could fund the research and development needed to find solutions to problems.[60]

Although Whittle argued that large private corporations devoted to education could improve teaching and learning, this remained a hope more than an achievement. For example, in 2006, the National Center for Education Statistics revealed the findings of a study comparing the achievement of students in charter schools to the levels achieved by students in public schools. The mean scores for charter school students in reading and mathematics were lower than the scores for students in public schools. Although the many different tests the researchers used reinforced this conclusion, U.S. Secretary of Education Margaret Spellings remained hopeful about charter schools. She claimed she had visited many high-performing charter schools. Thus, she refused to give up on charter schools because she believed that the schools were pioneering strategies to raise achievement.[61]

Although Whittle and Spellings asserted that private corporations could bring about innovation, it was not clear what improvements charter schools offered. For example, a critic of Edison Schools, Kenneth J. Saltman, complained that Whittle promised to build a new type of school. The early model of his schools offered a laptop computer to each student. The students and their families could track the students' progress through the computer. They could communicate with school faculty through email. In addition to the computers, the students were to learn to speak and read a foreign language. For basic instruction, the Edison Schools used standardized curriculums available in public schools, such as *Success for All* and *Everyday Mathematics.* Teachers whose students did well on the achievement tests would receive cash bonuses. Further, students and parents would take on many of the daily duties, thereby freeing the teachers to concentrate on instruction.[62]

Saltman complained that by 2005 most of these plans had failed. The teachers did not integrate the computers into the instruction. Many of the computers failed to work, and few teachers or parents knew how to operate the computers. The schools dropped the dual language programs because they were expensive and cumbersome. Few schools trusted the students to take up many administrative or instructional tasks. Further, Saltman argued that the lessons in the standardized curriculum programs such as *Everyday Mathematics* advanced simple consumerism, such as providing candy bars as prizes for successfully completing worksheets, rather than enhancing complex social understandings, such as encouraging the students to explore public health issues.[63]

When RAND Corporation conducted a study of Edison Schools, they found a complicated situation. In 2000, Edison Schools contracted with RAND to carry out a multiyear, comprehensive evaluation of its schools. Released in 2005, the RAND study found that Edison schools offered resources and accountability measures to promote student achievement. Because the company controlled its schools, it could demand that students demonstrate academic improvement. Further, the schools offered broad curriculums. Nonetheless, when the researchers visited twenty-three different Edison school buildings, they found significant variation. Some schools worked well, and others did not. The researchers credited the leadership of the principal for the successful schools. As far as student achievement, the researchers could not be sure whether Edison Schools were more successful than other schools. As a result, they called for further studies to determine what would be necessary to improve charter schools.[64]

Although most efforts to introduce parental choice or free enterprise into education began with pleas to help children whose families endured poverty, the movement spread to include families with more economic resources. According to Martin Carnoy, the effort to introduce the free market into schools had to move beyond helping low-achieving children. In Chile, he found that Catholic schools had produced higher levels of achievement than public schools because they spent more money per pupil. When the for-profit charter schools appeared in Chile, those schools produced the same results as the public schools because they sought to control costs. To boost their achievement scores, the Chilean for-profit schools attracted more academically advanced children by opening schools in affluent neighborhoods.[65]

Conclusion

As Chapter 14 showed, during the late 1940s and 1950s, federal officials recommended that schools adopt curriculum changes to meet pressures deriving from foreign affairs. These included reinforcing patriotism, preparing scientists to develop systems of military defense, and ending racial discrimination. With the war in Vietnam and the urban riots of the 1960s, many people attacked the efforts of desegregation and President Johnson's efforts to end poverty through education. They found support for their efforts in a series of legal decisions that restricted the spread of racial desegregation and in studies showing innovations such as Head Start had not fulfilled their promises.

Although Presidents Nixon and Reagan argued that local officials could best control the affairs in their schools, those presidents did not end federal involvement in local school affairs. They reversed its direction. For example, seeking to counter such foreign conditions as industrial competition from overseas that led to the reduction of domestic manufacturing, Reagan called together members of an influential panel who recommended that teachers stress the acquisition of abstract academic material rather than allow students to pursue projects that interested them. When these calls for increased rigor did not result in improved student performance, conservative politicians claimed the problems were that public schools represented monopolies. They turned to mechanisms to give parents more choices such as vouchers and charter schools, even though major studies showed that public schools were more effective.

As was the case in the previous chapter, the educational reforms inspired by federal officials in the 1980s and 1990s sought to meet foreign pressures although they aimed at imposing better educational techniques on schools. In these ways, the officials appeared to consider American schools as a means to rectify imbalances in foreign trade, among other things.

Endnotes

1. John A. Andrew III, *Lyndon Johnson and the Great Society* (Chicago: Ivan R. Dee, 1998), 181–199.
2. James L. Sundquist, *Politics and Policy: The Eisenhower, Kennedy, and Johnson Years* (Washington, D.C.: Brookings Institution, 1968), 495–497.
3. Sundquist, *Politics and Policy,* 498–499.
4. H. W. Brands, *The Wages of Globalism: Lyndon Johnson and the Limits of American Power* (New York: Oxford University Press, 1995), iii–viii, 259–264.
5. *Report of the National Advisory Commission on Civil Disorders* (New York: E.P. Dutton & Co., 1968), iii–vii, 534.
6. *National Advisory Commission on Civil Disorders,* 1–7.
7. *National Advisory Commission on Civil Disorders,* 1–2.
8. Michael Harrington, *The New American Poverty* (New York: Penguin Books, 1984), 20–23.
9. Jeffrey W. Helsing, *Johnson's War/Johnson's Great Society: The Guns and Butter Trap* (Westport, Conn.: Praeger, 2000), ix–xi, 255–256.
10. Gary Orfield, *The Reconstruction of Southern Education: The Schools and the 1964 Civil Rights Act* (New York: Wiley-Interscience, 1969), 162–206.

11. National Education Association. Commission on Professional Rights and Responsibilities, *Beyond Desegregation: The Problem of Power; a Special Study of East Texas* (Washington, D.C.: National Education Association, 1970).
12. Michael Eric Dyson, *I May Not Get There with You: The True Martin Luther King, Jr.* (New York: Free Press, 2000), 51–77.
13. Stokely Carmichael and Charles Hamilton, *Black Power: The Politics of Liberation in America* (New York: Random House, 1967), 83, 166–167.
14. Rosemary Salomone, *Equal Education under the Law: Legal Rights and Federal Policy in the Post-Brown Era* (New York: St. Martin's Press, 1986), 66–67; George R. Metcalf, *From Little Rock to Boston: The History of School Desegregation* (Westport Conn.: Greenwood Press, 1983), 267– 269.
15. Sundquist, *Politics and Policy,* 498–499.
16. Stephen Samuel Smith, *Boom for Whom? Education, Desegregation, and Development in Charlotte* (Albany: State University of New York Press, 2004), 24–25, 62–65.
17. Salomone, *Equal Education under Law,* 48–50.
18. *Bradley et al. v. Milliken et al.,* 338 F. Supp. 582; 1971 U.S. Dist. Lexis 11487.
19. *Milliken, Governor of Michigan, et al. v. Bradley et al.,* 418 U.S. 717 (1974).
20. Gary Orfield, *Must We Bus? Segregated Schools and National Policy* (Washington, D.C.: Brookings Institution, 1978), 391–420.
21. Gary Orfield, Susan Eaton, and the Harvard Project on School Desegregation, *Dismantling Desegregation: The Quiet Reversal of Brown v. Board of Education* (New York: New Press, 1996), 16–19, 54–55.
22. John R. Logan, Jacob Stowell, and Deirdre Oakley, "Choosing Segregation: Racial Imbalance in American Public Schools, 1990–2000," The Mumford Center, University at Albany, 29 March 2002, www.albany.edu/mumford.
23. U.S. Commission on Civil Rights, *Fulfilling the Letter and the Spirit of the Law: Desegregation of the Nation's Public Schools* (Washington, D.C.: Government Printing Office, 1976).
24. Michael Katz, *In the Shadow of the Poorhouse: A Social History of Welfare in America* (New York: Basic Books, 1986), 290.
25. Kenneth T. Jackson, *Crabgrass Frontier: The Suburbanization of the United States* (New York: Oxford University Press, 1985), 283–305.
26. Lewis Mumford Center for Comparative Urban and Regional Research, *The New Ethnic Enclaves in America's Suburbs,* www.albany.edu/mumford/census, 2002.
27. Myron Orfield, *American Metropolitics: The New Suburban Reality* (Washington, D.C.: Brookings Institution, 2002), 1–15.
28. John Ogbu, *Black American Students in an Affluent Suburb: A Study of Academic Disengagement* (Mahwah, N.J., 2003), ix–xiii, 252–260.
29. Charles T. Clotfelter, *After Brown: The Rise and Retreat of School Desegregation* (Princeton: Princeton University Press, 2004), 75–123.
30. Clotfelter, *After Brown,* 178–200.
31. Paul R. Dimond, "The Constitutional Right to an Education," *Hastings Law Journal* 24 (1973): 1087–1127; Erwin L. Levine and Elizabeth M. Wexler, *PL 94-142: An Act of Congress* (New York: Macmillan, 1981).
32. U.S. Commission on Civil Rights, *A Better Chance to Learn: Bilingual Bicultural Education* (Washington, D.C.: U.S. Commission on Civil Rights, 1975); Malcolm N. Danoff, *The Evaluation of the ESEA Title VII Spanish/English Bilingual Education Program: Overview of the Findings* (1978): fiche ERIC Document Number ED 162 524; Rachel F. Moran, "The Politics of Discretion: Federal Intervention in Bilingual Education," *California Law Review,* 1988 (Lexis-Nexus Academic Universe, 2002).
33. Edward Zigler and Susan Muenchow, *Head Start: The Inside Story of America's Most Successful Experiment* (New York: Basic Books, 1992), 1–4.
34. Zigler and Muenchow, *Head Start,* 5–55.
35. Sar A. Levitan, *The Great Society's Poor Law: A New Approach to Poverty* (Baltimore: Johns Hopkins Press, 1969), 133–155.
36. Levitan, *The Great Society's Poor Law,* 156–158.
37. Zigler and Muenchow, *Head Start,* 56–75.
38. James O. Miller, "An Educational Imperative and Its Educational Fallout," in *Disadvantaged Child Compensatory Education: A National Debate,* vol. 3, ed. Jerome Hellmuth (New York: Bruner/Mazel Publishers, 1970), 36–50.
39. Levitan, *The Great Society's Poor Law,* 161.
40. Barbara Beatty, *Preschool Education in America: The Culture of Young Children from the Colonial Period to the Present* (New Haven: Yale University Press, 1995), 197–198.
41. Beatty, *Preschool Education in America,* 198–199.
42. Zigler and Muenchow, *Head Start,* 173–175.
43. Henry M. Levin, "A Decade of Policy Developments in Improving Education and Training for Low-Income Populations," *A Decade of Federal Antipoverty Programs: Achievements, Failures, and Lessons,* ed. Robert H. Haveman (New York: Academic Press, 1977), 123–188.
44. Arthur Jensen, "How Much Can We Boost IQ and Scholastic Achievement," *Harvard Educational Review* 39, no. 1 (1969): 1–123.

45. John Ogbu, *The Next Generation: An Ethnography of Education in an Urban Neighborhood* (New York: Academic Press, 1974), 5–13.
46. Robert H. Haveman, *Poverty Policy and Poverty Research: The Great Society and the Social Sciences* (Madison: University of Wisconsin Press, 1987), 3–5; Martin Carnoy, *Faded Dreams: The Politics and Economics of Race in America* (Cambridge: Cambridge University Press, 1994), 215–217.
47. National Commission on Excellence in Education, *A Nation at Risk: The Imperative for Educational Reform* (Washington, D.C.: Government Printing Office, 1983).
48. Leonard Lund and Cathleen Wild, *Ten Years After Nation at Risk* (New York: Conference Board, 1993).
49. Maris A. Vinovskis, "Missed Opportunities," in *A Nation Reformed? American Education Twenty Years After a Nation at Risk,* ed. David T. Gordon (Cambridge: Harvard Education Press, 2003), 115–130.
50. Margaret Eisenhart and Lisa Towne, "Contestation and Change in National Policy on 'Scientifically Based' Education Research," *Educational Researcher* 32, no.7 (October 2003): 31–37.
51. Monika Williams Shealey, "The Promises and Perils of 'Scientifically Based' Research for Urban Schools," *Urban Education* 41, no. 1 (January 2006): 5–19.
52. Jaekyung Lee, *Tracking Achievement Gaps and Assessing the Impact of NCLB on the In-depth Look into National and State Reading and Math Outcome,* www.civilrightsproject.harvard.edu/news/pressreleases/nclb_reprot06php, accessed 16 June 2006.
53. Henry M. Levin, "Studying Privatization in Education," in *Privatizing Education: Can the Marketplace Deliver Choice, Efficiency, Equity, and Social Cohesion?* ed. Henry M. Levin (Cambridge: Westview Press, 2001), 3–19.
54. Martin Carnoy, "National Voucher Plans in Chile and Sweden: Did Privatization Make for Better Education?" *Comparative Education Review* 42, no. 3 (August 1998): 309–337.
55. Carnoy, "National Voucher Plans," 335–337.
56. *Susan Tave Zelman et al. v. Doris Simmons-Harris et al.* 536 U.S. 639 (2002).
57. Editorial, "Kids get a Lesson in Loopholes," *The Catholic Telegraph* (16 June 2006): 5.
58. Pearl Rock Kane and Christopher J. Lauricella, "Assessing the Growth Potential of Charter Schools," in *Privatizing Education: Can the Marketplace Deliver Choice, Efficiency, Equity, and Social Cohesion?* ed. Henry M. Levin (Cambridge: Westview Press, 2001), 203–233.
59. Erica Frankenberg and Chungmei Lee, "Charter Schools and Race: A Lost Opportunity for Integrated Education," *Education Policy Analysis Archives* 11, no. 32 (September 2005): 1–48, http://epaa.asu.edu/epaa/v11n32.
60. Chris Whittle, *Crash Course: Imagining a Better Future for Public Education* (New York: Riverhead Books, 2005), 1–42.
61. Henry Braun, Frank Jenkins, and Wendy Grigg, *A Closer Look at Charter Schools Using Hierarchical Linear Modeling,* http:/nces.ed.gov/nationreportcard//pubs/studies/2006460.asp, accessed 23 August 2006.
62. Kenneth J. Saltman, *The Edison Schools: Corporate Schooling and the Assault on Public Education* (New York: Routledge, 2005), 1–17.
63. Saltman, *The Edison Schools,* 16–17, 103–111.
64. Brain P. Gill et al., *Inspiration, Perspiration, and Time: Operations and Achievement in Edison Schools* (Santa Monica: RAND Corporation, 2005), 163–175.
65. Martin Carnoy, "School Choice? Or is it Privatization?" *Educational Researcher* 29, no. 7 (October 2000), 15–20.

16

Globalization and the History of American Education

Student from early twentieth century reading historical text

Historians encountered many difficulties as they sought to explain the relationship between globalization and education. One reason was the processes happened quickly. In a short period, towns changed into cities, railroads linked villages to cities, and ships connected distant countries. Another reason is that the changes influenced each other. While the rise of industrialism altered the political and economic geography of the world, ideas about curriculum and about teaching methods shifted and moved around the world. Faced with a wealth of information, historians interpreted the changes differently when they found information that called older views into question. In addition, they revised their theories as they considered their material in new ways.

At the same time, historians have their own opinions, and they pursue problems that interest them. They rely on records that people wrote to explain a particular way of thinking about things. Further, when the historians select parts of those records as important and ignore other parts, they compound the problems of bias. Although historians of education faced the same problems, they had an added difficulty. Because they wrote accounts of a field that became a profession, they had to help prospective teachers understand their fields and the methods that they would use. Thus, historians of education had to write texts that served the needs of the colleges and universities in which they worked.

As a result, the problems of bias interfered with the efforts of historians and of historians of education to explain the relationship between globalization and education. Nonetheless, the styles of work and the orientations of historians of education followed the patterns set by historians in general. The sections that follow may make this process of parallel development clear and show how both types of historians tried to illuminate the ways schools and societies influenced each other.

How Did Historians Seek to Illuminate Social Problems While Remaining Objective?

In the early nineteenth century, amateurs studied American history for personal reasons. For example, when Patrick Henry died in 1799, he had a reputation as a famous Virginian. This was inadequate for William Wirt, a lawyer in Virginia. Wirt wanted people to recognize Henry as a champion of liberty and to consider him a national hero. Thus, around 1805, Wirt decided to write Henry's biography. For the next twelve years, Wirt collected materials. Although he found that most Virginians regarded Henry as a wonderful public speaker, he could not find texts of Henry's speeches. Worse, Henry's service as a military commander and as a governor reflected badly on his abilities. According to Daniel Boorstin, the lack of evidence did not deter Wirt from glorifying Henry. To make Henry appear a hero for all time, Wirt fabricated events, debates, and such immortal utterances as, "Give me liberty or give me death."[1]

Boorstin suggested that Wirt wrote as he did because Wirt wanted to encourage native Virginians to have feelings of pride for their home state. Boorstin added that patriots from other sections such as New England tried to create their own heroes in similar ways. The result was that authors competed with each other in telling tales to make their own areas appear the cradle of liberty.

By the late nineteenth century, historians sought to do more than glorify their past heroes. According to Peter Novick, the study of history became a professional activity. American scholars traveled to Germany to study, and they returned to teach in universities where they developed a fetish for objectivity. They believed that careful attention to documents made their historical researches scientific. Praising Leopold von Ranke for originating this practice in Germany, many American scholars sought to avoid philosophical thinking, to make no interpretations, and to provide no generalizations in historical writing. Although Novick suggested that Ranke never expressed this intention as strongly as Americans interpreted it, Novick added that these historians thought their task was to present the facts they had found in various documents in the hopes that these truths would align themselves in ways that enabled readers to recognize wider truths about the nature of social change. The scholars claimed this was what Francis Bacon and Charles Darwin had done in other fields.[2]

By depending on incontrovertible evidence, these historians corrected the fault found among earlier authors, such as Wirt, who had invented events to fit their preconceptions. They took historical research out of the realm of propaganda. Unfortunately, when historians tried to be objective, they had difficulty using their research to influence affairs in their own time. Searching for incontrovertible facts, historians pursued trivial information, such as whether a building stood on the northeastern corner of an intersection of streets or which strategy a group of soldiers used in an insignificant battle.[3]

In 1884, the first president of the American Historical Association, Andrew Dickson White, suggested a way to avoid these problems. In his presidential address, White urged historians to follow the European standards of scholarship, but he added that historical studies should lead to some sort of philosophical synthesis offering insights into the types of social arrangements that could lead to the ethical improvement of humankind. Although he wanted scholars to develop the historical knowledge of their own country, he thought the researchers should relate their findings to wider concerns. Thus, he urged historians to recognize the need for two types of work. One type focused on the accumulation of accurate information about limited subjects, such as the development of a particular town or the strategies involved in battles. The other type compared broad tendencies such as industrial developments in several different areas over many years. Concluding that each type had to aid the other, he hoped the association's meetings would offer opportunities for different types of scholars to share their findings showing how humankind could improve.[4]

Despite White's view that studies of particular events could contribute to broader understandings, historians may not have followed his suggestions. As early as 1900, James Harvey Robinson complained that historians spent their time collecting details. For example, Robinson quoted six pages from a text about Italy whose author claimed to present the essential facts in due order. The pages presented a list of minor kings who succeeded each other from 1309 until 1435. Not only were these facts presented in an unappealing fashion, the list gave no indication that a renaissance was taking place at that time.[5]

Robinson's view was that historians should select events or tendencies that illuminated contemporary conditions or problems. Thus, the needs of the present would determine what the historians thought about the past. Not only did Robinson gain fame using this approach, he influenced the curriculum in twentieth-century high schools. In 1892, he was a member of the Madison Conference of the National Education Association's Committee of Ten that made recommendations for teaching subjects such as history and civics in high schools. This group approved of what the report called the topical method, wherein students made reports about specific issues of social importance. In 1916, the Committee on the Social Studies quoted Robinson extensively in its report to the National Education Association's Commission on the Reorganization of Secondary Education. This report urged that teachers organize history courses in ways that helped students understand contemporary social problems.

In 1929, Robinson delivered his presidential address to the American Historical Association. Entitling his speech "The Newer Ways of Historians," he acknowledged that he had adjusted paragraphs in his textbook history of Europe to justify the fury of World War I. Although Robinson argued that, at the time, his actions were justified, he accepted the criticism that he had written in ways that conformed to national propaganda rather than objectively assessing the emotional crisis as a historian should do. Thus, Robinson acknowledged that historians should be able to stand apart from mass hysteria. Despite this need for objectivity, he maintained it was correct to use the past to interpret the present. He suggested that historians might be able to do this if they gathered as much evidence from as many sources as possible. He suggested that historians should include works of literature and art that seemed to reflect the perspectives of the artists. Robinson's hope was that, by using many different interpretations, historians might be able to distinguish the difference between the intentions expressed in policy statements and the effects those policies had.[6]

In 1931, Carl Becker used his presidential address to the American Historical Association, entitled "Everyman His Own Historian," to defend Robinson's idea that history had to have social functions. Becker compared the writing of history to the way people keep records of the events in their lives. Defining history as the record of things said and done, Becker claimed that historical efforts included people looking in their checkbooks to determine if bills were correct. From this metaphor, Becker decided that historians had to select facts that suited what people wanted to be and what they wanted to achieve. Further, he argued that historians could recall some facts incorrectly to suit specific purposes. For example, Becker thought it made no difference that Americans celebrate the signing of the Declaration of Independence on the wrong day. What mattered to Becker was that historians selected the facts they used and arranged them in ways to help people understand what they were doing as a society and what they hoped to do.[7]

In 1933, a coauthor of Robinson's, Charles A. Beard, defended the new history approach in his address as president of the American Historical Association. Beard defined history as contemporary thought about the past. Although his definition implied that all interpretations of what had happened were equally acceptable, Beard did not stretch his point this far. Instead, he claimed that historians should build their thought about the past on a study of records. They should subject their ideas to criticism and order them with some form of the scientific method.[8]

After Beard made his speech, Theodore Clarke Smith criticized the progressive model of historical thinking. In a paper entitled "The Writing of American History in America from 1884 to 1934," Smith contended that most historians followed what he called a scientific historical technique, wherein they sought positive evidence and fashioned their conclusions from those findings. Smith complained that Robinson abandoned this notion by seeking to bring the accumulated findings to bear on the problems of contemporary society. Smith added that Beard made the problem worse when he considered the movement of society toward a collectivist democracy as the only valid historical narrative.[9]

Beard replied that Smith had misrepresented the work of the American Historical Association by separating it into the majority of the historians who followed scientific historical techniques and another group, led by Robinson, who were more subjective. Beard could not find any such split among the members of the Association. In fact, Beard quoted the founder of the Association, Andrew D. White, as saying in 1884 that the historians ought to provide works that opened the possibility of improving the society. In this way, Beard accused Smith of misusing facts in the same way that Smith contended Robinson had ignored historical truth. Although Smith claimed White's ideas had differed from those of Robinson, Beard noted that White's pleas sounded like the hopes that Robinson had expressed.[10]

How Could Educational Histories Inspire Teachers While Illuminating the Relation of Schools and Societies?

Whereas historians debated the way they should conduct their studies, some authors used history to advance the profession of teaching. In general, these authors were educators or trained in fields other than history. In their texts, they offered information about the profession that they thought prospective teachers could use.

According to Sol Cohen, there were few available texts in the history of education during the last years of the nineteenth century. Many programs of teacher training relied on texts that offered chronologies, compilations of facts about educational institutions, lists of laws, and descriptions of administrative codes. Such mind-numbing treatises could not provide insights into the problems and developments in the United States.[11]

Other authors concentrated on changes in philosophical thinking in Europe to portray educational advances. For example, in 1900, Thomas Davidson published *A History of Education.* Davidson was a prolific author who wrote about a wide range of topics, such as Greek philosophy, medieval thought, poetry, and art. William Knight recalled that Davidson had attended King's College, Aberdeen, where he won prizes for his abilities in Greek, logic, and moral philosophy. Coming to the United States, he taught at Harvard, and he began traveling the world. His fame came from establishing a summer school of philosophy in the Adirondack Mountains and a lecture series for working people in New York City.[12]

In his text, *A History of Education,* Davison quoted Herbert Spencer to indicate that history was a record of evolution. Positing that evolution stemmed from the desire for greater depth and variety to their feelings, Davidson claimed that all creation shared this desire. Because education was a human effort aimed at self-improvement, it represented the highest form of evolution. According to Davidson, education appeared when people became conscious of the evolution they were pursuing. Despite the importance of education, Davidson found that people thought of teaching as a low and profitless profession. Thus, he wanted to impart a dignity to teaching by helping people recognize that teachers were the chief agents of social progress. In turn, he hoped that his account would encourage people who were devoted and enthusiastic to enter the profession.[13]

In *A History of Education,* Davidson focused on the ways that people at different times conceived of correct instruction. Beginning his account with what he called savage education, he moved to what he called barbarian education. Instruction in these societies sought to produce individuals who conformed to social restraints, and he claimed that education in Asia and Africa conformed to this model. In his next section, Davidson contended that humanism had opened the possibility for individuals to have freedom. This quest began with Hellenism and came to fruition in the nineteenth century with such figures as Horace Mann. According to Davidson, Mann had created the noblest form of education in the world during the twelve years when he served as secretary to the Massachusetts Board of Education. In line with the sentiments he found in Mann's reports, Davidson concluded by noting the teachers earned the highest honors from society when they changed students from selfish creatures into honest citizens.[14]

Other authors of educational history imitated Davidson's praise of education. For example, in 1906, Paul Monroe of Columbia College in New York City published *A Textbook in the History of Education.* Monroe had received his Ph.D. from the University of Chicago where he had studied sociology and political science. On graduating, he studied in Heidelberg, Germany, returning to the United States to join the faculty at Columbia. He had been a high school teacher and principal for four years before he began graduate studies. At Columbia, he taught in the school of education and became the school's director in 1915.

In his text, Monroe sought to supply enough information to enable the students to understand the challenges that awaited them as teachers. As a result, Monroe admitted that he limited his descriptions to educational figures who represented typical movements and who influenced contemporary schools. Monroe hoped that prospective teachers could gather enough information from his text to guide their own practices. Above all, he wished to give teachers the fundamentals of a faith in the importance of their work.[15]

To direct the students' attention to the ways that teachers had operated in the past, Monroe divided his book into chapters that explained how adults in particular cultures or epochs taught children to embody the qualities needed to live with other members of the society. Beginning with what he called primitive education, Monroe classified this as the nonprogressive adjustment to group demands. Moving to what he called oriental education, he explained this as the recapitulation of wisdom handed down from ancestors. He described education in the middle ages as a type that imparted discipline through monastic life and the study of the humanities. During the Reformation, the religious conception of education dominated. With Rousseau came a naturalistic education. Three other models followed: the psychological tendency led by Pestalozzi and Herbart, the scientific movement led by Herbert Spencer, and the sociological tendency from educators such as Horace Mann. It was Monroe's belief that teachers could use their understanding of these different forms to arrive at what he called an eclectic tendency that combined aspects of each model in an intelligent fashion.

When Monroe wrote his text, he combined information about philosophy of education and sociology of education with material on the history of education. According to Lawrence Cremin, this combination was one of convenience. In the program at Columbia where Monroe worked, prospective teachers studied these fields together. Further, at Columbia, the teacher-training component imparted practical instruction and teacher-training courses were separate from academic departments. Consequently, Cremin acknowledged, it was not surprising that Monroe wrote a didactic and narrow history of education.[16]

In 1919, another author, Ellwood P. Cubberley published *Public Education in the United States: A Study and Interpretation of American Educational History.* Like Davidson and Monroe, Cubberley designed his text to aid prospective teachers in understanding the problems of education in the twentieth century in light of their historic evolution.

Cubberley was a professional educator rather than historian. He had been the superintendent of schools in San Francisco. As a professor and dean at Stanford University, Cubberley sought to make educational administration a profession. In his texts on the history of education, Cubberley used the history of education to show the development of public education.

In *Public Education in the United States,* Cubberley treated public schooling as a product of what he called the "Protestant Revolt" of the sixteenth century. After a short chapter on the transmission of education from Europe to the United States, Cubberley described such nineteenth-century controversies as tax support for schools, the effort to make schools without cost to the students, the elimination of sectarianism, and the evolution of graded school instruction.[17]

In his account of the growth of public education, Cubberley sought to impart a sense of mission to the beginning teachers whom he expected to be his readers. His chapters led to the conclusion that schools were the most important means to promote the welfare of the nation, because teachers could awaken children to the difference between freedom guided by law and license, and they could teach the young to shoulder responsibility and to develop self-control. Most important to Cubberley, the schoolteacher could blend the children's different heritages into a national mold.[18]

Cubberley's book enjoyed considerable popularity. Published shortly after every state then in the Union adopted laws for compulsory education, creating a need for trained teachers, Cubberley's text fit the attitude of the times because it appeared during the movement to Americanize the immigrants. Perhaps most important, Cubberley's former students taught similar classes in other universities where they could use the text.

In fairness to Cubberley, he provided some objectivity to his research. For example, in 1920, when Cubberley wrote a text about the history of education in the Western world, he published a separate book with selections of original documents that ran parallel to the subjects developed in the text. In keeping with his aim in the text, Cubberley selected documents dating from Ancient Greece to the early twentieth century to illustrate the ways that schooling spread Western civilization throughout the world.[19]

Thus, although the educational historians—Davidson, Monroe, and Cubberley—had different backgrounds and different interests than the historians—White, Robinson, Becker, and Beard—both groups of authors shared two important ideas. First, they believed that history should serve the present. Second, both groups held that authors should select and interpret material about the past in ways that made social improvement possible.

At the same time, the two groups followed different directions. The educational authors wanted their historical studies to glorify contemporary schools whereas historians often criticized present trends. In addition, because the educational authors limited their studies to formal instruction, they focused on one institution whereas the historians considered broader social issues.

In the Great Depression, educational historians followed more closely the ideals of progressive historians. In 1939, R. Freeman Butts recommended that books and courses in the history of education contribute to understanding problems in education and to the development of American intellectual history. Butts's ideas about educational history fit closely with what George S. Counts called the social foundations of education. According to Counts, prospective teachers should learn this combination of the disciplines of history, philosophy, sociology, and economics because it illuminated the social changes influencing schools.[20]

Thus, with the Great Depression, historians of education wanted to encourage prospective teachers to assist in the reconstruction of society. Not only did this shift put educational historians in line with progressive historians, it asked them to loosen their ties of loyalty to their professions. As social reconstructionists, teachers might learn to criticize the organization of schools. Although Counts's aim was consistent with Davidson's desire to impart to teachers the inherent nobility of their calling, Counts did not want teachers to impart virtue to the students as much as to lead movements of social reform. Although Counts helped to create a field of study called social foundations of education, the other more conservative models of educational history persisted.

How Could Historians Describe Schools as Part of Wider Institutional Networks?

In the years that followed World War II, historians considered the social concerns of progressive historians, such as Robinson and Beard, to be narrow. According to Gene Wise, the historians who worked in the 1950s tended to view events and personalities as being complicated. Describing the historians of the 1950s as counterprogressives, Wise claimed they were less sympathetic to figures that progressives had cheered, such as Andrew Jackson and Woodrow Wilson, and they were more sympathetic to personalities that the progressives considered conservative, such as John Winthrop and many American business leaders. Wise added that some of these historians, such as Daniel Boorstin, felt there was no unifying ideology to American life. Boorstin focused on the varied efforts of different individuals who kept trying to succeed at assorted tasks.[21]

At the same time, educational historians retained their connections with progressive ideas of the social foundations of education. This bias remained although various educational historians wanted to align the historical study of education more closely with the academic discipline of history. In 1953, Arthur Bestor, a professor of history, criticized the tendency of educational history to focus on school systems.

Bestor argued that colleges of education violated principles of academic responsibility by setting up courses of their own that dealt with other disciplines. Although Bestor agreed that prospective teachers should become acquainted with the historical forces that shaped school systems, he complained that colleges of education set up their own courses in the history of education. The instructors in courses in teacher preparation taught as if the teaching practices from the past were errors that led to the present practices found in classrooms. Thus, the history of education lost any claim it had to objectivity. It became a way to indoctrinate students into accepting the instructional plans that the faculty thought were best.[22]

Other American historians joined the criticism of educational historians. In 1959, Bernard Bailyn delivered a paper entitled "Education in the Forming of American Society" to the Institute of Early American History and Culture. Expanded and reprinted as a book, Bailyn's paper described the history of education as a special type of history that began in 1900. According to Bailyn, a rising class of professional educators fastened on to Thomas

Davidson's *A History of Education* published at this time, because it portrayed modern education as a force advancing human evolution and showed teachers to be the missionaries who brought civilization wherever they worked.[23]

Bailyn argued that Davidson's belief that education was a cosmic force leading human beings into full realization of themselves fit the social Darwinism of the day. Most important, the view suited the professional educators who believed that prospective teachers had to have a sense of mission to succeed in their work. He claimed that professional educators wanted new teachers to understand how modern scientific teaching techniques had come into being and why teachers had to use them. As a result, the history of education became an important introductory course in programs of teacher training. Using a religious metaphor, Bailyn complained that courses in the history of education became some sort of initiation for the beginners who wanted to become teachers in the same way that prospective priests had to learn what to believe to advance their faiths. In this effort, educational history texts advanced the ideological perspective teachers needed for their jobs. The books did not encourage thought about education.[24]

Bailyn believed that one problem was that these texts conceived of schools as self-contained entities whose development followed an internal logic. Although the authors related the schools to the environment, Bailyn found the social connections to be so weak that the authors could not show how the schools' burdens had changed over time.[25]

A second problem Bailyn found with authors such as Monroe and Cubberley was that they interpreted the past as being similar to the present. This violated Bailyn's view that some elements in the present never existed in the past. For example, although Monroe and Cubberley wrote as if private and public schools evolved from the eighteenth century, Bailyn argued that public schools began anew in the late nineteenth century with no relation to earlier forms of education. To him, public education was an unexpected institution that had troubled many intelligent people.[26]

Bailyn approved of Edward Eggleston's *The Transit of Civilization from England to America in the Seventeenth Century*, published in 1901. What intrigued Bailyn about Eggleston's view was that he included several aspects of the culture as education. Some of these educative forces were ideas of medicine, approved models of speech and literature, expectations of correct conduct, and types of labor. To Eggleston, these factors were parts of education that functioned beside schools. Although Bailyn believed that many of Eggleston's constructions were crude or unbalanced, he admired the way that Eggleston sought to place education, broadly conceived, in the center of historical change.[27]

Following Eggleston's ideas, Bailyn contended that the way to cure educational history of its narrowness was for historians to consider education as an entire process by which one generation transmitted culture to another generation. This meant that the role of schools would fade when compared to other social agencies such as the family. Further, he asked historians to recognize that the past was different from the present. In this way, historians could more accurately trace what changed and how those changes took place.[28]

Some historians of education agreed with Bailyn. In 1965, Lawrence Cremin wrote an essay on the historiography of American education. He noted that Cubberley's text, *Public Education in the United States,* had been an immediate and lasting success. By 1934, almost 80,000 readers had bought copies. Cremin added that colleges across the country used Cubberley's text until 1965 as critics such as Bailyn pointed out its weaknesses.

Although Cremin agreed with Bailyn, he noted that many other educational historians shared Cubberley's faith about the mission of teachers; they believed that public schools spread civilization. They thought that the schools developed out of institutions begun in the past. Claiming these views were misleading, Cremin called for educational historians to follow Bailyn's suggestions. First, rather than focus on schools, Cremin thought that authors should investigate a wide range of institutions involved in shaping human character. Second, Cremin called for educational authors to work more closely with other historians. Noting that historians were changing their methods and their ideas, he suggested that educational authors should do the same. Third, Cremin called for authors to reconsider the ways that education, broadly conceived, influenced people's thinking.[29]

In 1970, Lawrence Cremin produced the first of his three-volume series on the history of education. In the bibliographic essay of this work, Cremin praised Bailyn's concern for broader definitions of education, and he noted that many institutions besides schools provided education. In addition, Cremin tried to determine what practices were in place within educational institutions rather than consider the types of policies that appeared in official documents. Finally, Cremin sought to determine how changes in cultural practices related to education, such as childrearing, influenced the characters of adults.[30]

Could History Enable People to Improve Social Conditions?

Some educational historians such as Cremin sought to expand the focus of studies of education to include many elements in the wider society; however, other historians narrowed their approaches and abandoned the drive for objectivity in favor of the cause of social regeneration. For example, in 1970, Howard Zinn offered a radical interpretation of the obligations of historians. He claimed that historians should sharpen the readers' perceptions of how much victims suffered in the world. Calling his approach radical history, Zinn argued that when historians made problems vivid and real, they could lead citizens to take actions to improve the society. To achieve this aim, Zinn urged historians to take the perspectives of the underdogs and eschew the traditional tendency to be objective. Although such accounts were biased, Zinn felt that the proliferation of studies would reduce this problem. For example, Zinn contended that historians had used plantation diaries to write histories of slavery and wrote histories of slavery from the perspectives of the plantation owners. Telling the story from the perspectives of the slaves would provide another perspective. It could balance the accounts, and it might cause readers to engage in social action.[31]

A group of educational historians took on Zinn's idea of radical history by reversing Cubberley's conclusions in an effort to bring about social change. Although they focused on the public schools as Cubberley had, they argued that public schools were instruments by which powerful elites controlled other less fortunate groups. Thus, while Cubberley contended in the 1920s that education was the means of spreading Western civilization, educational historians in the 1970s argued that public schools were instruments enabling powerful groups to dominate weaker social classes.

In 1968, Michael Katz published the conclusions of his study of the records of an election held in Beverly, Massachusetts, in 1860 to determine whether to close the town's high school. After determining the social classes of the voters, Katz concluded that upper-class citizens wanted to maintain the high school whereas lower-class citizens did not. From this evidence, Katz argued that the common school movement served social class interests.[32]

In 1973, Clarence J. Karier, Paul C. Violas, and Joel Spring collaborated in writing a book of essays entitled *Roots of Crisis.* Claiming that history writing was an art, they quoted Carl Becker to argue that historians should explain the meaning of present conditions. As times changed, historians had to create new visions of the past. In the early years of the twentieth century, historians such as Cubberley could write favorably of schools because they believed that people who occupied lower-class status benefited from the expansion of schooling. Karier, Violas, and Spring argued that that Cremin accepted Cubberley's vision. They criticized Cremin for holding to a liberal bias that caused him to praise schools during the 1960s when urban rioters burned cities and schools. Concluding that the riots of the 1960s indicated that times had changed, they asserted that views of history should change as well. Thus, Karier, Violas, and Spring wanted their histories to show how the society was racist, materialistic, and elitist.[33]

Although Karier, Violas, and Spring criticized the conclusions they attributed to Cremin, they followed his idea of considering a wider range of institutions than schools. For example, in *Roots of Crisis,* the authors published essays on such issues as the items on U.S. Army intelligence tests, the settlement movement, and the youth culture. In the final essay, Spring called for an examination of the writings of people he called anarchists, such as William Godwin, Leo Tolstoy, and Emma Goldman. Arguing that educational historians had blinded themselves through a devotion to public schooling, Spring claimed that a study of the fears these anarchists expressed could restore the radical tradition in education. He added this would help people understand that the schools operate as machines directing students in ways to aid the modern industrial state.[34]

The aim of radical historian was not new. Several historians had described what Zinn called the perspective of the underdog. For example, the African American historian, John Hope Franklin, had pursued Negro history since 1947. By 1967, white novelists such as William Styron entered the field with such books as *Confessions of Nat Turner.* These books offended some African Americans who accused the novelists of perpetuating racism with the images of famous black people that they created. The African Americans claimed that only black authors could write about black people. As this idea spread, every group supplied its own historians.[35]

In the case of education, African American authors presented revisionist perspectives of the history of the education of black people. In general, the authors who wrote educational histories of different groups appeared sympathetic to Zinn's ideas; they sought to demonstrate the discrimination the different groups had suffered. Their hope was that such explanations would cause people to ameliorate those problems.

In 1988, James D. Anderson published *The Education of Blacks in the South, 1860–1935.* Framing his argument to show the unfairness black people suffered, Anderson turned around the arguments of Karier and Violas. Anderson claimed that the former slaves were the first native Southerners who campaigned for universal state-supported education. Claiming that African Americans contributed from their poverty to create schools, Anderson argued that the white teachers turned the desire the African Americans had for education to serve the white establishment. In making this point, Anderson complained that some of the missionary teachers during Reconstruction taught black children to be subservient to white people. He added that a more effective method of subverting African Americans' desire for self-control came in 1868 with the Hampton model. According to Anderson, these industrial training schools, such as Booker T. Washington's in Tuskegee, taught black adolescents to work hard and accept the inequalities of Southern life.[36]

How Did Educational Historians React to the Revisionists?

Educational historians tried to meet the criticisms of the revisionists. In 1974, R. Freeman Butts complained of two forms of revisionism then popular. He found the first form in Cremin's work. According to Butts, when Cremin explored the constellation of institutions and cultural pursuits that educated people, he engaged in *culturalism* because, by widening the focus beyond schools, he caused people to underestimate the importance of the formal institutions in bringing about social change. In this regard, Butts contended that schools were the most important educational institutions in the United States during the nineteenth and early twentieth centuries. The second form of revisionism Butts called radical revisionism. He included the authors Katz, Karier, Violas, and Spring in this category. To criticize their work, Butts quoted such educational historians as Ronald Goodenow and Wayne Urban, who claimed that these authors depended on overgeneralizations, they used confusing categories, they selected their evidence to fit their complaints, and they oversimplified the problems. Butts argued that the radical revisionists failed to offer a fair portrayal of both the good and the bad effects of public schools. He contended that the radical revisionists held the same narrow perspective as did historians such as Cubberley. Whereas Cubberley presented information that showed the schools to be the source of social improvement, the radical revisionists selected information that blamed the schools for social problems.[37]

For Butts, the solution was for historians of education to link their studies of the United States with understandings of what he called an international and comparative perspective. Butts claimed that Cremin acknowledged the importance of a comparative view but did not include it in his works. He noted that the radical revisionists ignored such a comparative perspective. Butts claimed studies employing this perspective would show that the motivating force in educational change since the eighteenth century has been the trend that he called *modernization.*[38]

In his book, *Education of the West,* Butts described what he called the eight aspects of modernization that have most influential in the United States. These included increasing power of the central government, expanding urban industrialization, enhancing secular and technical knowledge, spreading the modern ways throughout the world, expanding popular participation in public affairs, searching for religious and cultural pluralism, seeking racial and ethnic integration, and believing that education will solve practical human problems. For Butts, an intelligent interpretation of the history of American education came from the interaction of these trends with their contradictions and tensions.[39]

For Butts, such a comparative approach would help determine the political role of American education. Since Butts claimed that the greatest need was for improved civic education, he thought the concept of modernization and the way the notion placed concepts in opposition to each other offered possibilities for greater understanding. For example, the concept turned historical research away from labeling certain actors as evil. According to Butts, when researchers viewed public education as a phase of modernization, they could consider educational reformers in the first years of the twentieth century as seeking to spread the benefits of modern industries to impoverished immigrants from pre modern societies rather than trying to impose their culture on weaker groups. Thus, ideas about unintended consequences could replace simple conspiracy theories. In addition, a conception of modernism could indicate to researchers that calls for greater pluralism with increased alternatives for individual life styles might lead to increased social control. Lacking coherent reference groups, people would be unable to resist advertising campaigns.[40]

While Butts believed that the drift of education since the eighteenth century has been toward increasing modernization, he did not oppose it. Butts wanted to guide modernistic tendencies, such as expanding popular participation in public affairs or searching for religious and cultural pluralism, toward increased freedoms of all people. Thus, Butts shared the faith in evolution that Davidson expressed in 1900 in his text *A History of Education,* although he did not use the same language.

Butts did not convince historians to use modernization as an organizing concept. Although the term appeared in social sciences since the nineteenth century, historians did not refer to modernization. By the end of the twentieth century, historians referred to aspects of modernization theory rather than to the concept itself. The problem was in defining the essential aspects of modernism. At first glance, the concept appeared simple because it implied a Darwinist view that societies should follow similar patterns as the members moved away from religious precepts and came to accept scientific rationalism. Thus, the basic distinction was between traditional and modern. The questions became complicated when historians asked when a traditional practice changed into a modern one. Furthermore, a tradition could change to fit new circumstances and remain traditional.

As far as Butts' plea for comparative history, such approaches had a place and advocates within the American Historical Association. For example, C. Vann Woodward championed the comparative approach and used it to make fruitful discoveries about the pattern of relationships between African Americans and white southerners.[41] Similarly, Cyril Edwin Black urged historians to use comparative approaches to classify and organize complex materials and to explain changes in institutions or functions.[42]

Despite the opportunities that comparative methods offered, Black noted that historians had difficulties using them. One problem was that the members of different groups could exhibit such variations that researchers making the comparisons found similarities that were so general they offered no explanatory value. Another difficulty was that the effort to make comparisons among dissimilar societies eliminated the rich detail available from close studies of available documents about particular events. Such problems warned against the use of comparative methods and the search for generalizations.[43]

Despite the difficulties with comparative methods and the search for generalizations, historical study became increasing interdisciplinary through such combined specialties as historical sociology or economic history. This tendency influenced educational historians. For example, in 2002, John Rury offered a text that sought to illuminate the relationship between education and social change. In his several chapters, Rury did not focus on events, names, or dates. Instead, Rury preferred to use concepts and terms from other social sciences to illuminate his discussion of schools and social progress. He found that the most helpful terms were *industrialization, urbanization*, and *ideological change.* Showing the increases in school attendance that took place over the twentieth century, he concluded that the trend is for education to be a significant fact in American life. To Rury, this suggested that schools could be important facts in American life and significant forces in social change.[44]

Rury's book illustrated the willingness of historians to do comparative or interdisciplinary studies such as Butts had urged. Although Rury did not organize his book around the concept of modernization, he used components of that concept such as urbanization, industrialization, and human capital. Unlike Butts, he did not use his investigations to suggest what political role schools could play. He sought to ask the broader question of whether schools affect social change or social change influences schools.

On the other hand, many historians of education focused on traditional concerns and avoided broad generalizations about education and the social order. For example, in 1975, the National Academy of Education invited Diane Ravitch to review the works of the radical historians of education. In the spirit of Butts, she divided the revisionists into the same two types. Praising the revisionism of Bailyn and Cremin, Ravitch claimed that their criticisms of such authors as Monroe and Cubberley broke down artificial barriers that had separated educational history in the United States from the mainstream of American history. On the other hand, she disparaged the radical revisionism she found in such authors as Katz, Karier, Violas, and Spring because she thought the authors focused excessively on schools to show the harm those institutions caused and the authors misled educational policy makers by making simplistic analyses. For example, Ravitch claimed that when historians wrote that schooling served only to sort people for jobs, policy makers reduced the academic standards allowing more students to attain degrees. The result was schools became diploma mills that ignored their aim of encouraging literacy. Her answer was for historians to portray the complexity of events and the tenuousness of connections. In this way, history could enable educational policy makers to think in modest but appropriate terms.[45]

Other historians looked more closely at the evidence the radical revisionists used to determine if schools served the interests of social efficiency and control. For example, in 1985, Maris Vinovskis went to Beverly, Massachusetts, and used the same data Katz had considered. Vinovskis claimed that the division among the social classes was not as clear as Katz had argued. Many more issues were involved so that the results of the election about the high school did not reflect the voters' attitudes about high schools. For example, Vinovskis claimed that the town leaders held another election for school committee and people who voted against the high school voted for candidates who had supported the high school.[46]

An important educational historian in the 1960s was Edward Krug. Although neither Butts nor Ravitch considered Krug to be a revisionist, he was the teacher of Joel Spring, whom Butts and Ravitch criticized. Spring had worked as Krug's research assistant and found Krug to be an able critic of American liberalism. Spring noted that under Krug's tutelage, he learned how education was an instrument of social control.[47]

In 1964, Edward A. Krug completed the first volume of his history of the high school curriculum in the United States. He argued that high schools took on the role of the universal custodian of American youth and processed them in ways that ensured the society functioned efficiently. Thus, Krug argued that, by the 1920s, the high school offered a range of programs in addition to academic studies. According to Krug, the advocates of these new programs viewed education as social control. By this he meant that school people wanted the subject matters to serve practical functions in social life, and they wanted to offer programs that separated youths and trained them for their probable destinies.[48]

Because such programmed differentiation could cause high schools to maintain social inequality, Krug's student, Spring, could label the high school as a sorting machine. At the same time, critics claimed that the comprehensive high school, a building that housed vocational programs, general classes, and college preparatory courses, came from an effort to create democracy's high school.

In the main, the development of the comprehensive high school had come from the 1918 report of the National Educational Association's Commission on the Reorganization of the High School. In 2001, William Wraga reviewed the surviving documents about deliberations of the commission members and the published sources. He found evidence to contradict Krug's account. Thus, he claimed that the planners had not tried to create machines to maintain inequality. They hoped that the high school would avoid the problems of trade schools and academic schools in separate buildings because the comprehensive high school allowed students to choose programs and transfer among programs frequently. If these things did not happen, Wraga added, the fault did not fall on the intentions of the planners as Krug and his followers suggested.[49]

How Did Historians Influence Teacher Training?

Radical revisionists of educational history enjoyed considerable popularity. The criticism the revisionists received may have contributed to their popularity. For example, in 1986, Joel Spring published a textbook, *The American School, 1642–1985: Varieties of Historical Interpretation of the Foundations and Development of American Education.* Designing his text for use in programs of teacher preparation, Spring claimed that historians disagreed about the role of public schools in American society. According to Spring, prospective teachers and other readers should become aware of these controversies because historical interpretations shape people's image of the past and influence their choices for future actions. Spring contended that there were two general sets of interpretations. On one side, historians such as Cubberley considered the public schools as beneficial forces. On the other side, Spring claimed there were historians such as Katz who portrayed the school as maintaining the social and racial distinctions in society. Spring wanted to show that both views were partly correct. To him, it appeared that elite groups had wanted to use education to maintain their power and control while underclass groups had sought to use schools as avenues of social improvement. He hoped that such a presentation would enable readers to clarify their opinions about the relationship of schools to social events.[50]

In 1987, Donald Warren reviewed Spring's text for the *History of Education Quarterly.* Warren found Spring's work to be important because it was part of what he called a revisionist history of education that added depth, candor, and complexity to people's understanding of schools. Warren noted that Spring claimed there was such a thing as an American school and it had extended from the colonial period to the present. Further,

Warren quoted Spring as contending that although this school served contradictory purposes, those purposes tended to be less democratic aims. Although underclass groups wanted the schools to provide a means of liberation, Spring showed how elites used schools to dominate the nation's political, economic, and intellectual life.[51]

Although Warren admitted that he shared Spring's sympathies, he complained that Spring left out a considerable amount of information that would have deepened and complicated his story. Warren felt that Spring portrayed most of the historical figures that appeared in the book as agents or categories. Spring did not consider these people as thinking and feeling men and women. Most important, Warren accused Spring of tailoring history to fit his interpretation, of posing uncomplicated questions to the readers, and of offering simple either/or answers. These difficulties meant that Spring failed to achieve his aims.[52] Warren's criticisms did not dissuade instructors in teacher-training programs from adopting *The American School* for their courses. By 2005, Spring had published six editions of this text.

Authors such as Wayne Urban, who had raised complaints about the radical revisionists, published texts that competed with Spring's *American School.* In 1996, Urban joined with Jennings L. Wagoner, Jr. to publish *American Education: A History.* Claiming the important characteristic of their text to be the avoidance of one-sided views of schools, Urban and Wagoner presented multiple views explaining how educators at the times had thought and felt. They wrote that they adopted this strategy because the issues were sufficiently complex, and they wished to avoid the simplistic orientations of those textbook authors who had declared the public schools to be wonderful and the one-dimensional view of authors who deplored the schools.[53]

When Edith Nye MacMullen reviewed Urban and Wagoner's book, she found that the authors' efforts to present multiple views caused two problems: the text lacked conviction and it did not have a cohesive view. As a result, she could not recognize the organization of the text. She complained that the book devoted an entire chapter to education in the South during the nineteenth century and spent few pages on the Northwest, the Southwest, or the Midwest. She found that the book offered little about the treatment of European immigrants or Asians or Hispanics. Acknowledging that it would be difficult to describe the social, political, and economic context within which schools developed, she thought prospective teachers should recognize the cultural context within which schools operate. In Urban and Wagoner's book, she could not understand why the authors chose to describe some elements of the culture while ignoring others. Despite these flaws, MacMullen thought the scholarship was sound, and the book would serve for introductory courses in the history of education. It could inspire class discussions and research projects for students.[54]

American School by Spring and *American Education* by Urban and Wagoner focused on formal education rather than relating schools to the wider culture as Cremin urged, and the authors of both books ignored Butts's call for more comparative studies to offer new understandings about American education. If they considered the culture, it was to illustrate more clearly the workings of formal education. At the same time, although both texts noted the increasing influence of the federal government in local school affairs, they did not direct readers to recognize the contradictory elements in the trend toward what Butts called modernization. While Spring suggested that the tendency toward central control served the industrial state, Urban and Wagoner mentioned it as one change among many reforms.

How Did Postmodernism Change the Field of History?

Whereas radical historians and revisionists championed what they called the underdog, other historians followed a movement that had spread among literary critics. This was the tendency to deny that anyone could draw general conclusions from any study. The argument was that knowledge was local and directed to a specific culture. It did not reveal some wider social change. In 1979, Jean-François Lyotard called this tendency *postmodernism.* According to Lyotard, the grand narratives that came from any scientific study seemed to reinforce the institutions that made these studies. Because knowledge justified the power that created it, Lyotard argued that the concepts of justice and truth served special interest groups because institutional studies showed how to achieve those ideals. Consequently, Lyotard urged people to turn to specific narrative elements that did not extend beyond their local situation.[55]

Although critics point to many influences that made the idea of postmodernism popular, many advocates of postmodernism contend what they call the crisis of 1968 made the issues important. During the summer, assassins killed Martin Luther King, Jr. and Robert Kennedy, damaging the civil rights movement. Riots broke out in American cities. In Chicago, police attacked antiwar demonstrators who were protesting the nomination of Hubert Humphrey as U.S. President. In Europe, students and workers undertook massive waves of strikes protesting the advent of rational systems of industrial relations that reinforced management policies. As a result, many people embraced conservative institutions and governments, and in the United States, conservative Richard Nixon won the election.

According to Thomas Docherty, intellectuals embraced the term *postmodern* after they lost faith in progressive reform. He contended that critics such as Lyotard distrusted the optimistic narratives of Marx, Freud, or the liberalism of John Dewey, because these grand theories ignored the uniqueness of particular situations as they pushed a wider notion of truth. Docherty noted that other authors, such as Zygmunt Bauman, pointed to the Holocaust to illustrate the barbarous side of modern thought, because the Nazi government began the genocide in a rational effort to solve what they called the Jewish problem.[56]

Despite the popularity of postmodernism in literary circles, by 1995, historians in the United States had not adopted what Robert F. Berkhofer, Jr. called the infection of postmodernism. Nonetheless, he believed that traditional historians faced three challenges. First, few audiences appreciated what he called great narratives. Second, multiculturalists complained that Eurocentric studies obscured the alternative cultures existing in the world. Third, stories about progress and liberation no longer provided guidance for contemporary actions. According to Berkhofer, postmodernist theory exacerbated these challenges by raising questions about the ways knowledge served social groups and the ways it reinforced existing elites. Most important, postmodernism suggested that the only things historians can know are texts; they cannot find a correspondence between the descriptions and the events that took place in the world.[57]

Instead of accepting the nihilistic perspective of postmodernism, Berkhofer urged historians to seek ways to unite the traditional approach to history with postmodern theory. To illustrate the possibilities and the problems of including postmodernism in historical studies, Berkhofer pointed to Simon Schama's book, *Citizens: A Chronicle of the French Revolution.* Instead of an overall description of the events, Schama presented chronologically arranged vignettes hiding what Berkhofer called the "Great Story" in the text. In *Dead Certainties (Unwarranted Speculations),* Schama added fiction to his technique of presenting distinct voices and perspectives. In this case, he invented a diary by one of the protagonists and described the person's inner thoughts in the way a novelist might. Although Berkhofer approved of the inventions Schama used, he noted that this form of history writing would not be appreciated until reviewers and readers learned to think differently about history.[58]

In his conclusion, Berkhofer suggested there were four steps that historians had to take if they were to move beyond what he called normal history. First, they had to explain how they had come to think about their topics as well as explain what they had decided. Second, they should be willing to present a variety of voices in dialogue with the author's voice. Third, they had to avoid representing the past with terms and concepts of the present. Finally, they had to accept new forms of representation without forming rules defining what was acceptable in historical studies.[59]

The reviews of Berkhofer's book ranged widely. Michael Roth praised Berkhofer in *The American Historical Review* for writing an intelligent and well-researched book. Roth complimented Berkhofer for questioning the assumptions of historical writing. He thought Berkhofer's complaints might make historical accounts more exciting and less likely to reinforce the present arrangements of social institutions. In the *Journal of American History,* Bryan D. Palmer called Berkhofer's book well researched and balanced in its presentation of postmodernism. Nonetheless, Palmer added that Berkhofer overlooked the wide variety of traditional historical orientations, lumped them together, and showed them lacking in the face of postmodern challenges. According to Palmer, such oversights caused Berkhofer to underestimate the different perspectives that historians take and the flexibility that they demonstrate.[60]

Interestingly, in the 1990s, traditional historians reacted against the tendency of multiculturalism and postmodernism. Complaining that the focus of radical historians on such areas as feminist studies or on gay and lesbian concerns replaced research on the changes of governments, traditional historians sought to reassert the focus of historians on the rise and fall of empires, states, and republics. They argued that the radical historians presented a series of vignettes about everyday life that did not help people understand the wider transformations in society. As a result, in 1998, several prominent historians joined together to form The Historical Society, dedicated to restoring what these individuals considered more traditional approaches to historical study.[61]

In a volume dedicated to the formation of this new group, Elisabeth Lasch-Quinn complained that radical historians had removed any sense of public verifiability from historical research. According to Lasch-Quinn, universities and learned societies adopted the view that each speaker from a particular perspective had a viewpoint as valid as any other viewpoint. Thinking this advanced social equality, the institutions set up different areas or ways that such spokespeople could work. Lasch-Quinn complained that this arrangement caused interest group politics to replace reasoned discussion. She contended that the members of these groups did not engage in dialogue. Instead, the members of the various groups sought to bar some teachers from working in certain areas and to coerce students to reach particular conclusions.[62]

Although The Historical Society called upon historians to return to traditional historical orientations, the members of the society sought to overcome the division that had existed between mainstream history and educational history. For example, Diane Ravitch, who appeared above as a critic of the radical revisionist view, contributed an essay to the volume commemorating the emergence of the new historical society. Writing about school curriculums, she complained that the controversy over national history standards in 1994 weakened the possibility of teaching history in a credible academic manner in high schools. Ravitch claimed that the contracts to work on these standards had come from her office in the U.S. Department of Education. As a result, she blamed herself for some of the problems. More important, though, she blamed some of the problems on social studies educators who disdained the instruction of historical content and preferred to teach children to solve problems of contemporary interest.[63]

In 2000, she published a text that continued the general complaint she made in her essay for The Historical Society. Narrowing her study to progressive reforms, she accused the progressives of causing educational policy makers to dilute subject matter requirements to the point that students could not acquire the skills of literacy. Entitling her book *Left Back: A Century of Battles over School Reform*, Ravitch aimed her book at a narrow audience although one that differed from the readers Spring and Urban and Wagoner sought to engage. Whereas texts such as Spring's were for prospective teachers, Ravitch wanted to appeal to parents, educators, policy makers, and citizens. She appeared on national television advancing the arguments in her book, telling parents it offered a rationale for improving academic standards in public schools. Such a fight was important, she contended, because all students should have the opportunities to enrich their lives as citizens and as individuals with understandings of what she called the varieties of human experiences.[64]

The basis of Ravitch's complaint was that, throughout the twentieth century, progressive educators sought to meet students' needs and interests. She argued that, in this quest, they substituted the ideal of utility for the aim of knowledge. Labeling such a tendency as anti-intellectual, she claimed that academic studies offered practical benefits such as advancing everyone's civic intelligence, providing a forum for creating shared values, and protecting the public from irrational belief systems.[65]

Without intending to be ironic, Ravitch complained that progressive educators who sought to relate school lessons to children's experiences weakened the practical values that the children could derive from academic study. Although such a point may be true, Ravitch did not explain this idea. She asserted it, and critics found the lack of explanation to be a flaw in her work.

In 2001, William G. Wraga wrote a review of *Left Back* for the journal of the American Educational Research Association, *Educational Researcher*. In his review, Wraga accused Ravitch of omitting material from documents she quoted that weakened her case or opposed it. For example, Wraga claimed that Ravitch extolled the 1893 report of the Committee of Ten for its affection for academic studies while ignoring the fact that the report did not expect many students to attend high schools. He added that Ravitch cited from authors selectively in ways that discredited their suggestions. For example, he wrote that Ravitch asserted John Dewey had found Rousseau's ideas to be correct. Although Wraga acknowledged that Dewey approved of the freedom Rousseau wanted children to have, he added that Dewey thought Rousseau's theories were incomplete because they lacked any standard toward which the learner could move. Wraga noted that Ravitch excluded reform efforts, such as the Harvard report, *General Education in a Free Society,* written in 1945, that would contradict her thesis. In all, Wraga labeled Ravitch's book a failure study. He defined such studies as books that led people to reject some course of action because it apparently did not work. Although such studies may be valuable, Wraga wrote, they do not suggest how to organize schools. For example, Wraga contended that most studies of contemporary schools show that teachers consider academic instruction to consist of forcing students to memorize information that they will forget. Although Wraga thought these studies implied that some aspects of progressive education's efforts to connect learning to life experiences were necessary, he concluded that Ravitch could not describe which parts of progressive approaches to retain because she refused to provide a balanced view of progressivism.[66]

Conclusion

When scholars of history and of the history of education sought to explain social change, they followed similar methods. In general, historians sought to write in ways that helped people understand what they were doing and historians of education sought to inspire prospective teachers by showing what practices teachers should follow.

Over time, these groups changed their methods and their aims. Nonetheless, historians and historians of education changed in similar directions. For example, in times of social stress, such as the Great Depression, both groups tried to help people reshape society. During the civil rights movement, both groups tried to champion disenfranchised groups.

The efforts of historians that most closely fit the aim of this book were those who called for comparative views of social development. Unfortunately, historians had difficulty making the general comparisons that comparative studies required.

Educational historians who linked schools to the forces of modernization tried to accomplish aims similar to those of this text. In taking such a direction, they tended to see the schools as enhancing opportunities for all people. This was the view that revisionist historians challenged strongly. Incorporating some of those criticisms of school development, some educational historians adopted interdisciplinary approaches. In this effort, they sought to map wider social and educational changes that offered broad general conclusions, and they used descriptions of specific dates, events, or people to illuminate those conclusions.

Instead of a comparative approach, this text uses descriptions of specific educational movements and the writings of various educators to trace the ways that ideas spread around the United States and from America to some other countries. As a result, the book offers an account of the ways people thought about education by considering such matters as curriculum proposals, ideas about teaching methods, and suggestions about appropriate school architecture. These documents appear as indications of the relation between schools and societies. Thus, this book does not concentrate on concepts from fields such as sociology as much as it tries to find the links with globalization through descriptions of what leading spokespeople recommended.

Postmodernists may complain that such a history describes the views of influential social groups. Although the complaint may be correct, it does not invalidate the effort. The ideas of educational theorists offer important pictures of educational change when these suggestions appear against each other in comparison to the social settings in which they appeared. This is a reasonable approach to history, and even postmodernists write history. They think of it as something personal and everchanging. Authors who want to be as objective as possible may find the postmodern perspective reasonable. Although the quest to determine how societies and schools influence each other may not lead to definite conclusions, the effort can improve the perspectives that people hold.

Endnotes

1. Daniel J. Boorstin, *The Americans: The National Experience* (New York: Vintage Books, 1965): 356–359.
2. Peter Novick, *That Noble Dream* (Cambridge, U.K.: Cambridge University Press, 1988), 25–40.
3. Herman Ausubel, *Historians and Their Craft: A Study of the Presidential Addresses of the American Historical Association, 1884–1945* (New York: Russell and Russell, Inc., 1965), 17–18.
4. Andrew D. White, "On Studies in General History and the History of Civilization," *Papers of the American Historical Association,* vol. I (New York: G. P. Putnam's Sons, 1886), 49–72.
5. James Harvey Robinson, *The New History: Essays Illustrating the Modern Historical Outlook* (1912; reprint, Springfield, Mass.: Walden Press, 1958), 3–4.
6. James Harvey Robinson, "The Newer Ways of Historians," *The American Historical Review* 35 (January 1930): 245–255.
7. Carl Becker, "Everyman His Own Historian," *American Historical Review* 37 (January 1932): 221–236.
8. Charles A. Beard, "Written History as an Act of Faith," *The American Historical Review* 39 (January 1934): 219–229.
9. Theodore Clarke Smith, "The Writing of American History, 1884–1934," *The American Historical Review* 40 (January 1935): 439–449.
10. Charles A. Beard, "That Noble Dream," *The American Historical Review* 41 (October 1935): 74–87.
11. Sol Cohen, "The History of the History of American Education, 1900–1976: Uses of the Past" *Harvard Educational Review* 46, no. 3 (August 1976): 298–330.
12. William Knight, *Some Nineteenth Century Scotsman: Being Personal Recollections* (London: Oliphant, Anderson, and Ferrier, 1903), 351–362
13. Thomas Davidson, *A History of Education* (1900; reprint, New York: AMS Press, 1970), v–vi.
14. Davidson, *A History,* 248–276.
15. Paul Monroe, *A Textbook in the History of Education* (1905; reprint, New York: Macmillan Co., 1930), vii–x.
16. Lawrence Cremin, *The Wonderful World of Ellwood Patterson Cubberley: An Essay on the Historiography of American Education* (New York: Teachers College, 1965), 43–45, 72.
17. Elwood P. Cubberley, *Public Education in the United States: A Study and Interpretation of American Educational History* (Boston: Houghton Mifflin Co., 1919), vii–viii.
18. Cubberley, *Public Education,* 504.
19. Ellwood P. Cubberley, *Readings in the History of Education: A Collection of Sources and Readings to Illustrate the Development of Educational Practice, Theory, and Organization* (Boston: Houghton Mifflin Co. 1920), vii–viii.
20. Cohen, "The History of the History of American Education," 310–311.
21. Gene Wise, *American Historical Explanations: A Strategy for Grounded Inquiry* (Homewood, Ill.: Dorsey Press, 1973), 83–84, 103.
22. Arthur Bestor, *Educational Wastelands: The Retreat from Learning in our Public Schools* (Urbana: University of Illinois Press, 1953), 143–145.
23. Bernard Bailyn, *Education in the Forming of American Society* (New York: Vintage Books, 1960), 5–7.
24. Bailyn, *Education,* 7–9.
25. Bailyn, *Education,* 9.
26. Bailyn, *Education,* 11.
27. Bailyn, *Education,* 6.
28. Bailyn, *Education,* 13–14.
29. Cremin, *The Wonderful World,* 4–5, 42–52.
30. Lawrence Cremin, *American Education: The Colonial Experience, 1607–1783* (New York: Harper and Row, 1970), xii–xiii.
31. Howard Zinn, *The Politics of History* (Boston: Beacon Press, 1970), 35–41.

32. Michael B. Katz, *The Irony of Modern School Reform* (Cambridge, Mass.: Harvard University Press, 1968), 19–20, 80–85.
33. Clarence J. Karier, Paul C. Violas, and Joel Spring, *Roots of Crisis: American Education in the Twentieth Century* (Chicago: Rand McNally and Co., 1973), 1–5.
34. Karier, Violas, and Spring, *Roots of Crisis,* 215–231.
35. Novick, *Dream,* 473–475.
36. James D. Anderson, *The Education of Blacks in the South, 1860–1935* (Chapel Hill: University of North Carolina Press, 1988), 4–33.
37. R. Freeman Butts, "Public Education and Political Community," *History of Education Quarterly* 14 (Summer 1974): 165–183.
38. Ibid.
39. R. Freeman Butts, *The Education of the West: A Formative Chapter in the History of Civilization* (New York: McGraw-Hill Co.), 295–334.
40. Butts, "Public Education and Political Community," 172, 180.
41. C. Vann Woodward, *Thinking Back: The Perils of Writing History* (Baton Rouge: Louisiana State University Press, 1986), 121–133.
42. Cyril Edwin Black, *The Dynamics of Modernization: A Study in Comparative History* (New York: Harper and Row, Publishers, 1966), 35–37.
43. Black, *The Dynamics of Modernization,* 37–38.
44. John Rury, *Education and Social Change: Themes in the History of American Schooling* (Mahwah, N.J.: Erlbaum Associates, 2002), 1–21, 226–227.
45. Diane Ravitch, *The Revisionists Revised: A Critique of the Radical Attack on the Schools* (New York: Basic Books, 1977), 20–31, 164–173.
46. Maris Vinovskis, *The Origins of Public High Schools: A Reexamination of the Beverly High School Controversy* (Madison: University of Wisconsin Press, 1985), 109–113.
47. Joel Spring, *The Sorting Machine Revisited: National Educational Policy Since 1945* (1976; revised, New York: Longman, 1989), ix–x.
48. Edward A. Krug, *The Shaping of the American High School* (New York: Harper and Row, 1964), xiii–xv.
49. William G. Wraga, "A Progressive Legacy Squandered: The Cardinal Principles Report Reconsidered," *History of Education Quarterly* 41, no. 4 (Winter 2001): 494–519.
50. Joel Spring, *The American School, 1642–1985: Varieties of Historical Interpretation of the Foundations and Development of American Education* (New York: Longman, 1986), ix–x.
51. Donald Warren, "Review of *The American School, 1642–1985: Varieties of Historical Interpretation of the Foundations and Development of American Education,*" *History of Education Quarterly* 27, no. 1 (Spring 1987): 113–118.
52. Warren, "Review," 113–118.
53. Wayne J. Urban and Jennings L. Wagoner, Jr., *American Education: A History* (Boston: McGraw-Hill, 1996), xxi.
54. Edith Nye MacMullen, "Review of American Education: A History," *History of Education Quarterly* 37, no. 1 (Spring 1997): 78–81.
55. Jean-François Lyotard, "Excerpts from *The Post Modern Condition: A Report on Knowledge,*" in *A Postmodern Reader,* ed. Joseph Natoli and Linda Hutcheon (Albany, N.Y.: SUNY Press, 1993), 71–89.
56. Thomas Docherty, "Introduction," in *Postmodernism: A Reader*, ed. Thomas Docherty (New York: Columbia University Press, 1993), 10–13, 33–37.
57. Robert F. Berkhofer, Jr., *Beyond the Great Story: History as Text and Discourse* (Cambridge, Mass.: Harvard University Press, 1995), 4–25.
58. Berkhofer, *Beyond the Great Story,* 280, 282.
59. Berkhofer, *Beyond the Great Story,* 283.
60. Michael Roth, "Review of *Beyond the Great Story: History as Text and Discourse,*" *The American Historical Review* 102, no. 2 (April 1997): 427–428; Bryan D. Palmer, "Review of *Beyond the Great Story: History as Text and Discourse,*" *The Journal of American History* 83, no. 1 (June 1996): 167–168.
61. Eugene D Genovese, "A New Departure," in *Reconstructing History: The Emergence of a New Historical Society*, ed. Elizabeth Fox-Genovese and Elisabeth Lasch-Quinn (New York: Routledge, 1999), 6–8.
62. Elizabeth Lasch-Quinn, "Democracy in the Ivory Tower," in *Reconstructing History: The Emergence of a New Historical Society,* ed. Elizabeth Fox-Genovese and Elizabeth Lasch-Quinn (New York: Routledge, 1999), 23–34.
63. Diane Ravitch, "The Controversy over National History Standards," in *Reconstructing History: The Emergence of a New Historical Society,* ed. Elizabeth Fox-Genovese and Elizabeth Lasch-Quinn (New York: Routledge, 1999), 242–252.
64. Diane Ravitch, *Left Back: A Century of Battles over School Reform* (New York: Touchstone Books, 2000), 13–18.
65. Ravitch, *Left Back,* 466.
66. William Wraga, "Left Out: The Villainization of Progressive Education in the United States," *Educational Researcher* 30, no. 7 (October 2001): 34–39.

Epilogue: A Summing Up

When scholars seek to understand the relation of education to globalization, they confront the question of whether schools changed society or the society changed the schools. Educators such as Horace Mann, W. T. Harris, and John Dewey thought that both changes took place. On the one hand, societies created schools to support the social order. On the other hand, schools appeared to support the society, changing the social order. During the nineteenth century, these men argued that social changes had made different educational reforms necessary. They added that the reforms would enable the schools to reinforce a harmonious society of free people.

In the 1830s, Mann acknowledged that Northwestern cities had to establish schools to teach the many newly arrived immigrants how to prosper in their new homes. Without proper education, those immigrants could turn to crime and become social menaces. At the same time, he disapproved of the then popular Lancaster schools because these did not allow teachers to impart a proper sense of values to the students. Thus, he advocated better teacher training to help students acquire the attitudes that would help them succeed in their new environment, and he wanted the curriculum to teach the rules of health so the children could learn to take proper care of their bodies. In this way, Mann wanted the schools to respond to social change and lead to the creation of a better society by teaching students to be good and healthy citizens.

In the 1880s, W. T. Harris advanced similar hopes for schools. Although Harris disagreed with Mann about the proper curriculum, he held that schools should teach children about the ways in which society had changed. Harris wanted students to master academic subjects because these reflected the ways that people in the society had learned how to think. Mastering the different models of thought enabled students to learn about learning and thereby recognize how to help society continue its movement toward the creation of institutions that advanced personal freedom and understanding.

Adopting Harris's love of dialectics, Dewey became famous for avoiding dualisms. He made no exception when it came to the question of whether society changed schools or schools changed society. Both things happened, he believed. Thus, in the 1890s, in his laboratory school, Dewey had the children learn by doing. This meant that students would begin with interesting activities, which Dewey called occupations. To accomplish their goals, the students had to turn to the academic subject matters for assistance. In the process, they learned how to plan and solve problems. For Dewey, there was only one way to think. The scientific method had shown itself to be superior to other ways of thinking because it had led to the growth of large industries and advanced means of transportation that had changed the world. Thus, through their occupations, the children learned to think in a manner similar to the scientific method and, thereby, to participate intelligently in this newly created social order.

Although some historians contend that the ideas of Harris and Dewey did not pervade American schools, the idea that schools were essential to democracy did prevail in various forms. For example, when educational missions joined the forces of occupation in Japan and Germany after World War II, the educators who served on the missions advanced the American model of a system made up of a single track ending in a comprehensive high school as the antidote to domination by an emperor or to dictatorship. In this way, educators equated a particular model of American schooling with democracy.

Some authors consider the spread of American democracy to be an aspect of globalization. As noted in the introduction, several authors agreed that the important aspects of globalization include industrial development with concurrent expansion of a bureaucratic organization, spread of a free economy, and increased popular concern for material satisfactions over spiritual achievements. Although these characteristics of globalization appeared in most historical epochs, historians noted that those factors expanded to change the quality of social life. Thus, the important change was not that new things appeared. Instead, the quantity or extent to which those aspects appeared may have been sufficient to change the quality of life in the society. For example, a small rural village contains houses and streets. A large city has the same things. Although the difference between the village and the city is the number of houses and streets, the quantity in the city changes the quality of life into an urban pattern. Calling this transformation Engel's law, John Wilkerson warned that there did not have to be a particular threshold for this transformation to take place because every change in quantity caused a change in quality. At the same time, he suggested that changes could go in the opposite direction so that quantity could become a measure of quality. Such reversals took place when people considered anything bigger to be better.[1]

Taking Wilkerson's position, this book seeks to combine two stories. In describing the ways that the drive to establish or change schools advanced or retarded the characteristics of globalization in the United States, the book explains how America shared those characteristics with several other countries. This raises two problems. Such a system of organization implies that globalization resulted from the extension of an American empire or hegemony and that education shaped the various societies. Fortunately, the book's thesis does not depend on demonstrating those possibilities. Although there may be an American empire, its existence may not have depended on any educational model. As suggested in the introduction, military force and consumer goods could have been more important. At the same time, although the model of schools that people preferred followed social movements, there was not a clear cause and effect relationship. The descriptions indicate that, at times, societies influenced schools and, at other times, schools influenced society.

This book begins with the period of colonization by considering the work of two European powers. Although the process of colonization was a part of the transition from a feudal economy to a more modern economy, the methods used by Spain and England fell on opposite sides of a possible continuum. For example, Spain began its efforts after Ferdinand and Isabella and united the Iberian peninsular under their control. When these Catholic rulers wrote to the Pope, they offered religious reasons for the quest. Nonetheless, they included the desire for exotic trade goods. In England, the drive for profit mingled with the urge to spread the Gospels. Some English colonists sought to avoid forms of state control of religion that derived from the Renaissance. Once these countries established colonies, the settlers developed different approaches to education. Because the Spanish wanted to use

Native Americans to advance the goals of the empire, they built missions. The New England colonists had more complicated goals because they had looser ties to their mother country. Although the English Puritans established schools to reinforce the English culture, education may have weakened the hold of religious leaders in the colonies.

The next two chapters concentrate on the development of central control of schools in different parts of the country on the assumption that the development of central state authority is an aspect of modernization or globalization. For example, Chapter 3 suggests that schools served as a means to attract settlers to the Northwest Territories. Although the Continental Congress allocated sections of land for the support of education, the funds from these lands disappeared. As a result, although the policies of land grants implied that there should be central control of local schools, they did not lead to the creation of such administrations.

Chapter 4 follows the efforts of advocates such as Horace Mann and Henry Barnard to establish the office of a state superintendent of schools and a system of common schools. Instead of advancing their cause directly, these advocates complained that children suffered in poorly built district schools, that untrained teachers abused the children, and that the children wasted time with inappropriate curriculums. Chapter 5 shows that advocates of common schools followed the same process in the South before the American Civil War but the rise of abolitionism in the North by 1830 enabled critics to ignore their pleas for common schools.

In Chapter 6, the book considers Northern efforts after the American Civil War to rebuild the South to establish racial justice. When the complicated situation made success difficult, the North withdrew. By the 1890s, boosters claimed that racial antagonisms had ended and a New South was prepared to share industrial prosperity. Although African Americans faced intense segregation that denied them access to the education they needed to participate in a democratic, industrial society, the South was able to mount an impressive effort to increase industrial production and adopt the methods of school organization found in other parts of the country.

Chapter 7 describes the late nineteenth-century efforts to build a new order in the North and the Midwest to open insular communities to a national society. Confronting the same devotion to localism that frustrated common school advocates of the 1830s, educators sought to create a federal organization that would spread the ideas they accepted as the best practices. At the same time, educators in the rapidly growing cities sought to consolidate the schools to enhance the training of teachers and to expand the curriculums.

The rise of bureaucratic organizations is the topic of Chapter 8. With this chapter, the book turns from regional concerns and devotes attention to issues that confronted school people as they sought to consolidate their institutions and follow a model commonly considered progressive. In the next four chapters, the topics include the rise of educational philosophies, the growth of educational psychology, the development of a unified system of schools that led to the comprehensive high school, and the spread of the activity movement. Although these chapters cover the last years of the nineteenth century and the first years of the twentieth, they treat each topic independently. Although these developments unfolded together, they had different trajectories. To make sense of the differences, the chapters present them separately. Together, these chapters describe the development of modern American conceptions of education.

Chapter 13 shows how American educators tried to spread the views they had of education once they had solidified them. Independent commissions of educators took the ideas across the United States and to the different parts of the globe after World War II, spreading the idea that schools had to be bureaucratically organized, that education should bring together the different groups in a society, and that training in vocations was an important part of learning. In these ways, the American commissions spread components of globalization.

With the rise of the Cold War, federal officials sought to change local schools in the United States to meet threats arising from foreign affairs. As a result, Chapter 14 explains the efforts to instill patriotism in youth, to end racial discrimination in schools, and to train scientists needed to develop methods of military defense. Chapter 15 shows how federal officials in the 1970s sought to end efforts for racial integration and to turn the curriculum toward the study of basic academic skills for all children. Although these chapters describe two different sets of policies that took place sequentially, the chapters suggest that both types of reforms derived from federal officials' views of how schools could offset problems with other nations.

Chapter 16 is a description of the ways that historians have tried to explain the nature of social change and the ways that educators sought to use similar models to explain changes in schools. By offering an overview of the work of historians, this chapter explains that this book offers an intellectual history that traces changes in ideas of school practices and educational thought to locate the relation between social change and educational reforms. Although the chapter notes that postmodernists claim such an interpretation is beyond the reach of human minds, the chapter suggests that this criticism should stand as a warning to historians, not as a dismissal. Historians may not be able to point to the absolute truth. They can offer important insights when they realize their limits.

An example of how simple conclusions can be misleading derives from the descriptions in Chapters 14 and 15. These explanations showed that, during the last half of the twentieth century, federal officials encouraged schools to adopt programs that would meet national concerns by passing legislation that offered considerable monies to the local schools. Although these descriptions are correct, they might lead a person to conclude that federal support of local schools caused education to influence globalization. This would be a simplistic answer even for the period covered by those chapters. First, some programs began as efforts to advance uniquely American ideals. In this case, the effort to end racial segregation extended the ideal of bringing together children from different social groups through systems leading to the comprehensive high school. Second, American educators continued to develop and to export ideas for school arrangements to other parts of the world. For example, U.S. economist Milton Friedman created the idea of schools vouchers in 1955. When Friedman visited Chile, he recommended that the president, Augusto Pinochet Ugarte, adopt a free market economy that included vouchers. Thus, Chile and Sweden implemented the American idea of school vouchers and free market model of school finance before any state in the United States could offer them.

Although the text avoids simple conclusions, it offers valuable observations. For example, in the twentieth century, when reformers adopted a change, they tended to emphasize one aspect of democracy at the expense of other aspects. The reformers described in Chapter 11 advanced the comprehensive high school as a model to help children learn to work together for the common good. The educators depicted in Chapter 12 believed the project method allowed children to pursue what they wanted to do, thereby emphasizing the essential element of the pursuit of happiness. The reforms considered in Chapter 14 derived from efforts to end racial discrimination and to overcome the disadvantages of poverty in ways that extended the ideal of equality and freedom. The movement to make students master the subject matters in Chapter 15 seemed to fulfill the ideal of an intelligent citizenry, and the efforts to use vouchers or charter schools applied principles of the market system allowing everyone to make free choices.

In each of the cases, difficulties occurred when educators pursued their ideas beyond the points that they were reasonable. Comprehensive high schools may cause harm when they imply that vocational pursuits are superior to intellectual ones. Projects may cause harm when they prevent children from developing proficiencies in the subject matters. Racial integration may cause harm if it implies that minorities lack certain strengths. Compensatory education may cause problems when it leads teachers to categorize children inappropriately. Finally, the free market approaches may allow large corporations to run schools in ways that will end the free market that created them.

There may not be answers to these problems beyond calling for intelligence and moderation. Nonetheless, historical studies can help people develop those qualities.

Endnote

1. John Wilkerson, translator's introduction to *The Technological Society,* Jacques Ellul (New York: Vintage Books, 1970), xv–xvii.

Index